The Visible Hand

ALFRED D. CHANDLER, JR.

The Visible Hand

The Managerial Revolution in American Business

The Belknap Press of
Harvard University Press
Cambridge, Massachusetts
and London, England

£8.50.

Library of Congress Cataloging in Publication Data

Chandler, Alfred Dupont.
   The visible hand.

   Includes bibliographical references and index.
   1. Business enterprises—United States—Management—
History. 2. Industrial organization—United States—
History. 3. United States—Industries. I. Title.
HF5343.C584   658.4'00973   77-1529
ISBN 0-674-94051-2 (cloth)
ISBN 0-674-94052-0 (paper)

To Fay—with love

Acknowledgments

This book had its beginnings some fifteen years ago, when the late Arthur C. Cole, Thomas C. Cochran, and I agreed to write a three-volume series on the history of American business. Cole was to review the evolving structure of the American business system. Cochran was to examine the place of business in its broader culture, and in 1972 published *Business in American Life*. I was to study changing business practices, particularly those concerned with the management of the firm.

My own study acquired its first focus when I received a grant from the Alfred P. Sloan Foundation to examine the rise of big business and the public response to it. By concentrating on the coming of modern business enterprise I believed that I could broaden my contribution to the series by describing the changing processes of production and distribution in the United States and the ways in which they have been managed, since the eighteenth century. The second part of the Sloan Foundation project, that dealing with the public response to big business, was carried out by Louis Galambos, who published his results in 1975 in *The Public Image of Big Business in America, 1880–1940*. The work I began under the Sloan Foundation grant was completed with assistance from the Division of Research, Graduate School of Business Administration, Harvard University. I am greatly indebted to the officers of the Sloan Foundation and to Dean Lawrence E. Fouraker and the heads of the Division of Research at the School who provided funds to pay for time and facilities so necessary to the completion of such an extended study.

The research and writing of this history was carried out in a traditional manner. It has been pieced together from reading business records and secondary works, and from countless discussions with students and colleagues. No teams of scholars or computerized data were involved. I learned much from graduate students, particularly those who wrote dissertations on topics related to the themes in this book. These included William H. Becker, Charles N. Cheape III, Russell I. Fries, Harold Livesay, Edwin J. Perkins, P. Glenn Porter, and Mary A. Yeager. I am especially grateful to Chuck Cheape who, as my research assistant, carried out the laborious work of compiling and collating the data for Appendix A and other tables. Without the major contributions of these young scholars the study would have been far less complete.

As valuable were those long talks with academic colleagues, many of whom were willing to plow through parts or all of the lengthy manuscript at different stages of its completion. Fred V. Carstensen, Herman Daems, Louis Galambos, Thomas K. McCraw, H. Thomas Johnson, and P. Glenn Porter read large parts of the manuscript. Stuart Bruchey, Alfred S. Eichner, Stanley Engerman, Max R. Hall, Albro Martin, and Peter Temin read it from beginning to end. All provided invaluable suggestions that corrected errors of fact, refined interpretations, and improved the presentation of the data. I am especially indebted to Stuart Bruchey who, in giving the manuscript its final going-over, forced me to sharpen and define more precisely my terms and concepts and to Max Hall who worked with such care and patience to improve the organization of the chapters and the clarity of the prose.

Essential too were the many persons who transcribed pages of rough, almost illegible typescript and checked and rechecked the final pages. Jane Barrett, Eleanor Bradley, Violette Crowe, Rose Giacobbe, Peter Grant, Hilma Holton, June Kingsbury, William La Piana, and Anne O'Connell carried out these onerous tasks with great cheerfulness and care.

Without the constant encouragement of my wife, Fay, and her ability to assure the best of working conditions at home where all but the basic archival and library research was done, I could never have completed this or any of my other historical studies.

Many have contributed, but the final product is mine and for it I take full responsibility.

Alfred D. Chandler, Jr.

Cambridge, Massachusetts

Contents

ix

Tables

Figures

Maps

Introduction: The Visible Hand

The title of this book indicates its theme but not its focus or purpose. Its purpose is to examine the changing processes of production and distribution in the United States and the ways in which they have been managed. To achieve this end it focuses on the business enterprise that carried out these processes. Because the large enterprise administered by salaried managers replaced the small traditional family firm as the primary instrument for managing production and distribution, the book concentrates specifically on the rise of modern business enterprise and its managers. It is a history of a business institution and a business class.

The theme propounded here is that modern business enterprise took the place of market mechanisms in coordinating the activities of the economy and allocating its resources. In many sectors of the economy the visible hand of management replaced what Adam Smith referred to as the invisible hand of market forces. The market remained the generator of demand for goods and services, but modern business enterprise took over the functions of coordinating flows of goods through existing processes of production and distribution, and of allocating funds and personnel for future production and distribution. As modern business enterprise acquired functions hitherto carried out by the market, it became the most powerful institution in the American economy and its managers the most influential group of economic decision makers. The rise of modern business enterprise in the United States, therefore, brought with it managerial capitalism.

Modern business enterprise defined

Modern business enterprise is easily defined. As figure 1 indicates, it has two specific characteristics: it contains many distinct operating units and it is managed by a hierarchy of salaried executives.

Each unit within the modern multiunit enterprise has its own admin-

Figure 1. The basic hierarchical structure of modern business enterprise (each box represents an office)

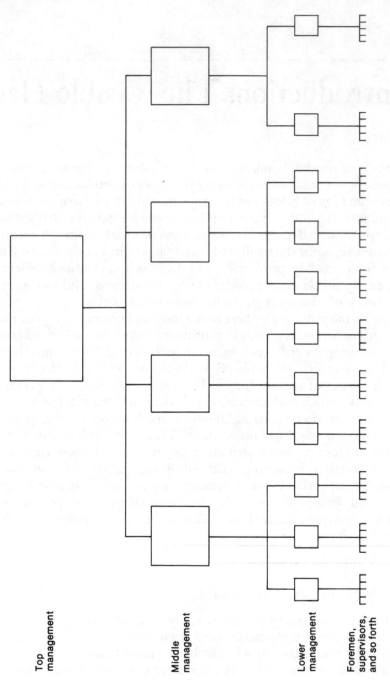

Top management

Middle management

Lower management

Foremen, supervisors, and so forth

istrative office. Each is administered by a full-time salaried manager. Each has its own set of books and accounts which can be audited separately from those of the large enterprise. Each could theoretically operate as an independent business enterprise.

In contrast, the traditional American business firm was a single-unit business enterprise. In such an enterprise an individual or a small number of owners operated a shop, factory, bank, or transportation line out of a single office. Normally this type of firm handled only a single economic function, dealt in a single product line, and operated in one geographic area. Before the rise of the modern firm, the activities of one of these small, personally owned and managed enterprises were coordinated and monitored by market and price mechanisms.

Modern enterprise, by bringing many units under its control, began to operate in different locations, often carrying on different types of economic activities and handling different lines of goods and services. The activities of these units and the transactions between them thus became internalized. They became monitored and coordinated by salaried employees rather than market mechanisms.

Modern business enterprise, therefore, employs a hierarchy of middle and top salaried managers to monitor and coordinate the work of the units under its control. Such middle and top managers form an entirely new class of businessmen. Some traditional single-unit enterprises employed managers whose activities were similar to those of the lowest level managers in a modern business enterprise. Owners of plantations, mills, shops, and banks hired salaried employees to administer or assist them in administering the unit. As the work within single operating units increased, these managers employed subordinates—foremen, drivers, and mates—to supervise the work force. But as late as 1840 there were no middle managers in the United States—that is, there were no managers who supervised the work of other managers and in turn reported to senior executives who themselves were salaried managers. At that time nearly all top managers were owners; they were either partners or major stockholders in the enterprise they managed.

The multiunit enterprise administered by a set of salaried middle and top managers can then properly be termed modern. Such enterprises did not exist in the United States in 1840. By World War I this type of firm had become the dominant business institution in many sectors of the American economy. By the middle of the twentieth century, these enterprises employed hundreds and even thousands of middle and top managers who supervised the work of dozens and often hundreds of operating units employing tens and often hundreds of thousands of workers. These enterprises were owned by tens or hundreds of thousands of shareholders and carried out billions of dollars of business annually. Even a relatively small business enterprise operating in local or regional markets had its top and middle managers. Rarely in the history of the world has an institution grown to be so important and so pervasive in so short a period of time.

Describing and analyzing the rise of an institution and a class of such immense historical and current significance provides a fascinating challenge to a historian of the American economy. Because this institution is so easy to define and because it came into being so recently, the scholar has little difficulty in answering the historian's special questions of when, where, and how. He can record with precision at what dates, in what areas, and in what ways the new institution first appeared and then continued to grow. In so doing, he can document the rise of the new subspecies of economic man—the salaried manager—and record the development of practices and procedures that have become standard in the management of American production and distribution. Once he has answered the historical questions of when, where, and how, he can begin to suggest the reasons why this institution first appeared and then became so powerful.

The challenge is particularly attractive because it has not yet been taken up. For all its significance, the history of this institution has not been told. Scholars have paid surprisingly little attention to its historical development. Before the 1930s economists only grudgingly acknowledged its existence, and since then they have looked on large-scale business enterprise with deep suspicion. Much basic economic theory is still grounded on the assumption that the processes of production and distribution are managed, or at least should be managed, by small traditional enterprises regulated by the invisible hand of the market. According to such theory, perfect competition can only exist between such single-unit enterprises, and such competition remains the most efficient way to coordinate economic activities and allocate economic resources. The modern, multi-unit enterprise, by its very act of administrative coordination, brings imperfect competition and misallocation of resources. Since many economists have for so long considered the modern business enterprise as an aberration, and an evil one at that, few have taken the trouble to examine its origins. For them the desire for monopoly power has provided an adequate causal explanation.

Until recently historians as well have concentrated little systematic attention on the rise of modern business enterprise and the managerial class that came to administer it. They have preferred to study individuals, not institutions. In fact, few businessmen have appeared in general American histories except those who founded modern business enterprises. Historians have been attracted by entrepreneurs, but they have rarely looked closely at the new institution these entrepreneurs created, at how it was managed, what functions it carried out, and how the enterprise continued to compete and grow after the founders had left the scene. Instead they have argued as to whether these founding fathers were robber barons or industrial statesmen, that is, bad fellows or good fellows. Most historians, as distrustful as the economists about the enterprises these men built, agreed that they were bad. These same historians, however, made few value judgments either way about the new class of managers whose actions were so influential in the continuing development of the American economy.

In recent years economists and historians have increasingly turned their attention to modern economic institutions. Economists such as Edward S. Mason, A. D. H. Kaplan, John Kenneth Galbraith, Oliver E. Williamson, William J. Baumol, Robin L. Marris, Edith T. Penrose, Robert T. Averitt, and R. Joseph Monsen, following the pioneering work of Adolph A. Berle, Jr., and Gardiner C. Means, have studied the operations and actions of modern business enterprise. They have not attempted, however, to examine its historical development, nor has their work yet had a major impact on economic theory. The firm remains essentially a unit of production, and the theory of the firm a theory of production.

Economists with a historical bent have only just begun to study institutional change and its impact on industrial organization. Douglass C. North has been the innovator here.[1] In his work with Lance E. Davis he outlined a most useful theory of institutional change and applied it to American economic growth. In his study with Robert Paul Thomas he demonstrated how the changing industrial organization affected the rise of the west. The works of North and his colleagues use this sweeping panorama of history to test, buttress, and refine their theory. They have not yet focused on a detailed analysis of the historical development of any specific economic institution.

Historians of the American experience have also moved to the study of institutions. Such scholars as Robert H. Wiebe, Morton Keller, Samuel Hays, and Lee Benson have taken a close look at the changing nature of political, social, and economic organizations. They have pioneered in what one analyst of recent writing in American history has called the "new institutionalism."[2] Few historians, however, have tried to trace the story of a single institution from its beginnings to its full growth. None have written about the rise of modern business enterprise and the brand of managerial capitalism that accompanied it.

This study is an attempt to fill that void by concentrating on a specific time period and a specific set of concerns. It centers on the years between the 1840s and the 1920s—when the agrarian, rural economy of the United

States became industrial and urban. These decades witnessed revolutionary changes in the processes of production and distribution in the United States. Within this time period I examine the ways in which the units carrying out these changing processes of production and distribution—including transportation, communication, and finance—were administered and coordinated. I have not tried to describe the work done by the labor force in these units or the organization and aspirations of the workers. Nor do I attempt to assess the impact of modern business enterprise on existing political and social arrangements. I deal with broad political, demographic, and social developments only as they impinge directly on the ways in which the enterprise carried out the processes of production and distribution.

Some general propositions

This study is a history. It moves chronologically. It is filled with details about men and events, about specific processes, policies, and procedures, and about changing technologies and markets. It attempts to carry out the historian's basic responsibility for setting the record straight. That record, in turn, provides the basis for the generalizations presented. The data have not been selected to test and validate hypotheses or general theories. I hope that these facts may also be useful to scholars with other questions and concerns other than those relevant to the generalizations presented here.

Before I enter the complexities of the historical experience, it seems wise to outline a list of general propositions to make more precise the primary concerns of the study. They give some indication at the outset of the nature of modern business enterprise and suggest why the visible hand of management replaced the invisible hand of market mechanisms. I set these forth as a guide through the intricate history of interrelated institutional changes that follows.

The first proposition is that modern multiunit business enterprise replaced small traditional enterprise when administrative coordination permitted greater productivity, lower costs, and higher profits than coordination by market mechanisms.
This proposition is derived directly from the definition of a modern business enterprise. Such an enterprise came into being and continued to grow by setting up or purchasing business units that were theoretically able to operate as independent enterprises—in other words, by internaliz-

ing the activities that had been or could be carried on by several business units and the transactions that had been or could be carried on between them.

Such an internalization gave the enlarged enterprise many advantages.[3] By routinizing the transactions between units, the costs of these transactions were lowered. By linking the administration of producing units with buying and distributing units, costs for information on markets and sources of supply were reduced. Of much greater significance, the internalization of many units permitted the flow of goods from one unit to another to be administratively coordinated. More effective scheduling of flows achieved a more intensive use of facilities and personnel employed in the processes of production and distribution and so increased productivity and reduced costs. In addition, administrative coordination provided a more certain cash flow and more rapid payment for services rendered. The savings resulting from such coordination were much greater than those resulting from lower information and transactions costs.

The second proposition is simply that the advantages of internalizing the activities of many business units within a single enterprise could not be realized until a managerial hierarchy had been created.

Such advantages could be achieved only when a group of managers had been assembled to carry out the functions formerly handled by price and market mechanisms. Whereas the activities of single-unit traditional enterprises were monitored and coordinated by market mechanisms, the producing and distributing units within a modern business enterprise are monitored and coordinated by middle managers. Top managers, in addition to evaluating and coordinating the work of middle managers, took the place of the market in allocating resources for future production and distribution. In order to carry out these functions, the managers had to invent new practices and procedures which in time became standard operating methods in managing American production and distribution.

Thus the existence of a managerial hierarchy is a defining characteristic of the modern business enterprise. A multiunit enterprise without such managers remains little more than a federation of autonomous offices. Such federations were formed to control competition between units or to assure enterprises of sources of raw materials or outlets for finished goods and services. The owners and managers of the autonomous units agreed on common buying, pricing, production, and marketing policies. If there were no managers, these policies were determined and enforced by legislative and judicial rather than administrative means. Such federations were often able to bring small reductions in information and transactions costs, but they could not lower costs through increased productivity. They could not provide the administrative coordination that became the central function of modern business enterprise.

The third proposition is that modern business enterprise appeared for the first time in history when the volume of economic activities reached a level that made administrative coordination more efficient and more profitable than market coordination.

Such an increase in volume of activity came with new technology and expanding markets. New technology made possible an unprecedented output and movement of goods. Enlarged markets were essential to absorb such output. Therefore modern business enterprise first appeared, grew, and continued to flourish in those sectors and industries characterized by new and advancing technology and by expanding markets. Conversely in those sectors and industries where technology did not bring a sharp increase in output and where markets remained small and specialized, administrative coordination was rarely more profitable than market coordination. In those areas modern business enterprise was late in appearing and slow in spreading.

The fourth proposition is that once a managerial hierarchy had been formed and had successfully carried out its function of administrative coordination, the hierarchy itself became a source of permanence, power, and continued growth.

In Werner Sombart's phrase, the modern business enterprise took on "a life of its own."[4] Traditional enterprises were normally short-lived. They were almost always partnerships which were reconstituted or disbanded at the death or retirement of a partner. If a son carried on the father's business, he found new partners. Often the partnership was disbanded when one partner decided he wanted to work with another businessman. On the other hand, the hierarchies that came to manage the new multiunit enterprises had a permanence beyond that of any individual or group of individuals who worked in them. When a manager died, retired, was promoted, or left an office, another was ready and trained to take his place. Men came and went. The institution and its offices remained.

The fifth proposition is that the careers of the salaried managers who directed these hierarchies became increasingly technical and professional.

In these new business bureaucracies, as in other administrative hierarchies requiring specialized skills, selection and promotion became increasingly based on training, experience, and performance rather than on family relationship or money. With the coming of modern business enterprise, the businessman, for the first time, could conceive of a lifetime career involving a climb up the hierarchical ladder. In such enterprises, managerial training became increasingly longer and more formalized. Managers carrying out similar activities in different enterprises often had the same type of training and attended the same types of schools. They read the same journals and joined the same associations. They had an approach to their work that was closer to that of lawyers, doctors, and ministers than that of the owners and managers of small traditional business enterprises.

The sixth proposition is that as the multiunit business enterprise grew in size and diversity and as its managers became more professional, the management of the enterprise became separated from its ownership.

The rise of modern business enterprise brought a new definition of the relationship between ownership and management and therefore a new type of capitalism to the American economy. Before the appearance of the multiunit firm, owners managed and managers owned. Even when partnerships began to incorporate, their capital stock stayed in the hands of a few individuals or families. These corporations remained single-unit enterprises which rarely hired more than two or three managers. The traditional capitalist firm can, therefore, be properly termed a personal enterprise.

From its very beginning, however, modern business enterprise required more managers than a family or its associates could provide. In some firms the entrepreneur and his close associates (and their families) who built the enterprise continued to hold the majority of stock. They maintained a close personal relationship with their managers, and they retained a major say in top management decisions, particularly those concerning financial policies, allocation of resources, and the selection of senior managers. Such a modern business enterprise may be termed an entrepreneurial or family one, and an economy or sectors of an economy dominated by such firms may be considered a system of entrepreneurial or family capitalism.

Where the creation and growth of an enterprise required large sums of outside capital, the relationship between ownership and management differed. The financial institutions providing the funds normally placed part-time representatives on the firm's board. In such enterprises, salaried managers had to share top management decisions, particularly those involving the raising and spending of large sums of capital, with representatives of banks and other financial institutions. An economy or sector controlled by such firms has often been termed one of financial capitalism.

In many modern business enterprises neither bankers nor families were

in control. Ownership became widely scattered. The stockholders did
not have the influence, knowledge, experience, or commitment to take
part in the high command. Salaried managers determined long-term policy
as well as managing short-term operating activities. They dominated top
as well as lower and middle management. Such an enterprise controlled
by its managers can properly be identified as managerial, and a system
dominated by such firms is called managerial capitalism.

As family- and financier-controlled enterprises grew in size and age
they became managerial. Unless the owners or representatives of financial
houses became full-time career managers within the enterprise itself, they
did not have the information, the time, or the experience to play a dominant role in top-level decisions. As members of the boards of directors
they did hold veto power. They could say no, and they could replace
the senior managers with other career managers; but they were rarely in
a position to propose positive alternative solutions. In time, the part-time
owners and financiers on the board normally looked on the enterprise in
the same way as did ordinary stockholders. It became a source of income
and not a business to be managed. Of necessity, they left current operations and future plans to the career administrators. In many industries and
sectors of the American economy, managerial capitalism soon replaced
family or financial capitalism.

The seventh proposition is that in making administrative decisions,
career managers preferred policies that favored the long-term stability
and growth of their enterprises to those that maximized current profits.

For salaried managers the continuing existence of their enterprises was
essential to their lifetime careers. Their primary goal was to assure continuing use of and therefore continuing flow of material to their facilities.
They were far more willing than were the owners (the stockholders) to
reduce or even forego current dividends in order to maintain the long-
term viability of their organizations. They sought to protect their sources
of supplies and their outlets. They took on new products and services in
order to make more complete use of existing facilities and personnel. Such
expansion, in turn, led to the addition of still more workers and equipment.
If profits were high, they preferred to reinvest them in the enterprise
rather than pay them out in dividends. In this way the desire of the
managers to keep the organization fully employed became a continuing
force for its further growth.

The eighth and final proposition is that as the large enterprises grew
and dominated major sectors of the economy, they altered the basic
structure of these sectors and of the economy as a whole.

The new bureaucratic enterprises did not, it must be emphasized, replace the market as the primary force in generating goods and services. The current decisions as to flows and the long-term ones as to allocating resources were based on estimates of current and long-term market demand. What the new enterprises did do was take over from the market the coordination and integration of the flow of goods and services from the production of the raw materials through the several processes of production to the sale to the ultimate consumer. Where they did so, production and distribution came to be concentrated in the hands of a few large enterprises. At first this occurred in only a few sectors or industries where technological innovation and market growth created high-speed and high-volume throughput. As technology became more sophisticated and as markets expanded, administrative coordination replaced market coordination in an increasingly larger portion of the economy. By the middle of the twentieth century the salaried managers of a relatively small number of large mass producing, large mass retailing, and large mass transporting enterprises coordinated current flows of goods through the processes of production and distribution and allocated the resources to be used for future production and distribution in major sectors of the American economy. By then, the managerial revolution in American business had been carried out.[5]

These basic propositions fall into two parts. The first three help to explain the initial appearance of modern business enterprise: why it began when it did, where it did, and in the way it did. The remaining five concern its continuing growth: where, how, and why an enterprise once started continued to grow and to maintain its position of dominance. This institution appeared when managerial hierarchies were able to monitor and coordinate the activities of a number of business units more efficiently than did market mechanisms. It continued to grow so that these hierarchies of increasingly professional managers might remain fully employed. It emerged and spread, however, only in those industries and sectors whose technology and markets permitted administrative coordination to be more profitable than market coordination. Because these areas were at the center of the American economy and because professional managers replaced families, financiers, or their representatives as decision makers in these areas, modern American capitalism became managerial capitalism.

Historical realities are, of course, far more complicated than these general propositions suggest. Modern business enterprise and the new business class that managed it appeared, grew, and flourished in different ways even in the different sectors and in the different industries they came to dominate. Varying needs and opportunities meant that the specific substance of managerial tasks differed from one sector to another and from one industry to another. So too did the specific relationships between managers and owners. And once a managerial hierarchy was fully estab-lished, the sequence of its development varied from industry to industry and from sector to sector.

Nevertheless, these differences can be viewed as variations on a single theme. The visible hand of management replaced the invisible hand of market forces where and when new technology and expanded markets permitted a historically unprecedented high volume and speed of materials through the processes of production and distribution. Modern business enterprise was thus the institutional response to the rapid pace of tech-nological innovation and increasing consumer demand in the United States during the second half of the nineteenth century.

PART
one

The Traditional Processes of
Production and Distribution

Most histories have to begin before the beginning. This is particularly true for one that focuses on institutional innovation. A history of the modern business enterprise has to start by examining the ways in which the processes of production and distribution were carried out before it came into existence, before administrative coordination became more productive and more profitable than market coordination. It has to identify the specific conditions that led to the rise of the institution and its continuing growth. An analysis of innovation requires a close inspection of the context in which it occurred.

Let us therefore first look at the changing processes of production and distribution from the 1790s to the 1840s, from the time when the ratification of the Constitution provided the legal and political underpinnings of a national economy until the decade when a new source of energy, coal, began to be used extensively in production and the railroad and telegraph began to provide fast, regular, all-weather transportation and communication. Let us begin by examining changes in distribution broadly conceived as commerce and then focus on the management of production.

Although the American economy grew rapidly between 1790 and 1840, the size and nature of business enterprises were little changed. As the population rose from 3.9 million to 17.1 million and as Americans began to move west across the continent, the total volume of goods produced and distributed and the total number of transactions involved in such production and distribution increased enormously. Nevertheless the business enterprises carrying out these processes and transactions continued to be traditional single-unit enterprises. Their numbers multiplied at an impressive rate, and their activities became, as Adam Smith would have predicted, increasingly specialized. Yet they were still managed by their owners. They operated in traditional ways using traditional business practices. Little institutional innovation occurred in American business before the 1840s.

Why was this so? As long as the processes of production and distribution depended on the traditional sources of energy—on man, animal, and wind power—there was little pressure to innovate. Such sources of energy simply could not generate a volume of output in production and number of transactions in distribution large enough to require the creation of a large managerial enterprise or to call for the development of new business forms and practices. The low speed of production and the slow movement of goods through the economy meant that the maximum daily activity at each point of production and distribution could be easily handled by small personally owned and managed enterprises.

C H A P T E R 1

The Traditional Enterprise in Commerce

Institutional specialization and market coordination

In the half century after the ratification of the Constitution American business enterprise became increasingly specialized in commerce and production. The trend was particularly evident in commerce. As commerce expanded and as commercial activities became more specialized, the dependence on market mechanisms to coordinate these activities increased proportionally. In the 1790s the general merchant, the businessman who had dominated the economy of the colonial period, was still the grand distributor. He bought and sold all types of products and carried out all the basic commercial functions. He was an exporter, wholesaler, importer, retailer, shipowner, banker, and insurer. By the 1840s, however, such tasks were being carried out by different types of specialized enterprises. Banks, insurance companies, and common carriers had appeared. Merchants had begun to specialize in one or two lines of goods: cotton, provisions, wheat, dry goods, hardware, or drugs. They concentrated more and more on a single function: retailing, wholesaling, importing, or exporting.

Economic expansion and business specialization greatly increased the number of business enterprises operating in the economy. In the 1790s a relatively few merchants living in the eastern ports carried on the major share of the trade beyond local markets. By the 1840s the much larger flows of a greater variety of goods were guided from the producers of the raw materials through the processes of production and distribution to the ultimate consumer by hundreds and thousands of businessmen who had little personal acquaintance with others. The motives of the businessmen were to make a profit on each of the many transactions and such motivation seemed to be enough to assure the successful operation of the economy. Although, as Adam Smith wrote, each businessman "intends

15

only his gain, he is . . . led by an invisible hand to promote an end which is not his intention."[1] In fact, Smith continued, "by pursuing his own interest he frequently promotes that of society more effectively than when he really intends to promote it."

If the expansion of the economy brought specialization in the activities of business enterprise, it did little to alter the internal operation or organization of these enterprises or their methods of transacting business. In the 1790s American businessmen still relied entirely on commercial practices and procedures invented and perfected centuries earlier by British, Dutch, and Italian merchants. Stuart Bruchey, in his study of the Olivers, Baltimore merchants of the 1790s, points to the "remarkable" similarities between the nature of their activities and those of the Venetian merchants. The Olivers' "form of organization, and their method of managing men, records and investments would have been almost immediately understood by the fifteenth century merchant of Venice."[2] The Americans of the 1790s and the Italians of the 1390s used the partnership form of business and the same double-entry bookkeeping records, records in which Adventure and Merchandise accounts were conspicuous features. Both sold on their own account and on consignment for standardized commission rates and employed ship captains and supercargoes as consignees. Americans also made use of institutional arrangements perfected by the Dutch and British, such as formal exchanges to carry out market transactions, more sophisticated instruments of credit, and concepts and usages of commercial law.[3]

The practices that Americans had inherited remained quite satisfactory until after the 1840s. The Americans adjusted commercial law to meet the needs of a rapidly expanding economy and a federal polity. They made increasing use of the incorporated stock company developed in the sixteenth century by the British to promote overseas trade and colonization and used in the eighteenth century to manage ancillary or utilities operations such as docks, water works, and the like. Traditional forms were refined, but the practices, instruments, and institutions of commercial capitalism which had evolved to meet the growth of trade and the coming of market economies in the Mediterranean basin in the twelfth and thirteenth centuries were not fundamentally altered. Before the 1840s there was no revolution in the ways of doing business in the United States. The great transformation was to await the coming of new technologies and markets that permitted a massive production and distribution of goods. Those institutional changes which helped to create the managerial capitalism of the twentieth century were as significant and as revolutionary as those that accompanied the rise of commercial capitalism a half a millennium earlier.

The general merchant of the colonial world

In 1790 general merchants still ruled the economy. In this economy the family remained the basic business unit. The most pervasive of these units was the family farm. In 1790 only 202,000 out of the 3,930,000 Americans lived in towns and villages of more than 2,500, and of the 2,881,000 workers, 2,069,000 labored on farms.[4] Only in the south, where crops were cultivated by slave labor, did the production of staples become more than a family affair. In the production of crops, only on the plantation did a class of managers appear.

The small amount of manufacturing carried on outside the home was the work of artisans in small shops. In the towns, the artisan often had the assistance of one or two apprentices or journeymen, who were usually treated as part of the family. In the ports, somewhat larger, though still very small, shipyards, ropewalks, candle manufactories, and rum distilleries operated. As Sam Bass Warner wrote of Philadelphia on the eve of the American Revolution: "The core element of the town economy was the one-man shop. Most Philadelphians labored alone, some with a helper or two."[5]

Other resources besides land were exploited, but on a limited scale. Lumbering continued to be a by-product of land clearing, although Maine and North Carolina supplied timber regularly for both the Royal Navy and the West Indian trade. Local farmers provided most of the lumber that went into the making of masts, spars, barrels, staves, as well as beams, shingles, and paneling for houses, churches, warehouses, and other buildings. The output of the only coal mines in the colonies, in Virginia, was hardly 1,000 tons a year.[6] Except for some iron, all metals were imported. The largest business unit either in mining or manufacturing was the "iron plantation," where the iron ore was mined, wood converted into charcoal, iron ore refined into pigs, and the pigs forged into wrought iron. These plantations, with their rural setting, the seasonal nature of their work, and the use of indentured servants and occasionally slaves, were operated in many ways like the rice and tobacco plantations of the southern colonies.

The activities of these producing units were coordinated through the business transactions of the merchants who resided in the port and river towns. The resident merchant distributed and marketed the products of these small enterprises and supplied them with raw materials, tools, and furnishings. For this reason, this all-purpose businessman dominated the economy.[7] He exported, imported, and sold all types of products at retail and at wholesale. He took title to the goods he purchased for his regular customers. He also acted as correspondent or agent for merchants in other ports, taking their goods on consignment and selling for a fixed commission.

The resident general merchant acted as the community's financier and was responsible for the transportation as well as the distribution of goods. He provided short-term loans to finance staple crops and manufactured goods when they were in transit, and he made long-term loans to planters, farmers, and artisans to enable them to clear land or to improve their facilities. Usually in cooperation with other merchants, he arranged for the handling of ships needed to carry these goods and often, with other partners, was a shareholder in these ships. With other merchants, he also insured ships and cargoes. Again with others, he built wharves for the ships. In the same port town, he helped to finance the construction, both by himself and with others, of rum distilleries, candle works, ropewalks, and shipyards—that is, those manufacturing industries not carried on by craftsmen in small family shops.

In all these activities, the colonial merchant knew personally most of the individuals involved. He tried, where possible, to have members of his own family act as his agents in London, the West Indies, and other North American colonies. If he could not consign his goods and arrange for purchase and sale of merchandise through a family member or through a thoroughly reliable associate, the merchant depended on a ship captain or supercargo (his authorized business agent aboard ship) to carry out the distant transactions. Even then, the latter was often a son or a nephew. The merchant knew the other resident merchants in his town, who collaborated with him in insuring and owning ships, as he did the shipbuilders, ropemakers, and local artisans who supplied his personal as well as his business needs. Finally, he was acquainted with the planters, the farmers, and country storekeepers, as well as the fishermen, lumbermen, and others from whom he purchased goods and to whom he provided supplies.

Between Baltimore and Charleston, where there were few ports with resident merchants, a somewhat different pattern of commerce developed.[8] In Maryland and Virginia, and to some extent farther south, planters bought directly from the British merchants. Factors in London arranged for the sale of their tobacco and rice and at the same time purchased any supplies they needed. The planters, in turn, often provided their smaller neighbors with the same type of services they received from the British factors. As tobacco planting moved inland in the mid-eighteenth century, Scottish merchants began to send factors and agents to set up permanent stores, where tobacco could be collected and finished goods sold to the upland farmers and planters. Farther south, the resident merchants in the towns of Charleston and Savannah began to handle the trade of their region in much the same way as did northern merchants.

With the coming of political independence, this personal family business world began to change. The break with Britain disrupted old trading patterns and led to the opening of new areas to American merchants, including the Baltic, the Levant, China, India, and the East Indies. The continuing growth of population and the rapid expansion west into Kentucky and Tennessee, north into Maine, and southwest into Georgia enlarged domestic markets, as did the growing seaport towns themselves. After the outbreak of the wars of the French Revolution, trade with Europe and the West Indies, which had been cut off since the Revolution, again boomed. Far more important, however, for the American economy than the after-effects of the political revolution in France was the advancing industrial revolution in Great Britain. For the new United States became almost overnight the major source of supply of the raw material and the major market for the products of the new machine-made textiles. The coming of these new trades was the most important single factor in bringing specialization to business enterprise and impersonalization into business activities.

Specialization in commerce

Even without the boom in cotton and textiles, specialization in commercial business enterprises certainly would have come to the United States in the fifty years after 1790. Before the Revolution specialization was already appearing in the distribution of goods in New York, Philadelphia, and other large towns. The distinction between merchants and shopkeepers was becoming clear. The former continued to sell at retail as well as at wholesale, but the shopkeepers sold only at retail, buying from the merchants rather than directly from abroad.[9] By 1790, the merchants were also beginning to specialize in certain lines of trade. Specialization was coming, too, in manufacturing in New England, and possibly parts of the middle states, with the beginning of a domestic or "putting-out" system, and the first use of simple machines.[10] Well before the 1790s, shoes, boots, and even furniture were being manufactured for the West Indian and other distant markets by entrepreneurs who "put-out" work into the homes of farmers and town dwellers. Nevertheless, the rapid reorientation and expansion of American commerce and the rapid development of specialized business institutions resulted directly from the new and unprecedented high volume of cotton exports and new machine-made imports.

The impact of cotton on American commerce did not become fully apparent until after 1815, although it had begun to make itself felt in the 1790s. The French Revolution and the Napoleonic Wars kept the older West Indian and European carrying trades booming until 1807. Then, for the next eight years, embargoes, trade restrictions, and wars shut down practically all trade except for a brief period in 1810 and 1811. The wars and wartime commerce overshadowed the rise of the brand new and profoundly significant cotton trade.

As the new cotton textile machinery in Britain went into production, Americans responded quickly.[11] Cotton was first grown commercially in the United States in 1786. By 1793, the year Eli Whitney invented the cotton gin, annual exports were already 488,000 pounds. By 1801, they reached 20.9 million pounds, by 1807, 66.2 million, and by 1810 (the year when trade restrictions were temporarily lifted), 83.8 million. In 1815, 83.0 million pounds exported was valued at $17.5 million. By 1825, the value of cotton exports had risen to $37 million, and by 1840 to $64 million. Between 1821 and 1850, the United States provided over 75 percent of Britain's annual supply of raw cotton. The volume and value of these exports contrast sharply with the modest expansion of the older crops, namely, tobacco, rice, sugar, and wheat. Exports of tobacco, for example, were valued at $8 million in 1815 and only $10 million in 1840.

Cotton brought commercial agriculture to broad regions of the south where, because of climate and soil, other staple crops were unable to grow. Moreover, cotton moved westward in the south a generation before wheat moved west in the north. As the cotton plantations in the lower Mississippi Valley were coming into production, they provided an important initial market to the farmers in the new western settlements at a time when the lack of transportation facilities made it costly to ship whiskey, hogs, horses, and mules to the east or to Europe.[12]

The spread of commercial agriculture in the south encouraged commercial specialization in the east. The unprecedented volume of the cotton trade helped to make New York the nation's leading city and initiated the swift decline of the all-purpose general merchant.[13] The cotton trade was handled increasingly by specialized firms that preferred not to take title to the goods (except when they wanted to speculate) and were instead paid for their services by fixed commissions. Because they had no control over the fluctuating prices set by the international forces of supply and demand, these and other merchants who were becoming specialized disliked the risk of taking title to the goods, preferring the more certain 5 percent commission. For the first time in the United States merchants began to sell much more on commission than on their own account.

The first cotton traders were new rather than existing merchants.[14] In

New York they were at the start agents of British textile firms who came to sell cloth and to make arrangements for obtaining raw cotton. They were soon joined by young men, many of them New Englanders, who began their business life in this trade. New Englanders also went to the south. There they and local merchants in the cotton ports and in the new towns in the interior—Columbia, Augusta, Macon, Montgomery, Jackson, and Natchez—became factors for planters who had recently cleared the land in the rich black belt of Alabama and Georgia and the bottom lands along the Mississippi River.

Although the distinction between commission and commercial houses is often not a clear one, the census figures suggest the importance of the commission business to the foreign trade.[15] In the census of 1840, 381 commission houses and only 24 commercial houses were listed as engaged in foreign trade in Louisiana where commodities completely dominated. For New York (where the commodity trades were major) the division was 1,044 commission houses and 469 commercial houses; in Boston (where such trades were of much less significance), there were 241 commercial houses and only 123 commission houses. By 1840, too, the older, less specialized houses had come to concentrate on cotton or some other commodity and to trade on commission.

The first man in the chain of the new middlemen from the planter to the manufacturer was the cotton factor.[16] He not only marketed the planter's crop, but also purchased his supplies and provided him with credit. Relations between the two were close and personal. In purchasing supplies, equipment, and household goods for the plantation, the factor purchased locally and normally traveled twice a year to buy in New York and other commercial centers of the northeast. In marketing the planter's crop in the impersonal international market, the factor sold directly to the agents of manufacturers or shipped on consignment to other middlemen in nearby river or coastal ports, or to others in New York and other coastal cities, and still others in Liverpool and continental ports. These middlemen, in turn, sold directly or on consignment to manufacturers in the United States as well as in Britain or often to yet another set of middlemen. In addition, the factor made arrangements for the transportation of the crop, the payment of insurance, storage, drayage, and, where necessary, the payment of duties, wharf fees, and the like. On all of these different transactions, he received a commission. And in the process both of buying and of selling, the factor usually made the credit arrangements.

The distribution system was also a credit network, with the credit based on the crop in transit. The cotton trade was financed largely by advances. Cotton moved in one direction and the advances against its shipment in the other. On the American side, as Harold Woodman, the historian of the factor, has written: "Anyone with cotton on hand could easily get an advance from the merchant to whom he chose to consign it, be that merchant in the interior, in the port cities, or in the North, or in Europe." On the British side, a commission merchant in 1833 stated that it was virtually impossible to get goods on consignment without giving advances.[17] These advances were usually from two-thirds to three-fourths the value of the current crop. The providing of advances did, therefore, carry a certain risk, for if the price fell during transit, as it often did while the annual harvest was being completed, the house providing the advance might have to sell at a loss.

The credit system, a complex one, relied on traditional instruments: the promissory note and the bill of exchange. Planters, factors, or river or coastal port merchants were rarely paid in cash but in promissory notes or bills of exchange payable in 60, 90, or even 120 days at 7 or 8 percent interest. If the advance was given before the delivery of the crop, it was made in the form of a promissory note, which was often renewed if it became due before the actual sale was transacted. If the payment was made at the time of delivery, it was made in the form of a bill of exchange, drawn on the house providing the credit. Such transactions were further complicated by the need to convert pounds sterling into dollars. A simple sale, involving two middlemen, could give rise to as many as four different transactions and four different bills of exchange. Woodman provides a revealing example from the correspondence of William Johnson, a Mississippi planter, and his factor, Washington Jackson & Company of New Orleans:

In the 1844–1845 season, Johnson had the New Orleans firm sell part of his cotton in Liverpool through Todd, Jackson and Company, the Liverpool branch of the firm. After shipping his cotton to New Orleans, Johnson drew on Washington Jackson and Company, thereby creating a domestic bill for discount. The New Orleans firm reimbursed itself for this advance by drawing on the Liverpool house after shipping the cotton there, thus creating a second bill for discount. When a sale was made in Liverpool, Todd, Jackson and Company sent a sterling bill for the proceeds over and above the advance drawn upon them. The New Orleans firm sold the sterling bill to a bank for local currency and then authorized Johnson to draw another bill to cover his returns over the advance he had drawn originally.[18]

It was in providing advances and in discounting bills of exchange that the older resident merchants came to play their most important role in the new cotton trade. Some, indeed, soon became specialists in finance. Those with the largest resources became, through the financing of the cotton trade, the most influential businessmen of the day. They were, for the most part, British business houses in Liverpool and London. They stood at the end of the long chain of credit stretching from the banks of the Mississippi to Lombard Street.

In the major ports, the volume of trade was large enough to permit the rise of another type of specialized enterprise—the brokerage house. Not attached to any specific set of clients, it brought together buyers and sellers of cotton for a commission.[19] The basic distinction between the broker and the factor was that the former did not, as did the latter, buy or sell on his principal's account or, more precisely, did not make contracts in his own name that were binding on his principal. The broker's function was to help factors or other merchants or manufacturing agents obtain the cotton necessary to fill out a shipment or order and dispose of odd lots after the completion of a major transaction.

As the farming frontier moved west across the mountains into the Mississippi Valley, a somewhat different network evolved to move provisions (corn, pork, and whiskey), some cotton, and then wheat and other grains from the west to the south and east. Where the soil was tilled by many small farmers rather than a few large planters, the country storekeeper took the place of the plantation factor as the first businessman on the chain of middlemen from the interior to the seaport.[20] These storekeepers, the economic descendants of the pre-Revolutionary Scottish factors in Virginia and of the storekeepers scattered in the interior of colonial Pennsylvania and New England, marketed and purchased for the farmer much as the factors did for the planters. They differed from the factors, however, in that they bought and sold primarily on their own account.

In the early years of western settlement the outgoing crops and the incoming goods moved along different routes. Tobacco, hemp, lead, and produce went down the river to and through New Orleans to the east and the finished goods came westward across the mountains to Pittsburgh and then down the Ohio. Storekeepers, and at first even farmers, accompanied their crops south. In a short time, however, they made arrangements with commission merchants in New Orleans and other river ports —Cincinnati, Louisville, St. Louis, Memphis, and Nashville—to receive their crops and sell them, or to forward them to other merchants, to provide advances, and to send payments.[21] The storekeepers, like the plantation cotton factors, went east normally twice a year to purchase their stocks of finished goods, coffee, tea, sugar, and other staples. There they had to work out complex arrangements for the transportation of their goods west and for their warehousing, drayage, and loading at the different transshipment points along the way. The western storekeepers were soon relying on credit more from the eastern wholesalers from whom they purchased their supplies than from the commission houses through which they sold their produce.

With the opening of the Erie Canal in the mid-1820s and the completion of the Ohio and Pennsylvania canal systems in the next decade, a new trade sprang up, creating still another string of middlemen to handle the transactions and transshipments involved in moving the crops. Prior to 1830, little wheat had been raised in the Mississippi Valley. Tobacco, hemp, provisions, horses, and mules, rather than wheat and flour, were the region's major exports. Then, since the canal provided a shorter route through a cooler part of the country (wheat and flour sent via New Orleans often rotted or soured), production expanded. In 1839 Cleveland received 2.8 million bushels of wheat and flour, or 87 percent more than New Orleans.[22] In the same year, New York received three times as much wheat as New Orleans.

The pattern of specialization in the grain trade followed that of the provisions and cotton trades, yet because of its smaller volume before 1840, it was less systematized and specialized than that of cotton. Cleveland, Buffalo, and other lake ports, including the new village of Chicago, became transshipping centers similar to New Orleans and the other cotton ports. As in the cotton trade, advances and the discounting of notes on goods in transit came to play critical roles in financing the movement of crops. Western millers, storekeepers, local merchants who built warehouses, and occasionally the farmers themselves consigned their grain or flour to commission houses and more specialized freight forwarders in the lake ports, particularly Buffalo. In return they received advances which they usually discounted for cash. The Buffalo merchants, in turn, sent grain to the millers of Rochester, or grain or flour to New York merchants—such as Eli Hart & Company; Suydam, Sage & Company; or Chouteau, Merle & Standford—who had previously provided advances. Whenever the final purchase was not designated, the shipment was sent on to a commission house or appointed agent in the east for final sale.[23] That agent might ship it on consignment to a commission house in Liverpool or Rio de Janeiro for sale on the foreign market. These merchants shipping overseas obtained funds for advances from international merchant banking houses such as the Barings. The grain trade differed from the cotton trade, however, in that it marketed primarily in the United States and therefore was financed by American rather than British capital. Moreover, the trade had hardly been fully established before it was radically transformed in the 1850s by the coming of the railroad and the telegraph. The cotton trade, on the other hand, continued to operate relatively unchanged for several decades.

The rise of specialized commercial enterprise to handle the flow of agricultural products out of the interior to the east and Europe was paralleled by a comparable specialization of enterprise to bring finished goods and staples into the coastal ports and thence to the interior. After 1815, imports of manufactured products—dry goods, metals, hardware, and drugs—grew to an impressive volume. The expanding economy also increased the demand for coffee, tea, sugar, and molasses, products that grew in tropical or semitropical countries, and wines and spirits that were produced in Europe.[24] Before 1815 many of the commission houses which exported cotton also imported a wide variety of goods from Europe and the West Indies. But as the new patterns of trade evolved, they tended to concentrate on cotton exports and a smaller variety of more specialized imports.[25] In importing standardized goods, they increasingly gave way to the specialized importer who purchased directly in Europe and sold to local manufacturers, retailers, and wholesalers. Importers differed from exporters, since they often took title to goods, rather than selling them on consignment or commission.

The experience of Nathan Trotter of Philadelphia provides a good example of the new specialized importer.[26] When Trotter joined a family partnership in 1802, the firm was still importing and exporting a wide variety of goods. During the Napoleonic Wars the partnership concentrated on importing from Europe dry goods, felt, leather, and metals, much of which was reshipped and sold to the West Indies and Latin America. The firm also shipped sugar, molasses, rum, and coffee to the United States and to Europe. Then, in 1816, when Nathan Trotter took over the firm, he began to concentrate on importing a single line of goods —iron, copper, and other metals. These he purchased directly in Britain and northern Europe. As domestic tariffs appeared, raising the price of metals, he began to buy in the United States. He sold some of the more finished goods to local retailers and jobbers. But the largest share of his trade went to traditional artisans (blacksmiths, tinsmiths, and coppersmiths), to artisans who were beginning to specialize in making a single line of goods (stoves, grates, furnaces, lamps, gas fixtures, and steam engines), and to new types of craftsmen (roofers and plumbers). Elsewhere in the metals trade, Trotter's story was paralleled by that of Anson G. Phelps, James Boorman, and Joseph Johnson in New York, and David Reeves and Alfred Hunt in Philadelphia.[27]

In the years after 1815 a new type of specialized middleman appeared in the eastern seaports. This was the jobber who, unlike the importer, purchased at home and who, more than the importer, sold his goods to plantation factors and storekeepers from the south and west. Jobbers were, in the words of an 1829 report of the New York state legislature, "an intermediate grade of merchants, between the wholesale and importing merchants and the retail shopkeepers."[28] They "purchased largely at auctions, at package sales, or wholesale importers, and in other such ways that they can obtain merchandise in reasonable ways." They then broke down large lots into smaller more varied ones, to meet the needs of local retailers and of country storekeepers and plantation factors who made semiannual purchases in their shops.

As the quotation suggests, the rise of the jobber was closely related to the use of auctions in the marketing of imported goods.[29] Auctioning began on a large scale when the British dumped their textiles in New York and, to a lesser extent, other ports upon the reopening of transatlantic trade at the end of the War of 1812. In Philadelphia and Boston established merchants were able to restrict the use of auctions by means of local and state ordinances. In New York similar attempts failed. The extensive use of auctions during the 1820s helped to make New York a mecca for the country trade and brought a concentration of jobbers to that city. Although used primarily in the marketing of textiles, auctions became employed in the other basic trades as well. During the decade 1821–1830 auction sales in New York City amounted to $160 million or 40 percent of the value of that port's total imports and one-fifth of the value of the entire nation's imports. In 1820, for example, out of a total of $10.4 million worth of goods sold at auction in New York, $7.0 million were textiles ($0.7 million of which were American made); $1.9 million groceries, hardware, and drugs; $1.0 million teas, silks, and chinaware from distant seas; and $0.4 million wines and spirits largely from Europe.[30] In the 1830s and 1840s jobbers began to rely less on auctions and began to purchase more directly from agents of manufacturers, at first buying from domestic and then foreign producers.

A check of city directories emphasizes how predominant specialized business enterprise had become by the 1840s in the marketing and distributing of goods in the eastern ports. It also shows in which trades the jobber had become most influential. For example, *Dogget's Directory for New York City in 1846* indicates that the number of specialized business enterprises was highest in dry goods and groceries, with 318 establishments in the first and 221 in the second. China, glass, and earthenware came next with 146, hardware with 91, drugs with 83, wines and spirits with 82, silks and fancy goods with 74, and watches with 40.[31] There were more jobbers than importers in dry goods, groceries, china, glass, and earthenware, and about the same number in drugs and wines and spirits. On the other hand, importers continued to dominate the hardware, fancy dry goods, and clothing trades. All 40 watch dealers were importers. A quick and relatively superficial check of directories in other cities indicates that, until the 1850s, jobbers and importers—that is, wholesalers who took title to their goods instead of selling on commission—were concentrated in the eastern ports of New York, Philadelphia, and Baltimore.

In these many ways the specialized impersonalized world of the jobber, importer, factor, broker, and the commission agent of the river and port towns replaced the personal world of the colonial merchant. Cotton had paced the transformation. The massive exports of the new crop provided payments for greatly expanded imports of manufactured goods and of foods and beverages that could not be grown or produced in this country. The flows in and out of the nation and across the ocean came to be handled by a network of specialized middlemen. Nearly every plantation, farm, and village in the interior came to have direct commercial access to the growing cities of the east as well as to the manufacturing centers of Europe. The output of millions of acres moved every fall over thousands of miles of water. Dry goods from Manchester, hardware from Birmingham, iron from Sweden, the teas of China, and the coffees of Brazil were regularly shipped to towns and villages in a vast region which only a few years before was still wilderness.

This quickly created continental commercial network was coordinated almost entirely by market mechanisms. Goods produced for other than local consumption moved through the national and international economy by a series of market transactions and physical transshipments. The cotton, as it traveled from the plantation to the river ports (Memphis, Natchez, Huntsville, Montgomery, and Augusta), to the coastal ports (New Orleans, Mobile, Savannah, Charleston), to the northeastern ports (New York and Boston), to the continental ports (Liverpool, Le Havre, Hamburg), and finally to the cotton textile manufacturers in New England, old England, and the continent, required at the very least four transactions (between planter, factor, manufacturer's agent, and manufacturer), and often several more. And it passed through at least four transshipments and often several more. Provisions from the west moved south and east through a similar network. Grain from the northwest also went through a comparable number of transactions and transshipments as it traveled from the farmer to the country store, to the interior town, river, or lake port, to the eastern seaport, and then sometimes overseas. The flow of finished goods involved similar sets of buyers, sellers, and shippers in European cities, American seaports, and river towns. The granting of credit and the making of payments required a still different and even more complex set of transactions and flows.

In the agrarian economy of the first decades of the nineteenth century, the flow of goods was closely tied to the planting and harvesting of the crops. The merchants who carried out the commercial transactions and made the arrangements to move the crops out and finished goods in did so in order to make a profit on each transaction or sale. The American economy of the 1840s provides a believable illustration of the working of the untrammeled market economy so eloquently described by Adam Smith.

Specialization in finance and transportation

The expansion of trade in the first decades of the nineteenth century caused business enterprises to specialize in the financing and transportation of goods as well as in their marketing and distribution. Specialization in finance and transportation, unlike that in distribution, led to an important institutional development: the growth of incorporated joint-stock companies. Merchants continued to use the partnership as the legal form for shipping and financing ventures, as they did for their trading firms. Only when they found it advantageous to pool large amounts of capital to improve financial and transportation services by setting up banks, turnpikes, and canals did they turn to the corporation. At first they looked on the corporation as the proper legal form for what they considered to be "private enterprise in the public interest."[32] They used it to provide essential specialized ancillary services to support their profit-making commercial activities. When the pooling of local capital in a corporation was not enough to provide these services, the merchants did not hesitate to seek funds from public sources.

Specialization in finance was a natural concomitant of specialization in other commercial activities. As trade expanded, the older resident general merchants often turned to finance. The alternative was to specialize in trade with more distant regions, particularly China, India, and the East Indies, where the low volume of trade and high value of goods made it possible to continue the old patterns of commerce. For some years after the War of 1812 the Perkinses, Forbeses, and Lees of Boston, and the Griswolds, Howlands, and Grinnells of New York continued to reap profits from these more exotic trades. For most general merchants the old ways were no longer rewarding. They suffered from the same experience as the Browns of Rhode Island. As James B. Hedges has recorded: "The story of the shipping interests of Brown and Ives from 1815 to 1838 is anti-climactic, a doleful story of gradual decline and decay."[33]

For many, the more profitable alternative was to concentrate on finance. John Jacob Astor, Nathaniel Prime, Stephen Girard, Samuel Ward, the Browns of Providence, and the Browns of Baltimore were resident general merchants whose business increasingly became that of granting credit to and discounting exchanges for other merchants.[34] Later,

even successful specialized merchants like Trotter carried on such banking activities. And by the 1820s younger men were entering business as
specialized private bankers and brokers. Fitch & Company of New York,
Thomas Biddle & Company of Philadelphia, and Oelrich & Lurman of
Baltimore were from their beginnings specialized banking enterprises
rather than general mercantile firms.

The most powerful financiers in the American economy after 1815
were, however, those same men who had once held the most influential
partnerships in trade: moving cotton out of and, to a lesser extent, finished
goods into the United States. These were the enterprises that provided
the credit advances so essential to the financing of the cotton trade. As
Britain was the center of finance and had greater capital resources, these
firms were British rather than American. At first they were Liverpool
enterprises, including such firms as Cropper, Benson & Company;
Crowder, Clough & Company; Bolton Ogden & Company; and Rathbone
& Company.[35] After 1820, leading London firms like Baring Brothers and
the three W's (Thomas Wilson & Company, George Wildes & Company, and Thomas Wiggins & Company) entered the trade. The only
American-based firm to become one of the leading Anglo-American
merchant bankers was the Browns of Baltimore, and this firm's central
partnership was housed in Liverpool.

With the merchants and merchant bankers financing interregional and
international movements of trade, the incorporated bank served local
needs. By pooling of local capital in state chartered banks, businessmen
increased sources for long-term loans, based on mortgages, securities,
and even personal promissory notes (if the latter had the additional signa-
ture of a co-maker). In the United States early commercial banks became,
therefore, more providers of long and medium capital needs than sources
of short-term commercial loans. As one British commentator noted in
1837 about American banks: "Their rule is our exception, our rule their
exception. They prefer accommodation paper, resting on personal security and fixed wealth, to real bills of exchange, resting on wealth in
transition from merchants and manufacturers to consumers."[36] In addition
state chartered banks issued bank notes which became the standard circulating medium in the United States. This was because the United States
government issued almost no paper money until 1862 and only a limited
amount of coin and because bills of exchange were not as abundant as they
were in Europe where they served as the basic medium of exchange. Banks
provided other services. They were relatively safe places to deposit funds.
Their stock could be purchased as an investment at a time when investment opportunities in other than land and nonliquid assets were limited.
Finally, by incorporating a bank, local merchants were able to turn over

the day-to-day work in providing specialized financial services to a full-time salaried employee, who usually had the title of cashier.

The need for such services was strong enough to bring the incorporated bank quickly to all parts of the nation. The first was the Bank of North America in Philadelphia chartered in 1781. In 1790, six more banks were operating in the major American ports: New York, Philadelphia, Boston, Baltimore, and Charleston. In 1791, Congress approved Alexander Hamilton's proposal for a federally chartered bank with headquarters in Philadelphia and branches in the larger towns. The chartering of banks boomed in the 1790s and again after the charter of the First Bank of the United States expired in 1811. Between 1811 and 1815 the number increased from 88 to 206.[37] With the expansion of the economy after 1815, the number jumped again. In 1816 alone, 40 banks were chartered, and by 1820 there were 307. In the late 1820s and the early 1830s, a period during which the Second Bank of the United States was providing excellent services, the number leveled off. In those two decades, however, local banking business had expanded enough to encourage the opening of even more specialized financial institutions in the United States, including savings banks and trust companies.[38]

By 1830, the Second Bank of the United States was not only providing high quality local banking services but also operating on a national and indeed international scale. For a brief period it competed most successfully with the merchant bankers in the financing of the flow of domestic and international trade. It did so because it was the only commercial institution to have a number of branches—twenty-two located in all parts of the country by 1830. No other financial institution operated on this scale. Merchant bankers often had interlocking partnerships but these partnerships rarely operated in more than three commercial centers. Merchant bankers continued to handle their business in distant ports almost wholly through correspondents, other merchants who were paid by commission.

Nicholas Biddle, who became the Second Bank's president in 1823, fully appreciated the value of using its branches to finance American trade. He realized that the branches provided an administrative network that permitted the transfer of funds and credit throughout the country by means of a series of accounting transactions between branches controlled and supervised by the Philadelphia headquarters. He indicated how this was accomplished when he described the activities of the New Orleans branch to a congressional committee in 1832.

The course of the western business is to send the produce to New Orleans, to draw bills on the proceeds, which bills are purchased at the various branches, and remitted to the branch at New Orleans. When the notes issued by the several branches find their way in the course of trade to the Atlantic branches, the western branches pay the Atlantic branches by drafts on their funds accumulated at the branch at New Orleans, which pay the Atlantic branches by bills growing out of the purchases made in New Orleans on account of the northern merchants or manufacturers, thus completing the circle of operations. This explains the large amount of business done at that branch.[39]

Foreign exchanges were handled in much the same way. Payments made by the British and Europeans for American cotton and other commodities were deposited, normally with London merchant bankers, and became the source of funds and credit for American merchants purchasing goods abroad. The Second Bank is an early and highly successful example of the administrative coordination of monetary flows. Such coordination permitted Biddle to increase the bank's domestic exchange business from $1.8 million a month in 1823, to $5.02 million in 1828, and $22.6 million in 1832. At the same time, the bank came to dominate the nation's foreign exchange business.[40]

The Second Bank was, however, short-lived. Its concentrated economic power and its role as the federal government's banker made its activities and even its very existence a major political issue. In 1832, Andrew Jackson vetoed a bill to recharter the bank in 1836. The veto, which probably helped to re-elect Jackson to the presidency, assured the end of the Second Bank of the United States. After its demise in 1836, merchants, particularly the more specialized merchant bankers, continued to finance the long-distance trades. The state incorporated banks continued to serve local communities and domestic trade, increasing in number from 506 in 1834 to 901 in 1840. The Barings, the Browns, and a small number of lesser survivors handled the financing of a major portion of American imports and exports after the financial panics of 1837 and 1839 destroyed several of the British merchant banking houses, including the three W's.[41]

The history of insurance companies in the United States parallels closely that of the state incorporated banks. By pooling resources in an incorporated insurance company, resident merchants, importers, exporters, and a growing number of specialized shipping enterprises were able to get cheaper insurance rates. At the same time, salaried employees of the new insurance firms (appraisers and inspectors) could concentrate on the more technical and routine aspects of the business. Again, as in the case of banks, the insurance companies provided a source for long-term loans, primarily based on mortgages, and their stocks were held as investments. Their number grew quickly. The first American company to insure ships and their cargoes was incorporated in 1792. By 1800, there were twelve marine insurance companies in the United States and by 1807, forty.[42] As in the case of the banks, the numbers leveled off in the 1820s, with New

York supporting around twenty and other ports a somewhat smaller number. Nearly all these companies handled only the business of local shippers and ship owners. Fire insurance was slower in developing. Until the great New York fire of 1835, fire insurance was written on a small local scale, often by marine insurance companies. As for life insurance, scarcely a handful of firms operated in the United States before the mid-1840s, when the first mutual life insurance company was formed. Only after the country began to industrialize and urbanize rapidly did the issuing of life insurance become a significant business.

In the early years of the republic, merchants regarded transportation companies as they did financial institutions. They were primarily vehicles for providing services vital to the furtherance of their commercial activities. The incorporation of turnpike and canal companies made possible the pooling of capital required to improve overland rights of way. And when the capital pooled by incorporation was not enough to complete the new overland rights-of-way, American businessmen quickly turned to local, state, and national governments for the necessary funds. On the other hand, they rarely suggested that the government operate the common carriers that used the turnpikes and canals. These enterprises continued to be operated by individuals and partnerships but not by corporations.

In the colonial period, the only common carriers (that is, enterprises specializing wholly in transporting goods and passengers, with services available to any user) were a small number of ferries, stagecoaches, and wagon lines. The stagecoaches, carrying passengers and mail, but very little freight, ran on the most informal schedules. The wagon lines were even more unscheduled. Teamsters, usually located in country towns, picked up loads from storekeepers and brought them to the larger ports. There the teamsters waited until the city merchant had a return shipment to their home towns. This method continued to be used until the early 1830s even in Philadelphia, a city whose large hinterland was served by the best turnpike system in the nation.

As the roads were relatively few and travel over them a bone-shaking experience, most passengers and nearly all freight moved by water. The most impressive growth of common carriers came, therefore, in the development of shipping lines on waterways. During the colonial period, there were no common carriers on water routes except for an occasional ferry. Merchants who owned or who had shares in ships often "rented" space to other merchants. The former, however, were under no obligation to carry another merchant's goods and did so only when they themselves had no need of the space. Moreover, in the eighteenth century, ships did not follow any specific schedules or ply between two termini. They normally moved between regions, such as between New England or the middle colonies and the West Indies or between these colonies and Great Britain or southern Europe. Within these areas the ships went from port to port as trading opportunities appeared.[43]

As the transatlantic trade expanded, ships became "regular traders" running between ports, say New York and Liverpool, or Philadelphia and London.[44] And as ships became regular traders, merchants began to meet their carrying needs by chartering rather than by building or purchasing vessels. They were soon relying on the services of a regular ship's agent or husband who owned and operated several vessels.[45] The ship's husband made arrangements with merchants, received and loaded cargoes, laid down the ship's route, and arranged for payment of customs and port duties. These services were developed so swiftly and so effectively for the cotton trade that by the 1820s the leading mercantile firms handling the flow of cotton to Liverpool owned no ships of their own.[46]

The step from the regular trader to the scheduled packet line came quickly. In January 1818, a small number of close associates in the cotton and textile trade who owned four regular traders decided to operate them between New York and Liverpool on a regular schedule departing on stated days and at stated times. This enterprise, the Black Ball Line, soon had its imitators. By 1822, two other packet lines were running between New York and Liverpool and the year before one had started between Philadelphia and that British port. Within a short time, sailing packet lines appeared on coastal routes south from New York and Philadelphia, to Charleston, Savannah, Mobile, and New Orleans, and north to the New England ports. The merchants who started these lines soon became shipping specialists, or else they sold their interest in the lines to specialists who owned and operated these sailing ships.

Steamships were not used on the high seas until the 1840s. On rivers, lakes, and bays they ran from the beginning on regular routes and, when carrying passengers, on some sort of schedule, although unscheduled tramps became common on the Mississippi.[47] Because the steamboat was a new and patented invention, the early lines were less the promotions of merchants and more those of inventors and their financial backers. The country's first steamboat line was set up by inventor Robert Fulton and his financial supporter Robert Livingston after the successful trial run of the Clermont on the Hudson in 1807. For some years, the two were able to maintain a monopoly in New York, but they had no success in preventing competition on the western waters, where one of their boats made its first run from Pittsburgh to New Orleans in 1813.

After 1815, the number of steamboats on the western rivers grew swiftly, from fourteen (totaling 3,290 tons) in 1817 to sixty-nine (totaling

13,890 tons) just over three years later. Even before 1824, when the Supreme Court in the case of *Gibbons v. Ogden* brought to an end the Fulton-Livingston monopoly, steamboats had appeared on Long Island Sound and other eastern sounds, bays, and rivers and, to a lesser extent, on Lake Erie. After the court's decision, steamboat lines boomed in the east. One of the most aggressive operators was Cornelius Vanderbilt, who had been Gibbons' captain on a New York to New Brunswick line before and during the famous case. As canals came to be built in the 1820s and 1830s, similar canal boat lines, powered, of course, by horses and mules rather than by steam, came into being.

In building these canals, and the turnpikes as well, Americans increasingly relied on state funding.[48] The early turnpikes in New England and the middle states were built and maintained by private corporations. But those constructed somewhat later in the south and west, and also in Pennsylvania, were state funded and often state maintained projects. The few canals built before 1820—the Middlesex Canal connecting Boston and the Merrimack and the Blackstone connecting Providence and Worcester being the most important—were also privately financed and maintained. It was only after the completion in 1825 of New York's great Erie Canal connecting the eastern and western waters that canal construction became popular in the United States. Then the merchants of the other Atlantic ports began to insist on having their own connections with the west. In the west, businessmen wanted to connect the lakes with the Ohio and Mississippi rivers. Far too costly to be financed by local capital, even if pooled through incorporation, the new canal systems of Pennsylvania, Maryland, Virginia, and Ohio were financed almost wholly by the states and the port cities. Their operation then became managed by representatives of these political bodies. Only a government had the credit rating needed to raise the required funds; for their ability to pay interest on their bonds was based on the power to tax, as opposed to private corporations, which depended merely on anticipated profits from providing rights-of-way. The one significant exception to public construction was the system of canals built in eastern Pennsylvania to transport anthracite coal to the tidewater. However, the private corporations carrying out these projects were able to attract investors on the basis of the natural resources they controlled, rather than from expected toll profits.

Again except for the coal canals, the private corporations building and maintaining the canals and turnpikes rarely operated the transportation lines that used them. The states never did. The stage and wagon lines using the new turnpikes differed little from those of colonial days; and the canal boat lines ran in much the same fashion as did other shipping enterprises. Some held to schedules; others moved when they had full loads.

The first canal lines were organized by merchants who needed the facilities to transport their goods. But they quickly came to be owned and operated by specialists. The freight forwarders were (writes Harry Scheiber of those on the Ohio canals) "men engaged in the transportation business only, including small-scale operators of one or two boats as well as owners of large fleets, maintaining regular through-freight arrangements with the Erie Canal, Pennsylvania Mainline and river boat lines."[49]

These specialized ancillary enterprises—the merchant bankers and the incorporated bank; insurance, turnpike, and canal companies; the ship's husbands; the scheduled shipping lines; and the freight forwarders—all facilitated the flow of goods through the economy. They made it easier for the merchants to specialize in handling one set of products and functions and to carry out their specialized tasks more efficiently. They helped to create at that time one of the world's most effective "transaction sectors," to use a term of Douglass North. The number of transactions, the volume of goods moved, and the speed and distances carried were as great as any in history.[50] The efficiency of this sector must have played an important role in maintaining the per capita income of Americans at a time when the population was growing fast.[51] It must have been critical in sustaining the continued economic development of the country in the decades before 1840.

Nevertheless, by modern standards the movement and distribution of goods were hardly efficient. Many transactions and transshipments were required to move a single shipment from the producer to the ultimate consumer. The flow of goods was slow and its pace irregular. The movement of goods still depended on the vagaries of wind and weather. A sailing ship could leave on schedule but one could never predict the precise time of arrival. A transatlantic voyage might take from three weeks to three months. Droughts and freshets delayed shipments along rivers and canals in the summer, spring, and fall. Winter freezes stopped movement of goods completely for several months in all but the southern parts of the country. Snows isolated even the largest cities for days, and heavy rains kept smaller interior towns and villages mud-bound for weeks.

Of even more significance, the movement of goods still relied, as it had for centuries, on wind and animal power. The traditional transportation technologies offered little opportunity for improvement. By 1840 the speed of a stagecoach, canal boat, or sailing ship, or the volume carried by these facilities, could not be substantially increased by improving their design. By 1840 steam power was just beginning to be used in overland transportation. (The nation's first railroads only began to go into operation in the 1830s.) And steamboats were still used only on quiet rivers, bays, and lakes. They were not yet technologically advanced enough to be employed in the coastal or transatlantic trades. In 1840, well over 90 percent of the Post Office's mail routes were still dependent on the horse.[52] New technology had not yet lifted the age-old constraints on the speed a given amount of goods might be moved over a given distance. Such constraints, in turn, put a ceiling on the volume of activity a commercial enterprise was called upon to handle.

Managing the specialized enterprise in commerce

Because of these technological constraints on the speed and volume of moving goods through the economy, not even the rapid expansion of that economy and its resulting specialization in business activities brought specialization within the business enterprise itself. Nor did the expanding economy lead to the integration of several operating units into a single large firm. No managerial hierarchies appeared. The size of business enterprise did not grow beyond traditional limits. Its internal administration continued to be carried out along traditional lines. Therefore, although the increased volume of American commerce brought modifications and improvements of existing business methods, instruments, and institutions, it did not stimulate the invention of new ones.

Until well after 1840 the partnership remained the standard legal form of the commercial enterprise and double-entry bookkeeping its basic accounting system. The partnership, normally a family affair, consisted of two or three close associates. It was a contractual arrangement that was changed when a partner retired, died, or decided to go into another business or join another associate. A partnership was often set up for a single voyage or venture. And one man could be involved in several partnerships. The partnership was used by all types of business, from the small country storekeepers to the great merchant bankers who dominated the Anglo-American trade.

The most powerful business enterprises of the day were international interlocking partnerships. Thus, the Brown family was represented by Brown, Shipley & Company in Liverpool; Brown Brothers & Company in New York; Browns and Bowen in Philadelphia; and Alexander Brown & Sons in Baltimore. The Ogden New York connection was Ogden, Ferguson & Company; the Liverpool representative, Bolton, Ogden & Company.[53] The name and makeup of all these interlocking partnerships changed constantly over time. Even John Jacob Astor's American Fur Company, one of the few incorporated commercial enterprises, remained a partnership. Astor held the large majority of the shares in this company. His partners received payments from profits in accordance with the number of shares held. The contractual arrangements between partners in incorporated companies were for a specific period of time, usually five years. In the case of the American Fur Company, the partners and shares held changed at each renewal. Except in forming enterprises that provided supplementary services requiring the pooling of capital (namely banks, insurance, turnpike, and canal companies), American merchants did not yet feel the need for a legal form that could give an enterprise limited liability, the possibility of eternal life, or the ability to issue securities. Even when an enterprise was incorporated it remained a small single-unit firm run in a highly personal manner. In the commercial capitalism of the 1840s, owners managed and managers owned their enterprises.

Not even in New York City, which by 1840 was one of the most active commercial centers in the world, was the press of business enough to cause a merchant to delegate any of his tasks. J. A. Scoville, a New York merchant and chronicler of his class, indicates the pace and nature of a merchant's activities by sketching a particularly busy day:

To rise early in the morning, to get breakfast, to go down town to the counting house of the firm, to open and read letters—to go out and do some business, either at the Custom house, bank or elsewhere, until twelve, then to take a lunch and a glass of wine at Delmonico's; or a few raw oysters at Downing's; to sign checks and attend to the finances until half past one; to go on change; to return to the counting house, and remain until time to go to dinner, and in the old time, when such things as "packet nights" existed, to stay down town until ten or eleven at night, and then go home and go to bed.[54]

Inside the counting house—the term first used by the Italians for a merchant's office—a business was carried on in much the same manner as it had been in fourteenth-century Venice or Florence. The staff included only a handful of male clerks.[55] There were two or three copiers, a book-keeper, a cash keeper, and a confidential clerk who handled the business when the partners were not in the office. Often partners became responsible for handling one major function. At N. L. & G. Griswold, one of the most active of the older New York mercantile partnerships, one brother was responsible for the buying and shipping of goods, and the other took care of financial affairs. The organization and coordination of work in such an office could easily be arranged in a personal daily conversation.[56]

The partners' task was, of course, to initiate and carry out the commercial transactions involved in the buying, selling, and shipping of goods. Transactions with local businessmen were negotiated in the counting house or on the merchants' exchange, a building designated as a place to carry out such business dealings. For those carried out in distant commercial centers, partners had to rely on their correspondents, merchants with whom they contracted to do their work on a commission. If the partnership still owned or chartered ships, its ship captains or supercargoes, who usually owned shares and were partners in the voyage or venture, handled the transactions. Although merchants wrote long and detailed letters of instruction to correspondents, captains, or supercargoes, they had little control over the actions and decisions of their agents in distant ports or on distant seas. Letters took weeks and sometimes months to reach their destinations. Only the man on the spot knew how to adjust to changing local market conditions. For these reasons the choice of agent had been for centuries one of the most important decisions a merchant had to make. Since loyalty and honesty were still more important than business acumen, even the more specialized merchants continued to prefer to have sons or sons-in-law, or men of long acquaintance, as partners or agents handling their business in a distant city.

The specialization of business in the early nineteenth century actually eased the merchant's tasks. He handled more transactions and dealt with more suppliers and customers than did the older general merchants, but the transactions were more of the same kind and with men in much the same business. Transactions became increasingly routinized and systematized. Information on a single trade in a few ports was easier to come by than that for many trades in many ports. Specialization in this way reduced transactions and information costs.

The function of a merchant's system of accounts was to record the transactions he carried out. The most advanced accounting methods in 1840 were still those of Italian double-entry bookkeeping—techniques which had changed little over five hundred years. The major difference between the accounting practices of colonial merchants and those of the more specialized mercantile firms of the nineteenth century was that the larger number of transactions handled by the latter caused them to keep their books in more meticulous manner.

There were still three standard accounting books used.[57] Actual transactions were recorded in the day, work, or waste book at the time that they were made. At the end of each month these figures were transferred to the journal where accounts for sums paid out or goods sold were credited and the goods and monies received were debited. This chronological record of transactions was, in turn, transferred to appropriate accounts in the ledger including those for "adventures" or voyages, for "vessels," for "commodities," as well as those for each individual or firm having transactions with the enterprise. Often, too, there were "merchandise" accounts for miscellaneous items carried in smaller quantities as well as pages for "notes receivable," "notes payable," and "commission sales." Under the normal accounting practices of the day, the partners' household effects and property were also included in the list of assets.[58] The ledger was generally "balanced" by "being closed to profit and loss" at the end of each year. Such closings were often made at the end of a voyage or planting season, or when a partnership was being dissolved. The resulting profit was then listed for each partner in proportion to his share in the business.

Accounts of the traditional enterprise provided a historical record of financial transactions, together with information essential for orderly housekeeping routine. As stated in one of the most widely used late-eighteenth-century texts on accounting: "A merchant . . . ought to know, by inspecting books, to whom he owes, and who owes him, what goods he purchased; what he has disposed of, with the gain or loss upon the sale, and what ready money he has by him; what his stock was at first; what alterations and changes it has suffered since, and what it now amounts to."[59] If he were acting as a factor or an agent, his accounts for his principal should show: "What commissions he has received, how he has disposed of them, what returns he has made, what of his employer's goods are yet in his hands, or in the hands of debtors."

By checking his accounts a merchant knew his operating income and outgo and the working capital he had on hand, but he would have found it difficult to calculate his net gain or loss. From the special "venture," commodities, and ship accounts, he could determine the outcome of single ventures, ships, or commodities, but only by utilizing information from a number of interrelated accounts. The Olivers of Baltimore, for example, followed standard practice when they listed the value of cargo, insurance, and loading expense in the venture accounts, and the cost of a ship and its outfitting and insurance under a separate account.[60] Their commodity accounts listed price received and paid, but often included certain expenses as well. All three accounts—venture, vessel, and commodity—were closed separately to profit and loss. These merchants made no attempt to determine the precise cost, say, of shipping coffee from a given Latin American port to Baltimore. Not surprisingly, then, early and even mid-nineteenth-century texts on accounting said practically nothing about cost accounting or capital accounting, but concentrated almost wholly on the proper way to record financial transactions.[61]

One reason merchants made so little effort to analyze their costs was because such information could have little effect on their business decisions. Since commodity prices fluctuated, a look at the past year's records could tell little about next year's gains. Prices were set by current supply and demand. Markets could be quickly glutted, and sources of supplies and commodities just as quickly depleted. The business information the merchants wanted came from external sources not internal records. To quote Stuart Bruchey: "Experience was of far lesser importance than fresh news."[62]

In the early nineteenth century, therefore, businessmen were more innovative in reducing information and transactions costs than in refining traditional accounting practices or developing new ones.[63] The existing exchanges in the older commercial cities set up rules and regulations to further routinize transactions. The merchants in the new centers organized their exchanges along the same lines as earlier American exchanges, which were patterned after those set up in Holland and Britain centuries earlier. The demand for fresh news contributed to the success of the packet lines. It caused merchants to press for faster mail service which was steadily improved after reforms in the postal system in the Jacksonian administration.[64] In the 1830s, too, shipping and mercantile firms built private semaphore systems at various landfalls for relaying messages from incoming ships to counting houses in the port cities.

This mercantile demand for quicker, cheaper information was reflected in the nature of American newspapers.[65] Until 1815 the small number of newspapers had been more political than commercial organs. Then as they grew in number they began to devote an increasing amount of space to commercial news. Besides listing ship arrivals, departures, sales, auctions, and prices, they also included advertisements of merchants, giving types, amounts, and prices of goods for sale. The very names of the papers indicate what had become their primary function: *The Commercial Advertiser*, *The Mercantile Advertiser*, and *The Journal of Commerce* in New York City; the *Daily Advertiser* and *Commercial Gazette* in Boston; the *North American Advertiser* and the *Commercial and Maritime Register* in Philadelphia. By the 1830s, *Prices Current* and *Shipping Lists* were published in those three cities as well as in Baltimore and New Orleans. Similar to those first printed in Amsterdam in the early sixteenth century, the papers gave prices of a wide variety of goods and commodities and listed the shipping movements in local ports.

By adopting and perfecting long-established business institutions and procedures, American merchants lowered transactions and information costs and further reduced the cost of distributing goods in the United States. Improved market mechanisms permitted "the invisible hand" of market forces to coordinate and monitor more effectively the flow of goods through the economy. American merchants, however, felt no need to alter the ancient ways of doing business.

Managing the specialized enterprise in finance and transportation

In managing the specialized enterprise in transportation and finance, American businessmen were somewhat more innovative, although their practices did not differ greatly from those of their British and Dutch predecessors. In the operation of private banking firms and shipping lines, they continued to use the partnership form and the same types of internal record keeping used in mercantile firms. Even more than the British, however, they made use of incorporated joint-stock companies to organize and operate enterprises calling for a pooling of capital. In these firms one or two full-time salaried managers, rather than the owners, came to administer the enterprise.

In incorporated banks, the cashier and sometimes the president was a full-time executive. From the start he was responsible for the routine activities involved—handling withdrawals, paying and receiving interest, and redeeming notes and loans. At first the board of directors, consisting of local merchants and manufacturers, made decisions, in consultation with the cashier, on those matters which required business judgment and discretion. These included making loans on mortgages and other securities or even discounting bills of exchange based on goods in transit.[66] Because board members were busy with their own affairs, these decisions were soon turned over to committees of the board which met weekly or often only once a month. Normally such committees were established to review discounts, exchange, and dividends. It was not long before the full-time cashier or president took over the making of loans, dividends, and the like, with the committees becoming little more than ratifying bodies.

Because bank cashiers and presidents were responsible for other peoples' money, they had to have a more accurate and continuing current view of their enterprise's financial situation than did the merchants themselves. Traditional double-entry bookkeeping, however, proved quite satisfactory in recording their banking transactions.[67] The journal provided a chronological record of all daily transactions. The ledger listed the separate accounts of individuals dealing with the bank and, in addition, had separate accounts for deposits, withdrawals, discounts, loans, bills in circulation, bills of other banks held, amounts deposited in other banks, capital stock paid in, specie and other reserves, cash on hand, profit and loss, and dividends. Instead of annual balances the banks made monthly ones. By the first years of the nineteenth century, monthly balances were already being summarized in tabular form. The systematic tabulation and review of the accounts of banks were further encouraged by state legislation. Massachusetts, for example, as early as 1792, required its banks to make semiannual reports to its governor and Council of the Commonwealth. In 1806, the legislature called for monthly reports.[68] Yet, while the banks kept a close watch on their general accounts, they did not seem to use this information in making policy decisions such as increasing or decreasing specie or other reserves, expanding or contracting notes, or even changing the mix between mortgage and commercial paper. These decisions appeared to have been made almost entirely on evaluation of current business conditions and the personal knowledge of the borrowers and markets.

Much of what has been said about the management of banks before 1840 applies to insurance companies as well. They too, found double-entry bookkeeping quite adequate for their needs.[69] The day books, journals, and ledgers listed the individuals who paid premiums and received payments. In addition, they listed amounts invested or loaned out to firms, and the "disaster books" enumerated the details of each major casualty. Since a month-to-month knowledge of the company's financial situation was less important, and since states did not require monthly reports, these accounts were not summarized as regularly as those of banks.

As in the case of banks, insurance companies also were administered by salaried managers, usually a president, secretary, and inspector.[70] These men came to make important decisions even earlier than did bank cashiers, for the setting of insurance rates required specialized knowledge. To help provide such information, New York insurance firms in 1820 organized the first Board of Underwriters in the United States, which set rates for ships, cargoes, and even prospective freight earnings between New York and other ports throughout the world. Insurers in other cities soon had their Boards of Underwriters. In determining rates, these boards concentrated on obtaining, in Robert G. Albion's words, "the freshest information possible, since that was highly essential to the business." With such information, insurance executives were able to consider the age and condition of the ship, the reputation of the masters, and other factors in setting rates. Success in insurance depended even more than it did in banking on outside information rather than on accurate and detailed internal accounting.

Of all the financial institutions operating in the first half of the nineteenth century, the Second Bank of the United States was the most complex to administer. It involved the management of not one but many units. Its numerous branches made it the first prototype of modern business enterprise in American commerce. During the brief period when it played a dominant role in the financing of American long-distance trade, it carried on a huge volume of business for its day. In January 1832 the bank had loans outstanding on real estate and other personal securities at $49.7 million.[71] Its domestic exchange accounts amounted that month to $16.7 million. In addition, it held $2.1 million worth of real estate acquired from foreclosed mortgages. In January 1833 its *monthly* profit on loan and domestic exchange reached $1.8 million. It did more business in a month than leading mercantile houses did in a year. For example, the consolidated profits of the five senior partners in the several interlocking units of the house of Brown, the largest American mercantile house, were for 1831 and 1832, $391,465 and $393,541.

Nevertheless, a very small number of men had little difficulty in managing this high volume of business. The Second Bank's president, Nicholas Biddle, had only two assistants.[72] One reviewed and coordinated the bank's exchange business, the other was responsible for suspended and other unpaid debts, and for the bank's real estate holdings of foreclosed mortgages. Biddle and these two salaried managers supervised the work of the cashiers of the twenty-two branches. These cashiers were salaried managers who were selected by and were subject to dismissal by Biddle. The tiny headquarters staff reviewed the detailed weekly statements sent in by the cashiers, made regular inspection trips, and took action on the evaluation of the information they received. Biddle, after consulting with his assistants, met with his board of directors to set up general policies for the bank as a whole. He did not, however, have comparable contact with local boards of directors who worked with the local cashiers in managing their branches. These autonomous local boards could and often did act on their own. The volume of business carried on by the biggest and most powerful financial institution of the day was not yet large enough to require the creation of a managerial hierarchy.

Nor was this the case in transportation. As has been emphasized, two types of transportation enterprises appeared in the early nineteenth century: common carriers that moved goods and packages, and turnpike and canal companies that built and maintained rights-of-way. The first were operated by partnerships; the second by a corporation or by the state. Until the 1840s, the investment in sailing ships, steamboats, canal boats, stagecoaches, and wagons remained small enough to be easily funded by a small number of partners. On the Mississippi and on other western waters, Louis Hunter has pointed out, "the construction costs of a single mile of a well-built railroad was enough to pay for a new and fully equipped steamboat of average size."[73] By 1840 the normal Mississippi steamboat cost about $30,000 and the largest, most elaborate ones ran as high as $60,000. The initial cost of steamboats on the Hudson River and Long Island Sound was about the same. The largest and best appointed vessels in Commodore Cornelius Vanderbilt's fleet ran about $60,000.[74] Crews on the river and sound steamboats included a captain and a mate (the only two supervisory personnel) and averaged just over twenty hands. Occasionally crews ran as high as fifty. Half of these were involved in serving passengers. The annual operating expenses of a Mississippi steamboat, Hunter estimates, were one and one-quarter to two times initial cost.[75] The initial costs of the fast and rugged packets, the most expensive of the sailing ships on the transatlantic run, were somewhat more than the river and sound steamboats. Robert Albion estimates that the packet boats were built in the 1820s at about $30,000 apiece. In the 1830s they cost over $40,000 and approached $100,000 by the end of the 1840s.[76] The crews on the Atlantic sailing ships were larger and operating expenses were somewhat higher than those on the steamboats plying river and sound. The expenses of manning and operating freight barges and packet boats on the canals were, of course, much less. The most elaborate canal packet, fully furnished, cost $1,500. It was manned by a crew of seven and pulled by two horses.[77] Stagecoaches and wagons were even less expensive to build and operate.

Normally steamboats on rivers, lakes, bays, and sounds, the ocean-going sailing ships, and even the horse-drawn canal boats were owned by more than one individual. On the Mississippi in 1830 the majority of steamboats were owned by two to four businessmen (56.8 percent, while 18.9 percent were owned by single individuals and 24.3 percent had five or more owners).[78] The pattern was much the same in the coastal and transatlantic trades. The owners on river or ocean were normally merchants in river ports and seaports who benefited by having their carriers available. The ship's captain was usually one of the owners, so too was the line's business manager, and, in the case of tramps, the ship's husband.

Before the 1840s these transportation enterprises operated a relatively small number of ships or vehicles. Most freight-carrying sailing ships, steamboats, and even canal boats were tramps moving only when they had a load, but following fairly regular routes. The scheduled packet lines on all waterways were loosely organized affairs. On the Mississippi, boats participating in a shipping line were owned separately and, except for maintaining a schedule, were operated independently.[79] Even these schedules were subject to repeated changes. In the east, the Hudson River Steamboat Association, which Vanderbilt effectively challenged in the 1830s, was a similar organization. Few of these lines ever operated more than three or four ships on one route. Vanderbilt himself, who became one of the largest and most successful steamship operators in the country, rarely ran more than four ships at one time.[80] The transatlantic packet lines normally operated four ships, but some occasionally had as many as eight.[81]

On the canals, some freight forwarders owned fleets of a dozen or more boats. Rarely, however, were the total expenses of obtaining and operating such fleets as much as those of a single steamship or a mile of railroad.[82] Very few lines remained permanent enterprises, since partners changed and ships serviced different routes and trades. Traditional double-entry bookkeeping was adequate for their operating needs. Throughout the first half of the nineteenth century common carriers were operated by small personal enterprises whose management was similar to that of other commercial firms.

On the other hand, a great deal more money and many more men were required to build and operate the overland rights-of-way—the turnpikes and the canals. Also, much more capital, professional skill, and specialized management were needed for the canals than for the turnpikes. On a canal a professional engineer had to lay out the route of a canal, estimate its cost, supervise construction, and, once built, repair and maintain the right-of-way. The engineer in charge of construction usually reported to a board of directors or a state canal commission. After he had located the route and estimated the cost, he normally continued to advise the board or the commission on the writing of contracts. He then kept his eye on the construction done by contractors who were hired by the corporation or the state.[83]

Before the 1840s turnpikes and canals, even the largest of them, were built by small contractors, who at first were local farmers, merchants, and even professional men. They built one or two short stretches of a project, using local labor.[84] Only on the Chesapeake and Ohio was imported labor used to any significant degree. By the mid-1830s some small contractors had become specialists, moving from place to place as new projects were undertaken. They ran their businesses much as did the merchants and shippers of the day. "Contractors often formed partnerships," the historian of the Ohio canal system has noted, "and one man might have different partners for each of several bids on various jobs."[85]

The operations of a turnpike or canal required a far smaller work force and far less working capital than did the construction. Toll keepers, lock tenders, and other operating employees were usually supervised directly by the corporate board or state commission; maintenance crews reported to a salaried manager, often a trained engineer, who was in turn responsible to the board or commission.[86]

The management of the nation's largest and one of the earliest canals, the Erie, set the pattern for others. A board of five canal commissioners appointed by and responsible to the New York state legislature administered the canal. Of these five, three were "acting commissioners" each with special responsibility for one of the canal's three geographical divisions. A fourth was the state comptroller, traditionally a leading politician who controlled and allocated state patronage. The fifth had no specific duties. The commissioners set tolls and regulations for boats and cargoes, hired employees, and were responsible for allocating funds for construction and repair. However, they left the financing of new construction and the handling of profits made by the enterprise to still another board, the commissioners of the canal fund, headed by the state comptroller. Until

1840, all employees, except those involved in maintenance and construction, reported to the comptroller. These toll collectors, inspectors of boats, weigh masters, and lock tenders were expected to keep the comptroller, in the words of the canal's most recent historian, Ronald E. Shaw, "informed of breaks in the canal, the progress of repairs, the balances of canal deposits in local banks, conflicts with local authorities, and infractions of the rules and penalties imposed."[87]

Employees must have reported to the comptroller on monies received and spent. The canal commissioners apparently did not develop any systematic reporting or auditing of accounts kept by the toll keepers and other employees. One commissioner angrily complained in 1833 to the comptroller that: "In the history of public expenditures I do not believe there is such an instance of want of system and accountability."[88] Nor were the relations between the operating employees and the repair crews clearly defined. One or two repair crews of from five to ten men working from a "State skow" reported to the acting commissioner responsible for their division. At the same time, the canal engineer and his subordinate resident engineers (there was one for each division) were responsible for major construction and repair.

The only significant administrative change on the Erie Canal came in 1841 when the comptroller—a post held by such eminent politicians as William L. Marcy, Silas Wright, and Azariah C. Flagg—was relieved of his supervisory duties. These were handed over to a Canal Department which consisted of a chief clerk and four assistants.[89] Even the members of this tiny group and the canal engineer and his three division engineers, who together formed the total managerial force of the canal, had little permanency. All jobs on the canal continued to be patronage at the disposal of the party in power. "Every shift in political power in the state," Shaw emphasizes, "brought new engineers, collectors, weigh masters, boat inspectors, superintendents, and lock tenders to the entire line of the canal."[90]

The management of the Pennsylvania and Ohio Canal systems, as well as Maryland's Chesapeake and Ohio, was similar to that of the Erie.[91] The commissioners in Pennsylvania were elected, those in Ohio and Maryland were appointed. On the Pennsylvania and the Ohio systems the operating employees (toll collectors, lock tenders, and so forth) and the maintenance staff were supervised by the acting commissioner in charge of one of the canal's three or four major geographical divisions. On the Chesapeake and Ohio all but the heads of the maintenance crews reported to the "superintendent" in charge of each geographical division. The maintenance crews reported directly to the commissioner. There appears to have been as little systematic reporting and auditing of accounts on these canals as there were on the Erie. No large canal adopted a formal internal organizational structure, for the commissioners had little diffi- culty in maintaining personal contact with the very small number of managers involved in operating and maintaining the canal. And since all jobs on these canals were looked on, as they were on the Erie, as political patronage, no major state canal system developed a set of experienced workers, to say nothing of a cadre of career managers.

Yet neither a more efficient work force nor a larger and more effectively organized managerial staff would have increased the speed or enlarged the volume of goods transported through these canal systems. More sys- tematic accounting and controls might have reduced operating and maintenance costs and, therefore, lowered tolls by a small amount. Such controls might have prevented some delays in the movement of goods. But the speed and size of canal boats were limited by the amount a team of draft animals could pull. Sustained speeds of four miles an hour were rare. Such low speeds required little careful scheduling and control. More- over, the weather, droughts, freshets, and ice shut down parts or all of the canals far more often and for longer periods of time than any manage- ment error or dilatory work force. Careful internal organization, so absolutely essential for safety and efficiency in moving railroad traffic, was far less necessary in canal or water transportation.

Except in the financing of long-distance trade there was as little need and as few opportunities in banking as in transportation to depart from traditional methods. In funding those trades, the use of branches did provide for the internalizing of activities of several business units and the transactions between them. Only the Bank of the United States, however, with its unique federal charter and its special relationships with the federal government, had the facilities to coordinate administratively the high-volume flow of funds used to finance the movement of commodities and finished goods through the economy. Because this coordination in- volved accounting transactions on notes payable within two or four months, it was not affected by the slow and uncertain movement of mail that in the 1830s still required, at the very least, two weeks to go from Washington to New Orleans.[92] Even so such coordination was only possible by a national institution with massive financial resources. The largest of the newly specialized merchant banks did not yet find it neces- sary or profitable to set up branches manned by salaried employees. They continued to rely, as had mercantile enterprises for centuries, on inter- locking partnerships and other merchants acting as their agents to handle their distant financial transactions. In these specialized ancillary trans- portation and financial enterprises, as well as in the increasingly specialized primary mercantile enterprises which distributed goods in America, there was still no call to create anything comparable to the modern business enterprise with its many units and its hierarchy of managers.

Technological limits to institutional change in commerce

The specialization of enterprise in commerce, finance, and transportation is, then, the central theme of the institutional history of the American economy during the first half century after the ratification of the Constitution. Such specialization brought an end to the personal business world of the general merchant of the colonial era and replaced it with the increasingly impersonal world of the commission merchant. Although personal relations remained important in arranging specific shipments and sales and above all in the extension of credit, the importer, exporter, jobber, auctioneer, bank cashier, insurer, and broker dealt daily with buyers and sellers with whom he had little personal contact. Rarely did a merchant know both the producer and consumer at either end of the long chain of middlemen, transporters, and financiers who moved the goods through the economy.

The concomitant of such specialization was thus a reliance on impersonal market coordination. Between the 1790s and the 1840s the mechanisms for such coordination were steadily improved. As commercial centers grew in size, their businessmen set up exchanges similar to those in the larger coastal ports. Their newspapers were filled with commercial information. Their merchants were served by a growing number of specialized ancillary enterprises—banks, insurance companies, shipping lines, and freight forwarders. Specialization lowered information and transactions costs as well as the costs of financing and transporting the flow of goods through the American economy.

On the other hand, expansion and specialization in trade and commerce failed to bring institutional innovation.[93] Existing procedures and practices remained fully adequate for handling the activities within the commercial enterprises and the transactions between them. Even the most significant institutional development—the widespread use of the corporation to permit the pooling of capital in banks and insurance companies and in those constructing and operating transportation rights-of-way—did not lead to new ways of doing business between or within enterprises. These corporations came to be administered by one or two salaried managers, who stayed in close personal contact with representatives of the owners, or the state, or the boards of directors, or the commissioners.

Business enterprises remained small and personally managed because the volume of business handled by even the largest was not yet great enough to require the services of a large permanent managerial hierarchy. The overall management of the Second Bank of the United States, the nation's foremost financial firm and its most powerful economic institution, required only the services of Nicholas Biddle and two assistants. On the largest and most used canals, only the canal engineer and possibly the canal clerk could qualify as middle managers. Before 1840, two or three men could administer all the activities any enterprise involved in the distribution of goods might be called upon to handle.

Modern multiunit business enterprise did not make its appearance before 1840 for technological reasons. A steadily increasing population was spreading across the continent. The volume of trade through the economy increased concomitantly, but the speed or the velocity of the movement of that trade did not. As a result, as the population grew in numbers and expanded geographically, the number of units handling the trade grew rapidly and became increasingly specialized. The number of transactions between units multiplied. But the amount of goods and the number of transactions handled by an individual unit within a given time period remained much the same. As long as the movement of goods through the economy continued to be powered by the traditional sources of energy—wind and animal power—the volume of business an individual enterprise was called to handle was not extensive enough to bring either a subdivision within the firm or the internalization of several small units within a larger enterprise.

Theoretically, technological limits on speed and volume of movement of goods did not have to limit the size of the firm. Theoretically, the volume generated by the market could have been extensive enough to bring into being the large multiunit enterprise. Indeed, in Europe, where the urban markets were bigger and closer together than they were in the United States and where water transportation—coastal and inland— was more regular and more reliable, such subdivided and integrated enterprises had begun to appear. Even so, the large multiunit enterprise was still a rarity in the Europe of the 1840s. In the rural, agrarian economy of the United States, where cities were small and commercial centers far apart, and where inland transportation was closed down during the winter months, slow speed of movement remained the most powerful constraint on the growth of business enterprise and on the coming of institutional change in commerce.

CHAPTER 2

The Traditional Enterprise in Production

Technological limits to institutional change in production

Until the 1840s traditional enterprise remained as all-pervasive in production as in commerce, and for the same reason. The volume of activity was not large and owners had no difficulty in administering their enterprises. In farming, lumbering, mining, manufacturing, and construction the enterprise remained small and personal. In nearly all cases it was a family affair. When it acquired a legal form, it was that of a partnership.

In production, the relative scarcity of labor in the United States was a more significant constraint on the size of the enterprise than it was in distribution, simply because more men were usually needed to produce a given quantity of goods than to distribute them. In the early years of the republic, rapid geographical expansion and growth meant that hired labor was difficult to find and costly to keep. In agriculture, except where crops were suitable for cultivation by slave labor, the output of a farm was limited by the amount a family and a small number of hired hands could plant and harvest.[1] In manufacturing, workers who were not members of the family were normally apprentices and journeymen who were working as part of their training to become independent producers.

Nevertheless, the technological limitations on output appear to have been even more of a constraint to the growth of the enterprise than the scarcity of labor. Until the 1840s farmers continued to rely almost completely on traditional tools. So too did the builders of ships, wharves, houses, and commercial buildings, and the extractors of ores and other materials from the ground. In manufacturing, simple machines began to replace men in a number of operations, but these machines continued to be moved by the traditional sources of energy. As long as the processes of production remained powered by humans, animals, wind, and water,

50

the volume of output was rarely large enough to require the creation of subunits within the enterprise or to call for the services of a salaried manager to coordinate and monitor the work of these subunits. In production as in distribution, existing institutions were more than adequate to manage the basic processes.

Before the 1840s manufacturers expanded output in three ways. Craftsmen added more apprentices and journeymen to their work force. Entrepreneurs distributed work for processing in the homes of neighboring families. Other manufacturers used simple machinery powered by the flow of small creeks and streams. The large industrial establishment, with its battery of machines, foundries, or furnaces that relied on a central source of power and heat and was operated by a large number of workers who had no other source of income than their wages, remained a rarity in the United States until the 1840s. Before then the factory—as such establishments will be termed in this study—appeared in substantial numbers only in the textile industry. The one other type of manufacturing enterprise to have similar characteristics was that producing firearms for the American army. The textile manufacturers overcame technological constraints by harnessing the power of large rivers. The firearms manufacturers were willing to pay the high costs of production and distribution because the army guaranteed their market in order to have a domestic supply of arms.

The expansion of prefactory production, 1790–1840

In 1790 nearly all the families who raised or processed crops or goods lived on the same premises on which they worked. The largest group of producers who lived and worked in the same place were, of course, the farmers, who accounted for close to 90 percent of the labor force in 1790. In the early nineteenth century the family farm which produced crops for the market also raised much of its own food and manufactured its own furniture, soap, lye, candles, leather, cloth, and clothing.[2] In fact, goods manufactured in the home were often sold to neighbors and nearby towns. In 1810 the secretary of the treasury, Albert Gallatin, estimated that "about two-thirds of the clothing, including hosiery, and of the house and table linen, worn and used by the inhabitants of the United States, who do not reside in cities, is the product of family manufactures."[3]

In the seaboard cities and the small towns of the interior, manufacturers were largely artisans who lived above or near their shops.[4] They worked at a specialized trade such as the making or processing of cloth (spinners, weavers, tailors, and makers of stockings, gloves, hats, and sails), leather (tanners, shoemakers, and harnessmakers), wood (makers of furniture, carts, wagons, carriages, paneling, and clocks), metals (smiths of gold, silver, copper, tin, blacksmiths and whitesmiths, gunmakers and iron-mongers), or clay and glass. Some artisans, especially journeymen who had not yet set up their own establishment, became itinerants during the warmer months, traveling from village to village and farm to farm in the practice of their trade.

Those few producers who worked outside the home lived in the towns and were concentrated in the building trades, constructing homes, ware-houses, commercial edifices, ships, and wharves. They too were artisans— painters, carpenters, masons, shipfitters, riggers, caulkers, and the like. Normally their work was supervised by a master carpenter or shipbuilder. In the ports, ropewalks and copper-sheeting works supplemented ship construction. Like the small city breweries, rum and sugar refineries, and tanneries, they were usually operated by a master artisan and a small number of assistants.

Other industries were rural in nature and often tied closely to farming. Lumbering and potash making remained primarily part of the process of land clearing. Farmers became lumbermen in the winter, providing wood for fuel and lumber for the growing seaports and for the West Indian trade. Trapping, too, provided additional "cash crop" for the frontier farmers. However, until the expansion of John Jacob Astor's American Fur Company, after 1815, large-scale fur trading in the United States was dominated by the British in Canada. After 1815, Astor's fur company carried out trapping on a continental scale, but its trappers were working in areas that were not yet settled by American farmers.

Until the 1840s mining continued to be carried out on a small scale. Before the opening of the anthracite fields in Pennsylvania, the only place coal was mined extensively in the United States was along the James River in Virginia.[5] There much of the mining was done by farmers and planters who leased pits. As early as the 1790s, however, a few large enterprises employed as many as forty miners, usually slaves, supervised by an overseer or two. The total output of the James River coal mines remained small and was for many years measured in bushels rather than tons. In the years after 1790, iron mining continued to be carried on as part of iron processing in the rural iron plantations. These iron plantations worked largely by slaves and indentured servants were, before the coming of the integrated textile mills, the largest industrial enterprises in the United States. Lead mines in the frontier districts of Missouri, Wisconsin, and Illinois were leased out under government supervision to individuals or partnerships who rarely employed more than a score of men. No copper was mined in any quantity until after 1840, and what little gold and silver was extracted was done so largely by individuals rather than partnerships.

Of the three ways to expand output in manufacturing or processing—the enlargement of existing shops with the traditional work force, the "putting-out" system, or the use of machinery and other capital equipment—the first was used primarily to meet local demand. After 1790, the artisans enjoyed growing local markets and had access to local supplies of yarn, leather, and wood and easily obtained cloth and metal from importers of British products. Although they became somewhat more specialized, they expanded their output to make their suits, dresses, hats, furniture, tableware, copper, brass, and pewterware by employing more apprentices and journeymen who continued to work in the traditional manner with traditional tools. The same could be said for the makers of sails, ropes, and glassware, and rum, whiskey, and beer. In all these trades new machinery was not extensively developed or used before the 1840s. The enlarged shop was still a small personal enterprise. Work continued to be done in or near the home of the master who remained responsible for feeding and housing his apprentices and journeymen.

In the same way, the building and construction enterprises expanded to meet the growing demand by employing and training younger craftsmen.[6] As the cities grew, master carpenters and builders often contracted to construct a series of houses at one time, and so kept a number of journeymen and apprentices at work under their direction.[7] This was the case, too, in shipbuilding, where master shipwrights took charge of bringing together and supervising a group of skilled shipwrights, riggers, caulkers, and the like. Contractors, who took over the task of laying down and paving city streets, worked in much the same manner as those who were building turnpikes and canals. They were small local contractors using local labor. Normally an engineer or a city official supervised the work of these contractors. Their workers continued to use traditional tools and skills.

Where artisans, shipbuilders, and building contractors expanded their output to meet growing local demand by adding apprentices and journeymen to their work force, those producing for distant markets turned to putting-out work to be processed by workers in their homes, a method of production widely used in Europe. To produce the needed volume, an artisan or a merchant would purchase materials—yarn, leather, cloth, wood, or metal—deliver them to workers in their homes, pick up the completed article, and then arrange for its sale, either outright or, more often, on commission to merchants in the nearest major port or commercial center. In the 1790s, shoes, straw hats, lace, stockings, other clothing, woven cloth, chairs, clock cabinets, other furniture, cards for cleaning wool, and nails were produced through putting-out to households. Of these, shoes and chairs were the items made on the largest scale for distant markets.

The history of the shoe industry best illustrates how the putting-out system in the United States evolved to meet a growing demand.[8] From the late eighteenth century until the 1840s, shoes for markets in the West Indies and then in the south and west were produced in homes or on farms. After the turn of the century, an increasing number of specialized workers received leather, thread, and other supplies from a merchant or a master "cordwainer." The makers of shoes carried out their tasks in tiny shops attached to their homes (mostly farmsteads), known as "ten footers." As the demand expanded in the 1820s, the entrepreneurs tried to supervise and coordinate production more effectively by setting up a "central shop."[9] There, the leather was cut into soles and the upper part of the shoes. The latter was sent out to out-workers. After the completed uppers came back to the shop, they and the soles were sent out to other workers, the "fitters," who completed the shoe.

Under this system, shoemaking was all done by hand, at the individual's own time and pace. "Up to the forties," Blanche Hazard, the industry's leading historian has written, "the shoemaker had used mainly [hand] tools, and just such as had been used for centuries . . . The domestic worker had enjoyed all the latitude that he needed or wished. He sowed his fields and cut his hay when he was ready. He locked up his ten footer and went fishing when he pleased, or sat in his kitchen reading when it was too cold to work in his little shop."[10] In the forties, improved metal machinery began to replace the older, traditional tools, and, in the fifties, the invention of steam-powered, relatively expensive shoe-making machines brought the factory form of production to the shoe industry and quickly brought to an end the putting-out system.

In other industries the putting-out of goods in homes was not as widespread as in the shoe trade. Leather manufacturing, such as saddlery and belting, continued to be done in the artisans' shops. In clothmaking, putting-out was used only between the Embargo in 1807 and the adoption of the power loom. How long this system continued in the making of chairs, cabinet work, and other wood products is not clear. It was used in its most simplified form (that is, having the workers make the complete product at home) in the production of straw and palm leaf hats, cloth bonnets, and gloves until well after 1840.[11] Indeed, the invention of the sewing machine, though ending its use in the making of shoes, expanded it in the apparel industry. In all these trades, the entrepreneurs sold the finished wares through the wholesaling networks that had developed after 1815 on the east coast to market British goods.[12]

In the United States, more than in Britain or on the Continent, machinery was used oftener than the putting-out system to produce goods for distant markets. Some machines came from Britain; many were developed by Americans, especially New Englanders. Until the 1840s, however, the machines were simple, made largely of wood. Metal was used only in the critical cutting parts or where friction occurred. These machines were, therefore, easily built and repaired by local carpenters, blacksmiths, and tinsmiths, or by the manufacturers themselves. Their initial cost and maintenance were low. They were nearly all powered by water from small streams. As these streams froze in the winter, flooded in the spring, and often ran dry in the summer and early fall, the volume of the output of the machines they powered was small and varied with the seasons.

The use of machinery came early in the processing of products of the field and forest.[13] As early as 1795, Oliver Evans constructed a continuous process flour mill on the Brandywine Creek in Delaware. This mill annually milled 100,000 bushels of wheat into flour. It employed six workers who spent most of their time closing barrels. Similar mills soon appeared along the towns on the fall line, where streams and rivers reached tide water, particularly Baltimore and Richmond. With the opening of the New York and Ohio canals, Rochester and Buffalo in the 1830s and 1840s surpassed the more southern cities as the nation's leading mill centers. Although output increased, the mills remained small and operated only during and immediately after the harvest season.

Machinery also was used increasingly in the wood and lumber trades. Sawmills employing either imported or locally made saws began to sell to specialized dealers, who in turn marketed lumber for fuel and supplied finished woods to local builders and manufacturers. Such manufacturers used water-powered planes, presses, and simple cutting machinery to make clapboards, flooring, and mill work (paneling, mantels, doors, window frames, and so forth), furniture, clocks, buttons, and other notions, as well as axe and hoe handles, gun stocks, hat blocks, and shoe lathes. Although most such production was winter's work for local consumption, an increasing amount went for distant markets.

Clockmaking provides a revealing example of the expansion of production by the application of machinery in the woodworking industries. Here Eli Terry of Plymouth, Connecticut, was a pioneer. After inventing a machine for cutting the teeth of wood clockworks, and another for cutting the leaves of pinions, Terry, in 1806, built a shop twenty feet square, using water conveyed "through a hole six inches square." After enlarging his shop and developing more machines, ten men and two women were able to produce 1,100 clocks annually; these sold for $25 and $30 apiece. The materials for these clocks could be obtained from nearby forests and fields. Only small amounts of special woods—cherry and mahogany—and brass and glass came from nonlocal sources. Only the weights, pendulum bob, and crown wheel were made of brass.[14] Other Connecticut clockmakers soon followed Terry's lead. By 1820, similar small manufacturing establishments in the Bristol-Litchfield-Waterbury area of the state were producing 15,000 clocks a year. Comparable production by machinery in small shops became quite widely used in the making of chairs and other furniture, buttons, combs, and notions. In southern New England machine-made products often replaced hand-manufactured items.

The example of Eli Terry and of others manufacturing by means of fabricating and assembling wooden interchangeable parts suggest the scale of operations in the woodworking industry before the 1840s. The work force was tiny—a dozen or so people—power came from small streams, materials were close at hand, and those few items that came from a distance were required in only small amounts. While the output of a mill greatly exceeded that of a single artisan, or that of a number of home workers, it still could be easily marketed by a few peddlers, who drove their carts as far west as Buffalo and as far south as Richmond, selling to farmers and to general stores along the way. As the number of producers increased in the 1820s, the clockmakers and woodmakers continued to use peddlers, but relied increasingly on local merchants and distant storekeepers to sell their goods and to provide credit. By 1840, clocks came to be sold almost entirely through commission agents and then jobbers in New York and other eastern cities.

Metal products were manufactured and sold in much the same way as wood products. Buttons, razors, cutlery, locks, pots and pans, and other consumer goods were produced for consumer markets in small shops using simple but specialized cutting, stamping, and polishing machinery.[15] The metalmakers also sold through peddlers and then through commission agents and jobbers in New York and other eastern ports.

They differed from the wood processors in other ways, however: their materials came from a greater distance and cost much more. Nearly all their copper, tin, and much of their iron came from abroad. In New England even the blacksmiths, the largest consumers of wrought iron in an agrarian economy, imported their materials.[16] In 1832, 161 out of 167 blacksmiths in Maine used European iron. The largest ironworks in New England—makers of nails, hoops, wire bars, axes, and shovels—were in that year receiving 70 percent of their requirements from abroad, even after the high tariff of 1828 (the notorious Tariff of Abominations). So too were manufacturers on the Delaware River. Until the 1830s these works continued to use charcoal for the heat needed to work their iron, despite rising costs as local wood supplies were depleted.

The production of American pig and wrought iron remained concentrated in eastern Pennsylvania. Its price stayed high, not only because of transportation costs (iron was rarely mined near tidewater), but because its producers relied wholly on an ancient form of production.[17] As Peter Temin has pointed out, "the American iron industry in 1830 operated almost exclusively on the basis of traditional technology, despite the very successful new technology in Britain."[18] Pig iron was still produced by charcoal-fired blast furnaces, and wrought iron was still made by water-driven hammers. Even as late as 1832, much of the American iron was produced on iron plantations similar to those of the colonial period, located in isolated rural areas where ore, wood for charcoal, and water power for the forges were to be found on a single large tract of land. The output of these plantations remained small, with the furnaces producing at best twenty-five to thirty tons a week.[19] Both the furnaces and forges were normally shut down during the cold (and freezes) of winter and the heat (and droughts) of summer.

As their ore supply was depleted, iron plantations were often abandoned. Their owners, if they stayed in the business, located ore in more distant areas. The blast furnaces usually followed mining into the hills, but forges remained closer to the markets.[20] Although ironworks became more specialized in function, they continued to make a variety of products. The pig-iron processors made stoves and other cast-iron products; while the makers of wrought iron produced nails, wire, and fittings, as well as bar and sheet iron.[21] In the making and processing of iron, as in nearly all other manufacturing, the enterprise remained small and personally managed. In the blast furnaces, forges, and finishing mills, a work force of as many as fifty men was uncommon.

It was only in the making of cloth that the factory employing a permanent force of more than fifty workers had become common before 1840. And even in clothmaking the new type of manufacturing establishment did not appear until 1815, when the machinery for both spinning and weaving was placed within a single mill. Before that date, machinery had been used only in spinning; weaving continued to be done entirely by hand. Although in 1790 the design of Richard Awkwright's water-powered spinning mules had been brought by Samuel Slater from England to Rhode Island, the adoption of spinning machinery came slowly. Only fifteen cotton spinning mills were in operation before the passage of the Embargo Act of 1807.[22] All were located in southeastern New England, all were powered by the flow of small streams, and nearly all used crude Awkwright frames.[23] Their owners depended on local families for the labor force, with the children tending the machines and the adults doing the heavy work. The heads of the family were paid in goods—yarn, food, and supplies—supplemented by some cash. The manufacturers sold their yarn at first to local householders and weavers and then to commission merchants in Boston, New York, Philadelphia, and Baltimore. These spinning mills were managed by partners, or often by a single owner.

In the years between 1807 and 1815, when embargoes, trade restrictions, and wars cut off the normal British imports of thread and cloth, the domestic textile trade boomed. By 1809 Albert Gallatin noted that sixty-two spinning mills were already in operation and twenty-five more were being constructed, with the greatest concentration still being in southeastern New England.[24] The demand for yarn and for cloth woven from that yarn not only remained high but also moved westward as the population migrated into the Mississippi Valley. In 1806 the Providence firm of Brown and Almy (the mercantile enterprise that marketed the products of Slater's mill) sold 16 percent of its total products through Philadelphia and 8 percent through Baltimore. By 1808 the proportions had jumped to 30 percent and 14 percent. At the same time, Brown and Almy shipped an increasing amount of woven cloth with its yarn. By 1814, 67 percent of the firm's total output was sold through Philadelphia.[25] To meet the demand for cloth, Slater and other spinning mill operators began to have yarn put out to be woven by hand looms in homes. Then, in 1809, these manufacturers moved the workers into central shops in order to supervise more effectively the processes of production.[26]

The growing demand for cloth encouraged the mechanization of weaving. The resulting integration of weaving and spinning within a single mill led to the construction of the first large factories in the United States.[27] In 1814 a Bostonian, Francis Cabot Lowell, who had smuggled the plans of a power loom out of Britain, built a factory on the Charles River at Waltham, Massachusetts. There he placed spinning machinery to feed his new weaving machines. By integrating all the activities involved in these two basic processes, Lowell's Boston Manufacturing Company was able to turn out a far greater volume of cloth at a much lower unit cost than any other American textile producer. The integrated factory, with its initial capitalization of $100,000 (raised quickly to $300,000 and then to $600,000) and its work force of three hundred workers, was far larger than any existing mill in the nation. Because of its size, the work force could no longer be paid irregularly and in kind. Monthly cash wages provided the mill hands with their only source of support. Unlike the workers in the spinning and other small mills, they no longer looked to agriculture for part-time work and subsistence.

Because of the volume of its operations, the success of the Boston Manufacturing Company demanded more than technological innovation. To build and to repair the large number of machines needed, Lowell and his associates constructed their own machine shops. To obtain a permanent work force of the size they needed, Lowell reached out to that yet-unused supply of labor, New England farm girls who had finished their schooling but who were not yet married. To provide the unprecedented amount of working capital needed to pay regular wages and to buy cotton in volume, Lowell and his associates incorporated their enterprise. They did so in order to tap the funds of Boston mercantile families who, because of trade restrictions and wars, had not been able to continue their investment in commerce. Finally the Boston Manufacturing Company placed the marketing of its output in the hands of a single agent. Because of the high volume involved, the agent readily accepted a commission of only 1 percent. The marketing firm, B. C. Ward & Company, with which Lowell's associates were closely connected, sold most of the factory's output through the growing dry goods jobber network in New York City. Aided by the mildly protective Tariff of 1816, Lowell's enterprise was able to compete easily with the output of British factories whose low prices were at that time driving many American textile enterprises out of business.

In fact, the integrated mill proved highly profitable. The profits of the Boston Manufacturing Company, reflecting the productivity of its factory, ranged from 16 percent to 26 percent annually, even during the period of price-cutting caused by the depression following the panic of 1819.[28] After seven years of operation, the stockholders received more than 100 percent return on their original investment.

Eager to expand, the entrepreneurs associated with Lowell were keenly aware of the need for a more powerful and steady source of power than was available from the Charles, Blackstone, Brandywine, and Schuylkill, the small streams that powered existing mills in the United States. To keep more than a single integrated mill going, they needed not only to harness a major river but to do so where a large drop in the riverbed promised a powerful force of water. They selected a site on the Merrimack River where a canal had been built around a thirty-foot fall. By enlarging the canal to a width of sixty feet and a depth of eight feet, and by building the largest waterwheels in the country, they obtained the power to run, winter and summer, a dozen mills the size of the one at Waltham. There they set up an industrial town named for Lowell.[29]

By the end of the decade, ten of the largest corporations in the United States, capitalized at between $600,000 and $1,000,000 were using the water power that flowed through the hydraulic system at Lowell. Other manufacturers began to build similar integrated mills powered by the same technologies on the Merrimack, Connecticut, Passaic, and other large rivers where they took major drops as they flowed to the sea.[30]

These men used much the same types of labor force, and they organized their enterprises as corporations. The shares of these firms were closely held. In nearly all cases, the controlling shares remain in the hands of three or four close associates and their families.[31]

Yet such industrial sites were limited. Lowell, Manchester, Lawrence, Holyoke, Springfield, and Patterson were among the few industrial cities in the United States whose growth was based on water power. It was not until the steam generated from anthracite coal became available that similar large integrated mills were built in southern New England and the middle states.[32] Appropriately enough, Samuel Slater, the founder of the spinning industry in America, built the first integrated steam mill in 1828, in Providence. Until that time he and most of the other textile producers in southern New England continued to rely on hand weavers to process their yarn. Only after coal became available to generate inexpensive steam power were the southern New England enterprises able to compete efficiently with the river-powered mills to the north or the steam-powered factories of Great Britain.

The cotton industry set the example for the wool manufacturers, but for no others. By the 1830s both the spinning and weaving of wool were being handled first by water-powered and then by steam-powered machinery.[33] The very first woolen mill to adopt the full panoply of the techniques developed at Waltham began operation in Lowell in 1830.

A survey of American manufacturing authorized in 1832 by the secretary of the treasury, Louis McLane, documents the concentration of the factory form of production within textiles.[34] Of the 106 manufacturing firms listed in the *McLane Report* that had assets of $100,000 or over, 88 were textile companies (of these, 10 were producers of wool fabrics, and 2 made both cotton and wool cloth). Twelve were ironmakers, the majority of which were still the ancient type of "iron plantation." (The assets of these firms were as much in land and mines as in buildings and machinery.) The remaining 6 enterprises in the largest 106 included manufacturers of nails and hoops, of axes, of glass, of paper, of flour, and of hydraulic equipment. Of the 36 enterprises reporting 250 or more workers, 31 were textile factories, the remaining were 3 ironworks, the nail and hoops works, and the axe factory.

If smaller amounts of capital and smaller numbers of workers are used to define the large manufacturing establishments of the 1830s, the pattern remains the same. Of the 143 firms having capital assets of between $50,000 and $100,000, the greatest number were textile firms with iron enterprises following in about the same proportion as they did on the list of 106 firms with assets of $100,000 or more. The enterprises in the $50,000 to $100,000 range in other industries included nailmaking firms, a producer of steam engines in Pittsburgh, a firearms maker in Connecticut, a gunpowder company and a flour mill in Delaware, and a saddlery establishment in Pennsylvania. If one looks at the enterprises with fifty or more workers (which were not included in the other categories), the concentration remains in textiles, with ironworks second in number, but a good way behind. There are a number of industries in which one or two enterprises reported hiring more than fifty workers. But in only six industries were there as many as three to seven firms with a work force of over fifty: books and printing with seven, cordage with five, shipyards with five, buttons with three, combs with three, and glass with three. (The button and comb firms listed workers working at home.) The overwhelming majority of the enterprises listed in the *McLane Report* had assets of only a few thousand dollars and employed at the most ten or a dozen people.

The *McLane Report* is incomplete. It covers only ten states, all in the northeast (with a short and very incomplete statement on Ohio). Although the returns for some states, especially Maine, Massachusetts, Rhode Island, Pennsylvania, and Delaware are most detailed, those for others have gaps in capitalization, employment, and other data. Nevertheless, the information covers those states in which, as late as 1850, 75 percent of all American manufacturing was concentrated. Much of the data provided on individual enterprises is very detailed, giving a wealth of information on wages, sources of raw materials, locations of markets, and types of power used, as well as on assets, working capital, and employees. Moreover, scattered data in the censuses of 1830 and 1840 and studies of individual firms and industries support the generalizations indicated by the 1832 survey. Although other enterprises with assets of more than $50,000 and with employees of more than fifty workers not listed in these reports or studies certainly existed, it seems hardly likely that new information would alter the profile of American industry given in the *McLane Report*.[35]

The *McLane Report* also emphasizes that as late as 1832 American manufacturing was still powered almost exclusively by water. If enterprises in the Pittsburgh area where coal was plentiful are excluded, only 4 of the 249 firms capitalized at $50,000 or more relied on steam for power. Three more supplemented water power with steam. A check of the firms with assets of less than $50,000 but with fifty or more workers shows only one using steam and that was a machine and iron works in New Britain, Connecticut. Peter Temin, in his study of steam and water power, located as many as 100 steam engines in the *McLane Report*, but the majority of those were often low-horsepower auxiliary engines.[36] With the exception of Pittsburgh, more firms reported the use of wind and mule power than steam.[37] In the great majority of cases, water power was generated by small streams rather than large rivers. This meant not only that the volume of power generated was relatively low but also that most machinery in the United States was subject to seasonal periods of shutdown because of ice, drought, and freshets.

The profile of American industry delineated in the *McLane Report* and other sources is, then, one of production being carried out by a large number of small units employing less than fifty workers and still relying on traditional sources of energy—water, wind, animal, and human. The resulting products, when sold beyond local markets, were marketed through the growing specialized distribution network, initially created to market the goods produced by British factories in the United States. Investment decisions for future output, as well as those for current production, were made by many hundreds of small producers in response to market signals, in much the way Adam Smith described. Before 1840 the traditional form of enterprise remained quite satisfactory for the management of production in the American environment.

Managing traditional production

As this profile suggests, the management of production was no more complex than that of commerce. Artisans, craftsmen, shipbuilders, house builders, distillers, and refiners who relied on the labor of apprentices and journeymen found the age-old methods of accounting completely adequate. Like the merchants, they kept records of their financial transactions by using the double-entry system. However, they paid much less attention to improving information on markets and sources of supply than did the merchants.[38]

The same was true of manufacturers who expanded production by adopting machinery. Their simple machine required neither heavy investment nor a large work force. Few manufacturing enterprises operated full time. Even when they remained active all year, they were closely tied to the seasonal variations and routines of a still overwhelmingly agrarian economy.

Nor was the management of putting-out work any more complicated. In the United States the organization of the putting-out or domestic system of manufacturing was never as sophisticated as it was in sixteenth-century Florence or eighteenth-century Britain.[39] Tasks were rarely subdivided; instead the complete product was manufactured in the home. Even in the making of shoes, where the putting-out system was used most extensively, the worker did only two different tasks: the making of the "uppers" and the fitting of the "uppers" to the soles. In carrying out this method of production, the merchant or artisan who owned the materials and was responsible for the sale of the finished goods kept the books. He debited the worker's account with the value of materials received and credited it with the pieces of finished goods returned at the agreed-upon price. The books show that the worker was often charged for the household supplies he needed, and then credited with farm produce, as well as for the completed shoes or cloth that he returned to the entrepreneur.[40]

These accounts were not used to control the worker's activities as they were in the eighteenth and early nineteenth centuries in Great Britain. There, according to Sidney Pollard, they were used as a "check on materials handed over to the outworkers, on rent on their equipment (if any), and on the workmanship of the finished goods handed back."[41] In the United States, the entrepreneur made few attempts to see if the materials he handed out were efficiently used. In fact, the shoemakers usually had enough leftover leather from their production to make and sell shoes for their own profit. Much the same was true of the cloth weavers.[42] An Englishman who visited Rhode Island in 1815 deplored the unsystematic nature of American methods. He urged that the distribution of yarn and the receiving of cloth be done on specific days, and that the use of weavers' tickets, so common in England, be adopted.[43] Instead, Americans often turned to the central shop where the work could be supervised by a single overseer. As the merchant who handled the yarn produced in Slater's mill wrote to a correspondent as early as 1809, "We have several hundred pieces now out weaving, but a hundred looms in families will not weave so much cloth as ten at least constantly employed under the immediate inspection of a workman."[44]

All in all, the domestic system of production, so important in the processing of goods in Europe, had little impact on the evolution of a business enterprise or its management in the United States. It did strengthen the tradition of paying by the piece, and the central shop in shoemaking and cloth weaving had some similarities to the factory. But since the entrepreneur who allotted the materials had little fixed capital to account for and no permanent work force to discipline and control, his business activities were much closer to those of a contemporary merchant than to those of a factory owner.

Before the 1840s the relative scarcity of labor and the continuing use of traditional technologies thus sharply limited the amount an enterprise was able to produce and the size to which it might grow. Before that decade very few enterprises in either production or distribution had acquired an internal organization as complex as a single operating unit of the many that make up a modern business enterprise. Only the southern plantations and the northern textile and gunmaking factories had managerial needs at all comparable to those of a single unit at the lowest level of modern management (see figure 1 in the Introduction). The plantations, which were able to enlarge their output by employing slaves, represented an ancient form of production. The textile factories, which expanded their output by developing the technology to harness power from large rivers, and the gun factories, whose guaranteed markets permitted them to pay the costs of traditional technology, were the pioneers of a basic new form of production. The plantations and early textile and arms factories in the United States were as large and as complex to manage as all but the biggest agricultural and industrial enterprises in Europe. An analysis of their operation indicates the nature of management in the largest private businesses at home or abroad before the coming of the railroads. This analysis emphasizes the limited managerial experience on which the later builders of modern business enterprise could draw.

The plantation—an ancient form of large-scale production

Until the nineteenth century, in both the United States and Europe there were many more large-scale enterprises in agriculture than in industry. In Europe the large landed estates with their salaried land agents or managers had some influence on the evolution of industrial management.[45] In the United States this was not the case.

One reason may have been that the great majority of southern planters directly managed the property they owned. They were not absentee landlords, as was so often the case in Europe.[46] They hired overseers to assist them and not, as did many Europeans, to replace them in managing their estates. And as Robert Fogel and Stanley Engerman have argued, many owners of large plantations did not employ a resident salaried overseer.[47]

The managerial tasks of the planter were not complex. Close supervision of the work force was necessary only during the planting, initial cultivation, and harvesting. Between December and March, before the planting, and in the summer when the crops were maturing, planters often left the plantation in charge of trusted slaves. In fact the social seasons in southern towns were arranged with this calendar in mind.

Moreover, the plantation work force was small by modern standards. Indeed, it was smaller than in contemporary New England textile mills. As late as 1850 the census reported that only 1,479 plantations had more than 100 slaves. Of these, 187 had more than 200, 56 more than 300, 9 more than 500, and 2 more than 1,000.[48] Normally a third of the slaves on a plantation were either children under ten years of age or too old for regular field work; a few did only housework. Therefore, less than a dozen plantations in the south in 1850 had a work force of 300 full-time field hands, in other words, a work force comparable in size to that of the first integrated textile mill in New England. And few had capital assets (excluding the value of slaves) of $300,000, the capitalization of the Boston Manufacturing Company when it began production in 1815.

Nevertheless, as the first salaried manager in the country, the plantation overseer was an important person in American economic history. The size of this group (in 1850 overseers numbered 18,859) indicates that many planters did feel they needed full-time assistance to carry out their managerial function.[49] Where they did not have white overseers, many may have relied on black "drivers" to carry out these tasks. Such tasks remained almost wholly the supervision of workers. The overseer rarely handled money or accounts and had little acquaintance with complex machinery. The written rules that the planters issued to the overseers "for the governance of a plantation" dealt almost wholly with the handling of slaves and the working of crops. Even though plantations usually had a mill or gin on them, for use in the first step of processing the crop, the instructions say little about machine maintenance. These rules called for, as William K. Scarborough has written, "firm discipline, tempered with kindness, and a uniform, impartially administered system of justice."[50] The overseer was expected to know the strengths and weaknesses of his foremen, or "drivers," and even of many of the field hands themselves.

The organization of the work force that planters and overseers supervised followed a traditional pattern. On the older tobacco and sugar plantations and the newer cotton ones, the slaves worked in gangs led by a "driver."[51] Each gang was assigned an allotted task to be completed during a day or even a week, and particularly during planting the work of these gangs was carefully coordinated. In rice growing and often in the harvesting of cotton, where teamwork and coordination were less necessary, the planters used the "task system," under which each hand was assigned a daily task and could leave the field when it was completed. Whether done by piece (task) or by day (gang), the sowing, tending, and harvesting of crops followed time-tested procedures. Only at those critical periods of planting and harvesting, or when a storm or flood endangered the crops, did the work of the planter, the overseer, and the drivers become more than routine.

Neither the overseer nor the planter himself kept detailed financial accounts. They maintained a "plantation book" that recorded births, deaths, and as one guide for overseers put it: "the daily picking of each hand; the mark, number, and weight of each bale of cotton, and the time of sending the same to market; and all other such occurrences, relating to the crop, the weather, and all other matters pertaining to the plantation, that he may deem advisable."[52] The plantation book was similar to a ship's log. As in the case of a log, its contents were only occasionally transcribed or summarized in a systematic way. The overseer or owner was rarely able to make a comparative analysis of the output of different hands, gangs, or fields over an extended period of time.

On most plantations, account books were usually kept by the planter's factor, and not by the planter himself. Some planters, however, did keep fairly accurate consolidated books when they had accounts with more than one storekeeper, factor, or banker. These double-entry accounts, like those kept by factors and merchants, were only records of external transactions. In accounting for their income and outgo, the planters included their own personal expenses and those of their families—as did the merchants. At the annual balancing of the books, or for an evaluation of property for taxes or sale, a planter drew up inventories that provided a rough estimate of the value of his property including slaves. A few even computed a 7 percent charge on these estimates, and recorded them as an expense. Such accounting sophistication was, however, rare. Planters made little effort to analyze their overall cost or the unit cost of raising a bale of cotton or a hogshead of sugar. Indeed, one student of plantation operations has written that an analysis of cost must be "hypothetical, and cannot be ascertained from surviving records. It was seldom taken into consideration by the planters themselves who usually were content with the simplest records and figured profits or losses on the basis of cash income and expenditure."[53]

This lack of concern for costs did not mean that the plantations were mismanaged. As in the case of contemporary mercantile enterprises, financial success or failure hardly depended on accurate cost accounting. The factors' abilities to market the crop and the overseers' to grow it were far more important. The planter had as little control over the drought, rain, and frost that affected the size and quality of his crops as he had over forces of supply and demand that set the prices he received in the international market. Even if costs could have had been accurately estimated, the planter could do little with the information except to shift to the production of other crops. When prices dropped, he might plant less of a staple crop and more food. He was, however, rarely in a position to shift from one staple cash crop to another. If he had surplus to invest he almost always put it into land and slaves.

Thus the southern plantation, although it required some subdivision of labor and some coordination of the activities of the work force, had little impact on the evolution of the management of modern business enterprise.[54] In agriculture, as in commerce, the use of traditional tools to carry out traditional tasks meant that the traditional ways of organization were wholly adequate. There was little the planter could do to increase productivity or to speed up the processes of the crop cycle.

Only after 1850 were the processes of agriculture to be altered by the application of new technologies. Then, instead of adding more manpower to increase output per acre, farmers turned to using mass-produced farm machinery, new types of fertilizers, and new strains of crops and cattle. Once the Civil War brought the abolition of slavery, the family farm using the new machines and techniques remained the basic unit of enterprise in American agriculture. The processes of agricultural production long remained the prerogative of personally owned and personally managed enterprises.

The integrated textile mill—a new form of large-scale production

Unlike the operation of the plantation, the management of the integrated textile mills, the largest industrial establishments of their days, did create new challenges. Owners and managers paid close attention to expanding output and increasing productivity. Nevertheless, their managerial methods adhered to those of the mercantile world that spawned them. The transition from mercantile to industrial management came slowly.

Within a single mill the integration of all the processes of production involved in making cloth stimulated innovation in each of the specific processes. Close coordination of the flow at first put a premium on speeding up the spinning processes so that the thread could be fed into the weaving machines as fast as the latter could consume it. Then came the development of leather belting to transmit power faster than was possible with the cumbersome and costly iron gearing. Soon throstle-spinning (and later ring-spinning) frames replaced the slower mule-spinning frames. Besides permitting a much faster and therefore much larger output for each machine, throstle-spinning and ring-spinning frames were easier for women and children to operate. In Britain, on the other hand, where spinning and weaving were not integrated and male labor was more extensively used, the mule continued to be used well into the twentieth century.[55] The increase in velocity of output encouraged by the integration of the processes of production thus helped to make the three decades after the War of 1812, in the words of an expert in the field, a "seminal period in the history of American textile technology." The resulting increase in speed caused output per spindle to rise by almost 50 percent.[56]

Organizational innovation came more slowly. The merchants who founded the mills and those who came to control them, as well as those who marketed their output, held to traditional ways. Although they incorporated these manufacturing enterprises in order to pool capital, they continued to manage them like partnerships. The manufacturing firm had one full-time officer, normally the treasurer, who resided and worked in Boston or another commercial center and was a major stockholder.[57] The day-to-day operations of the distant mill were left to a salaried agent or to a superintendent. To the treasurer and members of the board, the mill agent was a technician similar to an engineer on a canal or an inspector in an insurance company. He was not, as was the overseer to the planter, a close personal assistant helping him to supervise the enterprise as a whole. The treasurer kept in touch with the agent through the accounts the agent sent him and through weekly visits to the mill.

As the mills were designed to facilitate the coordination of flow through the processes of production, the mill agent's administrative task was relatively routine. Each process was normally carried out on a separate floor. In the early mills the raw cotton entered at the bottom floor and the finished cloth emerged at the top.[58] On the first floor, raw cotton was picked and cleaned by machines, "lapped" on to wooden cylinders, and then carded. The cleaned and carded cotton went by elevator to the second floor where it was spun into yarn. Next the yarn was dressed—sized, brushed, and dried—and wrapped on to a lap or heavy wooden bobbin, while the fill (undressed yarn) was also wound on another set of bobbins. The warp (the dressed yarn) and the fill were woven into cloth on the third floor. The cloth was then moved to the next floor where it was dressed, and then sent to the cloth room, where it was trimmed, measured, and folded. Some of the finished product went to a nearby bleachery to be bleached and, as facilities were added, to be dyed and printed. Such a factory embodied, it must be stressed, an integration, not a subdivision of work.

Each process was, then, carried on within a subunit of the factory, mostly on one floor, and was supervised by two or three foremen or overseers, as they were then called. The machine tenders were usually women, since the tasks required dexterity and certain manipulative skills and not heavy manual labor. The work was far more routine than even that of plantation slaves. Indeed, the mill workers were the first sizable group of Americans to be totally isolated from seasonal variations in the tempo of their work. Although the rooms were large, with many workers, the foremen had little difficulty in keeping a close watch on their employees. The mill agent had no trouble either in maintaining constant personal touch with the overseers and maintaining an eye on the flow of materials from one floor to another. In fact, when the owners put up a new mill on the same site, their agent normally had the time to take charge of both mills.

The agent's concern was almost wholly with the processes of production. He had to manage workers, as did the plantation overseer, but he also had to have an intimate knowledge of machines. James Montgomery, a British textile manager with American experience, wrote that the mill agent must "have a thorough knowledge of the business *in all* its details."[59] To Montgomery these details were technological not entrepreneurial. He advised agents to permit their overseers or foremen to carry out the detailed supervision of their departments, even to the hiring and firing of workers, and the processing of payrolls. The agent's task was, Montgomery emphasized, to concentrate on maintaining a high steady flow of materials through the mill. He was to "be expert in performing all kinds of *calculations* connected with the business . . . First, in regulating the *speed* of the various machines; second, in adjusting the *draughts* of the different machines; and third, in making *changes* in the qualities of the cotton and size of the yarn." Most of Montgomery's treatise on the management of textile mills was devoted to methods of machine tending. In handling workers, Montgomery's advice was much the same as that which the planter gave to his overseer. To assure "good feeling and good understanding" within the factory, Montgomery urged that, "while guarding against too much *lenity* on the one hand, to be careful to avoid too much *severity* on the other; and let him [the agent] be firm and decisive in all his measures, but not overbearing and tyrannical;—not too distant and haughty, but affable and easy of access, yet not too familiar."

In his treatises on mill management Montgomery said nothing about accounts. The mill agent did, however, keep a set of reports which went to the treasurer. Assisted by a clerk or bookkeeper, he recorded the amounts of raw cotton received at the mill, from where and by what means it had been transported, and from what mercantile firms it had been obtained.[60] The actual buying of the cotton remained the province of the treasurer. The agent also kept an account of the cloth manufactured and then shipped to the company's selling agent.

In addition the mill agent maintained the payrolls. At first most mill workers were paid by the piece.[61] By the 1830s, however, daily payment was becoming more common. This shift occurred because day work was easier to compute. Carding and weaving tended to be paid by the day, while dressing and winding remained by the piece. Weaving was paid both ways. The operators, whether paid by the piece or by the day, received their wages monthly. These monthly payrolls went to the treasurer who maintained the financial accounts of the company.

The treasurer's accounts show clearly that these factories were run by merchants for merchants.[62] The journals and ledgers differed little from those that were used for the sale of the firm's finished goods. They relied on double-entry bookkeeping, and made increasing use of "trial balances" which were presented semiannually to the board of directors. These balances, drawn from the company's ledger, were cast into four sets of accounts and then into a "final balance." One of these four was the cotton account; another the cloth account. The first listed the amounts paid for cotton and cotton on hand; the second, cloth on hand which had not yet been shipped to the marketing firm. The third was the "general expense" account including all wages, all supplies and materials (including oil, starch, flour, wood, burlap, paper, but not cotton), cartage within the mill town, repair charges, and miscellaneous items. The fourth "balance" listed accounts receivable and accounts payable. Some firms also had special sets of treasurer's accounts for taxes, insurance, and transportation of raw cotton.

All this information was then placed in the "final balance." The credit side listed bills receivable, cotton and cloth on hand, the amount listed as sold in the selling agent's account, and the value of property (mills, houses, bleacheries, machines, and land). The debit side listed stock out-standing, bills payable, and finally profit and loss (income received minus general expenses and the cost of cotton). Paul McGouldrick, who re-viewed the accounts of many Lowell mills, gained "a strong impression that valuation [of cotton and cloth] at market (minus an arbitrary per-centage as insurance against the fall of cloth prices) was customary," and that the valuation of capital facilities was usually set at cost.[63]

There was little uniformity in the accounting practices of the leading textile mills, even among those that leased their water power from the same company, sold through the same agents, and had some of the same stockholders. In accounting for depreciation, directors wrote down the value of mills and machinery and other assets in an ad hoc, unsystematic way. The amount and timing was purely at the discretion of the board. Some mills kept reserve funds for specific contingencies including fire and bad debts, and occasionally for renewal and repair, but others did not. None had a surplus account as such. Surpluses were listed under profit and loss or in the contingency accounts. As McGouldrick discovered, fixed assets, insurance, bad debts, and even payments of dividends were accounted for separately by the different companies with mills in Lowell. Nor was there any public discussion (comparable to that carried on after 1850 in the railroad world) on ways to increase uniformity and accuracy on accounting problems and procedures.

This lack of interest in accounting suggests that textile executives were not using their accounts to assist them in the management of their enterprises. As in the case of commercial firms, accounting remained merely a recording of past transactions. It was not until the 1850s that the owners and managers began to use their accounts to determine unit costs.[64] By then they had a fair picture of their prime costs but little information on overhead or capital costs. In any case, the mill agents rarely, if ever, looked at the company's financial books in Boston, and the treasurer and part-time president and members of the board had an up-to-date picture of their company's finances only twice a year.[65]

As in the case of the plantation owners, there was little pressure on the textile manufacturers to improve cost data. As labor and cotton were by far the major costs, they had little incentive to compute indirect and overhead cost. McGouldrick estimates that cotton represented over 90 percent of the costs of all purchased materials.[66] And the manufacturers had as little control over the price of cotton as they did over that of their finished cloth. Both were determined by the forces of supply and demand in the international markets. Moreover the treasurer and the board came to rely increasingly on their selling agent to make critical decisions as to output, quality, and style.[67]

These selling agents included some of the best-known mercantile partnerships in Boston. By the 1830s Benjamin C. Ward & Company, and its successor, James W. Paige & Company (Nathan Appleton, a founder of the Boston Manufacturing Company and several of the Lowell firms, was a senior partner in both), A. & A. Lawrence, Mason & Lawrence, J. K. Mills, and Francis Skinner & Company were all specialists in selling textile products. Each of these enterprises, serving as exclusive marketing agents for several large mills, sold their products through the distributing network which had been created after 1815 and remained centered on New York.[68] Mason & Lawrence, for example, had accounts with 105 firms in New York, 16 in Philadelphia, 15 in New Orleans, and a few in other scattered towns. These selling agents came to provide the textile companies with the credit needed for working capital in much the same way as the factors aided the plantation owners, and as other middlemen assisted the small shop and mill owners. They also paid the insurance and most of the transportation costs of the finished cloth. They, of course, determined the terms of sale, including discounts and time of payment. It is hardly surprising, therefore, that they were soon also deciding what styles, quantity, and quality of cloth the different mills should produce.

Thus, in the textile industries long after 1840, the basic functions of marketing, production, finance, and purchasing remained under the control of different men often in different enterprises who rarely lived in the same place and who at most saw each other briefly once a week or less. In a word, no central management yet existed. Indeed, the selling and production remained in the hands of two legally different enterprises. There was, of course, some coordination, for often merchants who were partners in the selling company were on the board of the manufacturing firms. Once in a while a man like J. K. Mills came to head both manufacturing and selling firms and so managed the enterprise as a whole. Yet even for Mills this arrangement proved only temporary. More normal were the conflicts that occurred during the 1850s and 1860s between the mill agents, treasurers, and selling agents of the mills of Lowell and Lawrence.[69] In many Boston owned and managed companies and in those of other areas, a single set of executives did not become responsible for the basic activities of an industrial enterprise—marketing, manufacturing, purchasing, and finance—until well after the Civil War. Despite the fact that the integrated textile mills were the first large factories in this country, the new textile industry had little impact on the development of modern industrial management. This was in large part because traditional businessmen had not yet been pressed to alter their traditional ways.

The textile mills were, nevertheless, pioneers in the technology of modern production. They did internalize and integrate all or nearly all the processes of production involved in making a product within a single mill. Such integration provided a basic model for later mass production. It is significant, in light of later developments, that the factory first came to the United States as a result of internalizing several processes of production and not from the specialization and subdivision of labor within the industrial establishment.

The Springfield Armory—another prototype of the modern factory

Before the mid-1830s the only industrial enterprises in the United States to have an internal subdivision as extensive as that of Adam Smith's famous pin factory were a small number of gunmaking establishments. Even here integration preceded specialization and subdivision. Only after the integration of production of all parts of a gun within a single establishment did specialization come in the manufacture of each part of the gun: the lock, stock, and barrel. Of the handful of establishments producing guns for the army, the United States Army's Armory at Springfield, Massachusetts, was the most important. With its work force of 250 men, the armory was for decades the largest metalworking establishment in the country. Because it was the first works in the United States to develop extensive internal specialization, and because it was in the metalworking industry, the industry where so many of the techniques of modern factory management were first to appear, the armory became an even more important prototype of the modern factory than the integrated textile mill.

However, its organization and operation, like those of the Second Bank of the United States, were unique. It had even closer relations with the federal government than did the bank, and was much less of a private business enterprise. Its large market was guaranteed. It could and did pay more for fuel and scarce raw materials than private metalworking enterprises. As part of the nation's military organization, its managers and supervisors were accountable to both the War Department's Ordnance Department and to Congress. Finally, the single military officer who was accountable for the armory's performance had an awareness of organizational and bureaucratic procedures that was still totally foreign to the American merchants.

Even so, the contribution of the Springfield Armory was as much the result of the administrative capabilities of its superintendent, Colonel Roswell Lee, as of its special and unique condition.[70] The other large federal armory located at Harpers Ferry continued to be operated in a personal way along traditional craft lines. When Lee took command at Springfield in 1815, his first move was to centralize authority and responsibility in the office of the superintendent. He then reorganized the administration of the armory. He devised and put into operation a set of controls that assured accountability for material used and for the quality of the product, and at the same time permitted the piecework wages to be accurately determined.

Lee used these accounting controls to monitor and supervise work done in four departments—three sets of "shops" where the metal and wood parts were fabricated and the central building where they were assembled. The central building also housed the forge, casting furnaces, and a magazine. In the shops fabricating the lock mechanisms, barrels, and stocks, the subdivision of labor had increased rapidly after 1815. In 1815 the different occupational specialties at Springfield numbered thirty-six. In 1820 they had increased to eighty-six, and by 1825 to one hundred.[71]

Each shop had its foreman and an inspector. They, and apparently the several foremen responsible for the furnaces, forges, and assembling the guns, reported to the master armorer. That manager was directly responsible to Lee for the production of firearms. Lee had other assistants who handled the purchasing and shipping of materials and the deliveries of the finished guns. The management of the armory was thus effectively centralized.

Lee achieved control over production and accountability for work done in two ways. One was through careful inspection. Each worker placed his "private mark" on each piece he made. After the assistant master armorer had inspected and passed the piece, he put his mark on it next to that of the worker. The supervisor also submitted a monthly office report which listed pieces passed and rejected.

The second method of control was through bookkeeping, that is, by accounting for each transaction carried on within the enterprise involved in production through the use of the standard double-entry accounts. The master armorer and each foreman had a day book in which he entered the amount and value of wood, coal, and supplies (cutting steel, files, emory, and the like), which the workers had received. These amounts were transcribed monthly into a ledger or "abstract book," the debit side of which listed the total of items received and the credit side the parts produced, materials still on hand, and scrap. The foreman, in turn, had similar books for each worker under his control. In his monthly abstract, the foreman credited each worker with units completed, units on hand, scrap, waste, and tools returned as worn out. "All these must equal each workman's debit [for materials taken] or he is made to pay for the deficiency," reported an army officer who reviewed the work of the armory in 1819.[72] In addition, each worker submitted each week and each month a statement of amount and value or "return," as it was called, of materials he had on hand. These accounts were consolidated monthly in tabular form for each shop or other operating unit by its foreman, and for the armory as a whole by the master armorer. Through these accounts Lee reviewed in detail the work of each subunit. As the 1819 report noted: "Complete accountability is established and enforced throughout; and if there is any error committed, it will be discovered on a comparison with the books and it can be traced to its source."

The accounting and inspection controls Lee set up at the Springfield Armory were certainly the most sophisticated used in any American industrial establishment before the 1840s. Precisely how Lee employed the data so generated to assist in the management of his work is uncertain. He and his master armorer surely used them to monitor and evaluate the performance of the departmental foreman and even of workers within the subunits. There is little evidence, however, that Lee developed accurate figures on the cost of making a single gun, bayonet, or other product. At least present-day historians have found it necessary to compute such data in analyzing the performance of the armory. Nor did Lee use his information to obtain more effective internal coordination and so speed up the flow of materials through his establishment. The output of guns remained steady, and production continued at the same relatively slow pace for the two decades after Lee took over the arsenal.[73]

Nevertheless, in later years, the organizational innovations at Springfield came to be used in the management of metalworking factories whose processes of production involved the fabricating and assembling of interchangeable parts. The systems and controls developed at the armory were as critical to the development of what became known as "the American system of manufacturing" as the new metalworking machinery and machine tools. They began to be used in the production of axes, shovels, and other simple implements in the mid-1830s and 1840s, and in the making of sewing machines and firearms for the commercial market in the 1850s.[74] Finally in the 1880s, over half a century after Lee devised his methods, the practices and procedures developed at Springfield were taken up and perfected by the practitioners of modern scientific factory management.

Modern factory management (but *not*, it must be stressed, the management of large modern multiunit enterprises) had its genesis in the United States in the Springfield Armory. Although the practices and procedures developed there became significant after 1840, they had little relevance for contemporary manufacturers or other producers. The small shops, mills, farms, and plantations that accounted for an overwhelming share of American production had little need for such methods of internal accounting and inventory and quality control. Their output was small enough and the pace of their work slow enough so that production was easily supervised by their owners.

Lifting technological constraints

Until the 1840s, then, the armories and textile mills remained the exception. In all other manufacturing enterprises the volume of production was not enough to bring the subdivision of labor nor the integration of several production processes within a single establishment. The primary constraint on the spread of the factory in the United States appears to have been technological; the demand for such volume production existed. In fact, steam-driven factories in Manchester, Birmingham, and other European industrial cities were satisfying this demand.[75]

The armories were able to become large integrated and subdivided factories because their guaranteed markets permitted them to pay the high costs of production and distribution. Even so, the private contractors had difficulty in fulfilling their contracts and in remaining solvent.[76] The textile manufacturers were able to set up factories by harnessing the power of large rivers, by relying on wooden equipment and leather belting, rather than on iron machinery and gearing. Yet the water power sites generating the needed head of water were limited. By 1840 industrial establishments using such sources of power were relatively few, and the class of managers that operated them was still small.

Of all the technological constraints, the lack of coal was probably the most significant in holding back the spread of the factory in the United States. The opening of the anthracite coal fields in eastern Pennsylvania lifted this constraint.[77] Anthracite first became available in quantity for industrial purposes in the 1830s. Before that time the only source of domestic coal for the American northeast, where manufacturing was concentrated, remained the limited output of mines on the James River. The value of the hard or stone coal of eastern Pennsylvania was first recognized during the War of 1812. Owners of coal lands first began to build canals into the anthracite regions in the 1820s. As the Schuylkill, the Lehigh Valley, and the Delaware and Hudson canals came into operation, output of anthracite coal soared. It rose from almost nothing before 1825 to 91,100 tons in 1828, to 290,600 in 1830, to 1,039,000 in 1837. Moved by canal to New York and Philadelphia, coal was then transported by small coastal ships to Boston and the smaller New England ports. By 1831, 563 vessels carried 56,000 tons of anthracite from Philadelphia to Boston. By 1836, 3,285 vessels moved 345,000 tons. By the mid-1830s the price of anthracite had dropped from close to $10 a ton to less than $5 a ton. By the mid-1840s production had risen to over 2 million tons, and the price fell to $3 a ton. Anthracite, first used for heating houses and other buildings in the seaport cities, thus became increasingly available for industrial purposes.

The metal-working and metal-making industries were among the first to expand output on the basis of the new fuel. In the early 1830s, fabricators of wrought iron were just beginning to use anthracite in the shaping of axes, shovels, wire, and similar finished products. In the mid-1830s ironmakers devised the anthracite reverberatory furnace to replace the charcoal-heated, water-driven forge to make wrought iron bars, sheets, and rods. In 1840 the first anthracite coal blast furnace to make pig iron went into blast. By 1849, 60 such furnaces were in operation, and by 1853 their number had doubled to 121. In 1849 the average work force of these furnaces numbered eighty and their average capital assets were valued at $83,000.[78]. By 1854, 45 percent of all the iron made in the United States was produced by anthracite coal—303,000 tons as compared to 306,000 tons produced by charcoal and 49,000 by bituminous coal. The coming of anthracite coal thus quickly assured American manufacturers for the first time of an abundant domestic supply of iron.

Inexpensive iron and coal permitted the factory to spread quickly in a wide variety of metal-working industries. Not only did the output of establishments making axes, scythes, hoes, and plows increase, but for the first time the fabricating and assembling of interchangeable parts became widely used in making metal goods besides guns for the United States army. Locks, safes, clocks, and watches were produced in large departmentalized factories. In the small-arms industries, new men and new firms —Colt, Remington, Sharpe, Lawrence and Robbins, and the forerunners of the Winchester Arms Company—all of whom had built large factories in the late 1840s and 1850s, replaced the older private contractors and armories as the industry's leaders. During the late 1840s manufacturers first began to use the technology of interchangeable parts in factories to produce newly invented machines, such as sewing machines and reapers. The need for specialized machinery in all these industries led to the creation almost overnight of the American machine tool industry. By the 1850s the Ames Manufacturing Company in Chicopee, Pratt and Whitney in Hartford, Browne & Sharp in Providence, and Sellers & Bancroft in Philadelphia were already established machinery-making enterprises.[79]

By mid-century the availability of coal, iron, and machinery transformed the processes of production in other industries. Coal not only provided heat so essential for large-scale production in foundries and furnace industries and also in the refining and distilling trades, but it also provided an inexpensive and efficient fuel for generating steam power. Cheap coal permitted the building of large steam-driven factories in commercial centers close to markets and existing pools of labor. In the heat-using industries the factory quickly replaced the artisan and craftsman in the making of sugar, spirits, beer, chemicals, glass, earthenware, plated ware, and India rubber.[80] In the non-heat-using industries the coal-powered steam engines encouraged the relocation of industries. One significant example was the building of integrated textile mills along the coast from New London to Portsmouth. Comparable factories came, though more slowly, in the cloth, wood, and leatherworking industries. Coal, then, provided the source of energy that made it possible for the factory to replace the artisans, the small mill owners, and putting-out system as the basic unit of production in many American industries.

In the decade and a half before the Civil War, as the availability of coal and the introduction of coal-using technologies brought fundamental changes in the processes of production, the railroad and the telegraph were also beginning to transform the processes of distribution. They made it possible for middlemen to receive and distribute goods in a far greater volume than ever before. These basic changes in production and distribution reinforced one another. The factory could only maintain high levels of production if materials flowed steadily in and out of the factory site in volume and on schedule. And the new factories provided the goods that railroads carried in unprecedented volume to be distributed by jobbers and other marketers. The new sources of energy and new speed and regularity of transportation and communication caused entrepreneurs to integrate and subdivide their business activities and to hire salaried managers to monitor and coordinate the flow of goods through their enlarged enterprises. The almost simultaneous availability of an abundant new form of energy and revolutionary new means of transportation and communication led to the rise of modern business enterprise in American commerce and industry.

PART
two

The Revolution in
Transportation and
Communication

The railroad and the telegraph provided the fast, regular, and dependable transportation and communication so essential to high-volume production and distribution—the hallmark of large modern manufacturing or marketing enterprises. As important, the rail and telegraph companies were themselves the first modern business enterprises to appear in the United States. They were the first to require a large number of full-time managers to coordinate, control, and evaluate the activities of a number of widely scattered operating units. For this reason, they provided the most relevant administrative models for enterprises in the production and distribution of goods and services when such enterprises began to build, on the basis of the new transportation and communication network, their own geographically extended, multiunit business empires.

The history of the new technologies in transportation and communication and of the enterprises that came to operate them is as complex as it is significant. It calls not only for a review of the introduction of the railroad, steamship, electric street railway, and the telegraph and telephone, but also for a description and analysis of the institutional innovations generated by their operating requirements. Part II therefore focuses on how these new enterprises were financed, organized, and administered; how they competed with one another; and how and why they then enlarged their domains to become the largest business enterprises the world had ever seen.

Of the new forms of transportation the railroads were the most numerous, their activities the most complex, and their influence the most pervasive. They were the pioneers in the management of modern business enterprise. They therefore receive the most attention. Other new forms of transportation and communication—the steamship, the electric urban street railway, the telegraph, and the telephone—underwent comparable, if less dramatic, developments. By the early twentieth century modern business enterprise, with its large staff of salaried managers and its clear separation of ownership and control, completely dominated the American transportation and communications networks—networks that were so necessary for the coming of mass production and mass distribution and for the rise of modern business enterprise in other sectors of the economy.

CHAPTER 3

The Railroads: The First
Modern Business Enterprises,
1850s-1860s

Innovation in technology and organization

Modern business enterprises came to operate the railroad and telegraph networks for both technological and organizational reasons. Railroad companies were the first transportation firms to build and to own rights-of-way and at the same time to operate the common carriers using those rights-of-way. Telegraph companies also both built the lines and ran the messages through them. The enterprises, both public and private, that constructed and maintained the canals and turnpikes rarely operated the canal boat companies, stage lines, or mail routes that used them.[1] Even when they did, their rights-of-way were used by many other independent transportation companies.

On the railroad, however, the movements of carriers had to be carefully coordinated and controlled if the goods and passengers were to be moved in safety and with a modicum of efficiency. The first railroads—those using horses for motive power—were often able to allow common carriers operated by other individuals and companies to use their rails.[2] But as soon as the much faster steam locomotive began to replace the horse-drawn vehicles, operations had to be controlled from a single headquarters if only to prevent 'accidents. Considerations of safety were particularly compelling in the United States, where nearly all railroads relied on a single line of track. For a time railroad managers experimented in hauling cars owned by local merchants and freight forwarders. However, the coordination of the movement of cars and the handling of charges and payment proved exceedingly difficult. By 1840 the railroad managers

81

found it easier to own and control all cars using their roads. Later, express companies and other large shippers operating on a national scale came to own their own cars; but only after the railroads had devised complex organizational arrangements to handle the movement of and charges for such "foreign" cars.

Because they operated common carriers, railroads, unlike the major canal systems, became privately rather than publicly owned enterprises. In the early years of the Republic, American merchants and shippers gave strong support to government construction and operation of costly rights-of-way.[3] On the other hand, these businessmen rarely, if ever, proposed that the government operate the common carriers. Only a small number of American railroads were initially operated by the state, and by 1850 with very few exceptions these had been turned over to private business enterprises. These same merchants and shippers who distrusted government ownership were also fearful of private monopoly. Therefore, the charters of the early roads generally provided for close legislative oversight of these new transportation enterprises.

The railroads did not begin to have a significant impact on American business institutions until the nation's first railroad boom which began in the late 1840s and 1850s. Before that time railroad construction did not fundamentally alter existing routes or modes of transportation, since the first roads were built in the 1830s and 1840s to connect existing commercial centers and to supplement existing water transportation. The lines from Boston to nearby towns (Lowell, Newburyport, Providence, and Worcester); from Camden to Amboy in New Jersey (the rail link between New York and Philadelphia); from Philadelphia to Reading, Philadelphia to Baltimore, and Baltimore to Washington, were all short, rarely more than fifty miles.

This was also true of those lines connecting the several towns along the Erie Canal. In the south and west, railroads were longer because distances between towns were greater, but they carried fewer passengers and smaller amounts of freight. Until the 1850s, none of the great lines planned to connect the east with the west were even close to completion. Before 1850 only one road, the Western, which ran from Worcester to Albany, connected one major regional section of the country with another. Except for the Western, no railroad was long enough or busy enough to create complex operating problems.

During the 1840s the technology of railroad transportation was rapidly perfected. Uniform methods of construction, grading, tunneling, and bridging were developed. The iron T rail came into common use. By the late 1840s the locomotive had its cams, sandbox, driver wheels, swivel or bogie truck, and equalizing beams. Passenger coaches had become "long cars," carrying sixty passengers on reversible seats. Boxcars, cattle cars, lumber cars, and other freight cars were smaller but otherwise little different from those used on American railroads a century later.[4]

As technology improved, railroads became the favored means of overland transportation. They not only quickly captured the passenger and light-weight and high-value freight traffic from the canals and turnpikes but also began soon to compete successfully as carriers of textiles, cotton, grain, coal, and other more bulky products. Indeed, some of the first roads in the north, such as the Boston and Lowell and the Reading, were built by textile manufacturers and anthracite coal mine owners to replace canals they had already constructed to carry their products to market; while railroads in the south and west were constructed specifically to carry cotton and grain.[5] In the decade of the 1840s, only 400 miles of canals were built to make the nation's total mileage at the end of the decade just under 4,000. In that same decade, over 6,000 miles of railroads went into operation providing a total of 9,000 miles of track by 1850.[6]

As the country pulled out of the long economic depression of the late 1830s and early 1840s, railroad building began in earnest. The railroad boom came in the mid-1840s in New England and then in the late 1840s in the south and west. In the decade of the 1850s, when more canals were abandoned than built, over 21,000 more miles of railroad were constructed, laying down the basic overland transportation network east of the Mississippi River. As dramatic was the almost simultaneous completion between 1851 and 1854 of the great intersectional trunk lines connecting east and west (the Erie, the Baltimore and Ohio, the Pennsylvania, and the New York Central) and the building of a whole new transportation network in the old northwest. In 1849 the five states of the old northwest, a region endowed with a superb river and lake system, had only 600 miles of track. By 1860 the 9,000 miles of railroad covering the area had replaced rivers, lakes, and canals as the primary means of transportation for all but bulky, low-value commodities.

The reason for the swift commercial success of the railroads over canals and other inland waterways is obvious enough. The railroad provided more direct communication than did the river, lake, or coastal routes. While construction costs of canals on level ground were somewhat less than for railroads, the railroad was cheaper to build in rugged terrain.[7] Moreover, because a railroad route did not, like that of a canal, require a substantial water supply, it could go more directly between two towns. In addition, railroads were less expensive to maintain per ton-mile than canals. They were, of course, faster. For the first time in history, freight and passengers could be carried overland at a speed faster than that of a horse. The maps emphasize how the railroad revolutionized the speed of

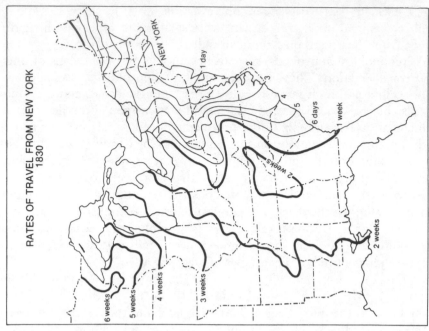

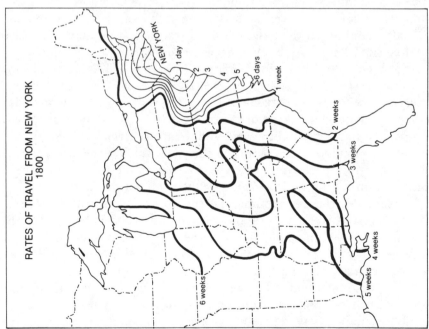

Rates of travel, 1800, 1830, 1957. Adapted from Charles O. Paullin. *Atlas of the Historical Geography of the United States* (Washington, D.C.: Carnegie Institute and American Geographical Society, 1932), plate 138A, B, C.

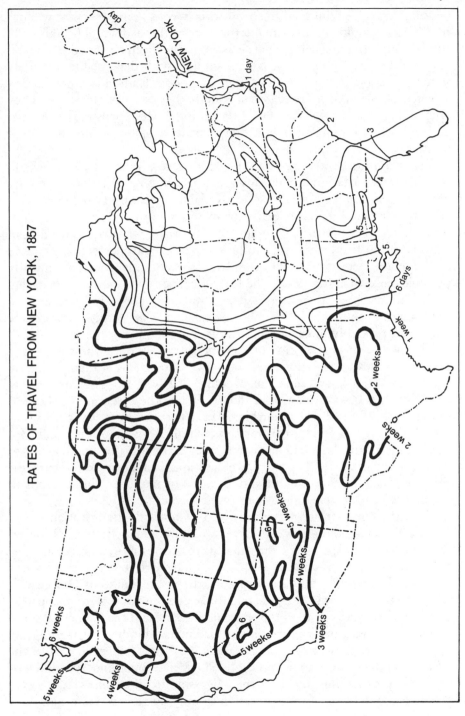

RATES OF TRAVEL FROM NEW YORK, 1857

travel. A traveler who used to spend three weeks going from New York to Chicago, could by 1857 make the trip in three days. The railroad's fundamental advantage, however, was not in the speed it carried passengers and mail but its ability to provide a shipper with dependable, precisely scheduled, all-weather transportation of goods. Railroads were far less affected by droughts, freshets, and floods than were waterways. They were not shut down by freshets in the spring or dry spells in the summer and fall. Most important of all, they remained open during the winter months.

The steam locomotive not only provided fast, regular, dependable, all-weather transportation but also lowered the unit cost of moving goods by permitting a more intensive use of available transportation facilities. A railroad car could make several trips over a route in the same period of time it took a canal boat to complete one. By 1840, when the new mode of transportation had only begun to be technologically perfected, its speed and regularity permitted a steam railway the potential to carry annually per mile more than fifty times the freight carried by a canal. Even at that early date, Stanley Legerbott writes, "railroads could provide at least three times as much freight service as canals *for an equivalent resource cost*—and probably more nearly five times as much."[8]

The history of competition on specific routes supports these estimates. For twenty years, the trip from Boston to Concord, New Hampshire, by way of the Middlesex Canal, the Merrimack River, and ancillary canals, took five days upstream and four down. When the extension of the Boston and Lowell reached Concord in 1842, the travel time was cut to four hours one way.[9] A freight car on the new railroad made four round trips by the time a canal boat had made only one. To handle the same amount of traffic, a canal would have to have had approximately four times the carrying space of the railroad and, because of ice, even this equipment would have had to remain idle four months a year.

With the completion of the railroad to Concord, the historian of the Middlesex Canal points out "the waterway is immediately marked for defeat; in 1843 the expenses of the canal were greater than its receipts. The end has come."[10] The end came almost as quickly to the great state works of Pennsylvania and Ohio. For example, the net revenues of Ohio canals which were $278,525 in 1849, were only $93,421 in 1855; they dropped to a deficit of $107,761 in 1860.[11] For a time the Erie and the Chesapeake and Ohio canals continued to carry bulky products—lumber, coal, and grain —primarily from west to east. By the 1870s they had even lost to the railroad on the grain trade. And in the 1850s river boat lines lost much of the rapidly expanding trade of the Mississippi to the railroads.[12] Never before had one form of transportation so quickly replaced another.

The swift victory of the railway over the waterway resulted from organizational as well as technological innovation. Technology made possible fast, all-weather transportation; but safe, regular, reliable movement of goods and passengers, as well as the continuing maintenance and repair of locomotives, rolling stock, and track, roadbed, stations, roundhouses, and other equipment, required the creation of a sizable administrative organization. It meant the employment of a set of managers to supervise these functional activities over an extensive geographical area; and the appointment of an administrative command of middle and top executives to monitor, evaluate, and coordinate the work of managers responsible for the day-to-day operations. It meant, too, the formulation of brand new types of internal administrative procedures and accounting and statistical controls. Hence, the operational requirements of the railroads demanded the creation of the first administrative hierarchies in American business.

The men who managed these enterprises became the first group of modern business administrators in the United States. Ownership and management soon separated. The capital required to build a railroad was far more than that required to purchase a plantation, a textile mill, or even a fleet of ships. Therefore, a single enterpreneur, family, or small group of associates was rarely able to own a railroad. Nor could the many stockholders or their representatives manage it. The administrative tasks were too numerous, too varied, and too complex. They required special skills and training which could only be commanded by a full-time salaried manager. Only in the raising and allocating of capital, in the setting of financial policies, and in the selection of top managers did the owners or their representatives have a real say in railroad management. On the other hand, few managers had the financial resources to own even a small percent of the capital stock of the roads they managed.

Because of the special skills and training required and the existence of an administrative hierarchy, the railroad managers came to look on their work as much more of a lifetime career than did the plantation overseer or the textile mill agent. Most railroad managers soon expected to spend their life working up the administrative ladder, if not on the road with which they started, then on another. This career orientation and the specialized nature of tasks gave the railroad managers an increasingly professional outlook on their work. And because they had far greater personal, if not financial, commitment to the continuing health of their enterprise, they came in time to have almost as much say about financial policies and the allocation of resources for future operations as did the owners and their representatives. The members of the administrative bureaucracy essential to the operation of the railroad began to take control of their own destinies.

The construction of the nation's new transportation network and the evolution of the nation's first modern business enterprise—as well as the first modern managerial class—fall into two distinct chronological periods. External changes in each period had a significant impact on internal organizational and managerial development. The first period extended from the beginning of the railroad boom in the late 1840s to the coming of the economic depression of the 1870s. It was a period of almost continuous growth of the network (except of course during the Civil War) and a period of impressive organizational innovation. By the start of the depression of the 1870s, the 70,000 miles of track in operation provided the nation with the basic overland transportation network that would serve until the coming of the automobile and airplane in the twentieth century. By the 1870s the large railroads of over 500 miles in length had perfected complex and intricate mechanisms to coordinate and control the work of thousands of employees, the operations of tens of millions of dollars' worth of roadbed and equipment, and the movement of hundreds of millions of dollars' worth of goods. By that time, too, the railroad had worked out complicated intercompany arrangements so that a carload of goods or produce could be moved from almost any sizable town in the country to another distant commercial center without a single transshipment. In other words, goods placed in a car did not have to be reloaded until they reached their destination.

The second period of American railroad history, extending from the depression of the 1870s to the prosperous first years of the new century, was one of competition and consolidation, although railroad building continued apace. By 1900 close to 200,000 miles of line were in operation. Except along the disappearing frontier in the west, this new mileage filled in the existing network. Indeed, much of the construction was not needed to meet the existing demand for rail transportation. This overbuilding was one consequence of the creation of the giant consolidated systems, the managers' response to increasing competition. These managers adopted the strategy of consolidation because they wanted to have their own tracks into all the major commercial centers of the areas they served. They were unwilling to rely on potential competitors to provide outlets for the freight and passenger traffic they carried. By the beginning of the new century not only had the American railroad network been virtually completed but the boundaries of the major railroad systems had also become fixed. The systems would continue to operate in much the same areas and in much the same ways until the second half of the twentieth century, when the automobile, truck, and airplane had reoriented American transportation. For several decades the consolidated railroad systems remained the largest business enterprise in the world.

The early history of the business enterprises created to operate the telegraph and then the telephone was quite similar to that of the railroads. As the railroads marched across the continent, so too did the telegraph. Invented in 1844, it began to be used commercially in 1847. Railroad managers quickly found the telegraph an invaluable aid in assuring the safe and efficient operation of trains; and telegraph promoters realized that the railroads provided the only convenient rights-of-way. Because the telegraph was easier and cheaper to build than the railroad, it reached the Pacific first, in 1861. By the beginning of that decade 50,000 miles of wire were in operation. Two decades later, according to the census of 1880, 31,703,000 messages had been sent per year over 291,000 miles of wire.[13]

The telephone, commercialized in the 1880s, at first only supplemented the telegraph. It was used initially almost wholly for local conversations. Then with the development of the "long lines" in the 1890s the telephone became increasingly employed for long-distance calls. Thus, where the railroad improved communication by speeding the movement of mail, the telegraph and then the telephone permitted even faster—indeed almost instantaneous—communication in nearly every part of the nation.

The enterprises that built, owned, and operated these new instruments of communication soon governed a large number of units scattered over a wide geographical area. The coordination of a large number of messages to all parts of the country called for even tighter internal control than did the movement of railroad transportation traffic. Not surprisingly, the nation's telegraph network was by 1866 dominated by a single enterprise, Western Union. Nor is it surprising that its administrative and accounting procedures were very similar to those of the railroads. As the telephone network began to expand in the 1890s, the pioneering group—the Bell interests—maintained its control of the industry "through traffic" by means of the American Telephone and Telegraph Company, which built and operated through or long-distance facilities. In modern communication, as in modern transportation, the requirements of high-volume, high-speed operations brought the large-scale managerial enterprise and with it oligopoly or monopoly.

The impact of the railroads on construction and finance

Any detailed analysis of the history of modern business enterprise in the United States must, therefore, pay particular attention to the 1850s. There was some preliminary activity in the 1840s. Not until the 1850s, however, did the processes of production and distribution start to respond in strength to the swift expansion of the new forms of transportation and communication and the increasing availability of a new source of energy—coal. During the 1850s, railroad and telegraph enterprises began to devise the organizational structures and accounting procedures so central to the operation of the modern firm. In that decade, too, the demands of railroad building led to a fundamental change in the nation's financial and construction industries. Before considering the broader impact of the railroad and telegraph on transportation, communication, production, and distribution, it seems well to indicate how the railroads helped to centralize the American capital market in New York City and at the same time revolutionize the construction industry.

The demands of the railroads during the 1850s on American financial intermediaries and on construction contractors were unprecedented. Railroads required far larger amounts of capital to build than did canals. The total expenditures for canals between 1815 and 1860 reached $188 million, of which 73 percent was supplied by state and local governments with funds raised through sales of state and municipal bonds.[14] By 1859 the investment in the securities of private railroad corporations had passed the $1,100 million mark; and of this amount close to $700 million had been raised in the previous ten years. In that decade many large railroads were being constructed simultaneously. Before 1850 the largest railroad enterprise, the Western Railroad between Worcester and Albany, had cost $8 million to build. In the short period between 1849 and 1854 more than thirty large railroads were completed. Many cost more than the Western. The great east–west trunk lines—the Erie, the Pennsylvania, the Baltimore and Ohio, and the New York Central—were capitalized at from $17 to $35 million.[15] Major roads in the west—the Michigan Central, the Michigan Southern, and the Illinois Central—cost from $10 to $17 million. Other roads in the west and those in the south that went through less populated territory rarely required less than $2 million and often more than $5 million. By comparison, during the same decade of the 1850s, only a few of the largest textile mills or ironmaking and metalworking factories were capitalized at over $1 million. In fact, during the 1850s there were only forty-one textile companies capitalized at $250,000 or more; and these mills had been financed over a thirty-year period.[16]

The railroads were the first private business enterprises in the United States to acquire large amounts of capital from outside their own regions. The textile mills of New England, and the iron and other metalmaking enterprises of Pennsylvania, had been financed locally or in Boston or Philadelphia. The state and municipal bonds used to finance canals were sold abroad through large mercantile houses, through the Second Bank of the United States, and by personal visits of canal commissioners to Europe.

With the coming of the railroad boom of the late 1840s, capital required for railroad construction could no longer be raised, as it had been earlier, from farmers, merchants, and manufacturers living along the line of the road or by having the railroad president go to European money markets. This was particularly true in the transallegheny west, where much of the territory had only recently been opened to settlement. Funds for the simultaneous construction of so many large railroads had to come from the older commercial centers of the east. Soon only the largest financial communities of Europe could provide the vast amount of capital required.

Those seeking funds for the new roads in the late 1840s came increasingly to New York City. After the demise of the Second Bank in 1836, Boston replaced Philadelphia as the major source of capital for the modest railroad construction of that time. During the 1840s Boston capital supplied funds to build New England roads, the first roads in the west, and even those in the Philadelphia area. By 1847, however, Boston merchants had little more surplus to invest. As a result, money rates were higher in Boston than in New York. By the early 1850s even the largest and most prosperous Massachusetts roads were relying on New York for capital for new construction.[17]

At the same time Europeans, troubled by the political unrest which culminated in the Revolution of 1848, began for the first time since the depression of the late 1830s to look for investment opportunities in the United States. First they purchased United States government bonds—those issued to finance the Mexican War. Next they began to buy state bonds. Then finally in 1851 and 1852 the Germans and the French, and a little later the British, began to purchase American railroad securities in quantity. To meet the needs of American railroads seeking funds and those of Europeans looking for investments, a number of importing and exporting firms located in New York, particularly those concentrating on the buying and selling of foreign exchange, began to specialize in handling railroad securities. By the mid-fifties such partnerships as Winslow, Lanier; Duncan, Sherman; Meyer and Stucken; De Coppet and Company; Cammann and Whitehouse; De Launay, Islin and Clark; and De Rham and Moore were on their way to becoming the nation's first specialized investment banking firms. As agents for a railroad they sold its securities for a straight fee or on commission, acted as its transfer agent in New York, and advised their railroad client on financial matters. Occasionally they even purchased rails, locomotives, and other equipment. At the same time, they became agents for larger European investors who had purchased or were planning to buy American railroad stocks and bonds.

As soon as the American capital market became centralized and institutionalized in New York City, all the present-day instruments of finance were perfected; so too were nearly all the techniques of modern securities marketing and speculation. Bonds became the primary instrument to finance railroad construction. The promoters of the American roads and those initial investors who lived along their lines preferred to maintain control over their investment by owning stock; the eastern and European money men, however, believed that bonds assured a safer and more regular income. Railroad builders inevitably underestimated the cost of construction, causing first mortgage bonds to be followed by second and third mortgage bonds. Then came income and debenture bonds. At the same time, to attract a somewhat different set of customers, bonds which could be converted into stock appeared, as did a variety of preferred stocks.

The great increase in railroad securities brought trading and speculation on the New York Stock Exchange in its modern form. Before the railroads the volume of stocks in banks, insurance companies, and state and federal bonds was tiny. One day in March 1830 only thirty-one shares were traded on the New York Stock Exchange.[18] By the mid-1850s the securities of railroads, banks, and also municipalities from all parts of the United States were being traded in New York. Where earlier hundreds of shares had been traded weekly, hundreds of thousands of shares changed hands weekly in the 1850s. In a four-week period in the 1850s transactions totaled close to a million shares.

The new volume of business brought modern speculative techniques to the buying and selling of securities. Traders sold "long" and "short" for future delivery. The use of puts and calls was perfected. Trading came to be done on margin. Indeed, the modern call loan market began in the 1850s, as New York banks began to loan to speculators on call in order to provide funds to cover the interest they were beginning to pay on their deposit accounts. In the 1850s skillful securities manipulators were becoming nationally known figures. Jacob Barker, Daniel Drew, Jim Fiske, and Jay Gould, all made their dubious reputations by dealing in railroad securities.

By the outbreak of the Civil War, the New York financial district, by responding to the needs of railroad financing, had become one of the largest and most sophisticated capital markets in the world. The only significant innovations after the Civil War were the coming of the telegraphic stock ticker to record sales and the development of the cooperative syndicate of several investment bankers to market large blocks of securities. For more than a generation this market was used almost wholly by the railroads and allied enterprises, such as the telegraph, express, and sleeping car companies. As soon as American manufacturers had comparable needs for funds, they too began to rely on the New York markets. However, except for the makers of electrical equipment, few manufacturers felt such a need until the 1890s. When they did begin to seek outside funds, the institutions to provide such capital were fully developed. No further innovation was needed. New York provided an even more efficient national market for industrials than it did for railroads. In American industry the lack of a well-organized national capital market cannot be considered a constraint on the rise of modern business enterprise.

The simultaneous construction of many large railroads during the 1850s modernized the construction trade as much as it did the business of finance. Before the railroad boom of that period, construction companies were still small partnerships. The earlier railroads, built in much the same manner as turnpikes and canals, were largely constructed by local part-time contractors: usually farmers, merchants, or even professional men who lived along the line of the road. Each contracted to build a small section, working under the supervision of the road's chief engineer. By the 1840s more full-time professional contractors began to make a career of railroad and canal construction. Their enterprises, however, remained small. They continued to rely on local labor and materials. The building of one road required the services of many small firms.

The railroad boom created new needs and opportunities. On the large roads it became increasingly difficult for the engineer and his assistants to oversee the work of many small contractors. Labor and equipment often became hard to find at the time they were most critically needed. As a result, in the late 1840s and early 1850s engineers like Horatio C. Seymour (the former state engineer of New York), Alvah C. Morton of Maine, and Joseph Sheffield and Henry Farnum from Connecticut formed companies to build railroads.[19] These great contractors handled all aspects of construction and were often engaged in building more than one road. They supplied all necessary equipment, including rails and even locomotives and rolling stock. They recruited labor and often subcontracted parts of the construction. They did all this for a flat fee, either on a per mile or total cost basis, receiving at least part of their payment in railroad stocks or bonds. One contractor, Horatio Seymour, on his premature death in 1853, was reported to have on hand more than $30 million worth of business.[20] Such contractors thus became heavily involved in railroad finance. Some railroad promoters used the contracting firm as a way to make higher profits than they might by simply operating the road. These large contractors relied increasingly on immigrant labor. Even though the Irish and German famines had brought a flood of immigrants into the United States in the late 1840s and early 1850s, these firms soon had agents overseas recruiting workers in Britain and western Europe.

The new labor supply and the railroad experience brought the large contracting company quickly into urban construction. After the 1840s, mayors and councils in the growing American cities let out contracts similar to those of the railroads (though usually smaller) for the paving of streets, the building of schools, and the construction of water and sewage systems. By the Civil War the letting of such contracts had become a valuable piece of political patronage, and urban contractors were becoming ever more closely tied to city politics.

In these ways, then, the nation's first railroad boom provided a basic impetus to the rise of the large-scale construction firm and the modern investment banking house. However, these firms created no new problems of internal management in their operation. Neither the construction company nor the investment banking house built a large geographically extended administrative network of operating units. They were not yet full-fledged modern business enterprises. Although the investment banking houses had partners and occasionally salaried managers in other American cities and European financial centers, most of their day-to-day buying and selling activities were handled in a small office near or on Wall Street. And although construction companies carried out a number of multimillion dollar jobs in different parts of the country, each project was managed locally by a handful of managers. None was permanent. When the road was completed that contracting unit moved on to another job in another place. Only the home office had a permanent staff. There the senior partner of the firm with one or two associates negotiated contracts and provided general supervision of operations from a single office. That office too was normally located in New York City. The management of such enterprises did not require the constant, almost minute-to-minute supervision that operation of the railroads demanded.

Structural innovation

Such constant coordination and control were, however, fundamental to the management of the railroads. Once a large road was financed, constructed, and in operation, the next challenge was that of management. Without the building of a managerial staff, without the design of internal administrative structures and procedures, and without communicating internal information, a high volume of traffic could not be carried safely and efficiently. Obtaining the full potential of the new technology called for unprecedented organizational efforts. No other business enterprise, or for that matter few other nonbusiness institutions, had ever required the coordination and control of so many different types of units carrying out so great a variety of tasks that demanded such close scheduling. None handled so many different types of goods or required the recording of so many different financial accounts.

The men who faced these challenges were a new type of businessman. It is worth emphasizing again that they were salaried employees with little or no financial interest in the companies they served. Moreover, most had had specialized training. The pioneers of modern management—George W. Whistler of the Western, Benjamin Latrobe of the Baltimore & Ohio, Daniel C. McCallum of the Erie, Herman Haupt and J. Edgar Thomson of the Pennsylvania, John B. Jervis of the Michigan Southern, and George B. McClellan of the Illinois Central—were all trained civil engineers with experience in railroad construction and bridge building before they took over the management of their roads.[21] Because they worked for a salary and not a share of the profits, because they had professional training and had developed professional expertise, their way of life was much closer to that of the modern manager than to that of the merchants and manufacturers who owned and operated business enterprises before the coming of the railroads.

To meet these unprecedented challenges these engineers had little to go on. The operation of the early canals and turnpikes provided few clues. The first railroads with their small size and light traffic developed only a modicum of useful experience. Nor did the managers of the first large roads borrow directly from the practices and procedures of military or other nonbusiness bureaucracies. Of the pioneers in the new managerial methods, only two—Whistler and McClellan—had military experience, and they were the least innovative of the lot.

The military model may, however, have had an indirect impact on the beginnings of modern business management. Because the United States Military Academy provided the best formal training in civil engineering in this country until the 1860s, a number of West Point graduates came to build and manage railroads. Some of these West Point trained engineers had served in or had an acquaintance with the Ordnance Department or the Corps of Engineers, two of the very few professionally manned, hierarchical organizations in antebellum America.

Yet even for such officers, engineering training was probably more important than an acquaintance with bureaucratic procedures. There is little evidence that railroad managers copied military procedures. Instead all evidence indicates that their answers came in response to immediate and pressing operational problems requiring the organization of men and machinery. They responded to these in much the same rational, analytical way as they solved the mechanical problems of building a bridge or laying down a railroad.

These administrative challenges first appeared in the 1850s when the railroads grew large enough to require the coordination of the activities of several geographically contiguous operating divisions. The operations of the early small roads remained relatively simple, although even the earliest railroads required the management of more varied activities than did a contemporary textile mill or armory. An early road from thirty to fifty miles in length with relatively heavy traffic employed about fifty workers and was administered by a superintendent who had under him a manager responsible for each of the road's major functional activities: transportation and traffic, maintenance of way, and maintenance of locomotives and rolling stock. On lightly traveled roads the superintendent himself often supervised the functional activities and arranged for and maintained train schedules.

On these early roads personal management was easy; the superintendent and his functional assistants worked out of the same office. As in a New England textile mill, the superintendent conferred weekly with the treasurer or president, and occasionally with the board of directors. The treasurer maintained the books which were, in the words of the Boston & Worcester directors, "kept in a strictly mercantile style, according to the Italian method of bookkeeping by double entry."[22]

The coordination of the movements of trains and the flow of traffic did not yet raise complex scheduling problems. For example, on the busy forty-four-mile Boston & Worcester Railroad, passenger trains left each terminal at precisely the same time—6:00 A.M, 12:00 noon, and 4:00 P.M.[23] One daily freight train departed immediately after the morning passenger train. The trains would meet at the mid-point, Framingham. Neither train would move on to its destination until the other had pulled into the station. On the longer but more lightly traveled roads to the south, trains ran one way one day and the other way the next. Except for the Western, which in 1840 became the first intersectional railroad in the country by connecting Worcester and Albany, no road before 1850 demanded a complicated operating structure.

As the Western neared completion, the inadequacies of the traditional, personal methods of management became clear. That road, which was just over 150 miles in length, had been built in three different sections or divisions. As each came into operation, each became a separate operating division with its own set of functional managers. Because of the road's length, the morning passenger train that started from Worcester at 9:30 A.M. did not reach the western terminal on the Hudson River until late that afternoon. As the company ran three trains a day each way (two passenger trains and one freight), the trains moving in opposite directions met twelve times daily. Since they ran on a single track, without the benefit of telegraphic signals, through mountainous terrain, such scheduling threatened tragedy. It came quickly. Even before the road had reached the Hudson River, the Western suffered a series of serious accidents, culminating in a head-on collision of passenger trains on October 5, 1841, killing a conductor and a passenger and injuring seventeen others.

The resulting outcry helped bring into being the first modern, carefully defined, internal organizational structure used by an American business enterprise. After the accident, the Massachusetts legislature launched an intensive investigation into the operations of the Western. *The American Railroad Journal and Mechanics Magazine* called for administrative reform. The company's directors, fully agreeing, appointed a committee of three directors (two Boston businessmen and a physician) and the engineer in charge of construction, Major George W. Whistler, to find a remedy.

The solution outlined in the committee's "Report on Avoiding Collisions and Governing the Employees" was, in the words of the road's historian, to fix "definite responsibilities for each phase of the company's business, drawing solid lines of authority and communication for the railroad's administration, maintenance, and operation."[24] The new organizational structure called for a comparable set of functional managers on each of the three geographically contiguous operating divisions and then the creation of a headquarters at Springfield to monitor and coordinate the activities of the three sets of managers. Each division had its assistant master of transportation (later called division superintendent), its roadmaster, and its senior mechanic or foreman in charge of roundhouses and shops.

On each division the assistant masters of transportation were responsible for the movement of trains and of freight and passenger traffic, the roadmasters for the maintenance of way, and the mechanics for the repair and maintenance of locomotives and rolling stock. The assistant masters of transportation reported to the master of transportation at Springfield headquarters, the mechanics to the master mechanic, who headed the main shops in Springfield and who also reported to the master of transportation. The roadmasters, on the other hand, reported directly to the superintendent and not to the master of transportation as did those in the other functional departments. The superintendent (soon to be the general superintendent) was responsible to the president and directors for the operation of the road. All managers were to make regular reports based on the information received from their subordinates: station agents, conductors, locomotive engineers, the shop foreman, and the foreman of repair gangs. To prevent accidents, precise timetables were determined by the division superintendents working with the master of transportation and the general superintendent. These were given to the conductor who had "sole charge of the train," and who was given detailed instruction about how to handle delays or breakdowns.[25] No changes could be made in the schedules without written permission from the master of transportation and then only after consultation with his three division managers.

The need to assure safety of passengers and employees on the new, high-speed mode of transportation made the Western Railroad the first American business enterprise to operate through a formal administrative structure manned by full-time salaried managers. This embryonic modern business enterprise included two middle managers—the master of transportation and the master mechanic—and two top managers—the superintendent and the president. The latter, who became in 1852 a full-time officer, was the link between the full-time salaried managers and the part-time representatives of the owners elected to the board of directors.[26]

When other long and heavily traveled lines came into operation in the early 1850s, the most important of these being the lines that connected the east and the west and the first major lines in the west, they began to create organizational structures similar to that of the Western Railroad. By then it was the volume and velocity of traffic rather than the need for safety that demanded better organization. The coming of the telegraph in the late 1840s, as well as the perfection of procedures first developed on the Western, helped to make rail travel relatively safe. But the great increase in the volume of the railroad's business made a smooth and efficient coordination of the flow of trains and traffic increasingly difficult. Where the Western as late as 1850 ran freight trains for a total that year of 453,000 miles, the Erie in 1855 ran a total of 1,676,000 miles; and where the Western carried 261,000 tons of freight in 1850, the Erie moved 842,000 in 1855. By 1855 the Erie was operating 200 locomotives, 2,770 freight, and 170 passenger and mail cars.[27] Freight had become a more important source of income than passengers or mail for all the large roads.

Rising costs of moving freight underlined the problems of operating these longer lines efficiently. To their surprise, the managers and the directors of the larger roads quickly realized that their per mile operating costs were greater than were comparable costs on smaller roads. The basic reason, argued Daniel C. McCallum, general superintendent of the New York and Erie, was the lack of proper internal organization:

A Superintendent of a road fifty miles in length can give its business his personal attention, and may be constantly on the line engaged in the direction of its details; each employee is familiarly known to him, and all questions in relation to its business are at once presented and acted upon; and any system, however imperfect, may under such circumstances prove comparatively successful.

In the government of a road five hundred miles in length a very different state exists. Any system which might be applicable to the business and extent of a short road, would be found entirely inadequate to the wants of a long one; and I am fully convinced that in the want of system perfect in its details, properly adapted and vigilantly enforced, lies the true secret of their [the large roads] failure; and that this disparity of cost per mile in operating long and short roads, is not produced by a *difference in length,* but is in proportion to the perfection of the system adopted.[28]

In perfecting such a system the senior managers on three of the four east-west trunk lines, none of whom had had military experience, made significant innovations in the management of modern, multiunit business enterprise. Benjamin Latrobe of the Baltimore & Ohio concentrated on the needs of financial accounting as well as operational precision. McCallum of the Erie articulated the principles of management for this new type of business enterprise; while J. Edgar Thomson of the Pennsylvania worked out the line-and-staff concept as a means of integrating more effectively the functional activities of several regionally defined operating units. The fourth trunk line, the New York Central, which had not been constructed like the others as a single work, but formed by a consolidation of many small lines, continued to be operated by merchants and financiers rather than by engineers. That road contributed almost nothing to the development of modern management.

The Baltimore & Ohio first reshaped its organization when it began to complete earlier plans to cross the mountains and reach the Ohio at Wheeling. In 1846 its president, Louis McLane, and its chief engineer, Latrobe, decided that the rapid growth of traffic, particularly from the newly opened coal mines, "the great augmentation of power and machinery demanded by the increasing business," as well as the anticipated further expansion of traffic when the Ohio was reached, demanded "a new system of management."[29] Assisted by a committee of the board, Latrobe outlined a new set of regulations "after diligent investigation, with the aid of the experience of other roads in New England and elsewhere." The objectives of the new plan were clearly defined:

[They] consisted in confining the general supervision and superintendence of all the departments nearer to their duties, and, by a judicious subdivision of labor, to insure a proper adaptation and daily application of the supervisory power to the objects under its immediate charge; in the multiplication of checks, and to effecting a strict responsibility in the collection and disbursement of money; in confining the company's mechanical operations in their shops to the purposes of repairs, rather than of construction; in promoting the economical purchase and application of materials and other articles needed in every class of the service; and in affecting a strict and more perfect responsibility in the accounting department generally.[30]

The plan itself as set forth in a printed manual, *Organization of the Service of the Baltimore & Ohio Railroad*, began by departmentalizing the road's functions into two basic activities: "First, the working of the road. Second—the collection and disbursement of revenues."[31] The second task was far more complicated than it had been in the early factories where only the mill agent or his clerk handled money, or on a canal where toll masters and senior engineers did the same. On a large railroad, scores of individuals—conductors, station agents, freight and passenger agents, purchasing agents, managers and foremen in charge of shops and round-houses and of the repair of track and roadbed—all had sizable sums of money pass through their hands each day.

Under the new system of management on the Baltimore & Ohio, financial responsibility was centralized in the company's treasurer, who not only supervised internal transactions but also handled external financing, including making the routine arrangements for assigning shares of stocks and bonds to the merchants and bankers who had agreed to market them, assuring the proper recording of sales and other transfers of securities, and sending out dividends and interest payments. Directly subordinate to the treasurer was the secretary who was wholly concerned with internal transactions. (In a short time the secretary's duties became those of the comptroller.) He inspected all passenger and freight accounts and supervised those who routinely handled the company's monies. Under the secretary was the chief clerk, into whose office in Baltimore flowed receipts and reports from all agents and conductors who received or disbursed funds along the road line. The chief clerk's office not only compiled and audited these accounts but also began to issue "daily comparisons of the work done by the road and its earnings with the monies received therefor." Daily figures were in turn summarized into monthly reports. These data thus became tools of the management as well as checks on the honesty and the competence of railroad employees. The reports remained, however, only records of financial transactions. Though detailed and numerous, they were not yet consolidated and reorganized to permit a realistic analysis of the costs involved in operating the road.

In organizing the operating department, Latrobe set up a structure similar to that of the Western to integrate the three major types of functional activities in the two (and when the road reached Wheeling, three) geographical divisions.[32] He reshaped the lines of responsibility for operation "by confining the departments of transportation, of construction and repairs of the road, and of repairs of machinery to a separate superintendency, each being subject to the immediate supervision of a professional engineer, under the direction of the President."[33] The heads of these departments were responsible for carrying out their carefully defined duties and for appointing subordinate managers and employees, usually with the "concurrence of the General Superintendent and the President." The functional managers of the Baltimore & Ohio then reported directly to their superiors in the central headquarters. As on the Western, the managers in the transportation department became responsible for the movement of traffic as well as the movement of trains.

The general superintendent was the key administrator. The organizational manual described this manager as "an officer of general duty . . . who besides duties peculiar to himself is charged with the supervision and control of the whole system, subject to the President and Directors." Into his office flowed a series of reports. Each of the operating departments forwarded weekly and monthly statements. The master of machinery, for example, was to report on "the condition and performance during the week of each locomotive and engine in service or under repair—the condition of the cars, and also the stationary machinery and workshops— and will present a monthly estimate of the probable expenses of their repair during the ensuing month." Besides reading reports, the senior operating executive maintained constant communication with department heads regarding problems and policies, inspected the road's facilities, and conferred with the president and the road's financial officers.

Daniel C. McCallum of the Erie further shaped the organizational form developed on the Western and the Baltimore & Ohio. After its completion in 1851 the Erie had been plagued by high operating costs. These threatened to become intolerable when, in the spring of 1853, the short lines along the Erie Canal consolidated to form a single enterprise, the New York Central, and so make that route a much more effective competitor for through traffic. That autumn Erie's board sought to reorganize its administrative structure in order to insure a more precise accountability and control over expenses and a more effective appraisal of men and managers. The directors hoped to achieve this objective by making available "comparisons of the expenses of the various operations with those of similar roads, with the several divisions of the road itself; and the expense of different conductors, engine-men, etc. with each other."[34]

To carry out this task the directors promoted McCallum from superintendent of one of the road's five operating divisions to general superintendent. When McCallum took office, the Erie had already adopted a structure similar to that of the Western and the Baltimore & Ohio.[35] Although he did define more precisely the lines of authority and responsibility, McCallum's major contribution consisted, first, of enunciating "general principles" of administration and, second, of perfecting the flow of internal information so essential for top and middle management to coordinate complex widespread activities and to monitor and evaluate the performance of the large number of managers handling them. McCallum emphasized that a definition of "general principles" was particularly necessary because "we cannot avail ourselves to any great extent of the plan of organization of shorter lines in framing one for this, nor have we any precedent or experience on which we can fully rely in doing so."[36] For McCallum the six basic principles of general administration were these:

(1) A proper division of responsibilities.
(2) Sufficient power conferred to enable the same to be fully carried out, that such responsibilities may be real in their character [that is, authority to be commensurate with responsibility].
(3) The means of knowing whether such responsibilities are faithfully executed.
(4) Great promptness in the report of all derelictions of duty, that evils may be at once corrected.
(5) Such information, to be obtained through a system of daily reports and checks, that will not embarrass principal officers nor lessen their influence with their subordinates.
(6) The adoption of a system, as a whole, which will not only enable the General Superintendent to detect errors immediately, but will also point out the delinquent.

In putting these principles into practice, McCallum gave the superintendents in charge of geographical divisions the power to carry out their responsibilities for the day-to-day movement of trains and traffic by an express delegation of authority. These regional officers were to be:

held responsible for the successful working of their respective Divisions, and for the maintenance of proper discipline and conduct of all persons employed thereon, except such as are in the employment of other officers acting under the directions from this office, as hereinafter stated. They possess all the powers delegated by the organization to the General Superintendent, except in matters pertaining to the duties of General Ticket Agent, General Freight Agent, General Wood Agent, Telegraph Management, and Engine and Car Repairs.

This power included control over the hiring and firing of subordinates, subject to the veto of top management. In McCallum's words, each officer had "the authority with the approval of the President and General Superintendent to appoint all persons for whose acts he is held responsible, and may dismiss any subordinate when, in his judgment, the interest of the company will be promoted thereby." The Erie's general superintendent stressed the value of adhering to explicit lines of authority and communication. "All subordinates should be accountable to and be directed *by their immediate superiors only;* as obedience cannot be enforced where the foreman in immediate charge is interfered with by a superior officer giving orders directly to his subordinates."

McCallum, nevertheless, failed to define precisely the relationship between the geographical division superintendent and the other functional managers of the division who reported to the general superintendent. He saw the problem clearly enough, pointing out that there were "some exceptions" to the rule that subordinates can communicate only through their senior officers. For example, "Conductors and station agents report, daily, their operations directly to the General Superintendent," and not to their division superintendents. He thought that the general superintendent would have the time and information needed to coordinate these activities. To illustrate more clearly these lines of authority, McCallum drew up a detailed chart—certainly one of the earliest organization charts in an American business enterprise.[37]

McCallum stressed that channels of authority and responsibility were also channels of communiation. He paid close attention to improving the accuracy of the information and the regularity and speed with which it flowed through these channels. Hourly, daily, and monthly reports were more detailed than those called for on the Baltimore & Ohio. The hourly reports, primarily operational and sent by telegraph, gave the location of trains and reasons for any delays or mishaps. "The information being edited as fast as received, on convenient tabular forms, shows, at a glance, the position and progress of trains, in both directions on every Division of the Road." Just as important, the information generated on these tabular forms was filed away to provide an excellent source of operational information which, among other things, was useful in determining and eliminating "causes of delay." McCallum's use of the telegraph brought universal praise from the railroad world both in this country and abroad. What impressed other railroad managers was that McCallum saw at once that the telegraph was more than merely a means to make train movements safe. It was a device to assure more effective coordination and evaluation of the operating units under his command.

Daily reports, the real basis of the system, were required from conductors, agents, and engineers. These were then consolidated into monthly statements. Reports on each locomotive, for example, included miles run, operating expenses, cost of repairs, and work done. Such data, flowing regularly from the division superintendents and other operating officers to the general superintendent, were supplemented by further detailed information provided both by the divisional managers and the heads of the functional departments. This information, so essential for regular and economical flow of trains and traffic, also made possible the comparison of work of the several operating units with one another and with those of other railroads. It provided the comparative statistics that the directors had asked for in the 1853 report. In order to have a constant and impersonal evaluation of the performance of the road's operating managers, "it is very important," McCallum insisted, "that principal officers should be in full possession of all information necessary to enable them to judge correctly as to the industry and efficiency of subordinates of every grade." In order to permit a more effective evaluation McCallum called for each of the five operating divisions to have its own separate and detailed set of accounts.

Central to coordinating flows and evaluating performance, these statistical data were also, McCallum pointed out, essential in understanding and controlling costs and in setting rates. The Erie and other roads had recently raised their rates, which they had found to be "unremunerative," only to discover that in so doing higher rates had threatened to "destroy this business."[38] By cutting traffic they had reduced net revenue. "To guard against such a result, and to establish the mean, between such rates as are unremunerative and such as are prohibitory, requires an accurate knowledge of the cost of transport of the various products, both for long and short distances." Important too was an understanding of the traffic flows along the line, for prices should be "fixed with reference to securing, as far as possible, such a balance of traffic in both directions as to reduce the proportion of 'dead weight' carried." Unused or excess capacity on a return trip warranted lowering prices for goods going that way. McCallum's concern, however, was almost wholly with operating costs and revenues. He said little about what costs should be allocated to construction or capital accounts. Nor did he consider ways to account for long-term depreciation of engines, rolling stock, rails, and other equipment.

McCallum's organizational innovations received wide attention. Henry Varnum Poor, the editor of the *American Railroad Journal*, was particularly impressed by his achievements and devoted much space to them. For example, Poor noted in 1854 that McCallum was already increasing the Erie's efficiency at the same time he reduced the size of its work force. Moreover, he continued:

By an arrangement now perfected, the superintendent can tell at any hour in the day, the precise location of every car and engine on the line of the road, and the duty it is performing. Formerly, the utmost confusion prevailed in this department, so much so, that in the greatest press of business, cars in perfect order have stood for months upon switches without being put to the least service, and without its being known where they were. All these reforms are being steadily carried out as fast as the ground gained can be held.[39]

Poor had McCallum's organization chart lithographed and offered copies for sale at $1 apiece. Douglas Galton, one of Britain's leading railroad experts, described McCallum's work in a parliamentary report printed in 1857. So too did the New York State Railroad Commissioners in their annual reports. Even the *Atlantic Monthly* carried an article in 1858 praising McCallum's ideas on railroad management.[40]

McCallum's principles and procedures of management, like his organization chart, were new in American business. No earlier American businessman had ever had the need to develop ways to use internally generated data as instruments of management. None had shown a comparable concern for the theory and principles of organization. The writings of

Montgomery and the orders of plantation owners to their overseers talked about the control and discipline of workers, not the control, discipline, and evaluation of other managers. Nor does Sidney Pollard in his *Genesis of Modern Management* note any discussion about the nature of major principles of organization occurring in Great Britain before the 1830s, the data at which he stops his analysis.[41]

McCallum's methods and concepts of administration were tested and further rationalized on the Pennsylvania rather than on the Erie. Before the end of the 1850s the Erie had fallen into the hands of unscrupulous financiers who, like its notorious treasurer Daniel Drew, cared little about efficient administration. McCallum soon left the road to develop a profitable bridge-building business. On the Pennsylvania, however, engineers rather than financiers continued to run the road. J. Edgar Thomson, the builder and first superintendent of the Georgia Railroad, had come to the Pennsylvania in 1849 to take charge of its construction. In 1852, he became its president and controlled its destinies until his death in 1874. When Thomson took command, he modified the centralized administrative structure set up by Herman Haupt, a highly successful civil engineer who had been the general superintendent of the road since 1849. Thomson's first move was to follow the example of his competitors and to separate the road's financial and operating departments.[42] The modified organization remained quite adequate until 1857.

Then increasing traffic plus rising costs and the onslaught of a business depression brought a major reorganization. Thomson enlarged his central office, this time separating the accounting from the treasury department and creating a secretary's office and a legal department.[43] The legal department was similar to one Latrobe had set up on the Baltimore & Ohio. The two were among the first such departments to be established in an American business firm and handled the ever-increasing legal work involved with contracts, claims, and charters. Thomson appointed a new middle manager "controller and auditor" as the head of the new accounting department and placed under him two "assistant auditors" and several senior clerks. At the same time, Thomson set up a purchasing department to handle the centralized buying of supplies for the company as a whole. Finally he greatly expanded the staff of the general freight agent. Both the new purchasing and the enlarged freight office were placed in the transportation department.

Thomson's major achievement was to clarify relations between the functional offices of the division and those of the central office. In so doing he relied heavily on the Erie model. The organization manual which Thomson signed in December 1857 included many of McCallum's words and phrases. Thomson's plan, however, differed from McCallum's because he centralized the authority, as well as the responsibility for the moving of trains and traffic, and put this authority in the hands of the division superintendents in charge of transportation. They were explicitly delegated the authority to give orders to men and managers in the other functional departments. In the words of the 1857 manual:

The Division Superintendent shall, *on their respective Divisions* (subject to the directions and approval of the General Superintendent), exercise all the powers delegated by the organization to the General Superintendent, for the control and the use of the road, its branches and connections, for the transportation of Freight and Passengers, including the movement of Motive Power employed thereon, whether engaged in the transportation of Freight and Passengers, or in the construction and repairing of the road, or the supply of fuel and materials. They shall also have general charge of all employees connected with Motive Power and Transportation on their respective divisions, and see that they perform the duties assigned them, and shall render such assistance to the Master of Machinery in preserving discipline, in the arrangement of the Locomotives to their particular service, in securing the services of competent engine men, and other responsible persons for the Motive Power, as the General Superintendent and the best interests of the company may require. They shall be furnished with copies of all rules and regulations, and orders to foremen of shops, and others holding positions of responsibility and trust connected with the Motive Power or Transportation of the company, and shall enforce their observance.

Thus the division superintendent was on the direct line of authority from the president through the general superintendent. All orders concerning the movement of trains and traffic went out of the division superintendent's office to workers in the motive power, maintenance of way, and transportation departments. The master of machinery set rules and standards for "the discipline and economy of conducting the business of the shops," and he or his divisional assistants hired, fired, and promoted people in their departments. But even in these activities, they were to have, as the new organizational manual emphasized, the "assistance" of the division superintendents.[44] In a short time the same became true for the chief engineer and his subordinate engineers responsible for the maintenance of way.[45] This line-and-staff concept, by which the managers on the line of authority were responsible for ordering men involved with the basic function of the enterprise, and other functional managers (the staff executives) were responsible for setting standards, was first enunciated in American business by the Pennsylvania Railroad in December 1857.

The decentralized line-and-staff divisional form of organization initially put into operation on the Pennsylvania became, in the years after the Civil War, widely used, though often in a modified form, by other large American railroads, including the Michigan Central, the Michigan Southern, and the Chicago, Burlington & Quincy.[46] On these and other roads the division engineers (responsible for maintenance of way) reported at first to the chief engineers who remained primarily responsible for completing the construction of the road. Once the road was built the chief engineer joined the staff of the general superintendent as a "consulting engineer" and the division engineers reported directly to their division superintendent. Once construction was completed, large American railroads had two major departments: one for operations and one for finance. Only in the 1870s did they add a third—the traffic department. Figure 2 is an organization chart showing the line-and-staff structure on a large railroad in the 1870s. By then full-time vice presidents headed the major functional departments. (The largest roads might have as many as nine divisions and three general superintendents.)

Not all railroads adopted this decentralized divisionalized structure. Indeed, a more "natural" form of organization was generally used by the British and European railroads.[47] In what became known as the "departmental" structure, the president and general superintendent did not delegate their authority. Instead, the functional managers on the geographical divisions—transportation, motive power, maintenance of way, passenger, freight, and accounting—reported directly to their functional superiors at the central office. This was true of the New York Central and a number of other American roads, particularly those where managers gave little attention to the problems of organization.[48] In time, however, nearly all the railroads in the United States carrying heavy traffic over long distances came to use the divisional line-and-staff type of organization.

By the coming of the Civil War the modern American business enterprise had appeared among American railroads. The needs of safety and then efficiency had led to the creation of a managerial hierarchy, whose duties were carefully defined in organizational manuals and charts. Middle and top managers supervised, coordinated, and evaluated the work of lower level managers who were directly responsible for the day-to-day operations. In the 1850s large roads were already employing from forty to sixty full-time salaried managers, of whom at least a dozen and often more were middle or top management.[49] In the 1850s top management included the president, the general superintendent, and the treasurer. By the 1870s it also included the executive in charge of the traffic department and a general manager who supervised the work of two or three general superintendents. By then middle management included the general superintendents, their assistants, and the heads of machinery (motive power and rolling stock), maintenance of way, telegraph, freight, passenger, and purchasing offices within the transportation department; the controller and his assistants and the treasurer's assistants within the financial depart-

Figure 2. Simplified organization chart of a large railroad, 1870s

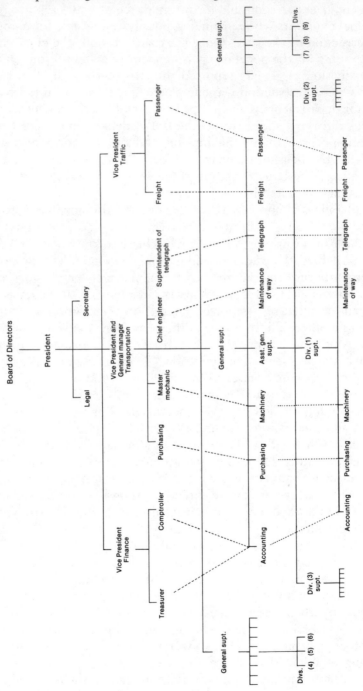

ment; and the heads of the legal department and secretary's office. In addition, on the roads still being built, there were the chief engineer and his assistants who had charge of construction. No private business enterprise with as many managers or with as complex an internal organization existed in the United States—nor, except for railroads in Britain and western Europe, in any other part of the world.

Accounting and statistical innovation

As Latrobe, McCallum, and Thomson so clearly understood, a constant flow of information was essential to the efficient operation of these new large business domains. For the middle and top managers, control through statistics quickly became both a science and an art. This need for accurate information led to the divising of improved methods for collecting, collating, and analyzing a wide variety of data generated by the day-to-day operations of the enterprise. Of even more importance it brought a revolution in accounting; more precisely, it contributed substantially to the emergence of accounting out of bookkeeping. The techniques of Italian double-entry bookkeeping generated the data needed, but these data, required in far larger quantities and in more systematic form, were then subjected to types of analysis that were new. In sum, to meet the needs of managing the first modern business enterprise, managers of large American railroads during the 1850s and 1860s invented nearly all of the basic techniques of modern accounting.

Of all the organizational innovators, J. Edgar Thomson and his associates on the Pennsylvania Railroad made the most significant contributions to accounting. Their work and that of other managers received much public attention. Investors, shippers, and railroad directors were as much concerned about the accuracy and value of the new procedures as were the managers themselves. Railroad trade journals, particularly Henry Varnum Poor's *American Railroad Journal*, and the new financial journals (first the *Banker's Magazine*, and then the *Commercial and Financial Chronicle*) carried articles, editorials, and letters about the subject. Comparable public discussion of accounting methods had never occurred before in the United States; and it would be another thirty or forty years before similar accounting discussions took place in manufacturing and marketing.

The new accounting practices fell into three categories: financial, capital, and cost accounting. Financial accounting involved the recording, compiling, collating, and auditing of the hundreds of financial transactions carried out daily on the large roads. It also required the synthesizing of these data to provide the information needed for compiling the roads' balance sheets and for evaluating the company's financial performance. Where the largest of the textile mills had four or five sets of accounts to process and review, the Pennsylvania Railroad had, by 1857 (the year Thomson reorganized his accounting office), 144 basic sets of accounting records.[50] Of these accounts, the passenger department had 33, the freight department 25, motive power 26, maintenance of cars 9, and maintenance of way 22. Eight more were listed under general expenses, while construction and equipment had 21. Moreover, where the textile company's accounts were compiled only semiannually, those of the Pennsylvania were summarized and tabulated monthly, and were forwarded in printed form by the comptroller to the board of directors by the fifteenth of the following month. The totals of the monthly reports were then consolidated in the road's annual report.

In the preparation of these reports the accounting office collected, summarized, and printed detailed operating as well as financial data. As early as 1851 the Pennsylvania's annual report showed for each month the number of passengers entered at each station, as well as the tonnage on local and through freight to Pittsburgh and Philadelphia and from each of the way stations. By 1855 traffic data of over two hundred major products were listed.[51] This mass of printed information on expenses and receipts, and on passengers and products moved, remains a magnificent and little-used source for the flows and costs of American transportation at mid-century.

The processing and analyzing of these data required the Pennsylvania and other large railroads to build extensive comptrollers' departments and to hire full-time internal auditors. By 1860 the railroads probably employed more accountants and auditors than the federal or any state government. In any case, after 1850 the railroad was central in the development of the accounting profession in the United States.

In reviewing the balance sheets and other condensed information provided by the new comptrollers' department, railroad managers, directors, and investors quickly employed these data to evaluate and compare the performance of the different roads. In addition to the balance sheets themselves, they began in the late 1850s to use the "operating ratio" as a standard way to judge a road's financial results. Profit and loss were not enough. Earnings had to be related to the volume of business. A better test was the ratio between a road's operating revenues and its expenditures or, more precisely, the percentage of gross revenue that had been needed to meet operating costs.[52] Such ratios had never before been used by American businessmen. They remain today a basic standard for judging the performance of American business enterprise.

In drawing up their balance sheets, the railroads were the first American businesses to pay close and systematic attention to capital accounting. Again the problem was unprecedented. No other type of private business enterprise had ever made such huge investments in capital, plant, and equipment. In discussing capital accounting in the 1850s, railroad managers, stockholders, and journalists at first gave the most attention to defining clearly the distinction between the construction or capital account and the operating account.[53] On the one hand, by charging operating expenses to construction accounts, promoters and managers could give the appearance of making profits that were not really earned. This they did to improve their chances of raising funds for completing or continuing construction.

On the other hand, by charging construction costs to operating costs, the investors in the road benefited at the expense of its users. Railroad reformers, such as Henry Varnum Poor in the 1850s and Charles Francis Adams, the chairman of the Massachusetts Railroad Commission, in the 1860s and 1870s, repeatedly urged the railroad officials to delineate clearly these two sets of accounts. To see that they were properly differentiated, the reformers proposed that outsiders—either groups of investors or railroad or legislative commissions—have the opportunity to review a railroad's books.

Once a road was completed and the construction account closed, its total amount was recorded on the asset side of the consolidated balance sheet as a capital or property account. The problem then arose as to how to account for depreciation and even obsolescence of the road's capital assets. For not only were such capital assets of far greater value than those of the factory, but they depreciated at a more rapid rate. The early roads, such as the Boston & Worcester, began by following the textile mill procedures. They put money aside in contingency funds or in their profit and loss or their surplus accounts, in order to have it available for expensive repairs or the purchase of new equipment. Every now and then, usually in good years, the financial officers wrote down the value of their plant and equipment. During the 1850s, however, the managers on the new large roads began to find it easier to consider depreciation as an operating cost and did so by charging repairs and renewals to the operating accounts.

The directors of the Pennsylvania Railroad explained these new concepts of renewal accounting in their annual report of 1855. By charging repairs and renewals to operating expenses, the property accounts would continue to reflect the true value of the capital assets. "The practice of the Company in relation to its running equipment is to preserve the number of cars and locomotives charged to construction account, in complete efficiency; thus, if a car or locomotive is destroyed, or has become old and worthless, a new one is substituted in its place, and its cost charged to the expense account."[54] The same was true for rails, cross ties, and bridges.

Such a procedure neatly avoided the complex problem of determining depreciation, but it did not assure the availability of funds for extensive renewal and repairs. The company estimated that the charge for "the annual decay" of the roadbed was $110,000 and the "depreciation" on "running machinery" was $40,000. "If the Company had been declaring dividends from its profits, it would be prudent to carry a portion of the year to a reserved fund." After balancing receipts with expenditures, the company deducted for taxes, interest, and other expenses; then it set dividends at 6 percent. The balance or surplus went into a "contingent fund," part of which was used to invest in bonds of connecting roads.[55] The funds in these contingency accounts, as those in sinking funds set up for the payment of bonds, were to be placed in "safe" investments. These accounts, however, quickly became mere bookkeeping devices with funds "loaned" out to other accounts of the road itself. After the Civil War, even the Pennsylvania dropped the use of separate contingency accounts, and merely kept the surplus account high enough to meet anticipated demands for repair and renewal of rails and equipment.

By the 1870s this type of renewal accounting had become the standard form of capital accounting used by American railroads. Repair and renewals were charged to operating expenses and not to the capital or the property accounts. These two accounts—one for construction and the other for equipment—were to be altered only when new facilities were added or existing ones dropped. A convention of state railroad commissioners meeting in June 1879 to set up uniform accounting methods for American railroads defined the procedure in this manner: "No expenditure shall be charged to the property accounts, except it be for actual increase in construction, equipment, and property, unless it be made on old work in such a way as to clearly increase the value of the property over and above the cost of renewing the original structures, etc. In such cases only the amount of increased cost shall be charged, and the amount allowed on account of old work shall be stated."[56] In the model financial statement proposed by the commissioners (table 1) such additions (or subtractions) were to be listed under a separate heading "Charges and Credits to Property During the Year." Under that heading was also listed changes in the value of real estate and other property held by the company.

By charging repairs and renewals to operating expenses, the value of the property was theoretically maintained at its original value. The method of renewal accounting meant the profit would continue to be

Table 1. Form of accounts recommended by the convention of railroad commissioners held at Saratoga Springs, New York, June 10, 1879

General Exhibit

Total income
Total expense, including taxes
Net income
Interest on funded debt
Interest on unfunded debt
Rentals
Balance applicable to dividends
Dividends declared (percent)
Balance for the year
Balance (profit and loss) last year
    Add or deduct various entries made during the year not included above (specifying same)
Balance (profit and loss) carried forward to next year

CHARGES AND CREDITS TO PROPERTY DURING YEAR

Construction and equipment (specifying same)
Other charges(specifying same)
Total charges
Property sold or reduced in value (specifying same)
Net addition (or reduction) for the year

ANALYSIS OF EARNINGS AND EXPENSES

Earnings:
From local passengers
Through passengers
Express and extra baggage
Mails
Other sources, passenger department
Total earnings passenger department
Local freight
Through freight
Other sources, freight department
Total earnings freight department
Total transportation earnings
Rents for use of road
Income from other sources (specifying same)
    Total income from all sources

Expenses:
Salaries, general officers and clerks
Law expenses
Insurance
Stationery and printing

Table 1. (*continued*)

Outside agencies and advertising
Contingencies
Repairs, bridges (including culverts and cattle guards)
Repairs, buildings
Repairs, fences, road crossings, and signs
Renewal rails
Renewal ties
Repairs, roadway and track
Repairs, locomotives
Fuel for locomotives
Water supply
Oil and waste
Locomotive service
Repairs, passenger cars
Passenger-train service
Passenger-train supplies
Mileage, passenger-cars (debit balance)
Repairs, freight cars
Freight-train service
Freight-train supplies
Mileage, freight cars (debit balance)
Telegraph expenses (maintenance and operating)
Damage and loss of freight and baggage
Damage to property and cattle
Personal injuries
Agents and station service
Station supplies
    Total operating expenses
    Taxes
    Total operating expenses and taxes

ASSETS AND LIABILITIES

   Assets:
Construction account
Equipment account
Other investments (specifying same)
Cash items:
  Cash
  Bills receivable
  Due from agents and companies
Other assets:
  Materials and supplies
  Sinking funds
  Debit balances
    Total assets

Liabilities:
Capital stock
Funded debt
Unfunded debt, as follows:
    Interest unpaid
    Dividends unpaid
    Notes payable
    Vouchers and accounts
    Other liabilities
Profit and loss or income accounts
        Total liabilities

PRESENT OR CONTINGENT LIABILITIES NOT INCLUDED
IN BALANCE-SHEET

Bonds guaranteed by this company or a lien on its roads (specifying same)
    Overdue interest on same
    Other liabilities (specifying same)

Source: *Proceedings of the Convention of Railroad Commissioners Held at Saratoga Springs, New York, June 10, 1879* (New York, 1879), Appendix IX, no. 21.

considered, as it always had been in American business, as the difference between operating income and expenses but not as the rate of return on investment on actual capital assets. In fact, the use of renewal accounting made it impossible to know how much capital had been invested in road-bed, plant, and equipment since so much of the cost of capital equipment had been absorbed as operating expense. Such accounting methods thus, of necessity, made the operating ratio, rather than the rate of return, the basic tool for analyzing the financial performance of railroad enterprises. Finally, this method of defining depreciation also meant that American railroad accounting overstated operating costs and understated capital consumption.[57]

The basic innovations in financial and capital accounting appeared in the 1850s in response to specific needs and were perfected in the years after the Civil War. Innovations in a third type of accounting—cost accounting—came more slowly. In making his recommendations for detailed divisional accounts, McCallum had emphasized the need to develop comparative cost data for each of the operating divisions on a large road. "This comparison [of division accounts] will show," McCallum wrote in 1855, "the officers who conduct their business with the greatest economy, and will indicate, in a manner not to be mistaken, the relative ability and fitness of each for the position he occupies. It will be valuable in pointing out the particulars of excess in the cost of management of one Division with another, by comparison of details; will direct attention to those matters in which sufficient economy is not practiced; and it is believed, will have the effect of exciting an honorable spirit of emulation to excell."[58] Not until the late 1860s, however, did cost accounting become a basic tool for railroad management.

The railroad manager who most effectively developed McCallum's proposals for cost accounting and control was Albert Fink, a civil engineer and bridge builder. Fink, after receiving his training on the Baltimore & Ohio, joined the managerial staff of the Louisville & Nashville, becoming its general superintendent in 1865 and the senior vice president in 1869.[59] Fink's aim was to determine with much more precision the basic measure of unit cost, the ton mile. His first step in obtaining accurate cost of carrying one ton for one mile in each of his divisions was to reorder the financial and statistical data compiled by his accounting and transportation departments.[60] He consolidated some of the existing accounts and subdivided others. Most important of all, he recategorized existing accounts according to the nature of their costs rather than according to the departments in which the functions were being carried out.

Table 2 shows how Fink reordered his accounts into four fundamental categories. One included those costs which, within limits, did not vary with the volume of traffic. Here he placed twenty-seven accounts involving primarily the maintenance of roadway and buildings and "general superintendence" or overhead. A second category included nine sets of accounts that varied with the volume of freight but not with the length of road or train-miles run. These were largely station expenses "incurred at stations in keeping up an organized force of agents, laborers, etc. for the purposes of receiving and delivering freight, selling tickets, etc." A third class of thirty-two sets of items, "movement expenses," varied with the number of trains run. But, as Fink pointed out, since the trains rarely ran fully loaded, the expenditures did not vary precisely with the volume of business. The accounts in these categories were determined for each division on a per-train-mile run basis. In addition to these operating expenses Fink had a fourth category, the interest charges that, of course, had no relation to traffic carried or trains run. Interest charges increased only when expanding business called for new construction and an enlarged debt. Table 2 gives the complex formula Fink used to convert these sixty-eight sets of accounts into costs per ton-mile. A comparison of these internal accounts (and the methods devised to use them to ascertain and control costs) with those employed in the textile mills, armories, shipping, and merchant enterprises, emphasized dramatically how much more complex railroads were to manage than any other contemporary business enterprise.

Fink stressed how costs varied on the different divisions or "branches," as they were then called, on the Louisville & Nashville. Movement expenses, for example, went from a high of 41.3 percent of total expenses on the main stem to a low of only 17.6 percent on the less-traveled Richmond branch. Station expenses ran from only 4.3 percent of all expenses on the Knoxville branch to 18.1 percent on the main stem, maintenance of road from 9.3 percent on the Glascow branch to 22.5 percent on the Bardstown branch, and the interest account from 26 percent on the main stem to 59.2 percent on the Richmond branch. By developing a time series on the costs of the different divisions and by knowing the division's physical and economic characteristics, the general superintendent was able to identify with some precision the reasons for the differences in costs. Such historical data and constant reviewing of current financial and operating data permitted him to evaluate performance of different divisions and their operating executives.

In addition, Fink emphasized that such cost analysis was fundamental to ratemaking. The "mere knowledge of average costs per ton mile of all expenditures" was of "no value," for "no freight is ever transported under the average condition." If rates are to be based on costs, then "we must classify freight according to conditions affecting the cost of transportation, and ascertain the cost of each class separately."[61] And Fink knew, as did every railroad manager, that costs were only one factor in the complex calculus that determined rates.

Cost per ton-mile rather than earnings, net income, or the operating ratio thus became the criterion by which the railroad managers controlled and judged the work of their subordinates. One reason was that revenues, particularly those from through traffic, could not be easily allocated to separate divisions. Also, many factors completely out of the division superintendent's control affected the amount of revenues his jurisdiction produced. Thus while financial and capital accounts remained primarily the concern of the financial officers, cost accounting became increasingly the province of the transportation department and came to be used as an operational rather than a financial control.

The volume of financial transactions handled by a large railroad, as well as the volume of traffic and passengers carried, encouraged, indeed forced, railroad managers to pioneer a modern business accounting. This sharp increase in the business activity of the firm thus revolutionized accounting practices. The new methods, devised in the 1850s and perfected in the following years, were quickly adopted by the first large industrial enterprises when they appeared in the 1880s. They remained the basic accounting techniques used by American business enterprise until well into the twentieth century. Only in cost accounting did the large industrial enter-

Table 2. Albert Fink: classification of operating expenses and computation of unit costs

---

Headings of Accounts

MAINTENANCE OF ROADWAY AND GENERAL SUPERINTENDENCE

Road repairs per mile of road—
1. Adjustment of track
2. Ballast
3. Ditching
4. Culverts and cattle-guards
5. Extraordinary repairs—slides, etc.
6. Repairs of hand and dump-cars
7. Repairs of road tools
8. Road watchmen
9. General expense of road department
10. Total
11. Cross-ties replaced—value
12. Cross-ties, labor replacing
13. Cross-ties, train expenses hauling
14. Total cost of cross-ties per mile of road
15. Bridge superstructure repairs
16. Bridge watchmen
17. Shop-building repairs
18. Water-station repairs
19. Section-house repairs
20. Total cost of bridge and building repairs per mile of road
21. General superintendence and general expense of operating department
22. Advertising and soliciting passengers and freight
23. Insurance and taxes
24. Rent account
25. Total per mile of road
26. Salaries of general officers
27. Insurance and taxes and general expense
28. Total per mile of road
29. *Total cost per mile of road for maintenance of roadway and buildings*
29½. Total cost per train mile for maintenance of roadway and buildings

STATION EXPENSES PER TRAIN MILE

30. Labor loading and unloading freight
31. Agents and clerks
32. General expense of stations—lights, fuel, etc.
33. Watchmen and switchmen
34. *Expense of switching—*
    Engine repairs
    Engineers and firemen's wages
    Expense in engine-house
    Supervision and general expense
    Oil and waste
    Water supply
    Fuel
35. Total per train mile
36. Stationery and printing
37. Telegraph expenses
38. Depot repairs
39. Total per train mile
40. *Total station expenses per train mile*

MOVEMENT EXPENSES PER TRAIN MILE

41. Adjustment of track
42. Cost of renewal of rails—value
43. Labor replacing rails
44. Train expenses hauling rails
45. Joint fastenings
46. Switches
47. Total cost of adjustment of track and replacing rails per train mile
48. Locomotive repairs
49. Oil and waste used on locomotives
50. Watching and cleaning
51. Fuel used in engine-house
52. Supervision and general expense in engine-house
53. Engineers and firemen's wages
54. Total engine expenses per train mile
55. Conductors and brakemen
56. Passenger-car repairs

57. Sleeping-car repairs
58. Freight-car repairs
59. Oil and waste used by cars
60. Labor oiling and inspecting cars
61. Train expenses
62. Total car expenses per train mile
63. Fuel used by locomotives
64. Water supply
65. Total fuel and water expense per train mile
66. Damage to freight, and lost baggage
67. Damage to stock
68. Wrecking account
69. Damage to persons
70. Gratuity to employees
71. Fencing burned
72. Law expenses
73. Total per train mile
74. *Total movement expenses per train mile*
75. GRAND TOTAL for maintenance and movement per train mile.

Formula for Ascertaining the Cost of Railroad Transportation per Ton-Mile

---

$$\text{Movement expenses per ton-mile} = \frac{\text{Movement expenses per train mile (items 41 to 74)}}{\text{average number of tons of freight in each train}} = a$$

$$\text{Station expenses per ton-mile} = \frac{\text{Cost of handling freight (items 30 to 40) at forwarding station} + \text{at delivery station}}{\text{length of haul}} = b$$

$$\text{Maintenance of road per ton-mile} = \frac{\text{Cost of maintenance of road per mile per year (items 1 to 29)} \times \frac{\text{total miles run by freight-trains per year}}{\text{total revenue trains, pass. and freight, per year}}}{\text{average number of tons of freight transported over one mile of road per year}} = c$$

$$\text{Interest per ton-mile} = \frac{\text{Cost of road per mile} \times \frac{\text{rate of interest per annum}}{100} \times \frac{\text{number of freight-train miles per year}}{\text{number of revenue-train miles, freight and pass., per year}}}{\text{average number of tons of freight transported over one mile of road per year}} = d$$

$$\text{Total cost per ton-mile} = a + b + c + d.$$

In order to make use of this formula it is necessary to know . . . fifty-eight items of expense [above], all of which vary on different roads, and enter into different combinations with each other. Some of the items of movement expenses (41 to 74) change with the weight of trains, and have to be ascertained in each individual case. The average cost for the year can be made the basis of the estimate. Besides the items shown [above], the following other items enter into the calculation: the average number of tons of freight in train per mile of the round trip of the train, the average length of haul, the number of miles run over the road with freight and passenger-trains per annum, the cost of the road, the rate of interest, and the total number of tons of freight carried during a year over one mile of road. Without these data it is impossible to make a correct estimate of the cost of transportation on railroads.

Source: Albert Fink, *Cost of Railroad Transportation, Railroad Accounts, and Government Regulation of Railroad Tariffs* (Louisville, 1875), pp. 47–48.

prises modify and adjust the methods initially devised by the railroads in the mid-nineteenth century, and this because the operations being costed were so different from those in transportation.

Organizational innovation evaluated

The railroads were, then, the first modern business enterprises. They were the first to require a large number of salaried managers; the first to have a central office operated by middle managers and commanded by top managers who reported to a board of directors. They were the first American business enterprise to build a large internal organizational structure with carefully defined lines of responsibility, authority, and communication between the central office, departmental headquarters, and field units; and they were the first to develop financial and statistical flows to control and evaluate the work of the many managers.

In all this they were the first because they had to be. No other business enterprise up to that time had had to govern a large number of men and offices scattered over wide geographical areas. Management of such enterprises had to have many salaried managers and had to be organized into functional departments and had to have a continuing flow of internal information if it was to operate at all.

Nevertheless, the innovations made by the early large intersectional roads in organization, accounting, and control went beyond mere necessity. The railroads could have operated well enough with only rudimentary organizational structures, without the line and staff distinction, without an internal auditing staff, and without the development of the more sophisticated financial, capital, and cost accounting procedures devised by McCallum, Thomson, and Fink. Indeed, many roads continued to operate for many years in an ad hoc informal way. Lines of authority and communication remained unclear, and operational and accounting information imprecise and unsystematically collated and analyzed. This was particularly true on the shorter roads, on those with relatively light traffic, and even on the larger and more traveled ones where senior managers paid little explicit attention to organizational matters. In fact, on some roads the quality of the management and the attention paid to internal organization regressed. A dramatic example was the Erie, when speculators, whose interests were to manipulate securities rather than to provide transportation, took control of the road.

By the 1880s, however, the innovations of the 1850s and 1860s had become standard operating procedures on all large American railroads. Expanding traffic and the growth and size of the roads forced the senior railroad managers to pay attention to their administrative and informational procedures. Moreover, as railroad managers became more professional, information about these methods became disseminated more systematically. By the 1870s organization and accounting were topics for discussion at formal meetings of railroad managers. They were reviewed in such periodicals as the *Railroad Gazette,* and the *Railroad Journal* and such books as Marshall Kirkman's *Railroad Revenue: A Treatise on the Organization of Railroads and the Collection of Railroad Receipts.*[62]

The innovations of the 1850s and 1860s, which became standard practice in the 1870s and 1880s, increased the efficiency and productivity of transportation provided by the individual routes. Improved organization and statistical accounting procedures permitted a more intensive use of available equipment and more speedy delivery of goods by providing a more effective continuous control over all the operations of the road. These innovations also made possible the fuller exploitation of a steadily improving technology which included larger and heavier engines, larger cars, heavier rails, more effective signals, automatic couplers, air brakes, and the like. These improvements permitted the roads to carry a much heavier volume of traffic at higher speeds.

The organizational innovations described in this chapter, however, affected only the productivity and performance of the individual railroads and not necessarily the railroad system as a whole. The creation of an efficient national overland transportation network required close cooperation between railroad companies so that traffic might move easily from one road to another. As the railroad network grew, as it became more interconnected, through traffic passing from one line to the next was increasingly important to the profits of the individual railroad companies. In the years after the Civil War, external relations were becoming as critical to the successful operation of the new large railroads as were the development of internal organization and controls before the war.

CHAPTER 4

Railroad Cooperation and Competition, 1870s-1880s

New patterns of interfirm relationships

By the Civil War salaried middle and top railroad managers—the first representatives of this new economic group in this country—had created organizational and accounting methods that permitted their enterprises to coordinate and monitor a high volume of traffic at a speed and regularity hitherto unknown. A small number of large, managerially administered enterprises replaced a large number of the small personally run transportation, shipping, and mercantile firms that had previously carried goods from one transshipment point to another. The number of transactions and transshipments involved in the transportation of goods and passengers was sharply reduced. In 1849 freight moving from Philadelphia to Chicago had to pass through at least nine transshipments in the course of as many weeks: ten years later the journey took only three days and required only one shipment.

Nevertheless, by 1861 the American rail network was in no sense integrated. Except for the Mississippi at Rock Island, and the Ohio at Pittsburgh, the major rivers did not yet have bridges. Roads entering the same terminal city had no direct rail connections. Roads used different gauges and different types of equipment. Therefore, cars of one railroad could not be transferred to the track of another. In the early years this differentiation had been made purposely so that freight shipped on a railroad sponsored by the merchants of one city could not be syphoned off by those of another. For these reasons, railroad managers were by 1861 only beginning to develop organizational procedures to permit the movement of freight cars over the tracks of several different railroad companies.

As a result, transshipment costs were still high. In the late 1850s and early 1860s, the average cost of a single transshipment was estimated at from 7 to 25 cents a ton and required at least a day's delay.[1] In 1865 the Boston Board of Trade stated that the cost of unloading and reloading freight between Boston and Chicago was over $500,000 a year. Reduction of such costs and delays required interfirm cooperation of the highest order.

This type of cooperation between business enterprises was an entirely new phenomenon. The necessary standardization of equipment and operating procedures called for detailed and prolonged discussions among the managers of the many roads. They had to work out and then put into operation standardized operating procedures and equipment.

Such cooperation proved highly successful. By the 1880s a rail shipment could move from one part of the country to another without a single transshipment. By then the traffic departments of the major roads had become responsible for moving a large share of the long-distance traffic within the United States. This internalization of the activities and transactions previously carried out by many small units, well under way in the 1850s, was completed by the 1880s.

The very success of interfirm cooperation increased interfirm competition. As the nation's rail network expanded, as interconnected lines became completed, and as the roads became physically and organizationally integrated, through traffic grew rapidly. With this expansion, the volume of through traffic carried often made the difference between a road's financial success and failure. The need to assure a steady flow of traffic created a constant pressure for railroad managers to obtain through freight from other roads on parallel routes. They did so by cutting rates and by aggressive advertising and selling.

To control such competition railroad managers turned to cooperation. In order to obtain this constant flow of traffic across their lines, they made informal alliances with competing and connecting roads. When growing pressures to obtain through traffic weakened these alliances, railroad managers set up more formal federations, creating some of the largest and most sophisticated cartels ever attempted in American business. But these cartels rarely worked. If cooperation to expand the flow of through traffic proved to be a great success, cooperation to control competition was a resounding failure.

The new class of middle and top managers had the responsibility for defining the new types of interfirm relationships. The part-time members of the board of directors had neither the time, the training, nor the technical understanding and competence needed to decide complex questions of cooperation and competition. The managers at the lowest level, the divisional level, concentrated wholly on the functional tasks required to move trains and traffic safely and efficiently. The middle managers were the persons who devised the organizational procedures and worked out the technological standardization necessary to achieve a national railroad system. Constant consultation and cooperation on complex common problems brought these managers a sense of professionalism that had never existed before in American business.

The top level managers defined their relationships with other roads in more strategic terms. They decided when and where to make alliances and form cartels and when to abandon them. These decisions required the approval of the representatives of the owners on the board. Normally the top salaried managers and the members of the board agreed on strategies of alliance and cartels. But when they did not, the managers usually came to have their way.

Cooperation to expand through traffic

The integration of many different railroad enterprises into a single national transportation system required the managers to cooperate on three quite different sets of concerns. They had to arrange the physical connection of the many roads; they had to devise uniform operating, accounting, and other organizational procedures; and they had to agree on the use of a standardized technology. Until the roads were linked, and until procedures and equipment were made uniform, freight could not flow quickly and easily across the lines of several roads. Although managers had begun to cooperate on all three of these requirements in the 1850s, their major effort was concentrated in the 1860s and 1870s. The culmination of this cooperation in the 1880s gave the nation a fully integrated railroad network.

Of the three requirements, the physical integration linking the roads was the easiest to accomplish. Bridge building was often merely an internal matter. Where roads terminated at a river's edge, the two roads often formed a joint enterprise to build and maintain the connecting bridge. Similar joint enterprises were formed to build belt lines and facilities connecting the lines of different roads terminating in the same cities. By 1870 the Hudson, the Delaware, the Potomac, the Ohio, the Mississippi, and the Missouri had been crossed by railroad tracks, often in several places.[2] During the 1870s belt lines and other facilities to connect roads had been constructed in Chicago, Cincinnati, Indianapolis, Baltimore, Richmond, and a number of smaller cities.[3] In other commercial centers the managers worked out cooperative methods to move cars from the switching and marshaling yards of one road to those of another.

The creation of uniform operating procedures to permit the flow of through freight traffic and passengers across several connecting lines was much more complex than physically linking the roads. The first task was to set uniform classifications and rates for freight and to agree on through ticketing and schedules for passengers. Ways had to be found to allocate the amount to be paid and to make the payment for that share to each of the roads involved in carrying through shipments or through passengers to their destination.

Such initial procedures began to be worked out at the meetings of connecting and competing roads in the mid-1850s. The executives of the new longer roads began to confer as soon as their lines neared or reached completion. In August 1854, as the Pennsylvania entered Pittsburgh, its president and general superintendent met with those of the Baltimore & Ohio, the Erie, the New York Central, and their western connections.[4] That October, other roads in the old northwest had similar meetings. The senior executives of a number of southern roads met the following March. These meetings were called to work out arrangements for handling through traffic on connecting roads and, in the words of J. Edgar Thomson, the Pennsylvania's president, "with a view of agreeing upon general principles which should govern Railroad Companies competing for the same trade, and preventing ruinous competition."[5] At the first meetings and the many that followed, the railroad managers were concerned almost wholly with through traffic. Rates for local traffic were left entirely to the roads carrying that traffic.

In working out the general principles for determining rates, the railroad managers had almost as few precedents to go on as they had in devising their internal organizational structures and procedures. Merchants and manufacturers of the day had little opportunity to formulate systematic pricing policies. Except in local markets, prices were set by the forces of supply and demand. Only the canals provided a guide. The managers of both state and private canals set their tolls for boats using their rights-of-way on the basis of what the traffic would bear.[6] Boats carrying bulky freight paid proportionately lower rates than those moving more valuable, lighter goods. The first railroads had set up similar basic classifications for bulky and light freight.

At the railroad conventions of the 1850s, presidents and general superintendents accepted the principle of charging on the basis of the value of the product being transported rather than on the actual cost of transportation. Otherwise, they reasoned, as the canal officials had done earlier, the transportation charges for bulk freight would be prohibitive. The freight classifications adopted by the conventions followed those that had been devised by the Pennsylvania. That road placed more than two hundred articles into four overall classifications.[7] At one end of the scale were articles in the first class such as books, carpeting, clocks, cutlery, dry goods, fresh eggs and meat, wines, and woolens; at the other end those in the fourth class included coal, lumber, grain, lard, lead, looms, and similar products. Once the convention agreed on the basic classifications, the freight agents of these several roads worked out the official "tariffs" for each of the many different items carried.

If the first principle for setting rates was to charge what the traffic would bear, the second was flexibility. Rates had to be adjusted to meet the demands of large shippers for lower prices on volume shipments, to assure return cargo when a large share of the traffic went only one way (as occurred each fall with the movement of crops), and to fill only partially used cars. As Herman Haupt of the Pennsylvania put it in 1852, when it comes to ratemaking, "one principle . . . of universal application" exists "and that is, that changes must be made *when circumstances* require them; on no other, can the operations of the road be conducted with success."[8] At the conferences in the mid-1850s, railroad managers attempted to rationalize and formalize this principle of flexibility for each particular set of schedules. By definition this was an exceedingly difficult task. It led to differentiation in rates which, to many shippers, was arbitrary and discriminatory.

From their early years, therefore, American railroads, like those of all nations, determined the basic regional rate structure cooperatively. During the Civil War, railroad conventions were held only occasionally. The war disrupted traffic and, at the same time, greatly expanded it. After the war, meetings were again held regularly. The "official" rates on through traffic were adjusted and classifications were revised and expanded as new types of traffic appeared and as existing flows changed in volume and direction. At these conventions, the roads agreed to maintain the accepted rate structure. Individual managers, however, were constantly tempted to adjust through rates in order to attract traffic or meet demands of shippers, especially large ones. Rates were often lowered by means of secretly rebating to a shipper the difference between the official rate and the one agreed upon by the manager and his customer. At other times they were reduced openly. Nevertheless, except for a brief period after the panic of 1857, railroad managers adhered quite closely to the official rates. They continued to do so until the long depression (starting in 1873) ushered in the age of railroad competition.

Another task in coordinating the flow of through traffic was to improve arrangements for the movement of freight and passengers across the lines of several companies. Although the roads cooperatively worked out through passenger ticketing and scheduling in the early years, they made few attempts to coordinate the flow of through freight traffic. Until after the Civil War, railroad managers were too preoccupied with completing construction and working out their internal operating structures and procedures to do more than determine the official rates and classifications. In these years a new type of enterprise—the express and fast-freight companies—began to handle the movement of most light, valuable freight.

Express companies had first appeared in the late 1830s and early 1840s to deliver goods locally. In the late 1840s and the 1850s such pioneering firms as those headed by William C. Fargo, William F. Harden, and Alvin Adams saw the opportunity to profit from shipping goods across the nation's expanding but not yet integrated transportation network. As railroad mileage grew, their companies and other new express and fast-freight lines began to operate on a national scale. They also started to carry more standard goods that were shipped in volume lots.

In the mid-1850s the new large railroads and the fast-freight lines began to make mutually beneficial alliances. A railroad, by giving an exclusive contract to an express or fast-freight line, was able to assure itself of a more certain volume of traffic. Also, since the express lines often provided their own cars, the railroad's outlay for rolling stock was reduced. Express companies received special rates in return for the contract.

These arrangements began on the east-west trunk lines and were soon repeated in other parts of the country. Kasson's Dispatch (later the Merchants' Dispatch) and Wells, Fargo & Company made the first of such exclusive contracts with the New York Central.[9] Quickly the Erie signed a similar contract with the United States Express Company and the Great Western Dispatch. The Pennsylvania hesitated for some time before tying itself too closely to one or two express lines. On a more informal basis, it already enjoyed the business of the Adams Company and other leading concerns.

Then in the early 1860s the Pennsylvania followed suit by sponsoring new companies rather than relying on existing ones.[10] In 1863 it helped to organize and finance the Union Railroad and Transportation Company for carrying goods over its lines to and from the major commercial centers of the midwest. In 1865 it played a major role in setting up a second fast-freight line, the Empire Transportation Company, to attract traffic from the newly opened oil regions of western Pennsylvania to the Pennsylvania's recently completed lines from the oil fields to the seaboard.[11] Within a few years the Empire line became one of the largest express companies in the country, owning 4,500 cars including box, refrigerated, rack, and tank cars, as well as eighteen lake steamers and a number of elevators, warehouses, and oil yards in Erie, New York, Philadelphia, and other eastern ports. Its agents covered 20,000 miles of railroad in the east and midwest. As a pioneer in oil transportation, it even came to have its own pipelines.

By the late 1860s, after nearly all roads had allied themselves with large and increasingly powerful express or fast-freight companies, railroad managers began to feel that their own enterprises were being exploited.[12] Directors of their roads often became directors in the allied express companies. These men seemed to be using the express lines, as they did construction companies, as a device for siphoning off profits from the railroad itself. The express companies skimmed the cream of the high-value freight business; while the roads themselves were having difficulty in making a profit on the bulky less remunerative freight business. In addition, the express lines remained a serious threat to rate stability.

The response of the trunk lines and other major roads was to take over this business themselves by forming "cooperative fast-freight lines." The first, the Red Line, founded in 1866, ran between New York, Boston, and Chicago. A second, the Blue Line, opened in January 1867 to serve these same cities by using roads to the north of the Lakes. In 1868 the Green Line was established to move freight over most of the roads in the south. Soon there was a White Line that ran to the Pacific coast.

These lines were not legally separate enterprises, but rather freight-car pools, each managed by a separate administrative organization. The constituent railroads owned their cars individually. Each furnished the line (or pool) a quota in proportion to the revenue each received from through traffic. Each road was paid a mileage charge (normally 1½ cents a mile per car) for cars of other companies passing over its tracks. It also received a fee of 1½ cents for moving cars of roads which were not members of the cooperative. The line's central office kept a record of the movement of cars and drew up balances at the end of each month.

The cooperative schemes worked well. In 1874 a congressional investigation noted that "substantially all" traffic in the United States was carried by fast-freight lines. Most of these were cooperatives. By 1877 those that were not, including the Merchant's Dispatch, Great Western Dispatch, and the Empire had been purchased by the roads to which they had been allied. The few remaining independent express companies—Adams, American, United States, and Wells Fargo—concentrated as they had in their early years on the delivery of high-value freight rather than on handling through shipments of more standard cargoes.[13]

The cooperative arrangements for handling fast, dependable, scheduled shipments of through freight rested on two organizational innovations. One was the through bill of lading; the other was the car accountant office. The through bill of lading or waybill had not existed in the days of the packet lines, stagecoach lines, and other small personally operated shipping enterprises. It had its beginnings in the mid-1850s when the trunk lines and their connecting roads began to work out their procedures for billing shipments that moved across several lines.[14] The through waybill was perfected in the 1860s. It gave the details of the goods shipped, route sent, and charges levied. The shippers, receivers, and carriers responsible for the shipment—at first freight lines and later railroad companies—all retained copies of the waybill. By the 1870s the fast-freight lines were gauranteeing the accuracy of the quantity listed on the waybill. With such guarantees those bills quickly achieved the status of negotiable commercial paper and became used as a regular medium of exchange.[15]

At the same time that the bill of lading was being developed for through traffic, it was being improved for local trade.[16] Shipments for one town were placed in one or more cars and were left on the siding to be unloaded after the train had departed. The local stationmaster, who supervised the unloading, then notified local addresses of the arrival of their goods. Smaller lots were placed in "distributing cars" which were quickly unloaded while the train waited at the different stops. Copies of the bills of lading went to the road's auditor who credited the shipping agent and billed the receiving agent. These auditors' accounts were then checked with the daily reports of the station agents and so provided an improved control over shipments and the financial transactions involved.

Even before the railroads moved to cooperative pooling of their equipment through the fast-freight lines, the major roads had set up a car accountant office to keep track of the location and mileage run by "foreign" cars using its tracks and the location and mileage of its own cars on other roads.[17] In the 1870s such foreign cars included tank and coal cars owned by a small number of industrial companies, dining and sleeping cars operated by the Pullman Palace Car Company and its smaller competitors, and cars owned by other railroads and express companies. As the car accountant offices perfected their methods, the roads came to have less need for the joint fast-freight lines. In the 1880s and 1890s the coordination of flow of through traffic came to be handled increasingly by the traffic managers of the railroads themselves rather than through cooperative arrangements.

The growing importance of through traffic and the takeover from outside express and fast-freight companies of through freight greatly increased the duties of the railroad managers responsible for obtaining, moving, and delivering freight. With the intensified competition brought by the depression of the 1870s, the financial success of a railroad lay increasingly in these managers' hands. Therefore, during the 1870s, passenger and freight managers no longer reported to the general superintendent in the transportation department but were accorded a separate department of their own. The new traffic departments soon had the same status as the finance and transportation departments.

In this unplanned, ad hoc way American railroads internalized through a variety of organizational devices the activities and transactions that had been handled previously by hundreds of small enterprises. The fast-freight lines, the cooperatives, and finally the traffic departments of the larger roads had completed the transformation from market coordination to administrative coordination in American overland transportation. A multitude of commission agents, freight forwarders, and express companies, as well as stage and wagon companies, and canal, river, lake, and coastal shipping lines disappeared. In their place stood a small number of large multiunit railroad enterprises. As a result one shipment and one transaction had taken the place of many. By the 1880s the transformation begun in the 1840s was virtually completed.

The 1880s and early 1890s witnessed the culmination of technological as well as organizational innovation and standardization. In those years the United States railroads acquired a standard gauge and a standard time, moved toward standard basic equipment in the forms of automatic couplers, air brakes, and block signal systems, and adopted uniform accounting procedures.[18] On the night of May 31–June 1, 1886, the remaining railroads using broad-gauge tracks, all in the south, shifted simultaneously to the standard 4'8½" gauge. On Sunday, November 18, 1883, the railroad men (and most of their fellow countrymen) set their watches to the new uniform standard time. The passage of the Railroad Safety Appliance Act of 1893 made it illegal for trains to operate without standardized automatic couplers and air brakes. In 1887 the Interstate Commerce Act provided for uniform railroad accounting procedures that had been developing for a quarter of a century. All four of these events resulted from two decades of constant consultation and cooperation between railroad managers.

The cooperation required by the managers to integrate what had become by far the largest transportation network in the world stimulated a sense of professionalism among them. The middle managers who met regularly to discuss common problems in performing their different functions soon set up permanent quasi-professional associations. While some regional associations were formed before 1861, primarily in New England, nearly all the national societies appeared in the two decades after the Civil War. By the early 1880s, such associations had been formed for nearly every major railroad activity. They included the American Society of Railroad Superintendents, American Railway Master Mechanics Association, Master Car Builders Association (which included more members from railroad shops than from manufacturing companies), Roadmasters Association of America, National Association of General Passenger and

Ticket Agents, National Railroad Agents Association, American Ticket Brokers Association, General Baggage Agents Association, Society of Railroad Comptrollers, Accountants and Auditors (soon to be shortened to the Society of Railroad Accounting Officers), Railroad Traveling Auditors Association, Car Accountants Association, American Train Dispatchers Association, and the Association of Railroad Telegraph Superintendents. At the semiannual meetings, 100 to 150 of the railroad managers of each of these associations listened to papers and discussed technical problems of mutual interest. Between meetings of the national associations, the same executives and others often attended sessions with smaller regional affiliates.

In the 1870s and 1880s the papers and committee reports presented at these meetings were listed in the railroad press. Hardly a meeting passed without a discussion of national standardization of procedures and equipment. Thus, at the June 1885 meeting of the Master Car Builders Association, its president, Leander Garvey, opened the session, the *Railroad Gazette* reported, by pointing to "the many standards . . . now being acted upon. Out of the twelve committee reports to be acted on five were on proposed new standards. Mr. Garvey also especially dwelt upon the vital necessity of prompt action on the car coupler question."[19] That same month the train dispatchers met in Denver and "on the second day of the convention considered the question of a uniform system of rules and train orders." In late August, reporting on the Railroad Traveling Auditors meeting, the same journal noted: "An afternoon session was held, which was devoted to the discussion of various systems of railroad accounts, with a view to promoting uniformity in method. Several points in railroad practice concerning the interchange of business were also discussed." Similar comments on comparable meetings of other railroad specialists appeared in the pages of the *Gazette* and other railroad papers of this period. These associations had proliferated and become well established before professional academicians began to set up similar societies such as the American Historical Association formed in 1884, the American Economic Association formed in 1885, and the American Political Science Association formed in 1902.

The men who met together regularly at the meetings of associations devoted to their particular railroading activity developed a sense of professional expertise that was quite new to American businessmen. This professionalism was reinforced by reading the same journals and by following the same career lines. In the 1870s and 1880s the leading railroad journals —the *Railroad Gazette*, the *Railway World*, and the *Railroad and Engineering Journal* (a successor to Poor's *American Railroad Journal*)— came to concentrate on technical and professional matters. The great majority of the managers who read these papers and attended the meetings of their national societies had started at the lowest rung of the managerial ladder, usually serving an apprenticeship as a clerk, agent, messenger, telegraph operator, rodman, chainman, or machinist's assistant.[20] Most knew that, as they moved up the managerial ladder, they would remain in the same specialty and often would continue to be employed by the same company throughout their entire career.

Those who joined the managerial ranks in the construction, maintenance-of-way, or mechanical departments had usually taken a college course in civil or mechanical engineering. Indeed, the rise of American engineering education was, in part at least, a response to the needs of American railroads for trained civil and mechanical engineers. In the 1850s and 1860s leading institutions of higher learning such as Harvard, Yale, Columbia, Pennsylvania, and Virginia offered specialized four-year courses in engineering. So too did new schools such as the Massachusetts Institute of Technology and the new land-grant colleges. These trained engineers in 1867 revived the Society of American Civil Engineers which railroad men had attempted to found in the years before the Civil War.[21]

Thus by the 1880s American railroad managers had taken on the standard appurtenances of a profession. They had their societies and their journals. They moved through life along a well-defined career pattern. By then they saw themselves and were recognized by others as a new and distinct business class—the first professional business managers in America.

The interfirm cooperation that encouraged the professionalizing of the railroad manager increased the productivity of the American transportation system. Repeated discussions by the salaried managers of both organizational and technological innovations permitted their quick development and rapid adoption by American railroads. Professional exchanges encouraged improvements in locomotives, tracks, and other facilities, as well as standardization of couplers, air brakes, and signals, because these products were designed and improved by the railroad departments and not the manufacturers. The latter merely built to specifications set forth by the former. In addition, the constant consultation and cooperation of many salaried managers achieved for the national network what the pioneers of internal organization had done for the individual lines. Both made possible an administrative coordination of transportation that was much more efficient than prerailroad market coordination.

The productivity of American railroads increased impressively during the second half of the nineteenth century. Albert Fishlow has quantitatively defined and analyzed the great expansion in the volume and the "dramatic relative decline in the price of railroad services."[22] "Over the entire interval 1838 to 1910, railroad services grew at annual rate of

11.6 percent with [national] income and commodity output proceeding at a pace only one-third as rapid. Indeed, no single major sector grew as rapidly. With an 1870 benchmark, these same observations obtain, albeit with a somewhat narrowed margin of superiority."[23] At the same time "real freight rates fell more than 80 percent from their 1849 level, and passenger charges 50 percent." Fishlow credits this basic improvement to an increase in size and efficiency of locomotives and rolling stock and, most of all, to the adoption of heavy steel rails. He points also to the value of standardization of equipment made possible by "informal industry-wide associations and committees," and the normal economies of scale and specialization that came as the size of the firm increased. Yet all these improvements, he believes, account for only half of the productivity increase between 1870 and 1910.[24] He suggests that the importance of increased educational level and experience of the work force might help to explain the residual.

Certainly the organizational innovations perfected by the railroad managers and their increased training and professionalization must also have played a part. Some productivity increases surely came from the administrative arrangements that permitted a more intensive use of rolling stock and a greater velocity of traffic flow across the lines of individual roads and the nation's transportation system as a whole. Arrangements to permit freight cars to move without reloading across many lines lowered capital outlays needed for equipment and working capital required for fuel and labor. Constant discussions in the managerial associations of all types of technological and organizational innovation helped further to increase productivity and reduce costs. The close cooperation between the managers of the first modern multiunit enterprises in the United States contributed impressively to increasing the speed and regularity of transportation and decreasing its costs. And, as will be analyzed in later chapters, it was the economy and velocity of transportation that provided the basic underpinnings of the institutional changes in American production and distribution that occurred in the later part of the nineteenth century.

Cooperation to control competition

Before considering the central role that the new transportation system played in revolutionizing the processes of production and distribution, the story of the growth of the first modern business enterprises needs to be carried to its logical conclusion. Although the railroads had by 1880 been integrated into a single national network, the individual enterprises had not yet taken on their permanent form. The network was operated by a sizable number of lines of a few hundred miles in length. Then in the last two decades of the nineteenth century, the earliest and longest established roads created giant systems operating from 5,000 to 10,000 miles of track. By 1900 these systems had reached the geographical boundaries they would retain into the second half of the twentieth century. The rapid growth of the nation's first modern business enterprises was almost wholly a response to competition and the failure of interroad cooperation to control competition.

Competition between railroads bore little resemblance to competition between traditional small, single-unit commercial or industrial enterprises. Railroad competition presented an entirely new business phenomenon. Never before had a very small number of very large enterprises competed for the same business. And never before had competitors been saddled with such high fixed costs. In the 1880s fixed costs, those costs that did not vary with the amount of traffic carried, averaged two-thirds of total cost.[25] The relentless pressure of such costs quickly convinced railroad managers that uncontrolled competition for through traffic would be "ruinous." As long as a road had cars available to carry freight, the temptation to attract traffic by reducing rates was always there. Any rate that covered more than the variable costs of transporting a shipment brought the road extra income. Normally the only way a competing road could retain such traffic was to make comparable cuts. The weak roads whose lines were longer and less advantageously located and less efficiently managed tended to succumb first. They needed the traffic to remain financially solvent. If such tactics resulted in bankruptcy, a road actually had a competitive advantage. It no longer had to pay the fixed charges on its debt. Since American railroads were financed largely through bonds, these charges were high. To both the railroad managers and investors, the logic of such competition appeared to be bankruptcy for all.

From the start, railroad men had looked on interfirm cooperation as the way to control interfirm competition. As soon as they went into operation, the roads followed what has been aptly termed a "territorial strategy."[26] By making informal alliances with connecting and competing roads, railroad managers expected to maintain the flow of traffic necessary to assure a profitable return on the investment made in their facilities. Such alliances would permit the roads to provide the transportation services in the "natural territory" they had been built to serve. Feeder lines were constructed or bought only when such alliances failed to maintain a continuing flow of traffic across their lines.

As long as through traffic expanded, a territorial strategy carried out by informal alliances worked well. But once the volume of through traffic began to fall off and competitive pressures increased, railroad managers and owners found the informal alliances inadequate. They turned increasingly to employing closer and more formal methods of cooperation to control competition. Only after the most concerted and most sophisticated attempts at cooperation had failed did railroaders turn in large numbers to system building as a means of eliminating the threat of ruinous competition.

An understanding of the later efforts of formal cooperation to control competition requires a review of the earlier policy of alliances. In the 1850s many, though not all, major roads embarked on such a policy as soon as they had, and sometimes even before they had, completed construction. Alliances with connecting roads were usually cemented by purchasing securities in the feeder lines. The Pennsylvania, for example, began in 1852 to invest in roads then under construction westward from Pittsburgh. In 1858 it already had invested $1.6 million in the Pittsburgh, Ft. Wayne & Chicago, the Steubenville & Indiana, and the Marietta & Cincinnati.[27] The Baltimore & Ohio followed a similar strategy in the 1850s. So too did the first of the largest midwestern roads—the Michigan Central and the Michigan Southern. The investors in the first helped to organize and finance the Chicago, Burlington & Quincy and the New Albany & Salem; those in the second the Rock Island. Both groups next financed connecting lines across Iowa. Other lines out of Chicago, including the Chicago & Northwestern, the Milwaukee & St. Paul, and the Illinois Central, followed the same plan. In the south the Georgia and the Georgia Southern both placed funds in their westward connections.

Alliances with competing roads came as quickly as those with connecting ones. At the regional meetings in the mid-1850s where railroad executives grappled with the principles of ratemaking and first determined official rates for their territories, they also agreed not to cut rates or to make excessive use of agents or "runners" to drum up business.[28] However, they did little to provide means of enforcing these decisions. Only the east-west trunk lines set up an enforcing organization which was formed in 1858 after the panic of 1857 had reduced traffic and increased competition. However, it accomplished little before it was abandoned during the Civil War.[29]

After the war these informal alliances began to be strained. Not only did through traffic become increasingly critical for a road's profit, as has been indicated, but also there were often several alternate routes where before 1861 there had been one. Feeder lines felt less reliance on or allegiance to their sponsors. A desire for independence and financial needs led them to look to other sources for carrying their goods. At the same time, other major roads began to ally themselves to or even take over the feeder lines of competitors. In fact, the attempt of Jay Gould in 1869 to take control of the Pennsylvania's connections west of Pittsburgh caused the Pennsylvania's president to create the first great self-sustaining system in the United States. However, except for the Baltimore & Ohio, no other American road followed the Pennsylvania's example until the 1880s.

For more than a decade American managers continued to hope to control competition through cooperation. They preferred to stick with a strategy of alliances rather than turn, as had the Pennsylvania, to the building of a giant system. The managers opposed expansion because they considered any road much over five hundred miles in length to be too large and complex to manage. The investors were even more adamant. The cost of such expansion could only result in reducing the funds available for dividends. In addition, investors and managers agreed that there was another reason for not building giant railroad enterprises. They concurred with J. Edgar Thomson's arguments for maintaining the Pennsylvania system of alliances before 1869:

Sensible of the prejudice against large corporations since the failure of the United States Bank, the policy of this Company was first directed to the procuring of these connections by securing the organization of independent railway companies, and their construction by such pecuniary assistance as was required to effect this business. This course, it was confidently expected, would meet the objects desired without involving this company in the direct management of distant enterprises.[30]

Nevertheless, in the early 1870s many roads were having increasing difficulty in maintaining their strategy of alliances. In the trunk line territory competition was not yet a critical problem. Paul MacAvoy, the most careful student of trunk line competition, has noted that until 1874 there was "a general adherence to official rates in large volume shipments."[31] But in the south, roads found themselves buying or building more track than they wanted to in order to maintain their territorial position.[32] And in the west, where so much of the through freight consisted of the grain trade, some companies were devising new techniques to maintain rates. They had set up informal pools for allocating traffic and profits. Such allocations, they reasoned, removed the incentive for rate-cutting, since lower rates could not bring either increased traffic or more revenue. In 1870 the Burlington, the Rock Island, and the Chicago & Northwestern set up an informal unsigned money pool—the Iowa Pool—that divided equally between the three roads 50 percent of the income from freight, and 55 percent from passenger traffic.[33] In September 1874 the three roads connecting Chicago and St. Paul adopted similar pooling procedures. As business fell off, other roads in the country began organizing informal traffic and money pools.

With the onslaught of the depression after 1873 nearly all managers and investors agreed that informal cooperation was no longer adequate.

With the increasingly desperate search for traffic, rate agreement collapsed. Secret rebating intensified. Soon roads were openly reducing rates. Nor were the informal pools able to maintain rates. Their members took traffic that was not allocated to them and often failed to return income to be redistributed by the pool. Some railroad managers argued that the Pennsylvania had the right answer. They urged their boards of directors to build comparable large, self-contained interregional systems. To most managers, however, the problems of administering such a giant enterprise still appeared formidable. For nearly all investors, the costs of such system-building in the depressed years when dividends were already low seemed prohibitive. In the mid-1870s American railroaders grasped at another solution to meet the threat of ruinous competition. They decided to transform weak, tenuous alliances into strong, carefully organized, well-managed federations.

The great cartels

The answer to competition was better cooperation. Formal federations were created, and they were soon to have their own legislative, executive, and judicial bodies. The largest and most powerful of the roads—the trunk lines—were the first to organize formal cartels.

The move toward federation came in the summer of 1874, as falling traffic intensified the pressure to cut rates.[34] That summer the presidents and the general managers of the Pennsylvania, the Erie, and the New York Central (but not of the Baltimore & Ohio) met, together with the senior executives of their western connections, at Saratoga Springs. According to Thomas Scott, who had just replaced J. Edgar Thomson as the Pennsylvania's president, these men hoped, as had their counterparts twenty years earlier, "to abolish all commissions, agencies and outside expenses" involved in obtaining traffic. Of more importance the roads established an administrative office, the Western Railroad Bureau, to maintain rates between east-west competitive points. The bureau was to have the power of enforcement, including the dismissal of railroad employees who knowingly cut rates. In addition, the three roads set up a commission to provide what they hoped would be considered an objective outside agency to review and supervise the ratemaking process:

A commission to be composed of three gentlemen familiar with railway traffic, but disinterested and in no way officially connected with the Companies; this commission to have power to make such moderate rates from time to time as would be reasonable and just to the public, and give in the future equal and uniform rates to every shipper.[35]

The presidents of the three trunk lines traveled to Baltimore in November to try to persuade the conspicuously absent Garrett to agree to these proposals. The president of the Baltimore & Ohio hesitated. He wanted to see what effect the completion of a nearly finished line into Chicago would have on the business of his road. He hoped that the rounding-out of his self-contained system might forestall the need for joining the cartel. Before the end of the year, however, the Baltimore & Ohio had reduced its rates on grain and other fourth-class freight between Baltimore and Chicago, and its competitors followed suit. In 1875 a new contender, the Grand Trunk of Canada, operating from Portland, Maine to Detroit via Montreal entered the east-west competition. It did so by temporarily allying itself with the Michigan Central and the Vermont Central to give it connections into Chicago, Boston, and New York.[36] Immediately it cut its rates to obtain traffic. In the next year came the sharpest rate reductions the country had yet seen. In the drawn-out negotiations that followed, the merchants of Baltimore and those of Philadelphia had joined their railroads in demanding that the rates from the western cities to their ports be lower than those to New York, while New England businessmen supported the Grand Trunk in its call to keep rates to Boston and Portland the same as those to New York.[37]

Finally in the spring of 1877 the exhausted roads agreed to compromise.[38] On May 5 the trunk lines signed the Seaboard Differential Agreement and created a new interfirm organization to carry it out. The new rate structure followed the demands of New York City's rivals. Philadelphia and Baltimore received somewhat lower rates on westbound traffic than New York had, while Boston's remained much the same. On May 23 came a second agreement aimed at reducing the incentive to cheat on the newly established schedules by arranging for an allocation of traffic. The New York Central and Erie each were to carry 33 percent of the westward moving traffic, while the Pennsylvania took 25 percent, and the Baltimore & Ohio the remaining 9 percent. This time there was no opposition from Garrett. Then the presidents of these trunk lines asked Albert Fink to head the new Executive Committee of their Eastern Trunk Line Association. They proposed that he build the administrative offices necessary to carry out and enforce these agreements and to work with their western connections to do the same.

Fink was at that time managing a similar organization in the south. The southern roads differed from those north of the Potomac since there were fewer major competing roads between large cities. On the other hand, many alternative routes did exist for carrying through traffic which often moved to the seaboard ports and then by coastal steamer to New York and other northern ports. Even before the coming of the depression, these financially weak roads began to fight for the declining traffic by constant rate-cutting. At a meeting in Atlanta in 1875 a convention of southern transportation companies quickly accepted a proposal from Albert Fink, still a senior executive of the Louisville & Nashville, to set up an association or federation which would allocate traffic at points where competing roads met.[39] The allocation would be in accordance with already existing traffic patterns determined by a statistical bureau set up by the association. The presidents of the southern roads then persuaded Fink to become the first commissioner of the Southern Railway and Steamship Association.

When Fink went to work eighteen months later for the Eastern Trunk Line Association, he applied the methods he had already worked out in the south.[40] His first task was to formalize regional conventions of competing roads to meet at regularly specified times to determine local as well as interregional freight rates and classifications. At the same time, he built a large staff in New York, which soon included more than sixty clerks, to collect information on existing rates and traffic movements which the committees used in their deliberations. He also held conferences on ways to adjust and enforce rate and allocation decisions and to review complaints.

Fink next brought the connecting lines to the west and to New England into the association. In the summer of 1878 the midwestern roads, at Fink's suggestion, formed the Western Executive Committee to set rates for and to allocate eastbound traffic. Then, in an agreement signed in December, the associated roads set up a Joint Executive Committee, chaired by Fink, which would give final approval of all rates worked out by the regional subcommittees or associations in the east and the west. Continuing complaints and a burst of rate-cutting drove home the need for formal cooperative action.[41]

According to a new agreement all cases involving rates which were not decided unanimously were to be referred to the chairman, "who shall decide the case on its merits, and whose decision shall have the same force and effect as the unanimous vote of the Committee." Soon afterward the committee's power was further enlarged. At the same time, a Board of Arbiters was created to listen to the complaints about Fink's actions and to review and decide on all alleged violations of the agreement. The board was composed of three of the most able and respected railroad experts of the day: Charles Francis Adams, chairman of the Massachusetts Railroad Commission; David A. Wells, the economist; and John A. Wright, a Philadelphian who had long been a director on the Pennsylvania Railroad. For almost two years these new administrators were able to maintain the through rates on the trunk line routes.

In this way Albert Fink had by the end of 1878 created a federation of railroads which included nearly all the lines north of the Ohio and east of the Mississippi. As he reported to the Joint Executive Committee at its first annual meeting in Chicago in December 1879:

You have now for the first time established a practical method by which the competitive traffic of your roads can be properly managed and controlled. Heretofore this was impossible; the mere holding of conventions of railroad managers, passing resolutions, and then dispersing and letting things take care of themselves, each party acting as it sees fit, will not accomplish the purpose of intelligent joint management of the large property under your charge. You have now added to the legislative department—your conventions—also a permanent executive department the duty of which is to see that the resolutions passed and agreements made are faithfully carried out. In addition to this you have also established a judiciary department, consisting of a board of arbitration, whose duty it is to settle peaceably any question of difference, without resort to wasteful warfare, with all its injurious consequences. You have thus formed a complete government over this large competitive traffic over which it has heretofore been found impractical to exercise intelligent control.[42]

Such formal federations of railroads quickly became the order of the day. Cooperation appeared to be getting control of competition. In 1876 a number of western roads organized the Southwestern Railway Rate Association with an organization copied directly from that of the Southern Railway and Steamship Association.[43] John W. Midgley, formerly of the Chicago & Northeastern, became its secretary and full-time operating head. Although the new association had difficulties in carrying out its objectives, particularly after Jay Gould entered the area, other local federations were soon formed. They included the Iowa (the old "Iowa Pool" which would become in time the Western Traffic Association), the Colorado, the Texas, the Pacific Coast, and the Transcontinental Associations. Midgley soon acquired the same type of overall control of these several associations as Fink had as chairman of the Joint Executive Committee in the east. Such associations, railroad executives and experts agreed, were the only way to prevent, in Albert Fink's words, "centralization and absorption of the roads under the absolute control of one or a few persons. It makes the separate, individual existence of these roads possible, and puts a check on the consolidation of these roads . . . [It] secures all the advantages of consolidation without its disadvantages."[44]

Fink nevertheless feared that private federation would not in itself be able to maintain stability. To the paragraph cited above, the commissioner had added, "It must be remarked, however, that the only bond which holds this government together is the intelligence and good faith of the parties composing it."[45] He therefore urged the members of the committee and their roads to make a concerted effort to have "the operations of this committee . . . legally binding upon all parties by legislative action, provided it can be shown, as I believe it can, that its operation is beneficial to the public interests." Yet despite an energetic campaign before congressional committees, Fink and the many other railroad managers and directors who supported this proposal failed to get the national legislature to sanction the rulings of their private associations. And they soon found to their sorrow that they could not rely on the intelligence and good faith of railroad executives, particularly entrepreneurs or speculators who like Gould had little interest in the long-term profits or operational performance of the roads whose securities they controlled.

In 1880, Jay Gould, often allied with those able stock market manipulators Russell Sage and Sidney Dillion, was moving swiftly to put together a transcontinental railroad empire. In the east he invaded the trunk line territory by increasing his control over the Wabash and by buying stock of the Lackawanna, the Central of New Jersey, and the Boston, New York, and Erie.[46] In order to obtain traffic, Gould violated earlier agreements and provoked a passenger rate war with the Erie and the Central during the spring of 1881. Even Fink's threat to bring all rates down to the level to which Gould had reduced them had little effect until August 1884 when a temporary armistice was finally arranged.

By this time Fink had become discouraged. As early as August 1881, he told the executive committee that: "The late events . . . have convinced me that, even with the most sincere intention, it is impractical; and that if sincerity is wanting, it is impossible to maintain the established tariff."[47] In continuing to try to make the cartel work, Fink's organization had almost as much trouble with the weak cooperative roads (and even some of the stronger ones) as he did with the uncooperative ones controlled by speculators. Traffic managers and freight agents developed new subterfuges for evading the published rates. These included false billing regarding weight or amounts shipped or distances sent and improper classification of freight moved. To prevent such frauds Fink developed an inspection system. In 1882 the Joint Executive Committee agreed to appoint a joint agent at all places where traffic or revenue was allocated.[48] This official was to have the authority to examine books and bills of lading of all member roads, while the roads and soliciting agents were deprived of any power to alter or adjust rates. The prerogative was given solely to the commissioner and his agents.

At the very time that the association was being debilitated by its failure to get the necessary cooperation from the weaker roads and those in the hands of the speculators, it was also being attacked by farmers' granges and merchants' boards of trade for attempting to maintain rates at artificially high levels. New York merchants continued to be angered by the rate differentials agreed upon in 1877. They argued that the rates discriminated against New York in favor of the other ports. As a result, the effort of Fink and the other representatives of the railroads to legalize cartels had to encounter an ever-growing pressure to declare pooling completely illegal.

The situation failed to improve. The roads controlled by Gould and other speculators continued to maintain agreements only when it suited their immediate purposes. In 1884, with the rate structure in chaos, the association did little more than stand by helplessly. Charles Francis Adams reported of one of its meetings, "It struck me as a somewhat funereal gathering. Those comprising it were manifestly at their wit's end . . . Mr. Fink's great and costly organization was all in ruins . . . They reminded me of men in a boat in the swift water above the rapids of Niagara."[49] A more than temporary agreement between the eastern roads was not reached until November of 1885, when the weaker companies had become exhausted. In 1886 and early 1887 the joint executive committee had little success in maintaining rates. Nor were the federations in other parts of the country doing any better.

By 1884 nearly all the railroad managers and most investors agreed that even the most carefully devised cartels were unable to control competition. They could not be relied on to assure an equitable flow of through traffic. Railroad managers continued to press for state and national legislation to legalize pooling.[50] The regional associations—the Eastern Trunk Line, the Southern Steamship and Railway, the Southwestern Railway Association, and the others—continued in their efforts to set rates and classes, and they did so until the Supreme Court ruled that the Sherman Antitrust Act of 1890 had made such practices illegal. However, few railroad managers any longer expected the associations to assure them a continuing and paying flow of through traffic across their facilities. To attain this goal they turned instead, precisely as Fink had predicted, to the building of giant, self-contained interterritorial systems.

The causes for the failures of these first great cartels in the United States were many. To control and allocate the flow of traffic across the transportation network of a major region was a complex administrative task requiring more men and managers than Fink and his counterparts in other associations ever had at their disposal. The pooling and allocating of income, while a more modest effort, was still administratively difficult. Moreover, the roads continued to have great difficulty in determining what each considered an equitable allocation of either freight or revenue. In time of rapidly growing traffic, percentage shares agreed upon at the start of the year were outmoded by the end of the year. The more efficient roads, like the Pennsylvania, which increased their share of the traffic actually carried, resented having to pay large sums into the pool at the end of each accounting period. In addition, the activities of speculators and other businessmen who controlled the stocks of railroads for purposes of other than getting a return on their investment in transportation facilities made agreement on and enforcement of rate contracts difficult. Most important of all, however, was the relentless pressure of high constant costs. The need to meet these costs intensified the pressure to use excess capacity by subverting the cartel arrangements.

The managerial role

If a central theme can be found in the operation of American railroads during the 1860s and 1870s, it is cooperation. Interfirm cooperation was essential for the creation of an integrated national transportation network. Without such cooperation the standardization of equipment and operating procedures required to move through passengers and freight quickly and efficiently from one line to another would have been much slower in coming. This cooperation was also necessary, in the opinion of railroad men, to control competition. It was necessary to prevent a struggle for the growing through traffic from becoming, in their terms, ruinous. In carrying out both types of cooperation the middle managers played a critical role.

The middle managers provided the administrative coordination that replaced market coordination during these years. Their decisions coordinated the flow of goods not only across their own lines but also across the national network. They met in their professional associations to work out uniform operating procedures and to install standardized equipment. They were the men responsible for devising and perfecting a number of basic organizational and technological innovations so central to the efficient operation of the railroads. Albert Fishlow's statistics suggest how well they performed these tasks.

The middle managers were less successful in cooperating to control competition. Again, the top executives—the president, the treasurer, the general manager, and the heads of the transportation and traffic departments—decided on the basic strategies of alliances and federations. But it was the middle managers at the regional railroad conventions who determined the actual official rate schedules. They had the responsibility for maintaining these rates. Yet they were often the ones, particularly those in the traffic departments, who cut the rates in order to get or keep traffic. Or they looked aside when a subordinate received secret rebates from the shippers. And when traffic dropped off, they were also the ones who recommended to top management that the official rate structure be abandoned. Their willingness to subvert this structure resulted in part at least from the demands of their day-to-day tasks. Their success as managers depended on obtaining and holding customers. The surest way to do this was to shave a bit on the rates.

Yet such cooperation might have worked. The middle managers might have been more aggressive in maintaining rates and might have worked more closely with Fink's minions in searching out the violators of existing agreements. If the cartel agreements had been enforceable in courts of law—that is, if they had been drawn up in the form of a legal contract—the costs of breaking agreements would have been much higher. Given the basic nature of railroad competition—competition between a small number of large enterprises with high constant costs—legalization of the cartel arrangements was probably the only effective method to control competition and so remove the incentive for system-building. But the hopes of Fink and others for legalized pooling had little political support in the United States of the 1880s.

When the United States Congress finally defined public policy toward railroad competition in the Interstate Commerce Act of 1887, it failed to sanction pooling. Indeed, the Congress forbade it. For many years railroad men agreed that if pooling were legalized an impartial commission, even one appointed by the government, should oversee ratemaking.[51] Despite this proviso, shippers strongly opposed the proposal. As railroad rates were such a critical part of their profit calculus, these businessmen hesitated to give the railroads such economic power, even if a government-appointed commission did have the final say on rates. To Americans less involved in transportation, legalized pooling was merely legalized monopoly. Its approval by a majority of the voters would have called for a basic shift in American attitudes and values.

The railroad managers were sensitive to the growing political debate. Many were uncertain of the remedies. Some doubted that even legalized pooling could stablize the rates. Others were distrustful of government regulation. In any case, the political controversy helped to convince them further of the futility of relying on cartels to prevent ruinous competition. For most, the building of the large, self-sustaining systems was the only practical answer to interfirm competition. And in the 1880s, well before the passage of the Interstate Commerce Act, railroad managers turned with vigor to system-building. They turned from a territorial strategy to an interterritorial one. They moved beyond the area their roads were originally built to serve and began to connect the commercial centers and sources of natural resources of one of the nation's basic geographical regions.

C H A P T E R 5

System-Building, 1880s-1900s

Top management decision making

The 1850s were a time of building and of learning to manage the railroads as the nation's first modern business enterprises; the 1860s and 1870s were a period of coordinating and competing for the flows of through traffic; the 1880s and 1890s were the years of system-building. The perfecting of internal organization and the coordination of flows across and between roads had been largely the job of middle management; system-building was almost completely the task of top management.

The top managers of American railroads made the alliances with consulting and connecting lines. They decided when to join and how long to stay in the great cartels. And they established when and where to buy, lease, or build the small feeder lines in the 1860s and 1870s, and where and when to build the giant interterritorial systems in the 1880s and 1890s. In a word, top management determined the long-term objectives of the enterprise and allocated the resources in men, money, and equipment needed to carry out these goals.

The senior executives who made the decisions concerning the road's basic policies and its strategies of growth included two quite different types of businessmen: the manager who had made a lifetime career in railroad operation and the entrepreneur or financier who had invested capital in the road. The full-time, salaried executives on a large railroad included the president, treasurer, general manager, and heads of the transportation and traffic departments. Of these, the last three were almost always career managers. The president and treasurer, on the other hand, were often major investors or their representatives.[1] The policies and strategies decided by these top managers required the approval of the board of directors, particularly its chairman. These board members, successful businessmen in their own right who served the road on a part-time basis, were almost always either large investors or spokesmen for investors.

The goals of these two groups were not always the same. The managers, who rarely owned large blocks of stock, looked to the long-term health and growth of the organization in which they worked and to which they had often devoted their whole careers. They were willing and indeed usually preferred to reduce dividends to assure long-term stability. The representatives of the owners, on the other hand, gave priority to maintaining dividends that would assure a reasonable continuing rate of return on their investment. Investors were therefore reluctant to spend large amounts of capital for expanding a road's facilities. Such expenditures could reduce, often for extended periods of time, the dividends the road paid. In the formulation of strategic decisions, the financiers in top management were almost certain to have the support of the investors on the board of directors.

The types of investors whose representatives sat on the boards and became presidents and treasurers changed between the 1850s and the end of the century. At first, investors were merchants, farmers, and manufacturers, who initially promoted and financed their roads in order to improve the economic fortunes of their particular city or region. As the roads grew in size and required increasing capital, and as local funds had to be supplemented by those from the nation's oldest and largest commercial centers, presidents and boards came increasingly to represent general entrepreneurs who had access to pools of capital. In carrying out their territorial strategies of alliances through stock purchases and new construction, railroad companies, particularly those in the south and west, began to rely for funds on such eastern capitalists as the Vanderbilts, the Forbeses, Nathaniel Thayer, Erastus Corning, Moses Taylor, John N. A. Griswold, William Osborn, and Henry Villard. These men invested their own funds and those of associates in the expectation that the railroads would continue to be profitable by helping to develop the territory they served. Then as roads began to build their interterritorial systems, they had to rely increasingly on the specialized investment bankers with close ties to British and European sources of capital to supply the massive amounts of money needed. In this latter period the members of the powerful investment banking firms of J. P. Morgan; August Belmont; Kuhn, Loeb; Lee, Higginson; Kidder, Peabody; Speyer; and E. W. Clark came to dominate the boards of the new railroad systems.

There was yet another type of businessman who determined railroad strategy and served on boards or as president or treasurer. This was the speculator. The speculators differed from the managers and the investors; they had no long-term interest in their enterprise. They did not expect to make their livelihood or receive an income by providing transportation services. Their profits came instead from exploiting ancillary operations such as construction and express companies, from obtaining land and mineral rights along the line of the road, and, most often, from making money by manipulating the price of the roads' securities.

The centralization and institutionalization of the capital market during the 1850s, so essential to the raising of the large sums of money required for railroad building, provided the instruments and procedures that made possible a new style of speculation. The most renowned of the speculators —Drew, Fiske, Russell Sage, Sidney Dillon, George I. Seney, Calvin Brice, and Samuel Thomas—would never have been able to buy and sell large blocks of stock, control roads, and manipulate their securities had not these new institutions and methods for the large-scale transfer of securities been perfected on Wall Street.

The strategies resulting from the interplay of speculators, investors, and managers reveal much about the process of growth in the first modern business enterprises. These strategies involved the allocation of much more capital and personnel and affected the economic lives and activities of many more Americans than did the investment decisions of any other type of nineteenth-century business firm. And they led to the creation of giant enterprises that consolidated and internalized the property, personnel, and activities of a number of already large bureaucratic corporations.

The formulation of the strategies that created these "megacorps"[2] indicates much about the motives of the managers, investors, and speculators who guided the destinies of American railroads. The systems were not built to reduce costs or increase current profits. The strategies of growth were not undertaken to fill any need for or to exploit the opportunities resulting from improved administrative coordination. By the 1880s such coordination had already been achieved for the American railroad network through interfirm cooperation. Other economies of scale brought some cost reductions, but they were far outweighed by the large expense of building and buying facilities which could not yet be fully used by existing traffic. The basic motive of system-building was, therefore, defensive: to assure a continuing flow of freight and passengers across the roads' facilities by fully controlling connections with major sources of traffic.

System-building proved costly to individual roads and to some extent to the national economy as well. The great growth of the individual enterprises often led to a redundancy of facilities. During the 1880s more miles of track were built than in any other decade in American history, and in the 1890s more mileage was in bankruptcy than in any decade before or since. The overconstruction resulting from system-building was on a much greater scale than the overbuilding stimulated earlier by the optimism of promoters or the lure of land grants. In time, however, most of the new roads became fully used. Many redundancies were temporary ones.

In the interplay between the three types of businessmen who determined railroad strategy, the investors played a passive role and the managers and speculators an active one. Once the investors and managers agreed on a strategy of expansion, the managers planned and carried it out. But it was the speculators who normally convinced the investors to permit the managers to embark on such a strategy. Given the steady pressure of high constant costs and the legal and administrative difficulties involved in maintaining cartel arrangements, the large systems would probably have appeared even if the speculators had not been active. By the 1880s the managers were becoming convinced of the inadequacies of the existing policies of alliances and federations. Investors were beginning to agree, even though they still balked at paying the cost of system-building.

It was, however, the speculators who shattered the old strategies. They were the first to disrupt the existing alliances. They undermined the viability of the regional railroad cartels since they often had more to gain from violating than from maintaining rate agreements. Sudden price wars and unexpected peace treaties effectively depressed and raised security prices. The speculators had none of the "good faith" Fink insisted was essential to make the cartels work. It was the speculators, then, who precipitated system-building in American transportation.

The interplay in the top management of railroads between the salaried managers, the investors, and the speculators affected the roads' organizational structure as well as grand strategy. In designing structures needed to manage these new megacorps, managers, investors, and speculators sought different solutions that reflected their different experiences and aims. After 1900, however, when the systems were completed and strategic planning was no longer of major significance, the American railroads nearly all came to have much the same type of internal structure.

Building the first systems

No man had a greater impact on the strategy of American railroads than Jay Gould, the most formidable and best known of the late nineteenth-century speculators. It was Gould who forced the Pennsylvania to abandon its long-held territorial strategy and to build the nation's first interterritorial railroad empire. And it was Gould who finally convinced William Vanderbilt to transform the New York Central into a similar giant system. Then, a decade later, it was the same "Mephistopheles of Wall Street" who pushed the top managers of the Burlington, the Chicago and Northwestern, and other western lines into a strategy of expansion and consolidation. A review of Gould's actions thus provides a useful focus for describing and analyzing system-building in American transportation.

Gould first acquired national notoriety when he joined Daniel Drew and Jim Fiske early in 1868 to prevent Cornelius Vanderbilt from taking over the Erie.[3] Vanderbilt, who had obtained full control of the New York Central only a year earlier, had moved quickly to acquire his nearby weak, and therefore, in his opinion, dangerous competitor. The three speculators were able to successfully stave off Vanderbilt's attack by the ingenious illegal and extralegal tactics that Henry and Charles Francis Adams dramatized in *Chapters of Erie*. After the battle, Drew and Fiske sold out. Gould became the road's largest stockholder and its president.

Gould needed traffic if the securities of the Erie were to have any value. One way to obtain this traffic was to obtain full control of roads to the west. Except for the financially shaky and poorly managed Atlantic and Great Western, the Erie had no alliances with western connections. By capturing those of either the Pennsylvania or the New York Central he could both assure traffic for his road and at the same time weaken a major competitor.

What precisely Gould's long-term goals were cannot be documented. He may have been planning to integrate the roads he acquired into a consolidated system. On the other hand, given the pattern of his whole career, it is much more likely that he expected these purchases to raise the price of Erie stock, which he could then dispose of at a high profit. Or possibly he merely planned to sell these lines back to the Pennsylvania or the New York Central at a comparable gain.

In any case, late in 1868 Gould, after he had leased the Atlantic and Great Western, began his campaign to obtain control of the Pennsylvania's western allies.[4] He started by negotiating with the Indiana Central, which would have connected the Atlantic and Great Western with St. Louis. Thomas A. Scott, the Pennsylvania's vice president in charge of external affairs, was able to parry Gould's try for the Indiana Central by offering a higher price to lease it. Gould's attempts to win control of both the Cleveland & Pittsburgh and the Pittsburgh, Ft. Wayne & Chicago were more novel. He purchased proxies to be voted at the roads' annual meeting. With these proxies in hand he could appoint the roads' directors and then arrange for their sale to the Erie. Scott prevented Gould from controlling the meeting of the Cleveland & Pittsburgh by challenging the legality of the proxies in the Ohio courts. He turned aside the threat to the Ft. Wayne by proposing that the Pennsylvania legislature alter the road's charter so that only one quarter of the directors could be appointed at each annual meeting. A sympathetic legislature quickly approved. Its members fully realized that Gould's control of the Ft. Wayne could divert much of the western traffic from Philadelphia to New York City.

Gould's swift and unexpected attack forced the Pennsylvania to adopt a new strategy.[5] "In view of these extraordinary movements, it became evident to your Board," its president, J. Edgar Thomson, reported to the stockholders, "that this Company must depart from the policy that had heretofore governed it, and obtain direct control of its western connections." By July 1, 1869, the Pennsylvania had leased the Ft. Wayne and then the Cleveland & Pittsburgh and the Indiana Central on reasonable terms. Their directors preferred Thomson and Scott as associates to Jay Gould.

Blocked by the Pennsylvania, the Erie's president immediately turned his attention to obtaining the lines running along the southern shores of Lake Erie.[6] Early in April he renewed an agreement with the Michigan Southern to obtain access to Chicago. By summer Gould had merged that line with others along the shore of Lake Erie between Toledo, Ohio, and Erie, Pennsylvania, into the Lake Shore and Michigan Southern. Here he had the help of Legrand Lockwood, a Wall Street speculator who had earlier tried to prevent Vanderbilt from obtaining the New York Central. At the same time, Gould began to buy stock in the Toledo, Wabash, and Western, a through road connecting Toledo to St. Louis. In August, he was elected to its board. Vanderbilt, who had been echoing the views of the Pennsylvania's executives by saying he had no interest in controlling or managing lines to the west, suddenly realized these vital western connections were about to fall into the hands of his arch rival, Jay Gould.

It was only Jay Gould's other speculations that permitted Vanderbilt to save the situation by reversing his earlier policies and obtaining control of the Lake Shore. In October 1869, Gould joined Jim Fiske for their most daring speculative coup, the attempt to corner the gold market. In the resulting stock market shakeup that followed the failure of the corner, Lockwood was forced to sell his shares in the Lake Shore. And, as Gould's biographer has pointed out, "It was Vanderbilt, the businessman with funds, and not Gould, the speculator without funds, who bought the distressed stock." Besides obtaining control of the Lake Shore, Vanderbilt picked up blocks of Wabash stock and soon had his representatives on its board, including his son-in-law, Horace F. Clark.

For all his energy and unscrupulousness, Gould lost the Erie's campaign for western connections. He failed to put together a railroad system. His strategic actions, however, had a lasting impact on two of three major east–west competitors. The responses of the presidents of these roads is revealing. J. Edgar Thomson, the professional engineer who built and then managed the Pennsylvania, immediately decided to build a self-contained system. In the words of a later stockholders' report, he and his senior managers "with grand ideas, formed a plan or policy to reach all important points in the West with their lines."[7] Robert W. Garrett of the Baltimore & Ohio, an experienced manager who was also a major stockholder, began to construct a smaller, less ambitious system. Cornelius Vanderbilt, the capitalist par excellence, merely made his son-in-law president of the lines Gould had forced him to buy.

The career managers of the Pennsylvania planned their strategy with care and carried it out with speed. Significantly by the 1860s these managers, who owned relatively little stock in their company, completely dominated its board. The board which in the early years of the company had met almost weekly now convened less than twice a month. Thomson was board chairman as well as company president. The four other top managers sat on the board with him. The remaining members, according to the findings of a stockholders' investigation, "are virtual appointees of the president."[8] Not surprisingly, the directors approved almost without discussion the plans for expansion.

These plans called for obtaining access to the major commercial centers and the natural resources—coal, oil, and lumber—in the nation's heartland between New York and Philadelphia and Chicago and St. Louis.[9] The Pennsylvania leased or purchased control of roads into Columbus, Cincinnati, Indianapolis, Louisville, Maysville, and Cairo. Simultaneously it purchased control of lines to the lake ports and the lumber region of Michigan. Then in 1871 it leased for 999 years the "Joint Companies" in New Jersey in order to insure absolute control of the routes from Philadelphia and other Pennsylvania rail centers into New York City.[10] It soon had its own lines into Buffalo and Toledo, as well as Detroit and Chicago, and its connections to Washington and Baltimore. In less than five years the Pennsylvania had grown from a line of 491 miles of track to one of just under 6,000 miles, or 8 percent of the total mileage of railroads operated in the United States. Its capitalization stood at just under $400,000,000, a fraction less than 13 percent of the total capital invested in American railroads. By 1874 the total mileage it directly administered equaled that of the railroad network of Prussia. Only two nations in the world, Great Britain and France, had more miles of railroad than the Pennsylvania system.

As they built their self-contained system, Thomson and his associates let their enthusiasm for empire-building get somewhat out of hand. In

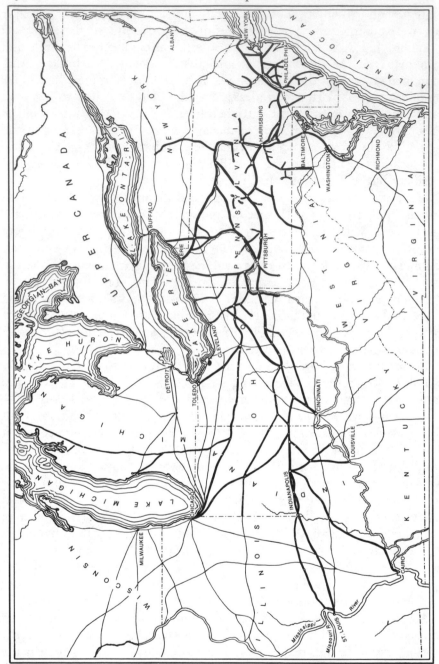

The Pennsylvania Railway System, 1876. Adapted from Joseph Nimmo, *First Annual Report on the Internal Commerce of the United States* (Washington, D.C., 1877), map G.

1871 they organized the American Steamship Company to run from Philadelphia to Liverpool, as a way of lessening their road's obvious dependence on the New York City outlet, and then invested over a million dollars in the International Navigation Company which ran ships to Antwerp and other continental ports.[11] In the following year its managers obtained full control of the fast freight lines they had earlier sponsored: the Union Railroad and Transportation Company and the Empire Transportation Company.[12] During the same period, the Pennsylvania entered mining and manufacturing. In 1872 and 1873 it bought large mining properties in the state's anthracite region. Again the managers stressed that its motives were defensive. Since the Reading and other carriers of anthracite coal had begun to obtain coal mines and lands, Thomson therefore felt obliged to do the same.[13] "To retain some of this traffic for its railroads, the Pennsylvania Railroad Company was compelled," read his annual report for 1873, "to follow the example of the other railroad companies by securing, in the vicinity of its lines, the control of coal lands that would continue to supply transportation for them."[14] The book cost of carrying out this defensive plan came close to $4 million. Shortly thereafter the road spent three quarters of a million dollars to finance the Pennsylvania Steel Works Company to assure it of a steady supply of steel rails produced by the recently invented Bessemer process.[15] Finally, to encourage the cooperation of the supplier of the nation's sleeping and parlor cars, it invested still another million in the Pullman Palace Car Company. Even so, the Pennsylvania's holdings in nontransportation enterprises were only a small part of its total $400 million worth of assets.

Despite pronouncements to the contrary, the Pennsylvania in these same years looked to its connections beyond the Mississippi and south of the Ohio.[16] But outside of "the country which your Company thought belonged to them geographically," the executives relied more on the older policy of alliances than of the newer one of direct legal and administrative control.[17] In 1871, the company formed a holding company to purchase securities of railroad corporations connecting Cairo, Illinois, with New Orleans, and of roads south of Washington connecting Richmond, Danville, Charlotte, Raleigh, and Atlanta. To the west, the Pennsylvania's interest was more personal than corporate. Tom Scott (and probably other senior executives) invested his own funds in the Kansas Pacific and in the Union Pacific. For a brief period during 1871–1872, Scott was the president of the latter.[18] After retiring from the Union Pacific, he became president of the still-to-be constructed Texas and Pacific.

The coming of the depression of 1873 dampened the expansive mood of the Pennsylvania and its senior executives. In the interest of long-term stability, they decided to sell the corporation's interest in the roads to the south of the Ohio and west of the Mississippi, and to concentrate instead on the more efficient management of the system they directly controlled. The annual report for the year 1874 announced that the company had completed its expansion—an expansion that conformed to the basic strategy decided upon in 1869:

Your company, having secured lines and extensive terminal facilities at Philadelphia and New York and, through roads controlled by it, at Baltimore and Washington, in the east; the control of roads to Erie, Ashtabula and Toledo, on Lake Erie, with good connecting roads working in harmony to Buffalo; and the control of lines through the lumber region of Michigan; and in the west having terminals at Chicago, St. Louis, Louisville, Cincinnati, Wheeling and other important commercial centers, with good connections beyond those points; and having also perfected communications with the entire oil region of Pennsylvania, the Connellsville [sic] coke region, the city of Cumberland and the Cumberland coal region; and with Frederick and Hagerstown in Maryland, and Martinsburg in West Virginia—your Board have concluded to adopt as general policy that no further extension of lines should be made or obligations be assumed by your Company, either by lease or otherwise, except to complete the several small branches and extensions now in progress in Pennsylvania and New Jersey. The best energies of your Board and its officers will hereafter be devoted to the development of the resources of the lines now controlled. They believe these lines have a great future for the shareholders.[19]

The directors and managers of the Pennsylvania also began to draw back from their steamship, coal, and steel ventures. They had decided that the operation of a self-contained railroad system joining the midwest with the seaboard and reaching the major areas of natural resources was the maximum size enterprise they could profitably administer. The peripheral activities had not paid off. Through perfecting their administrative structure, they hoped to manage efficiently a single, unified transportation system.

The creation of the nation's first interterritorial railroad system—its first megacorp—required significant financial, legal, and administrative innovations. These innovations would be taken over by other railroads when they, a decade later, turned to building their systems, and still later by giant industrial enterprises when they grew large by integrating mass production with mass distribution.

The Pennsylvania's completed system was a huge business enterprise. In a period when very few industrials had assets of over $1 million, the Pennsylvania's were valued at $400 million. The actual cost of obtaining the system was much less than the value of its assets because many of the properties were leased rather than purchased. Also, when a company was purchased, only 51 percent of the stock was needed to assure certain control. Leases normally guaranteed the bonds of the road being leased and the payment of a rental to its stockholders equal to its current dividends. These charges the Pennsylvania's managers expected to pay from the current income of the leased roads.

Nevertheless, the cost of building the system was unprecedented. In the five years from 1869 through 1873, the Pennsylvania sold or otherwise disposed of $87 million worth of securities.[20] No other private enterprise in the United States had ever raised so much capital so quickly. Of the securities, $41.1 million were shares of stock. Their disposition increased the par value of stock outstanding from $27.0 million to $68.1 million. A sizable share of the new issues was sold to existing stockholders and nearly all the rest to other American investors. By May 1871 only 7.3 percent of the stock was owned by foreigners. A much larger share of the $26.3 million worth of bonds was sold abroad.

In marketing these bonds, and to a lesser extent the new stock, the Pennsylvania's managers relied on the services of the nation's foremost investment bankers. In 1870 Jay Cooke, who had made his reputation by mass marketing government bonds during the Civil War, formed the first modern underwriting syndicate in the United States to sell the Pennsylvania's bonds. He arranged for eight financial houses to guarantee the sale of a block of bonds, with each member of the syndicate accepting responsibility to sell an agreed upon amount. The syndicate paid all the costs of distribution, including advertising. The Pennsylvania received "90 flat" for the bonds for a total of $1.8 million.[21] And it agreed not to offer any bonds on its own account until the syndicate had completely disposed of the issue. After 1870 Thomson turned from Cooke to Drexel and Company to assist in marketing the road's securities.[22] Obtaining the Pennsylvania's account, the largest in the country, may have been the reason Anthony Drexel was able to persuade the young and financially well-connected J. Pierpont Morgan to become his New York agent. In 1871 Drexel, Morgan & Company opened its doors at 23 Wall Street. In any case, the Pennsylvania's career managers were allied with the leading investment bankers from the very beginning of their system-building.

Legal innovation accompanied financial innovation. To assure legal control of their many properties, the Pennsylvania perfected the modern holding company. In 1870 it obtained from the Pennsylvania legislature a charter for the Pennsylvania Company and in the next year one for the Southern Railway and Security Company.[23] The managers planned to use the Southern Railway to hold the securities of its southern allies. They wanted the Pennsylvania Company to control its unified system between the Atlantic coast, the Great Lakes, and the Mississippi River. Thomson had the Pennsylvania Company acquire from the Pennsylvania Railroad Company the leases and securities of the Ft. Wayne, the Cleveland & Pittsburgh, and other lines northwest of Pittsburgh and the Indiana Central, the Pittsburgh, Cincinnati & St. Louis (the latter was known as the Panhandle line), and other lines running southwest from Pittsburgh. In return for these leases and securities, the Pennsylvania Company paid the Pennsylvania Railroad Company $8.0 million of its total preferred stock issue of $11,360,900. The rest of that issue went to the Union fast-freight line to pay for its rolling stock, warehouses, depots, and other facilities. The Pennsylvania Railroad Company continued to hold the securities of the lines running east of Pittsburgh as well as those of its coal, shipping, and steel subsidiaries and those of the other fast-freight line, the Empire Transportation Company. On the basis of three large regional legal units (the Panhandle to the southwest, the Pennsylvania Company to the northwest, and the Pennsylvania Railroad Company to the east of Pittsburgh) Thomson and his associates then fashioned a carefully defined decentralized management structure through which over 1,000 managers supervised the work of at least 50,000 to 55,000 employees.[24] This administrative innovation is described later in this chapter when the development of the structures to manage the great systems is considered.

John Work Garrett, the president of the Baltimore & Ohio since 1858, followed the moves of Gould at the Erie and then Thomson at the Pennsylvania with keen interest.[25] A strong advocate of alliances, Garrett had been willing to obtain control of a connection if it was necessary to maintain his territorial strategy. He built a feeder into Pittsburgh and in 1866 leased the Ohio Central in order to connect Wheeling with Columbus. Early in 1869, as Gould began to negotiate with the Ohio roads, Garrett moved quickly to purchase full control of a line north to Lake Erie at Sandusky. At the same time, the Baltimore road substantially increased its stockholdings in the Cincinnati and Marietta (connecting Wheeling to Cincinnati), and made its vice president, John King, the Marrietta's president.

Then Garrett stopped. He and other investors on the board were becoming troubled by the cost of expansion. The road continued to be financed largely by the family mercantile and banking firm of Robert Garrett and Sons which had, since the 1840s, close connections with the two leading American financiers in Britain: George Peabody and Junius S. Morgan, J. Pierpont's father. These and other investors were represented on the board.

Nevertheless, the defensive need for assured connections to major commercial centers overcame the reluctance of president and board to expand. In 1874 the board agreed that the company could no longer rely on the Pennsylvania or other roads for entry into Chicago and authorized the construction of a 263-mile line connecting that city with the Sandusky road. Garrett also incorporated the Cincinnati and Marietta into the Baltimore & Ohio's management structure. Then in 1878 he obtained full control of and began to operate the old but often obstreperous ally, the Ohio & Mississippi, when that road went into receivership. Garrett's growing system now had direct connections with St. Louis, Louisville, and Chicago and with roads west of Chicago at Peoria. After the Pennsylvania purchased the Philadelphia, Wilmington and Baltimore in the early 1880s, the Baltimore & Ohio responded and built its own road into Philadelphia. Even then it continued for several years to rely on the Reading and the Central to carry its traffic into the New York area.

The Baltimore & Ohio moved, as had the Pennsylvania, into nonrailroad enterprises.[26] The road purchased coal properties and in 1872 built and operated a steel rolling mill. It had close ties with coastal steamer lines to Philadelphia and New York. After an unsuccessful venture with its own steamship line to continental ports, Garrett turned to an alliance with the powerful North German Lloyd Steamship Company to provide shipping to Britain and the Continent. He also built a chain of hotels along the line of the road. Moreover, Garrett insisted on manufacturing his own sleeping and parlor cars, even at the cost of a lengthy patent dispute with Pullman and others. As the road's historian has emphasized, by the late 1870s Garrett "very much preferred to run the company in every way as a self-contained and highly independent unit."[27] Nevertheless, strong investor influence on the board had slowed and limited expansion. The system always remained much smaller than that of the Pennsylvania.

The Vanderbilts, owners of the third great trunk line, were even more cautious than Garrett and his associates. After Gould forced Vanderbilt to take over the Lake Shore, the Commodore did little to integrate the operations of that road with those of the New York Central.[28] When Clark, his son-in-law, died unexpectedly in 1873, Vanderbilt sold the family holdings in the Wabash and in other midwestern roads in which Clark had purchased stock, turned over the operation of the Lake Shore to a professional manager, James H. Devereaux, and made it clear that he had no intention of enlarging his railroad properties.[29] William H. Vanderbilt, who took charge of the family interests after his father's death in January 1877, was even more conservative.

William Vanderbilt was an administrator, not an empire-builder.[30] He hired first-rate managers and installed advanced procedures and technology. But he had no enthusiasm for expanding his holdings. What purchases he did make were instigated by the speculative schemes of Jay Gould. In the summer of 1878, as part of a deal with Gould, Vanderbilt obtained the controlling shares of the Michigan Central.[31] Gould had organized a telegraph company to compete with Western Union, and Vanderbilt was one of the largest investors in the established telegraph enterprise. Gould was able to have Vanderbilt persuade the Western Union board to pay the price Gould wanted for his company by promising to provide Vanderbilt enough shares in the Michigan Central to control that road, which was the Lake Shore's foremost competitor. Then in the next year the Canadian Southern, the road connecting the Michigan Central to the New York Central, went bankrupt. Vanderbilt picked up this key connecting line at a small price. Almost in spite of himself, Vanderbilt was beginning to build a system.[32]

Bargains though the purchases were, they did require funds, particularly as the facilities on both roads had deteriorated. These expenses plus the cost of improving the roadbed and equipment of the New York Central itself, and the further stock purchases needed to maintain the alliances with the Central's eastern connections—the Boston & Albany and the Boston, Hoosac Tunnel and Western—helped to convince Vanderbilt of the futility of trying to maintain personal control over a major railroad. So in 1879 he arranged with the junior partner of Drexel, Morgan and Company to sell off a sizable portion (225,000 shares) of his New York Central stock.[33] J. P. Morgan formed a syndicate to sell these securities in London, then became an active member of the Central's board of directors.

One reason Vanderbilt had so little taste for system-building was his faith in the alternative strategy to assure the continuing flow of traffic across his properties. He believed that the cartels would work. He remained one of Albert Fink's strongest supporters. In this view he was supported by the presidents and directors of many other American roads. The leading capitalists and investors of the lines running west from Chicago, including John Murray Forbes of the Burlington, William Osborn of the Illinois Central, David Dows and Peter Geddes of the Northwestern, backed the regional associations that imitated and worked closely with the Eastern Trunk Line Association.

Although the large investors continued to believe that cartels provided a less expensive alternative to system-building, a number of younger managers, particularly in the west, were beginning in the late 1870s to speak out against the conservative policies of their boards.[34] Both Charles E. Perkins of the Burlington and Ransom R. Cable of the Rock Island maintained that the current economic depression of the 1870s was providing an opportunity for their roads to build their "defenses" by obtaining lines into key cities at low prices. In 1878, in a number of detailed reports, Perkins outlined an explicit strategy. He urged that the Burlington take over its ally in Nebraska, the Burlington and Missouri, and that it purchase adjoining roads, some of which were still unfinished, in order to assure it of its own entrance into Kansas City and St. Joseph.[35] "If we do take them now, when they are bankrupt," Perkins wrote Forbes, "and before others awake to the value of that region, we control that country and can extend the roads at our leisure."[36] Perkins planned to round out this network by obtaining the Hannibal and St. Joseph. As he told Peter Geddes:

> I have long been of the opinion that sooner or later the railroads of the country would group themselves into systems and that each system would be self-sustaining or in other words that any system not self-sustaining would cease to exist and be absorbed by those systems near at hand and strong enough to live alone . . . Each line must own its feeders.[37]

But Forbes, Geddes, and other directors continued to maintain that such a consolidated system would become too large for effective internal management, and too expensive for its stockholders. By the early 1880s, however, these investors both in the east and in the west were beginning to change their minds. The great cartels were clearly becoming inadequate. Again Gould was the catalyst.

System-building in the 1880s

As the decade of the 1880s opened, Jay Gould was embarked on a venture in railroad combination that dwarfed his attempt of more than a decade earlier to expand the Erie. This enterprise was the outcome of his success in 1874 in obtaining the Union Pacific, the road which, with the Central Pacific, formed the first transcontinental railroad. The depression that began in the fall of 1873 had weakened the Union Pacific's financial condition. Its stock was selling at a very low price. Sniffing a speculation, Gould began to buy. By the spring of 1874 he had control. At first, Gould concentrated on reorganizing the Union Pacific's finances and management.[38] During this time he became increasingly dissatisfied with the three roads which carried the Union Pacific's traffic eastward, and which at that time formed the Iowa Pool. To improve his eastern connections, he purchased stock in two of these three roads, the Northwestern and the Rock Island. Once on their boards, he attempted in March 1877 to work out with them and the Burlington, an agreement which included joint ownership of the Burlington and Missouri in Nebraska. Perkins made a strong stand against the proposal, causing its rejection. Perkins had Gould in mind when he urged on Forbes a change in strategy in 1878. Unable to assure himself of eastern connections, Gould then turned, as he had done in the east in 1869, and as Perkins had anticipated, to building a system of his own.

Moving swiftly and relying on his expert skill as a stock market trader, Gould soon put together a system that was for a short time far more extensive than the Pennsylvania.[39] The details of Gould's most intricate campaigns provide a fascinating inside view of speculative techniques. They were so complex that a biography of Gould devotes eleven chapters to the process. All that needs to be said here is that by 1881 Gould controlled the Kansas Pacific, the Missouri Pacific, the Missouri, Kansas & Texas, the Wabash, the Lackawanna, the Central of New Jersey, and the New York and New England, and once again the Erie. The railroad empire he controlled was the largest in the nation. It reached Boston, New York, Toledo, Chicago, St. Louis, Kansas City, Omaha, and Denver. Gould next began a quest for more connections to the southwest. By 1882 he had lines into Fort Worth, Dallas, El Paso, Laredo, Galveston, and New Orleans. He soon owned a total of 15,854 miles of roads, or 15 percent of the nation's mileage.[40]

But his control proved tenuous and short-lived. He made no attempt to coordinate, integrate, or efficiently administer the activities of his various properties. Some of his roads actually did not connect with the others, so shipments of system-generated through freight were hampered. Nor did his system, particularly in the east, run over the more favorable transportation routes. His was a speculative not an operating business enterprise.

So the Gould empire fell as quickly as it rose.[41] By 1882 he had pulled out of the Union Pacific, using the proceeds to build up the newly acquired network south and west of St. Louis. By 1884 the serious business recession and plummeting prices of securities forced him to dispose of most of his eastern lines. From the mid-1880s on, Gould concentrated on building a regional system in the southwest. There by 1890 the Gould system included the Missouri Pacific, the smaller Texas & Pacific, the St. Louis Southwestern, and the International and Great Northern.

Short-lived as his empire was, it had a lasting impact on American railroad history. His rapid purchases, his moves into territorial domains of other lines, his delight in breaking rate or freight allocation agreements forced the directors of the major roads in the west and William Vanderbilt in the east to embark on a strategy of system-building.

Gould's moves in the trunk line territory, in the anthracite coal region, and in New England, as well as his deliberate sabotage of Fink's Eastern Trunk Line Association, finally goaded William Vanderbilt into taking the offensive. Vanderbilt now fully agreed with his career managers, Henry B. Ledyard of the Michigan Central, John Newall of the Lake Shore, and James H. Rutter of the New York Central, that they must have a self-sustaining system of their own. The Vanderbilt group turned first to the southwest, obtaining their own routes into Indianapolis, the Ohio River cities, and St. Louis. First they secretly obtained control of the Bee Line, hitherto an Erie connection from Cleveland to Columbus and Indianapolis. Since that road controlled only 50 percent of the dominant stock of the line connecting Indianapolis to St. Louis, Vanderbilt and his associates persuaded the Pennsylvania to sell him the remaining 50 percent. At the same time, to forestall Gould's drive into the anthracite region, Vanderbilt secured a large though not controlling amount of stock in the Reading and built a costly connection between that road and the New York Central.

In 1882 Vanderbilt made another move which was also instigated by the actions of competitors. This was the purchase of the New York, Chicago and St. Louis, a new road which had just opened, paralleling the Lake Shore from Buffalo to Chicago.[42] The experienced speculators— Calvin Brice, George I. Seney, and Samuel Thomas—had built the road, which went by the name of the Nickel Plate, to sell either to Vanderbilt or to Gould. Again, Vanderbilt felt forced to buy before Gould did, in order to maintain railroad peace. In that same year he bought out minority stockholders of the Canada Southern and integrated that road into the Michigan Central's administrative structure.

Then in May 1883 Vanderbilt retired. His operating managers became presidents of their roads and his two sons, Cornelius and William K., divided the chairmanship of the several boards between them.[43] The elder Vanderbilt, however, kept a close watch on the affairs of his companies until his death in December 1885. After 1883, the expansion of the Vanderbilt system continued on an ad hoc basis as its managers and financiers responded to changing competitive conditions in 1885.[44] In 1885 the Vanderbilts agreed, at the urging of J. P. Morgan, to buy the West Shore, a road that had been built to parallel the New York Central. The purchase was part of the peace treaty Morgan had engineered between the Central and the Pennsylvania by which the Pennsylvania in its turn purchased the partially built South Pennsylvania. At the end of the decade, the Vanderbilt group, aided by Morgan, obtained a large block of stock in the Cleveland, Cincinnati, Chicago & St. Louis, the road known as the Big Four. They then incorporated the Bee Line legally and administratively into the Big Four. During the 1890s the Vanderbilts increased their stock ownership in the Big Four and in the Chicago and Northwestern. However, they did not acquire complete control of the Boston & Albany until the 1900s or of the Big Four until the 1930s, while the Chicago and Northwestern never became more than a loyal ally.

Even after Gould had convinced Vanderbilt of the need for a self-sustaining system, neither William H., his sons, or their managers ever outlined a precise strategy of expansion comparable to that of Thomson's for the Pennsylvania in 1869. Expansion continued to be more of an ad hoc response to current competitive pressures than the result of specific long-term planning. Nor was the completion of the Erie's system—the fourth eastern trunk line—more carefully planned.[45] On the other hand, the heads of western roads moved more deliberately. In nearly all cases the more aggressive young professional managers became their presidents. They defined and implemented the strategic expansion of their roads. Only on the Chicago & Alton did the restraining hands of financiers, particularly its president, T. B. Blackstone, effectively limit expansion. In carrying out their strategies, these career managers were soon responding to each other's moves more than those of Gould or other speculators.

On the Burlington, Perkins, who had written Forbes that "Gould moves so rapidly that it is impossible to keep up with him with Boards of Directors," was given a relatively free hand.[46] Perkins first merged the Burlington and Missouri in Nebraska with the parent line. He then purchased control of an essential, if indirect, connection with Council Bluffs and Kansas City at a cost that must have shocked many a Boston stockholder.[47] In 1882, in retaliation for Gould's move into Iowa, Perkins built his own line to Denver, paralleling that of the Union Pacific (and also that of the Rock Island). In the next year he regained full control of the Hannibal and St. Joseph and, during this time, continued to build into Wyoming, Montana, Colorado, and Nebraska. Finally, in 1885 he financed and had built a road into St. Paul. The Burlington, which operated a little over 600 miles in 1870 and was administering 2,772 miles by early 1881, operated close to 5,000 miles by 1887.

The Burlington's experience was repeated on the other major roads operating to the north and west of Chicago.[48] The president of the Chicago, Milwaukee & St. Paul, who was a local Milwaukeean, tended to be sympathetic to the plans of the general manager, Shelburne S. Merrill, and the assistant general manager, Roswell Miller, who defined and pushed through the strategy of expansion. The Milwaukee, for example, reacted to Perkins' decision to build into St. Paul by constructing its own line through Burlington territory to Kansas City. Even before Miller, who became president in 1887, completed that expansion, the road had become an interterritorial system operating more than 5,000 miles of track. After 1882, when the general manager Ransom R. Cable replaced Riddle as the Rock Island president, that road grew rapidly to become a large integrated system that ranged from Chicago to Kansas City, Denver, and Fort Worth.[49] At the Chicago & Northwestern, Marvin Hughett, the senior career manager, was able to convince conservative president Henry

Keep of the necessity to expand.[50] Although more cautious than his rival, Hughett, who soon became the road's president, expanded its mileage from under 1,000 miles in 1880 to close to 5,000 miles in 1885. Once Gould had begun to build his western railroad empire, in the words of Gould's biographer, "each road suddenly realized that a policy of aggressive invasion was the only safe defense."[51]

In precisely the same short stretch of years, similar strategies led to the formation of similar systems in the sparsely settled far west, the more populous old south and urban New England. Everywhere, railroad men gave up their faith in informal alliances, lost hope in the effectiveness of more formal federations, and turned to winning their own "self-sustaining," interterritorial systems. The managers, assisted by the speculators, had won the day. Regional variations, reflecting economic and historical differences, had relatively little effect on the overall pattern of system-building.

The history of the transcontinentals is instructive. Except for the Northern Pacific, no road was initially planned to be managed by a single enterprise operating between the Mississippi Valley and the Pacific Coast. During the decade of the 1880s, however, these roads decided, usually against the better judgment of their major investors, to have their own lines from the interior to the ocean. Under Gould, the Union Pacific had added nearly 1,250 miles of new lines. His successor, Charles Francis Adams, Jr., a conservative representative of Boston investors, was soon convinced by his managers that there was no alternative to responding to Gould's continuing activities in the southwest, and those of Perkins and the other roads in the midwest, except to build a system of his own. Adams purchased and constructed almost twice as much mileage as had his predecessors to protect his eastern flank from Perkins and his southwest flank first from Gould and then from Collis P. Huntington's Southern Pacific.[52] Unable to obtain control of the Central Pacific, his company's original outlet to the Pacific Coast, Adams felt forced to build the Oregon Short Line to the northeast to connect with Henry Villard's Oregon Railway and Navigation Company. (Its construction, in turn, caused the Burlington to build a line to Billings, Montana.) The resulting through trackage and traffic agreements gave Adams an alternative outlet to the coast. Nevertheless, the Union Pacific quickly found these agreements uncertain and unsatisfactory. So in 1889 Adams, working with Greenville M. Dodge, obtained control of the Oregon Railway and Navigation Company by a skillful Wall Street maneuver that assured his system its own tracks to the Pacific.

To the south the Santa Fe, through a series of defensive moves, became by 1887 the largest railroad system in the world.[53] In 1880, the Santa Fe had reached its original goal by completing its line to Albuquerque, New Mexico. It then built an extension from Albuquerque to the Southern Pacific at Deming, New Mexico. At that time, Huntington's Southern Pacific had no ambitions outside of California. Huntington's strategy was still a territorial one. "Its two objectives were to secure and maintain its control of California business," Robert Riegel has noted, "and to monopolize the transcontinental entrances to the state."[54]

But neither Huntington nor William B. Strong, the new president of the Santa Fe, was satisfied to rely wholly on one another for connections. Strong, who had worked up the managerial ladder on the Burlington before going to the Santa Fe as vice president and general manager in 1877, was able to convince his Boston-based directors that their road must have an alternative route west. They agreed to purchase a half interest in a second road planned to connect Albuquerque to the coast. Early in 1882 Huntington joined forces with Gould to buy most of the other half of the stock in this second road. The Santa Fe temporarily retreated by agreeing that its new road west from Albuquerque would go no further than the Colorado River, where it could connect with the Southern Pacific. Meanwhile Huntington, even more reluctant to rely on Gould for connections to the Gulf, started to construct and purchase his own lines to the growing Texas cities and to New Orleans. At the same time, he obtained steamship lines operating out of the Gulf ports. In 1884 Huntington and his associates combined all these rail and steamship lines into a single system headed by a holding and operating concern, the Southern Pacific Company of Kentucky.

In that same year, Strong persuaded the directors of the Santa Fe that they must have their own line to the Pacific coast. After obtaining full control of the road from Albuquerque to the Colorado River, Strong purchased lines from the Southern Pacific which, after some additional building, provided the Santa Fe its own route into Los Angeles and San Diego. Next, Strong decided that he could not rely on Huntington or Gould for connections to the southwest, so in 1886 he purchased a route into Fort Worth and Galveston. Finally, in 1886, the Santa Fe's president decided to build his own road from Kansas City to Chicago.[55] By 1888 the Santa Fe was operating a system of over 8,000 miles and was on the brink of financial bankruptcy.

To the north of the Union Pacific the story was much the same. At first James J. Hill's Manitoba Railroad had no transcontinental ambitions. Until 1883 it was satisfied to serve the wheat region of the Red River Valley of the north and to rely on the government-subsidized Canadian Pacific to carry its traffic westward. It began to build across the Rockies to the Pacific only after the Canadian Pacific began to move eastward to become an all-Canada transcontinental.[56] That same year, financier Henry Villard completed the Northern Pacific. Villard had obtained control of the Northern Pacific in 1881 in order to assure that his Oregon Railway and Navigation Company had an outlet to the east. From that time until the rounding-out of the two systems, the location and timing of construction and purchases reflected the interaction of the strategy and tactics of Hill, the experienced railroad entrepreneur and manager, and Villard, the able financier. When the systems neared completion in the early 1890s Hill had by far the superior system.

System-building in the south followed the pattern of that in the west. Light local traffic intensified the pressure to maintain through traffic by building and buying. Although maintaining territorial strategies, the southern roads were more aggressive than those in the north and even the midwest in assuring control over their feeders and connections. And those roads headed by career managers were the most aggressive. By 1880 contemporaries were already able to identify seven leading roads in the south —the Danville, the East Tennessee, the Central of Georgia, the Norfolk & Western, the Louisville & Nashville, the Savannah, the Florida and Western (which was controlled and operated by Henry Plant), and the southern extension of the Illinois Central.[57] Of these seven roads five had career men for presidents. These included the Louisville & Nashville, which grew first under the guidance of Albert Fink and then under that of his protégé Homer Smith; the Plant road, which would become the Atlantic Coast Line; the Central of Georgia, under William Wadley; the Norfolk & Western, under Frederick J. Kimball; and the Illinois Central, under William K. Ackerman and then James C. Clarke. Except for the Central of Georgia these roads became by 1900 major southern systems.

In the south a group of speculators including Calvin Brice, George O. Seney, John Inman, and William P. Clyde played the same role that Gould had played in the west. Working together, but sometimes at cross purposes, they used the Richmond and West Point Terminal and Warehouse Company in the mid-1880s to combine the Danville, the East Tennessee, and then the Central of Georgia into a single system. The Richmond Terminal ended in a spectacular bankruptcy, but its formation spurred its neighbors to build their interterritorial systems, connecting major cities in the south. After a thoroughgoing legal, financial, and administrative reorganization by J. P. Morgan & Company, the Richmond Terminal emerged as the Southern Railroad Company. The other systems, by developing close connections with the leading investment bankers, including Kuhn, Loeb; E. W. Clark; August Belmont; and Morton, Bliss remained financially sound. Of the new southern systems the Norfolk & Western was the least affected by the actions of the Richmond Terminal.

In building its empire, its president was responding more to the actions and counteractions of other coal carrying roads, particularly the road's chief rival, Collis P. Huntington's Chesapeake & Ohio.[58]

System-building in New England during the 1880s differed from that in the south in that heavy local traffic made through freight less important for financial solvency and so lessened the pressure to expand by buying and building. By the end of the 1870s the four centrally located lines—the Boston & Albany, the Boston & Maine, the New York, New Haven & Hartford, and the New York & New England—were carrying more traffic but still not operating much more mileage than the Vermont Central, the Fitchburg and its ally, the Boston, Hoosac Tunnel & Western, the Eastern, the Old Colony, the New York, Providence & Boston, and other major roads. By 1893, however, two roads, the New Haven and the Boston & Maine, had come to dominate completely the New England railroad network.

Consolidation came in the following manner.[59] In central New England the Boston & Albany was formed in 1869 as a consolidation with the Boston & Worcester and the Western. It remained closely allied to the New York Central, but was not formally leased by the Central until 1900. In northern New England the Boston & Maine fell into the hands of speculators who, by the end of the decade, had legally and financially consolidated but not administratively unified most of the roads in that area. To the south the speculative New York & New England controlled first by Gould, Sage, and Sidney Dillon, and later by Jabez A. Bostwick, a former Standard Oil partner, constantly threatened the traffic of the New Haven. This challenge permitted a career manager, Charles P. Clark, to convince his directors to make the New Haven into the leading road between New York and Boston.

System-building in New England came to a climax in the early 1890s when A. A. McLeod of the Reading decided to make his coal road into a major interterritorial system. He purchased both the Boston & Maine in the north and the New York & New England in the south at prices which delighted the speculators who then controlled them. These purchases, however, helped to bankrupt the Reading which was then reorganized by J. P. Morgan. Morgan, in March of 1893, brought together Clark of the New Haven and the financial men who had obtained control of the Boston & Maine. As Edward C. Kirkland has pointed out, they "divided New England between them; the route of the Boston and Albany became a sort of Mason and Dixon Line."[60]

This briefest of reviews of system-building by American railroads cannot possibly suggest the vast complexities or the constant drama involved.

It can only indicate what systems were built in the 1880s and the men who built them. An appreciation of the conflicting personalities, goals, and strategies that determined precisely where and when a system grew can only come from a reading of the works of Grodinsky, Overton, Riegel, Stover, Klein, Lambie, Kirkland, Martin, and others. Yet from a careful review of these works, a number of important generalizations can be drawn.

First, and most significant, the large enterprises that were to operate the American railroad network throughout the twentieth century took their modern form in the 1880s. They appeared after the senior executives of railroads in all parts of the country shifted almost simultaneously from a territorial or regional strategy to an interterritorial one in order to obtain self-sustaining systems. By the coming of the depression of the 1890s, the railroad map of the United States had taken the form that would remain relatively unchanged until the railroads began to become technologically obsolete in the years after World War II. The largest systems in 1893 were practically the same as those in 1906 and 1917 (See tables 3 and 4 and Appendix B). Later attempts to build or even to redefine systems were few and rarely successful.

Second, the roads that built the new systems were in nearly all cases the first large roads to be constructed in their regions. Their managerial hierarchies became the "core" to which other large operating enterprises were added through purchase, lease, or construction. By 1893 the managers of these new megacorps had become responsible for the management of most of the American railroad network. By that date the thirty-three railroad corporations with a capitalization of $100 million or more operated 69 percent of the railroad mileage in the United States. In addition, their managers coordinated and scheduled the flows of smaller connecting systems.

Third, salaried career executives played a critical role in the system-building of the 1880s. The managers, far more than the speculators and investors, defined strategic plans and directed tactical maneuvers. The strongest of the American railroad systems were those created by such managers as Thomson, Perkins, Cable, Miller, Merrill, Hughett, Ackerman, James Clarke, Strong, Fink, Smith, Plant, Kimball, Charles Clark, and the career presidents of the Vanderbilt roads—Ledyard, Newell, Rutter, and Depew. And the large capitalists or their representatives who helped to create successful systems, such men as William Vanderbilt, Garrett, Hutington, Hill, and Charles Francis Adams, were experienced railroaders. Among such financiers only Villard had no training in railroad operations. On the other hand, those lines controlled largely by

Table 3. Railroad systems with capitalization in excess of $100 million, 1893

Road	Mileage[a] (length of line)	1893 capitalization ($ million)
Atchison, Topeka & Santa Fe	9,328	647
Richmond Terminal, including		
E. Tenn., Va. & Ga. and Central of Ga.	8,697	329
Union Pacific	8,148	427
Chicago & Northwestern	7,955	314
Pennsylvania, including		
Pennsylvania Company	7,950	842
Chicago, Burlington & Quincy	6,533	274
Southern Pacific	6,461	643
Chicago, Milwaukee & St. Paul	6,128	225
Missouri Pacific, including		
St. Louis, Iron Mt. & So.		
Kansas & Colo. Pacific	6,114	309
New York Central, including		
Michigan Central, Lake Shore,		
N.Y., Chicago & St. Louis,		
Boston & Albany, and West Shore	5,662	553
Northern Pacific, including		
Wisconsin Central	5,216	370
Louisville & Nashville	4,732	218
Reading, including		
N.J. Central, Lehigh Valley,		
and Del., Lack., & Western	3,944	670
Great Northern	3,682	147
Illinois Central	3,681	215
Chicago, Rock Island & Pacific	3,456	123
Baltimore & Ohio	3,347	313
Denver & Rio Grande	2,381	148
Cleveland, Cincinnati, Chicago & St. Louis	2,281	118
Erie	1,966	386
Wabash	1,933	140
Boston & Maine	1,900	130
Missouri, Kansas & Texas	1,670	134
Texas & Pacific	1,499	106
Norfolk & Western	1,457	120
Chesapeake & Ohio	1,290	125
N.Y., New Haven & Hartford	644	110

Source: Mileage data is from S. F. Van Oss, *American Railroads as Investments* (New York, 1893). Capitalization is the total of each parent company and its subsidiaries in Interstate Commerce Commission, *Statistics of Railways in the United States, 1893* (Washington, D.C., 1894).

[a] The first track mileage operated by the above roads (118,055) was 69 percent of the total first track mileage operated in the United States (169,780) in 1893.

Table 4. Railroad systems with capitalization in excess of $100 million, 1906

Road	Mileage[a] (length of line)	1906 capitalization ($ millions)
Chicago, Rock Island & Pacific, including St. Louis–S.F.	14,816	842
Atlantic Coast Line, including Louisville & Nashville	11,634	470
Pennsylvania	11,390	1,218
Southern	10,700	609
Southern Pacific	9,781	515
Atchison, Topeka & Santa Fe	9,624	502
Chicago, Burlington & Quincy	9,142	220
New York Central	9,073	853
Union Pacific	7,720	636
Chicago & Northwestern	7,660	266
Chicago, Milwaukee & St. Paul	7,341	230
Missouri Pacific	6,962	340
Northern Pacific	6,614	444
Great Northern	6,114	347
Illinois Central	6,107	320
Baltimore & Ohio	4,760	489
Cincinnati, Hamilton & Dayton	3,593	178
Boston & Maine	3,369	187
Denver & Rio Grande	3,117	232
Seaboard	3,031	141
Missouri, Kansas & Texas	2,886	231
Wabash	2,801	325
N.Y., New Haven & Hartford	2,763	316
Cleveland, Cincinnati, Chicago & St. Louis	2,699	177
Erie	2,533	442
Reading, including N.J. Central	2,359	354
Colorado & Southern	2,133	102
Norfolk & Western	1,893	134
Chesapeake & Ohio	1,755	148
Lehigh Valley	1,479	158
Chicago Great Western	1,444	134
Delaware, Lackawanna & Western	1,035	120

Source: Interstate Commerce Commission, *Intercorporate Relationships in the United States as of June 30, 1906* (Washington, D.C., 1908). Mileage is the sum of its subsidiaries. Capitalization is from "Supplement to Tables I & II—Totals from Fifty Selected Railway Systems," p. 473.

[a] The first track mileage operated by the above roads (178,328) was 80 percent of the total first track mileage operated in the United States (222,340) in 1906.

speculators—such as the Erie, the Wabash, the Missouri Pacific, the Richmond Terminal, and the Boston & Maine—suffered financially and managerially from their early exploitation.

In building their systems the successful managers used the speculators
to obtain the support of reluctant investors to spend the funds needed for
system-building. To complete their systems they soon developed alliances
with investment banking firms like J. P. Morgan; Kuhn, Loeb; August
Belmont; and Speyer & Company in New York; Kidder, Peabody & Company and Lee, Higginson & Company in Boston; and Drexel & Company
and E. W. Clark in Philadelphia. Only those specialized banking enterprises had the facilities and the connections to attract the huge sums of
capital needed. By the early 1890s the local investors and even individual
capitalists rarely had a say in railroad affairs. The Vanderbilts and Villard,
for example, turned over investment decisions on their roads to J. P.
Morgan & Company. It was the local investors and more distant capitalists
who had initially financed the roads who paid a substantial part of the
cost of the overbuilding in the 1880s. In subsequent reorganizations the
value of their shares was usually greatly reduced and too often completely
obliterated.

The managers overcame the opposition of the investors to expansion
partly because they were on the spot. They had the time, the information,
and, above all, the long-term commitment to the road in a way that was
often not true of the investors and their representatives on the board.
They had much more to gain by expansion. They were willing to risk
bankruptcy to assure the continuing, long-run flow of traffic across their
tracks. Even if the investors lost their investment, the managers had their
system. Once the moves of the speculators helped to emphasize the futility
of depending on cooperation to assure continuing traffic and dividends,
and once the pools had demonstrably failed, the investors had little choice
but to delegate the making of strategy and its execution to their managers.

In building their systems the managers based their strategic planning far
more on the moves of their rivals than on any careful estimate of the demand for transportation. In short-term pricing, as well as long-term investment decisions, the railroad managers were the first to face the realities
of modern oligopolistic competition. For them the actions of a small
number of competitors were of more concern than market demand.
When the managers were unable to control oligopolistic pricing through
means of formal associations, they decided to become as self-sufficient as
possible. This new strategy, in turn, led to an even more costly competition
in building and buying capital facilities. For many roads the drive to self-
sufficiency led to bankruptcy. However, except for one or two at the
top, the managers did not lose out. Their organizations remained intact.

The major difference was that they now had to share their most critical decisions with the investment bankers who supplied the funds necessary to build the systems.

Reorganization and rationalization in the 1890s

It was therefore in the years immediately after 1893 that the investment bankers came to play their most influential role in American railroading. During the 1880s, 75,000 miles of track had been laid down in the United States, by far the greatest amount of railroad mileage ever built in any decade in any part of the world.[61] And between 1894 and 1898 foreclosure sales alone aggregated over 40,000 miles of track, with a capitalization of over $2.5 billion, the most massive set of receiverships in American history. Only the leading American investment bankers had the financial resources to reorganize bankrupt or otherwise weakened roads. J. P. Morgan had already reorganized the Reading in 1886, the Baltimore & Ohio and the Chesapeake & Ohio in 1888. After 1893 his firm refinanced the Santa Fe, the Erie, the Northern Pacific, the Richmond Terminal (which became the Southern), and once again the Reading.[62] Other leading investment bankers accomplished similar reorganizations, though on a smaller scale than did the colossus of 23 Wall Street.

For a short period before 1893 Morgan and other bankers hoped, as had investors and financiers before them, that a policy of cooperation might prevent the continuing high costs of system-building. They looked for help from the provisions of the new Interstate Commerce Act that called for "just and reasonable rates" and prohibited temporary, short-lived rate changes.[63] The Eastern Trunk Line and the Southern Railway and Steamship Association drew up new agreements to use these provisions to assist in the enforcement of rates and even to allocate traffic.[64] When the Southwestern Association failed to do the same, Morgan brought the presidents or general managers of the leading western roads and representatives of leading banks to a series of meetings in New York. At these meetings a new Western Association was formed; this association agreed to follow the lead of the other associations. At that same time Morgan emphasized his determination to discipline competitive construction as well as competitive ratemaking. He told the group that his firm and the other banking houses represented at the meetings were "prepared to say that they will not negotiate, and will do all in their power to prevent negotiation of any securities for the construction of parallel lines, or the extension of lines not unanimously approved by the Executive Committee [of the association]."[65]

But Morgan's hopes were in vain. Strong systems such as the Burlington and Illinois Central failed to join the new Western association and the Southern Pacific soon moved out.[66] So too did the largest of the Gould roads—the Missouri Pacific and the Wabash. In the east, the Trunk Line Association helped to maintain rates briefly from 1891 to the onslaught of the 1893 depression. Then they were sharply cut in all parts of the country. The cartels once again disintegrated.[67] At the same time, court decisions weakened the Interstate Commerce Commission's authority and so made it less useful in maintaining rates. Then in March 1897 the Supreme Court found the Trans-Missouri Freight Rate Association (a constituent part of the Western Traffic Association) in violation of the Sherman Act for attempted rate fixing.[68] With this decision the regional associations still in operation quietly went out of existence. The Court's ruling thus brought to a final and complete end the great interfirm federations set up by Albert Fink more than twenty years earlier.

Well before the announcement of the decision, Morgan and the other bankers had become fully convinced of the futility of relying on cooperation to control competition, even with government support. By 1893 they accepted the logic of consolidation. Their role in the reorganizations of the depression years gave them the opportunity to rationalize the boundaries, as well as the financial and administrative organizations, of many existing systems. Then as the country pulled out of the depression, the bankers encouraged still further consolidation. The Interstate Commerce Commission reported that between July 1899 and December 1900 over 25,000 miles of track, equivalent to one-eighth of the total mileage of the United States, were "brought in one way and another under control of other lines."[69] A few new but relatively small systems appeared including the Seaboard Air Line, the Cincinnati, Hamilton & Dayton, and the Colorado & Southern, but the great majority of the mileage was added to long-established "core" enterprises.

The final railroad merger movement, therefore, did little to alter the structure of the industry. The number of railroads in the United States with capitalization of over $100 million remained almost the same as in 1893. The thirty-two roads, however, now operated close to 80 percent of the nation's railroad mileage (see table 4). Except for a few midwestern roads, all these systems connected the seaboard and the interior. And most of those that did not had firm alliances with those that did. After 1900 the major changes in the boundaries of American railroad systems came when those interior systems moved to get their own outlets to the seaboard. The later unhappy, often speculative, financial histories of the Rock Island, the Alton, the Cincinnati, Hamilton & Dayton, the Wabash, the St. Paul, and Missouri Pacific were closely tied to their efforts to obtain coastal connections, for these moves exposed them to exploitation by prominent Wall Street speculators.

To tighten control over rate-cutting and competitive construction, the bankers and managers in the top management of the leading systems developed in the years immediately following the depression what they described as "community of interests" between systems operating in the same areas. This they accomplished by having one system buy stock in neighboring ones, much as the earlier roads had cemented alliances with their major connecting lines.[70] In the east one of the first and certainly the most important of such arrangements was a secret contract negotiated at the end of 1899 between the Pennsylvania and the New York Central systems. By this agreement the Pennsylvania made "substantial investments" in the Baltimore & Ohio, the Chesapeake & Ohio, and the Norfolk & Western. The Baltimore & Ohio then bought into the Reading. At the same time, the New York Central purchased stock of the Lehigh Valley, the Erie, the Lackawanna, as well as the Reading, and through the Reading obtained an interest in the Central of New Jersey. These moves were guided in part by the house of Morgan, which was still the dominant influence on the Central's board and the reorganizer of several of the companies involved in these stock transfers. In the south, too, Morgan used his influence to have the Atlantic Coastline purchase 51 percent of the Louisville & Nashville, which in turn jointly owned the Georgia and a road from Louisville to Chicago. In the west, the speculator William H. Moore and his brother James arranged for the interlocking stock purchases of the Rock Island, the Alton, the St. Louis, the Santa Fe, and some smaller roads.

Edward C. Harriman, with the aid of the banking house of Kuhn, Loeb, and James J. Hill, with the backing of J. P. Morgan, were the major architects of the intersystem alliances in transcontinental territory.[71] Harriman, who had long held a large block of stock in the Illinois Central, became in 1898 chairman of the executive committee of the Union Pacific's Board after that road's financial reorganization by his banking house and that of Kuhn, Loeb & Company. In 1901, after Huntington's death, Harriman bought 46 percent of the stock of the Southern Pacific. A few months earlier he tried to convince Perkins and the board of the Burlington to sell him control of that road. In May 1901, however, Hill, who had built the Great Northern and refinanced the Northern Pacific, purchased the Burlington. Half its stock was turned over to the Great Northern, the other half to the Northern Pacific. Then Harriman made a concerted effort to get control of the Northern Pacific and with it half the stock of the Burlington. The result of this conflict was the formation of the Northern Securities Company, which held the stock of Great Northern and the Northern Pacific, whose stock was in turn held by both Harriman and Hill. When the Supreme Court ruled in 1904 that that holding company violated the Sherman Act, the company was dissolved. The Hill interests continued to control the Burlington as well as the Great Northern and Northern Pacific and the Harriman interests the Union Pacific, Southern Pacific and Illinois Central.

The purposes of these stock deals was not to create supersystems. Only Harriman built any sort of organization apparatus to supervise his two major systems, the Southern Pacific and the Union Pacific. Rather, they were meant to help control rate-cutting and to prevent further competitive construction. As a result of the consolidations and the development of these community interests, two-thirds of the nation's mileage was operated in 1906 under the surveillance of seven groups: the Vanderbilt roads including the Chicago & Northwestern (22,000 miles); the Pennsylvania group including the B. & O. and the C. & O. (20,000 miles); the Morgan roads including the Erie, as well as the Southern and the Atlantic Coast Lines, but not as yet the New Haven (25,000 miles); the Gould roads including the Wabash, the Missouri & Pacific, the Denver & Rio Grande, and others in the southwest (17,000 miles); Moore's Rock Island group which also included the Santa Fe (25,000 miles); the Hill roads (22,000 miles); and the Harriman lines (25,000 miles).[72] The systems not included in these groups were the two in New England and several, largely in the midwest, which remained quite dependent on others for through traffic. Well before the passage of the Hepburn Act strengthened the powers of the Interstate Commerce Commission, consolidation of administrative and financial control had practically eliminated rate and building competition between major railroads.

Since the bankers and managers had found a solution to such competition through financial and administrative arrangements, they no longer pressed as they had in the 1880s to legalize pooling and to have the government help in maintaining agreed-upon rate structures. However, they still felt the pressure from large shippers who demanded special rate reductions. So the railroad men supported the campaign of Robert M. La Follette and other Progressives to eliminate rebates as enacted in the Elkins Act of 1903.[73] On the other hand, railroad men had little enthusiasm for increasing the power of the Interstate Commerce Commission. In 1905 they mounted a massive publicity campaign against regulation. At the hearings in that same year on a bill to give the commission power to fix rates, twenty-one representatives of major systems and four other spokesmen for the railroads testified.[74] Of these twenty-four, only one, A. B. Stickney of the Chicago & Northwestern, favored the proposal.

None of the others saw any advantages in the bill to their roads in particular or to the railroad network in general. Nor were they much more enthusiastic for the more moderate Hepburn Act that Theodore Roosevelt pushed through Congress in the following session. Indeed Roosevelt had to use his great political skill to steer the bill past the opposition of a large block of senators who had the support of much of the American business community as well as its railroad leaders.[75]

The completion of the consolidated systems, the building of communities of interest, and the passage of the Hepburn Act, marked the end of an era. Construction and purchases continued, but largely to fill out existing systems, or to provide those without them connections to the seaboard. Ratemaking became as much a political process as an economic one. It involved increasingly routinized negotiations between the roads, two or more sets of shippers, and the commission. Once the boundaries of the systems became defined and their operations became relatively routine, the need for formulating grand strategy disappeared. Railroad managers concentrated on maintaining their systems and coordinating the ever-increasing flow of traffic across their lines.

For American railroad executives the answer to competition for through traffic between a small number of large, heavily capitalized enterprises was thus the building of self-sustaining systems. It was the response to competition and not the needs or opportunities to reduce costs through administrative coordination that led to the internalizing of activities and transactions of the already large, bureaucratic enterprises within a single giant megacorp. If the federal government had sanctioned pooling, the response might have been different. Although railroad men had lobbied for such legislation in the 1870s and 1880s, they and the investment bankers as well had, by the 1890s, come to agree on the futility of controlling competition through cartels even if those associations were supported and regulated by a government commission. After 1893 very few railroad men considered government regulation a more practical method than system-building for controlling competition.[76]

Structures for the new systems

The managers and financiers who built the systems that came to dominate American railroad transportation also collaborated in devising the structures to manage them. The speculators, smaller investors, and larger capitalists contributed little. In the 1880s railroad men employed two alternative structures for the management of the huge new consolidated megacorps. One, which was entirely the creation of the most able senior career managers, was strikingly similar to those adopted by the largest industrial corporations in the mid-twentieth century. However, it was the other, the one favored by the financiers and the specialized operating executives, which became by 1900 the standard for large American railroad systems.

A memorandum Charles E. Perkins wrote his managers in May 1883 outlining a proposed organizational structure for managing the many properties he had recently obtained for the Chicago, Burlington & Quincy outlined these two alternatives: "There are essentially two different methods practiced by large railroad systems. One method is to spread the working organization so to speak, over the entire system; the other makes a number of different working organizations, or units of management, each complete in itself."[77] Perkins preferred the latter. "It involves a somewhat more expensive management; but I believe this is far more than made up by the greater efficiency and economy in details."

This second form, invented by the Pennsylvania and enthusiastically endorsed by Perkins, had proved a brilliant success. One British railroad expert writing in 1893 stressed that the Pennsylvania's administration was the best in the country, and indeed in the world. "The Pennsylvania is in every respect the standard railway of America," he wrote. "Its rails and rolling stock, its ballast and bridges, its stations and service are regarded as embodying a state of perfection to equal which should be the highest ambition of every railroad company in the country."[78] On this point few railroad men disagreed. Yet despite the success and the convincing arguments made by its advocates, relatively few systems adopted this "decentralized" type of government. Instead they spread their existing centralized structure over their greatly enlarged domains.

The Pennsylvania began to plan a new administrative structure for its system, as it was still carrying out its strategy of expansion. The initial legal changes, which have already been described, placed the control of the system in three interlocking corporations—the Pittsburgh, Cincinnati & St. Louis Railroad known as the Panhandle Company, the Pennsylvania Company, and the Pennsylvania Railroad Company. These three legal entities became the basis for three self-contained administrative networks. The Panhandle or "southern system," which operated 1,150 miles of road in 1873, included the lines legally held by the Panhandle. The "northern system" of 1,564 miles took the lines controlled by the Pennsylvania Company. The third, the "eastern or Pennsylvania" system, totaling 2,408 miles in 1873, was administered directly by the Pennsylvania Railroad Company.[79] As Thomson told his stockholders early in 1873, the object of the new administrative and legal changes was:

to secure, by a single management of these works, harmonious action throughtout the entire system of railways that we control, and at the same time to obtain the best results from the large amount of rolling stock upon them, by transferring, as occasions may require, portions of that on one line to another, where the demand for its use was more urgent and important to the interest of the Company and the public.[80]

The administration of each of these three systems (each much larger than the Pennsylvania Railroad had itself been in 1870) was placed under a general manager, who had full responsibility and authority for the "*safe* and *economical* operation of the Roads committed to his charge." He directly controlled the transportation, traffic, and purchasing department of his territorial unit, and was responsible, with the assent of the president, for the hiring, firing, and promotion of all administrative personnel.[81] The general managers of the two western units reported to the same set of senior executives, since the Pennsylvania Company and the Panhandle had identical top management.[82] One man was the first vice president of both enterprises, watching over traffic and transportation, another was the second vice president of both, responsible for finance, and a third was the third vice president and comptroller of both. The president of the Pennsylvania Railroad was also the president of these two companies.

The internal organization of the three subsystems was similar. The largest, the eastern system, was divided into three large administrative subdivisions and two smaller ones.[83] All five were built around what had been independent railroad managements before 1870, the three major units being the Philadelphia and Erie, the United Railroads of New Jersey, and the original line between Philadelphia and Pittsburgh. Their boundaries were now reshaped to meet more satisfactorily the needs of traffic and administrative oversight. So too were their internal subdivisions. The Philadelphia and Erie with relatively little traffic had two such divisions. The United Railroads of New Jersey had three, while the old Pennsylvania Division reached seven.

The general managers, then, supervised, appraised, and coordinated the daily operations of the major subunits within their large territorial administration. They took the initiative, working closely with each other, on ratemaking within the framework set at the regional interfirm conferences.[84] They also determined capital requirements for their divisions and appointed managerial personnel. In all three operating systems, the general managers, who had a great deal of freedom, remained responsible for financial performance. They operated, however, within a set of general policies and procedures in whose definition they often played a role. The duties of the general superintendents who reported to the general managers involved, in the words of a contemporary, "constant supervision rather than independent direction."[85] Finally, the division superintendents at the fourth level of management were involved completely in the routine, day-to-day movement of trains and traffic. At all levels, the line and staff distinction prevailed.[86]

The system's top managers had their offices in the company's headquarters in Philadelphia. The president and the three (soon four) vice presidents were responsible for coordinating and evaluating the performance of the three autonomous subsystems and for planning and allocating resources for the system as a whole. Although these vice presidents had some supervision of operating activities on the lines east of Pittsburgh, they were expected to concentrate their attention on the larger system. When the new structure was first installed, the first vice president handled external strategy for the system as a whole and the relations with all connecting roads.[87] The second vice president, in addition to maintaining an oversight of the traffic and the comptroller's departments on the lines east of Pittsburgh, was to advise on and review the recruitment and selection of executive personnel throughout all three systems. In addition, the second vice president was particularly charged with assisting the first vice president "in all matters relating to connecting railroads west of Pittsburgh." The third general officer had supervision over construction and acted as a consulting engineer for the three autonomous systems. He also was assigned the task of keeping a close watch on the "financial condition" and performance of the parent company and its many subsidiaries, including steamship, express, and coal companies. He was to "obtain from the books and accounts in the general offices of such companies periodical statements of their business operations, and report them quarterly in clear and concise form to the President." In 1882, a number of the duties of the third vice president were given to a fourth vice president.[88] On the whole, however, the duties of the general officers in the Philadelphia headquarters and of the general managers and the middle managers in the operating units remained relatively unchanged from the early 1870s until after World War I.

The general officers who determined the strategies of expansion and competition and who appraised and coordinated the work of their major units of management did so by constant consultation and correspondence with general managers and department heads of the three primary operating units. They also relied heavily on accounting and statistical data provided by the comptroller's department. In addition the general office had a staff, including a legal department and a testing and standards laboratory. Since the general executives and staff officers were housed in the same building on South Fourth Street in Philadelphia as were the senior operating officers of the Pennsylvania Railroad Company, they consulted one another with little difficulty when the occasion arose. However, they undoubtedly did have regularly scheduled meetings to consider the allocation of resources, promotion of personnel, and so on.

On the other hand, their oversight of the two western subsystems followed carefully planned agenda. On the first Tuesday of each month the president and vice presidents met in Pittsburgh with general officers of the western companies as the Finance Committee of both the Pennsylvania and the Panhandle Companies to review their financial policies and performance and to approve or disapprove of expenditures for capital equipment. On the following day they met, this time as the Executive Committee of both enterprises, to review "all matters relating to the business (except the matter of rates), police, and working of the railways or lines of traffic, owned or controlled by the Company."[89]

This structure, with its autonomous subsystem responsible for day-to-day operations and its general office to handle long-term supervision and planning, was as sophisticated as any modern giant industrial enterprise. It was not, it must be stressed, the result of an evolutionary process. It was instead an almost immediate response to a totally new managerial challenge. Contemporaries credited the innovation to one man, J. Edgar Thomson. As a stockholders' investigating report noted in 1874: "Your corporation has grown to its present status under the inspiration and guidance of one mastermind—a man of honest intentions and remarkable ability."[90] And in the words of one Pennsylvania executive: "We are specialists, that is, pygmies. Thomson was great in everything—operating, traffic, motive power, finance; but most important of all in organization." Thomson was indeed one of the most brilliant organizational innovators in American history.

In adopting Thomson's decentralized structure at the Burlington, Perkins had much to say about the advantages of this type of organization. His road, though somewhat smaller than the Pennsylvania, had four autonomous operating divisions including "lines east of the Missouri," "lines west of the Missouri," the Hannibal and St. Joseph Railroad, and the "Kansas City lines." Each had its own transportation, traffic, legal, accounting, and purchasing departments. Only the accounting and purchasing departments had direct contact with the general office—the first to provide effective financial controls through uniform accounting and reporting, and the second to take advantage of the economies of large-scale purchasing. The other three units reported directly to the general manager in charge of the subsystem.

These general managers, Perkins stressed, must be generalists rather than specialists. Such an executive should not be simply a "train and track" man, wrote the Burlington's president, rather "he ought to be more of a man of business experience who can come into contact with businessmen of the community."[91] Perkins considered "a sound head and good judgement" more necessary than engineering and technical skills.[92] Such managers must avoid becoming involved, Perkins repeatedly pointed out, in operating details.[93]

For Perkins the most important duties of the top managers in the general offices were strategic planning and recruitment of senior managerial personnel. "In the administration of so large a property as we now have, the chief business of a President and the Vice President must be with questions of policy and in *selecting and keeping the good men in important places*."[94] Perkins himself concentrated on the second, for, in his opinion, "nothing is more important in the management of our large railroad properties than to make and keep good men."[95] The president and the first and second vice presidents were to maintain a watch on policy and strategy, while the second vice president was also to specialize in the coordination and appraisal of the operating units. In the early 1880s strategy was critical. Perkins reminded his managers that:

Every mile of railroad added to the system anywhere is just so much more property exposed to the attacks of our enemies; the country we now serve is so large that we are exposed to attacks in a great many directions. All this wants careful watching, so that we may provide against such attacks, where it is possible to do so. Then, too, the country is growing; and the opportunities for building profitable lines in connection with those which we now have, has to be watched. This particular branch of our business, taking care of our geographical relations, is, in itself, of so much consequence, and involves so much study, and so much going on and about from one place to another, that it should be the duty of one man, acting under the Second Vice-President, and also coming in more or less direct contact with the President, when necessary, to look after it.[96]

The second vice president was also to keep in touch with all "pooling arrangements, especially the important pools of through business." In coordinating and appraising the activities of the different units of management, he and the president were not only to review regularly the accounts and statistics of the different units but also to spend "a certain number of days every month or two with each General Manager, on the ground, for the purpose of observing him and his methods of dealing with questions that come before him."

To Perkins an organization of regionally autonomous "systems" had obvious advantages over the centralized functionally departmentalized structure. It "made possible obtaining the advantages of the large property and organizations, without losing the advantages of the small property and the small organization."[97] It brought responsible senior management closer to the firing line. In addition "the local population in the country or towns through which the road passes can more readily know and often more readily see in person the General Manager."[98] Such an organization encouraged initiative and independent thought. "Men's minds and abilities grow and expand with use and responsibility."[99] Finally the decentralized structure aided in "preparing and educating men" for top managerial positions. Much the same arguments would be made again in the mid-twentieth century by advocates of comparable decentralized structures in large multiunit industrial enterprises.

The decentralized structure with its autonomous operating divisions and its policy making, evaluating, and coordinating in the general office was adopted by a few large roads whose managers paid close attention to organization matters. In the 1880s the Baltimore & Ohio, the Rock Island, the Sante Fe, the Union Pacific (under Adams), the St. Louis & Southwestern (before Gould took it over), and the Plant lines were using this type of organization.[100] On the other hand, in the same decade those roads where financiers had a strong influence on top management turned to another model. They looked instead to the New York Central, the Pennsylvania's major rival in trunk line territory. One reason was that J. P. Morgan, the nation's most powerful investment banker and foremost railroad reorganizer, received his practical knowledge of railroading as a director with many years of service on the New York Central's board.

In May 1883 William H. Vanderbilt, on deciding to retire from active business, brought forward to the Central's board of directors a plan of government for the properties it had recently obtained.[101] Each of the roads that Vanderbilt and his associates had acquired remained administratively as well as legally independent entities. The operating heads, normally their presidents, were carefully selected career managers. The roads were unified by means of interlocking directorates and a common financial office in New York City. In the memorandum to the central board outlining his plan Vanderbilt noted: "Under the reorganization, each of them [the roads controlled by the Central] will elect a Chairman of the Board, who in connection with the Executive and Finance Committee, will have immediate and constant supervision of all the affairs of the companies, and bring to the support of the officers, the active assistance of the Directors."[102] The executive and finance committee of the New York Central referred to here was a single committee and acted as the central office of the system. But unlike that of the Pennsylvania it consisted not of salaried managers but part-time representatives of investors with other business activities of their own. Vanderbilt's two sons then became chairmen of the boards (or in the case of smaller companies, presidents) of the several roads. Cornelius took the chairmanship of the

New York Central (which also operated the Harlem) and the Michigan Central (which also operated the Canada Southern). William K. became the chairman of the Lake Shore (which also operated the Nickel Plate). E. D. Worcester, secretary of the New York Central, became treasurer of the Michigan Central (and the Canada Southern) and the Lake Shore (which operated the Nickel Plate). On the other hand, Vanderbilt did not create similar arrangements for those roads in which the Central had large blocks of stock but did not fully control. On the Chicago & Northwestern, the Bee Line, the Boston & Albany, and later the Cleveland, Cincinnati, Chicago & St. Louis, members of the Vanderbilt family and their associates did no more than sit on their boards, usually as members of their finance committees.

As a result, the New York Central system had no general office or general command comparable to that of the Pennsylvania or the Burlington. The third vice president of the New York Central had the responsibility for calling the meetings of the presidents of the roads in the system to consider rates and connections, but he did so only occasionally. The chairmen of the boards appeared to have met on a somewhat regular basis. But no full-time executive or set of executives had the responsibility for planning and coordinating the system as a whole.[103] The one group entrusted with this function, the members of the Central's executive and finance committee, were all active businessmen in their own right and could devote only part of their time to the affairs of the system. Even the younger Vanderbilts were part-time executives, spending much more of their time on leisure and social affairs than on railroading.

One result of this loose organization was that the New York Central was unable to obtain the economies of scale provided by the staff units in the general office. There were no standardization or testing laboratories for the system as a whole comparable to those set up on the Pennsylvania in 1875 and on the Burlington in 1876.[104] Nor could the Vanderbilt system benefit from the advantages derived from centralized purchasing, a centralized legal staff, or a centralized management of insurance and pension funds for workers.

More serious was the lack of a central office to evaluate the performance of the operating units and to plan and allocate resources for the system as a whole. The statistical data reviewed by the board and its committees were financial rather than operating. The finance and executive committee looked at the balance sheets and operating ratios provided by Worcester's office but not at the operating figures or cost accounting data that flowed into the office of the different presidents and on which evaluation of managerial performance had to be based.

In allocating the funds for several roads, the Central's board appears to have acted in an ad hoc manner. As renewal and repairs were considered operating expenses, capital expenditures for such items remained completely under the control of the operating managers. But all expenditures for new equipment and construction required the approval of the local boards and apparently the Central's executive and finance committee. There is no evidence that that committee developed any systematic procedures to review carefully the financial needs of the system as a whole. It merely responded to individual requests from the career managers. Thus Cornelius Vanderbilt replied to a proposal by John Newall of the Michigan Central with a brief note saying: "Newport, R.I., 31 Aug. 92: You can proceed with freight house, Cleveland: also the grading for second track Pettisville to Stryker and Kennelsville to Goshen."[105] The financiers on the board had a powerful veto power over the proposal of the managers to improve or expand facilities, but they had neither the time nor the information to make their own constructive suggestions about capital investment.

This division of labor in top management in which the professional managers supervised operations but the financiers controlled financial policy became standard on American railroads. For those roads controlled by speculators like Gould, Sage, Brice, Clyde, and the Moore brothers, the gap between operations and finance was greater than on the Vanderbilt roads. The speculators paid almost no attention at all to operating needs, nor were they particularly concerned about the caliber of the managers operating their lines. Not surprisingly the Gould roads became, in Robert Riegel's words, "a synonym for bad management and poor equipment."[106]

On those roads financed or refinanced by the investment bankers (and these included most of the major systems in the country), the relations between the boards and the operating managers came to be similar to those on the Vanderbilt roads. Morgan, trained in the Vanderbilt school, carefully picked experienced, tested career managers as presidents of the roads he reorganized. He gave them almost complete autonomy in operating matters, while having the board retain a close oversight of financial affairs including dividend policy and the allocation of financial resources. Members of the Morgan firm chaired the boards and sat on their executive and finance committees. (On most roads these became separate committees.) Kuhn, Loeb; Lee, Higginson; Kidder, Peabody, Belmont; and Speyer all acted in much the same manner. So too did such financiers as Harriman and Hill, although because both had long experience in railroading they paid closer attention to operating data than did the others. No financier, not even Harriman who did build an abbreviated superstructure to oversee the Union Pacific and Southern Pacific, created a structure comparable to the Pennsylvania to administer the systems they financially controlled.[107]

In their railroad reorganizations Morgan and the other financiers did much more than merely appoint presidents and members of boards of directors. They instituted financial and administrative reforms within the systems they refinanced.[108] On the financial side they lowered the fixed charges on the bonded debt by converting bonds into preferred stock. Common stock issues were reduced through exchanging four, five, or more shares of old for one of new and even then assessing the stockholders to provide new capital. In issuing new securities the amounts were based on the earning power of a road as indicated by its operating ratio. Bonds to be used for new capital equipment were to be expended in specified amounts over a specified period of time. In most cases the bankers insisted on setting up a voting trust which gave them the power to vote the majority of the stock for a period of normally five years or up to the time when the preferred stock began to pay its 4 or 5 percent dividend regularly. This last provision was adopted as much to prevent speculators from obtaining control of reorganized roads, as those companies became once again financially viable, as it was to assure the bankers of a continuing oversight of the road's finances.

In their administrative reorganizations the bankers adopted the centralized operating structure rather than the decentralized one used on the Pennsylvania and the Burlington. In making this move they often had the support of the more specialized operating managers. The experience of the Illinois Central indicates why both financiers and middle managers favored the centralized structure.

In the mid-1880s, the managers and investors of the Illinois Central who went east to find funds to cover the costs of system-building, obtained the support of a group of conservative and respected New York bankers including August Belmont, Robert Goelet, Sidney Webster, and young Edward H. Harriman.[109] In 1887 these financiers appointed as president Stuyvesant Fish, who had for the previous ten years worked in the road's financial department, and they appointed Harriman to Fish's former position of vice president in charge of finance. The executive committee then set up a subcommittee to outline a "plan adequate for conducting the present and prospective business of the Company."[110] In the resulting discussions the financiers relied heavily on the operating men for suggestions. The acting general manager favored a scheme of autonomous territorial units similar to that of the Burlington.[111] The traffic manager, however, argued strongly that he should have full control over all traffic activities of all the lines incorporated into the system.[112] He wanted to report directly to the president instead of to the general manager. By his plan, the president would coordinate and decide disagreements between traffic and transportation departments. The executive who had worked under Fish in the financial office wanted similar centralized control over the road's accounting, auditing, and purchasing officers, and strongly supported the traffic manager's proposal. So the centralized structure was adopted.

The new organization thus concentrated all decisions regarding traffic, transportation, and finance in Chicago.[113] The three major functional departments remained quite independent. Even their regional subdivisions did not cover the same geographical areas. In addition, the central office at Chicago housed the chief engineer who was in charge of new construction and acted as a staff engineer to the transportation department, and the smaller legal, secretary's, and land offices, as well as the relief (employee benefits) department. Only the president residing in Chicago coordinated all these activities. Since nearly all the board members lived in New York and were involved in other tasks, they had little time to review past operations or plan for future ones.

The New York financiers preferred this plan for several reasons. By having fewer managers, administrative costs were reduced. By having all the senior executives housed in one Chicago office, these managers were able to consult with one another and to be easily reached by the New York directors. Finally, the traffic department's autonomy permitted it to adjust its schedules swiftly to meet continuing rate changes. To many managers, as well as to many bankers, these considerations outweighed the advantages that Perkins had outlined for the decentralized structure with its possibilities for increased managerial efficiency and better training.

By the beginning of the new century, nearly all American railroad systems were using this type of internal organization structure. Those roads that had adopted the Pennsylvania's decentralized form reverted, usually during financial reorganizations, to the centralized form. These first modern megacorps thus came to be administered by career managers who used operating structures similar to those devised by McCallum and Thomson in the 1850s, structures which were, in Perkins' phrase, "spread . . . over the entire system." Because of the increased size these organizations had at least two levels of middle management between the division superintendent and the president. Some roads even moved away from the divisional form with its line and staff differentiation to the departmental one. Most, however, continued to use the line and staff device to help assure effective coordination of movement of trains and traffic. Other matters requiring coordination between the transportation, traffic, and financial departments had to be decided by the president.

The bureaucratization of railroad administration

Top management of American railroads remained truncated. The Pennsylvania had created a structure that permitted top managers working as a group to evaluate, coordinate, and allocate resources for the system as a whole. In the centralized form, however, no place existed in which such executives, relieved of day-to-day functional operating activities, could carry out these critically important activities. Top level evaluation as well as coordination of middle management and the units they administered became the task of one man, the president.

The third top management function—the allocation of capital and personnel—continued to be divided between the president, who by the end of the century was almost always a career manager, and the financiers on the board. Although Morgan and the other bankers hired an independent certified public accountant to provide an outside check on their companies' financial and capital accounts, they made no comparable audit of costs and operating statistics. Nor did the bankers allocate resources systematically. There is some evidence that they asked for operating budgets from their managers, but there is little indication that they used capital budgets in planning and allocating funds.[114] Morgan and the others often set broad limits on the amounts the managers could spend over an extended time, but they did not develop careful capital appropriation procedures, nor did they use financial forecasts in order to coordinate capital needs and capital supply.[115] Until well into the twentieth century capital allocations on these large railroad systems continued to be carried out on an ad hoc, piecemeal way with the managers proposing and the financiers disposing.

One reason that the railroads could afford such a truncated top management was that, by the first years of the twentieth century, they had achieved control over competition. With the rounding out of these large systems and development of a community of interest, strategic planning no longer required close attention. At the same time, the process of rate-making was being shared with the Interstate Commerce Commission, which handled the negotiations between sets of shippers and the railroad. Without competitive pressure there was less need for long-term planning of future activities and careful evaluation and coordination of existing ones.

As both pricing and investment decisions became relatively routinized, railroad administration became increasingly bureaucratized. The tasks of management at all levels concentrated almost wholly on the coordination of traffic and trains. One result was that promotion in the managerial hierarchy became based more on seniority than on talent.[116] Nearly all managers remained functional specialists during their entire career. Few reached the top of their departments before they were almost ready to retire.

Such growing bureaucratization of railroad enterprises had little impact on the ability of the roads to move a massive volume of traffic with speed and regularity, since required techniques for such movement had become well systematized and routinized. It may, however, have made railroad top management less flexible in meeting nonroutine situations such as the unexpected and novel transportation demands created by the nation's entry into World War I. It may, too, have made the roads ill-prepared to respond to post-World War I competition when new forms of transportation based on the internal combustion engine challenged the railroads.

In this way, then, the basic structure of the large railroad enterprise reflected the process of its growth. From the start, the technical needs of providing fast, reliable, high-volume transportation required the services of trained career managers who held at most only a small portion of the stock in the companies in which they served. From the start, too, the investors who provided the funds to build and expand the roads had neither the training nor the information to participate in management decisions, except those involving the allocation of funds generated by the roads' operations and those requiring new capital. As the importance of through traffic increased, and after the cartels failed to control competition for this traffic, the managers were able to convince investors of the need to build self-sustaining systems. In nearly all cases the career managers became responsible for the strategy of growth; but in order to finance this growth they had to make alliances with specialized investment bankers who had access to large amounts of capital. In return for their support these bankers continued to have a say or at least a veto on managers' plans involving the obtaining and allocation of capital.

The railroad systems thus became and remained the private business enterprises that most closely exemplified financial capitalism in the United States. No other enterprises required such large sums of outside capital. On a few—the Pennsylvania is the best example—the managers were able to control the board. On most, however, financiers outnumbered managers at the board meetings. In few other types of American business enterprise did investment bankers and other financiers have such influence.

Yet even on the railroads the power of finance was a negative one. Except in the promoting of communities of interest, bankers rarely defined strategic plans and were even less involved in operating matters. Financiers may have had some say in the organization and management of American railroads, but full-time, salaried, career managers had a great deal more. The American railroad enterprise might more properly be considered a variation of managerial capitalism than an unalloyed expression of financial capitalism.

CHAPTER 6

Completing the Infrastructure

Other transportation and communication enterprises

As the first modern business enterprises, the railroads became the administrative model for comparable enterprises when they appeared in other forms of transportation as well as in the production and distribution of goods. The railroads were highly visible; the American businessman could easily see how they operated. Railroad managers, even at the lowest, the division management level, were men of high status in their business communities. These men often compared notes with friends and neighbors about the nature of their work. Of more importance, every businessman who produced or distributed goods in volume had to work closely with railroad managers. In carrying out their own businesses they daily observed the operations of the railroads.

No enterprises were more intimately related to the railroads than those operating in other transportation and communication activities—that is, in other parts of what economists term the infrastructure of a modern advanced economy. In the United States the railroads were at the center of a basic and fast growing transportation and communication infrastructure. Besides providing the rapid all-weather transportation so essential to the emergence of modern processes of production and distribution of goods, they provided the right-of-way for the telegraph and telephone lines. Their coming also led to the formation of a modern postal system. In addition, by the end of the century the railroads had come to operate nearly all the country's domestic steamship lines. Finally, their stations were central points in the new urban traction systems.

Precisely because the other new forms of transportation and communication intensified the speed and volume of the flow of goods, passengers, and messages, they too came to be operated through large modern business enterprises. Like the railroads their operation called for careful administrative coordination provided by a hierarchy of full-time salaried managers. A small number of steamship lines, where coordination was less necessary to efficient operation, remained the exception. In urban transportation, the new electric-powered equipment was costly and technically complex to operate and passenger traffic was dense, so a small number of large managerial enterprises came to administer a city's traction lines. In communication the increased speed and volume of mail made possible by the railroads led to the reorganization of the postal service. The far greater speed and volume of the new electrical telegraphic communication brought the telegraph network under the administration of a single business enterprise, Western Union. That company's managerial hierarchy was soon coordinating the flow of hundreds of thousands of messages generated daily by thousands of operating units. And not long after the invention of the telephone, a single enterprise, American Telephone and Telegraph, built, operated, and coordinated the flow of long-distance telephone calls. The operational requirements of the new technology in communication and transportation thus brought, indeed demanded, the creation of modern managerially operated business enterprises.

Nevertheless, neither American Telephone and Telegraph, Western Union, the urban traction systems, nor the largest steamship lines ever became as complex to manage as a railroad system. Although the two communication enterprises were as large in terms of assets and employees as a large railroad system, they were involved in handling only a single kind of traffic. This was also true of the postal service that carried only mail, and of the urban traction systems that moved only passengers. The steamship lines handled a larger variety of goods, but the volume carried and the number of transactions handled by the largest of the profitable steamship lines were much smaller than those of a major railroad system. Managers of the other forms of transportation and communication, therefore, often adopted the procedures of railroad management rather than creating new ones of their own.

Transportation: steamship lines and urban traction systems

Steam revolutionized ocean-going transportation and the new lines became a significant part of the modern infrastructure, but of all the new forms of transportation and communication, steamship lines had the least impact on the development of modern business enterprise.

Steam power began to alter ocean-going transportation in the 1850s, at almost exactly the same time the railroads were beginning to transform overland transportation and the telegraph overland communication.[1] Before Samuel Cunard moved the terminus of his four ship lines from Boston to New York in 1848, only a tiny number of steamships traveled the North

Atlantic routes. In the following decade, Cunard, Edward A. Collins, William Inman, and other entrepreneurs expanded service with improved ships using iron hulls and screw propellers. In the early 1850s scheduled steamship lines were operating from New York, Philadelphia, and New Orleans to France and Germany as well as to Great Britain. At the same time, steamships began to replace sailing vessels in the coastal trade.

The new steam driven ships with their iron hulls carried larger cargoes and were faster and more regular than sailing packets. Whereas the westbound trip of a sailing ship ranged from three weeks to three months, with an average of thirty-five days, the steamship reduced the time to ten days or two weeks. On the eastbound trips, where the prevailing winds meant an average sailing voyage of about twenty-five days, the steamship still far outpaced the fastest clipper. By the coming of the Civil War, the steamship had taken over the best paying routes from the sailing packets. After the war the steamship steadily replaced sailing ships on the less-used routes, where unscheduled tramps moved from port to port picking up and discharging cargo.

The post-Civil War shipping enterprises on the most heavily traveled routes grew to unprecedented size. John B. Hutchins, the historian of the American maritime industries, has pointed out how the volume and cost of operations affected the size and organization of shipping enterprises:

> To provide frequent freight sailings, large firms often found it necessary to use a score or more of ships. It became important to reduce the port time of these costly fleets as much as possible in order to increase earnings capacity. Office staffs for the solicitation of passengers and freight, the quoting of rates, and the rapid collection and distribution of mixed cargoes became essential. In order to contact shippers and passengers and to ensure a steady supply of business it became even necessary to establish inland offices and agencies and build up elaborate organizations at all ports touched by the line. Advertising designed to differentiate the service of each line and to build up good will became an important element in the economic arsenal. It also became necessary to create shore staffs to handle the problems of repairing, outfitting, provisioning, and otherwise operating the ships economically, and to rationalize many other activities. Such matters, which were formerly handled by the shipmaster, could no longer be cared for quickly and economically by them.[2]

To meet these many needs, British, German, Dutch, and French entrepreneurs, usually with subsidies from their governments, formed large enterprises manned by salaried middle and top managers.

American entrepreneurs and financiers, however, made little effort to compete in the international ocean-going trades. The high costs of American ships and labor as well as the lack of subsidies prevented Americans from seriously competing in the transatlantic and other ocean trades.[3] Only seven American shipping enterprises operated in international trade at the beginning of the twentieth century. These lines relied primarily on ships flying foreign colors. Of these seven, two were owned by industrial firms—United Fruit and Anglo-American Oil (a subsidiary of Standard Oil of New Jersey)—and a third by a railroad—the Chesapeake and Ohio.[4] None was the size of even a small railroad system.

In the American coastal, river, and lake trades that were reserved for American shipping companies by congressional legislation, most lines by 1900 were owned and operated by railroad systems. System-building, as the experience of the Pennsylvania and the Baltimore & Ohio indicated, entailed the acquisition of connecting steamship lines to Europe and South America as well as to other American ports. In most cases the roads dropped their transocean enterprises but did continue to operate the coastal ones.[5] Thus in the northeast the New Haven was by 1900 operating much of the shipping along the New England coast. On the west coast the Southern Pacific controlled and operated the Pacific Mail Line established in the 1850s. It also owned a shipping line in the Gulf. The Southern Railroad, the Central of Georgia, and the Atlantic Coast Line all had their own ships operating in the Gulf and along the southeast coast. As a prominent shipowner, Henry Mallory, wrote in 1903: "There are but two independent lines doing business on the coast [south of New York], the Mallory and Clyde lines. All others are owned by railroad companies." Even those two independent lines were closely allied to major railroad systems.[6] In this way American shipping became closely integrated into the national railroad network.

Not surprisingly, the merger movement in shipping was only a pale imitation of that which occurred in railroads and industry. There were only two mergers of any note, one in the coastal trades and the other in international shipping. Both were less than successful. In the coastal trades Charles W. Morse, a Wall Street speculator, formed in 1906 a combination of six independent lines operating on the east coast and in the West Indian trade. These included the Mallory and Clyde lines, two lines serving northern New England and the Maritime provinces, and two lines serving the West Indies.[7] The combination, however, lasted only a few months, for Morse was forced into bankruptcy during the panic of 1907. In the resulting reorganization the four lines operating in the coastal trades south of New York to the West Indies were administered by the Mallorys. That enterprise, the Atlantic, Gulf & West Indies Steamship Lines, made little attempt to centralize the administration or to coordinate the activities of these four operating units. Such an enterprise required only a handful of middle and top managers; thus, the Mallorys and their associates who owned the line continued to manage it.

Inspired by his successes in railroad consolidations, J. P. Morgan attempted a comparable merger in ocean-going shipping.[8] In 1902 his firm formed the International Mercantile Marine Company, capitalized at $130 million. It soon owned 136 ships, or one-third of the dry cargo vessels employed in the North Atlantic carrying trades. Although it became the largest shipping enterprise in the world, at least thirty American railroad systems were larger in terms of assets and employees. Unlike the railroad systems, it never was profitable. The new combination made little attempt to centralize its administration, but remained a federation of autonomous lines. Since it failed to benefit from any gains of administrative coordination, it rarely paid a dividend even on its preferred stock. In 1914 it defaulted on its bonds. Financial reorganization and wartime demands only temporarily revived the enterprise. After World War I it managed to limp along until the depression, and finally ceased to exist as an operating company in 1937.

Thus no successful giant shipping concern appeared in the United States. The gains from administrative coordination were on a much smaller scale in shipping than in railroading, and the services of career middle and top managers were therefore much less needed. On the lines that became parts of larger railroad systems, these functions were carried out by the railroad managers.[9] The few remaining independent lines, such as the Grace Lines that shipped to South America and the Matson Lines that served Hawaii, continued, like the Mallory Lines, to be operated by their founders and their families. Modern managerial enterprises never fully developed in American shipping. Nor did American shipping enterprise ever play a significant part in worldwide shipping or on the American business scene.

On the other hand, managerial enterprise became the dominant form in the operations of another quite different type of transportation—mass transit in American cities. Here a new technology brought an amazingly swift transformation in the structure of the industry and of the enterprises providing these services. The new technology, in turn, was a response to the almost desperate need to find a substitute for the slow, expensive horse-drawn streetcar.[10] The first substitute was the cable car, initially put into operation in San Francisco in 1873. Moved by steam-powered cables, such cars moved faster and cost less per passenger mile to operate than horse-drawn cars. But the cable car system was expensive to install and to run, and difficult to operate except in a straight line between two points. Although at least nine major American cities had cable cars by 1890, such systems still made up only 6 percent of the street railway mileage operated in the United States in that year.[11]

Electric power provided the solution. The electric streetcar system was cheaper to install than cable car systems and almost as flexible to operate as the horse-drawn car. After the first system installed in Richmond, Virginia, in 1887 had proved itself, electric traction quickly replaced other modes of urban transportation. By 1890, 15 percent of urban transit lines in the United States were already using electric-powered streetcars and by 1902, 94 percent were. By then only 1 percent still employed horses and another 1 percent cable cars. The remaining 4 percent was either steam-driven elevated roads or new electric-powered subways.

The new technology brought an immediate organizational response. Before the invention of the electric streetcar, ten to twenty different transit lines operated horse-drawn cars in major American cities. These enterprises were relatively small and required little in the way of experienced managers. They continued to be operated by their owners. Often these lines competed in the traditional ways, along the same route. Only in larger cities such as New York and Boston were several horse-drawn car lines merged to create a unified transportation network for at least one section of the city.

Electric traction brought consolidation and centralized administration to urban transportation. The new equipment was costly, requiring the installation of new track and repair and maintenance facilities, as well as the purchase of more expensive cars. Operation was technically far more complex. Since the cars moved at greater speed and could carry greater loads, careful scheduling became essential. Faster, cheaper service in turn led to a more rapid increase in passenger traffic and so further intensified the need for careful administrative coordination. Both operational and financial requirements thus caused mass transit in American cities to be operated by a small number of large enterprises. In most cities, urban transit was monopolized by a single enterprise.

The full-time salaried managers hired to administer these enterprises established organizational structures and accounting and statistical controls. These they borrowed directly from the railroads. In Boston, for example, the West End Street Railway Company in 1887 merged seven out of the eight street railways in Boston to form a single transportation network connecting the city with Brookline, Cambridge, and other suburbs. In the next year its promoter, Henry Whitney, began to install electric power, and its general manager, Calvin Richards, set up a line and staff type of organization to supervise the eight operating divisions, each headed by a division superintendent.[12] Its staff offices included a master mechanic's department to service the equipment, a roadmaster's department to build and repair the lines, a purchasing office, and a legal office. One office that differentiated this structure from that of the railroad was the department of inspection. Its function was to assist the general manager and the division superintendents in coordinating operations. This department trained and checked on the work of employees, made studies of local traffic patterns, and adjusted schedules on the basis of changing demands. At rush hours, departmental supervisors were placed in charge of loading, unloading, and moving cars. As the largest New York enterprise, the Metropolitan Street Railway Company, began to shift from cable and horse to electric-powered cars in 1893, its senior managers adopted a similar structure. The dominating systems in Philadelphia, Chicago, and other major cities soon followed suit.

At first the salaried managers of these traction companies had to share top-level decisions with the entrepreneurs who created the consolidated system. In the nation's largest cities, a small group of men who knew each other personally—Peter A. B. Widener, William I. Elkins, William and Henry Whitney, Thomas Fortune Ryan, and Charles T. Yerkes—became specialists in negotiating mergers, in raising the needed funds, and in making the political arrangements to transfer franchises to the new consolidations. In Boston, New York, Philadelphia, and Chicago, these entrepreneurs were able to reduce fares so that 5 cents carried a passenger to nearly all parts of the city. At the same time, they made huge fortunes by skimming off the profits resulting from the technological and organizational innovations. But as the cost of construction and maintenance increased, and as public pressure prevented the raising of the 5 cent fare, these promoters sold out. They were replaced on the boards of directors by investment bankers whose firms sold the bonds to finance expansion, and by the representatives of the public commissions or municipal governments which increasingly took the responsibility for financing and constructing the growing systems.[13] By World War I, urban transportation was operated by salaried career managers who shared their decisions about capital outlays and pricing with investment bankers and representatives of the public.

By the beginning of the twentieth century, therefore, the small personally owned transportation enterprise had all but disappeared. It continued to exist only in the livery, cab, and wagon businesses that still relied on the horse for motive power. A very small number of steamship lines not owned by the railroads remained entrepreneurial enterprises, that is, their owners employed salaried middle managers, but the owners still made top management decisions. The rest of American transportation had become administratively coordinated by managerial hierarchies. Fewer than forty giant railroad systems operated over 80 percent of domestic rail and water interurban facilities. Within a city one or occasionally two or three managerial enterprises handled the movement of passengers.

Communication: the postal service, telegraph, and telephone

A communication revolution accompanied the revolution in transportation. The railroad permitted a rapid increase in the speed and decrease in the cost of long-distance, written communication; while the invention of the telegraph created an even greater transformation by making possible almost instantaneous communication at great distances. The railroad and the telegraph marched across the continent in unison. As has been pointed out the telegraph companies used the railroad for their rights-of-way, and the railroad used the services of the telegraph to coordinate the flow of trains and traffic. In fact, many of the first telegraph companies were subsidiaries of railroads, formed to carry out this essential operating service. The second basic innovation in communication technology, the telephone, was used at first only for local calls. However, it too soon began to be used for long-distance communication. When it did, it was administered through a national enterprise similar to that operating the telegraph.

All three of the communications networks—postal, telegraph, and telephone—came to be administered by career salaried managers. The top managers in the postal services had to share their decisions with the representatives of Congress. Those in the telegraph and telephone companies did so with the same type of investors, speculators, and investment bankers who served on the boards of railroads. Indeed those names so influential in American railroad history—Vanderbilt, Forbes, Gould, and Morgan—all appeared in the building of the nation's new communication networks.

The initial growth of railroads had a powerful impact on the United States postal system. As the railroad network expanded, it increasingly carried the long-distance mail. In 1847 railroads carried only 4.2 million (or 10.8 percent) of the 38.9 million miles of mail moved by the federal postal service. Steamboats accounted for another 3.9 million miles (10.0 percent). Stagecoach and horseback riders carried the rest.[14] By 1857 mail mileage had almost doubled to 74.9 million miles. Of these the railroad carried 24.3 million (or just under a third). The steamship's share had only increased to 4.5 million (or 6 percent).

The increase in speed of mail and the improved regularity of its transportation helped to bring the sharpest reductions of rates in postal history. In 1851, first-class mail rates of 5 cents an ounce up to 300 miles carried, and 10 cents beyond, were reduced to 3 cents up to 300 miles and 5 cents up to 3,000 miles. Then in 1855 the rate became 3 cents an ounce up to 3,000 miles.[15] Three years before that the Post Office made its first general use of postage stamps to facilitate mailing. The drop in rates and the speed and certainty of transportation greatly facilitated long-distance business communication. It also encouraged a much greater use of the mails for personal correspondence as well as business correspondence.

It was this increase in volume and particularly speed that brought a reorganization of the postal service. For the first thirty years of the nineteenth century, the Post Office Department had been administered as a personal domain of two brothers, Albert and Phineas Bradley. During the Jackson administration, Postmasters William T. Barry and Amos Kendall reshaped the department's Washington headquarters by setting up three divisions each supervised by an assistant postmaster general.[16] One was for finance, a second—a vital political post—handled the appointment and supervision of local postmasters, and a third supervised mail contracts and contract performance. Until the changes in the 1850s, three assistant postmaster generals, assisted by a few clerks, made up the department's administrative staff. There were no middle level administrators between Washington and the operating units, which by 1849 numbered 16,749 post offices.[17]

In that year Selah R. Hobbie, one of the three assistant postmasters appointed by Jackson, proposed reorganization. He pointed to the need to set up new procedures and facilities to handle "the immense and intricate business of intercommunication between 17,000 post offices," for "arrangements of this character our system has never possessed."[18] In the following year's annual report, Hobbie was more specific. He urged the creation of a number of distribution centers from which mail for specified regions could be collected, sorted, and then sent directly to its ultimate destination.[19] Such a reform involved setting up distribution centers at post offices in larger towns and cities and appointing a set of managers to administer them. It also required the formulation of systematic procedures to carry out "the complicated operation of opening the mail [bags], resorting the letters, remailing them, with new post bills and new entries on the accounts, and rewrapping, tying, and bagging it." Hobbie further urged that such a distribution system be supplemented by having the railroad companies use specialized mail cars where mail could be sorted as it traveled.

The Congress provided funds to carry out Hobbie's proposals. By 1855 the Post Office had set up some fifty distribution units manned by salaried middle managers and had carefully defined the detailed procedures and controls needed to coordinate the flow throughout the country.[20] At the same time, the railroads increased their use of the specialized mail car. As in the case of comparable arrangements devised by the railroad to coordinate the flow of freight, these procedures took time to carry out. By the 1870s, however, they had been perfected. By then, American postal service was the largest and among the most efficient in the world.

It remained efficient even though the postal service provided the lion's share of federal patronage available to politicians of both parties. The reason was that middle and top managers were less subject to political change than local postmasters in charge of individual operating units. The managers who coordinated the flow of mail across the land became the professional cadre of the federal government's largest operating organization in terms of employees and number of business transactions handled.

In the same decade that the postal service began to be reorganized along modern lines, the organization as well as the technology of telegraphic communication was being perfected.[21] At its inception the invention had strong government sponsorship. In 1844 Congress appropriated $30,000 to build an experimental line from Washington to Baltimore. In 1845 the Post Office took over the operation of this successful line employing the inventor, Samuel F. B. Morse, as its superintendent. In the next year, however, because of the difficulties of public financing and management, the Post Office turned the telegraph over to private development. Then, under the guidance of Amos Kendall (who became Morse's agent), Ezra Cornell (who built the first line to Baltimore), and others, the construction of telegraph networks spread swiftly across the nation. By 1852, 23,000 miles were in operation.

Because of the importance of through traffic, the patterns of competition, cooperation, and consolidation were compressed into a much shorter time period in the history of the telegraph than they were in that of the railroads. By the mid-1850s, the managers of telegraph companies began to work out the cooperative arrangements required to send messages directly from one part of the country to another across the lines of several different companies. In August 1857, the six leading telegraph companies signed a treaty that divided the nation into six regions. Each company was given a specific area of operation. Where their lines still overlapped, the business was pooled. These pools, however, proved ineffective. Soon there were only "the big three." In 1866 these three merged into a single company, Western Union, thus creating the first nationwide multiunit modern business enterprise in the United States. The men who engineered these consolidations, Amos Kendall, Ezra Cornell, Hiram Sibley, Norwin Green, William Orton, and others, now looked to leading capitalists, particularly the Vanderbilts, to help them finance the continuing expansion of their system.

Their first task, however, was to set up an organizational structure to manage their transcontinental network. By the end of 1866 they had all but completed the organization that continued to operate the system until well into the twentieth century. For administrative purposes they divided the nation into four regional divisions—the Eastern, Southern, Central, and Pacific—each headed by a general superintendent. These four senior executives supervised a total of thirty-three divisions in the United States and Canada, whose division superintendents, in turn, administered the activities of 3,219 stations.[22] The company's annual report for 1869 described the structure:

> Each station is in charge of a Manager, who has control of his office, and is accountable to the District Superintendent for the proper performance of his duties and those of his subordinates. The District Superintendents are accountable to the General Superintendents, and the latter to the Executive Committee. On the first of every month each office forwards to the District Superintendent a report, showing the number of messages sent and received, the gross receipts, the amounts received on messages for each office with which business was done; the amounts received at all other offices with which messages were exchanged; the amounts received for or paid to other lines, and all expenditures in detail.

The general and the division superintendents had on their staff repair and maintenance managers, auditors, and purchasing agents. In defining the relationships between the functional and regional units, Western Union relied on the same line and staff distinctions as those used for the railroads. In addition, the company had as part of its corporate headquarters a large legal staff, an "electrician" whose office appears to have had charge of testing and development laboratories, and managers who supervised two factories that produced, according to the company's 1869 annual report, "every variety of instruments required in the service."

The managers of the major territorial divisions were, as the report pointed out, responsible not to a president but to an executive committee of the board. This top committee was large, including the president, the treasurer, and the three and later five vice presidents. The vice presidents were, however, not operating executives, as they were on the Pennsylvania, but holders of large blocks of stock. Three—Hiram Sibley, Norwin Green, and William Orton—had built the leading early companies. A fourth, Alonzo Cornell, was the son of another pioneer, and the fifth was a representative of the Vanderbilts, the largest outside investors. As many of the committee members had spent their life in developing the industry, they were able to speak with authority on operational as well as financial matters. And although the company required some outside capital, especially in its initial growth, it was able to rely, much more than had the railroads, on the retained earnings to finance expansion. Therefore the financiers never became as prominent in top management decision making at Western Union as they did on many railroads. Nor in the early years did full-time salaried managers dominate the board of Western Union as they did on the Pennsylvania.

The existence of the national network of offices gave Western Union a powerful competitive advantage. Because the building of telegraph lines required relatively little capital, competitors appeared. They had small chance of success, however, unless they created an operating network comparable to that of Western Union. It required a speculator with the imagination and talent of Jay Gould to mount a serious competitive challenge.

Gould developed such a threat by using the telegraph subsidiaries of railroad companies under his control—subsidiaries that were operated by Western Union under contracts signed in the 1850s and 1860s.[23] After acquiring the Union Pacific, Gould canceled that road's contract with Western Union. He then began to expand the railroad's telegraph subsidiary, the Atlantic & Pacific Telegraph Company, by making contracts with the telegraph subsidiaries of the Baltimore & Ohio and other railroads. He enlarged his system further by obtaining control of the International Ocean Telegraph Company with cable lines to Latin America. By 1878 these moves were enough to frighten Western Union into buying the Atlantic & Pacific at Gould's price. Gould sealed the bargain by offering Vanderbilt, the largest stockholder in Western Union, a controlling share in the Michigan Central if Vanderbilt persuaded the Western Union board to purchase the Atlantic & Pacific.

The speculator's success only whetted his appetite further. During the next year Gould formed the American Union Telegraph Company and gave it the contracts for the telegraph subsidiaries of the roads he controlled in the southwest. He then renewed his alliance with the Baltimore & Ohio, purchased a Canadian company, Dominion Telegraph, and announced plans for building a new transatlantic cable. As the price of Western Union stock once again plummeted under this new attack, Gould began to buy. Soon he was his competitor's largest stockholder. In this position he again convinced Western Union to purchase his American Union at a properly inflated price. He then became the controlling member of Western Union's board.

After obtaining control Gould had little difficulty in successfully staving off competition. The most serious threats came from the Baltimore & Ohio's subsidiary, which under Garrett began to build a national system, and from Postal Telegraph, an enterprise financed by George F. Baker and John W. Mackay that provided the domestic pick-up and outlet for Mackay's Commercial Cable Company. Gould obtained Garrett's system in 1887 when the Baltimore & Ohio suffered a financial crisis. At the same time, he made an agreement with Postal Telegraph, which permitted the two companies to have mutual use of each other's equipment and allowed his competitor to operate on a limited scale within the United States.

In all these financial manipulations Gould left operations completely to the career managers. When he acquired control of the company in 1881 Gould appointed a general manager, Thomas T. Ecker, with full responsibility for all operations.[24] Eckert, in turn, enlarged the central offices. His department heads became vice presidents. As these senior executives were able to finance continued expansion from retained earnings, they had relatively little connection with Gould. Gould took part in management decisions only when the possibility of competition appeared.

The history of the telegraph demonstrates even more vividly than that of the railroad how the requirements of maintaining a high-volume, high-velocity flow of business forced the rapid growth of the multiunit managerial enterprise. Since the greatest value of the telegraph to its customers lay in long-distance rather than in local communication, cooperation between connecting lines was essential to handle such through traffic efficiently. Because such a large share of the traffic was through messages, competitors often cut rates to get business. The result was rapid consolidation. System-building came so quickly that the telegraph companies never looked to government support of cartel arrangements to control competition. On the other hand, Western Union provided rates and services that were sufficient and inexpensive enough to soften demands to break up or even to regulate this powerful monopoly.[25] The telegraph company was a natural target for criticism. Businessmen had to use its wires to send confidential information; newspaper reporters depended on it to send their stories; and the notorious Jay Gould controlled it. Yet the managers were careful not to exploit their position. As a result the telegraph business was not placed under federal regulation until 1934.

Telephone communication also was soon dominated by a single national enterprise.[26] If it had not been for Gould's challenges in the late 1870s, Western Union probably would have taken over the new communications instrument shortly after Alexander Graham Bell invented the device in 1876. Aware of its competitive potential, Western Union executives late in 1877 hired Thomas A. Edison to develop an instrument that was different enough to avoid patent infringements and improved enough to get the business away from Bell. Edison did, in fact, contribute even more than Bell to the design of the modern telephone. However, because Gould's second attack on Western Union came just at this time, and because the executives of the Bell company made it clear they would make a determined fight to uphold their patents, the telegraph company agreed in November 1879 to sell the patent rights to its instrument to the National

Bell Company for a fixed royalty and retire from the telephone business. A few months later National Bell was reorganized as the American Bell Company and refinanced to meet the clear demand for the new form of communication.

To continue to grow, the Bell Company required in 1880 a large injection of capital, a long-term strategy, and a rational structure. William H. Forbes, the son of John Murray Forbes, and other Boston capitalists, who had been closely associated in railroad finance, provided the funds. At the same time, Theodore N. Vail, who joined the company in May 1878, defined the strategy and the structure. Vail, a telegraph operator who joined the postal service in 1868, had already had a brilliant career. He was so successful in improving operations and routing that by 1876, at the age of thirty, he had become general superintendent of the United States Rail Mail Service. This career manager then became to American Bell what J. Edgar Thomson had been to the Pennsylvania Railroad.

In planning the company's strategy and in building its structure, Vail focused on the still-to-be-created long-distance traffic.[27] In the battle with Western Union, he persuaded his colleagues to refuse the telegraph companies' compromise offer to let the Bell interests have the patents if Western Union was allowed to build and operate the long-distance lines. Once the settlement was made, Vail had the company's technicians begin developing the technology of long-distance voice transmission, while he started to obtain the rights-of-way for the proposed long lines.

Vail always stressed the importance of legally protecting the existing patents and, through research and development, generating new patents. From the start, however, he insisted that an even more certain way to dominate was to control the through traffic between local operating enterprises. In addition, Vail argued that American Bell must continue to maintain and if possible expand its stock ownership in the major operating companies that licensed its phone and switchboard equipment. When such an operating company expanded its facilities, the parent company's investment should increase proportionately.

These policies, particularly the last, soon brought Vail into conflict with the investors, their representatives on the board, and above all with William H. Forbes, the president.[28] Vail, the professional manager, urged rapid and continuing expansion. He emphasized the advantages of having the Bell-sponsored companies the first to provide telephone service in an area. Forbes and other investors held back. The costs would reduce dividends and threaten loss of control. Since profits on existing business were satisfactory, why pay this price? Frustrated, Vail submitted a letter of resignation in May 1885. After much discussion, Forbes and the board members were able to get him to stay on as head of the new subsidiary, the American Telephone and Telegraph Company, formed to build and operate the long lines. Two years later, after completion of the nation's first long-distance line from New York to Albany and Boston, Vail left the company.

Vail's forecast proved correct. Despite the lengthy legal suits and continuing research and development, the number of local, independent companies grew, particularly after the basic Bell patents expired in the 1890s. The number of instruments in the hands of independent companies rose from 30,000 in 1894 to 656,000 in 1899.[29] It was only because of its control of through traffic that American Bell was able to keep the new companies from growing large. Finally, in 1902, Forbes and his associates agreed that Bell-sponsored operating subsidiaries and the parent company must expand their activities. In that year they authorized a consortium of J. P. Morgan & Company, George F. Baker's First National Bank, the Manhattan Trust, and the Old Colony Trust of Boston to market a block of 50,000 shares at $7.7 million. Then in 1906 investment bankers following a proposal of Vail, who had returned to the board in 1902, embarked on a major expansion program by selling $100 million of convertible bonds in the next two years. Finally, early in 1907, Vail was made president once again.

To operate his national enterprise, Vail quickly created an administrative structure based on legal changes instituted in 1900. By those changes American Telephone and Telegraph, which had been formed to build and operate the long lines, became the parent company for the system as a whole. It held the company's patents, the stocks of local operating companies, and those of Western Electric. The last, wholly owned by AT&T, manufactured and installed the equipment used by its subsidiaries. Vail first reshaped the boundaries of the operating subsidiaries, the Associated Companies as they were called, so that they more rationally met current commercial needs. Then he set up the "central administration" at American Telephone and Telegraph to provide common services and evaluate and appraise operating performance, as well as to define policy and determine long-term plans for the operating companies and the enterprise as a whole.[30] Central administration had, in turn, eight and then ten regional divisions which supervised a number of local districts. This structure, perfected by 1910, remained relatively unchanged until the 1970s.

In the creation of the nation's communication network, monopoly rather than oligopoly became the pattern. The postal service, operated by the central government since colonial times, remained a public monopoly. The enterprises operating the telegraph and the telephone became privates ones. The speed and volume of messages made possible by the new electric technology forced the building of a carefully defined administrative organization, operated by salaried managers, to coordinate their flow and to maintain and expand transmitting facilities. The first enterprise to create a national organization to handle through traffic obtained an almost unassailable position. To achieve that position, however, required more careful planning in the building of the telephone system than in the creating of the telegraph system, because through traffic for the telephone was for many years only a technological potential.

Nevertheless, monopoly was not inevitable. Gould's speculative skills helped to maintain the Western Union control and certainly Vail's strategic vision and organizational talents were central to obtaining control in the telephone field. In both companies career middle managers remained responsible for administering the work of operating units and coordinating the day-to-day flow of traffic through what were the world's largest communication networks. Until the basic systems were built, financiers had some say in top management decisions. Once the basic outline of the system was completed, the communication enterprises became even more managerial enterprises than the railroads. Their career managers came to make nearly all long-term investment decisions as well as short-term operating ones.

The organizational response

The organizational response to the new technologies in communication was comparable to that in transportation. Both came to be operated through modern business enterprises with career middle managers coordinating flows and top managers allocating resources. In the railroads, in urban transit enterprises, and to a lesser extent in the telephone and telegraph companies, top managers shared decisions concerning the raising and spending of money with investment bankers or representatives of their institutional investors. Owners continued to manage their enterprises only where administrative coordination was not essential for safe, efficient movement of traffic—that is, in the operation of steamship lines on the less-traveled routes and of horse-drawn vehicles carrying local freight and passengers.

With these same exceptions, American transportation and communication companies no longer competed in the traditional manner. The operational requirements of the new technologies had made obsolete the competition between small units that had no control over prices—prices that were set by the market forces of supply and demand. At the opening of the new century, economists, businessmen, and politicians were groping for a new theory of "natural monopoly," and for new methods of public control over and regulation of those enterprises that were no longer regulated by market mechanisms.

In the late nineteenth century, comparable business enterprises appeared to provide light, power, and heat in American towns and cities. In most urban areas, the generation and transmission of gas and electricity was carried out by a single privately owned enterprise operated by a full-time, technically trained manager who shared investment and pricing decisions with financiers and representatives of local public commissions or municipalities.[31] Such utilities were managed in much the same manner as urban transportation companies.

In the second and third decades of the twentieth century, both urban transit and urban power and light companies began to expand beyond their original localities. System-building in electric power and electric traction resembled, particularly in the 1920s, railroad system-building in the last two decades of the nineteenth century.[32] Investors, speculators, and investment bankers played much the same types of roles. Yet even when these local enterprises grew larger, they remained smaller and less complex than the older railroad systems. They employed less capital and fewer workers. Their operations involved only a single operating activity —the generation and transmission of electricity—or, in the enlarged traction systems, the movement of passengers. The administration of the flow of such traffic required less complicated statistical and accounting procedures and fewer administrative decisions than did coordinating traffic movements on large railroad systems.

The railroad was, therefore, in every way the pioneer in modern business administration. The great railway systems were by the 1890s the largest business enterprises not only in the United States but also in the world. As the century opened, each of more than thirty railroad systems had a capitalization greater than any urban transit system, greater than any power or light company, and greater than Western Union (and seventeen had a capitalization greater than American Telephone and Telegraph).[33] They employed more workers and carried out a greater number and variety of operations.

No public enterprise, either, came close to the railroad in size and complexity of operation. In the 1890s a single railroad system managed more men and handled more funds and transactions and used more capital than the most complex of American governmental or military organizations. In 1891 the Pennsylvania Railroad employed over 110,000 workers.[34] In the same year the total number of soldiers, sailors, and marines in the United States armed services was 39,492. The Post Office, the largest government office in terms of employees, had 95,440 workers in 1891, but the majority had jobs in one of the 64,000 post offices as payment for political services rendered. The permanent managerial staff in that department was smaller than that of the major railroad systems. Two years later when the expenditures of the federal government were $387.5 million and its receipts $385.8 million, those of the Pennsylvania were $95.5 million and $135.1 million. That year the total gross national debt of $997 million was only about $155 million more than the Pennsylvania's capitalization of $842 million. In the United States, the railroad, not government or the military, provided training in modern large-scale administration.

In Europe, on the other hand, the much larger military and governmental establishments were a source for the kind of administrative training that became so essential to the operation of modern industrial, urban, and technologically advanced economies. In Europe, too, the government played a much larger role than it did in the United States in financing, locating, and even operating the transportation and communication infrastructure. Except for Great Britain, the European nations gave their railroads more support and direction than did the American government. Even in Great Britain, the telegraph and telephone came under the ownership and operation of the central government. And all seafaring nations except the United States subsidized their shipping lines. One clear difference between the rise of modern business enterprise, and with it the rise of modern capitalism, in the United States and Europe was, therefore, the role the central government played in providing the transportation and communication infrastructure and in furnishing modern administrative procedures. In Europe, public enterprise helped to lay the base for the coming of modern mass production and mass distribution. In the United States this base was designed, constructed, and operated almost wholly by private enterprise. State and federal governments assisted in its financing. Yet by 1900 probably no more than 20 percent of the capital funds required to build the modern transportation and communications systems—those based on steam and electrical power—came from public sources.

P A R T
three

The Revolution in
Distribution and Production

The revolution in the processes of distribution and production rested in large part on the new transportation and communication infrastructure. Modern mass production and mass distribution depend on the speed, volume, and regularity in the movement of goods and messages made possible by the coming of the railroad, telegraph, and steamship. These changes in production and distribution began as soon as steam and electricity were used extensively in transportation and communication. As the basic infrastructure came into being between the 1850s and 1880s, modern methods of mass production and distribution and the modern business enterprises that managed them made their appearance.

In distribution the railroad and telegraph were primarily responsible for the coming of the modern mass marketer who purchased directly from the growers, manufacturers, and processors of commodities and goods and sold directly to the retailers or final customers. In manufacturing the railroad and the telegraph gave rise to mass production by encouraging the concentration within a single establishment of all or nearly all the processes involved in making of a product.

This increase in the volume of output produced daily by a processing unit and in the number of transactions handled daily by a distributing unit permitted business enterprises to subdivide their activities into several operating departments. Of even more significance, the new velocity of output and flows encouraged the integration of several units into a single enterprise. The managers of these new multiunit enterprises were able to monitor the processes of production and distribution and to coordinate the high speed, high volume flows through them more efficiently than if the monitoring and coordination had been left to market mechanisms.

Changes in demand were only partly responsible for this sharp increase in the volume of goods and the rate they flowed through the economy and through the business enterprises that operated it. Expanding markets were, of course, essential to maintaining mass production and mass distribution, and the United States had the fastest growing market of any industrializing nation. During most of the nineteenth century, American population, output, and income, the basic indicators of market expansion, grew at a faster rate per decade than those of Western Europe and Japan. Nevertheless the rates of growth did not rise markedly in the decades when modern business enterprise first appeared in American production and distribution. These decades, however, were those when the nation's modern transportation and communication networks were being laid down, and the procedures for their operations perfected, and when coal became available in huge quantities for industrial power and heat. These factors were, therefore, more directly related to the timing of when modern business enterprise appeared in commerce and industry than was market demand.

C H A P T E R 7

Mass Distribution

The basic transformation

Transformation in the size and activities of business enterprises came most swiftly in distribution. In the 1840s the traditional merchantile firm, operating much as it had for half a millenium, still marketed and distributed the nation's goods. Within a generation it was replaced in the sale of agricultural commodities and consumer goods by modern forms of marketing enterprises. In the 1850s and 1860s the modern commodity dealer, who purchased directly from the farmer and sold directly to the processor, took over the marketing and distribution of agricultural products. In the same years the full-line, full-service wholesaler began to market most standardized consumer goods. Then in the 1870s and 1880s the modern mass retailer—the department store, the mail-order house, and the chain store—started to make inroads on the wholesaler's markets.

All these mass marketing enterprises had the same internal administrative structure. Their buying and selling organizations, by using the railroads, the telegraph, the steamship, and improved postal services, coordinated the flow of agricultural crops and finished goods from a great number of individual producers to an even larger number of individual consumers. By means of such administrative coordination, the new mass marketers reduced the number of transactions involved in the flow of goods, increased the speed and regularity of that flow, and so lowered costs and improved the productivity of the American distribution system.

The modern commodity dealer

The transformation began, as might be expected, in the nation's most important business—the marketing of farm crops. It came most dramatically in the distribution of the two great crops, grain and cotton. The railroad and telegraph not only accelerated the movement of those crops to market but also, of equal significance, made possible the rapid growth of ancillary enterprises: grain elevators, cotton presses, warehouses, and, most important of all, commodity exchanges. The exchanges, based on new telegraphic communication, permitted cotton, grain, and other commodities to be bought and sold while they were still in transit and indeed even before they were harvested. The standardizing and systematizing of marketing procedures carried out by the exchanges transformed the methods of financing and reduced the costs of the movement of American crops.

The fundamental changes in marketing and financing came first in the grain trade. Here they began as the railroad and telegraph moved across the upper Mississippi Valley in the 1850s and opened up highly productive grain-growing areas. John G. Clark, in his history of the grain trade, tells what happened:

Improvements in transportation and communications, particularly the railroads and telegraph, effected a remarkable change in the marketing of grain. The telegraph put western markets in close touch with price changes in eastern centers, and the railroads facilitated delivery so that a favorable price change could be exploited. As a result, larger purchases of grain were made in markets such as Chicago and Buffalo. With the aid of telegraphic communication, a dealer in New York could also purchase directly at the point of production. The degree of risk, though still large, was lessened, and the long line of individuals making advances to other individuals farther along the line was reduced. More important, as the time required for a shipment of grain to arrive at its destination was reduced, so too was the time in which the purchaser was overextended by an advance. These improvements became operative in a full sense only after the Civil War, and largely in regard to the purchase of flour. Wheat [in 1860] still traveled the lake route to market.[1]

Then with the coming of the fast-freight line and the through bill of lading, the railroads in the 1870s captured the wheat and other grain as well as the flour trade from the lakes and canals. By 1876 five-sixths of the eastbound grain went by rail.[2] By then the revolution in the shipping and marketing of grain had been completed.

Central to this transformation was the building of storage facilities and the formation of exchanges. The first grain elevator was constructed in Buffalo in 1841.[3] Steam power greatly speeded the process of unloading and loading involved in the storage of grain. However, the demand for such facilities had not yet appeared. A second elevator was not built until 1847, and only in the 1850s did grain elevators begin to be constructed in any numbers. In that decade at least fifteen were built in Chicago alone. Over half of these were owned and operated by the recently opened grain-carrying railroads, including the Galena and Chicago Union, the Michigan Central, the Illinois Central, the Rock Island, and the Burlington. The elevators grew larger and adopted improved automatic equipment to increase the speed of loading. From the 1850s on, railroads and grain dealers began to build elevators for storing the grain purchased directly from the farmers along the lines of railroads in wheat-growing regions.

The new storage and shipment methods made necessary the standardized grading of wheat at the point of departure and storage. Wheat could no longer be shipped "as it was in the 1840s in separate units as numerous as there were owners of grain."[4] The high-volume sales required impersonalized standards. Buyers were no longer able personally to check every lot.

In the 1850s the need to standardize grading and the methods of weighing and inspection encouraged the establishment of grain exchanges. The Chicago Board of Trade, established in 1848 on the pattern of the older merchant exchanges of eastern and European cities, assumed this role in the following decade, before it became incorporated in 1859.[5] The Merchants Exchange of St. Louis took on the characteristics of a modern grain exchange in 1854; that in Buffalo did so at about the same time. The New York Produce Exchange, formed in 1850, soon took over these activities for grain and other commodities; it was incorporated in 1862. The Philadelphia Corn Exchange commenced its activities in 1854. In 1860 the Milwaukee and Kansas City Exchanges opened for business, and by the 1880s there were similar organizations in Toledo, Omaha, and Minneapolis.

These exchanges began to develop cooperative efforts to standardize grading, weighing, and other procedures on a national basis. Even before the Civil War, the exchanges at the great collecting points in the west were beginning to force the eastern ones to adopt their systems of weights.[6] It was not until 1874, however, that the New York Produce Exchange agreed to accept the western system of grading and inspection as the national standard.

One reason the existing boards of trade and merchant exchanges took on this new role was the emergence of "to arrive" contracts. Made practical by the telegraph and the assured delivery dates permitted by the railroad, this device quickly replaced the long-established "consignment" contract.[7] Such a contract for future delivery specified the amount, quality, price, and delivery date. It was paid for in cash. The new futures contract had many advantages. It permitted grain to be shipped and delivered at the moment when a manufacturer was ready to process it or when the retailer was ready to receive it. As there was less need to sell at a going price when the grain reached a commercial center, prices tended to be more stable.

As important, the new procedures lowered the credit cost required to move the crops. Because a shipment's price was set in the contract and because the time of transit was short, involving little risk, shippers were able to obtain short-term notes at low interest rates from local commercial banks. No longer did the financing of the movement of the crops require long and often risky negotiations between one commission merchant and another.

The significance of this revolution in financing was enthusiastically, if ungrammatically, noted in a report of the New York legislature in 1860:

While the railroad interest has been growing up, and extending all over our country, a most important change has been wrought thereby, in distributing trade through the whole year. Formerly all surplus productions of the western country were purchased . . . on the credit of large commission houses . . . It was, though necessary, always an uncertain mode of conducting business. The property must be held, and so held on the credit of some parties. If the value rose, it was maintained; then acceptances were met and all went well . . . If the value fell . . . then the commission house failed, and often the ruin extended widely into the interior. All this is now changed . . . It is the substitution of cash for credit . . . It is the practical working of actual correct business, for the slow and uncertain working of the old system. It is a great reform. It will never go back.

As the grading and inspection became standardized and as elevator and storage receipts and through bills of lading became negotiable, the use of "to arrive" contracts was quickly systematized into modern futures trading.[8] Immediately grain dealers began to use speculators' funds to finance the movement of the crops. They did this by the technique of "hedging." By this practice a grain buyer made four transactions in financing a single shipment. For example, he obtained the funds to purchase, say in September, a lot of 5,000 bushels of wheat at $2 a bushel by selling a futures contract for December wheat for that amount at that price. When he sold his 5,000 bushels, a month or six weeks later, he used the proceeds from the sale to purchase a futures contract for December wheat and so met his obligations on the contract he had sold in September. In this way he cut the cost of credit still more, for the many transactions handled by a dealer usually balanced out the slight rise and fall in price of futures during the time he held them. The techniques of hedging thus permitted commodity dealers to shift to speculators much of the cost of credit required in the shipment of grain, already greatly reduced by the speed and regularity of the new transportation and communication.

The procedures devised in the 1850s and 1860s were fully institutionalized by the 1870s. State regulation of grain elevators helped to standardize more precisely the grading and methods of inspection, while elaborate self-regulation of exchanges systematized and stabilized the high-volume trading made possible by the railroad and telegraph.[9]

Commodity dealers soon replaced the traditional merchant in the American grain trade. The new firms bought directly from the farmer, took title to shipments, and arranged for their transportation and delivery to the processors.[10] Such dealers as David Dows and Company, Jesse Hoyt and Company, Yale Kneeland, and John B. Truesdale had offices at the major grain centers, owned seats on the grain exchanges, and had their own buyers in the grain-growing regions. They made use of brokers who bought and sold on commission to fill in or complete orders received from processors and exporters. These new enterprises were able to ship a much larger volume of grain at a much lower cost than had traditional merchants.

A similar revolution occurred in the marketing of cotton in the years immediately after the Civil War. The complete dislocation of the cotton trade during the war delayed, but only for a brief time, development of procedures comparable to those in the grain trade. Once the cotton trade was reopened and the south's railroad and telegraph networks had been rebuilt, the change came swiftly.

The impact in the early 1870s of the new transportation and communication on the long-established factorage system for marketing cotton was similar to their impact on the grain trade in the late 1850s. In Harold D. Woodman's words:

> The railroad, through bills of lading, and improved cotton compresses were moving cotton-buying into the interior, thereby undermining the old cotton factorage system . . . The telegraph, the transatlantic cable, and later the telephone put merchants in every market in almost instantaneous touch with one another. Cotton prices in Liverpool and New York could be known in minutes not only in New Orleans and Savannah, but, as the telegraph expanded inland along with the railroad, in hundreds of tiny interior markets.[11]

Cotton dealers now began to buy directly from planters, small farmers, and general storekeepers. Buyers for New England and British mills (and soon for local ones in the south) purchased their supplies from those dealers who soon came to have large buying networks throughout the south. Cotton dealers, like grain dealers, supplemented their orders by purchasing from brokers on the new cotton exchanges. As a result, the cotton producers no longer needed the services of the cotton factor, particularly the seacoast factor, to market their crops or to provide essential credit.

Exchanges came to play the same role in the cotton trade as they did in the marketing of grain. The first cotton exchange was formed in New York less than a year after the formal organization of the Liverpool Cotton Brokers Association in 1869. Another began operations in New Orleans in 1871.[12] The exchanges immediately defined and standardized classifications and grades of cotton and arranged for their inspection. They also standardized contracts and set up procedures to adjust and arbitrate differences arising out of these contracts. Such standardization meant that a purchaser could sell or a buyer obtain a specific grade of cotton on a through bill of lading that would carry the shipment from the railroad station nearest the grower directly to the purchaser's warehouse.

Finally the cotton exchanges expanded and regularized the new trade in futures. Selling cotton "to arrive" had its beginnings in the 1850s when it was done on a small scale, largely as a speculation. After the war, dealing in futures contracts became increasingly acceptable to conservative businessmen, particularly after the new cotton exchanges systematized and regulated transactions. As soon as the transatlantic cable was completed, the practice of hedging developed in precisely the same way for precisely the same reason as it had on the grain exchanges. "Cotton purchased would be balanced by the sale of a futures contract and cotton sold, by the purchase of a contract."[13] The new procedures reduced the risk and lessened the cost of financing the movement of the cotton crop just as they had in the grain trade.

The coming of the exchanges and the increased speed and regularity of transportation and communication brought to an end that long and expensive chain of middlemen and advances that had run from Manchester and Liverpool through the seacoast ports to the cotton plantations. The cotton trade quickly became the province of dealers who, assisted by brokers at the exchanges, purchased directly from planters and farmers at rail heads and sold directly to textile mills and other manufacturers. After the 1880s the trade became increasingly concentrated in the hands of a small number of dealers who had their own buyers and their own presses and storage facilities in the cotton growing regions in the South and their own selling offices in northern and European cities.

These enterprises moved cotton by telegraphic orders throughout all parts of the world. The resulting high-volume flow helped to reduce costs of individual transactions and gave the larger firms a competitive advantage. By 1921, twenty-four firms with sales of over 100,000 bales annually handled 60 percent of the American cotton crop.[14] One such firm, Clayton & Company, established at the turn of the century, was by World War I the largest cotton dealer in the world. The fundamental changes in the marketing of the cotton crop came swiftly in the years immediately following the Civil War, as the impact of the railroad, telegraph, cable, and steamship was fully felt. Since then relatively few changes in the marketing of cotton have occurred.

In the post-Civil War years, other crops—corn, rye, oats, and barley —were distributed and marketed by commodity dealers and brokers using commodity exchanges.[15] However, when commodities were processed by large mass producers, these manufacturers rather than the commodity dealers took over the marketing and distribution of the product. Such developments occurred in the marketing of meat, tobacco, and imported foodstuffs such as sugar and cacao. But where processing did not become concentrated in the hands of a few mass producers, exchanges continued to play a major role in a commodity sale and distribution. For example, the only imported foodstuff to have an exchange was coffee, requiring no processing in the United States. It was shipped by dealers to wholesalers and then to retailers in the same bags in which it was originally packed in Brazil.[16] Where commodities were purchased from millions of farmers and sold to a sizable number of processors, then the coordination of the flow of goods between the two became the function of specialized commodity dealers who used the commodity exchanges to facilitate their work.

Although the administrative networks these dealers created were often worldwide in extent, they required only a few managers and a small investment in capital facilities. Much of the buying, selling, storing, and shipping was coordinated and controlled from a single, central office. Nevertheless, such organizations made possible an even more effective exploitation of the existing railroad and telegraph systems. They helped to reduce the number of transactions involved and the number of men needed to distribute a given amount of commodities. They lowered the cost of credit required in movement of crops and, finally, by improving information and scheduling they permitted a closer integration of supply with demand. In these ways the rise of the large commodity dealers contributed to the efficiency and productivity in the marketing of basic American commodities at a time when their export was still important to American economic growth.

The wholesale jobber

In somewhat different ways the new instruments of transportation and communication transformed the distribution of manufactured consumer goods as dramatically as they did the marketing of agricultural commodities. The wholesalers were the first to use the modern multiunit enterprise to mass market manufactured and processed goods. The new speed, regularity, and dependability of transportation and communication affected the wholesaler in several ways. First, and most important of all, the merchant handling consumer goods became a jobber. He no longer sold on commission. Like the grain and cotton dealer, he took title to the goods. By the 1870s nearly all wholesalers had become jobbers. Second, the jobber moved west. No longer did the middlemen on the eastern seaboard control the distribution of manufactured goods. Third, the new jobber created large buying networks through which he purchased directly from manufacturers at home and abroad, and he built extensive marketing organizations to sell to general stores in rural areas and specialized retailers in the cities. No longer did the storekeepers of the south and west have to make their semiannual treks to the eastern markets. The jobbers came to them. Finally, the reduction in the chain of middlemen, and the increased speed and regularity of transportation and communication, altered procedures of financing these trades.

This account of the impact of the new transportation on merchandizing in the midwest by Lewis Atherton is just as true for the south:

The railroad's penetration of the region completely revolutionized the techniques of wholesaling and ended the pioneer period of merchandizing in Mid-America. No longer did the merchant buy the bulk of his supplies for the year at one time; no longer was it necessary for him to visit the seaboard; no longer did he risk the loss of his goods. The railroad brought the goods he now could order as he needed; it brought the traveling salesman to him, so it was possible for him to spend all his time attending to business at home; and the greater safety of rail transport relieved him of the worries he had faced in the days of river transportation. Thus the railroad, as an improved means of transportation, ushered in the days of modern merchandizing.[17]

The wholesaler who supplied the country storekeeper benefited as much from the coming of the railroad and the telegraph as did the storekeepers themselves. Like the retailer, the wholesaler no longer needed to carry such large inventories as in the prerailroad days. Nor did the wholesaler have to worry about the high risks of losing shipments en route. He now ordered directly from the manufacturers by telegraph and was fairly certain of delivery on a specified schedule. The increase in speed and regularity made it possible for the merchant to handle a greater volume of goods. Expanded volume, in turn, reduced unit costs and promised higher profits. By taking title to and reselling goods, the wholesaler was normally able to obtain a markup higher than the usual 2 ½ to 5 percent commission. At the same time, the increased volume of business assured the jobber of a more certain cash flow and so reduced his credit needs. Thus commission merchants who handled relatively standardized products became full-time specialized jobbers.

Finally, the new arrangements pleased the manufacturers. They now obtained cash for their products instead of waiting for payment for six months to a year until the product was finally sold. Payment in cash substantially reduced the manufacturer's requirements for working capital and therefore his dependence on the merchants who supplied it.

Until the 1850s wholesaling was concentrated on the eastern seaboard and factors in the south and storekeepers in the west had to come east to get their stock. As soon as the railroad and the telegraph provided close and direct contact with sources of supply, the jobbers moved west. A citizen of Cincinnati, writing in 1859, makes the point:

Within the last eight or ten years Cincinnati has been gaining a position as a great centre of supply by wholesale, to country merchants of Ohio, Indiana, Illinois and Kentucky, of their dry goods, groceries, hardware, boots and shoes, hats, drugs, and fancy goods. In these various lines of business it is becoming very apparent to purchasers that they can deal here to greater advantage than our eastern cities. The effect of this has been to enlarge our sales to country merchants. For example—dry goods, from $4,000,000, in 1840 to $10,000,000, in 1850, and to $25,000,000, at this time. There is a corresponding increase, also, in all other descriptions of business which go to make up general sales to country merchants.[18]

What was true for Cincinnati was also true for St. Louis and even more so for Chicago. Chicago's rapid growth as a railroad terminus meant that it became a distributing center for manufactured goods as well as a transmitter of wheat, meats, and other agricultural products. By 1866 Chicago had fifty-nine jobbers with sales of over a million dollars, while Cincinnati and St. Louis had only fifteen apiece.[19] Nevertheless, the eastern wholesale centers—New York, Philadelphia, and Baltimore—did not give up the trade of the west without a struggle. They sent out a stream of traveling salesmen and catalogues to retailers in all parts of the old northwest. Throughout the 1870s the largest dry goods wholesaler in Chicago, Field, Leiter and Company (soon to become Marshall Field & Company), was more concerned with competition from New York than from other Chicago wholesalers.[20]

As the jobbers of New York and Chicago competed for the retail trade of the midwest, those in St. Louis and Cincinnati, as well as in Louisville and Baltimore, began to concentrate on the trade in the south.[21] There the Civil War, by ending the old plantation system and by turning slaves into freedmen, brought a rapid growth of country stores. The country store became, as it had long been in the midwest, the basic retail outlet. Planters set up stores where freedmen, now tenants, could get their supplies. Former Union as well as Confederate soldiers established new stores at rail crossings and country crossroads, often becoming planters themselves. So too did a number of Jewish peddlers who had replaced Yankee ones selling in the rural south during the late forties and fifties. In fact, the new stores, along with improved transportation and the rise of the modern wholesaler to supply them, all but ended the peddler as an instrument of distribution in the United States.

By the late 1860s the full-line, full-service wholesaler had taken over the distribution of the traditional consumer goods—that is, dry goods (including clothing and upholstered furnishings), hardware (including cutlery, tools, and implements), drugs, and groceries (including fruit and confectionary).[22] The jobber also became central in the marketing of boots and shoes, saddlery and other leather products, tobacco, liquor, jewelry, furs, watches, furniture, mill work and other wood products, china and glassware, stationery, paint, oil, and varnish. During the second half of the nineteenth century these enterprises continued to dominate the distribution of consumer goods in the American economy.

Such wholesalers handled a much greater volume of business than did any earlier middlemen. The sales of the largest importers in the 1840s, such as Nathan Trotter of Philadelphia, rarely rose above a value of $250,000 a year. And Trotter's staff consisted of only a son, two or three clerks, and a porter.[23] By contrast, Alexander T. Stewart, the nation's foremost dry goods distributor, had, by 1870, annual sales reported at $50 million (of which $8 million were retail). At that time his enterprise employed 2,000 persons.[24] In 1864 H. B. Claflin and Company, Stewart's leading New York competitor (and a wholesaler only), was reported to have sales of $72 million.[25] These figures do not come from internal records and certainly they grossly exaggerated. Nevertheless, once the railroad and telegraph permitted the wholesaler to market in a broad geographical territory, the volume of sales which a single firm handled jumped from an annual value of tens and hundreds of thousands of dollars to tens of millions of dollars.

Data on wholesalers in cities other than New York suggest that as soon as they reached out for the markets of the hinterland, they became as large as any mercantile enterprises in history. For example, two years after Marshall Field and his partner Levi Leiter joined Potter Palmer in 1865, their sales, concentrated in dry goods, reached $9.1 million, of which $1.5 million was retail. Five years later they had risen to $17.2 million, of which $3.1 million was retail.[26] By 1889 Field's sales were $31.0 million ($6.0 million retail), and by 1900 $36.4 million ($12.5 million retail). Field's largest Chicago competitor, James V. Farrell and Company, had a volume of sales close to Field's, with $7.1 million in 1867; $9.5 million in 1870; and $20 million in the early 1880s. Carson, Pirie and Scott; Charles Gosage and Company; J. B. Shay; and Hamlin Hale and Company were smaller dry goods houses but still of substantial size. In Philadelphia the largest dry goods enterprise, Hood, Bonbright & Company, was close in size to Field's and Farrell's. The great hardware houses of Hibbard, Spencer and Bartlett of Chicago, and Simmons and Company of St. Louis were not far behind.[27] McKesson & Robbins, Schieffelin Brothers & Company, and other large drug wholesalers in New York and Chicago grew quickly to comparable size and expanded at a comparable rate.

To handle such an unprecedented volume of trade the new enterprises had to build and staff managerial organizations. The new large wholesale houses, operating in quite different trades, came to be structured along much the same lines.[28]

Central to the success of the large wholesale jobbing enterprise was its sales force. Salesmen were the firm's primary competitive weapon and its basic source of marketing information. Wholesalers in New York and Philadelphia had first used "drummers" in the late forties to solicit trade of the country merchants when the storekeepers appeared in town.[29] Then, in the years after the Civil War, traveling salesmen began to swarm through the land.[30] They became familiar figures in rural America and the nation's folklore.

These salesmen went "by the cars" to the towns and villages on the railroads and then by horse and buggy to the smallest and most distant of country stores. They appeared at these stores at different times of the year and marketed their goods in different ways, depending on the lines they handled. The dry goods representatives sold largely by sample, spending much of their lives unpacking and packing trunks. The hardware and implement men relied, as did those selling groceries and drugs, more on catalogues.

Besides taking orders and drumming up new trade, the salesmen provided a constant flow of information back to their headquarters. They reported on changing demand, items particularly desired, the general economic conditions of different sections, and, above all, the credit ratings of local storekeepers and merchants. The salesmen also assisted the storekeepers in keeping a stable inventory, in improving their accounting, and even in enhancing their merchandise displays.

Normally the salesmen were monitored, evaluated, and directed by a general sales manager and his staff. If the enterprise was a particularly large one, there were assistant sales managers for different regions. The general sales department included a small advertising office, which prepared the firm's catalogues, sent regularly to customers, and arranged for some, though not extensive, advertising in local newspapers.

As essential to the success of the full-line wholesaler as a wide-ranging and aggressive sales force was its purchasing organization. It had two parts. One was the network of buying offices. The other, and more important, included the buyers who actually purchased the goods and who usually worked in the home office. Marshall Field, for example, after establishing offices in New York and other eastern cities, set up in 1871 an office in Manchester and, in the next year, one in Paris.[31] These overseas offices, in turn, kept in close touch with French and German agents who usually bought on commission. A. T. Stewart had an even larger overseas network. According to its historian, that house had by 1873 "branch purchasing offices in every important textile and apparel center in the British Isles and on the Continent."[32] Other wholesalers had similar though less extensive buying organizations.

The buyers quickly became the most important executives in the new jobbing houses. Each buyer and his assistants handled the purchases for one major product line. They determined the specifications of the goods they purchased, usually set the price to be paid as well as the selling price, and determined the volume of purchases. The buyers used the overseas purchasing organization and bought directly from manufacturers or manufacturers' agents at home. Working under the supervision of the general merchandising manager, each buyer was the senior executive of a sizable product department. In nearly all cases the buyers were managers who made a career of their specialty.

Because the requirements of each line were so different, buyers were given a great deal of autonomy. At Marshall Field's each department, in the words of that firm's historian, Robert W. Twyman, "was run as though it were an independent business firm. The department head was a merchant, completely and independently responsible for the results within his own separate department or 'store.'"[33] He purchased, priced, and advertised as he saw fit, and received a contracted for percent of the profits that his department produced. The buyers also had responsibility for developing private brands. Sometimes they did this by becoming exclusive distributors of one manufacturer's output. At other times they arranged for manufacturers to produce exclusively to their specifications. At still other times they did the branding and packaging at their own warehouses. The general merchandising manager who had supervision over the several buying departments also watched over the warehousing operations which often involved unpacking and repacking, as well as labeling, branding, and special packaging. He kept an eye too on any manufacturing activities that the firm had acquired.

Large wholesalers came to do some manufacturing, but such efforts were never extensive. The large dry goods jobbers often hired their own needle workers to make standard items such as underwear, shirts, collars, cuffs, suspenders, furs, and upholstering for furniture. More often, however, this work was contracted out.[34] Except for A. T. Stewart, very few dry goods wholesalers owned mills or factories and Stewart's ventures into manufacturing proved unsuccessful. The hardware wholesalers, while developing their own brands, nearly always had independent manufacturers make the product.[35] In drugs, some of the mixing of compounds was done by the wholesaler, but the compounds were processed by a manufacturer. In the late twentieth century, these large marketing enterprises still concentrate almost entirely on their basic function of merchandising.

The managers in the operating departments had the responsibility for the physical movement of goods from the supplier to the consumer, and for the flow of cash the other way.[36] The magnitude of this task is suggested by the fact that by the 1890s an individual hardware jobbing firm handled 6,000 items purchased from well over 1,000 firms and sold to many more customers. The traffic department concentrated on scheduling the shipments from the suppliers to company warehouses and then to the retailers. Often it made arrangements with the railroads to ship goods directly from the manufacturer to the customer. Managers in the traffic department bargained constantly with railroads to get the lowest possible rates and classifications for their goods and rebates for themselves and their customers. The traffic department had its own shipping office which handled the actual details of the movement of goods. Both shipping and traffic units worked closely with an order department responsible for seeing that the orders were properly filled.

Another functional department, credit and collections, played a critical role in determining the business success of the new wholesalers. Very short-term and tightly controlled credit greatly reduced credit costs. The standard terms in the dry goods, hardware, and drug trades were twenty days net with a 1 or 2 percent discount for cash paid in ten days, and somewhat longer terms for slower moving items.[37] Competition, however, often forced the granting of credit extension for more than twenty days. Marshall Field, for example, was particularly generous in extending credit to retailers who were just getting started. Credit extension clearly had its dangers. Unless carried out with care it could jeopardize the maintenance of high cash flow which was so essential to a wholesaler's success. In granting such extensions, wholesalers relied on information from their own sales force and from credit agencies which had by the end of the Civil War become an integral part of American marketing and distribution.

In fact, the needs of the wholesalers supplied a major reason for the rapid growth of this new type of service enterprise.[38] The Mercantile Agency, the first of the credit reporting firms, was formed by a New York dry goods jobber, Lewis Tappan. Founded in 1841, it began to expand its activities outside of the New York and New England area in the 1850s. In that decade a second firm, the Bradstreet Agency, began operations. By 1870, the older agency, which had been taken over by R. G.

Dun, had set up twenty-eight branch offices in the nation's major commercial centers. By the end of the decade it had added forty-one more. Bradstreet followed suit, though on a somewhat smaller scale. As was so often to be the case, the first two enterprises to create a branch office network in a business continued to dominate it. By the 1870s these two enterprises were doing an enormous volume of business. Dun's agency then employed over 10,000 reporters or investigators and received daily some 5,000 requests for information. The most successful competitors of the two giants (who later combined to form Dun & Bradstreet) were agencies that reported on specialized trades including dry goods, hardware, furniture, stationery, and jewelry. Marshall Field, for example, relied on two specialists in the dry goods field—Barlow and Company, and Huart, Garlock and Company—as well as on Dun and on Bradstreet.

At Marshall Field's the granting of credit was of such importance that it became an almost full-time responsibility for one partner, Levi Leiter. Leiter's abilities in this field made it possible for the enterprise to carry out most of its huge business on a cash basis. "With their carefully selected customers discounting their bills as regularly as a group of faithful employees punching a time clock, the two partners had little capital tied up in delinquent accounts, knew with reasonable certainty how much money was coming in each month, and were subsequently able to maintain an unsurpassed reputation themselves for prompt payment."[39] The resulting steady cash flow reduced the cost of credit per unit of merchandise obtained to a new low.

Managers in the credit and collection department worked closely with those in the accounting department. Both provided information essential to the overall management of the enterprise. The data kept by the accounting department included a record of all financial transactions and the receipts and expenditures of all funds. The several buying offices handling the different lines, and the functional departments, each had their own set of accounts. Although the number of entries was far greater than those in accounts of commission merchants in the 1840s, the method of double-entry bookkeeping remained much the same. In addition to departmental journals recording the transactions, and ledgers showing the accounts of each supplier, customer, or shipper, there was the general ledger that gave monthly summaries of each office and department and of the enterprise as a whole.[40] Since the financial transactions were straightforward and of much the same nature, the new mass marketers had less need than the railroads to develop complex procedures to record them and then to collect, collate, and analyze the resulting accounts. The wholesalers, therefore, had smaller accounting departments than did the railroads and less extensive internal auditing. As their capital investment was very small in relation to their total business, they were not pressed to consider depreciation and other matters of capital accounting.

In evaluating the performance of their operating managers, the senior executives used two types of information generated by the accounting department. One, somewhat comparable to that used by the railroads, was gross margins (income from sales minus cost of goods) to net sales. The other and more important was the rate of inventory turnover or "stock-turn," as the wholesalers termed it. This they defined as the number of times stock on hand was sold and replaced within a specified time period, usually annually.[41] Stock-turn was, indeed, an effective measure of the efficiency of a distributing enterprise, for the higher the stock-turn with the same working force and equipment, the lower the unit cost and the higher the output per worker and per facility.

Significantly the concept of stock-turn only appeared in American marketing after the coming of the railroad had permitted the rise of the modern wholesaler. I know of no example of a prerailroad merchant using that term. On the other hand, by 1870 Marshall Field's most repeated admonition to his managers was to keep "one's stocks 'turning' rapidly."[42] And he constantly urged the retailers to whom he sold to concentrate on the same goal.

By this criterion Marshall Field's company performed well. In 1878, the first year for which information exists, the average stock-turn in Field's wholesale operation was 5.9 and was kept about 5, except for one year, until 1883.[43] This record was excellent even by twentieth century standards. As the figures suggest, once a distributing network such as Field's was perfected, further increases in stock-turn and productivity were difficult to achieve. The quantum jump in the volume handled and productivity achieved by a single firm came at the moment when the railroad and telegraph made possible the rise of modern business enterprise in American marketing and distribution.

Many of the organizations the wholesalers created in the 1860s and 1870s continued on beyond the life of their founders. With some notable exceptions, such as the firm of A. T. Stewart, most lasted into the twentieth century.[44] After 1880, however, wholesalers began to be challenged by and then even to succumb to two brand new and very different types of enterprises. One was the mass retailer who purchased from the manufacturer and who sold directly to the final consumer. The other was the manufacturer who began to build his own wholesale marketing and distributing network as well as his own extended purchasing organization. Both proved successful competitors because they internalized the activities of the wholesaler and so extended the administrative coordination of the flow of goods from the manufacturer or processor directly to the ultimate consumer.

The mass retailer

The wholesalers' dominance in American distribution peaked in the early 1880s. Although the total number of wholesalers continued to grow, their market share fell off.[45] According to Harold Barger's estimates, $2.4 billion worth of goods went to retailers by way of wholesalers in 1879, and $1.0 billion went directly from manufacturers and processors to retailers.[46] Much of the latter were goods or produce grown or made locally for local markets. Between 1869 and 1879 the ratio between direct sales and sales via the wholesaler rose from 1:2.11 to 1:2.40. And after that date the ratio declined regularly for the ten-year intervals on which Barger made estimates. In 1889 it had declined slightly to 1:2.33; by 1899 to 1:2.15; by 1909 to 1:1.90; and by 1929 to 1:1.16. This reduction in the ratio came more from an increase in sales by mass retailers and large integrated mass producers than it did from sales by local producers selling to local consumers.

Mass retailers began to replace wholesalers as soon as they were able to exploit a market as large as that covered by the wholesalers. By building comparable purchasing organizations they could buy directly from the manufacturers and develop as high a volume of sales and an even higher stock-turn than had the jobbers. Their administrative networks were more effective because they were in direct contact with the customers and because they reduced market transactions by eliminating one major set of middlemen.

The first of the mass retailers, the department stores, had their beginnings in the 1860s and 1870s. They sold to the growing urban market in the largest American cities. The mail-order houses which appeared in the 1870s to serve the rural markets did not reach full flower until the end of the century. And the chains that moved into the smaller cities and towns and into the suburbs of larger metropolitan areas began to expand in size and numbers only after 1900.

The policies, practices, and administrative organization of these three types of retailers all had much in common and were often directly derived from those of the wholesale jobber. Like the jobber, their basic objective was to assure profits by maintaining a high velocity of stock-turn; and they did so by extending the administrative network so that they coordinated the flow of goods from suppliers to the ultimate consumers.

The department store. Modern department stores appeared almost simultaneously in many American cities, growing most profusely in New York City—the largest urban market in the nation. In all cities they evolved from much the same sort of background, carried on much the same strategies of expansion, and adopted much the same type of internal operating policies and administrative procedures.

Many of the first major department stores in New York and Chicago began as less profitable and smaller adjuncts to a wholesaling establishment. During the 1870s Marshall Field's palatial retail store accounted for only 15 percent of Field's total sales and about 5 percent of its profits. The same was reportedly true of Stewart's in New York. Throughout his lifetime Alexander Stewart concentrated on his wholesale activities. As late as 1876 his firm built a branch wholesaling establishment in Chicago. In Philadelphia John Wanamaker, after developing a highly successful retail store, considered wholesaling at least as promising. Wanamaker purchased Hood, Bonbright & Company, the largest wholesaler in that city and two other wholesale dry goods houses.[47] Nevertheless, after the 1880s retailing became more profitable than wholesaling. Stewart's venture in Chicago failed; retailing remained the center of Wanamaker's activities; and retailing became increasingly important to the prosperity and profits of Marshall Field.

The department store appeared when an establishment which retailed dry goods or clothing began to add new lines such as furniture, jewelry, and glassware.[48] Alexander T. Stewart built the first large dry goods retail store in 1846—the famous Marble Dry Goods Palace. Although he may have added a few lines, until 1862 the Palace remained essentially a store for selling cloth, thread, sheetings, ribbons, and other dry goods. Then when Stewart constructed a still larger establishment up Broadway between 9th and 10th Streets, he added other lines and became a full-fledged department store. While Stewart's business did not survive many years after his death in 1876, most of his imitators are still in operation over a century later. Arnold Constable built its Marble House in 1857 and a larger department store in 1877. In 1858 Lord & Taylor was completing "a new and elegant marble structure," and in 1872 it too moved further uptown above 20th Street and built a still more massive building to house a department store. Rowland Macy began as a retailer of fancy dry goods in New York in 1858 and expanded during the 1860s by taking over adjacent stores and adding new lines. Macy's had become a department store before 1870.

Macy's represents a second department store lineage, those that grew out of small retail clothing or dry goods enterprises rather than from large wholesaling establishments. Others to grow in this manner included

Bloomingdale's, which became a full department store in the late 1870s, and Abraham & Straus, which began to do a thriving business in Brooklyn after 1883 when the completion of the Brooklyn Bridge gave that borough direct access to Manhattan. Still other New York department stores to open in this period included B. Altman & Company (its large store was built in 1876), Best & Company (store built in 1879), and Stern Brothers (store in 1878). All of these survived into the second half of the twentieth century. Two that did not were John A. Hearn and Sons, and Bowen, McNamee & Company.[49] In a very short time—less than two decades—the largest department store complex in the world had been created in New York City. The stores founded in the 1860s and 1870s account for almost half of the leading department stores in New York a century later. Most of the others—Peck & Peck, Henry Bendel, Bonwit Teller, Franklin Simon, Bergdorf Goodman, Lane Bryant, and two branches of out-of-state stores, Wanamaker's and Gimbel's—were in operation by the first decade of the twentieth century.

The swift growth of the department store in the years immediately following the Civil War came first in New York precisely because it had become the largest concentrated urban market in the nation and one of the greatest in the world. In 1870 the population of New York (including Brooklyn) was 1,338,000, as compared to 674,000 for Philadelphia, 251,000 for Boston, and 299,000 for Chicago.[50] In these and other American cities, the timing of the coming of the department stores and the number established correlated closely to the growth of the city.[51] In Philadelphia, dry goods merchants Strawbridge & Clothier, and a men's clothing retailer, John Wanamaker, opened department stores in the years immediately after the Civil War, as did Jordan Marsh and R. H. White in Boston. At this same time Carson, Pirie, Scott & Company and the Mandel Brothers began to compete with Marshall Field in Chicago. In the late 1870s Hutzler's began operations in Baltimore and Woodward and Lothrop in Washington. In 1879 E. J. Lehman opened The Fair in Chicago which, with San Francisco's Emporium, was among the few major department stores that did not come out of the dry goods and clothing trades. In the 1870s and the early 1880s J. L. Hudson had its start in Detroit, F. & R. Lazarus in Columbus, and John Shillito in Cincinnati. In 1887 Adam Gimbel, who had built a Palace of Trade in the 1870s in Vincennes, Indiana, began his move to more profitable territory by building a similar store in Milwaukee, then in 1894 in Philadelphia, and finally in 1908 in New York. The Emporium and I. Magnum came to San Francisco, and the J. W. Robinson & Company to Los Angeles in the 1890s. The first decade of the twentieth century saw the opening of Bullock's in Los Angeles, Rich's in Atlanta, and Nieman-Marcus in Houston. In nearly every large city, and indeed in many smaller ones, the story was then much the same as New York. The first comers rarely faded away, but as the city grew, room was available for newcomers.

These establishments, which became department stores by adding new lines to their original ones, continued to grow by putting in still more lines and expanding the volume of existing ones. Their offerings remained, however, largely in clothing, dry goods, and household goods. Those that continued as wholesale houses moved more slowly into new lines than those that grew out of small retail shops. Thus Marshall Field, Chicago's largest mass retailer, carried only dry goods and ladies' clothing until 1872, when the firm added furs, men's clothing, carpets and rugs, and upholstered goods.[52] No more lines were added until 1889 when the able and innovative Harry Selfridge took charge of the enterprise's retail operations. On the other hand, Macy's was carrying, by 1869, all the lines that Field came to handle (except men's clothing), and also furniture, silverware, parasols and umbrellas, jewelry, hats, shoes, and toys. By 1877 books and stationery, china, glassware, crockery, flowers and feathers, and men's clothing had been added.[53] These were much the same lines of goods that came to be carried by the new department stores in New York and other American cities. Thus, in addition to selling directly to the ultimate consumer, the department store also differed from the wholesaler in carrying a much wider variety of offerings.

The internal policies, like the external strategies, were much the same from store to store.[54] They were aimed at maintaining the high volume, high turnover flow of business by selling at low prices and low margins. Profits were to be made on volume, not markup. All adopted a "one price" policy. This was, of course, the only feasible policy for an enterprise making thousands of sales by hundreds of sales people. Most followed the policy of accurate descriptions of goods advertised with money-back guarantees if the customer was dissatisfied. Some, like Macy's, for many years had no charge accounts at all. Others billed monthly, occasionally giving discounts for cash. With large and regular incoming cash flows, they bought, as did the wholesalers, on a cash basis. As they had less incentive to give credit to their customers than did the wholesalers, they probably had lower credit costs. Above all, the mass retailers concentrated on maintaining a high level of stock-turn. This they did by marking down slow-moving lines, by extensive local advertising, and by creating a clearly defined management structure.

Because they sold directly to the final consumer, the department stores spent more thought and more money on advertising than did the largest wholesalers. This need encouraged the growth of still another ancillary distribution institution, the advertising agency. Such agencies, which had their initial growth in the 1850s, concentrated, until the 1880s, on local rather than national advertising. They purchased advertising space and prepared copy for local newspapers and periodicals. They relied heavily on the patronage of the mass retailers. For example, the John Wanamaker account helped to give N. W. Ayer & Son its start in becoming one of the country's leading advertising agencies.[55]

The internal organization of a department store differed from that of a large wholesaler only in its selling activities. Because sales were made on the store's premises rather than through traveling salesmen, buyers had an even larger role than they did in the wholesale houses. They not only controlled the buying of different lines—that is, setting price and amounts and specifications of the goods they handled—but also had direct charge of the sales personnel who marketed their lines over the counter. They set up the displays and supervised the writing of advertising copy. Other operating divisions did little more than maintain the building; supervise employees, such as floorwalkers and janitors, who were not directly involved in selling; handle the delivery to customers' homes; process the advertising; and keep the accounts. Many of the new retail enterprises became, in the words of Edward A. Filene, little more than "a holding company for its departments."[56] Others, like Macy's, gave the store superintendents more authority. They were responsible for the employment of store personnel, for receiving and marking goods, and for returns and adjustments.

Yet even at Macy's, as its historian Ralph Hower points out, the purpose of the central organization was "to permit the department heads [buyers] to concentrate upon buying and selling of goods."[57] These department store buyers had, as did buyers in the wholesale houses, full responsibility for the performance of their departments. So "they generally arrogated to themselves complete command within their own bailiwicks and acknowledged no authority except the proprietor's."[58] At Macy's too, some of the newer departments—silver, china and glass, and shoes—were leased out. Indeed the lessee of the first two departments, L. Straus & Sons, wholesalers in china and glassware, handled similar departments at Wanamaker's, R. H. White's, Woodward & Lothrop's, Abraham & Straus's, and J. H. Walker's in Chicago. (They would become by the late 1880s senior partners at Macy's and in 1896 its sole owners.)[59] At Marshall Field's the buyers in the retail store differed from the heads of the wholesale departments because they were on straight salary rather than receiving a percentage of profit in addition to a small salary, and they had full responsibility over the sales force.[60]

For the stores which evolved, as did Field's, from wholesaling establishments, retail buyers bought through the wholesale organization.

Others like Macy's, with no wholesaling organization, built up comparable, though smaller buying networks with agencies abroad.[61] Again, as in the case of the wholesaler, the department stores often came to manufacture a portion of the clothing, upholstering, and other needlework products they sold, but they rarely took over the control and management of any other types of shops or factories.

The primary test of performance for the department store was exactly the same as it was for the wholesaler. Besides the ratio of gross margins to sales, stock-turn was a basic criterion. Monthly departmental stock-turn figures were compared to those of other lines and to those of the same departments for past months and years. By this test of the velocity of the flow, Field's retail stock-turn began to rise to about 5 in the late 1870s and 1880s. It fell to somewhat below 5 in the latter part of the decade and then rose and remained above 5 during most of the twentieth century. After 1890 retail stock-turn stayed consistently above that of Field's wholesaling business.[62] At Macy's the turn was higher, running 6 times for a half a year in 1887, indicating an impressive rate of stock-turn for the year of 12. That record doubled the average rate of stock-turn for department stores in the twentieth century.

Such velocity of stock-turn permitted mass retailers to take lower margins and to sell at lower prices and still make higher profits than small specialized urban retailers and the wholesalers who supplied them. In New England and comparable urban, industrial areas, department stores quickly made serious inroads into the trade of the jobbers and retailers. By the end of the century these stores had almost eliminated the middleman. One witness before the Industrial Commission of 1899 reported that, where there had been dozens of dry goods jobbers in the wholesale section of Boston in the 1880s, only four remained.[63] Not surprisingly, in the 1880s and 1890s such competition brought a strident protest from small urban retailers and their suppliers.[64] They demanded state legislation to protect them from the department stores' lower prices.

But they met with little success. The urban retailer was not yet a significant political force. In 1900 the rural population still outnumbered those living in towns and cities with over 2,500 inhabitants. Nor did the retailers have more than sporadic support from their suppliers, for the rise of the department store did not affect what was still the wholesalers' major market—the country store. As late as 1900, 60 percent of Marshall Field's profits and 75 percent of its sales still came from wholesaling primarily to the rural market. At the end of the century, however, the country store-keeper and the wholesaler who stocked his shelves were beginning to feel vigorous competition from another type of mass retailer, the mail-order house.

The mail-order house. A later and even more direct response to the new transportation and communication infrastructure than the department store was the mail-order house. Both relied, of course, on the railroad and telegraph for the effective operation of their purchasing organizations, but the department store customers came to their counters largely by horse car, carriage, or on foot. If the buyers did not carry off their purchases, the store delivered them by messenger or wagon. In the rural areas, however, mass retailers could reach their customers only by mail and could deliver their goods only by rail, first by express and then by parcel post.

The antecedents of the mail-order house appeared as soon as the new communication and transportation systems began to be integrated. The wholesalers themselves—especially those in hardware and drugs—sold many products through catalogues carried by salesmen and mailed to stores between salesmen's visits. After the Civil War other merchants began to retail goods by mail, for instance, jewelry, tea and foods, books, and implements. However, they sold only single lines of goods in small quantities. The first enterprise to market a wide variety of goods exclusively by mail was formed in 1872 by Aaron Montgomery Ward and his brother-in-law George A. Thorne.[65] Their Chicago company, which was supported by the Grange, the largest and most powerful farmers' association in the country, grew as rapidly as any of the department stores in the same decade. By the 1880s Montgomery Ward was doing a nationwide business. In 1887 its catalogue of 540 pages listed over 24,000 items.

Although specialized retailers and even department stores continued to sell through catalogues, the first serious challenge to Montgomery Ward came in the 1890s, when Sears, Roebuck & Company began to expand.[66] Sears had its beginning when Richard W. Sears and Alvah C. Roebuck joined forces in 1887 to sell watches by mail. Soon they were also marketing jewelry and silverware and, in 1893, added sewing machines, bicycles, and cream separators to their lines. Then in 1895, with Roebuck's retirement, Aaron E. Nusbaum and Julius Rosenwald, experienced Chicago clothing merchants, entered the firm as partners. With this new influx of talent and capital the company grew phenomenally. Dry goods and clothing lines were added. Then, following the example of Montgomery Ward, Sears took on a number of consumer durables, drugs, and, for a short time, even groceries. By 1899 the company had twenty-four merchandising departments. They included dry goods, men's clothing, men's furnishings, cloaks, shoes, notions, jewelry, groceries, drugs, hardware, carriage hardware, stoves, furniture and baby carriages, sewing machines, bicycles, buggies, vehicles, saddlery, sporting goods (including guns), musical instruments, gramaphones, optical goods, stereopticons, and books.[67] In other words, Sears and his new partners decided to sell nearly every product that was being retailed through the existing full-line wholesalers and some (such as sewing machines, bicycles, buggies, and musical instruments) that were being sold directly by the manufacturer. The results of this decision were phenomenal. Sales, which were $138,000 in 1891, soared from $745,000 in 1895 to $10,637,000 in 1900, and to $37,789,000 in 1905; and profits from $68,000 in 1895 to $776,000 in 1900, and $2,868,000 in 1905.[68]

Such astonishing success almost overwhelmed the enterprise. The greatest challenge did not come in creating a purchasing organization. Here the partners merely added new buyers for the new lines, closely following the pattern set a generation earlier by the wholesalers and department stores. Rather it came in building an operating organization that could administer the velocity of flow through the enterprise required by this huge volume of sales.

As in the case of other large-scale marketers, the buyers at Sears had full autonomy. In the words of the company's historians, Boris Emmet and John E. Jeuck: "Each merchandise department was a separate dynasty, and the buyer was in complete charge."[69] He set the specifications, prices paid, volume required, and then decided the price at which the goods would be listed in the catalogue. He even provided the necessary copy to describe and advertise his lines. Each department handled the complaints about its goods and all other correspondence involved in the purchasing and sale of its line. Each set its own wage scales and disciplined its employees. "Company officers were unlikely to interfere so long as the department prospered."

The buyers used the company's purchasing network as well as contacting manufacturers direct. Like the other mass marketers, Sears had a New York branch that concentrated on dry goods and clothing, and agencies abroad. Because it had a greater number and variety of lines than jobbers or department stores, Sears moved into manufacturing on a larger scale than did the other mass marketers. It did so in order to have an assured supply of goods at the volume, specification, and prices desired. By 1906 Sears owned wholly or in part sixteen manufacturing plants which produced safes, stoves, firearms, furniture, saws, farm implements, wire fence, wallpaper, cameras, shoes, vehicles, organs, furniture, plumbing goods, and cream separators.[70] Nevertheless, the Rosenwalds and their associates preferred to buy rather than to manufacture. When they did obtain a factory they made little attempt to go beyond providing necessary capital; they paid little attention to its day-to-day management.

The primary responsibility for coordinating the actual flow of goods from the manufacturer's door to the customer's mailbox belonged to the company's "operating organization." And it was this organization that fell into chaos and had to be drastically reorganized as the sales generated by mailing catalogues rose in geometric proportions. The operating department was "responsible for the receipt of all incoming shipments, storage of goods, filling of all orders, and shipment of all merchandise and catalogues."[71] Under the guidance of Otto Doering, an improved system for handling the massive volume of orders was worked out during the first years of the new century.

Increased speed in handling orders was made possible by the use of machinery and mechanical devices and the creation of an intricate scheduling system. The first was well described in the 1905 catalogue:

Miles of railroad tracks run lengthwise through, in and around this building for the receiving, moving and forwarding of merchandise; elevators, mechanical conveyors, endless chains, moving sidewalks, gravity chutes, apparatus and conveyors, pneumatic tubes and every known mechanical appliance for reducing labor, for the working out of economy and dispatch is to be utilized here in our great Works.[72]

The heart of the new processes was, however, the scheduling system based on a complex rigidly enforced timetable which made it possible to fill a steady stream of orders from a number of different departments. Each department was given a fifteen-minute period in which to send to the assembling room items listed on a specific order. If those items failed to appear in that time period the order was shipped without them. The delayed part of the order was mailed as soon as it was ready by prepaid express, with the negligent department being charged for the extra express costs and paying a fine of 50¢ per item. The new system permitted the filling of over 100,000 orders a day. That involved as many transactions as most traditional merchants in prerailroad days handled in a lifetime.

This kind of organization made possible coordination of the swift growth of the business that recorded annual sales of close to $40 million within a decade of its initial expansion.[73] By then, Sears' volume of sales more than doubled that of Macy's $15 million, and was substantially ahead of the wholesale and retail volume of Marshall Field ($28,480,000). Moreover, Sears' profits of $2,868,000 compared favorably with the $960,000 for Macy's and $1,450,000 for Fields. By 1900 Sears' sales already exceeded Ward's. Since that time, "Sears has been the leader and Ward's the chief competitor."[74]

The ability of Sears and its chief competitor to lower margins and prices by increasing the velocity of flow brought a resounding protest from rural retailers and wholesalers who served them—a protest similar to that raised against the department stores in the 1880s and 1890s.[75] As those stores had concentrated on handling lines in only a few major trades such as dry goods, clothing, and household furnishings, and as they had come early in the fast-growing urban market, the outcry remained local and sporadic. On the other hand, the mail-order houses carried all the goods handled by the country retailers and wholesale jobbers and their great expansion had come at the moment when the growth of the rural market was dropping off. The protest of the country retailers and the wholesale jobbers against the mail-order houses became nationwide during the middle of the first decade of the twentieth century. It reached a crescendo during the debate over the bill to extend parcel post service. Congress finally passed this bill in the summer of 1912. Its opponents fought the proposal bitterly, emphasizing how it would bring ruin to jobbers, retailers, and traveling salesmen. Farm, labor, and consumer groups (spokesmen for catalogue users) pressed for the legislation, while Sears and Montgomery Ward remained discreetly quiet. As the arguments in this debate emphasized, the efficiency of the mass retailing enterprises in reducing margins and prices was one reason for the loud outcry of small businessmen against big business in the Progressive period of American history.

The chain store

Although the chain store had its beginning and first growth in the post-Civil War years, it did not become a significant retailing institution until the first decade of the twentieth century. By the 1920s, however, such stores were established widely enough and had become efficient enough to receive the brunt of the political protest and its legislative manifestations that had been directed against the department store in the 1880s and 1890s and the mail-order houses in the decade after 1900.[76]

Chain stores appeared first in trades and sectors where the existing mass retailers were not yet strongly established. They moved into grocery, drug, and furniture trades rather than into dry goods and apparel. And they located in small towns and cities and on the outskirts of metropolitan areas rather than in large urban centers or in rural areas. At first the chains remained, with a few notable exceptions, regional rather than national. By World War I, however, they were operating nationally and were competing directly with other mass retailers. In the 1920s mail-order enterprises began to build chains of their own. By the 1920s, therefore, the chain store had become the fastest growing type of mass marketer and was becoming the standard instrument for mass retailing in the United States.

The first chain store of any size came in the grocery trade.[77] The Great

American Tea Company, founded in 1859 by George F. Gilman and George Huntington Hartford, was by 1865 operating twenty-six stores, all in the area of lower Broadway and Wall Street. They sold only tea. In 1869 the firm changed its name to the Great Atlantic and Pacific Tea Company and began to extend its chain of stores into the northeast and across the Appalachians. By 1880 it was operating one hundred stores in an area ranging from St. Paul, Minnesota, to Norfolk, Virginia. By then Gilman had retired and Hartford had brought into the enterprise his two sons, George L. and John A., who continued to manage their enterprise until the mid-twentieth century. By 1900 the company had spanned the continent between the Atlantic and the Pacific, though its branches were still concentrated in the northeast. It had sales of $5.6 million and sold a line that included coffee, cocoa, sugar, extracts, and baking powder, as well as tea. In the next decade it began its real growth.

Success brought imitation. Other tea wholesalers built chains and then others did the same in different grocery lines. In 1872 the Jones Brothers Tea Company of Brooklyn was formed; this became the Grand Union Company of today. Ten years later came the Great Western Tea Company, a forerunner of the Kroger Company, and in 1899 the present Jewel Tea Company was founded. By then more than half a dozen grocery chains were in operation in the United States, including the predecessors of American Stores and the First National Stores.

The story was much the same, although on a smaller scale, in the variety store business. Here Woolworth's was the first.[78] In the early 1880s, Frank W. Woolworth opened seven variety stores in southeastern Pennsylvania, that is, small department stores selling low-priced goods. By 1900 the Woolworth enterprise was operating five-and-ten-cent stores with sales over $5 million. Growth quickened and by 1909 the chain had 318 stores in the United States and was beginning to open branches in Britain. Others followed Woolworth's lead. John G. McCrory began a chain also in southeastern Pennsylvania in 1880. S. H. Kress started a similar one in Memphis in 1896, and S. S. Kresge in Detroit in 1899.

Before the turn of the century similar chains had appeared in mass retailing of drugs, shoes, jewelry, furniture, and cigars.[79] Although some, such as United Drug and United Cigar became national, even international in scope, these chains normally had fewer stores, and covered a smaller territory than did Woolworth's, the A & P, and their imitators. In all these trades the chains continued to grow rapidly during the first years of the twentieth century.

The chains in these different trades used variants of the same general organizational structure adopted by other mass marketers.[80] In the chains, each major line had its buyers who made the decisions about specifications of price and volume of orders. As in the department stores and the mail-order houses, the buyers were usually responsible for the private branding of a product and its advertising. As in department stores, they made good use of the advertising agencies. Either the buying department or traffic or shipping department had charge of the shipment of goods and produce from the producers to the branch stores.

The basic difference between the structure of the chain and the other two mass retailers came, of course, in their sales organization. The chains had to administer a number of geographically scattered units. Nearly all the larger chains acquired regional managers with a staff of accountants and "inspectors" or "road men" who kept a constant check on the sales and financial performance of the managers of the individual stores in their own territories. For all these middle managers stock-turn remained the basic criterion for success. The regional officers also advised on marketing policies, displays, personnel, and purchasing, and they made sure that the flow of goods moved into stores as scheduled.

Because they covered a broader and a faster growing market than did either of the other two types of mass retailers, the chains began in the twentieth century to grow more rapidly in number and in volume of sales than did either the mail-order house or the department store. The chains were better suited to respond to the changes in consumer buying resulting from the increased mobility made possible by the coming of the automobile and from the rapid growth of the suburbs. Faced with a declining rural market in the 1920s, the two great mail-order houses—Sears Roebuck and Montgomery Ward—organized chains of several hundred retail stores between 1925 and the coming of the great depression in 1929. Earlier both had constructed new mail order plants in different parts of the country. By the 1930s, department stores, though only in a most tentative way, had begun to build branches in the suburbs of the cities they served. The chains with their geographically widespread network of branches completed the retailing revolution begun by the department stores in the 1860s and the 1870s. They did so because they created administrative organizations that coordinated a higher volume flow of goods from the manufacturer to the largest number of final consumers in an increasingly urban and suburban economy.

The economies of speed

The coming of mass distribution and the rise of the modern mass marketers represented an organizational revolution made possible by the new speed and regularity of transportation and communication. These new enterprises, in turn, made it possible to increase the speed and lower the cost of distribution of goods in the United States even more. Whereas the railroads and telegraph coordinated the flow of goods from the train and express company stations of one commercial center to another, the new mass marketers handled the myriad of trasactions involved in moving a high-volume flow of goods directly from thousands of producers to hundreds of thousands of consumers.

The mass marketers replaced merchants as distributors of goods in the American economy because they internalized a high volume of market transactions within a single large modern enterprise. They reduced the unit costs of distributing goods by making it possible for a single set of workers using a single set of facilities to handle a much greater number of transactions within a specific period than the same number of workers could if they had been scattered in many separate small facilities. At the same time, high-volume stock-turn assured a steady cash flow that permitted the enterprises to purchase larger quantities in cash and so greatly reduce the cost of credit needs and finance distribution of goods. Such savings were, however, possible only if the flow of goods through the enterprise was carefully coordinated. The internal transactions had to be made more quickly and at a greater volume than if they were made in the external market. Economies of scale and distribution were not those of size but of speed. They did not come from building larger stores; they came from increasing stock-turn. To maintain and continue a high volume of flow demanded organizational innovation. It could be achieved only by creating an administrative hierarchy operated by many full-time salaried managers.

To assure a continuing high stock-turn the different types of new mass marketers created much the same sort of organizational structure. All handled the buying and shipping of goods the same way. Only in their marketing organizations did they vary according to the differing nature of their businesses. The sale of agricultural commodities to processors, of finished goods to country general stores and urban retailers, obviously required different methods than over-the-counter sales to urban customers, or catalogue sales to rural buyers.

These new marketing enterprises grew by making maximum use of the administrative networks they had created to coordinate the flow of goods and cash. This they could do by increasing the volume of existing lines, adding new lines, and setting up new outlets. Commodity dealers and the wholesalers were restricted to the first of these strategies of growth, that of increasing volume. The commodity dealer might handle different varieties of grain or of cotton, but his facilities and managers were all trained and organized to handle one basic trade. This too was basically true of the wholesaler, even though the wholesaler in dry goods, hardware, drugs, and the like carried many more different items than the commodity dealer.

The mass retailers, on the other hand, had less difficulty in adding new lines that might use more intensively their buying networks and operating organizations. In addition, they were able to expand volume by building new outlets. As cities and suburbs grew rapidly in the first years of the twentieth century, the mass retailers' markets expanded far more quickly than did those of the commodity dealer or the full-line wholesaler. The profitability of expansion through the building of new outlets caused the chains after 1900 to become the fastest growing type of marketer in the United States.

Because they internalized more market transactions than did the wholesalers, the new mass retailers still further increased the productivity and reduced the costs of the distribution of consumer goods in the United States. Although no measures of productivity have been developed for the distribution sector comparable to those worked out by Albert Fishlow for the railroads, rough indicators emphatically make this point. The new mass retailers were able to reduce their prices below those of the smaller retailer who bought from the wholesaler and were still able to generate higher profits than the wholesalers. The mass retailers' prices were so low that the growth of each type—the department store, mail-order house, and chain store—quickly led to a protest by the wholesalers and the small retailers. These outcries were strong enough to bring state and national legislators to introduce and often pass legislation aimed at protecting wholesalers and small retailers from such price competition. At the same time, the builders of the new retailing enterprises amassed impressive fortunes. The Wanamakers, the Strauses of Macy's, the Gimbels, the Bambergers, the Filenes, the Hutzlers, the Rosenwalds, the Thornes, the Hartfords, the Woolworths, the Kresges, and the Kresses soon ranked among the wealthiest families in the land.

In making their fortunes these entrepreneurs, their closest associates, and their families had to rely on the services of a phalanx of managers. The managerial staff of these enterprises differed, however, from those of railroad and telegraph companies in that there were proportionally a smaller number of middle and top managers. The middle managers—the buyers, department heads, regional supervisors, and the senior advertising, traffic, shipping, and accounting executives—normally made lifetime careers out of their specialities. Only a few owned stock in the company in which they spent most of their lives.

At the top, however, the owners did continue to manage. Unlike the railroads, the new mass marketers remained what I have termed entrepreneurial enterprises. Top policy decisions continued to be made by the builders of the firm and their families who remained the major stockholders. They made the long-term plans and allocated the resources to carry them out. Ownership did not become separated from control because the entrepreneurs who built these enterprises had little need to raise capital through the sale of securities. The large volume of cash flow, supplemented by short-term loans from commercial banks, not only paid for inventory but also provided funds needed for plant and equipment.

In such entrepreneurial enterprises the owner-managers carried out top management functions in a personal and intuitive manner. These senior executives made little effort to develop sophisticated cost and capital accounting methods or to develop long-term planning through capital budgeting and other procedures. On the operating level, the top managers in these mass marketing firms were not innovators in accounting and inventory control. Nor did they, before World War I, attempt to make even short-term systematic forecasts of market demand. Their buyers purchased largely on the basis of past experience and their own intuitive feeling about what the customers would continue to want.

The rise of the mass marketers and the revolution in distribution which they created was of critical importance to the institutional development of the modern American economy. Nevertheless, these enterprises affected the distribution of only part of the goods produced in the American economy. Local farm products and manufactured goods continued to go directly to local customers without passing through the hands of wholesalers or mass retailers. The commission merchant and the commission agent continued to buy, sell, and ship producers' goods which were manufactured on special order for other business enterprises. Such producers' goods as rails, bars, wire, castings, beams, other metal shapes, and a wide variety of machinery continued during the nineteenth century to be sold by the manufacturers directly or by manufacturers' agents selling on commission. Metals, chemicals, and other raw materials purchased by manufacturers from mining and other enterprises were bought either directly or through commission agents.

The marketing revolution based on the coming of the railroad and telegraph came, it cannot be too strongly stressed, only when the output of a large number of producers went to a large number of customers. It came in the marketing of the basic crops and in the production of traditional standardized goods, in such trades as dry goods, clothing, and other cloth products, in shoes, saddlery, and other leather products, in furniture, mill work, and other wood products, in groceries, confectionery, and other food products, in pharmaceutical and other drugs, and in jewelry and tableware. It came primarily in the older industries where the processes of production were labor intensive and technologically simple, and where manufacturing enterprises continued to remain small in size. In the newer industries, those using more complex, high-volume processes of production, the mass producer rather than the mass marketer took over the role of coordinating the flow of goods through the economy.

CHAPTER 8

Mass Production

The basic transformation

The revolution in production came more slowly than did the revolution in distribution, for it required further technological as well as organizational innovation. The new methods of transportation and communication, by permitting a large and steady flow of raw materials into and finished products out of a factory, made possible unprecedented levels of production. The realization of this potential required, however, the invention of new machinery and processes. Once these were developed, manufacturers were able to place within a single establishment (that is, to internalize) several processes of production.

Such mass production techniques came first in industries processing liquids or semiliquids, such as crude oil. They came a little later in a number of mechanical industries, including those processing tobacco and grain. They appeared more slowly in the metal-making and metal-working industries, because there high-volume production required more technological breakthroughs. But when those breakthroughs came, the increases in the speed of output were spectacular. In all these manufacturing establishments, the coordination of high-volume flow through several processes of production led to the hiring of a staff of salaried managers and the development of modern factory procedures and organization.

The basic difference between the coming of mass production and mass distribution lies, therefore, in technology. Mass distribution came primarily through organizational innovation and improvement, using the new forms in transportation and communication. Mass production, on the other hand, normally called for technological as well as organizational innovation. Although technological change has often been defined to include organizational change, it does seem useful to distinguish between them. Technological change in production and distribution refer, for the purposes of this study, to innovations in materials, power sources, machinery, and other artifacts. Organizational change refers to innovation in the ways such artifacts are arranged and the ways in which the movements and activities of workers and managers are coordinated and controlled.

In production an increase in output for a given input of labor, capital, and materials was achieved technologically in three ways: the development of more efficient machinery and equipment, the use of higher quality raw materials, and an intensified application of energy. Organizationally, output was expanded through improved design of manufacturing or processing plants and by innovations in managerial practices and procedures required to synchronize flows and supervise the work force. Increases in productivity also depend on the skills and abilities of the managers and the workers and the continuing improvement of these skills over time. Each of these factors or any combination of them helped to increase the speed and volume of the flow, or what some processors called the "throughput," of materials within a single plant or works. (Hereafter, "plant" means a large facility and "works" means an establishment of many facilities.) For managers of the new processes of production a high rate of throughput—usually in terms of units processed per day—became as critical a criterion of performance as a high rate of stock-turn was for managers of mass distribution.

Where the underlying technology of production permitted, increased throughput from technological innovations, improved organizational design, and perfected human skills led to a sharp decrease in the number of workers required to produce a specific unit of output. The ratio of capital to labor, materials to labor, energy to labor, and managers to labor for each unit of output became higher. Such high-volume industries soon became capital-intensive, energy-intensive, and manager-intensive.

Mass production industries can then be defined as those in which technological and organizational innovation created a high rate of throughput and therefore permitted a small working force to produce a massive output. Mass production differed from existing factory production in that machinery and equipment did more merely replace manual operation. They made possible a much greater output at each stage in the overall process of production. Machinery was placed and operated so that the several stages were integrated and synchronized technologically and organizationally within a single industrial establishment. As a result, the speed of throughput was faster at each stage than if each stage had been carried on in separate establishments.

The possibility of achieving high-speed throughput, or mass production, depended on the basic technology of the production processes. Agriculture offered little potential for a sharp accleration of the flow of materials through the processes of production. There, speed and volume rarely reached a level high enough to stimulate organizational and managerial innovation. In the raising of corn, cotton, wheat, and other crops, biological constraints determined the time of preparing the soil, sowing, cultivating, and harvesting, and so set the speed of the overall processes of production. Improved strains of crops and better fertilizers increased output per acre worked; improved machinery made it possible to carry out the different processes of production at a somewhat greater speed. But the need almost never arose to devise organizational procedures to integrate and coordinate the processes. Therefore, the family was able to remain the basic agricultural working unit; and the farmer, his family, and a handful of hired helpers relied, until the twentieth century, on human and animal power to work farm implements and machines.

Much the same could be said of the building and construction trades and the mining industries in the nineteenth and early twentieth centuries. Improved machinery increased output and permitted some integration of tasks. In the building industries, however, the tasks remained the traditional ones of the carpenter, bricklayer, plasterer, and the like. The working of mines involved little more than having small teams of men doing much the same thing in different parts of the mine. Until the twentieth century the workers in both these industries relied largely on hand tools. Here, as in agriculture, there was little opportunity to speed up the processes of production by a more intense application of energy. There was little need to build a complex organization to coordinate the flow of goods from one process to another. These industries long remained labor-intensive.

In the mechanical industries (those where machinery replaced men, as in the production of cloth, leather, and wood and products made from such materials), improved technology and the application of nonhuman energy played a larger role. The need for internal organization was more obvious. As the output of the enterprise grew, each process of production was organized into a major department, with its own specialized machines, which were normally operated from one central source of power. Coordination and control of the subunits therefore required close supervision of the machines and the men who tended them.

Yet in these mechanical industries the possibilities of accelerating the velocity of production was limited. Essentially, machines took the place of manual operations. A machine did a task comparable to that of a worker in spinning, weaving, sewing, cutting, and fabricating. The maximum speed of cutting or shaping wood, cloth, or textile products by machinery was quickly reached. Nor did the spinning and weaving of natural fibers or the tanning of natural leather lend itself to massive increase of throughput by a greater application of energy. Since the speed of production was limited and since this energy was used for little more than powering the machines, the requirements for coordination and control remained relatively simple. These mechanical industries continued to be labor-intensive, and the type of organization developed by the early textile mills remained satisfactory. The only important change was the centralization of management in a single office, usually at the mill site.

In some mechanical industries, however, machinery did more than merely replace the manual operations in each process of production. Machines also integrated these processes. The application of continuous-process machinery and nearly continuous-process factories to the production of tobacco, grain products, canned foodstuffs, soap, and film greatly increased the volume of output and sharply decreased the labor force required in processing. The new high-speed operations brought fundamental changes in the enterprises that adopted them and the industries in which they were located.

The furnace and foundry and the distilling and refining industries lent themselves more readily to mass production than did the mechanical industries. In those industries, where the processes of production required the application of heat and involved chemical rather than mechanical methods, improved technology, a more intensified use of energy, and improved organization greatly expanded the speed of throughput and reduced the number of workers needed to produce a unit of output. Enlarged stills, superheated steam, and cracking techniques all brought high-volume, large-batch, or continuous-process production of products made from petroleum, sugar, animal and vegetable fats, and some chemicals, and in the distilling of alcohol and spirits and the brewing of malt liquors. In the furnace industries (those producing iron, steel, copper, other metals, and glass), better furnaces, converters, and rolling and finishing equipment, all of which required a more intensive use of energy, did much the same. The resulting increase in the speed and volume of production put a premium on developing plant design to assure the maximum use of equipment in order to assure a steady and smooth flow of the maximum amount of materials through the processes of production.

In the metal-working industries, the requirements of high-volume output brought the most significant technological and organizational innovations. In metal-working, production involved a greater number of processes (both chemical and mechanical) than in other industries. It used a wider variety of machinery and equipment and of raw and semi-finished materials. Metal was more difficult to cut and shape than cloth, leather, or wood. Much finer tolerances were needed in the making of machinery and other metal products than in the production of apparel and furniture. Therefore, the coordination of the flow of materials through a metal-working establishment was highly complex. Not surprisingly, the most significant innovations in machine tools appeared in these industries, and it was here that the practices and procedures of modern systematic or scientific factory management were devised and perfected.

In modern mass production, as in modern mass distribution and modern transportation and communications, economies resulted more from speed than from size. It was not the size of a manufacturing establishment in terms of number of workers and the amount and value of productive equipment but the velocity of throughput and the resulting increase in volume that permitted economies that lowered costs and increased output per worker and per machine. The savings resulting from the use of the same light, power, and maintenance facilities were tiny compared with those achieved by greatly increasing the daily use of equipment and personnel. Central to obtaining economies of speed were the development of new machinery, better raw materials, and intensified application of energy, followed by the creation of organizational designs and procedures to coordinate and control the new high-volume flows through several processes of production. In industries where the processes of production had the potential for such technological innovation—and this was not the case in many industries—a manufacturing establishment that exploited such a potential was able to produce a greater output at lower cost than could a larger plant or works that had not adopted similar improvements. In such mass production industries, organizational and technological innovators acquired a powerful competitive advantage.

An analysis of the rise of mass production and the enterprises that came to manage it requires a general look at the changing technology of production after the 1850s, with special consideration of those industries where technological and organizational innovation permitted a sharp increase in throughput and so led to the rise of the modern factory. For the modern factory was as much the specific organizational response to the needs of the new production technology as the railroad and the telegraph enterprises were responses to the operational needs of the new technologies of transportation and communication, and as the mass marketing firm was to the opportunities created by those same technological advances.

Expansion of the factory system

As emphasized earlier, the beginnings of factory production in industries other than textiles had to wait for the opening of the anthracite coal fields in Pennsylvania. Before the mid-1830s, when coal became available in quantity for industrial purposes, nearly all production was carried on in small shops or at home. American manufacturing was still seasonal and rural. Workers were recruited when they were needed from the local farm population and paid in kind as well as wages. There was as yet only a tiny industrial proletariat and a minuscule class of industrial managers.

Coal provided the energy to power the new machines. More important, it generated the high and steady heat needed in the more advanced methods of production in the refining and distilling and in the furnace and foundry industries. The new availability of coal, in turn, permitted the rise of the modern iron industry and with it the modern machine-making and other metal-working industries in the United States.

Whereas coal, iron, and machines provided the energy, materials, and equipment required for modern factory production, the coming of the railroad and the telegraph encouraged the rapid spread of this form of production. The railroad and the telegraph became themselves large new markets for the metal-working industries. During the 1850s, rails, wheels, spikes, and other railroad products consumed over 20 percent of pig iron produced; the rerolling of worn rails provided rail mills with another substantial business.[1] Railroads also came to be the major markets for wood, glass, upholstery, and even India rubber springs. The demand for wire, both iron and copper, rose sharply as the telegraph network was thrown across the country in the 1850s and 1860s. Rarely has a single market become so important so quickly to an industry as the new and rapidly growing transportation and communication networks did in the primary metals industries during the 1850s.

But of far more importance to the expansion of the factory system was the reliability and speed of the new transportation and communication. Without a steady, all-weather flow of goods into and out of their establishments, manufacturers would have had difficulty in maintaining a permanent working force and in keeping their expensive machinery and equipment operating profitably. Moreover, the marketing revolution based on the railroad and telegraph, by permitting manufacturers to sell directly to wholesalers, reduced requirements for working capital and the risk of having unsold goods for long periods of time in the hands of commission merchants. Reduced risks and lower credit costs encouraged further investment in plant, machinery, and other fixed capital.

On the basis of cheap power and heat and of quick and reliable transportation and communication, the factory spread rapidly during the 1840s and 1850s. It became the standard form of production in the metal-making and metal-working and in the refining and distilling industries. It replaced the home and the shop in the making of carriages, wagons, furniture, and other wood products, as well as in the production of cloth. The improvements in the sewing machine brought the factory into the production of shoes and clothing. By the 1870s the one remaining vestige of the older putting-out system was in the making of clothing in or near some of the largest cities.[2] After the Civil War the factory system expanded even more rapidly. As Carroll D. Wright pointed out in the introduction to the census of manufactures for 1880:

Of the nearly three millions of people employed in the mechanical industries of this country at least four-fifths are working under the factory system. Some of the other remarkable instances of the application of the system [besides those in textiles] are to be found in the manufacture of boots and shoes, of watches, musical instruments, clothing, agricultural implements, metallic goods generally, fire-arms, carriages and wagons, wooden goods, rubber goods, and even the slaughtering of hogs. Most of these industries have been brought under the factory system during the past thirty years.[3]

In the refinery and distilling and the furnace and foundry industries the proportion of workers employed in comparable industrial establishments was probably even higher.

In those mechanical industries where heat was not used in the processes of production, the management of new factories remained relatively simple. Coordination of operations and supervision of workers required little more attention to plant design and organizational procedures than in the textile factories at Lowell during the 1830s. The machinery needed to fabricate and assemble products made of wood, leather, and cloth was relatively easy to operate. Normally, the set of machines used to carry out one stage of several specialized operations was placed in a single room, floor, or building, and the machine tenders and their supervisors formed a department. Each department was then located so that the product moved seriatim through several processes. The final packing or packaging of the materials required little in the way of complex machinery. In such establishments the factory manager was able to supervise personally the foremen or overseers responsible for the operations of each department and to coordinate the flow of materials through them. Neither he nor the owners felt the need for a formalized administrative procedure.

Nor were they pressed to improve their accounting and other statistical controls. Prime costs—those of labor and materials—made up the greater part of total expenses and were easy to determine. Raw and semifinished materials were few in number. Small overhead costs were allocated in the same rough manner as they had been in the 1830s in the large textile factories. Depreciation on capital equipment was handled in the same informal ad hoc way.

During the 1850s and again in the 1870s, depressed years in their industry, leading textile manufacturers, the largest enterprises in American mechanical industries, began to pay closer attention to cost accounting. From the 1850s on they developed "mill accounts," which permitted them to obtain an accurate picture of prime costs every six months. The Lyman Mills in Holyoke, Massachusetts, for example, began in the fifties to set up mill accounts for cotton, payrolls, and overhead.[4] In the last category charges for starch, fuel, and other supplies, as well as "teaming" (that is, local transportation) were allocated to each of Lyman's mills at the Holyoke site according to its floor area, number of looms, and rated horsepower. These factory accounts were sent to Boston, where the treasurer and directors computed profits on the basis of these costs.

Not until 1886, however, did the company begin to analyze unit costs for their specific products. Then, as on the railroads, these cost data became managerial tools. They were used to rationalize internal operations, to check on the productivity of the workers, to control the receipt and use of cotton, and to check the efficiency of minor improvements in machinery or plant design. On the other hand, these statistical data were not used in pricing or in making investment decisions concerning the expansion or contraction of existing lines. Such decisions remained almost entirely with the firm's selling agent.

One reason that plant design and organization changed relatively little in the non-heat-using (and so less energy-intensive) mechanical industries was that, after the initial creation of the factory, technological innovation failed to increase dramatically the speed and volume of throughput. Once the new power-driven machines were perfected, increases in output and productivity came in an incremental manner. Machines were speeded up, but only at a relatively slow rate.

The major innovations in textile machinery were completed even before 1850.[5] The giant steps came in the earlier decades with the spread of the large innovative mills that integrated all the processes of weaving with those of spinning. After that, the growing skills of workers and foremen may have been as important as improved machinery in increasing the speed of production and the output per worker and per unit of capital invested.[6] According to one estimate, such incremental improvements in skills and machinery permitted a factory of 30,000 spindles making print cloth to have in 1891 the output equivalent to one of 40,000 spindles twenty years earlier. In the cutting and shaping of cloth and leather, few significant innovations occurred after workers and facilities in the factories were adjusted to the sewing machine.

Much the same pattern occurred in the woodworking industries. For example, G. & D. Cole Company of New Haven in 1850 expanded its small carriage-making activities from a brick building 28 feet by 50 feet to a "mammoth" establishment. By concentrating on a single style, by obtaining the advanced wood-cutting machinery, and by carefully designing the works, with each process in its appropriate room, the firm increased production from 3 to 25 carriages a week and soon to 2,500–3,000 a year.[7] After that, growth came primarily by adding more men and machines. By the outbreak of the Civil War, nearly all the machines needed to mass produce wooden products had been perfected.[8] The factories of the nation's largest carriage manufacturers in the 1890s were similar in appearance, nature of work, technology, plant design, and organization, as those of the Cole Company in the 1850s. The speed and volume of throughput increased steadily but slowly. After forty years the nation's largest carriage makers, using the most sophisticated wood-cutting machinery, the minutest subdivision of labor, the most carefully designed plants, and nationwide marketing agencies, had an output of 40,000 to 50,000 carriages a year. When the metal automobile replaced the wooden carriage, output in the production of transportation vehicles increased at a much greater rate to a much greater volume.

The processes of production in other non-heat-using industries had the same characteristics as those making cloth, leather, and wood products. Total output was increased more by adding men and machines than by continuing technological and organizational innovation. For this reason the increased size of the enterprise brought few advantages in terms of increased productivity and decreased costs.

Changes in the organization of enterprises in these mechanical industries were more a response to marketing than to technological developments. The ability, after the coming of the railroad and telegraph, to sell directly to jobbers for cash simplified both marketing and finance. As a result, management tended to become centralized in the hands of two or three partners or large stockholders. No longer did the president and treasurer of an enterprise reside in the large commercial center and the partner or agent in charge of production at the distant mills. The offices were usually in one place, normally at the mill, with one partner handling finances and another production; either of them or a third partner bought materials from commodity dealers and sold finished goods to jobbers. In the late nineteenth century even the New England textile mills centralized control of these three basic functions at a single headquarters.

Beyond centralizing their activities there was relatively little change in the technology or organization of production in these mechanical industries after the substitution of machinery for manual operation. In these industries, until well into the twentieth century, the relatively labor-intensive and simple mechanical technology created few pressures or opportunities to develop new types of machinery, new forms of factory or plant design, or new ways of management. Small incremental improvements continued in technology and organization and in the skills of workers and their managers. As a result neither the technology nor the organization of the modern factory evolved out of the production processes in the older mechanical industries of textiles, apparel, and other clothing products, of shoes, saddlery, and other leather products, of furniture, wagons, and other wooden products.

The mechanical industries

In the late 1870s and early 1880s, however, mass production did come to some mechanical industries not using heat. Machines did more than replace manual operations. They were used to integrate several processes of production. Such innovations came in several industries at almost precisely the same time, and they appeared primarily in those processing agricultural products rather than cloth, leather, or wood.

The innovations were of two types. They resulted in either the adoption of continuous-process machines that turned out products automatically or the building of factories or plants in which materials flowed continuously from and through one stage to the next. Both greatly increased the ratio of output to workers and reduced the number of laborers involved in the production process within a single establishment. Workers did little more than feed materials into the machines, keep an eye on their operations, and, in some cases, where it was not yet done automatically, package the final product. The new machinery was rarely expensive. Therefore, although the industries in which they were used became capital-intensive—that is, the ratio of capital to labor became high—the new process of production did not require a heavy capital investment. Because these machines and plants sharply lowered unit costs, they gave the enterprises that first adopted them impressive market power.

One of the most dramatic examples of the new continuous-process machinery came in the tobacco industry. In 1881, James Bonsack patented a cigarette-making machine that could, even in its experimental stage, produce over 70,000 cigarettes in a ten-hour day.[9] By the late 1880s, one machine was turning out over 120,000 a day. At that time the most highly skilled hand workers were making 3,000 a day. Fifteen such machines could fill the total demand for cigarettes in the United States in 1880, and thirty could have saturated the 1885 market.

The machine integrated the processes of production in the following way. It swept the tobacco onto an "endless tape," compressed it into a round form, wrapped it with tape and paper, carried it to a "covering tube," which shaped the cigarette, pasted the paper, and then cut the resulting rod into the length of cigarette desired. According to the consultant who tested the machine for the leading British tobacco company, W. D. and H. O. Wills, it cut the cost of wages from 4 shillings to 0.3 pence per thousand cigarettes. When the initial costs of the machine, royalties, and depreciation were taken into account, the total cost of producing a thousand cigarettes was reduced from 5 shillings (60 pence) to 10 pence. Costs were further reduced when Bonsack, James B. Duke, and others perfected machinery to make the packages for cigarettes and then to place them into the package automatically. Not surprisingly, the first two firms to adopt the Bonsack machine—those of James B. Duke in the United States and Wills in Britain—dominated the cigarette industry and then the larger tobacco industry in their own countries. Within a decade they were joined in battle for the world market.

The invention of comparable machines revolutionized other industries. In 1881, four enterprises using the most efficient match-making machines combined to produce a machine that made matches by the billions and also automatically packed them in boxes.[10] Their company, Diamond Match, at once dominated the world match trade and continued to do so until well into the twentieth century. In the early 1880s, Procter & Gamble, using a new high-volume mechanical crusher for soap-making, registered the Ivory brand that made the firm the leader in its industry. In 1884, George Eastman invented, and by the end of the decade perfected, a continuous-process method for making photographic negatives by using gelatin emulsion on film instead of glass plates. His company dominates the photographic industry to this day.

The creation of a continuous-process or automatic factory was more complex than the invention of a single machine. It involved a number of inventions, each of which had to be synchronized with the others; it also required perfection in plant design. Probably the most important of these continuous-process factories was "the automatic all-roller, gradual-reduction mill" used to process wheat and other grains.[11] The first such mill was completed on an experimental basis in Minneapolis in 1879. Its creator, Cadwallader Colden Washburn, and his leading rivals, the Pillsbury brothers, improved and perfected these mills in the next decade.

Flour mills had used continuous-process machinery since Oliver Evans built his mill on Brandywine Creek near Wilmington, Delaware, in 1787. Such mills were small and operated seasonally. Only after the grain-growing regions had expanded and after the railroad and ancillary storage facilities permitted high-volume year-round operation did demand for the large automatic mill appear. The need to find more efficient ways to process the hard-grain spring wheat of the northern prairies intensified the search for processing innovations in the Minneapolis area. The result was a series of innovations, some borrowed from Hungarian and other European millers and others invented at home. They involved gradual reduction, multiple grinding, steel rollers to replace grindstones, purifiers and aspirators, and reels for scalping, grading, and dressing the flour. Central to this development, of course, was the design of the plant to make the maximum use of all this machinery. Figures 3 and 4 indicate how the first such plant was designed to assure continuing high-speed throughput.

The "new process" mills, as they were known, produced high-quality flour in high volume and at low unit cost. Theirs quickly became the standard processing technology in Minneapolis and then in other milling centers. The daily average output for the Minneapolis mills was 274

Figure 3. Floor plan of Washburn automatic, all-roller, gradual-reduction mill, June 1879

All extraneous matter has been left out of the drawing, including partitions, elevators, some shafting, and shafting supports. On the lowest machine floor stood the four break-roller assemblies (1, 8, 17, 31) and the ten reduction assemblies; on the intermediate floor, the purifiers; on the top floor, the bolting chests with their round reels and aspirators (e.g., 29). The machines are numbered to correspond to the flow chart (figure 4). Of the roller assemblies, 1, 4, 7, 11, 14, 16, and 31 were belt-run; the remainder were gear-paired. Though this mill is called experimental, it produced flour until 1899.

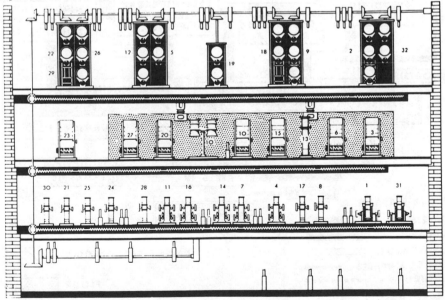

Source: John Storck and Walter Dorwin Teague, *Flour for Man's Bread: A History of Milling* (Minneapolis: University of Minnesota Press, 1952), p. 248.

Figure 4. Flow chart of Washburn experimental flour mill, June 1879

The numbers correspond to the machines in the floor plan (figure 3). As indicated at the upper left corner, the tailings of all purifiers were treated along with other stocks to make low-grade flour.

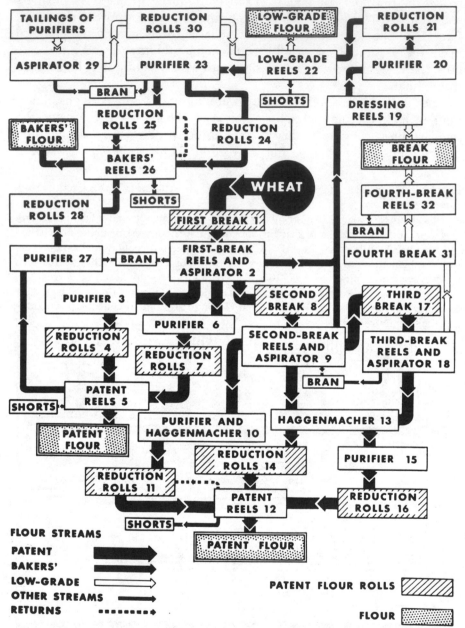

Source: Storck and Teague, *Flour for Man's Bread*, p. 250.

barrels in 1874; it had risen to 1,837 by the end of the 1880s, with some mills having a much larger capacity.[12] By 1882 Minneapolis was already producing 3 million bushels of flour annually. By 1885 the output had risen to 5 million and by 1890 over 7 million. Comparable developments occurred in the milling of oats, barley, rye, and other grains. In the milling of oats, the output was so high that the leading processors had to invent the modern breakfast cereal industry in order to dispose of their surpluses.

A comparable continuous-process factory for processing agricultural crops came in 1883, when two brothers, Edwin and O. W. Norton, put into production the first "automatic line" canning factory.[13] Their new machinery was so arranged that cans were soldered at the rate of 50 a minute, while other machines added tops and bottoms at the rate of 2,500 to 4,400 an hour. The firms that first came to use the new machinery on a year-round basis—Campbell Soup, Heinz, and Borden's Milk—at once became and still remain, nearly a century later, among the largest canners in the country.

In all these industries the new continuous-process technology appeared very quickly after the railroad and telegraph created the potential for mass production. Clearly, as Jacob Schmookler has pointed out,[14] demand is a basic stimulant to technological innovation; but the precise timing of such innovations in production, like the organizational innovations in marketing, can be related more closely to the new speed and volume at which materials and goods could flow through the economy than to any change in demand resulting from an obvious shift upward in the rate of growth of population and income.

The adoption of the new machinery and improved plant design, by sharply increasing output and decreasing unit costs, had a profound effect on the enterprises and the industries in which they were used. Although these innovations were central to the rise of the large modern industrial enterprise that integrated mass production with mass distribution, they had much less impact on the organization of the modern industrial factory. As in the case of other mechanical industries, once the new machinery and equipment and plant design were perfected, increases in output and decreases in cost leveled off. Continuing growth and productivity came after the initial innovations in a slower, incremental manner.

The refining and distilling industries

Mass production came in much the same way in the refining and distilling industries as in continuous-process mechanical industries, though in a less dramatic manner and at an earlier period in time. It appeared earlier because of the ease in integrating the flow of liquids through the processes of production and because the chemical nature of these processes permitted the application of more intense heat to expand the volume of throughput from a set of facilities. As in the case of the mechanical industries, these new high-volume, large-batch, or continuous-process production methods had a profound impact on the growth and organization of the enterprises and the structure of the industries in which they were used. But precisely because of the ease of controlling and coordinating throughput, their operation had only a little more impact on the development of modern systematic or scientific management methods than did the supervision of the processes of production in the non-heat-using mechanical industries.

Of all the refining and distilling industries, the development of the technology of mass production is best documented in petroleum. A review of the history of petroleum technology helps to identify the elements of mass production. The decade following Colonel Edwin L. Drake's discovery of oil in 1859 in Titusville, Pennsylvania, was, understandably, the most innovative in the improvement of the refining process. In the 1860s, the rapid building of railroad lines into the oil regions of northwestern Pennsylvania and the equally quick development of the railroad rack car permitted bulk movements of refined and crude petroleum.

The refiners initially increased output per facility by applying heat more intensively. They developed the use of superheated steam distillation, which they borrowed from recent innovations in the refining of sugar.[15] Next they devised the "cracking" process, a technique of applying higher temperatures to higher boiling points to reshape the molecular structure of crude oil. Such cracking permitted as much as a 20 percent increase in yield from a single still. The output of stills was further expanded by the use of seamless, wrought iron and steel bottoms; by improving cooling as well as heating operations; and by changing the fundamental design of stills so as to increase further the temperature used.

As the individual units were enlarged and made more fuel-intensive, the operation of the units within a single refinery was more closely integrated. Steam power was increasingly used to move the flow of oil through the plant from one refining process to another. In the late 1860s and early 1870s P. H. Van der Weyde and Henry Rogers began to develop and then Samuel Van Sickle perfected continuous-process, multiple-stage distillation. This innovation permitted petroleum to flow through the refinery at a steady rate and separate products to be distilled out at different stages—first gasoline, then kerosene, and then the heavy fuels and lubrication stock. Because so much of the demand for refined petroleum in the 1870s was for kerosene, Van Sickle's innovation was not fully used by

American refineries. Instead, refineries continued to handle one line of products, with the large stills producing kerosene and heavy fuels and lubricants being made in smaller ones. Although most American refineries continued to use what was essentially a large-batch rather than a continuous-process, they were designed to permit a regular and steady flow of material through the works (see figure 5). Labor was needed only to package the product. As the industry's historians, Harold F. Williamson and Arnold Daum, have explained:

Figure 5. Flow chart, Pratt Refinery, 1869

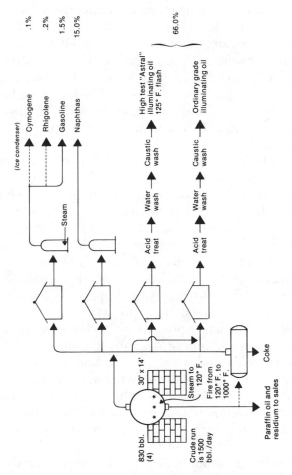

Source: Harold F. Williamson and Arnold R. Daum, *The American Petroleum Industry: The Age of Illumination, 1859–1899* (Evanston, Ill.: Northwestern University Press, 1959), p. 280.

By 1870, elimination of nearly all manual movements of oil distinguished not only large refineries like Charles Pratt's in New York City. The smallest decently appointed refinery with less than 1,000 barrels weekly capacity likewise had six steam pumps: to move the crude from tank car to storage tank and all other points; to pump water, distillate, and refine oil; and to power the air compressor for treating.[16]

Increased size of still, intensified use of energy, and improved design of plant brought rapid increase in throughput. Early in the decade, normal output was 900 barrels a week; it reached 500 barrels a day by 1870. Large refineries already had a charging capacity of 800 to 1,000 barrels a day and even more. At the same time, unit costs fell from an average of 6¢ to 3¢ a barrel, and cost of building a refinery rose from $30,000–$40,000 to $60,000–$90,000.[17] The size of the establishment was still small, in terms of capital invested, costing no more than two miles of well-laid railroad track. But the economies of speed were of critical importance. And one does not need to be an economic historian to identify the senior partner of the fastest refinery in the west in 1869. The high speed of throughput and the resulting lowered unit cost gave John D. Rockefeller his initial advantage in the competitive battles in the American petroleum industry during the 1870s.[18]

Similar, though less dramatic, developments occurred in other distilling and refining industries in these same years. The coming of steam refining and the expansion of the railroad network brought a revolution in sugar-making during the 1850s.[19] The innovation of superheated steam and a vacuum process (both were borrowed by petroleum refiners) and a steam-driven centrifugal machine for crystallizing sugar all greatly accelerated the velocity and volume of throughput in a single refinery. Many new large refineries were built in the 1850s and 1860s to use the new processes. Output soared, prices dropped, but until the 1870s an expanding market assured continuing profits.

Comparable high-volume production technology appeared for the processing of cotton and linseed oil; for the production of alcohol, sulphuric and other acids, and white and red lead and other pigments; for the distilling of liquor; and for the brewing of ale and beer. According to the testimony of one producer of sulphuric acid, a product essential in the refining of petroleum, output in 1882 had "increased nearly a 1,000 percent in the past ten years. In 1866, the price was 5 cents per pound, today it is 1¼ cents."[20] Coal and railroad transportation permitted enormous expansion in the output of individual breweries producing beer and ale. In 1860 the largest breweries averaged an output of 5,000 to 8,000 barrels a year. By 1877 they were producing over 100,000 and by 1895 from 500,000 to 800,000 barrels a year.[21] Careful use of piping and then

assembly-line bottling machines helped to make the process more continuous. In the making of beer and distilled liquors, as in the production of
sugar and margarine, taste requirements demanded sets of skills by the
brewmaster, sugar master, and their counterparts. Such requirements put
a constraint on the volume permitted by the application of new technology, the intensified use of energy, and improved plant design.

The history of these distilling and refining industries demonstrates the
basic axiom of mass production. Economies and lower unit costs resulted
from an intensification of the speed of materials through an establishment
rather than from enlarging its size. They came more from organization
and technological innovations that increased the velocity of throughput
than from adding more men and machines. The potential for mass production thus reflected the basic nature of the processes of production.
Cost savings comparable to those achieved by increased velocity of
throughput in the petroleum, sugar, and other large-batch, continuous-
process industries were not possible in apparel, wood-working, leatherworking and similar small-batch and craft industries. By 1883, two-fifths
of the world's production of petroleum products was being produced in
three large refineries. An attempt to place two-fifths of the nation's production of cotton textiles, men's suits or shoes, or furniture in three facilities would have been absurd. The diseconomies of scale would have far
outweighed any possible economies.

As in the case of continuous-process mechanical industries, such as
cigarettes, matches, milling, and canning, increased velocity of throughput in refining and distilling made production capital-intensive and energy-intensive. In oil refineries, where workers were employed primarily
to package the product, the average number of laborers rose from 110 in
1880 to 189 in 1899, and the total number of workers in the industry from
9,869 to 12,199; in the same two decades, the number of refineries dropped
from 89 to 75 and value of the output rose from $43.7 to $123.9 million.[22]

In these industries, too, efficient production resulted more from organizational improvements in layout of plants and works than from the
development of new administrative structures and procedures. Supervision of the working force required little more in the way of systemic procedures than with the much larger force in textile and shoe factories. Nor
was costing much more of a problem. Crude oil, coal, and sulphuric acid
were the main materials used by an oil refinery. Their costs were easily
calculated. The overall capital investment and fixed costs were still only
a small part of the total costs. They were tiny compared with those of a
railroad. So although the leading refiners appeared to have kept a close
watch on prime costs, they paid little attention to accounting for overhead
costs or determining depreciation. For example, after the formation of the

Standard Oil Trust in 1882, senior executives received monthly cost statements of prime costs that permitted calculation of unit costs.[23] They were soon using comparative costs-and-yield statements to evaluate the performance of their refineries and to make their decisions to concentrate production in large units. Yet there is no evidence that they began to develop sophisticated methods to account for overhead expense and for depreciation in their costs calculations. Nor do the excellent records of the Pabst Brewing Company, the largest brewing enterprise in the United States, reveal the use of modern accurate cost accounting, although in the 1880s executives gave some thought to depreciation in evaluating the worth of plant and equipment for inventory, tax, and insurance purposes.[24]

Mass production came even more quickly and at an earlier period in refining, distilling, and other industries employing chemical processes than it did in mechanical industries able to adopt continuous-process machinery. The resulting increase in output led to the formation of giant integrated enterprises. In both types of industries, however, the fact that effective coordination and control could be achieved by improved design of plants and works lessened the challenge to innovate in methods and procedures to regulate and systematize the movement of workers and managers, that is, lessened the challenge to innovate in factory management.

The metal-making industries

Modern factory management was first fully worked out in the metal-making and metal-working industries. In metal-making, it came in response to the need to integrate (that is to internalize) within a single works several major processes of production previously carried on in different locations. In metal-working, it arose from the challenges of coordinating and controlling the flow of materials within a plant where several processes of production had been subdivided and were carried on in specialized departments. In both metal-making and metal-working, the processes of production became increasingly mechanized, capital-intensive, and energy consuming. But because the materials were so hard to process and more difficult to work than in the mechanical or refining industries, mass production came in a slower, more evolutionary manner. In the metal-making and metal-working industries the drive to mass production required far more intricate and costly machinery, a more intensive use of energy, an even greater attention to the design of works and plants, and for the first time, concentration on the development of systematic practices and procedures of factory management.

In metal-making, the challenge of scheduling, coordination, and controlling the flow of work came only after more than one process had been placed in a single works. On the old "iron plantations" facilities had been too small and the technology too crude to create a need for internal scheduling and control or to permit a greater increase in output through careful plant design and improved management procedures. Then, the iron industry began to "disintegrate" in the 1830s and 1840s, when the availability of coal permitted a greater and steadier output and when many of the plantations had exhausted their ore supplies. Blast furnaces, forges, and rolling and finishing mills were soon operating in different establishments.

The reintegration of the iron-making processes came quickly. It first appeared with the building of the earliest large rail mills in the 1850s. As one rail mill normally consumed the output of two or three blast furnaces, there was an obvious advantage to placing the blast furnaces and final shaping mills within a single works.[25] By 1860 the four biggest integrated rail mills were the largest enterprises in the iron industry. Soon they were producing wire, beams, and merchant bar iron as well as rails. The capitalization of each was over $1 million. Not only was equipment costly but also the labor force in these mills was large. The ratio of capital to worker was still relatively low; the mills remained relatively labor-intensive. In 1860 the Mountour Iron Works at Danville employed close to 3,000 employees; the Cambria Iron Works at Johnstown, 1,948; the Phoenix Iron Company at Phoenixville, 1,230 (all three were in Pennsylvania); and the Trenton (New Jersey) Iron Works, 786.[26] During the Civil War the number of large integrated iron-making works increased, though they remained about the same in size.

In such integrated rail mills the Bessemer steel process—the first to produce that metal on a massive scale—was introduced into the United States in the late 1860s and early 1870s. And it was in these same mills that the open-hearth process made its appearance in the 1880s. Between 1865 and 1876 eleven iron and steel enterprises installed Bessemer converters.[27] In most cases the converters worked alongside or took the place of the existing puddling and rolling mills. However, Andrew Carnegie's Edgar Thomson Works in Pittsburgh and one or two other rail plants were entirely new ones.

One man, Alexander Lyman Holley, was responsible for the design of these eleven new steel works. This brilliant and versatile engineer had found his calling in bringing to fruition the ideas and plans of Henry Bessemer for the mass production of steel.[28] Holley's achievements were less in technological innovation than in the designing of equipment and facilities and their arrangement within the works. He defined as his primary goal "to assure a very large and regular output." He improved machinery by placing removable bottoms in the converters to shorten the time needed to reline them and by reshaping the form of converters themselves.[29] In Holley's mind, however, the design of the works and the quality of its management were as important as machinery in increasing the velocity of throughput. He emphasized this point in an article printed in the *Metallurgical Review* in 1877, in which he compared steel-producing works in Great Britain and the United States:

In the United States, while the excellent features of Bessemer and Longsbon's plant have been retained, the very first works, and in a better manner each succeeding works, have embodied radical improvements in arrangement and in detail of plant, *the object being to increase the output of a unit of capital and of a unit of working expense.* . . . It will have been observed that the capacity of these works for a very large and regular output, lies chiefly in an arrangement which provides large and unhampered spaces for all the principal operations of manufacture and maintenance, while it at the same time concentrates these operations. The result of concentration which is realized is the saving of rehandling and of the spaces and machinery and cost required for rehandling. A possible result of concentration which has been avoided is the interference of one machine and operation with another. At the same time a degree of elasticity has been introduced into the plant, partly by the duplication and partly by the interchangeableness of important appurtenances, the result being that little or no time is lost if the melting and converting operations are not quite concurrent, or if temporary delays or failures occur in any department of manufacturing or maintenance.

The fact, however, must not be lost sight of that the adaptation of plant, which has thus been analyzed, is not the only important condition of large and cheap production; the technical management of American works has become equally improved. Better organization and more readiness, vigilance and technical knowledge on the part of the management have been required to run works up to their capacity, as their capacity has become increased by better arrangement and appliances.[30]

Holley considered the Edgar Thomson Works his finest creation. He was proud of the installation he had built at his Cambria works at Johnstown, Pennsylvania, but that involved only the placing of the Bessemer units within a large, already existing works (see figure 6).[31] In building the Edgar Thomson Works for Andrew Carnegie he could start from scratch. The comparison of the layout of the two works is illuminating. Cambria was originally built in the 1850s before manufacturers fully appreciated the importance of plant design to productivity. It was constructed with little attention to flow of materials within the works. This had been the case with the layout of other large early works, such as the Du Pont Company's establishment on the Brandywine Creek and the Springfield Armory on the Connecticut River. On the other hand, at Carnegie's new works the site itself, on the Monongahela River at the

Figure 6. Plan of the Cambria Iron Works, 1878

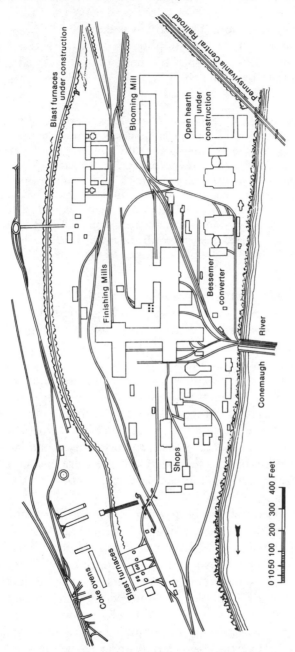

Source: A. L. Holley and Lennox Smith, "Works of the Cambria Iron Company,"
Engineering, 26:22 (July 12, 1878).

junction of three railroads—the Pennsylvania, the Baltimore & Ohio, and the Pittsburgh & Lake Erie—was selected to make the fullest use of existing railroad transportation. The plant was designed to assure as continuous a flow as possible from the suppliers of the raw material through the processes of production to the shipment of the finished goods to the customers. Holley described the works in 1878, three years after operations began, by saying:

As the cheap transportation of supplies of products in process of manufacture, and of products to market, is a feature of first importance, these works were laid out, not with a view of making the buildings artistically parallel with the existing roads or with each other, but of laying down convenient railroads with easy curves; *the buildings were made to fit the transportation.* Coal is dumped from the mine-cars, standing on the elevator track . . . , directly upon the floors of the producer and boilerhouses. Coke and pigiron are delivered to the stockyard with equal facility. The finishing end of the rail-mill is accommodated on both sides by low-level wide-gauge railways. The projected open-hearth and merchant plants have equally good facilities. There is also a complete system of 30-inch railways for internal transportation.[32]

The works relied at first on Carnegie's nearby Lucy and Isabella blast furnaces for their pig iron. Then in 1879 large blast furnaces were built at the plant site. The design of the works (figure 7) permitted the E. T. Works, as they were always called, to become the most efficient steel producer in the nation, and indeed the world.

In addition, Carnegie's blast furnaces—Lucy, Isabella, and then those at the E. T. Works—were the largest and most energy-consuming in the world. By "hard driving," through the use of more intense heat and improved and more powerful blast engines, the Lucy furnace increased production from 13,000 tons in 1872 to 100,000 tons in the late 1890s.[33] By 1890, other furnaces besides those of Carnegie were producing over 1,000 tons a week—an enormous increase over the 70 tons a week of the blast furnaces even as late as the early 1870s.

In the same period similar increases occurred in the output of the succeeding stages of the process and in quickening the flow from the blast furnace to the shipment of the final product. As Peter Temin has noted: "The speed at which steel was made was continually rising, and new innovations were constantly being introduced to speed it further." At the Carnegie works, for example, Bessemer converters became larger, the Thomas-Gilchrist process made possible a large output from open-hearth furnaces, and the Jones mixer accelerated the flow of materials from the blast furnace to converter. Here and at other works the cooling of ingots in the soaking pits was done faster and carrying rollers improved. "Steam and later electric power replaced the lifting and carrying action of human

Figure 7. Plan of the Edgar Thomson Steel Works, ca. 1885

1	Stoves	25	Pump house
2	Stacks	26	Baker blowers
H and I	Blast furnaces, Cast houses Boiler house	27	Boiler house
		28	Old rail mill
3	Boiler house	29	Ingot furnaces
4	Engine houses	30	Blooming mill
F and G	Blast furnaces, Cast houses	31–38	New rail mill
5,	Boiler house	31	Bloom furnaces
D and E	Blast furnaces, Cast houses	32	First roughing train
6	Boiler houses	33	Second roughing train
7	Pump house and tank	34	Finishing train
8	Engine house	35	Hot saws
A	Blast furnace, Cast house	36	Hot beds
B and C	Blast furnaces, Cast houses	37	Straightening and drill presses
13	Boiler houses		
14	Pump house	38	Loading beds
15	Engine house, Engine house wing	39	Boiler house
		39½	Pump house
12	Metal mixer	40	Roll shop
9	Offices and laboratory	41	Forge
10	Shops	42	Warehouse
11	Warehouse	43	Warehouse
16	Locomotive house	44	Office
18–22	Converting dept.	45	Machine, carpenter, and pattern shops
18	Boiler house		
19	Blowing engines and pumps	46	General offices, laboratory, drawing room
19½			
20	Converting house	47	Manganese shed
21	Ladle house	48	Boiler house
21½	Bottom house	49	Limestone crusher
22	Cupolas	50	Elevator
23	Electric light house	51	Switch tower
24	Boiler house		

Source: Carnegie Brothers and Co., *The Edgar Thomson Steel Works and Blast Furnaces* (Pittsburgh, nd).

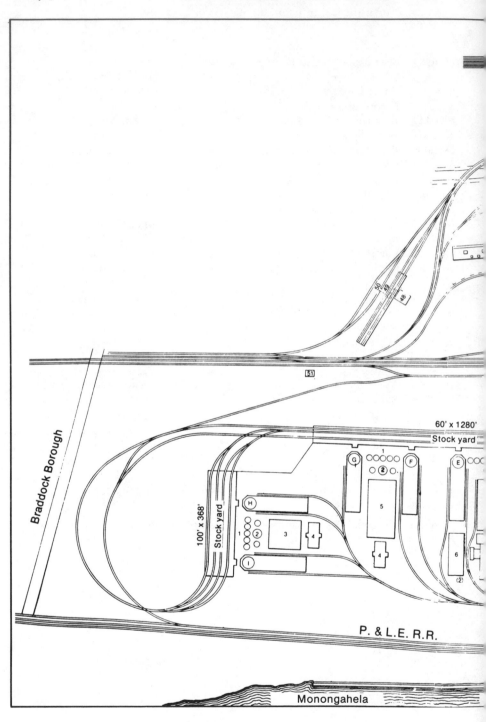

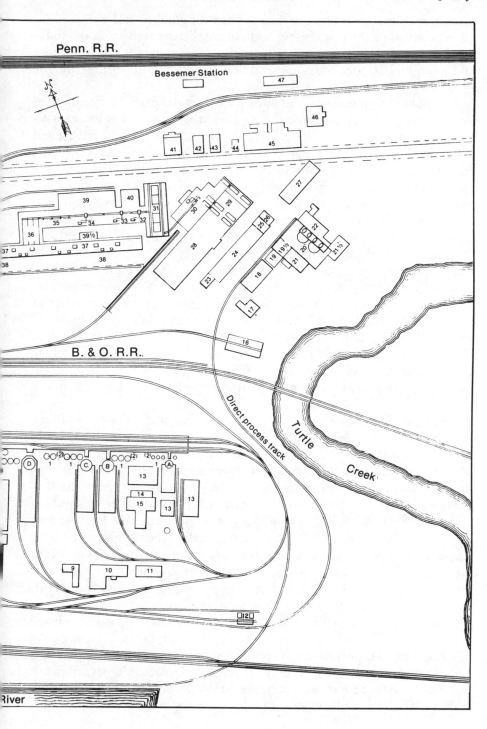

Penn. R.R.

Bessemer Station

B. & O. R.R.

Direct process track

Turtle Creek

River

muscle, mills were modified to handle the steel quickly and with a minimum of strain to the machinery, and people disappeared from the mills. By the turn of the century, there were not a dozen men on the floor of a mill rolling 3,000 tons a day, or as much as a Pittsburgh rolling mill of 1850 rolled in a year."[34]

Technological innovation and improved plant design, which continued to accelerate velocity of throughput, made the processes more capital-intensive and energy consuming. This was true not only of the largest and most efficient works, including those using the new open-hearth furnaces installed in the 1880s, but also of the industry as a whole. Between 1869 and 1899 the average annual output of the blast furnaces rose from 5,000 to 65,000 tons and that for steel works and rolling mills from 3,000 to 23,000 tons.[35] For the same period, the average capital investment for a blast furnace establishment increased four and a half times, from $145,000 to $643,000, and rolling mills eight times, from $156,000 to $967,000. The working force grew more slowly. That for a blast furnace increased from an average of 71 to 176, or two and a half times, and for rolling mills from 119 to 412, or three and a half times. In the same period the number of blast furnace establishments fell from 386 to 223, while the number of steel works and rolling mills stayed at about 400. This great expansion in the speed and volume of output required an immense amount of fuel. Coke, which was just beginning to be used in the United States as fuel in the 1850s, consumed 8.1 million tons of coal in 1885 and 49.5 million tons in 1905.

The greatly increased velocity of flow through these works, as Holley suggested, placed increased demands on their managers. Overall coordination and control was difficult, for unlike an oil or sugar refinery, each part of the production process involved different activities. Moreover, the subunits within the works—the coke ovens, the blast furnaces, the Bessemer converters or open hearths, the rail, wire, beam, and other finishing mills—were managed, in the words of one of the most able steel-makers, John Fritz, as "small principalities, each of them being governed by a despotic foreman."[36] These autocrats handled the day-to-day activities in their units. They hired, fired, and promoted the men who worked under them. Effective coordination of throughput required the placing of vigorous management controls over these despots.

In no metal-making enterprise were the techniques of coordination and control more effectively developed than in those of Andrew Carnegie. In building the administrative structure for his new steel works, Carnegie and his subordinates drew directly from the railroads. Carnegie himself was an experienced railroad executive before he entered iron- and steel-making. At the age of seventeen he had become an assistant to Thomas

Scott, who was then the first superintendent of the Western Division of the Pennsylvania Railroad.[37] When Scott moved up to be vice president, Carnegie succeeded him as division superintendent. He quickly proved himself a most effective manager on one of the busiest divisions of what was then the nation's best-managed railroad.

The Carnegie Company's close relation to the railroads was not unique. The entire output of the first Bessemer plants went into rails. "All of the Bessemer plants had ties of one sort or another with the railroads, usually through the medium of common ownership or directorships."[38] Railroads, in order to assure themselves of such essential supplies, provided much of the capital investment required in the new Bessemer works. The transfer of administrative techniques from the railroads to iron- and steel-producing plants was perfectly natural.

In organizing his steel company, Carnegie put together a structure similar to the one he had worked in on the Pennsylvania Railroad.[39] He appointed the nation's most accomplished steel-maker, Captain William Jones, as general superintendent to oversee the day-to-day work of the superintendents in charge of the blast furnaces, Bessemer converters, railroad mills, bridge-making plants, and other departments. As general managers, Carnegie selected William P. Shinn, a highly competent railroad executive who had been appointed the general agent of the Pennsylvania Company (the subsidiary that operated the Pennsylvania's lines north and west of Pittsburgh) when it was formed in 1871. "It was Shinn," notes Carnegie's biographer, Joseph Frazier Wall, "who had coordinated the various parts and created an effective unit of production."[40]

Shinn's major achievement was the development of statistical data needed for coordination and control. According to James H. Bridge, who worked in the Carnegie enterprises, Shinn did this in part by introducing "the voucher system of accounting" which, though it had "long been used by railroads, ... was not [yet] in general use in manufacturing concerns."[41] By this method, each department listed the amount and cost of materials and labor used on each order as it passed through the subunit. Such information permitted Shinn to send Carnegie monthly statements and, in time, even daily ones providing data on the costs of ore, limestone, coal, coke, pig iron (when it was not produced at the plant), spiegel, molds, refractories, repairs, fuel, and labor for each ton of rails produced.[42] Bridge called these cost sheets "marvels of ingenuity and careful accounting."[43]

These cost sheets were Carnegie's primary instrument of control. Costs were Carnegie's obsession. One of his favorite dicta was: Watch the costs and the profits will take care of themselves.[44] He was forever asking Shinn and Jones and the department heads the reasons for changes in unit costs.

Carnegie concentrated, as he had when he was a division manager on the Pennsylvania, on the cost side of the operating ratio, comparing current costs of each operating unit with those of previous months and, where possible, with those of other enterprises.[45] Indeed, one reason Carnegie joined the Bessemer pool, which was made up of all steel companies producing Bessemer rails, was to have the opportunity to get a look at the cost figures of his competitors. These controls were effective. Bridge reports that: "The minutest details of cost of materials and labor in every department appeared from day to day and week to week in the accounts; and soon every man about the place was made to realize it. The men felt and often remarked that the eyes of the company were always on them through the books."[46]

By 1880 Carnegie's cost sheets were far more detailed and more accurate than cost controls in the leading enterprises in textile, petroleum, tobacco, and other industries. In the metal-working industries comparable statistical data were only just being perfected. In addition to using their cost sheets to evaluate the performance of departmental managers, foremen, and men, Carnegie, Shinn, and Jones relied on them to check the quality and mix of raw materials. They used them to evaluate improvements in process and in product and to make decisions on developing by-products. In pricing, particularly nonstandardized items like bridges, cost sheets were invaluable. The company would not accept a contract until its costs were carefully estimated and until options had been obtained on the basic materials of coke and ore.[47]

Nevertheless, Carnegie's concern was almost wholly with prime costs. He and his associates appear to have paid almost no attention to overhead and depreciation. This too reflected the railroad experience. As on the railroads, administrative overhead and sales expenses were comparatively small and estimated in a rough fashion. Likewise, Carnegie relied on replacement accounting by charging repair, maintenance, and renewals to operating costs. Carnegie had, therefore, no certain way of determining the capital invested in his plant and equipment. As on the railroads, he evaluated performance in terms of the operating ratio (the cost of operations as a percent of sales) and profits in terms of a percentage of book value of stock issued.[48]

Although Carnegie had by the end of the 1870s created a plant organization at the E. T. Works that could be considered modern, the number of managers was still low and the staff was small. The staff executives included only the accountants who provided statistical controls, three engineers in charge of maintenance of plant and equipment, and a chemist, "a learned German, Dr. Fricke," whose laboratories played an important role in maintaining the quality of output and in improving the processes of production.[49] The enterprise was still very much an entrepreneurial one with Carnegie making nearly all the top management decisions.

The history of the American steel industry illustrates effectively how technological innovation, intensified use of energy, plant design, and overall management procedures permitted a great increase in the volume and speed of throughput and with it a comparable expansion in the productivity of operation. Carnegie's preeminence in the industry came from his commitment to technological change and from his imaginative transferral to manufacturing of administrative methods and controls developed on the railroads. Technological and organizational innovation paid off. Carnegie's prices were lower and his profits higher than any producer in the industry. As soon as the E. T. Works was opened in 1875 it recorded profits of $9.50 a ton.[50] In 1878 Carnegie's rail mill recorded a profit of $401,000 or 31 percent on equity. It rose in the next two years to $2.0 million. As the business grew, so did its profits. At the end of the 1890s Carnegie's larger and more diversified enterprise had profits of $20 million. For the year 1900 they stood at $40 million. By becoming a pioneer in the methods of mass production in steel, Carnegie quickly accumulated, as John D. Rockefeller had done in petroleum, one of the largest fortunes the world had ever seen.

Similar though less spectacular developments occurred in other steel companies and in the processing of iron, nonferrous metals, and glass. The new technology and organizational forms became well known. Carnegie, Jones, and other steel makers enjoyed describing their achievements. Many of their technical problems and procedures were written about in the pages of *Iron Age*, the *Engineering and Mining Journal*, the *Bulletin* of the American Iron and Steel Institute, and the *Proceedings* of the American Institute of Mining Engineers. These journals also reviewed the coming of new methods in the processing of copper, zinc, and other metals and in the production of plate glass. In all these industries expansion of output came more from increasing the velocity of throughput within the plant than from increasing the size of the establishment in terms of area covered and workers employed. Other metal-making industries became increasingly, though more slowly than in steel, capital-intensive, energy-intensive, and manager-intensive.

The metal-working industries

In the metal-working industries, the technical and organizational challenges were more difficult than those facing Carnegie and his competitors. Processing of materials required greater skills and more precision, the use of more complex machinery, and a greater variety of raw materials. For these reasons, major technological innovations took longer to be perfected and organizational improvements required more concentration on the design of the movements of men than on the layout of a plant or works.

The organizational challenges in the metal-working industries increased proportionately with the number of subunits within the enterprise. The making of simple fabricated products, such as castings, mouldings, nails, screws, and implements like axes, hoes, saws, knives, and other cutlery, required an establishment that differed little from Adam Smith's classic pin factory. Furnaces for welding and tempering, forges for stamping, machinery for grinding and polishing were lined up so that the materials moved easily from one part of the subdivided process to another. The making of stoves and plows added the extra dimension of assembling a relatively few interchangeable parts. This dimension became more complex in the production of harvesters and reapers, scales and safes, and still more intricate in the production of locks, clocks, and watches. Problems of overall coordination and control grew even more challenging where the production of goods involved a large number of different types of fabricated parts. Such was the case in the manufacturing of the new breechloading and repeating firearms, sewing machines, typewriters, electrical motors, and at the opening of the new century, automobiles.[51]

A brief description of the process of producing a sewing machine illustrates the complexity involved. This description is taken from Charles H. Fitch's introduction to the census of manufactures of 1880. He notes the many different materials used, including "pig-, bar-, and sheet-iron, iron and steel wire, bar- and sheet-steel, malleable iron, japan varnish, and power and machine supplies in general, woods for casing (largely walnut and poplar), besides a considerable range of other materials."[52] In the making of metal parts, the bulk of materials passed successively from one operating unit to another—from the foundry to the "tumbling-room, annealing, japanning, drilling, turning, milling, grinding and polishing, ornamenting, varnishing, adjusting, and proving departments." In addition, there were other metal-working departments producing tools, attachments, and needles. The "wood-working and cabinet-making departments constitute a separate and distinct manufacture" that was probably as complicated as any mass producing furniture factory of the period. Finally, a large assembling department was responsible for the completion of the product and its "gauging," inspection, and preparation for shipment.

In developing the technology and organizations essential for high-volume output in the metal-working industries, factory owners and managers relied more on their own industrial experience than did the first

mass producers of steel and kerosene. They borrowed less of their technology from other industries or from abroad, and less of their organizational methods from the railroads. The most innovative were the New
England manufacturers, particularly those of the Connecticut Valley,
where the mass production of firearms and, after the coming of anthracite
coal, simple tools and implements had their beginnings.

From the 1850s until the economically depressed years of the 1870s, the
manufacturers of mass-produced metal goods concentrated on improve-
ing their machinery for shaping metal. Skilled mechanics trained at the
Springfield Armory and other early metal-working establishments, such
men as the celebrated superintendent at the Collins Axe Factory, Elisha K.
Root, devised new types of machines and machine tools to produce recently invented breechloading and repeating firearms, agricultural implements, sewing machines, locks, scales, pumps, and, later, typewriters.[53]
Others trained in this type of manufacturing helped to establish Brown
and Sharpe, Pratt and Whitney, the Providence Tool Company, and other
enterprises specializing in the production of machinery so essential for
high-volume production in metal-working factories.

The initial concentration on technology left the manufacturers in these
establishments little time to improve management methods. They turned
the day-to-day operations of the new factories over to the foremen of the
several departments. As in the case of the iron and steel mills, these foremen controlled; they hired, fired, and promoted their working force. In
those departments requiring the most intricate processing techniques in
grinding, polishing, and other finishing of metal components, the foremen
were responsible for the profitability as well as the productivity of their
departments. They frequently became "inside contractors."[54]

By the "inside contracting" system of management, a skilled mechanic
or metal worker contracted to deliver a specified number of parts over a
specified period of time, usually a year. He paid as well as hired his labor
force. The owners agreed to provide the contractor with floor space,
machinery, light, power, heat, special tools, patterns, and the necessary
raw and semifinished materials. At first the contractor paid his men
directly; later payment was handled through the company's financial
office. Thus, as Harold Williamson has pointed out in his history of the
Winchester Repeating Arms Company: "The management credited the
account of the contractor so much for every hundred pieces of finished
work which passed inspection, and debited his account for the wages paid
to his men and the cost of oil, files, waste, and so on, used in production.
Anything left over was paid to the contractor as a profit."[55] In addition,
the contractor received a foreman's wage which assured him a minimum
income.

Such a system meant that the owners of these works had fewer problems of supervision of the working force than had the superintendent at the Springfield Armory in the 1820s. Nor did they have to work out accounting methods to assure proper payment for piece work. At the same time they knew relatively little about the precise costs of labor and materials used in the contracted departments and by the enterprise as a whole. Nor did they provide for careful supervision of the flow of goods from one department to another. Such coordination was left to informal cooperation of the foremen of departments with a modicum of supervision by the partner in the firm who had charge of manufacturing.

The beginnings of scientific management

When the prolonged economic depression of the 1870s brought a continuing drop in demand and with it unused capacity in metal-working, manufacturers began to turn their attention from technology to organization.[56] The new interest led to the beginnings of the scientific management movement in American industry. Organization and management improvement became a major topic of discussion at the recently formed American Society of Mechanical Engineers. In 1886, Henry R. Towne, the senior executive and major stockholder of the Yale and Towne Lock Company, made it the theme for that year's annual meeting of the society. In his presidential address, entitled "The Engineer as an Economist," Towne noted that:

The questions to be considered, and which need recording and publication as conducive to discussion and the dissemination of useful knowledge in this specialty, group themselves under two principal heads, namely: SHOP MANAGEMENT and SHOP ACCOUNTING . . . Under the head of Shop Management fall the questions of organization, responsibility, reports, systems of contract and piece work, and all that relates to the executive management of works, mills and factories. Under the head of Shop Accounting fall the questions of time and wages systems, determination of costs whether by piece or day-work, the distribution of the various expense accounts, the ascertainment of profits, methods of bookkeeping, and all that enters into the system of accounts which relates to the manufacturing departments of a business and to the determination and record of its results.[57]

Towne's address was followed by two other significant papers, one on cost accounting and the other on capital accounting. These two papers provide further insights into the state of factory management in the metal-working industries in the mid-1880s. The author of the second, Captain Henry Metcalfe, was an intellectual heir of Roswell Lee, the systematizer of the Springfield Armory early in the nineteenth century.

Metcalfe had served as superintendent of several of the federal arsenals and had the previous year published the first book to be written in the United States on cost accounting in manufacturing works. His analysis and proposals were based on modifications and refinements of the procedures that were first developed at the Springfield Armory after 1815. They had similarities to the voucher system of accounts that Carnegie borrowed from the railroads.

To Metcalfe the basic managerial problems were coordination and control. He began by describing "wasteful delay" in the process of manufacturing, which in many cases resulted from records "too often kept by memory." He then quoted the manager and owner of a large establishment employing 1,400 men as telling him:

The trouble is not foreseeing necessities, nor in starting the work to meet them; but in constantly running over the back track to see that nothing ordered has been overlooked, and in settling disputes as to whether such and such an order was or was not actually given and received. Superintendence . . . would be very different work if I were sure that an order once given would go of itself through the works, leaving a permanent trail by which I could follow it and decide positively where and by whom it was stopped. As it is, I spend so much of my time in "shooing" along my orders like a flock of sheep that I have but little left for the serious duties of my position.[58]

Metcalfe's answer was what he called a "shop-order system of accounts" which made it possible to control the flow and improve basic cost accounting. Each order, after it was accepted by the factory, received a number. That number was then put on what were essentially routing slips prepared at the plant's office. These indicated which departments the order would pass through and what parts were to be fabricated and assembled. These slips accompanied materials. On them, each department foreman placed the time and wages expended, as well as the machines and materials used on that order while it was in his department. The completed set of slips thus provided a record of the costs of labor and materials used to complete each order. They also gave an accurate account of the cost of operating each department. In addition, the ticket acted as an authority to do work and to requisition materials. It also became a "roll call or time check" on the working force.[59]

Metcalfe further used these data to determine for each department the "indirect expenses" or overhead costs as well as the "direct expenses" or prime costs. His procedures for computing the former appear to be more sophisticated than those used by the railroads or in Carnegie's steel works.[60] He had developed a formula to determine a "cost factor" based on each department's contribution to the work done by the enterprise as a whole. With this factor he allocated to each department a part of the general expenses such as rent, insurance, taxes, and what he termed "the standing order" charges, that is, heat, power, light, general foundry as well as general office and sales expenses. On the basis of the information provided by his routing slips Metcalfe produced monthly and even daily cost sheets for each department and for each order.

The speaker who took the platform after Metcalfe at the 1886 meeting, Oberlin Smith, the chief engineer of a New Jersey machine-tool company, rounded out the discussion by considering capital accounting.[61] For Smith, the purpose of such a valuation was to appraise the property accurately for tax and insurance purposes and to value properly the firm's assets on the annual balance sheets. Smith argued for using current replacement costs in making such valuation. However, neither Smith nor his contemporaries made any attempt to account systematically for depreciation. Most metal-working firms continued to use the railroad method of renewal accounting. They charged repairs and renewals to operating costs, and listed their assets either at original (historical) costs or at replacement costs.

The long discussion that followed these papers at the meeting in March 1886 indicated that other manufacturers were developing comparable control and accounting methods. Frederick W. Taylor of the Midvale Steel Company said that his firm had been using a technique "very similar" to Metcalfe's for the past ten years.[62] John W. Anderson, who operated a "large manufacturing establishment which embraced twelve different departments, each having a foreman," reported employing comparable ticket systems. Charles A. Fitch had observed the use of similar methods in sewing machine factories. While no one mentioned Carnegie's use of the comparable voucher system and of other examples of railroad accounting, Taylor in his later correspondence tells of his reliance on vouchers, in particular, and on railroad accounting, in general, in developing internal statistical controls.

Taylor and Anderson immediately pointed out the basic weaknesses in Metcalfe's proposed control system. Foremen and workers had neither the time nor interest to fill out the slips properly. For this purpose, metal-working firms were soon employing specialized clerks and timekeepers to collect, record, and disseminate the information needed for costing and coordination.[63] By the 1890s, these clerks had become the first "staff" employees in a number of metal-working factories.

Although metal-working manufacturers agreed to the value of the procedures proposed by Metcalfe and others, the inside contractors and other strong and independent foremen often stood in the way of getting the new systems installed. It has been noted that: "From the contractor's point of view any steps taken by the Company to obtain greater knowledge and control by expanding accounting procedures, greater inspection, or the introduction of rate cuts, represented a threat to his position and status."[64] This was true, too, of the foremen who operated furnaces and other major activities on a piece-rate basis.

Partly as a way to get the contractors and other foremen and their workers to accept the shop-order ticket system or similar control procedures, Henry Towne, Frederick W. Halsey, and other metal-working manufacturers developed what they termed gain-sharing plans. These plans, the manufacturers believed, provided incentives similar to those of inside contracting by assuring workmen as well as foremen higher pay for expanded output. At the same time they permitted the management to gain control over the processes of production.

In 1889, at the annual meeting of the ASME, Towne described a gain-sharing plan which had been used in his works since 1884.[65] It was essentially a contract with all the working force in a department or shop similar to that which his firm previously had had with individual inside contractors. By this scheme any reduction in unit costs achieved through improved equipment and plant design, more effective scheduling, fuller use of machines and materials, and more productive labor would be shared equally between the company and the workers. Thirty to 40 percent of the savings resulting from increased productivity was to go to the workers and 10 to 20 to the much smaller number of foremen.

Halsey's plan was a premium one. It was based on hourly rather than piece rate (thus assuring a certain minimum wage). Premiums, sometimes as high as a third of the hourly rate, were paid to workers who exceeded standard output. This scheme was widely used and copied.[66] In determining standard output, both Towne and Halsey had relied on past experience as shown in existing records and in the data collected through the installation of the new shop-order or voucher systems of accounts.

In 1895, Frederick W. Taylor delivered his first paper on what he soon termed "scientific management."[67] He explicitly addressed himself to improving the gain-sharing plans of Towne and Halsey.[68] First, he pointed out that the costs and the resulting savings to be shared should not be based, as they were in those plans, on past experience, but rather on a standard time and output to be determined "scientifically" through detailed job analyses and time and motion studies of the work involved. In addition, Taylor would apply the stick as well as the carrot. He would do this by returning to the piece rate and by paying a "differential piece rate." The workers who failed to meet this standard time and output received a lower rate per piece, while those who excelled received a much higher rate per piece.[69]

His efforts to determine scientifically standard time and output helped

Taylor to become the nation's best known expert on factory management. They also convinced him that shop or department foremen, the central figures in factory organization, must go. He became certain that no man could acquire the versatile competence needed by a general or "line" foreman to do his job properly.[70] He proposed to achieve this goal by forming a planning department to administer the factory as a whole and to do so through a number of highly specialized shop bosses, or, in his terms, "functional foremen." The activities of the general foreman were thus to be subdivided into parts. Instead of reporting to one boss the workers in one shop or department would report to eight. These included, as Taylor wrote in his major work, *Shop Management*, "(1) route clerks, (2) instruction card clerks, (3) cost and time clerks, who plan and give directions from the planning room, and (4) gang bosses." These four provide coordination and control. Three other functional foremen—the speed boss, the repair boss, and the inspector—were concerned with the performance and the result of work. An eighth, the shop disciplinarian, reviewed the workers' "virtues and defects," and aided them in more effectively carrying out their tasks.[71]

All eight of these functional foremen reported to the planning department. "The shop, and indeed the whole works," Taylor insisted, "should be managed, not by the manager, superintendent and foreman, but by the planning department."[72] The planning department was also to supervise job analyses and time and motion studies and to set the standards of output. After reviewing the orders received at the plant, it was, on the basis of its analyses and information, to schedule the flows of current orders and to set the daily work plan for each operating unit and for each worker in the factory. In addition, it was to refine the shop-order system of control and to keep a constant check on "the cost of all items manufactured with complete expense analysis and complete monthly comparative cost and expense exhibits." Its employment bureau was to have charge of recruitment and laying-off of workers. Finally, the planning department was to be responsible for "the maintenance of the entire system, and of standard methods and applicances throughout the establishment, including the planning room itself."[73]

Although Taylor's goal of extreme specialization proved unacceptable to American manufacturers, many of his basic concepts were incorporated into the organization of modern American factories. The weakness of the Taylor system was its failure to pinpoint authority and responsibility for getting the departmental tasks done and for maintaining a steady flow of materials from one stage of the process to the next. Responsibility for such activities was diffused among the several members of the planning department and among the functional foremen. Several of Taylor's contemporaries, including such writers on factory management as Alexander H. Church, Harrington Emerson, Leon P. Alford, and Russell Robb, pointed to this critical need in factory operations.[74] Church, for example, stressed that while Taylor focused on "analysis" of tasks, he failed to consider their "synthesis" into the organization as a whole. "Coordination," Church insisted, "is the keynote of modern industry."

No factory owner, even those who consulted Taylor or his disciples, adopted the Taylor system without modifying it. To provide the essential overall coordination and control of throughput and at the same time to benefit from the functional specialization proposed by Taylor, many installed an explicit line and staff structure. The operating departments or shops continued to be managed by foremen who were generalists and who were on a line of authority that came down from the president by way of the works manager or superintendent. The functions of Taylor's planning department and functional foreman became those of a plant manager's staff.[75] Overall coordination, control, and planning remained the responsibility of the works manager, who was now assisted by a staff of specialists.

The most articulate exponent of the line and staff type of factory organization was Harrington Emerson, who, not surprisingly, was an experienced railroad manager—first as a troubleshooter for the Burlington and then for the Santa Fe. In a series of articles in *Engineering News* in 1908 and 1909 and in two books, he proposed four major staff offices—personnel, plant and machinery, materials, and methods and procedures.[76] As had been the case on the railroads, the staff was to advise on but not have responsibility for carrying out day-to-day work. "It is the business of staff, not to accomplish work, but to set up standards and ideals, so that the line may work more efficiently."

In the first years of the new century many factories came to be organized along the lines set out by Emerson, Taylor, Towne, and other active members of the American Society of Mechanical Engineers. The contract system was eliminated; gain-sharing and incentive plans were adopted; cost accounting based on shop orders or a voucher system of accounts was introduced; time studies were carried out; route, time, cost, and inspection clerks were employed; and the manager's staff was enlarged.

The Remington Typewriter factory at Illion, New York, reorganized in 1910 by Henry Gantt, one of Taylor's most committed disciples, provides a good illustration.[77] All the units involved in the fabrication and assembling of parts were placed in the manufacturing department—the line department. Each subunit there had its own foreman responsible for its output. The other departments—purchasing, stock order, shipping, inspection, time and cost, works engineering, and labor—became staff departments, reporting directly to the works manager or his assistant and communicating to the operating units through these two senior executives.

In the structure Henry Towne finally adopted in 1905 for his lock-making enterprise, the line and staff distinction was more explicit and the staff offices more elaborate than at Remington. Here another Taylor disciple, Carl Barth, planned a new structure. In addition to the purchasing, the stock order and shipping, the power and plant, and employment departments, there were departments for product design, production efficiency, and methods. As at Remington, Towne's stock-order department supervised the flow of materials through the factory. It conducts, in the words of one report, "correspondence with customers concerning all entered orders, enters all orders for stock and from customers, controls all movement of material during manufacture, regulates the stock of all raw and finished materials, and supervises the packing and shipping of all finished products." The department of productive efficiency "is responsible for the working efficiency of all employees; supervises all time-study work, and establishes both piece and day wage rates," and the department of methods "studies and analyzes all manufacturing methods, covering both machine and assembling operations; keeps in touch with new developments of machine tools, and recommends their adoption where tending to increase economy or improve the quality of the product."[78] The reorganization of Yale and Towne, Remington, and other mass-producing metal factories in the early twentieth century marked the culmination of the movement for systematic and scientific management that had its beginnings in the economically depressed 1870s. Their line and staff form of organization became standard for the management of the processes of mass production in industries using increasing complex technologies in the years after World War I.

Immediately after 1900, much the same set of managers and consultants perfected modern factory accounting.[79] Here, innovations came primarily in determining indirect costs or what was termed the "factory burden," and in allocating both indirect and direct (or prime) costs to each of the different products produced by a plant or factory so as to develop still more accurate unit costs.[80] Of particular significance were the methods developed to relate overhead costs or burden to the fluctuating flow of materials through a manufacturing establishment. In a series of articles published in the *Engineering Magazine* in 1901, Alexander Church began to devise ways to account for a machine's "idle time," for money lost when machines were not in use. Henry Gannt and others then developed methods of obtaining standard costs based on standard volume of throughput. By determining standard costs based on a standard volume of, say, 80 percent of capacity, these men defined the increased unit costs of running below standard volume as "unabsorbed burden" and decreased unit costs over that volume as "over-absorbed burden." By 1910, these and nearly all other basic methods of modern factory cost accounting were being discussed at length in engineering and other professional journals. By then, the internal statistical data needed to control the flow of materials through several processes of production within a single industrial establishment had been fully defined.

These innovators in cost accounting, however, paid relatively little attention to financial or capital accounting. Because relatively fewer financial transactions were carried on within the plant, they did not develop as careful internal auditing as that initiated by the railroads fifty years before. Nor did they concern themselves with the problem of depreciation in determining their capital account. The reason was that, until well into the twentieth century, nearly all large industrial firms continued to use replacement accounting, which their managers had borrowed from the railroads. As on the railroads, they defined profits as the difference between earnings and expenses, and the latter included repairs and renewal.

While the factory managers were perfecting their organizational structure and statistical and accounting controls, they continued to improve the technology of production. They concentrated on three types of technological innovation to help expand further the volume of throughput: sustained development of multipurpose machine tools, improvement of metals in cutting tools to increase the speed at which machines worked, and increasing application of power to move materials more swiftly from one stage of production to the next. All three intensified the use of energy and increased the amount of capital required in the processes of production.

Many of the managers concerned with organizational innovation played a significant role in these technological developments. Taylor, for example, while still at Midvale received at least eleven patents on improved machinery and metals. In 1898 and 1899, with the aid of Maunsel White, he completed experiments begun at Midvale in the 1880s to perfect alloyed steels and other metals. Used at much higher temperatures than ordinary steel, these alloys permitted the cutting, grinding, and shaping of metal at speeds many times faster than had been possible before.[81] In his efforts to speed up machinery Taylor also worked to improve belting that transmitted power to the machines and carried materials to the machines and their operators. The accelerated speeds made possible by the new metals and new means of power transmission (here electricity was already replacing belting) helped to make obsolete shop methods based on older techniques of metal-working. This, in turn, made it easier to introduce further organizational changes to standardize and simplify the processes of production.

It was in the production of the automobile, the most complex product to be made in high volume in the metal-working industries, that the new technology was most fully applied. In that industry the use of multi-purpose machine tools, alloys, new forms of power transmission, with improved plant design and shop organization, made possible an integration of the processes of production that brought an enormously swift expansion in the output and productivity of a single factory. When Henry Ford and his associates produced the low-priced model T in 1908 and then created a worldwide sales organization to distribute their sturdy, reliable, cheap car, the resulting almost insatiable demand created a constant pressure to increase output by accelerating throughput. The building of the Highland Park plant to produce the "T" marked a culmination of earlier developments in the metal-working industries. Ford and his colleagues adopted the most advanced machinery, used the toughest alloyed steels, and followed the "line production system" of placing machines and their operators in a carefully planned sequence of operations.[82] Ford's factory engineers designed improved conveyors, rollways, and gravity slides to assure a continuing regular flow of materials in the plant. These engineers also began to experiment with the use of conveyor belts to move parts past the worker doing the assembly, with each man assigned a single highly specialized task. The moving line was first tried in assembling the flywheel magneto, then other parts of the engine, next the engine itself, and finally, in October 1913, in assembling the chassis and completed car. The innovation—the moving assembly line—was an immediate success. The speed of throughput soared. Labor time expended in making a model T dropped from 12 hours and 8 minutes to 2 hours and 35 minutes per car. By the spring of 1914 the Highland Park plant was turning out 1,000 cars a day and the average labor time per car dropped to 1 hour and 33 minutes. The moving assembly line quickly became the best-known symbol of modern mass production.

With the coming of the moving assembly line, the processes of production in the metal mass production industries had become almost as continuous as those in petroleum and other refining industries. The increased velocity of throughput permitted Ford to reduce the price of his product until it was half that of his nearest competitor, to pay the highest wages in the country for nonskilled work, and still to acquire a personal fortune that was larger than that of John D. Rockefeller, Andrew Carnegie, or James Buchanan Duke. As in steel, oil, and tobacco, the coming of mass production made the metal-working industries capital-intensive, energy-intensive, and manager-intensive. Because of the diffi-

culties of working the materials being processed, of the more intricate
nature of the processes themselves, and of the complexity of the finished
products, the development of mass production techniques in the metal-
working industries required more time, thought, and effort than it did in
others. And the additional effort required to make them more profitable
and productive meant, in turn, that these industries became the major seed
bed for modern factory technology and modern factory organization.

The economies of speed

The rise of modern mass production required fundamental changes in
the technology and organization of the processes of production. The basic
organizational innovations were responses to the need to coordinate and
control the high-volume throughput. Increases in productivity and decreases in unit costs (often identified with economies of scale) resulted
far more from the increases in the volume and velocity of throughput than
from a growth in the size of the factory or plant. Such economies came
more from the ability to integrate and coordinate the flow of materials
through the plant than from greater specialization and subdivision of the
work within the plant. Even in the metal-working industries, where increasing subdivision was possible, the primary impact such subdivisions
had on factory organization was to intensify the need for coordination
and control. As the fate of Taylor's functional foreman emphasizes,
specialization without coordination was unproductive.

This challenge of coordination and control that led to the development
of modern factory management initially appeared in those industries
where high velocity of throughput required careful control to assure
steady use of a plant's equipment and working force and where, at the
same time, such effective coordination could not be assured by the careful
designing of plants and works. In the mechanical industries, where
continuous-process machinery and plants permitted mass production,
and in the refining and distilling industries, where the materials were liquid
or close to liquid and the processes were chemical rather than mechanical,
improved plant design and machinery were in most cases enough to synchronize the processes of production and to assure intensive use of
equipment and personnel. But in the metal-making and metal-working
factories, organization and management of men became more critical than
plant design.

The organizational and technological challenges in the metal-making
and metal-working industries encouraged the professionalization of factory plant managers much as comparable challenges in the management

of large railroad systems led to the professionalization of railroad managers. The men who were in the forefront of designing and putting into
operation new machines, furnaces, factories, and works and in developing
new management techniques and structures were the moving spirits in the
new professional societies. Holley, Fritz, and Jones participated in the
founding and growth of the American Institute of Mining and Metalurgi-
cal Engineers.[83] Towne, Halsey, Taylor, and Oberlin Smith, were all
founders and became presidents of the American Society of Mechanical
Engineers. As late as 1907 the owners and managers of the metal-working
shops and factories dominated the membership of the ASME. In the national and local societies the members concentrated, as did their counterparts in railroading, on standardizing terminology, measurements, parts,
tools, and other equipment.[84] In the last two decades of the nineteenth
century mechanical engineers wrote about their technical problems and
common concerns in the pages of new professional journals like the
American Machinist, the *American Engineer, Engineering News, Engineering Magazine*, and the *Transactions* of the ASME.[85]

After 1880, training of factory and shop engineers also became more
professional. Mechanical engineering departments were founded and enlarged at Massachusetts Institute of Technology, Purdue, and Wisconsin.
Cornell opened a separate engineering school; Sibley College, Stevens
Institute of Technology, and Case Institute began to concentrate their
curriculum on mechanical engineering.[86] Although many mechanical
engineers continued to preach that the shop apprenticeship was of more
value than formal book learning, they looked on apprenticeship as the first
step to a full-time professional career, much as railroad men had viewed
comparable early training on the line of or in the shops of a road. By 1900
mechanical engineers operating shops, factories, and plants viewed themselves as professionals, as did many railroad executives. The difference was
that in railroading several functional specialties developed the paraphernalia of professionalism, but in factory management mechanical engineering was the only activity to do so.

As the new mass production industries became capital-intensive and
management-intensive, the resulting increase in fixed costs and the desire
to keep their machinery or workers and managerial staff fully employed
created pressures on the owners and managers to control their supplies of
raw and semifinished materials and to take over their own marketing and
distribution. The changing ratio of capital to labor and of managers to
labor thus helped to create pressures to integrate within a single industrial
enterprise the processes of mass distribution with those of mass production. By 1900 in many mass production industries the factory, works, or
plant had become part of a much larger enterprise. In labor-intensive,

low-level technology industries most enterprises still operated little more than a factory or two. But in those industries using more complex, high-volume, capital-intensive technology, enterprises had become multifunctional as well as multiunit. They had moved into marketing of the finished goods and the purchasing and often the production of raw and semifinished materials. These larger enterprises did more than coordinate the flow of goods through the processes of production. They administered the flow from the suppliers of raw materials through all the processes of production and distribution to the retailer or ultimate consumer.

PART
four

The Integration of Mass
Production with Mass
Distribution

The modern industrial enterprise—the archetype of today's giant corporation—resulted from the integration of the processes of mass production with those of mass distribution within a single business firm. The first "big businesses" in American industry were those that united the types of distributing organization created by the mass marketers with the types of factory organization developed to manage the new processes of mass production. They were the first enterprises to combine the economies of high volume throughput with the advantages of high stock-turn and generous cash flow. Such large integrated industrial organizations appeared as the nation's basic infrastructure—its railroad, telegraph, and steamship networks—were being completed and their operational procedures perfected. They grew and spread with surprising swiftness. Almost nonexistent at the end of the 1870s, these integrated enterprises came to dominate many of the nation's most vital industries within less than three decades.

By integrating mass production with mass distribution, a single enterprise carried out the many transactions and processes involved in making and selling a line of products. The visible hand of managerial direction had replaced the invisible hand of market forces in coordinating the flow of goods from the suppliers of raw and semifinished materials to the retailer and ultimate consumer. The internalizing of these activities and the transactions between them reduced transaction and information costs. More important, a firm was able to coordinate supply more closely with demand, to use its working force and capital equipment more intensively, and thus to lower its unit costs. Finally, the resulting high volume throughput and high stock-turn generated a cash flow that reduced the costs of both working and fixed capital.

The modern industrial enterprise followed two different paths to size. Some small single-unit firms moved directly into building their own national and global marketing networks and extensive purchasing organizations and obtaining their own sources of raw materials and transportation facilities. For others, mergers came first. A number of small, single-unit family or individually owned firms merged to form a large national enterprise. The new consolidated enterprise centralized the administration of production and then integrated forward and backward. In the 1880s most of the firms that grew large followed the first path. In the 1890s the merger route became more popular. At the end of the decade mergers became a positive mania. Yet as the history of the shakedown period after the merger movement demonstrated, these mergers were only successful if they were in industries where mass production could be integrated with mass distribution and if their organizers created the managerial heirarchies necessary to assure effective administrative supervision and coordination of the processes of production and distribution. By 1917 the integrated industrial enterprise had become the most powerful institution in American business and, indeed, in the entire American economy. By then, too, leading American industries and the economy as a whole had taken on their modern form.

C H A P T E R 9

The Coming of the Modern
Industrial Corporation

Reasons for integration

Integration of mass production with mass distribution offered an opportunity for manufacturers to lower costs and increase productivity through more effective administration of the processes of production and distribution and coordination of the flow of goods through them. Yet the first industrialists to integrate these two basic sets of processes did not do so to exploit such economies. They did so because existing marketers were unable to sell and distribute products in the volume they were produced. The new mass producers were keenly aware of the national and international markets opened up by the new transportation and communication infrastructure. The potential of that market had impelled them to adopt the mass production machinery. However, as long as merchandising enterprises were able to sell their goods, they saw little reason to build marketing organizations of their own. Once the inadequacies of existing marketers became clear, manufacturers integrated forward into marketing.

In the 1880s two types of mass producers embarked on such a strategy of vertical integration. One set was composed of those who adopted new continuous-process machinery that swiftly expanded the output of their industrial establishments. Such entrepreneurs found that the existing marketers were unable to move their goods quickly enough or to advertise them effectively enough to keep their high-volume production facilities operating steadily. Most of these manufacturers continued to distribute through wholesalers, but they assumed responsibility for the coordination of the flow from the factory to the customer.

The second set of pioneers were manufacturers who required specialized distribution and marketing services which wholesalers, mass retailers, manufacturers' agents, and other middlemen were unable to provide. These manufacturers were, in turn, of two sorts. One included a small number of processors who had adopted refrigerated or temperature-controlled techniques for the distribution of perishable products in the national market. The other included the makers of new complex, high-priced machines that required specialized marketing services—demonstration, installation, consumer credit, after-sales service and repair—if they were to be sold in volume. The marketing of these latter products demanded a continuing after-sales contact with the customer. Existing middlemen had neither the interest nor the facilities to maintain a continuing relationship. Nearly all of the firms in this last group manufactured standardized machines that were or could be mass produced through the fabrication and assembling of interchangeable parts.

Those manufacturers who found existing marketers inadequate to meet these needs created multiunit marketing organizations of their own. They set up branch offices headed by salaried managers in major commercial centers of the country and the world. Next, to assure a high-volume continuing flow of materials into their factories, they built large purchasing establishments and smaller traffic departments and often began to supply and transport their own materials.

Because they integrated production, marketing, and purchasing, the activities of the new firms were far more varied than those of other business enterprises of their day. Whereas the railroad, telegraph, marketing, financial, or existing manufacturing firms carried on a single basic economic function, the new integrated enterprise carried on several. Because they came to own and operate many factories, many sales offices, many purchasing units, mines, forest lands, and transportation lines, their operation required even more full-time salaried managers than did the railroad and telegraph companies of the late nineteenth century. These managers handled a far wider variety of tasks and faced even greater challenges in coordinating the flow of materials through their enterprises than did those in transportation, communication, or mass marketing. With the rise of the integrated industrial enterprise, the salaried manager became a major figure in the operation of the American economy.

The new administrative hierarchies, extending as they did from the supplier of raw materials to the ultimate consumer, were from their beginning national enterprises; many soon became multinational. The railroads by the 1890s covered large regions, but there was no single nationwide railroad enterprise. The mass marketers concentrated on local urban and larger rural regional markets. Before 1880, Western Union and Montgomery Ward were among the few large firms to operate on a national scale. By the end of the 1880s, however, a number of industrial enterprises were beginning to serve the entire nation. By 1900 the names of many integrated, multifunctional enterprises had become household words. By then they were beginning to play a significant role in the transformation of the nation from what Robert Wiebe had termed a distended society of "island communities" into a far more homogeneous and integrated community.[1]

As the twentieth century opened, the new integrated multifunctional, often multinational, enterprise was becoming the most influential institution in the American economy. It surpassed the railroad in size and in complexity and diversity of operations. The decisions of its managers affected more businessmen, workers, consumers, and other Americans than did those of railroad executives. It soon replaced the railroad as the focus for political and ideological controversy. In fact, in the first decade of the twentieth century the control of the new industrial corporations became the central domestic political issue of the day. Of more lasting importance, the techniques and procedures perfected in the first years of the century to manage these integrated enterprises have remained the foundation of modern business administration.

Integration by users of continuous-process technology

The most dramatic examples of the integration of mass production and mass distribution came in those industries adopting continuous-process machinery during the decade of the 1880s. Such machinery was, it will be recalled, invented almost simultaneously for making cigarettes, matches, flour, breakfast cereals, soup and other canned products, and photographic film. These innovations in mechanical continuous-process machinery and plant became the basis for a number of the first of the nation's giant industrial corporations. The creation of such enterprises drastically and permanently altered the structure of the industry in which they operated. The story of the organizational response to each of these technological innovations is told separately, in order to emphasize that this common response came simultaneously in different industries whose establishments were widely separated and whose entrepreneurs had little or no acquaintance with one another.

As has been suggested, innovation in these industries was in part a response to the rise of the mass market which emerged with the completion of the nation's basic transportation and communication infrastructure. By the 1880s railroad, steamship, and telegraphic networks were fully integrated. By then belt lines, standard gauges and equipment, and interroad administrative arrangements permitted the movement of goods in nearly all parts of the nation with the minimum of transshipment. And almost instantaneous communication existed between Western Union's 12,000 offices.

The potential of the national market was further enlarged by two new types of ancillary business institutions that had already become widely used by the mass marketers. The credit agency, operating on a national scale after the Civil War, permitted manufacturers to check the reliability of jobbers and retailers in all parts of the country. The advertising agency, which purchased advertising space for clients in newspapers, journals, and periodicals circulating throughout the nation, was of even more value to mass producers. Until after the Civil War such agencies concentrated on writing copy and buying space in their local communities. Until the 1870s their major customers were department stores and jobbers and wholesalers selling traditional lines of dry goods, hardware, groceries, jewelry, furniture, cards, and stationery in local and regional markets. In that decade only books, journals, and patent medicines were advertised on more than a regional basis. Nearly all other manufacturers left advertising to the wholesalers who marketed their goods.

The manufacturers adopting the new continuous-process technology differed from the producers of books, journals, and patent medicines in that the unit output of their factories was much higher. To enlarge and maintain a market for these goods, they embarked on massive advertising campaigns carried out through these advertising agencies. They learned soon, too, that the wholesaler could not be relied upon to order and maintain inventory so that the customer could be always sure of obtaining the product. So the manufacturer took charge of scheduling the flow of finished products from the factory to the customer and then of raw and semifinished materials from the suppliers to the factories.

The story of James Buchanan Duke effectively illustrates these general practices.[2] Duke's dominance in the cigarette industry rested on his appreciation of the potential of the Bonsack cigarette machine. Duke, a manufacturer of smoking tobacco in Durham, North Carolina, had decided in 1881 to produce cigarettes because he was having difficulty in competing with a well-established neighbor, Blackwell and Company. At that date cigarettes were still a new and exotic product just beginning to find favor in the growing urban markets. Cigarette smoking was only starting to take the place of pipe smoking, chewing tobacco, cigars, or snuff. In 1881 four cigarette firms produced 80 percent of the output, primarily for nearby markets.

As a newcomer, Duke was searching for a way to break into the market. In 1884, shortly after a sharp reduction in taxes on cigarettes permitted a major price cut to consumers, Duke installed two Bonsack machines.

With each machine producing 120,000 cigarettes a day, he could easily saturate the American market. To test the world market, Duke had sent a close associate, Richard M. Wright, on a nineteen-month tour overseas. In June 1885 Duke signed a contract with Bonsack to use the machine exclusively to make all his cigarettes, high-quality as well as cheap, in return for a lower leasing charge.

Duke's gamble paid off.[3] Output soared. Selling became the challenge. Even before Duke had made his basic contract with Bonsack, he built a factory in New York City, the nation's largest urban market, and set up his administrative offices there. He immediately intensified a national advertising campaign. Not only did Duke rely on advertising agencies but also his own staff distributed vast quantities of cards, circulars, and hand-bills—all proclaiming the virtues of his products.

He then began to build extensive sales organizations.[4] Duke followed up the contacts Wright had made on his trip abroad by signing marketing agreements with wholesalers and dealers in all parts of the globe. At the same time, he and one or two other associates established a network of sales offices in the larger American cities. These offices, headed by salaried managers, became responsible for both the marketing and distributing of the product. The office kept an eye on local advertising. Its salesmen regularly visited tobacco, grocery, drug, and other jobbers, and a few large retailers to obtain orders. Duke's local sales managers worked closely with New York headquarters to assure the effective scheduling of the high-volume flow of cigarettes to jobbers and a few large retailers.

At the same time that Duke and his close associates were building their sales organization, they were creating an extensive purchasing network in southeastern United States, where bright-leaf tobacco—that used in cig-arettes—was grown. Tobacco, after its annual harvest, was normally dried and cured before being sold to manufacturers. The timing of the process varied from several months to two or three years, according to the leaf and the quality desired. Because the supply of cured tobacco depended on both the size of the crop and the availability of curing facilities, prices fluctuated widely. By building its own buying, storing, and curing facil-ities, Duke's company was able to purchase directly from the farmers, usually at auctions, and so reduce transactions costs and uncertainties. What counted more was that the company was also assured of a steady supply of cured tobacco for its mass producing factories in Durham and New York City.

By combining mass production with mass distribution Duke was able to maintain low prices and reap high profits. By 1889 Duke was by far the largest manufacturer in the industry, producing 834 million cigarettes with sales of over $4.5 million and profits of $400,000 annually, despite heavy advertising costs. To compete, other cigarette manufacturers had little choice but to follow Duke's strategy. They quickly turned to machine production and began to build and enlarge their sales and purchasing organizations. As packages of cigarettes were priced in 5¢ increments—5¢ for the standard package and 10¢ to 25¢ for the better brands—there was little room for price cutting, particularly in the all-important cheaper brands. The manufacturers concentrated on advertising instead. In 1889 Duke's advertising cost rose to $800,000 a year. Here his high volume and resulting cash flow gave him an advantage, for he had a larger cash surplus than the others to spend on advertising. But the cost of these sales campaigns reduced profits.

The desire to control this competition caused Duke and his four competitors to merge in 1890, forming the American Tobacco Company.[5] For a brief time the constituent companies continued to operate independently; but after 1893 their functional activities were consolidated into the Duke manufacturing, sales, and leaf (purchasing) departments. As had been the case with the railroads and would be again in manufacturing, the largest of the early enterprises became the core organization for continuing growth. The enlarged centralized departmentalized company, operating from its New York corporate central office, proved extraordinarily profitable even during the economically depressed years of the 1890s.[6] Profits from cigarettes allowed Duke to install new methods of production and distribution in other branches of the tobacco trade. By 1900 the American Tobacco Company had come to dominate that industry completely, except for the making of cigars. These developments will be described in more detail in Chapter 12, which deals with the internal strategy and structure of a selected number of the pioneering integrated enterprises.

The history of the match industry parallels that of the cigarette, except that the development of a fully automated machine came more slowly. After the Civil War, machines began to replace hand production. By the early 1870s four machine-using firms accounted for 80 percent of the industry's output.[7] Each had its own specialized machinery, and each concentrated on a single regional market. After a brief period of competition for the national market, these four combined in 1881 to form the Diamond Match Company.

The leading entrepreneurs in the new firm, E. B. Beecher, William Swift, and Ohio Columbus Barber, then agreed on a strategy for improving the basic machinery by combining the best attributes of the different machines used by the erstwhile competitors. The result was, in the words of the firm's historian, "the beginning of the modern continuous, automatic, match machine . . . that revolutionized the match industry."[8] At the same time the company developed comparable machines for the manufacture of paperboard and strawboard boxes. By the early 1890s seventy-five workers could produce 2 million filled matchboxes a day, an output equivalent to that of five hundred workers prior to the introduction of the new machines. Production was then consolidated in large plants. In 1880 there were over thirty match factories. By 1900 production was concentrated in one giant plant at Barberton, Ohio, and three smaller ones. By then Barber, Beecher, and Swift had built a sales organization that, like Duke's, was responsible for establishing and maintaining contact with wholesalers, for handling local advertising, and for coordinating the flow of packages to the jobbers and often the retailers. Its buying organization began to purchase its wood paper and chlorate of potash directly from producers; the latter material came entirely from Europe. Soon the company had its own sawing and woodworking mills in Wisconsin and New England. In the 1890s it began to construct the largest match factory in the world in Liverpool. By the end of the decade it had plants in Germany, Canada, Peru, and Brazil.[9]

Until it began to move overseas, Diamond Match financed its impressive internal expansion from retained earnings alone. As was the case at American Tobacco, the cash flow generated by high-volume production and distribution along with some assistance from local commercial banks, covered the company's needs for both working and fixed capital. In 1889, assisted by a Chicago lawyer, William Henry Moore, the company acquired funds by increasing its capitalization from $7.5 million to $11.0 million.[10] During the depressed years of the 1890s it continued to pay a 10 percent dividend on common stock with no borrowing and with only a small increase in capitalization. The prices of matches did not rise, and the company had little difficulty in maintaining its monopoly position until well into the twentieth century.

New continuous-process methods of production had almost as great an impact on the processing and marketing of that ancient American industry, milling of grain, as it had on the nation's oldest commercial crop, tobacco. The innovative efforts of Cadwallader Colden Washburn and the Pillsbury brothers in the development of the automatic all-roller, gradual-reduction mill assured their enterprises leading position in the industry.[11] So, too, did a comparable mill built in 1882 by the oatmeal producer, Henry P. Crowell. That mill has been described as "the first in the world to maintain under one roof operations to grade, clean, hull, cut, package, and ship oatmeal to interstate markets in a continuous process that in some aspects anticipated the modern assembly line."[12]

These new continuous-process plants had more immediate impact on the structure of the oatmeal than the flour industry. For a while at least, the demand for flour was high enough and the costs reduced enough by the new machinery that the "new process" millers had little difficulty in disposing of their output by selling in bulk to wholesalers. On the other hand, the demand for oatmeal was more limited. A new market had to be found if the great volume of output from the new machines was to be sold. As a result, the modern breakfast cereal industry was invented.

The pioneer in developing this product was Crowell, the builder of the first continuous-process mill. While Ferdinand Schumaker, the largest producer, continued to market in the accepted way of selling in bulk through wholesalers, Crowell packaged and then advertised his brand, Quaker Oats, nationally as a breakfast cereal—a product that was even newer to American tastes than the cigarette. In advertising Quaker Oats, Crowell's staff used, much as Duke had done, box-top premiums, prizes, testimonials, scientific endorsements, and the like.[13] The company set up sales offices in the United States and abroad. Their managers were expected, as were Duke's, not only to maintain contact with jobbers but also to schedule flows from the factory to the jobbers. At the same time Crowell built a buying organization that soon came to include "fieldmen" who purchased directly from the farmers in the grain-growing states and buyers who had seats on the Minneapolis and Chicago grain exchanges.

The response of other manufacturers to Crowell's aggressive marketing campaign in oatmeal was similar to the response to Duke's in tobacco. In 1888 after a brief attempt at a cartel, Crowell, Schumaker, and a third large mass producer of oatmeal, Robert Stuart, formed the American Cereal Company. (It became the Quaker Oats Company in 1901.) Despite the determined opposition of Schumaker, who retained his preference for marketing in bulk, the new company took over and expanded Crowell's selling and purchasing organization. Production became concentrated in two giant plants—one at Akron and the other at Cedar Rapids—each using improved continuous-process machinery. After the turn of the century, to make fuller use of its marketing and purchasing facilities, the company added new lines of wheat cereals, farina, hominy, corn meal, specialized baby foods, and animal feed.

In the early 1890s, as the demand for roller mill flour leveled off, the Minneapolis and other millers began to follow the example of the American Cereal Company. Decline in prices at the beginning of the decade brought plans for large-scale mergers. These failed, as the leading companies preferred to remain independent. The Washburn firm was reorganized under the presidency of James S. Bell as the Washburn Crosby Company, and the Pillsbury family continued to operate through what became known as the Pillsbury-Washburn Flour Company. Bell and the Pillsburys quickly turned to the strategy of vertical integration.[14] They began to package their products rather than selling in bulk and to advertise their brands, Gold Medal Flour and Pillsbury, on a national scale. During the 1890s they created selling and buying networks similar to those of Crowell. From 1889 on, the Pillsburys had a chain of grain elevators in the wheat-growing regions. Because their product, flour, was so widely used and because the supply of wheat was so extensive, a single firm did not come to dominate the industry as in the tobacco, match, and breakfast cereal trades. On the other hand, Washburn-Crosby and Pillsbury continued to be the largest American flour millers well into the twentieth century.

The first enterprises to utilize fully the "automatic-line" canning factory were those that developed a product line which permitted more than seasonal operations.[15] The most successful of these were H. J. Heinz and Company of Pittsburgh and the Campbell Soup Company of Camden, New Jersey.[16] In 1880 Henry John Heinz, a small processor of pickles, relishes, sauces, and similar products for the local Pittsburgh market, was still recovering from his bankruptcy in 1876. In the early 1880s he adopted new, continuous-process methods of canning and bottling and built a network of sales offices to sell in the national market and advertise extensively his many brands. He created a large buying and storing organization to assure a steady flow of vegetables and other foodstuffs into his factories and contracted with farmers to provide these supplies to desired specifications. By 1888 Heinz had become one of Pittsburgh's most substantial citizens and the company remains to this day one of the largest food processors in the country.

Less is known about the beginning and growth of the Campbell Soup Company; but it appeared at almost the same time and grew in much the same way. It has long remained one of the major business enterprises in the Philadelphia area, and the Dorrance family, who had joined with Joseph Campbell to found and operate the firm, remains one of the city's wealthiest clans.

Other processors who used the large continuous-process canning plants were those who produced condensed canned milk and canned meats. In 1882 two of the smaller meat packers, Libby, McNeil & Libby and Wilson & Company, began volume production of canned meat in Chicago. At the same time the pioneer in the condensing of milk, the Borden Milk Company, greatly enlarged its operations and expanded and rationalized its marketing and purchasing organizations.[17] It did so partly because of the expanding market but also because foreign competitors had moved across the sea to exploit the American trade. In that decade both the Anglo-Swiss Condensed Milk Company (a forerunner of Nestle) and the Helvetia Milk Condensing Company (the precursor of two American firms, the

Pet Milk Company and the Carnation Milk Company) set up plants and sales organizations in the United States.

Only those companies who had earlier in their history developed products that could be produced year-round continued to remain large and dominant firms. Where canning remained seasonal, as was the case for most vegetables, fruit, and fish products, the large company did not appear. Instead, canneries came to buy their cans and canning equipment from two large can-making companies, American Can and Continental Can. American Can, whose first president was Edward Norton, the inventor of the "automatic-line" process, resulted from a merger in 1901. Continental Can was formed in 1906. Both soon had extensive marketing and servicing organizations. As late as the 1950s these two canning companies and Campbell Soup, H. J. Heinz, Carnation, Borden's, Pet Milk, and Libby, McNeil & Libby were still the leaders in the canning industry.[18]

Yet another industry, soap, adopted continuous-process machinery in the 1880s. Soap production for the commercial market had started as a by-product of the meat-packing industry, with small companies processing animal fats for regional markets. In the late 1870s mechanical improvements in the mixing and crushing process used in making bar soap greatly expanded output. British firms such as Pears and Pond advertised in the American market.[19] In 1879, a small Cincinnati soap maker, Procter & Gamble, developed by accident a soap that floated.[20] It was branded Ivory. By using the new machinery, Procter & Gamble was soon making 200,000 cakes of Ivory soap a day. To sell its volume, the firm began to advertise nationally and then to build a network of branch sales offices. At the same time it created an extended buying organization to assure itself of a steady supply of perishable raw materials—animal and vegetable oils, fats, and soda ash. By 1885, the company had constructed Ivorydale, a model industrial plant, which became a Cincinnati showplace. To make full and integrated use of its facilities, Procter & Gamble then moved into the production of laundry and other soaps, cottonseed and salad oil, and similar products. During the 1880s, other soap manufacturers, including Colgate & Company, N. K. Fairbanks, B. T. Babbit, and D. S. Brown, built integrated enterprises similar to Procter & Gamble.[21] These new large enterprises soon found themselves competing with meat packers and cotton-oil producers who had moved into soap production, as well as with leading European soap manufacturers who had continued to sell in the American market.

Another major innovation in continuous-process machinery to appear in the 1880s was in the photographic industry.[22] In 1884, George Eastman of Rochester, New York, one of the largest producers of photographic paper and plate, assisted by William H. Walker, began to study ways to mass produce the substance on which negative images were made. They devised a paper-based film using a gelatin emulsion to replace the existing glass plates. The film, attached to the camera by roll holders, could be produced by continuous-process machinery. However, because the new film required a new or rebuilt camera with holders and because the developing of the film was so complex that it had to be done at the Eastman factory, it found little favor with professional photographers.

Eastman then turned to a still untapped mass market, the amateur photographer. He and his associates concentrated on inventing a small, standardized camera which was easy to build and easy to operate and on finding a more satisfactory roll film to be used with the camera. In April 1888, Eastman patented and then immediately began to mass produce the Kodak. Then by 1889, he and his colleagues had perfected a celluloid-base roll film of high quality. Eastman combined the new film and camera for the mass market by selling each Kodak loaded with film for 100 exposures. Once the 100 pictures had been snapped, the camera (later the film) was returned to the Eastman factory in Rochester where the film was developed and printed and the camera reloaded.

To sell and distribute his new camera and film and to service their purchasers, Eastman immediately created a worldwide marketing network of branch offices with managers to supervise salesmen and demonstrators and to coordinate flows of cameras, films, and funds. In 1890, Eastman built production and servicing facilities in Great Britain. As the production of camera and film soared, the company set up a purchasing organization to buy massive quantities of paper, celluloid, lenses, and other material. Before 1900, Eastman Kodak, the towering giant of the industry, was beginning to manufacture several of these items in its own plants.

During a very short period in the 1880s, new processes of production and distribution had transferred the organization of a number of major American industries—tobacco, matches, grain milling, canning, soap, and photography. These changes were revolutionary, and they were permanent. The enterprises that pioneered in adopting and integrating the new ways of mass production and mass distribution became nationally known. By 1900, they were household words. Three-quarters of a century later the names American Tobacco, Diamond Match, Quaker Oats, Pillsbury Flour, Campbell Soup, Heinz, Borden, Carnation, Libby, Procter & Gamble, and Eastman Kodak are still well known.

These enterprises were similar in that they used new continuous-process machinery to produce low-priced packaged consumer goods. Their new processes of production were so capital-intensive (that is, the ratio of workers to the quantity of units produced was so small) that production for the national and global market became concentrated in just a few plants, often only one or two. In all cases it was the massive increase in output made possible by the new continuous-process, capital-intensive machinery that caused the manufacturers to build large marketing and purchasing networks.

The national and international network of sales offices took over from the wholesaler the functions of branding and advertising. Although advertising agents continued to be used to reach the national and world markets, the sales department became increasingly responsible for the content, location, and volume of advertising. As many of these products, like cigarettes, cereals, canned milk, and canned meat, were relatively new, advertising was important to enlarge demand. It was also a major competitive weapon because a relatively low unit price per package (usually 5¢ or 10¢) made demand inelastic. It was difficult to increase demand by reducing prices. Although in most cases, jobbers continued to be used to distribute goods to the retailers, the sales offices took over scheduling and coordinating the flow of goods from factories to jobbers and often to retailers. (At Eastman this involved the flow of exposed film for printing as well.) They also worked closely with the manufacturing departments to coordinate the flow from the suppliers of the raw material through the processes of production and distribution to the final consumers. A few of these firms, including Campbell Soup and Eastman Kodak, were soon selling and delivering directly to retailers. By the early twentieth century Eastman Kodak began to build its own retail stores in major cities.

In all these cases the high volume of output permitted by the integration of mass production with mass distribution generated an impressive cash flow that provided these enterprises with most of their working capital, as well as funds to expand capital equipment and facilities. These enterprises relied on local businessmen and commercial banks for both short-term and long-term loans. None, however, needed to go to the capital markets for funds to finance the expansion that so quickly placed them among the largest business enterprises in the world. For this reason the entrepreneurs, their families, and the associates who created these enterprises continued to control them. They personally held nearly all the voting stock in a company. Thus, although day-to-day operations had to be turned over to full-time salaried managers, long-term decisions as to investment, allocation of funds, and managerial recruitment remained concentrated in the hands of a small number of owners.

The administrative networks built to integrate the new processes of production and distribution gave the pioneering enterprises their greatest competitive advantage. Although capital-intensive in terms of the ratio of capital to labor inputs, the new machinery was not that expensive. The absolute cost of entry was not high, nor in most industries were patents a barrier to entry. The makers of cigarette, milling, canning, and soap-making machinery were eager to sell their products to as many manufacturers as possible. Nor was branding or advertising a barrier. Advertising agencies were just as intent as machinery manufacturers on finding new clients.

The most imposing barrier to entry in these industries was the organization the pioneers had built to market and distribute their newly mass-produced products. A competitor who acquired the technology had to create a national and often global organization of managers, buyers, and salesmen if he was to get the business away from the one or two enterprises that already stood astride the major marketing channels. Moreover, where the pioneer could finance the building of the first of these organizations out of cash flow, generated by high volume, the newcomer had to set up a competing network before high-volume output reduced unit costs and created a sizable cash flow. In this period of building he had to face a competitor whose economies of speed permitted him to set prices low and still maintain a margin of profit. Newcomers, of course, did appear. Kellogg and Postum in breakfast cereals and Colgate and Babbitt in soaps are examples. But all these industries were highly concentrated from the moment mass production methods were adopted. Except for flour milling, the industries in which these integrated industrial enterprises first appeared immediately became oligopolistic and have so remained.

Integration by processors of perishable products

Whereas many of the mass producers of semiperishable packaged products continued to use the wholesaler to handle the physical distribution of their goods—even after they had taken over that middleman's advertising and scheduling functions—the makers of more perishable products such as meat and beer, in building their marketing networks, began to sell and distribute directly to the retailers. The market for perishable products expanded as the railroad and telegraph networks grew. As early as the 1850s crude refrigerator cars were used to bring milk, butter, and meat to urban markets. In the 1870s, when the direct movement of cars over long distances became possible, western meat packers began to ship fresh meat to the eastern cities. Then, in 1881 the modern refrigerated car made its appearance. Gustavus F. Swift hired Andrew J. Chase, a leading refrigeration engineer, to design a car to carry Swift's dressed beef from Chicago to Boston. Again, the 1880s were the crucial years.

The refrigerator car, however, was not the reason Swift became the innovator in high-volume, year-round production of perishable products.[23] He became the first modern meat packer because he was the first to appreciate the need for a distribution network to store meat and deliver it to the retailers. He was the first to build an integrated enterprise to coordinate the high-volume flow of meat from the purchasing of cattle through the slaughtering or disassembling process and through distribution to the retailer and ultimate consumer.

When Gustavus Swift, a New England wholesale butcher, moved to Chicago in 1875, nearly all meat went east "on the hoof." Western cattle were shipped alive by rail in cattle cars to local wholesalers who butchered and delivered to retailers. The economies of slaughtering in the west and shipping the dressed meat east were obvious. Sixty percent of an animal was inedible and cattle lost weight and often died on the trip east. Moreover, the concentration of butchering in Chicago and other western cities permitted a high-volume continuous operation which not only lowered unit cost but also made possible fuller use of by-products.

To carry out his strategy, Swift, who had begun winter shipments in 1878, not only concentrated on improving the refrigerated car but also built a network of branch houses, first in the northeast and then after 1881 in the rest of the country. Each house included refrigerated storage space, a sales office, and a sales staff to sell and deliver the meat to the retail butchers, grocers, and other food shops. Swift soon supplemented this distributing and marketing network with "peddler car routes" which distributed dressed meat in small lots by refrigerator car to towns and villages.

In executing his plan, Swift met with most determined opposition. Railroads, startled by the prospect of losing their livestock business, which was an even greater producer of revenue than grain on the west to east routes, refused to build refrigerated cars. When Swift began to construct his own, the Eastern Trunk Line Association refused to carry them. Only by using the Grand Trunk, then outside of the association, was Swift able to bring his cars east. At the same time he had to combat boycotts by local wholesalers, who in 1886 formed the National Butchers' Protective Association to fight "the trust." These butchers attempted to exploit a prejudice against eating fresh meat that had been killed days or even weeks before, more than a thousand miles away.

High quality at low prices soon overcame this opposition. Though Swift did rely on advertising to counter prejudice against his product, it was clearly the prices and quality made possible by high-volume operations and the speed and careful scheduling of product flow that won the market. Once the market was assured, Swift had to expand his production facilities to keep up with demand. He increased his speed of throughput by subdividing the processes of butchering and by using moving "disassemblying" lines. In the 1880s and early 1890s, Swift & Company built new packing plants in six cities along the cattle frontier. The company then bought into adjoining stockyards where men from its purchasing department became experts in buying cattle in volume.

Other packers realized that if they were to compete with Swift in the national market they must follow his lead. By the end of 1882, Philip D. Armour of Chicago and George H. Hammond of Detroit were beginning to build comparable networks of branch houses and to compete with Swift for the best locations along the railroad lines. Nelson Morris of Chicago and the two Cudahy brothers of Omaha constructed similar networks in the mid-1880s.[24] The oligopoly was rounded out when the New York firm of Swartschild and Sulzberger completed a comparable integated national enterprise in the early 1890s. Except for Hammond who died in 1886, all these entrepreneurs enlarged their processing facilities, built new packing plants in other western cities, bought into the stockyards, and expanded their fleet of refrigerated cars. Well before the end of the eighties a small number of very large integrated meat-packing firms dominated the dressed meat business, and they continued to do so until well into the twentieth century.

Improved transportation also encouraged several brewers to enter the national market. In the 1880s a new pneumatic malting process increased speed and improved control in the process of brewing beer. At the same time the development of temperature-controlled tank cars made it possible to distribute their product nationally. In the 1870s brewers sold only within a relatively small radius of their plant, relying on traveling men to sell the product by the barrel to wholesalers. In the 1880s Pabst, Schlitz, and Blatz of Milwaukee, Lamp and Anheuser of St. Louis (the able Adolphus Busch took over Anheuser in 1880), and Moelin of Cincinnati all began to build a nationwide distributing network and to use advertising agencies to reach the national market. For example, in early 1879 Pabst had only one branch, in nearby Chicago. That year a second was set up in Kansas City.[25] Between 1881 and 1894 the company built thirty more branches in every part of the country. Although Pabst used wholesalers in some cities, an increasing proportion of sales came to be made through company offices that stored, distributed, marketed, and advertised the Pabst product. In 1887 Pabst went one step further by moving into retailing and purchasing saloons, which were rented to operators.[26] In the same years Pabst and the other national brewers expanded their purchasing organization, using them to buy high-quality malt, barley, rice, hops, and other materials in large quantities with precise specifications. They also set up barrel-making plants and purchased timberlands. By the 1890s these integrated enterprises were, like those of the meat packers, among the largest businesses in the land.

The growth of the large integrated enterprises in the meat-packing and brewing industries was similar to the pioneer enterprises in semiperishable packaged goods. The rise of the integrated enterprise and with it the reorganization of the industry came at almost precisely the same time. The pioneering firms long remained dominant in their industries. The names of the leading packers and brewers of the eighties are still familiar today. In both industries the new giants were financed from within. Cash flow generated by high-volume turnover and throughput provided nearly all the funds needed for working or fixed capital. As in the case of the new entrepreneurial enterprises in semiperishable industries, the founders and their families in meat packing and brewing continued to hold almost all the stock.[27] Even the Swifts, who had issued stock to the wholesalers who joined them to become branch houses, appear to have maintained full control of their company. These firms, in turn, became models for enterprises distributing similar goods—dairy products, bananas, and in more recent years, frozen foods.

Integration by machinery makers requiring specialized marketing services

The other manufacturers to by-pass the wholesalers were the makers of recently invented machines that were produced in volume through the fabrication and assembling of interchangeable parts. The marketing needs of these machinery makers were even greater than those of the meat packers and brewers. They found that the volume sale of their products required more than centralized advertising and coordinated flows. Their new and relatively complex products had to be demonstrated before they could be sold. Mechanical expertise was needed to service and repair them after they had been sold. And because the machines were relatively costly, buyers often could only purchase them on credit. Independent wholesalers were rarely able or willing to provide such demonstrations, maintenance and repair, and consumer credit.

The machines requiring these close and continuing services to the customer were of two sorts. Sewing machines, agriculture equipment, and office machinery were similar to present-day consumer durables, even though they were sold primarily to produce goods and services and not for consumption by the final consumer. They were produced at a high rate, often many thousands a week, and sold to individuals as well as to business firms. The second type—elevators, pumps, boilers, printing presses, and a variety of electrical equipment—were clearly producers' goods. They were complex, large, standardized machines that required specialized installation as well as sales and repair and long-term credit. In the eighties the makers of both sorts of machines began to expand output by pioneering in or adopting the new ways of systematic factory management. Both sold their products in national and world markets and created or reorganized extensive marketing organization in that same decade.

The first mass producers of machinery to build their own sales organizations were the makers of sewing machines.[28] These machines could be produced commercially in the early 1850s, but the manufacturers could not begin to make them in quantity until the legal battle over patents was settled in 1854 and a patent pool formed. The winner of the court trials, Elias Howe, insisted that the pooled patents be released to twenty-four manufacturers. Nevertheless, the industry was dominated within a short time by the three firms that first acquired marketing networks—Wheeler & Wilson Co., Grover and Baker, and I. M. Singer Company. These manufacturers at first relied on full-time but independent agents who, though receiving a small salary, were paid primarily on a commission basis and were solely responsible for marketing activities within their territories. But these agents had little technical knowledge of the machines and were unable to demonstrate them properly or service and repair them. Nor were the agents able to provide credit, an important consideration if customers were to pay for these relatively expensive goods in installments.

As an alternative, Grover and Baker began to set up a company owned and operated store or branch office to provide such services. By 1856 Grover and Baker had already established such branch offices, as they were called, in ten cities.[29] In that year Isaac Merritt Singer decided to follow suit. So, almost immediately, did Wheeler & Wilson. By 1859 Singer had opened fourteen branches, each with a female demonstrator, a mechanic to repair and service, and a salesman or canvasser to sell the machine, as well as a manager who supervised the others and handled collections and credits. Nevertheless, because finding and training personnel took time, these three enterprises continued to rely heavily on commission agents to market their goods. The swift selection of these agents and the building of branch stores permitted these three to dominate the trade. By 1860 they already produced three-fourths of the industry's output, with Wheeler & Wilson manufacturing 85,000 machines in that year and the other two 55,000 apiece.[30]

After 1860 Singer moved more aggressively than the other two in replacing regional distributors with branch stores supervised by full-time, salaried regional agents. Edward Clark, Singer's partner and the business brains of the partnership, had become even more convinced as time passed of the value of relying on his own sales force. The independent agents had difficulty in supplying the necessary marketing services, and their failed to maintain inventories properly. They waited until their stocks were low and then telegraphed large orders, requesting immediate delivery. They seemed to be always either understocked or overstocked. Moreover, the agents were frustratingly slow in returning payments made on the machines to the central office.

Therefore, Clark was constantly on the outlook for men he could hire as salaried "general agents" or regional managers of geographical districts to supervise existing branch stores and to set up new ones. Where such men could not be found, Clark continued to rely on independent agents; but he insisted that such dealers set up branch offices similar to those in a company managed district.

When Clark became president in 1876, a year after Singer's death, he decided to eliminate the independent agencies altogether, at home and abroad. Singer's central offices in New York and London had as yet little control over the branch stores of the independent distributors and, in fact, relatively little control over their own salaried agents. Scarcely any effort had been made to sell in any systematic or standardized way. Uniformity in sales, accounting, credit policies, and procedures was lacking. The techniques of administrative coordination had not yet been perfected. Moreover, in 1877 the last patents of the 1856 pool were to expire. After that year Singer would have to compete at home, as it had long done abroad, without patent protection.

Working closely with George Ross McKenzie, a Scotsman who helped to build Singer's overseas sales organization and succeeded him as president, Clark gradually reorganized and rationalized Singer's marketing and distribution network. First he completed the replacement of the independent distributors with regional offices manned by salaried executives. Then he installed everywhere similar branch offices with teams of canvassers as well as repairmen and accountants. Such offices had proved particularly successful in Great Britain, an area where Singer had never enjoyed patent protection.[31] The network made possible aggressive marketing, reliable service and repair, and careful supervision of credits and collections; it also assured a steady cash flow from the field to the headquarters in London, Hamburg, and New York.

In the period immediately after 1878, Clark and McKenzie perfected the procedures and methods needed to supervise and evaluate this branch office network.[32] In the United States twenty-five different regional "general agencies" reported to the central office in New York. In the United Kingdom, twenty-six regional sales offices reported to a London office. In northern and central Europe the managers of fifty-three more reported to headquarters in Hamburg. Nine others in the rest of Europe, Africa, and the Near East reported to London, while those in Latin America,

Canada, and the Far East were supervised by the central New York office.[33]

The expansion and then reformation of the marketing organization resulted in a constant increase in Singer's sales and, therefore, the daily output of its factories, and the overall size of the enterprise. In 1874 the company built by far the largest sewing machine factory in the world at Elizabethport, New Jersey. During the 1880s it grew in size; but its capacity was surpassed when the company constructed a plant in 1885 in Kilbowie, Scotland (a suburb of Glasgow). That plant, with a rated capacity of 10,000 machines a week, was constructed to replace a smaller Scottish plant built in 1867. Both plants were constructed to improve coordination between production and distribution. The filling of hundreds and then thousands of orders in Europe from the American factory became more and more difficult. Delays became the major cause for losing orders. In 1866, for example, the head of Singer's London office complained that the inability to deliver machines had "utterly ruined" the company's business in Britain.[34] All Singer's capital facilities—its two great factories, a small cabinetmaking plant in South Bend, Indiana, and a foundry in Austria—were financed out of current earnings.

Increased demand in these years caused Singer to expand and systematize its purchasing operations. By the 1890s the company had obtained its own timberlands, an iron mill, and some transportation facilities. These purchases were also paid for from the ample cash flow provided by sale of the machines. Indeed, the company often had a surplus which it invested in railroad and government bonds, and even in other manufacturing firms. Both insiders and outsiders credited Singer's business success to its marketing organization and abilities.[35]

Organization also appears to have been a critical element in the success of a leading manufacturer of the most complex agricultural machine, the mechanical reaper. According to Cyrus H. McCormick III, who wrote a detailed history of the family firm, the McCormick Harvesting Machine Company was able by the end of the century to lead the field because his grandfather "had at his back the best business organization."[36] During the 1850s, the rapid expansion of the railroads and the telegraph permitted the inventors of reapers, harvesters, and other agricultural machinery to build sizable factories for the first time. In marketing their products, Cyrus H. McCormick and his competitors, Obed Hussey, John H. Manny, and Lewis Miller, at first relied, like the sewing machine makers, on territorial agents or distributors. The agents received a small salary, usually $2.00 a week, plus a 5–10 percent commission. Fully responsible for all sales activities in their districts, they hired subagents or dealers who made the actual sales, handled service and repair, granted credit, and supervised collections. McCormick differed from his competitors in that he kept a closer surveillance over his distributors through "traveling agents" and constant correspondence.

Two factors caused McCormick to centralize his sales organization in the late 1870s. First the prolonged depression brought home the need for more effective control over inventories, payments, and sales personnel. Second the development of the binder, a more complex and expensive machine than the harvester, required a stronger sales service force. Therefore at about the same time as Clark and McKenzie began to phase out their independent distributors, McCormick decided to replace his regional agents with salaried managers. By that date the company had about fifty agencies concentrated in the midwest and plains states.

In the reorganization the subagents who had been hired and supervised by the distributors now became franchised dealers. These dealers, usually local livery men, storekeepers, and the like, signed a contract with the company directly. The contract stipulated a dealer's duties in the selling of machines, spare parts, wire, and later, twine for binding. It normally pledged the dealer to handle only McCormick reapers and harvesters, but permitted him to market other types of implements made by other manufacturers.

The primary task of the regional office manager was to keep a close watch on the dealers. He also supervised customer credit and collection and handled local advertising. That office had a number of salesmen who assisted the dealers and often made sales on their own account. Finally, the regional office included trained mechanics who assembled the machines when they arrived from the factory, demonstrated their operations, and serviced them when needed. In the mid-1880s the company employed 140 such "field experts." During the harvest season the factory normally curtailed production and sent out skilled men to the branches to assist in the servicing.

By creating a regional office network, McCormick pioneered in forming a sales organization to back up franchise dealers who did the retailing, much as Singer had innovated in developing its network of company owned and operated branch retail stores. McCormick continued to use independent distributors as his company began to sell beyond the midwest and plains states. By 1885, however, even these jobbers had been replaced by salaried managers and staffs. In the 1880s and 1890s McCormick began to extend its sales overseas to the wheat-growing regions of Europe, Australia, and New Zealand.[37] For foreign marketing, however, the company relied until the late 1890s primarily on local independent distributors.

As at Singer, the expansion of the marketing network increased factory output. Between 1879 and 1886, machines produced annually increased from 13,404 to 25,652. By 1891 it had reached 76,870.[38] To assure a continuing flow of goods into the factory the company systematized purchasing. To meet its requirements of 10 million feet a year of ash, hickory, oak, and poplar, it began in 1885 to buy timber tracts and sawmills in Missouri and Alabama.

In the late 1870s and 1880s other manufacturers of harvesters and other relatively costly agricultural machinery began to build or expand marketing organizations similar to those of the McCormick Company.[39] Walter A. Wood & Co., D. M. Osborne & Co., William Deering & Co., producing the new Appleby Twine Binder, and Warder, Bushnell & Glessner Co., makers of the Champion line, all created national branch office networks. So did the J. I. Case Threshing Company, Inc., and the three leading makers of modern steel plows—John Deere & Company, the Moline Plow Company, both of Moline, Illinois, and the Emerson Brantingham Company of Rockford, Illinois. The three plow makers quickly moved to marketing other less complex implements, including drills, wagons, mowers, and spreaders, in order to use their sales organizations more fully. All of these firms, like McCormick, began in the 1890s to integrate backward by obtaining timberlands and even mines, and in the case of the harvester companies twine factories and hemp plantations.

The integration of mass production and mass distribution of newly invented office machines followed much the same pattern as sewing and agricultural machinery. Scales, letter presses, typewriters, cash registers, adding machines, mimeograph machines, calculators—all required the building of a large marketing organization if the product was to be manufactured in volume. And so the first firms in the field continued long to be the dominant ones.

The experience of the first mass producer of the earliest business machines, E. & T. Fairbanks of St. Johnsbury, Vermont, paralleled McCormick's. Fairbanks, a manufacturer of weighing scales essential to the shipment and sales of goods, began in the 1850s to sell through regional agencies.[40] Like McCormick, "itinerant agents" supervised closely their activities. After the Civil War the firm built a network of regional branch offices with salaried managers, "scales experts," and canvassers to sell machines, provide consumer credit and continuing service, and also to assure steady flow of goods to and cash from the customers. To make full use of its marketing organization the company developed a broad line of products its marketing organization could sell, including letter and waybill presses, warehouse trucks, and "money drawers," the predecessors of the cash register.

The pioneering firms in the manufacturing of typewriters and cash registers which set up their sales forces in the 1880s relied more heavily on canvassers and small Singer-like branch offices than did Fairbanks. John H. Patterson of National Cash Register attributed the swift growth of his innovative enterprise after 1884—and with it the expansion of the industry as a whole—to the strength of his canvassing force, the training and competence of his salesmen, and the ability of his marketing organization to provide credit and service.[41]

The Remington experience underlines in a dramatic fashion the necessity of creating an extensive marketing organization to sell a new office machine in volume.[42] As the Civil War came to a close, E. Remington and Sons of Illion, New York, one of the first firms to mass produce the modern breechloading rifle, began to look for products besides military firearms that required their specialized metal-working manufacturing facilities and skills. In 1865 they set up the Remington Brothers Agricultural Works to make mowing machines and cultivators. As they did not attempt to develop the marketing organization, the enterprise failed. Next they were approached by a former Singer executive to produce an improved sewing machine. Again they failed. The machine was excellent, but, in the words of Remington's historian, "To sell it was another matter." They had little success in quickly creating an effective sales organization, and without it, Remington had little chance of competing successfully with Singer and the other established firms.

In 1873 the inventor of the typewriter, Christopher L. Sholes, came to the Remingtons and asked them to manufacture his typewriter at their Illion plant. This time they moved more slowly, selling the product at first though E. & T. Fairbanks. When in 1881 the typewriter proved a commercial success, the Remingtons hired a small team to build a sales force. Because these men concentrated on the home market, they asked Singer to sell their products abroad. When the Singer Company refused they began to set up their own marketing organization overseas. In 1886 difficulties in the gun business as well as other activities brought the Remington Arms Company into bankruptcy. Those men who were developing the typewriter sales organization then bought out the company's typewriter interests and set up a new firm, Remington Typewriter Company.[43] Soon their enterprise was as successful as Singer or National Cash Register. A number of rivals appeared, but only the Underwood Company and the Wagner Typewriter Company, which built similar sales organizations, succeeded in becoming major competitors.

As the experience of all the new mass-produced machinery companies emphasizes, they could sell in volume only if they created a massive, multiunit marketing organization. All their products were new, all were relatively complicated to operate and maintain, and all relatively costly. No existing marketer knew the product as well as the manufacturer. None had the facilities to provide after-sales service and repair. Few were willing to take the risk of selling on installment, a marketing device which these machinery makers had to invent. Nor were outsiders able to maintain close control over collections, essential to assure a continued cash flow on which the financial health of the enterprise rested. Finally, by using uniform sales techniques, bringing together regularly members of a nation-wide sales force, and comparing the activities and performances of the many different sales offices, the single, centrally controlled sales department was able to develop more effective marketing techniques. It was also able to obtain a constant flow of information on the changing shifts in demands and customer requirements.

Close and constant communication between the branch sales offices, the factory, and its purchasing organization made it possible to schedule a high-volume flow of goods from the suppliers of raw materials to the ultimate consumer, and so to keep the manufacturing facilities relatively full and running steadily. It also assured a steady flow of cash to the central office. Such coordination would have been exceedingly difficult if independent enterprises handled each stage of the processes of supplying, manufacturing, and marketing. The regular and increasing demand made possible in part by an aggressive sales force in turn created pressures to speed up the processes of production through improved machinery, plant design, and management. Increased speed of production in its turn reduced unit costs. The economies of speed and scale, and their national, often global, marketing organizations gave the pioneering firms an impressive competitive advantage and so made it easy for them to continue to dominate their industries.

All this was also true for the makers of new, technologically advanced, relatively standardized machinery that was sold to other manufacturers to be used in their production processes. Because these goods were even more complex and more costly, they required specialized installation as well as closer attention to after-sales service and repair. The sales force for such manufacturers required more professional training than persons selling light machines in mass markets. Salesmen often had degrees in mechancal engineering. Again, it was the decade of the 1880s when enterprises in these industries began to build or rationalize their national and global sales forces.

An excellent example of enterprises producing and marketing in volume for global markets were the makers of recently invented machinery to generate, transmit, and use electricity for power and light. The salesmen at Westinghouse, Thompson-Houston, and Edison General Electric (the last two combined into General Electric in 1892) all knew more about the technical nature of their equipment than did most of their customers.[44] Moreover, few independent distributors could obtain a firm grasp of the rapidly changing new technology. Because of the dangers of electrocution and fire, trained, salaried employees of these companies had to install and service and repair their products. Financing involved large sums, often requiring extensive credit, which independent distributors were unable to supply. Thompson-Houston and Edison Electric, and, to a lesser extent, Westinghouse, began to finance new local central power stations in order to build the market for their machinery.

In these pioneering years of the electrical equipment business, technology was developing fast. Coordination between the sales, production, and purchasing departments thus involved more than scheduling flows of material. It meant that salesmen, equipment designers, and the manufacturing executives had to be in constant touch to coordinate technological improvements with market needs so that the product could be produced at the lowest possible unit cost. It also lessened even more the opportunities for independent sales agencies to acquire the necessary skills to market the product.

Other manufacturers whose products were based on electricity developed in these same years similar marketing organizations with worldwide networks of branch offices. Such enterprises included Western Electric, the subsidiary of American Bell Telephone, which produced telephones and equipment necessary to relay calls, the Johnson Company, which built electric streetcar rails and switches, and the Otis Elevator Company.[45] Otis, established in 1854, began to expand after 1878 when it built its first high-speed hydraulic elevator for commercial buildings. The coming of electricity, a flexible source of power, helped the company expand its market. The branch office network created at Otis in the 1880s permitted it to dominate the business completely abroad as well as at home until well into the twentieth century, when Westinghouse became a major competitor.

Other makers of standardized machinery built comparable organizations in the 1880s.[46] One was Babcock & Wilcox, makers of steam boilers and steam machinery, incorporated in 1881 and financed in part by Singer Sewing Machine Company profits. Another was the Henry R. Worthington Company, maker of pumps and hydraulic equipment for urban water and sewage systems in all parts of the world. In this same decade Link-Belt Machinery Company, makers of conveying and transmission machinery, and the Norton Company, makers of grinding wheels and grind wheel machinery, set up their widespread sales and buying networks. And there were undoubtedly others.

The makers of the new machinery so central to the mechanization of American agriculture, business, and industry created similar integrated enterprises at about the same time and in about the same way. The organization, operation, and financing of these enterprises manufacturing durable goods were comparable to the procedures in the firms that pioneered in the mass production and mass distribution of semiperishable and perishable products. Nearly all of these machinery makers either built or perfected their marketing and then purchasing organizations in the decade of the 1880s. In nearly all cases production remained concentrated in a small number of large plants. To manage their multifunctional enterprises they built similar centralized, functionally departmentalized organizational structures. They differed from the manufacturers of perishable and semiperishable goods in that the purchasing organizations were smaller. The makers of the new sewing machine and agricultural and office machinery integrated backward to control supplies of raw and semifinished materials, but this was less common among the makers of electrical equipment and other heavy machinery. Like the producers of perishables and semiperishables, these machine companies were financed from within. Cash flow supplemented by short-term loans from local commercial banks provided the funds for working and fixed capital. In building this national and often global network they had no need to go to the capital markets for long-term credit. The one exception was the electrical equipment manufacturers who began to finance the construction of central power stations. As a result, all but these large electrical firms remained fully controlled by the entrepreneurs who founded them, their families, or a small group of associates.

All of the pioneering machinery firms continued to dominate their industries for decades. Administrative coordination brought lower costs and permitted manufacturers to have a more direct contact with markets. The technological complexities of their products, particularly those selling producers' goods, made their marketing organizations of trained engineers and other technical specialists even more powerful competitive weapons than were the sales departments of makers of consumer goods purchased for immediate consumption. The nature of their processes as well as products, led to the assigning of technicians to concentrate on improving both product and process and so to the formation of the first formal industrial research departments.[47] As in the case of the first integrated manufacturers of perishable and semiperishable products, the machinery firms soon had competitors. But to compete with the established enterprise demanded the creation of a comparable national and often international marketing network. And in competing, the new enterprise had to win customers before its organization could generate the volume necessary to provide low prices and high cash flow or develop its staffs of expert marketing and research technicians. Rarely did more than a handful of competitors succeed in obtaining a significant share of the national and international markets. These industries quickly became and remained oligopolistic or monopolistic.

Makers of volume-produced standardized machinery, processors of perishable products, and those that mass produced low-priced packaged goods, internalized the activities of the wholesaler or other middlemen when these distributors were unable to provide the marketing services needed if the goods were to be manufactured in the unprecedented volume permitted by the new technologies of production and distribution. The resulting enterprises, clustered in the food and machinery industries, were then the first industrial corporations to coordinate administratively the flow of goods on a national, indeed a global, scale. They were among the world's first modern multinationals. Their products were usually new. This was true not only for sewing, agricultural, and office machinery but also for cigarettes, matches, breakfast cereals, canned milk and soup, roll film and Kodak cameras, and even fresh meat that had been butchered a thousand miles away. In all these new industries the pioneers remained dominant enterprises. Because they were the first big businesses in American industry, they defined many of its administrative practices and procedures. Their formation, organization, and growth, therefore, have significant implications for the operation and structure of American industry and the economy as a whole.

The followers

The pioneers of the 1880s soon had their imitators. Nevertheless, the giant, integrated industrial enterprise remained the exception until after 1900. Nearly all American manufacturers, including those using the new mass production techniques, continued to employ existing marketers to sell and distribute their products. The makers of consumer goods relied on the wholesaler and increasingly on the mass retailer. The manufacturers of producer goods continued to depend on manufacturers' agents and other comparable middlemen.

The firms that did adopt the strategy of vertical integration in the 1890s did so for the same reasons as the pioneers in the 1880s. Middlemen were unable to provide for their marketing needs. In addition, a few firms which had for many years been well served by the existing marketers began to build their own selling and buying organizations. These were primarily metal-making and metal-working companies whose output reached unprecedented levels through continuing technological and organizational improvement.

For these reasons enterprises that grew large in the 1890s by building their own marketing and purchasing networks continued to cluster in the food and machinery industries. In the 1890s Andrew J. Preston created a refrigerated distribution network comparable to that of meat packers to sell bananas in the national market.[48] In 1899 his firm, the Boston Fruit Company, became the core enterprise in the United Fruit Company, which, in addition to its distribution system, came to own a fleet of refrigerated steamers and a vast acreage of plantations in the Caribbean region. In the same years William Wrigley and Asa Candler followed the model of American Tobacco and Quaker Oats to create giant business enterprises in the chewing gum and soft drink trade. Wrigley of Chicago made his fortune in chewing gum by integrating high-volume production with a global marketing organization and a supply department that became one of the world's largest buyers of chicle.[49] Candler of Atlanta became a multimillionaire from the making and selling of Coca-Cola in the same manner. The success of the Coca-Cola Company was based on his realization of the possibilities of high-volume sales by marketing syrup directly to druggists and other retailers rather than bottling the finished product.[50] His company quickly became an integrated enterprise with a global sales force and a purchasing organization that operated its own cooperage. In addition, the company began to build branch processing plants to supply distant markets at home and abroad.

In machinery the same pattern held. The makers of newly invented office machinery followed the examples of Remington Typewriter and National Cash Register. In the late 1890s, A. B. Dick & Company, the developers of the mimeograph machine, began to market their product on a national scale. Around 1900 William S. Burroughs began to mass produce and mass distribute his adding machines. Their integrated enterprises dominated their markets from the beginning.[51] In the next decade the two pioneering makers of time clocks and of computing and tabulating machines put together similar organizations. These were to merge in 1911 to form the Computing-Tabulator Recording Company, the forerunner of International Business Machines. It is safe to say that all office machines, from the typewriter to the Xerox duplicator, were from their initial development produced and marketed through large integrated enterprises.

In the 1890s makers of large, complex, standardized machinery set up marketing organizations similar to those of the electrical companies and Otis Elevator. These firms included Ingersoll Sergeant Drill (which in 1905 joined the Rand Company to become Ingersoll Rand), Mergenthaler Linotype, producers of a new form of typesetting machine, and E. W. Bliss, manufacturers of dies, presses, and similar machinery.[52] Comparable, too, was the Owens Bottle Machine and Crown Cork and Seal.[53]

Michael J. Owens had invented the bottle machine in Edward D. Libbey's glass factory, and by 1900 the machine produced a completely automatic high-speed bottling process for which Crown Cork and Seal provided the stoppers.

As the century came to an end, a small number of companies that had long relied on wholesalers or manufacturers' agents to sell their products also began to build their own marketing organizations. Manufacturers in the metal-making and metal fabricating industries, where the application of improved technology and factory design and the procedures of scientific management created a constant output, were among the first to adopt this strategy. In the late 1890s firearm manufacturers—Winchester, Colt, and Remington—began to set up a small number of regional sales offices of their own to contact wholesalers and retailers, to improve scheduling of deliveries, and to advertise more aggressively.[54] At about the same time the Yale & Towne Manufacturing Company, the leading producer of locks and building hardware, Waltham Watch and other watch and clock makers, and the Crane Company, makers of plumbing fixtures, created much the same type of multifunctional enterprise.

In the nineties leading iron and steel producers and fabricators began to replace independent manufacturers' agents who handled several accounts with salaried salesmen working out of branch offices. In that decade Washburn & Moen and the Trenton Iron Company (both prominent wire makers) set up several branch sales offices.[55] In the same decade the foremost iron and steel maker, the Carnegie Company, and smaller firms such as Lukens Iron and Steel did the same.[56] At Carnegie these sales managers and those agents who were still retained on a commission basis reported weekly to Alexander Peacock, who was appointed the company's general sales agent in 1893. Peacock kept a careful overview of sales and inventory so as to improve scheduling and flows through the Carnegie plants and to provide information on the changing demand and competitors' moves. In these same years, the wire companies and Carnegie began to expand their purchasing organizations and to integrate backward.

For these three companies, as in other large metal-making and metal-fabricating enterprises, such expansion and the beginnings of integration forward and backward quickly resulted in mergers with competitors. By 1901 all three of these firms had become part of the giant United States Steel Company. In the 1890s the primary route to size was becoming one of combination and consolidation. Their experience was part of another process of growth followed by American manufacturers.

C H A P T E R 10

Integration by Way of Merger

Combination and consolidation

American manufacturing firms became large, multiunit enterprises in two ways, by adding marketing and purchasing offices or by merger. The first embodied the strategy of vertical integration. The second was almost always an expression of the strategy of horizontal combination. The first aimed at increasing profits by decreasing costs and expanding productivity through administrative coordination of the several operating units. The second aimed at maintaining the profits by controlling the price and output of each of the operating units.

In the United States horizontal combination rarely proved to be a viable long-term business strategy. The firms that first grew large by taking the merger route remained profitable only if after consolidating, they then adopted a strategy of vertical integration.

Nearly all enterprises that grew by merger followed the same path. They had their beginnings as trade associations that managed cartels formed by many small manufacturing enterprises. These federations then consolidated legally into a single enterprise, taking the form of a trust or a holding company. Administrative centralization followed legal consolidation. The governing board of the merger rationalized the manufacturing facilities of the constituent companies and administered the enlarged plants from a single central office. The final step was to integrate forward into marketing and backward into purchasing and the control of raw or semifinished materials. By the time it completed the last move, the consolidated enterprise was employing a set of lower, middle, and top managers to administer, monitor, coordinate, and plan for the activities of its many operating units and for the enterprise as a whole. By then the visible hand of management replaced the invisible hand of market forces in coordinating the flow from the suppliers of raw materials to the ultimate consumer.

American manufacturers took this road at different speeds and in different ways. A few charted their courses with deliberation. A greater number moved from one step to the next in response to specific and immediate business problems. Some completed the course within a relatively short time. Others dawdled along the way for two or three decades. Nevertheless, very few American mergers remained large or profitable unless they followed this road to its logical end—that is, unless they moved beyond a strategy of horizontal combination to one of vertical integration. Even then they rarely became and remained powerful business enterprises unless they were in industries employing mass production technologies for mass national and global markets. Only in such industries did the advantages of administratively coordinating high-volume flows provide continuing market power.

In reviewing the history of the enterprises that followed the merger route, two points need to be kept in mind. First, mergers on a national scale appeared only as the railroad and telegraphic network went into full operation in the 1870s and 1880s. By lowering transportation barriers, the railroads permitted many small enterprises to compete in the national market for the first time. At the same time the telegraph and then the telephone helped to make possible centralized supervision of a number of geographically scattered operating units.

Second, until the passage of the Sherman Antitrust Act in 1890 and, indeed, until the act's interpretation by the Supreme Court, horizontal combination did not violate federal law. Until the 1880s only ill-defined and difficult to enforce concepts of common law provided any legal restraint to the formation of such cartels. In the 1880s a few states passed antimonopoly laws. It was, however, not until the Supreme Court handed down its decisions on the Sherman Act that effective legal action could be taken against nationwide combinations in restraint of trade.[1]

American manufacturers began in the 1870s to take the initial step to growth by way of merger—that is, to set up nationwide associations to control price and production. They did so primarily as a response to the continuing price decline, which became increasingly oppressive after the panic of 1873 ushered in a prolonged economic depression. That long-term price decline reflected the complex interaction between the supply of money (including the velocity with which it was used in making transactions) and the rapid expansion of output.[2] Industrial output soared as manufacturers widely adopted the new factory form of production. The wholesale price index on all commodities fell from 151 in 1869 to 82 in 1886, on farm products from 128 to 68 in the same span of years, and on metals and metal products from 227 to 110. To most manufacturers the only practical response to rising output and falling prices was to form national associations to maintain prices by curtailing production.

By the 1880s these federations had become part of the normal way of doing business in most American industries. Trade associations for the purpose of controlling price and production had appeared in the mechanical industries, including those making lumber, woodware, flooring, furniture, even caskets, and those producing shoes, saddlery, and other leather products. They came, too, in the refining and other chemically oriented industries—those producing petroleum, rubber footwear, explosives, glass, paper, and leather; and in the foundry and furnace industries—those making iron, steel, copper, brass, lead, and other metals. In addition, they occurred in industries fabricating metals into bars, wire, rails, nails, sheets, and all types of metal implements and machines. In the hardware industries alone, over fifty different trade associations managed cartels for as many specialized products (see table 5).[3] No industry appears to have been immune. Only in textiles, apparel, publishing, and printing were the number of trade associations small.

During the 1870s and 1880s, manufacturers working through their trade associations devised increasingly complex techniques to maintain industry-wide price schedules and production quotas.[4] The associations allocated specific markets to different firms. They followed the example of the railroads by forming money pools in which each was allocated a specific amount of income. Those that sold less than their quotas were paid the difference out of profits contributed to the pool by those that sold more than they had been allocated. They set heavy fines for making false reports or not providing complete records of sales and profits. In addition, the manufacturers' associations worked closely with individual wholesalers and selling agents and with the trade associations of wholesalers also being formed in these years.

But, as in the case of the railroads, the manufacturers and their marketing allies found these horizontal combinations difficult to maintain. The temptation always existed to increase returns by cutting prices through secret rebates, by falsifying reports, or by failing to record sales. Often after the association appeared to have successfully stabilized prices, manufacturers would leave the cartel, openly cutting prices to obtain more trade. Basically, the industrial cartels failed for the same reason as did those in railroads. The agreements did not have the binding effect of a legal contract. They could not be enforced in courts of law.

Whereas the railroads had responded to this problem by urging state and federal legislation to legalize pools or cartels, the manufacturers turned to developing tighter legal controls over the members of cartels. Owners of the leading firms in an industry purchased stock in each others' enterprises and in the smaller companies in their trade association. Stock ownership permitted them to look at the books of their associates and thus better enforce their cartel agreement.

Yet this strategy had its weaknesses. Buying into other companies was

Table 5. Manufacturers' trade associations in the hardware trades, 1870s and 1880s

1870s

Augurs, bits	Pumps
Door locks	Cast iron butts
Knobs	Rakes
Padlocks	Furniture hardware
Cast butts	Locks
Fluting machines	Hose
Stamped ware (common and deep fry pans)	Bench planes
Wood screws	Shears
Nuts, bolts	Brass
Table cutlery	Tacks
Hinges	Axes
Hollow ware (kettles, bellied pots, etc.)	Clothes wringers
Picks	Rules
Mattocks	Bit braces
Grub hoes	Sash weights
Sledges, hammers	Furniture casters
Strap, T. hinges	Carriage hardware
Cordage	Wrought butts, hinges
Nails	Stoves

1880s

Clocks	Bicycle tubing
Carriage bolts	Snaths
Curry bombs	Trunk locks
Wire	Wood planes
Soil pipe, fittings	Circular saws
Shovels	Sinks
Stove boards	Padlocks
Files	Boring implements

Source: William H. Becker, "American Wholesale Hardware Trade Association, 1870–1900," *Business History Review*, 45:183 (Summer 1971). This list makes no pretense at completeness. Associations came and went too quickly and the trade press was too limited to record them all. The major sources are *Iron Age*, 1873–1880, and the *Hardware Reporter*, 1879–1880. For the 1880s sources are rather limited, but what data there are indicate that there were a large number of associations. *American Artisan, Hardware*, and *Hardware Dealer* are the major sources.

expensive. Often, too, the new stockholders were still uncertain whether the company accounts they had access to were accurate. Moreover, firms were often still partnerships, whose control could not be obtained through the buying of shares. Nor did stock purchasing rectify the greatest weakness of the cartel. None of these trade associations could make decisions concerning the internal management of the individual firms. Nor could they decide where to build new plants or to shut down or modernize old ones. In other words, the associations managing cartels could not make either day-to-day operating or investment decisions for their members. They were merely federations of legally independent enterprises whose representatives met weekly and monthly to set price and production schedules.

More effective control over the companies in the combination required the merger of the constituent firms into a single legally defined entity. If this entity owned the majority of the stock of constituent companies, the board of the new overall enterprise could then institute and maintain more rigorous control over their operations. It could also consolidate and rationalize manufacturing facilities of the several subsidiaries.

The obvious legal form to meet these needs was the holding company—the device first used by railroads to merge hitherto independent corporations. The difficulty was that the formation of a company to hold stock in other companies required a special act of a state legislature. As many manufacturers were planning to use the device to strengthen existing cartels, they did not want to risk the publicity required in order to get a special act through a legislature. Nor could they expect legislators to endorse their plans with any enthusiasm.

So the trust was born. By this device a number of companies turned their stock over to a board of trustees, receiving in return trust certificates of equivalent value.[5] (Constituent companies that were still partnerships had to incorporate in order to have the stock necessary to make the exchange.) The board of trustees was then specifically authorized to act as a board of managers with the power to make operating and investment decisions for the constituent companies that had entered the consolidation.

The trust was, however, only a temporary expedient. It quickly came under attack in state and federal courts and in state legislatures.[6] What was needed was a general incorporation law that permitted the formation of holding companies simply by filing a few outline forms and paying a standard fee. The New Jersey legislature quickly obliged. In its session of 1888–1889, that body modified the state's general incorporation law to permit manufacturing companies to purchase and to hold stock in other enterprises within and without the state, and to pay for property owned outside the state with stock issued for that purpose. A year later the United States Congress, responding to the increasing protests against the cartelization of so many American industries, passed the Sherman Antitrust Act, declaring illegal "combinations in the form of a trust or otherwise in restraint of trade." Immediately the "New Jersey holding company" took the place of the trust as the legal form used to merge a number of single-unit enterprises operating facilities in several states into a single, large consolidated enterprise. The holding company, like the earlier trust, provided the legal form to maintain tighter control over a federation of small, single-unit, single-function manufacturing firms. Such legal consolidations also provided the first essential step in the transformation of such federations into modern industrial enterprises by means of administrative consolidation and centralization.

The mergers of the 1880s

During that formative decade of the 1880s a very small number of manufacturers first moved from cartels to legal consolidations. All the successful mergers of that decade went beyond legal consolidation to administrative centralization. Not all, however, went the whole course— that is, moved beyond administrative centralization of processing facilities to vertical integration.

Despite widespread use of the term trust (as distinguished from a trade association or holding company), I have been able to identify definitely only eight that were formed to operate in the national market.[7] Two—the cattle and cordage trusts—were short-lived. The other six—petroleum, cottonseed oil, linseed oil, sugar, whiskey, and lead processing—came to dominate their industries for decades. Though few in number, these succussful trusts, all in refining and distilling industries, pioneered in new legal and administrative techniques and are thus of great historical interest.

These processors, the first to grow large by merger, were those who had processes and products less technologically revolutionary than those manufacturers who attained great size in the same decade by internal growth. The latter built their modern business enterprises in response to the marketing needs resulting from adopting a new high-volume technology or from marketing a technologically complex product. In the refining and distilling industries new technologies of production evolved quickly but less suddenly than in those processing tobacco, matches, and cereals. Their products remained technologically simpler than those of the machinery makers, and they had little difficulty in marketing them through the existing wholesaler network. Those enterprises, therefore, did not feel the same pressures to integrate forward.

During the 1850s and 1860s the spread of the railroad and telegraph networks and the growing availability of coal to provide heat and fuel for machines permitted many small firms to adopt the new large-batch and continuous-process refining and distilling methods. Soaring output soon drove down prices. By the 1870s processing enterprises using these methods of production were under intense pressure to maintain profits by limiting production and controlling processes.

The first merger, or legal combination of many small manufacturers, came in the United States in the petroleum industry, the industry which by 1870 had most effectively perfected the new high-volume, capital-intensive technology. By the end of the 1870s the leading processors under the guidance of the largest refiner, the Standard Oil Company, had created one of the strongest industrial cartels in the nation.[8] It was so effective that its members no longer felt the need of the services of a trade association to administer it. The formation of the Standard Oil Trust was not, then, inspired by a need to tighten control over the members of the existing Standard Oil "alliance," as it was then called. It was rather the response to an opportunity to increase profits through concentration and centralization of production and then vertical integration. Yet the new giant legally and administratively centralized enterprise did not evolve from a carefully planned strategy but from short-term reactions to changing technology and markets.

In 1872, when their industry was little more than a decade old, the leading petroleum refiners decided on a strategy of horizontal combination. To control increasing output and decreasing prices they formed the National Refiners Association. John D. Rockefeller, whose Standard Oil Company operated in Cleveland, Ohio, the largest refinery in the nation, encouraged the creation of the refiners' association and became its first president. The association failed to maintain control of price or production. Such federations, Rockefeller quickly came to believe, were mere "ropes of sand." He and his associates then decided to obtain the cooperation of its rivals by relying on the economic power provided by their high-volume, low-cost operation. They began by asking the Lake Shore Railroad to reduce its rates from $2.00 to $1.35 a barrel on Standard Oil shipments between Cleveland and New York City if Standard provided sixty carloads a day, every day. The road's general manager quickly accepted, for assured traffic in such high volume meant he could schedule the use of his equipment much more efficiently and so lose nothing by the reduced rate. Indeed, the general manager, somewhat gratuitously, offered the same rates to any other oil refiner shipping the same volume.

The Standard Oil Company then invited the leading refiners first in Cleveland and later in other refining centers to join in benefiting from these rate agreements. The control of transportation provided a weapon to keep out new competitors and a threat to prevent those who joined Standard from dropping out of the cartel. Even so, Rockefeller and his associates in the Standard Oil Company—his brother William, Henry M. Flagler, Oliver H. Payne, and Steven V. Harkness—took the precaution of exchanging Standard Oil stock for that of their allies. By 1876 there were more than twenty-five firms in the Standard Oil group.[9] By 1880, when the number had reached forty, Rockefeller and his four associates

held four-sevenths of the securities of the alliance's members. Representatives of these firms met regularly to set price and production schedules,
but there was no central board with the power to administer the operations
of the constituent companies or to make plans and allocate resources for
the alliance as a whole.

In 1881 the alliance controlled close to 90 percent of the country's
refining capacity and had demonstrated its willingness to use its economic
power ruthlessly.[10] Any time its members desired, they could easily crush
the remaining few small refiners making kerosene or any of the growing
number of competitors producing lubricants and other specialized
products.

In Europe the discovery of the Russian oil fields by the Caspian Sea
posed a long-term competitive threat. This was a serious challenge, for
in 1880 Europe still took 70 percent of all the illuminating oil processed in
the United States.[11] To maintain their share of that market the Americans
would have to reduce costs in producing and distributing kerosene. Yet in
1881 the threat was still a distant one. The railroad connecting Baku to
the Black Sea was not scheduled for completion until 1883. After that,
rivals needed time to set up production and distribution facilities. In fact,
the competition in the European markets from Russian oil did not become serious for Standard Oil until the late 1880s.

Technology rather than markets triggered the decision of the Standard
Oil alliance to solidify legal control and to centralize its management.
The critical technological innovation was the long-distance crude oil pipeline.[12] It created cost-cutting opportunities that required the alliance as a
whole to make centralized investment decisions.

From the very beginning of the industry, pipelines had gathered stored
crude oil at railheads and terminals. But the construction of the first
long-distance pipeline was not begun until 1878. Then it was built by
producers of crude oil to break Standard's hold on railroad transportation.
These producers formed the Tidewater Pipeline Company that initially
built a line to connect the oil regions of western Pennsylvania (at that
time still the only major source of crude oil in America) with the Reading
Railroad. Since that road did not carry oil, it had no arrangement with
the Standard alliance. Despite all the efforts of the Standard Oil Company
to halt its construction, the pipeline was completed in July of 1879. The
Tidewater company then pushed its pipeline on to the coast. At first that
company sold to refiners in New Jersey and Pennsylvania, but soon it
built refineries of its own.

Once the long-distance pipeline had proved itself, Rockefeller and his
associates moved swiftly. Pipelines, they realized, transported crude oil
far more cheaply than railroads did. The lines also provided excellent

storage. Their existence made possible the scheduling of a much greater and steadier refinery throughput than was possible using rail shipments. Moreover, because the pipeline could carry crude oil to processing facilities but not refined products to markets, the completion of long-distance lines called for relocation of refinery capacity at centers close to the market, particularly at the ports where ships loaded the refined products for the great European markets.

The allies' initial move was to construct their own pipelines from western Pennsylvania to Cleveland to the west and to New York and Philadelphia on the coast. This required setting up a new large corporation, the National Transit Company, to build and operate the cross-country pipelines and to consolidate and operate the existing gathering and storage lines. Capitalized at $30 million (an impressive investment when the Standard Oil Company itself was capitalized at only $3.5 million), National Transit took over the stocks and properties of the pipeline companies controlled by members of the Standard Oil group and then began construction of a huge interregional pipeline network. The legal vehicle for this new pipeline company was a catchall charter issued by the Pennsylvania legislature ten years earlier that permitted the holding of stock in out-of-state companies. Originally obtained by Tom Scott in 1871 for possible use in the building of the Pennsylvania's railroad system, it had been forfeited by the road and much later purchased by Standard's lawyers from a state bureau.[13]

The next step—that of consolidating refining capacity in order to take advantage of the new pipeline network—proved more difficult. The owners of the forty enterprises forming the alliance now required a central authority to decide what refineries to close down, which ones to modernize, and where and when to build new ones.[14] To provide the necessary legal vehicle, their lawyers searched without success for another catchall charter similar to that used for the pipeline. At that moment, too, the Pennsylvania legislature was attempting to put a tax on the assets, including capital stock and dividends, of Standard Oil of Ohio as a "foreign" firm operating in Pennsylvania. As protests against Standard's power were growing, Rockefeller and his associates did not relish the legislative battle required to get a special holding-company charter.

Then the sharp mind of Standard's legal counsel, S. C. T. Dodd, conceived of the new trust form of organization. By the agreement signed on January 2, 1882, the shareholders of the forty companies exchanged their stock for certificates in the new Standard Oil Trust. The trust instrument authorized an office of nine trustees to "exercise general supervision over the affairs of the several Standard Oil Companies."[15] At the same time state-chartered subsidiaries were formed to take over the properties of the alliance operating in one state. As local enterprises, they were not subject to restrictions or excessive taxes levied on "foreign" corporations, similar to those Pennsylvania was seeking to place on Standard Oil of Ohio.

As soon as the new trust had set up its headquarters at 26 Broadway in New York City, the trustees began to consolidate refinery capacity.[16] Between 1882 and 1885 the trust reduced the number of refineries it operated from fifty-three to twenty-two. Over two-fifths of the trust's output came to be concentrated in three huge new refineries at Bayonne, New Jersey, Philadelphia, and Cleveland. The economies permitted by the greatly expanded volume and carefully scheduled throughput cut the average cost of producing a gallon of refined oil from 1.5¢ to 0.5¢, and the costs in the great new refineries were still lower. The administration of the refineries became centralized at 26 Broadway through creation of a committee for manufacturing and a supporting set of staff offices. In addition, committees and staff offices were set up to supervise packaging and transportation.

The coordination of throughput from the crude oil wells through the pipelines to the refineries became the responsibility of the Joseph Seep Agency. The former purchasing agent for Standard Oil of Ohio, it now handled all the buying of crude oil for the trust.[17] Because it purchased in such large quantities, it by-passed the oil exchanges, where crude oil had been bought and sold since the beginning of the industry. Because it purchased directly from crude oil producers, the exchanges went out of business in the 1890s.

Once the new trust completed its consolidation of refining, it moved into marketing.[18] Not planned when the trust was first formed, this move was primarily a response to the need to assure a steady flow of the high-volume output from the new centralized refining facilities to the consumer. The decision to go into marketing was also affected by the increasing power of the wholesalers of refined products. After 1875 the tank car began to replace the barrel and can for long-distance shipments of kerosene and other refined products. By doubling the load a train could pull, the tank car required wholesalers to increase storage facilities. Those wholesalers who invested in new equipment were able to sell at a much greater volume and cut their unit costs. Their new facilities not only gave them an advantage over small competitors but also put them in a better position to bargain with the trust. Moreover, many large wholesalers preferred to market their own brands, mixing kerosene from Standard with that of small independents. So their existence prevented Standard Oil's maintenance of the quality of its product as well as control over its price. A further argument for direct marketing was that it would improve the accuracy and lower the cost of market information.

The executive committee of the trust decided to build its marketing organization first at home and then abroad. In 1885, the committee set up two wholly owned sales subsidiaries—Continental Oil and Standard Oil of Kentucky. In 1886 it began to buy out the leading wholesalers. By the early 1890s it had a national sales organization managed through regionally defined subsidiaries. In 1888 it set up the wholly owned Anglo-American Petroleum Company to market in Britain; built a fleet of steam tankers for trans-Atlantic transportation; and then formed a joint venture with two German distributors to sell in central and western Europe.[19]

The process of vertical integration was completed in the late 1880s when Standard Oil began to produce its own crude oil. The move was a defensive one, largely in response to the changing supply situation.[20] Up to the late 1880s the Standard Oil alliance and then the trust felt little need to control its own crude oil supplies. There was always plenty available. As production declined in the Pennsylvania fields, the producers for the first time appeared to have a chance to control output and price. At the same time, the opening of new fields, which had been discovered near Lima, Indiana, raised the possibility of having the source of supply fall into the hands of a small number of crude oil producers. The Standard Oil trustees waited almost two years after the trust built pipelines into the Lima fields before they began to buy oil-producing properties. Then the trust moved quickly. Within three years Standard Oil was extracting 25 percent of the nation's crude oil.

By the early 1890s Standard Oil had become a fully integrated enterprise. Within a decade it had moved from a strategy of horizontal combination to one calling for legal consolidation, administrative centralization, and then vertical integration. As the firm centralized the administration of production and moved into new functions, its senior executives, the trustees, hired large numbers of middle managers to supervise and coordinate its many operating units. By the 1890s the large central office at 26 Broadway (whose activities are described in Chapter 13) coordinated flows of petroleum from the crude oil fields of Pennsylvania and Indiana through the processes of refining to markets in all parts of the nation and the world.

In the next two decades challenges to Standard's dominance came from other integrated enterprises. In Europe, the threat of competition finally materialized in the rise of major integrated enterprises managed and financed by such powerful business families as the Nobels and the Rothschilds. In the United States, the Tidewater Company, the consolidation of crude oil producers that built the long-distance pipeline, had made a deal as early as 1883 with the trust to divide pipeline shipments from the Pennsylvania oil regions to the coast. Tidewater continued to build its refining capacity, setting up in 1888 the largest refinery in the world at Bayonne, New Jersey.[21] It sold its product at home through its own marketing organization, but relied on Standard to market from 50 to 75 percent of its exports abroad.

A more serious domestic challenge to Standard came when the production of crude oil in the Pennsylvania oil fields had fallen off enough to permit the producers there in 1895 to combine to form the Pure Oil Company. That firm constructed a new transregional pipeline to Marcus Hook, Pennsylvania, on the Delaware River, built refineries there, and then set up its own marketing organization, which concentrated on the European market.[22] Within a decade of its founding the Pure Oil Company was an effective integrated competitor. By 1911, when Standard Oil was broken up by a Supreme Court decision, there were already at least eight other integrated American oil companies competing with Standard for national and international markets (see table 7).

Of the five other successful trusts, three—cottonseed oil, linseed oil, and lead processing—followed Standard Oil's example. Within less than a decade of their formation they had become fully integrated enterprises. The other two—sugar and whiskey—immediately consolidated production facilities and did their own purchasing, but did not move into marketing. They clung to the strategy of horizontal combination much longer than the other three.

Formed in 1884, the American Cotton Oil Trust had by 1889 consolidated production into seven refineries. (Seven more were added when the consolidation expanded in 1890.)[23] It also had obtained four soap works and four lard works. By 1889 it had an extensive buying network for purchasing cottonseed directly from farmers along the railroads of the south. By that same year it controlled some fifty cotton gins and fifty-two crude oil mills used in the initial processing. In the 1880s the trust also moved into transportation, acquiring a fleet of tank cars. By 1891 it owned and operated 326 tank cars. After 1890 it expanded its marketing organization of sales offices and storage facilities overseas. In 1892 the company had a tanker constructed and a major depot built at Rotterdam in order to exploit the large German market for margarine and food oils. By the early 1890s, the company was producing not only cottonseed oil and cake for cattle feed and fertilizer, but its own brand of "cottonlene" food oil and "Gold Dust" washing powder, lard, margarine, and soap. Then, to make use of the marketing organization it had developed to sell fertilizers, it purchased eight potash mines. Thus, by the early nineties the cotton oil trust had become a full-line, integrated, giant enterprise whose operation required the services of many salaried middle and top managers.

From 1888 on, the American Cotton Oil Company had strong competition from the Southern Cotton Oil Company, which also quickly became an integrated, full-line enterprise.[24] These two firms continued to dominate their industry until well into the twentieth century. Their competition, particularly in the European markets, came from large integrated British and Continental companies—Lever, Jurgens, and Van den Burgh. At home the competitors were Procter & Gamble and Armour, Swift, and other large meat packers who produced lard, soap, and fertilizers.

The National Lead Trust began to follow the same strategy of Standard Oil when William Thompson left the Standard Oil Trust to become the president of National Lead in June 1889.[25] The lead trust formed in 1887 was a merger of a large number of lead-processing firms, and it continued to concentrate on the chemical processing rather than the fabrication of lead. It soon produced 80 percent of the country's white lead capacity, 70 percent of red lead, 60 percent of lead acetate, and 15 percent of its linseed oil, and became the country's leading producer of paint. However, it accounted for less than 10 percent of the output of sheet lead, lead pipe, and other fabricated lead products. After consolidating production, Thompson, who had headed Standard's Domestic Trade Committee, began to build a national and global sales organization. At the same time he consolidated purchasing, setting up a special department to buy flaxseed for its linseed oil operation. Then he had the enterprise's smelting and refining works at Socorro, New Mexico, enlarged. From the early 1890s on, National Lead continued to dominate the industry, getting some competition from another trust, National Linseed.

The linseed oil trust was never as successful as the initial mergers in petroleum, cottonseed oil, and lead.[26] One reason was that it was smaller and had a less diversified product line than National Lead. Another was that it did not have the large markets, especially overseas, and ample sources of supply that Standard Oil and American Cotton Oil enjoyed. It did consolidate the original forty-nine mills that went into the merger. It came to own over forty storage elevators, a fleet of tank cars, and a number of tank stations, and it set up a number of branch sales offices. However, limited supplies of flaxseed led to speculation in the purchasing of its raw materials, and twice in the nineties such purchases almost ruined the enterprise. Only after the financial and administrative reorganization of the company in 1898, when it became the American Linseed Company, did it begin to achieve financial success. The appointment of Frederick T. Gates, Rockefeller's financial adviser, as its president and John D. Rockefeller, Jr., as a board member suggests that the Standard Oil experience may have been put to use in improving the performance of the reorganized company.[27]

In these four industries—petroleum, cotton oil, linseed oil, and lead processing—the leading mergers had by the 1890s adopted a policy of vertical integration and were soon competing with two or three other large vertically integrated enterprises. Two other trusts formed in the processing industries in the 1880s—the whiskey and sugar trusts—abandoned their strategy of horizontal combination only after it had proved itself increasingly costly and unproductive. The corporate successors to the whiskey trust, the Distillers Corporation, had by the early 1890s concentrated production so that eighty small plants had been reduced to twenty-one larger ones,[28] but they continued to operate with little overall control. Although the enlarged units permitted some reductions in costs, the enterprise kept prices high and so encouraged competition to grow. In 1895, just before it went into receivership, the company decided to spend a million dollars to build a selling organization in the urban east, its primary market. Only after passing through receivership did the company begin to alter its basic strategy. It first centralized the administration of its productive facilities, and then in 1898 purchased two leading liquor wholesalers. These wholesalers and the manufacturing enterprise were consolidated in 1903 into the Distillers-Securities Corporation. This integrated enterprise remained the largest distiller in the nation until the passage of the Eighteenth Amendment in 1919 drastically curtailed that trade.

The sugar trust also consolidated production and purchasing after its formation in 1887.[29] As in whiskey, such consolidation brought lower unit costs by making possible economies in the operation of the larger refineries. Once this was done, its most domineering founder, Henry O. Havemeyer, concentrated on using this economic power to drive out competitors by price cutting, exploiting railroad rebates, controlling supplies, and making rebate arrangements with wholesalers—all methods that the Standard Oil group had made notorious in the 1870s. Nevertheless, competition grew, particularly at those times when American Sugar made the error of raising the profit margin. Its share of the market fell from 75 percent in 1894 to 49.3 percent in 1907 and then by 1917 to 28 percent.[30] Even before 1900 two large competitors had appeared.[31] One was Federal Sugar Company, which provided an east coast refinery and marketing outlet for Claus Spreckels, the foremost Hawaiian and west coast sugar grower. The other operated a refinery set up by Arbuckle Brothers, one of the country's largest wholesale grocers, which wanted control over its own sugar supplies.

When beet sugar first came into production at the end of the 1890s, Havemeyer aggressively continued his strategy of horizontal combination. His company soon had control or near control over the largest of the new beet sugar companies, including American Beet Sugar formed in 1902,

Great Western Sugar in 1903, and Utah-Idaho in 1907.[32] In the same years Havemeyer came to invest on a much smaller scale in the Cuban-American Sugar Company.[33] Even so, neither Havemeyer nor his company had the resources needed to buy out new refining enterprises in Hawaii, California, Baltimore, and New Orleans.

During these years, the directors and managers of American Sugar were becoming increasingly unhappy with Havemeyer's expensive strategy of buying out competition. It cost the company over $20 million between 1902 and 1907. On Havemeyer's death in 1907 they shifted from horizontal combination to vertical integration. By 1909, when the federal government brought an antitrust suit against the sugar company, it had already begun to sell its holdings in other companies, to build up its own marketing organization, and to develop its own brand, Domino. By 1917 there were six large independent integrated sugar companies in the top 236 American manufacturing firms (see Appendix A), competing with each other in the modern oligopolistic way. In sugar, the concepts of a powerful entrepreneur delayed, but only by a few years, the shift from horizontal combination to vertical integration, and with it the coming of oligopolistic competition among a few large integrated firms.

Although the six trusts of the 1880s in the high-volume process industries were destined to dominate their industries for decades, the other two quickly failed. The American Cattle Trust, formed in 1887 as a means to give western cattlemen bargaining power with the Chicago packers, never got much beyond the organizing stage.[34] The trust purchased the Morris packing plant in Chicago, bought large feeding farms, and made contracts with the French and Belgian governments for canned beef. But as such an enterprise was in no way able to combine the advantages of mass production with those of mass distribution, it soon collapsed and was liquidated in the summer of 1890.

The National Cordage Association used the trust form to attempt to maintain an existing cartel.[35] It moved to centralize purchases and control sales, but it made no attempt to consolidate and centralize the administration of its constituent cordage and twine companies, nor did it try to consolidate or reorganize production facilities. The cordage trust (which became a New Jersey holding company in 1890), unlike the trusts in the processing industries, had to borrow large amounts of working capital because four-fifths of its production went into binder twine and therefore cash flowed in only at harvest time. With no economies of speed resulting from consolidation and with recurring heavy demands for working capital, the new enterprise had difficulty in making a return on the large amount of capital obtained to carry out its continuing strategy of buying out competition—a strategy that was weakened when a number of manufacturers who had joined the merger used their payments as capital to start new companies. In May 1893 the cordage company's sensational financial failure helped to precipitate the panic that ushered in the depression of the middle 1890s. Later attempts to revive the consolidation on a sound financial basis failed.[36] The cost-cutting advantages of consolidation and integration were few in the cordage industry.

The story of the trusts formed in the 1880s has been told in some detail, for they define the basic pattern of growth of the many mergers that followed. After 1890 the most successful mergers were in industries where technology and markets permitted reduction in costs. They became successful, however, only after their directors abandoned the costly strategy of horizontal combination for one of vertical integration—that is, after production facilities had been consolidated, their administration centralized, marketing and purchasing organizations built, and a staff of managers recruited to supervise, monitor, and coordinate these many different operating units.

The route to growth affected both the financing and the management of the new enterprises. Corporations that had integrated forward and backward without taking the merger path had been self-financed. But in these early mergers that had moved beyond legal consolidation the process of rationalization and concentration often called for the rebuilding as well as the reorganization of a major portion of their productive facilities. Such rebuilding, like the merger itself, required sizable amounts of capital. Except at Standard Oil and its smaller competitors who had an exceptionally high volume of production and global markets, current cash flow could not provide needed funds for industrial reorganization.

These early mergers were, then, the first American enterprises not involved in transportation, communication, or finance to go to the capital markets for funds. This need was one reason that the trusts, except for Standard Oil, quickly transformed themselves into corporations once the revision of the New Jersey statutes made this possible. Not only did the legal status of the holding company appear to be much sounder than the trust, but the investors preferred corporate securities to trust certificates.[37] Four of the reorganized trusts (American Cotton Oil, American Sugar, National Lead, and National Cordage) issued two types of securities: preferred stock based on earning capacity and secured by fixed assets and common stock based on anticipated growth in earnings resulting from the consolidation. The first was aimed to appeal to the conservative investor, the second to the more speculative one. And in going to the capital markets, the organizers of the first industrial mergers relied on the services of such leading railroad investment banking firms as Winslow, Lanier; Kidder, Peabody; August Belmont; and Poor and Greenough.[38]

This process of financing resulted in a significant difference in the relationship of owners and managers. Those firms that initially became large through internal expansion continued to have the stock ownership closely held by the founder, a few associates, and their families. On the other hand, the sale of securities to provide fixed and working capital for the new mergers further spread the ownership of capital stock, which the formation of the merger had already begun to disperse. Top executives in the central office of the first type were nearly always major stockholders or personally close to such stockholders; but those in the second type became salaried managers who held only a small amount of the total stock and had little personal acquaintance with the scattered owners. It was in the latter case that the separation of ownership and control first appeared in the United States in business firms other than the railroad and the telegraph.

Mergers, 1890–1903

All six of the successful pioneering trusts of the 1880s had been formed to concentrate and rationalize production. During the 1890s the number of consolidations increased rapidly. At the same time the motive for merger changed. Many more were created to replace the association of small manufacturing firms as the instrument to maintain price and production schedules.

The change reflected political and legal developments that occurred in the latter part of the 1880s. Most important were, on the one hand, the protests against the trade associations and trusts that culminated in 1890 in the passage of the Sherman Antitrust Act, and, on the other, the efforts of the manufacturers that led to the New Jersey general incorporation law for holding companies.[39] Following the advice of their lawyers, many of the existing associations, as well as the few existing trusts, incorporated themselves as holding companies. At first most of the new legal consolidations continued to operate as cartels with the holding company's board merely setting price and output quotas for the subsidiary companies. But as the decade of the 1890s passed, many legal consolidations embarked on a strategy of centralization and integration.

A second reason for the increasing number of mergers after 1890 was the growing market for industrial securities. New York City had been since the 1850s one of the world's largest and most sophisticated capital markets. Until the late 1880s, however, industrialists found little need to market large blocks of stocks. They raised the funds they required from local commercial banks. Nor did security dealers have much interest in industrials. By the early 1890s, however, railroad financing no longer offered the opportunities for profit it had earlier. The handling of railroad securities had become concentrated in the hands of a relatively few powerful Wall Street houses. Bankers, brokers, and investors were looking for new securities to buy and sell.[40] The manufacturers who organized the trusts were surprised by Wall Street's interest in obtaining their trust certificates. After 1890 buyers continued to take the securities of the new holding companies. Manufacturers soon realized that they could use the growing market as a source of funds for working and investment capital. They were also quick to appreciate that the demand for industrial securities enhanced the market value of their own companies. Expanded demand for industrial securities permitted manufacturers to obtain a handsome rate of exchange when they completed a merger by turning over the stock of their little-known small enterprises for that of a nationally known holding company. At the same time financiers began to take sizable blocks of stock as payment for arranging and carrying out a merger. Both manufacturers and financiers quickly learned how to profit from the actual process of legal consolidation.

The mergers of the 1890s came in two waves. One occurred between 1890 and 1893. The other and much larger surge began as the country recovered from the depression of the middle years of the decade. Beginning in 1898 it lasted until the end of 1902. The first wave, resulting from the legal attack on combinations, the passage of the Sherman Act, and the revisions of the New Jersey law, lasted as long as times were prosperous. Hans Thorelli lists the names of 51 holding companies or "tight combinations" formed between 1890 and 1893.[41] With the coming of the depression of 1893 the number of new mergers fell off sharply. Only 27 occurred for the next three calendar years, 1894 through 1896.

Then came the nation's first great merger movement. For 1898 Thorelli lists 24 legal consolidations. In 1899 the number shot up to 105—a number that almost equaled the total number (108) of all legal consolidations given by Thorelli for the years between 1890 and 1898. During the following three years the number dropped off, but remained substantial with 34, 23, and 26 for the years 1900, 1901, and 1902. For 1903 Thorelli records the names of only 7 tight combinations. The records cited by Thorelli are supported by Ralph Nelson's broader statistical study of firm disappearances. For example, his tables show that disappearance of firms through merger rose from 26 in 1896 to 69 in 1897, to 303 in 1898, to 1,207 in 1899.[42] For the next three years they ran 340, 423, and 370. In 1903 they dropped back to 79. By 1903 the merger movement had clearly run its course.

The sudden upsurge of mergers in 1899 reflected both the conditions

of the nation's financial markets and the Supreme Court's interpretation
of the Sherman Act. In the E. C. Knight case, a suit the federal government brought against the American Sugar Refining Company, the court's
decision, handed down in 1895, appeared to sanction the legality of the
New Jersey holding company.[43] It did so by making a sharp distinction
between manufacturing and commerce and by declaring that a manufacturing corporation (as opposed to a combination of separate manufacturing firms) was beyond the reach of the Sherman Act. Then the Supreme
Court in 1897 in the Trans-Missouri Freight Association case and in 1898
in the Joint Traffic case (involving the Eastern Trunk Line Association),
and in 1899 in the Addyston Pipe and Steel case, ruled clearly and precisely that any combination of business firms formed to fix prices or allocate markets violated the Sherman Antitrust Act. After 1899 lawyers
were advising their corporate clients to abandon all agreements or alliances
carried out through cartels or trade associations and to consolidate into
single, legally defined enterprises.

Financiers and speculators were delighted with the court's rulings. In
the prosperous years of the late 1890s, the capital markets had become
buoyant.[44] Investors, investment bankers, brokers, and promoters of all
types continued to look for new opportunities to obtain or to market new
security issues. Industrial mergers appeared to be the most promising. The
performance of railroads was improving but their business remained
spoken for. In the years immediately after 1898, the leading promoters of
industrial mergers were financiers and speculators who were not yet
closely involved with railroads. They included the Moore Brothers (W.
H. and J. H.), Charles R. Flint, and John W. Gates. They had instructed
manufacturers on the procedures of mergers in the early 1890s and had
little difficulty in convincing other businessmen to do the same later in the
decade. Whereas the mergers before 1897 had been initiated primarily by
the industrialists themselves, many more were now instigated by the
financiers and speculators.

By 1903 the market for industrial securities had become satiated. Investors, financiers, and bankers were becoming troubled by the poor performance of a number of the new consolidations. A few had already
undergone further financial reorganizations. Then, as the number of mergers dropped off, a circuit court decision in April 1903 in the Northern
Securities case upheld in the next year by the Supreme Court indicated
that the holding company might be vulnerable under the Sherman Act.
The decision which ordered the dissolution of the Northern Securities
Company (the company formed to hold the stock of the Northern Pacific
and the Great Northern railroad companies) did not overrule its decision
in the Knight case. It did not declare the holding company illegal. Each

holding company accused of violating the Sherman Act would be tried on the merits of the case. Nevertheless, it showed that the holding companies were clearly not immune from prosecution. Corporation lawyers began to advise their clients to eliminate constituent companies and place all their facilities in a single operating company.[45] Such a centralized enterprise could hardly be defined as a combination in restraint of trade, even if it might be accused of restraining trade.

Legal reasons were, however, of much less importance than business reasons in bringing administrative centralization. Whether the motive for forming legal consolidations had been to maintain and strengthen cartels or to profit financially from the process of merger, mergers quickly found themselves in financial difficulties if they remained merely holding companies. The depression of the 1890s had demonstrated how hard it was for a number of small, single-unit enterprises operating under a single legal roof to become viable business enterprises unless they were centrally controlled. If a loose knit holding company maintained prices at a level that provided even a reasonable margin of profit, competitors appeared. Often these competitors were the same manufacturers who had sold out to the trust. And if that company attempted to maintain its horizontal combination by cutting prices or buying out competitors, the price was high. The financial failures of the National Cordage, American Biscuit, United States Leather, National Wall Paper, National Starch, and the successors to the whiskey trust emphasized the costliness of a strategy of horizontal combination and the ineffectiveness of the holding company in carrying out that strategy. On the other hand, the financial success of Standard Oil, American Cotton Oil, National Lead, as well as American Tobacco, Quaker Oats, Singer Sewing Machine, Otis Elevator, the meat packers, and other integrated enterprises made clear the value of consolidating and centralizing the administration of their manufacturing facilities and moving forward into marketing and backward into purchasing and control of raw materials. The financial problems of several of the mergers occurring after 1897 reinforced these business lessons.

Some of the new horizontal combinations learned these lessons even more quickly than had Standard Oil and American Cotton Oil in the 1880s. Others, in the fashion of American Sugar Refining, moved slowly from horizontal combination to administrative centralization and to vertical integration. Others never made the transition at all.

The National Biscuit Company provides a particularly revealing example of a legal consolidation that realized the need for a change in strategy. That company, formed in 1898, was a merger of three regional consolidations—New York Biscuit, American Biscuit and Manufacturing, and the United States Baking Company. At first the new firm carried out the policies of its predecessors, but it soon decided that they did not pay. In its annual report for 1901 the company outlined the reasons for its shift:

This Company is four years old, and it may be of interest to shortly review its history . . . When the company started, it was an aggregation of plants. It is now an organized business. When we look back through the four years, we find that a radical change has been wrought into our business. In the past, the managers of large industrial corporations have thought it necessary, for success, to control or limit competition. So, when this company started, it was believed that we must control competition, and that to do this we must either fight competition or buy it. The first meant a ruinous war of prices and great loss of profits; the second, constantly increasing capitalization. Experience soon proved to us that, instead of bringing success, either of these courses, if perservered in, must bring disaster. This led us to reflect whether it was necessary to control competition . . . We soon satisfied ourselves that within the company itself we must look for success.

We turned our attention and bent our energies to improving the internal management of our own business, to getting the full benefit from purchasing our raw materials in large quantities, to economizing the expense of manufacture, to systematizing and rendering more effective our selling department, and above all things and before all things, to improving the quality of our goods and the condition in which they should reach the consumer . . .

It became the settled policy of this company to buy out no competition.[46]

In carrying out these plans the company's senior executives imitated the example of Quaker Oats and Pillsbury Flour. They shifted from producing in bulk for the retailers' cracker barrels to making distinctive packaged goods using the brand name "Uneeda Biscuit." "The next point," the same annual report continued, "was to reach the consumer. Knowing that we had something that the consumer wanted, we had to advise the consumer of its existence. We did this by extensive advertising." For this service the company relied on the services of an experienced advertising agency, N. W. Ayer & Son.[47] As it built its global marketing and purchasing organizations, it continued to carry out a policy of "centralizing" manufacturing in a small number of very large plants. After 1900 National Biscuit continued to compete in the new manner, relying on brand names, advertising, and scale economies. Its marketing organization and policies reduced unit costs and created barriers to entry. Its major competitors became comparable integrated enterprises, operating either on a regional or, like the Loose-Wiles Biscuit Company, on a national scale.

In corn products the integrated enterprise came only after a series of lamentable financial failures. The organizers of the leading mergers in that industry remained wedded to the concept of horizontal control. Significantly, those that favored the older strategy had a close association with Havemeyer and his fellow advocates of horizontal combination in sugar, while those who began to argue for vertical integration had had their business training at Standard Oil. The Corn Products Company, formed in 1903, was a merger of two unsuccessful combinations and three independent companies.[48] The combinations were the reincarnation of National Starch, originally formed in 1890 and financially reorganized in 1900, and the Glucose Refining Company, established in 1897 by the Matthiessen brothers, leading sugar refiners who had long been associated with American Sugar. Of the three independents, the largest and most successful was the New York Glucose Company headed by E. T. Bedford, who had spent many years as a senior executive in Standard Oil's overseas marketing office.[49] Despite the lack of success of the earlier consolidations and against the strong opposition of Bedford, C. F. Matthiessen as president of Corn Products continued to bear the costs of horizontal combination. Finally, in 1906, the merger was forced to undergo still another financial reorganization, which led to its reformation as the Corn Products Refining Company. Bedford then became its president. He immediately built up the enterprise's purchasing and sales organizations, moved aggressively into European and other overseas markets, and instituted new policies of packaging, branding, advertising, volume purchasing, and scale economies. The Corn Products Refining Company, the successor to four failures, quickly became, by the definition of a careful student of the merger movement, an "outstanding success."[50] Again the cost savings and barriers to entry raised by the strategy of vertical integration paid off.

By adopting such a strategy, Corn Products, like Distillers-Securities, turned failure into success. Most of the mergers that were unable to make such a transition failed. Some were liquidated after their first or second receivership. Others dissolved themselves before financial disaster struck. Thus the directors of the National Wall Paper Company, formed in 1892, agreed in 1900, "That the company be dissolved, and the factories be returned to their original owners or sold to the highest bidders." They had decided "that the manufacturer of wall paper is so dependent on such peculiar circumstances that independent plants can be operated to better advantage than can many plants under one control."[51]

The experiences of these companies suggest that successful mergers met two conditions. They consolidated production, centralized its administration, and built their own marketing and purchasing organizations. And they operated in industries where technology and markets permitted such integration to increase the speed and lower the cost of materials through the processes of production and distribution. For these reasons the long-lived mergers came to cluster in the same industries in which the first large integrated enterprise appeared in the 1880s.

The success and failure of mergers

The systematic analysis of success and failures of early mergers made by Shaw Livermore tells much the same story. Livermore selected from an initial list of 328 mergers occurring between 1888 and 1906 156 that were large enough to affect the market structures of the industries in which they operated. He defined success in terms of "earning power on capitalization," and then placed these companies into four categories: failures, successes, marginal successes, and those that were successfully rejuvenated.[52] He also distinguished between successes and outstanding successes and between early and late failures. Livermore's listings have been placed into the industrial categories that the U.S. Census defines as two-digit groups in its Standard Industrial Classification. The results, listed in table 6 (p. 340), indicate in what industrial groups mergers were concentrated and in which they succeeded or failed. Table 6 also indicates whether a company became integrated or remained a single-function activity by continuing only to manufacture. In that table a manufacturing company was considered integrated if it had its own branch sales offices and its own purchasing organization and/or controlled sources of raw and semifinished materials.

One fundamental fact emphasized by table 6 is that of the mergers Livermore studied, all but 8 were in manufacturing or processing. Three of the 157 were mergers of mining companies and 2 of these 3 were failures. Of the 4 others not in manufacturing, 1 was in distribution. That merger, Associated Merchants, resulted from the attempts of the heirs of H. B. Claflin, a pioneering mass marketer, to dispose of their holdings.[53] The other 3 included a New York realty company that dealt in business properties, the Bush Terminal Company, which operated railroad terminal facilities on the Brooklyn waterfront, and the Morgan-sponsored International Mercantile Marine Company. The last was a failure.

The basic finding indicated by table 6 is that which the historical narrative has already suggested. Successful mergers occurred in the same type of industries in which the integrated firm had appeared in the 1880s. There were fewer mergers and more failures in labor-intensive industries where the concentration of production did not significantly reduce costs and where distribution did not involve high-volume flows or did not require special services. Thus, Livermore lists no mergers in the apparel industry, only 1 in furniture, 3 in printing and publishing, and 3 in lumber.[54] In the textile group where nearly all the mergers failed, with 10 out of 12 failing quickly, only 1 was marginally successful. Another, American Woolen, Livermore characterized as a "limping" failure. In leather none of the 4 were successful; in asphalt (listed in group 29) 2 failed and 1 remained marginal. In the machinery trades failures dominated in industries that did not require specialized services in the selling of products or a complex technology in making them. These included mergers for the production of wringers, shears, bicycles, woodworking and laundry machinery, and simple agricultural implements such as forks, hoes, and seeders.

On the other hand, successful mergers were most numerous in the high-volume, large-batch, or continuous-process industries and in those needing specialized marketing services. These were particularly successful in food and in complex but standardized machines. They were also numerous in the chemical, stone-glass-clay, and primary metals groups—industries in which enterprises used capital-intensive, energy-consuming technologies and distributed standardized products to many customers.

Table 6 further emphasizes that mergers were rarely successful until managerial hierarchies were created—that is, until production was consolidated and its administration centralized and until the firm had its own marketing and purchasing organizations. As the table indicates, the successful firms had integrated. Moreover, the firms which Livermore lists as rejuvenated moved from failure to success only after they had changed their strategy and their structure. Nearly all the rejuvenations occurred after the managers failed to make profits through a strategy of horizontal combination. These enterprises, like Corn Products and Distillers-Securities, revived themselves by means of administrative centralization and vertical integration. Although information is not complete for all the mergers studied by Livermore, it does seem safe to say that by 1917 nearly all the successful consolidations had integrated production with distribution.

Livermore's review of successes and failures in the nation's first merger movement is based on limited data and is not conclusive. But it does emphasize that merger itself was not enough to assure business success. During the 1890s mergers had become a standard way of creating large multi-unit industrial enterprises. Those formed to control competition or to profit from the process of merger itself often brought short-term gains. But they rarely assured long-term profits. Unless the newly formed consolidation used the resources under its control more efficiently than had the constituent companies before they joined the merger, the consolidation had little staying power. Few enjoyed continuing financial success until they had followed the example of the pioneering mergers and created an organization that was able to coordinate a high-volume flow of materials through the processes of production and distribution, from the suppliers of raw materials to the ultimate consumers. By using resources more intensively and by improving information and cash flows, the managers of these enterprises reduced unit costs. At the same time, by assuring prompt delivery, by advertising, and by providing distributors and customers with specialized services, they created further formidable barriers to entry. Yet changes in strategy and organization were in themselves not sufficient. Unless the enterprise used the technologies of mass production and served mass markets, it had little opportunity to achieve such cost reductions and to raise such barriers to entry.

The experience of the early American mergers thus provides some suggestive documentation for a basic contention of this study. Modern business enterprise became a viable institution only after the visible hand of management proved to be more efficient than the invisible hand of market forces in coordinating the flow of materials through the economy. Few mergers achieved long-term profitability until their organizers carried out a strategy to make such integration possible and only after they created a managerial hierarchy capable of taking the place of the market in coordinating, monitoring, and planning for the activities of a large number of operating units. The history of the large industrial enterprises in the years between the merger movement of the turn of the century and the entry of the United States into World War I convincingly documents this basic proposition.

Table 6. The success and failure of mergers, 1888–1906

Firm	Classification[a]	Type[b]
Groups 10 and 12: Mining companies[c]		
Pittsburgh Coal	F	I
United Copper Mining	F	—[d]
U.S. Coal & Oil	S	I
Group 20: Food and like products		
American Beet Sugar	M	I
American Chicle	S	I
American Cotton Oil	S	I
American Fisheries	F	—
American Fruit Products	F	—
American Ice	S	I
American Malting	F	—
American Sugar Refining	S	I
A Booth & Co.	F	—
Continental Cotton Oil	F	—
Corn Products	F	—
Corn Products Refining	S	I
Distillers & Cattle Feeders	F	—
Distilling Co. of America	F	—
Glucose Sugar Refining	F	—
Great Western Cereal	F	—
National Biscuit	S	I
National Candy	S	I
Quaker Oats	S	I
Royal Baking Powder	S	I
United Fruit	S	I
U.S. Flour Milling (Standard Milling)	R	I (Inc.)
Group 21: Tobacco manufactures		
American Tobacco	S	I
Group 22: Textile mill products		
American Cotton	F	—
American Felt	F	—
American Grass Twine	F	—
American Thread	M	SF
American Woolen	F	I
Mt. Vernon-Woodbury Cotton Duck	F	—
National Cordage	F	—
New England Cotton Yarn	F	—
Standard Rope & Twine	F	—
U.S. Cotton Duck	F	—
U.S. Finishing	F	—
U.S. Worsted	F	—

Firm	Classification[a]	Type[b]
Group 23: Apparel and related products		
(None)	—	—
Group 24: Lumber and wood products, excluding furniture		
American Barrel & Package	F	—
Consolidated Naval Stores	S	— (Insuf.)
National Casket	S	I
Group 25: Furniture and fixtures		
American School Furniture	R	I (Inc.)
Group 26: Paper and allied products		
American Writing Paper	F	I
International Paper	M	I
National Wallpaper	F	—
Union Bag and Paper	M	I
United Box Board and Paper	F	—
U.S. Envelope	S	— (Insuf.)
U.S. Playing Card	S	— (Insuf.)
Group 27: Printing and publishing		
American Book	S	— (Insuf.)
American Colortype	R	— (Insuf.)
Butterick	S	— (Insuf.)
Group 28: Chemicals		
American Agricultural Chemical	F	I
American Coal Products (Barrett)	S	I
American Glue	F	I
Du Pont	S	I
General Chemical	S	I
National Carbon	S	I
National Lead	S	I
National Salt	R	I (Inc.)
New Jersey Zinc	S	I
U.S. Dyewood & Extract	F	—
U.S. Glue	S	— (Insuf.)
Virginia-Carolina Chemical	F	I (Inc.)
Group 29: Petroleum refining and related industries		
Asphalt Co. of America	F	—
General Asphalt	M	I
General Roofing	F	—
National Asphalt	F	—
Pure Oil	S	I

Table 6. *Continued*

Firm	Classification[a]	Type[b]
Group 30: Rubber and miscellaneous plastic products		
American Hard Rubber	S	— (Insuf.)
Atlantic Rubber Shoe Co. of America	F	—
Consolidated Rubber Tire	F	—
U.S. Rubber	M	I
Group 31: Leather and its products		
American Hide & Leather	F	I
American Saddlery & Harness	F	—
U.S. Leather	F	—
Central Leather	F	I (Inc.)
Group 32: Stone, clay, and glass products		
American Cement	F	—
American Clay Mfg. (American Sewer Pipe)	S	I
American Refractories	S	I
American Window Glass	M	I
Harbison-Walker Refractories	S	I
National Fire Proofing	M	I
National Glass	F	—
Pittsburgh Plate Glass	S	I
U.S. Glass	M	I
U.S. Gypsum	S	I
Group 33: Primary metal industries		
American Brass (Anaconda)	S	SF
American Smelting & Refining	S	I
American Steel Foundries	S	I
Anaconda Copper	S	I
Central Foundry	R	I
Colorado Fuel & Iron	M	I
Development Co. of America	F	—
International Nickel	S	I
Republic Iron & Steel	M	I
U.S. Cast Iron Pipe	R	I
U.S. Reduction & Refining	F	—
U.S. Smelting, Refining & Mining	S	I
U.S. Steel	S	I
United Zinc & Lead	F	—
Group 34: Fabricated metal products except ordnance, machinery, and transport equipment		
American Brake Shoe	S	I
American Can	S	I

Firm	Classification[a]	Type[b]
National Enameling & Stamping	M	I
Standard Sanitary	S	SF (Inc.)
Trenton Potteries (Crane)	S	SF (Inc.)

Group 35: Machinery, except electrical

Allis-Chalmers	R	I
American Fork & Hoe	F	—
American Laundry Machinery	F	—
American Lithographic (U.S. Printing)	M	— (Insuf.)
American Pneumatic Service	S	I
American Radiator	S	I
American Seeding Machinery	M	I (Inc.)
American Soda Fountain	R	I
American Type Founders	S	I
American Wood Working Machinery	F	—
American Wringer	F	—
Chicago Pneumatic Tool	S	I
Continental Gin	S	I (Inc.)
International Harvester	S	I
International Steam Pump	F	I
National Shear	F	—
Otis Elevator	S	I
Union Typewriter (Remington Typewriter)	S	I
United Shoe Machinery	S	I

Group 36: Electrical machinery

American Electric Heating	F	—
Electric Storage Battery	S	I (Inc.)
General Electric	S	I
General Railway Signal	S	I (Inc.)

Group 37: Transportation equipment

American Bicycle	F	—
American Car & Foundry	S	I
American Locomotive	M	I
American Shipbuilding	S	SF
Consolidated Railway Lighting & Equipment	F	—
Consolidated Railway Lighting & Refrigeration	F	—
Electric Vehicle	F	—
International Car Wheel	F	—
International Fire Engine	R	I
Pope Manufacturing (bicycle)	F	—
Pressed Steel Car	M	I

Table 6. *Continued*

Firm	Classification[a]	Type[b]
Pullman	S	I (Inc.)
Railway Steel Spring	M	I
U.S. Shipbuilding	F	—
Group 38: Instruments and related products		
Eastman Kodak	S	I
Group 39: Miscellaneous manufacturers		
Diamond Match	S	I
International Silver	S	I
National Novelty	F	—
United Button	F	—
Nonmanufacturing		
Associated Merchants	S	—
Bush Terminal	S	—
International Mercantile Marine	F	—
U.S. Realty & Improvement	R	—

Source: Shaw Livermore, "The Success of Industrial Mergers," *Quarterly Journal of Economics*, 50:68–95 (November 1935), supplemented by information from Moody's *Manuals of Industrial Securities* and company reports. See also note 53.

[a] F represents failure; R indicates rejuvenated company; M means marginal success; and S is a successful enterprise.

[b] I indicates integrated; SF indicates single function. (Inc.) means information incomplete but enough to suggest type. (Insuf.) means information not sufficient to indicate type.

[c] The two-digit groups used by the U.S. Bureau of the Census in its Standard Industrial Classification.

[d] Few attempts were made to learn whether a merger was integrated or remained solely a manufacturing enterprise if that merger failed.

C H A P T E R 11

Integration Completed

An overview: 1900–1917

As the new century opened, patterns of success and failure were only just beginning to appear. Manufacturers, financiers, investors, and other businessmen were entranced by the promise of large-scale industrial enterprise. They had differing reasons for creating these new empires and differing plans for keeping them profitable. Some still looked for profit through control of competition, others sought profit through the manipulation of securities. More were becoming aware of the profitability of rationalizing the processes of production and distribution. Few, however, considered the technology of production and the nature of markets to be the primary influences on the long-term success of their ventures. They saw much the same potential in textiles, leather, and bicycles as they did in biscuits, corn products, oil, chemicals, and automobiles. Contemporary economists and business analysts were no more perceptive.

By World War I, however, the broad patterns of growth of the large industrial enterprise were clear. The constraints of technology and markets on the growth of a firm were apparent. By the second decade of the century, the shakedown period following the merger movement was over. The successful mergers were established and the unsuccessful ones had failed. Modern business enterprises dominated major American industries, and most of these same firms continued to dominate their industries for decades.

Understanding the evolution of modern industrial enterprise during the critical years after the merger movement requires more than a review of the experience of individual companies. For the 1880s and 1890s, when the multiunit industrial corporation was new, the few individual pioneering enterprises provide the information necessary for an analysis of institutional developments. But after 1900 the modern multiunit industrial enterprise became a standard instrument for managing the production and distribution of goods in America. Hundreds of such companies came into

existence. Only a collective history of large industrial enterprises can reveal the outlines of institutional change in American industry after the
merger movement.

The companies that provide the base for this collective history are listed
in Appendix A. They include nearly every enterprise involved in the production of goods in the United States in 1917 that had assets of $20 mil-
lion or more. This list of 278 companies was taken from a compilation of
the 500 largest industrials in the United States made by Thomas R. Navin
and published in the Autumn 1970 issue of *Business History Review*.[1] In
compiling his list, Navin defined industrial enterprises as all those involved
in agriculture, forestry, fishing, mining, construction, and manufacturing.
He did not include those providing transportation, communication, and
light and power. Nor did he consider financial or marketing firms. In
Appendix A these industrial enterprises are grouped under the two-digit
Standard Industrial Classification industrial group in which they operated.
In each group they are listed by size, with the place among the top 500 indicated in the left column. The table also shows whether the firm became
an integrated, multifunctional firm or remained a single-function enterprise. An integrated firm is one that, in addition to operating its manufacturing facilities, had its own branch sales offices and purchasing organization or its own sources of raw and semifinished materials as well. Finally,
Appendix A indicates whether the integrated firms were managed through
departments or subsidiaries.

It is immediately apparent from Appendix A that the largest American
enterprises in 1917 involved in the production of goods were concentrated
in manufacturing and processing. There were none in construction. Only
5 were agricultural enterprises—1 in ranching, 1 in the growing of sugar
cane, and 1 in the growing and harvesting of crude rubber. A fourth was
United Fruit, a vast, integrated business empire that had adopted the new
techniques of the meat packers to transport, distribute, and market bananas. The fifth was one of its much smaller competitors, the Atlantic
Fruit and Sugar Company. A larger number, 30, were mining firms; 7
others produced only crude oil. But of the 278 largest industrials in the
United States in 1917, 236 manufactured or processed raw or semifinished
materials into finished products.

Further, of these 236 manufacturing firms, 171 (72.5 percent) clustered
in six two-digit SIC groups: 39 in primary metals, 34 in food, 29 in transportation equipment, 24 in machinery, 24 in petroleum, and 21 in chemicals. Twenty-three (9.7 percent) were scattered in seven groups: 7 in
textiles, 5 in lumber, 4 in leather, 3 in printing and publishing, 3 in apparel, 1 in instruments, and 0 in furniture. The remaining 42 were in continuous-process and large-batch four-digit industries within the seven re-

maining groups. In the paper group, the large firms were clustered in the production of newsprint and kraft paper; in the stone, glass, and clay group, in cement and plate glass; in the rubber group, in tires and footwear; in tobacco, cigarettes; in fabricated metals, cans; in electrical machinery, standardized machines and in miscellaneous, matches.

Thus the largest manufacturing firms in 1917, whether they grew large through merger or internal expansion, were clustered in industries with characteristics similar to those in which the integrated enterprise first appeared in the 1880s and 1890s, and those in which the turn-of-the-century mergers were most successful. The large industrial enterprise continued to flourish when it used capital-intensive, energy-consuming, continuous or large-batch production technology to produce for mass markets. It flourished when its markets were large enough and its consumers numerous enough and varied enough to require complex scheduling of high-volume flows and specialized storage and shipping facilities, or when the marketing of its products in volume required the specialized services of demonstration, installation, after-sales service and repair, and consumer credit. It remained successful because administrative coordination continued to reduce costs and to maintain barriers to entry.

The profile of American big business makes this point in another way. Modern industrial enterprise came more slowly and failed to thrive in industries where the processes of production used labor-intensive methods which required little heat, energy, or complex machinery. It was also slow to appear where the existing middlemen had little difficulty in distributing and selling the product. Few large firms can be found in the older, more traditional industries that produced and processed cloth, wood, and leather. Nor were they numerous in publishing and printing and in industries making highly specialized instruments or machinery. Most of the 23 firms listed in the seven groups whose processes of production were the most labor-intensive were at the lower end of the list of 236. Only 3 were in the top 100, and 2 of these firms—American Woolen and Central Leather—were weak, unprofitable companies.[2] In these industries the volume was rarely high enough or the marketing complex enough to encourage manufacturers to integrate the processes of production with those of distribution. In these industrial groups the mass marketers continued to distribute and sell consumer goods, and manufacturer's agents, usually selling on commission, arranged for the distribution of producer's goods.

Appendix A further emphasizes that by 1917 most large enterprises, by whatever route they took to size, had become integrated operating companies. Single-function firms (that is, those that had not integrated) were primarily in extractive industries. Information on the extent of integration is available on 269 of the 278 companies listed. Of these, 7 single-function, nonintegrated firms were in crude oil extraction, 16 in mining, and 2 in agriculture. Only 16 of the 236 manufacturing firms were not integrated. Of these, 4 were in textiles, 2 in book and publishing (neither of these 2 appear to have yet had branch sales offices of their own), 1 in primary metals, 2 in metal fabrication, and 7 others in production of transportation vehicles. So at least 85 percent of all industrials with assets of $20 million or over had by 1917 integrated production with distribution.

Finally, a review of the 236 manufacturing companies listed in Appendix A reveals that over 80 percent of the integrated enterprises managed their properties through functional departments (sales, production, and the like) rather than through autonomous operating subsidaries. By 1917, few large American industrials still administered their businesses by means of the holding company, although it remained an important device for maintaining legal control over far-flung activities.

Growth by vertical integration—a description

The companies listed in Appendix A provide an objective and comprehensive sample of big business in America. They are the corporate leaders in American industry in 1917. By that time those enterprises were already producing over a quarter of the net manufacturing output in the United States.[3] Their collective history reveals much about the growth of modern business enterprise and about the evolving structure of the industries in which they operated.

This review first describes the patterns of change between 1900 and 1917 and then analyzes them. The following sections describe developments by industrial areas in which enterprises capitalized at $20 million or over clustered. They focus on the six industrial (two-digit SIC) groups —food, oil, chemicals, primary metals, machinery, transportation equipment—in which 171 of the 236 operated, and on the four-digit industries in the two-digit tobacco, rubber, stone-glass-clay, paper, fabricated metals, and electric machinery groups in which 42 such firms were listed. The only industrial areas not considered in this description are those groups in which only 23 of 236 of the firms in Appendix A operated. These last were the groups in which a great majority of manufacturers remained small, single-unit enterprises that continued to rely on existing marketers to sell and distribute their products.

Food and tobacco. Food and tobacco provide a good starting point. In these groups (20 and 21 in Appendix A), along with the machinery group, the modern industrial enterprise had its beginning. In 1917 there were 35 food enterprises with assets of $20 million or over. Only primary metals, with 39, had more. The pioneering enterprises in the food industries were still strong and flourishing. In fact, most of the 35 firms had been formed before 1900 and a sizable number before 1890.

Among the largest in the group were the early processors of perishable products—meat packers (Armour, Swift, Wilson, Morris, and Cudahay), and brewers (Anheuser Busch and Schlitz). By 1917, United Fruit (listed under agriculture), American Ice, and Booth Fisheries operated comparable distributing networks with refrigerated facilities. However, the production processes at American Ice and Booth Fisheries were not of sufficient volume to give them an advantage over smaller local competitors. Both quickly lost their place among the nation's largest industrials. In fact, Booth Fisheries, according to Livermore, failed financially.

The pioneering producers of low-priced packaged goods manufactured by means of continuous-process machinery were still the leaders in their industries. Quaker Oats, Washburn-Crosby (flour), Heinz, Borden's, Libby, and Coca-Cola all continued to prosper. Indeed the only new firm of this type to be formed after 1900 was California Packing (Del Monte), a 1916 merger of local canning companies that built a nationwide marketing organization and an extensive—if more regional—purchasing network.[4]

The early mergers were also much in evidence. American Cotton Oil and its competitor, Southern Cotton Oil, still dominated their industries. Distillers-Securities remained the country's leading firm in its industry. By 1917 American Sugar Refining was competing with the 5 other large and integrated sugar companies on the list. By then, too, such turn-of-the-century mergers as Royal Baking Powder and United States Milling (later Standard Milling) had followed National Biscuit and Corn Products in transforming themselves from federations of single-function, family firms to centrally administered, integrated business empires. In chewing gum, American Chicle became Wrigley's major competitor, but only after it had put together its worldwide marketing and buying organization. Indeed, both American Chicle and Wrigley's became multinational in the sense of owning and operating facilities overseas.[5] For example, American Chicle held 3 million acres in Mexico where it produced raw materials, and operated factories in Great Britain and Canada.

Well before 1917, nearly all the large food companies in the United States had concentrated production in a few large plants and had their own extensive buying and marketing departments. Nearly all had an overseas sales network and several had built plants abroad. If they did not buy their raw materials from American farmers, they usually came to control part of their own sources of supply. Many, including the meat-packing, brewing, cotton oil, and sugar companies, owned their own ships, fleets of railway cars, and other transportation equipment. And in nearly all of their specific industries these leaders competed with each other in an oligopolistic manner—by advertising, branding, and assuring prompt and regular service rather than by price. In all these concentrated food industries the pioneers remained the leading firms.

In tobacco, the American Tobacco Company remained all-powerful until 1911, when it was broken up by a Supreme Court decision. Then the three new companies—Reynolds, Liggett & Meyers, and P. Lorillard—quickly built their own marketing and purchasing organizations. The four integrated firms continued to dominate the cigarette industry. In 1925 they accounted for 91.3 percent of the cigarettes produced in the United States, and they continued to increase their share of the market as the century passed.[6] Two other enterprises that were founded at the same time and for much the same reasons—Diamond Match and Eastman Kodak—continued to handle their giant's share of the industry's trade until long after 1917. (They are listed in groups 38 and 39 in Appendix A.)

Oil and rubber. In oil (group 29) and rubber (group 30) the story was much the same. The major difference resulted from the coming of a huge new market after 1900—that created by the automobile. The petroleum industry was particularly dynamic in the first two decades of the twentieth century.[7] The new demand for gasoline appeared just as the rapid spread of electricity for light was sharply reducing the demand for kerosene. And just as markets were being transformed, vast new sources of supply appeared. After 1900 the Gulf Coast, mid-continental, and California oil fields were simultaneously opened up.

New and expanding markets and sources of supply encouraged the growth of big business in oil. The pioneers were no longer able to dominate the industry completely. Standard Oil and its two smaller competitors—Pure Oil and Tidewater—continued to expand. But new entrants grew more quickly. Beginning as crude oil producers, they soon moved into refining and production. Before the Supreme Court ordered the dismemberment of Standard Oil in 1911, the Texas Company, Gulf Oil, Associated Oil, Union Oil, Shell Oil, and Sun Oil had already become large integrated enterprises operating in all basic functions of the oil industry (see table 7). Before 1911 a number of oil companies besides Standard Oil were among the largest business enterprises in the nation.

The breakup of Standard Oil created a number of single-function com-

Table 7. Petroleum companies with assets of $20 million or more, 1917[a]

Standard group	Independents before 1911	Independents after 1911
2. Standard Oil Co. (N.J.)	24. Texas Co.	37. Magnolia Petroleum Co. (no c) [Socony]
14. Standard Oil Co. of N.Y. (no c) [Socony]	26. Gulf Oil Co.	56. Sinclair Oil [Atlantic Refining]
	45. Pure Oil Co. [Union Oil, 1965]	
34. Standard Oil Co. of Ind.	69. Associated Oil Co. [Tide Water]	64. Pan American Petroleum & Transport Co. [Standard Indiana]
35. Standard Oil Co. of Calif.	71. Union Oil of Calif.	95. Midwest Refining Co. [Standard Indiana]
48. Prairie Oil & Gas Co. (c only) [Sinclair]	124. Tide Water Oil Co.	110. Cosden & Co. [Sunray-Mid Continent, 1955]
61. Ohio Oil Co. (c only)	160. Shell Oil of Calif.	
72. Vacuum Oil Co. (no c) [Socony]	229. Sun Co.	151. California Petroleum Corp. (c only) [Texas Co.]
84. Atlantic Refining Co.		162. Texas Pacific Coal & Oil Co. (c only) [Seagrams, 1965]
106. Pierce Oil Corp. (liquidated)		
205. South Penn Oil Co. (c only)		168. Houston Oil Co. of Texas (c only) [Atlantic Refining]
262. Standard Oil Co. (Ohio) (no c)		178. General Petroleum Corp. [Socony]
		261. Producers and Refiners Corp. (no marketing) [Sinclair]
		278. Skelly-Sankey Oil Co. (c only) [Getty Oil, 1967]

Source: Appendix A, Moody's *Manuals of Industrial Securities,* and company reports.
[a] Numbers indicate rank among the largest 278 industrials in 1917. Unless otherwise indicated the companies are fully integrated. The letter (c) indicates crude oil operations. Name in brackets is the company into which the firm merged. Dates are given for post-World War II mergers. The current name of Standard Oil (N.J.) is Exxon; Socony Vacuum is Mobil Oil; Ohio Oil is Marathon; and South Penn is Pennzoil United.

panies, because, except for Standard Oil of California and the recently formed Standard Oil of Louisiana, no Standard subsidiaries were fully integrated.[8] Even those that engaged in both marketing and refining concentrated on one of those two functions. By 1917, however, 8 of the former Standard companies with assets of more than $20 million had extensive marketing and refining facilities. Four of these had moved into crude oil production. A fifth, Standard Oil (Indiana), would follow in 1919. All had obtained tank cars, ships, and other facilities to transport their products. On the other hand, until World War I the 3 former Standard Oil pipeline and crude oil producers continued to find large enough markets, particularly with their former Standard associates, so that they did not feel pressed to integrate forward. In the years after World War I, however, the former Standard companies either became fully integrated enterprises or a part of another integrated company.

Eleven of the petroleum companies listed on table 7 were formed in the six years after the breakup of Standard Oil. Of these, only 4 were still solely crude oil producers in 1917, and one of these had made plans to build a refinery. One other produced and refined, but did not market, selling its product to other oil companies. The remaining 6 were fully integrated. After the war, nearly all the others became integrated or were merged into integrated enterprises. By World War I merger and acquisition became a more common route than internal growth to achieve size and integration.[9]

Although the number of large firms had increased, the swiftly growing oil industry remained concentrated. In 1917 the 23 firms listed in table 7 that owned refineries processed two-thirds of the petroleum products produced in the United States.[10] Even in crude oil production, one of the most competitive branches of the industry, the large integrated firm played a major role. A Federal Trade Commission report of 1919 indicated that 32 firms (not all listed in table 9) produced 59.4 percent of the nation's crude oil.[11] Fifteen of these, which produced 35.4 percent of the nation's total, were fully integrated; 8 more, which produced and refined but did not market, constituted 8.8 percent of the total; and 9 others produced only crude oil, accounting for 15.2 percent of the total crude oil. During the 1920s, the integrated firm came to play an ever larger role in crude oil production. And by 1931, the 20 major integrated oil companies produced 51.1 percent of the nation's crude oil and held 77.4 percent of its crude oil stocks.

As these figures indicate, the oil companies in 1917 had not achieved what might be termed a balanced integration; nearly all had to buy stocks from or sell products to other oil companies. And although nearly all these enterprises continued to integrate in the 1920s, few attempted to achieve a perfect balance in order to be completely self-sufficient. Their aim was to insure a continuing flow of materials through their capital-intensive facilities from the oil well to the retail gasoline dealers. Their purpose in acquiring control over production and distribution facilities was to assure, through administrative coordination, a high and steady use of their facilities. And this, not balanced integration, was the goal of most American companies, besides those in oil, that adopted a strategy of vertical integration before 1917.

Since World War I, an oligopoly of about twenty integrated enterprises has dominated the petroleum industry. Mergers and acquisitions in the 1920s and early 1930s completed the pattern of integration and concentration so firmly established before 1917. All of the independents formed after 1911 listed in table 7 became part of larger and older enterprises. On the other hand, nearly all of the independents formed before 1911 and nearly all of the old Standard Oil Company subsidiaries are still, in the 1970s, the industry's leading firms.[12]

During the 1920s the petroleum industry remained largely a domestic one. Both major markets and sources of supply were at home. Only Standard Oil of New Jersey and Socony marketed extensively abroad. It was not until the late 1930s that other companies began to sell overseas and to seek sources of crude oil more distant than the Caribbean area.[13]

In rubber a smaller number of firms than in oil came to dominate. Before the automobile created the demand for the tire, the major mass-produced products in that industry were rubber boots and gloves. In this business one of the two leading firms, Goodrich, had grown large through internal growth, while the other, United States Rubber Company, had begun as a merger. The other 3 rubber companies listed in Appendix A—Goodyear, Firestone, and Fisk—became large by building integrated organizations to produce and distribute tires. United States Rubber and Goodrich turned to the same new market. By 1917 both of these firms were beginning to move overseas, with United States Rubber operating rubber plantations in Sumatra and a plant in Canada and Goodrich a factory in France.[14] These firms competed through the use of brand names, heavy advertising, and more careful scheduling of flows through their producing and distributing facilities. In the mid-1970s the 4 leaders of 1917 (United States Rubber purchased Fisk in 1940) still dominated the rubber industry.

Chemicals, paper, and glass. The leading enterprises in the chemical, paper, and stone-clay-glass groups used large-batch and continuous-process methods of production similar to those of the oil and rubber companies. However, their markets differed. They manufactured primarily producer's rather than consumer's goods. Yet in nearly every case their producer's goods went to a large number and wide variety of users. They were sold to builders and contractors, as well as to manufacturing, mining, and other industrial enterprises. In many cases a small part of their output reached the consumer market through wholesalers. And in the specific industries within the larger industrial groups, where such mass producers had a mass market, the large integrated enterprise flourished.

The pattern is particularly clear in the paper group (26) and the stone-clay-glass group (32). Of the 7 paper companies with assets of $20 million or over, 5 produced newsprint and heavy kraft paper. Between 1900 and 1917 all 5 had extensive marketing organizations and owned tracts of timberland in Canada and the American south. The other two, American Writing Paper and Bemis Brothers Bag, had a broader line of products. They had their large buying and selling networks but did not integrate backward to control their raw materials. And although newsprint and kraft paper companies continued to dominate their industry, American Writing Paper and Bemis Bag found they had few advantages over small, nonintegrated competitors.[15] Their industries remained competitive at the time when newsprint and kraft paper were becoming oligopolistic.

In the stone-clay-glass group, 4 of the 6 largest firms in 1917 were in plate and window glass and the cement industries. All 4—Pittsburgh Plate Glass, American Window Glass, Lehigh Portland Cement, and Atlas Portland Cement—continued to lead their industry for decades, although the last operated as an autonomous subsidiary of United States Steel after 1930.[16] A fifth, Owens Bottle Machine, which became Owens-Illinois in 1965, is still a leader in this industry. The sixth firm, Harbison-Walker Refactories, was a merger of many small firebrick companies producing for local markets, largely in the middle Atlantic states. It was integrated from clay pits to sales to customers. However, given the nature of its production technology, it grew at a much slower rate than the other firms in this group and soon lost its place as one of the nation's largest industrial manufacturing firms.

The names of the enterprises in chemicals (group 28) are less familiar to present-day readers than those in the food, oil, rubber, paper, glass, and cement groups. The modern chemical industries did not come into their own in the United States until the 1920s. Rapidly changing technologies meant that the processes of some firms listed in Appendix A became obsolete, while other firms would develop a highly diversified product line. Even so, the basic structure of the American chemical industry was becoming clear.

By 1917 all the chemical companies with assets of $20 million or over had integrated production with distribution.[17] More had grown by merger than by internal expansion. Three of those that took the latter route—Grasselli Chemical, Sherwin-Williams (paint), and Procter & Gamble—had nineteenth-century roots. A fourth, Semet-Solvay, began in 1895 as a builder and operator of by-product coke ovens and was soon producing ammonium sulphate, benzene, toulene, and other chemicals. In the post-merger movement these older enterprises and the early mergers—National Lead and New Jersey Zinc—continued to thrive. Only American Linseed Oil, still suffering from National Lead's vigorous competition, returned to its early unhealthy financial condition. The mergers that had been formed between 1899 and 1902 moved, some much more quickly than others, from horizontal combination to vertical integration. These included Du Pont, 2 of the 3 fertilizer companies—Virginia-Carolina and American Agricultural Chemical—United Dyewood, Barrett, General Chemical, Union Carbide, and National Carbon. (The last 2 became part of Union Carbide and Carbon in 1917.) The mergers formed after 1903 (including International Agricultural Chemical, National Aniline, and United States Industrial Alcohol) centralized production and built extensive purchasing and sales networks. United Drug, a retail chain, moved the other way by investing in its own manufacturing facilities.

As in the case of the food and oil companies, the chemical firms integrated further backward to control part of their supplies of raw and semifinished materials.[18] Often these moves upstream were defensive. Managers did not want to pay exorbitant prices or shut down operations because of an inability to obtain adequate supplies. These firms, like food, petroleum, rubber, and glass companies, came to own or lease their own ships, rail cars, and other transportation facilities. Here the motive, a more positive one, was to improve the scheduling of flows. In most cases the marketing organization of chemical companies provided specialized services in addition to coordinating flow. They had storage facilities for volatile and often dangerous chemical products. As in electrical and machinery firms, their salesmen were technically trained engineers who instructed customers on the most efficient use of their industrial products. And like the leading companies in those technologically advanced industries, they pioneered in research and development to improve product and process.

In nearly all cases these firms dominated their particular industry or product market. When, as in the case of American Tobacco and Standard Oil, antitrust action split up Du Pont, the leader in the explosives industry, the response was similar. The spin-offs, Hercules and Atlas, adopted a strategy of vertical integration, building their own marketing and buying organizations.

All these firms continued to prosper, except for the 3 fertilizer companies, United Dyewood, whose processes became obsolete, and American Linseed, which never learned to compete successfully with other large integrated firms. All except for American Linseed and Aetna Explosives remain in operation today, either in their own right or as autonomous divisions of major chemical or other industrial companies. For example, Barrett, General Chemical, National Aniline, and Semet-Solvay became divisions of Allied Chemical when that merger was fashioned in 1920. The structure of the American chemical industry took on its modern form in the 1920s, after the formation of Union Carbon and Carbide and Allied Chemical; the shift of Du Pont, Hercules and Atlas from explosives to a large variety of chemical products; and the growth and diversification of smaller and more specialized companies such as Dow and Monsanto. These large, integrated, and increasingly diversified firms dominated their product markets.

The metal fabricators. In all the groups reviewed so far the large enterprise coordinated the flow of goods from the suppliers of raw materials to the final customer. In all, the volume of the flow was high, and its scheduling from many suppliers to still more numerous consumers was complex.

This was less true of the metal makers and metal users. Although they all integrated production with distribution, few came to control the flows through all the processes of production and distribution. The metal-fabricating and machinery-making companies purchased their materials from the metal makers, and the metal makers sold their finished products to the fabricators and machinery makers. This meant that the metal producers sold to a relatively few customers, and fabricating and machinery firms purchased from a relatively few buyers. This difference in the number of transactions affected the size and activities of the buying and selling departments in these enterprises. The fact that the metal makers and metal users did not integrate their operations suggests that there were few economic advantages in coordinating two processes that were so different technologically and required different types of working forces and managerial skills.

Although metal fabricators had larger and more costly manufacturing plants that did food or chemical companies, they rarely reached comparable size. They purchased from a few suppliers, and they often sold only to a relatively small number of buyers. The only firms in the metal-fabricating group (34) to have assets of $20 million or more by 1917 were those with large and varied markets. Only one in that group produced for the consumer market, and that was the Gillette Safety Razor Company. Its history follows closely that of the pioneering cigarette, oatmeal, and photographic film producers. In 1903 the inventor of the safety razor produced 51 razors and 168 blades. By the end of the next year his factory was turning out 90,000 razors and 2.4 million blades.[19] By the end of the decade the Gillette Company had, in addition to its worldwide marketing organization, factories in Britain, France, Germany, and Canada. Like similar earlier manufacturers, Gillette easily financed this sudden and massive expansion out of retained earnings.

The other metal fabricators listed in Appendix A used large-batch processes and sold to many and varied consumers. American Can and Continental Can, both the result of mergers, provided cans and canning machinery for small canners who normally operated on a seasonal basis throughout the country and much of the world.[20] Scovill Manufacturing, National Enameling & Stamping, Crane Co. and Standard Sanitary (both producers of standardized plumbing fixtures), and National Acme, makers of screws, sold to hundreds of contractors, builders, plumbers, manufacturers, and hardware dealers. Weirton Steel, producers of tin and roofing plate, and American Brake Shoe had a somewhat smaller set of customers, but still enough to make full use of a network of sales offices to obtain orders, assure prompt delivery, and take payments on thousands of orders.

Yet in 1917 these were the exception. Most metal-fabricating firms were like American Brass, an 1899 merger which produced semifinished materials for other manufacturers and was just beginning to build its own sales force. The makers of simple fittings, tools, and implements continued to rely on wholesalers to sell consumer goods and on manufacturers' agents to sell producers' goods. Even the largest of these had only a small sales force to keep in touch with dealers and customers. Though such firms had substantial manufacturing establishments, they did not grow to great size. Only 11, or 6.5 percent, of the manufacturing companies included in Appendix A are in the metal-fabricating group.

The machinery makers. On the other hand, the makers of complex machines had, almost from the beginning, built extensive marketing organizations and quickly became huge global enterprises. In fact, if the companies in electrical machinery (group 36) and transportation equipment (group 37) are added to those in machinery (group 35), they total 58, or one-quarter of all the manufacturing firms in the United States with assets of $20 million or more in 1917. Machinery making, thus, was the largest and, in many ways, the most representative big business in early twentieth-century America.

Except for the firearms makers, all the machinery firms in groups 35 and 36 and the majority in group 37 produced goods that required specialized marketing services—demonstration, installation, repair and service, and long-term credit. The firms in groups 35 and 36 include the makers of sewing machines, office machines, agriculture machines, standardized heavy machinery such as pumps, boilers, and elevators, and a wide variety of electricity-producing and -using machines. The pioneering firms are as much in evidence on the 1917 list of machinery makers as they are in the food group. Singer Manufacturing, Remington Typewriter, Burroughs Adding Machine, Deere and Company, Moline Plow, J. I. Case, Babcock and Wilcox, Worthington Pump, Otis Elevator, Mergenthaler Linotype, Westinghouse Electric, and Western Electric, all indicate the continuing permanence and power of the first enterprises to create extensive marketing networks in their industries. Moreover, Fairbanks, now part of Fairbanks Morse, was still the largest firm making scales and similar machines; National Cash Register was still the leader in its industry (both these had assets of $19.6 million, so are not included in the list of the largest 278); and A. B. Dick still dominated the manufacturing of mimeograph machines. In these industries very few new large competitors had appeared.

Although most of the early machinery firms had grown through internal expansion, a few on the list in Appendix A followed the route of legal consolidation, administrative centralization, and then vertical integration. These companies—United Shoe Machinery, American Radiator, and Electric Storage Battery—consolidated and rationalized production facilities and built worldwide marketing forces. The impressive and almost immediate success of United Shoe Machinery and American Radiator in European markets emphasizes the value of such a sales organization for increasing the size and market power of a machinery-making enterprise.[21]

There were also mergers of already integrated enterprises—more of this type of merger than in any other group. Such mergers included International Harvester, General Electric, Allis-Chalmers (makers of milling and other steam-powered machinery), Niles-Bement-Pond (machine tools), Ingersoll-Rand (mining machinery), Computing-Tabulating-Recording (the forerunners of International Business Machines), and Underwood Typewriter (a merger of Underwood and Wagner Typewriter). Except in the case of International Harvester, the mergers were usually carried out to obtain complementary lines that might use the same marketing and purchasing organizations. In nearly all of these mergers the personnel of the smaller companies were integrated into the functional departments (production, sales, engineering, or finance) of the larger. As was the case on the railroads, the oldest and largest firm normally provided the basic "core" organization.

In transportation equipment (group 37) the primary route to growth after 1900 was internal expansion. This was particularly true of the new and rapidly expanding automobile industry. These makers of cars, trucks, parts, and accessories grew in much the same way as the pioneering makers of sewing and agricultural machinery. At first they sold through independent distributors. Soon they were relying on franchised dealers to retail their products. The dealers were supported with an elaborate marketing organization that advertised, assisted in providing after-sales services and repair and consumer credit, and assured prompt, scheduled delivery. The first firms to build such extensive sales forces quickly led the industry. In fact, Henry Ford's well-organized global sales organization provided much of the incessant demand that pushed his engineers into evolving the moving assembly line. By 1917 Willys, Studebaker, Maxwell, Packard, Pierce Arrow, and White (trucks) had comparable, if smaller, sales departments. So, too, did the subsidiaries of General Motors— Buick, Oldsmobile, Cadillac, Chevrolet, and the parts maker, United Motors. In automobiles, as in sewing, agricultural, and business machinery, growth came from internal expansion. Mergers were few and unsuccessful. They made little attempt to consolidate their already integrated enterprises into a single centralized operating organization. Even the largest, General Motors, became a long-term profit maker only after its massive administrative reorganization in the 1920s.

The older companies listed in group 37 were either shipyards or builders of railroad equipment. Of the latter, Pullman, Baldwin Locomotive, Westinghouse Air Brake, and New York Air Brake had grown large in the late nineteenth century by internal expansion. The others—American Locomotive, American Car and Foundry, Pressed Steel Car, Standard Steel Car, and Railway Steel Spring—were all results of turn-of-the-century mergers. These firms moved from horizontal combination to vertical integration, setting up structures similar to those of competitors who had grown through internal expansion. Their sales departments were much smaller than those of the machinery makers, for they had fewer customers. On the other hand, these sales forces were global. They provided credit, maintenance, and other services that helped American manufacturers sell railway equipment in all parts of the world.

The shipbuilders were one of the few sets of manufacturers listed among the 278 largest enterprises in 1917 that were not integrated. Even though these firms were booming in 1917 because of the critical shortage of ships caused by unrestricted German submarine warfare, they remained single-function firms, usually operating in a single locality.[22] After the war they did not enjoy the growth that the integrated automobile, machinery, and fabricating companies did. In fact, they barely managed to stay alive.

Primary metals. The firms of this last industrial group differed from those in the other groups in which large enterprises clustered. Their manufacturing establishments were the most costly in American industry. (Indeed, because the criterion for size in Appendix A was assets, the sample is biased in favor of such heavy industry. If sales or value added had been used, fewer primary metal and more food and machinery firms would have appeared as the largest American enterprises.) The firms in the primary metal group also differed in that they made a much heavier investment in backward rather than in forward integration. Of the 26 iron and steel makers with assets of $20 million or over, 12 owned a full range of mines, transportation facilities, blast furnaces, open-hearth and Bessemer furnaces, and rolling mills (see table 8). Only 4 of these had integrated forward into fabricated finished products. As late as 1948 only 5.7 percent of the hot-rolled sheet steel produced in the United States was used by fabricating companies controlled by steel makers.[23] As table 8 indicates, the remaining 14 were even less integrated, with 5 making only pig iron and steel billets. Those that did integrate had done so,

Table 8. Iron and steel companies with assets of $20 million or more, 1917[a]

Integrated mine to rolling mill

1. U.S. Steel Corp. (f)
3. Bethlehem Steel Corp. (f)
6. Midvale Steel & Ordnance Co. (f) [Bethlehem]
19. Jones & Laughlin Steel
39. Republic Iron & Steel Co.
40. Lackawanna Steel Co. [Bethlehem]
53. Youngstown Sheet & Tube Co.
54. Colorado Fuel & Iron Co.
87. Inland Steel Co.
107. La Belle Iron Works (f) [Wheeling]
109. Brier Hill Steel Co. [Youngstown]
164. Pittsburgh Steel Co.

Blast to rolling mill

58. Crucible Steel of America
187. American Rolling Mill
203. United Alloy Steel Corp. [Republic]
248. Wheeling Steel & Iron Co.

Blast and open hearth only

137. Trumbull Steel Co. [Republic]
241. Mark Mfg. Co. [Steel & Tube Co. of America]
251. Otis Steel Co. [Jones & Laughlin]
276. Lukens Steel Co.
280. Whitaker-Glessner Co. [Wheeling]

Mine to blast

135. M. A. Hanna & Co. [Hanna Mining]
179. Woodward Iron Co.
206. Sloss-Sheffield Steel & Iron Co. [U.S. Pipe and Foundry]
250. Rogers Brown Iron Co. [Susquehanna Ore Co.]
270. Donner Steel Co. [Republic]

Source: Appendix A, Moody's *Manuals of Industrial Securities,* and company reports.

[a] Numbers indicate rank among the largest 278 industrials in 1917. The letter (f) indicates integration beyond rolling mills. Name in brackets is the company into which the firm merged.

much as Carnegie had done in the 1890s, to assure themselves of an adequate supply of raw materials for their costly production works.

Because the iron and steel companies purchased from so few sources and sold to a relatively small number of customers, their purchasing and sales departments were much smaller than those of most large American industrial enterprises. Nevertheless, all but 1 of the companies listed in the table had its own branch sales offices by 1917. Administrative coordination between production and distribution was a significant factor in reducing costs. Close cooperation between production and sales managers made possible tighter scheduling of the flow of materials through the furnaces and mills and also helped to assure the shipment of large and varied lots made to precise specifications and delivered on an exact schedule. The marketing of semifinished iron and steel products, however, did not require specialized installation, after-sales service and repair, or complex credit arrangements. A small sales force working out of a few regional offices was able to obtain orders, schedule them, and assure delivery.

The advantages of integrating production with distribution meant that the major mergers in iron and steel—Bethlehem, Crucible, United Alloy, Republic, and American Rolling Mill—consolidated their operations and administered them through functionally defined organizations. The last 2 had by 1917 gone one step further and set up integrated divisions to serve separate geographical markets.

The one major exception to administrative consolidation was the United States Steel Corporation. That huge consolidation formed by J. P. Morgan to control close to 60 percent of the industry's output resulted from the financier's concern for increased competition. His investment banking house arranged the merger in 1901 after Carnegie began to move forward into the making of finished products in response to backward integration by new combinations such as American Steel & Wire.[24] For many years after its formation the United States Steel Corporation continued to be a holding company that administered its many subsidiaries through a very small general office. Except for the Carnegie Company and, after 1907, the Tennessee Coal and Iron Company, these subsidiaries were single-function companies in mining, transportation, coke, metal production, and fabrication. The general office did little to coordinate, plan, and evaluate for the activities of the subsidiaries. Only in foreign purchases and sales was there any clear central direction. Until Myron C. Taylor began a massive administrative reorganization of the corporation in the 1930s, the Steel Corporation remained little more than a legal consolidation.

By 1917 the American iron and steel industry had acquired its modern look. Its major branches had become concentrated, and the same firms would long continue to be its leaders.[25] Of the 13 largest iron and steel companies in 1967, all but 1 was in operation in 1917. Of those 12, 8 were already among the 10 largest in the industry in 1917. The other 2 of the top 10 in that year—Midvale and Lackawanna—became part of Bethlehem in 1922. The only new company to appear by the 1970s was National—a merger of 3 firms, 2 of which already existed in 1917. As the table indicates, after 1917 the large steel firms grew by merger, and such mergers increased the extent of integration within the industry. By the 1930s nearly all the large firms came to coordinate the flow of materials from the mines through the rolling mill, but not further into fabrication.

In 1917 the copper enterprises were even less integrated than those in iron or steel. Anaconda had extended forward from mining to refining and fabricating of wire and sheet. American Smelting and Refining, a merger formed in 1899 of copper refiners and smelters, had reached backward into mining and soon had worldwide investments in copper mines. Kennecott and Phelps Dodge remained primarily mining companies, doing only a small amount of smelting and refining. And in 1917 Calumet & Hecla, Chile Copper, Utah Copper, Greene Cananea, and 6 other copper companies on the list of the 278 top companies were still only mining enterprises. On the other hand, one large copper-selling company, American Metal Company, was beginning to move backward into fabricating and smelting. So, by the coming of World War I the copper industry was just beginning to be dominated by a few large integrated firms. After World War I, integration of mining, smelting and fabricating of semifinished materials came quickly. By 1950 the big four—Anaconda, American Smelting and Refining, Kennecott, and Phelps Dodge—produced 90 percent of the nation's copper, and their subsidiaries processed 65 percent of the copper they produced.[26] Well after 1917 the sales organizations of the large copper companies were even smaller than those in iron and steel. Some continued to use manufacturers' agents to sell their products.

The producers of nickel, lead, and zinc who began as mining firms had by 1917 moved little beyond smelting and refining their ores. International Nickel, St. Joseph Lead, American Zinc, Lead, and Smelting, and United States Smelting and Refining had large refining facilities but did not fabricate standard shapes. As they sold to only a few customers, their sales forces remained tiny.

On the other hand, the first enterprise to commercialize the newly invented methods for the mass production of aluminum quickly created a large, global sales force to sell the output produced.[27] For when the Aluminum Company of America began operations, the market for aluminum products was small and specialized. The company found new uses for its goods in the older trades and still larger markets in the newer automobile and airplane industries. By developing a kitchenware line, it became the only large metal company to sell consumer goods in volume. The rapidly growing and varied demand engendered by its sales force quickly brought integration backward into bauxite mines and ore ships. By 1917 the Aluminum Company of America was coordinating the flow of goods from the sources of raw materials to the ultimate consumer much as the oil companies did. This powerful international organization with its high-volume, capital-intensive production and massive distribution gave the pioneering enterprise in the industry an enormous competitive advantage.

In the primary metals industry the motives for integration were largely defensive. Where a small number of mining firms controlled sources of supply, the processing companies wanted to have their own assured sources; and where mining firms sold to a small number of processors, they wanted to be sure of their outlets. The pattern in iron and steel was for manufacturing firms to move backward into mining and in the non-ferrous industries for mining firms to reach forward into manufacturing. Before World War I, however, few primary metal enterprises had integrated forward into the fabrication of finished products. When they did, the motive again tended to be largely defensive. Their aim was to have a more certain outlet for their products.

The relatively small size of the buying and selling organizations of primary metals companies and the fact that they did not coordinate the flow of materials from the supplier of raw materials to the final consumer meant that their managerial organizations were smaller than those in other industries. And possibly because they were smaller, the top companies in primary metals in the years after World War I made less effort than the leading firms in food, machinery, oil, rubber, and chemicals to diversify their product lines or to extend their activities overseas.

Growth by vertical integration—an analysis

This descriptive review of the experiences of close to 90 percent of all manufacturing companies with assets of $20 million or more in 1917 does more than document the fact that they grew to size through vertical integration. It reveals important generalizations about this process of growth. One is that the nature of the market was more important than the methods of production in determining the size and defining the activities of the modern industrial corporation. A second is that, although the strategy of vertical integration led to industrial concentration, it rarely resulted in monopoly. In nearly all cases these integrated firms competed with one another in an oligopolistic manner. Third, the review indicates that the large firms dominated their industries abroad as well as at home. Their reach early became global. Finally, the review emphasizes that the period between the great turn-of-the-century merger movement and the nation's entry into World War I completed the formative period in American industry. By 1917 most American industries had acquired their modern structure. For the rest of the century the large industrial enterprises continued to cluster in much the same industrial groups as they did in 1917. And the same enterprises continued to be the leaders in the concentrated industries in these groups.

The importance of the market. Technology of production was certainly the critical determinant in the growth of the firm. Nine out of 10 large manufacturing companies listed in Appendix A used capital-intensive, energy-consuming processes. But the use of such production methods did not in itself bring size to a firm or concentration of production to an industry. Enterprises in a number of fabricated metal, chemical, food, glass, paper, and rubber industries that used such processes remained relatively small and their industries relatively competitive.

Except in the production of primary metals, a manufacturing enterprise rarely became and remained large until it had built its own extensive marketing organization. Its owners took this step when the maintenance of high-volume output required precise and detailed scheduling of the flows of finished products to mass markets or the maintenance of specialized distributing facilities and marketing services. The creation of distributing and marketing networks to provide such coordination, facilities, and services caused the mass producers to internalize several processes of production and distribution and the market transactions between them within a single enterprise. Such internalization permitted the visible hand of administrative coordination to make more intensive use of the resources invested in these processes of production and distribution than could the invisible hand of market coordination.

Such administrative coordination in turn created formidable barriers to entry. High-volume throughput and stock-turn reduced unit costs. Advertising and the provision of services maintained customer loyalty. Rival firms were rarely able to compete until they had built comparable marketing organizations of their own.

The creation of a nationwide or global distribution marketing network further encouraged, indeed often forced, the integrated enterprise to build an extensive purchasing organization. The increasing volume of production intensified the need for assured supplies and for more careful scheduling of the flow of supplies into the processing plants. When the raw materials came from a large number of farmers, small processors, and suppliers, the purchasing organization grew as large as the marketing one. Its many buyers maintained contact with suppliers and dealers, and, in the manner of the comparable buying units of the mass retailers, set specifications for and price of materials purchased and scheduled flows to warehouses and factories. Like the mass marketers, they reduced costs by more efficient administrative coordination. When, on the other hand, the number of suppliers were few, the purchasing organization remained small.

Where the manufacturer's motives for backward integration into control over raw and semifinished materials were defensive, where they were to assure an availability of supply rather than to reduce costs, they were somewhat similar to those of the builders of railroad systems. Like the railroad managers, the manufacturers wanted to be self-sustaining. In some industries defensive integration by manufacturers, in turn, forced producers of raw and semifinished materials to integrate forward into manufacturing and marketing. Again, the parallels to railroad system-building are obvious.

Integration and concentration. In industries where administrative coordination provided competitive advantages, integration brought concentration. Even before 1900 a high degree of concentration could be found in many industries. Such industries became dominated by a few vertically integrated enterprises rather than by horizontal combinations of manufacturing firms. The first to integrate continued to dominate. Only those firms adopting a similar strategy continued to compete. In such industries small, nonintegrated firms filled the interstices by providing supplementary outlets for the large integrated firms.

On the other hand, in industries where technology did not lend itself to mass production, and where volume distribution did not benefit from specialized scheduling or services, vertical integration failed to bring concentration. In the labor-intensive, low-energy-consuming industries where administrative coordination did not result in sharp reductions of unit costs, or provide services, and so create barriers to entry, vertical integration did not provide a profitable alternative to horizontal combination. In such industries, small, integrated enterprises continued to prosper. Textiles, apparel, leather, shoes, lumber, and furniture; printing and publishing; and industries producing simple metal tools, implements, and fabricated shapes or highly specialized machinery remained unconcentrated. In these industries, as the history of American Woolen and Central Leather indicates, size might indeed be a handicap.

Table 9. Percentage of total product value produced by oligopolists within industrial groups,[a] 1909–1919

Type A groups: up to 3 percent of product value produced by oligopolists

	1909	1919
25 Furniture	<1(5)[b]	0(4)
27 Printing and publishing	<1(5)	<1(10)
31 Leather	<1(8)	<1(13)
24 Lumber and wood products	<1(11)	<1(14)
23 Apparel	1(18)	<1(22)
22 Textiles	<1(17)	<1(23)
26 Paper	<1(9)	2(11)
37 Transportation equipment	9(8)	3(12)
34 Fabricated metals	2(16)	3(28)

Type B groups: up to 25 percent of product value produced by oligopolists

	1909	1919
21 Stone, clay, and glass	2(16)	5(21)
28 Chemicals	9(25)	9(30)
35 Machinery	16(11)	20(17)

Type C groups: over 25 percent of product value produced by oligopolists

	1909	1919
20 Food	24(30)	28(36)
36 Electrical machinery	68(3)	40(7)
33 Primary metals	35(18)	40(25)
29 Petroleum	34(6)	44(6)
38 Instruments	10(5)	48(13)
30 Rubber	76(2)	69(2)
21 Tobacco	75(1)	80(2)

Source: Alfred D. Chandler, Jr., "The Structure of American Industry in the Twentieth Century: A Historical Overview," *Business History Review*, 43:259 (Autumn 1959).

[a] The two-digit groups used by the U.S. Bureau of the Census in its Standard Industrial Classification.

[b] Figures in parentheses beside the percentages give the total number of industries within an industrial group. <1 means less than 1 percent.

As table 9 suggests, the concentrated industries were clustered roughly in the same industrial groups as were the large enterprises. The table gives the total product value produced by the leading firms in the concentrated four-digit industries within the larger two-digit industrial categories.[28] For this table the concentrated industries were defined as those in which 6 or fewer firms produced 50 percent of the total value produced or 12 or fewer manufactured 75 percent of value produced or some number of firms between 5 and 12 produced a proportionate percent of the total product. The table indicates that the value produced by the oligopolists was the smallest in groups that had the smallest number of firms capitalized at $20 million or more. On the other hand, in those groups in which the large firms clustered, the oligopolists produced a much larger share of output. Instruments is the major exception. The correlation is only an approximate one. In the 1920s and 1930s with the continued growth of the automobile and chemical industries, the value produced by oligopolists became higher in those groups. This was also the case but to a lesser extent in the paper and the stone-clay-glass groups.

As the descriptive review of the companies listed in Appendix A further emphasizes, concentration meant oligopoly rather than monopoly. There were several reasons why so few monopolies appeared. One was the result of the very process of vertical integration. As has been stressed, backward integration by manufacturers caused producers of raw materials to move forward into processing and selling. Occasionally, marketers moved back into manufacturing. Such responses by firms operating in different parts of an industry were particularly significant in oil, sugar, chemicals, iron and steel, and copper.

A second reason for oligopoly was that two or more enterprises integrated forward and backward simultaneously. This was the case, for example, in meat packing, cotton oil, and agricultural implements. Often, too, leading firms refused to join horizontal mergers. As mergers consolidated their operations, centralized their administration, and began to integrate, such independents as Westinghouse Electric, Goodrich Rubber, Wrigley's Chewing Gum, Loose-Wiles Biscuit, and Jones & Laughlin Steel reacted by enlarging their marketing and purchasing organizations and by perfecting their internal structures.

Third, as the integrated firms began to make fuller use of their facilities by developing by-products and new products, they came to compete with other integrated enterprises. Thus, National Lead became a major competitor of National (later American) Linseed in the production of linseed oil; and American Linseed later competed in the fertilizer markets with the large cotton oil and fertilizer firms as well as with the giant meat packers. When cotton oil and meat-packing enterprises started to produce soap from their by-products, they provided new competition for Procter & Gamble. Competition also appeared when manufacturers such as the makers of agricultural equipment and other machinery decided to develop a "full line" of products in order to make more intensive use of their marketing organization.

A final reason for continuing competition between the large integrated firms was public policy. Antitrust legislation and its interpretation by the courts in these years discouraged monopoly but not oligopoly. Yet, it must be remembered that although such legislation was significant, it was only one of several reasons why concentrated industries became and remained oligopolistic rather than monopolistic.

The rise of multinational enterprise. Many of the large integrated enterprises became the nation's first multinationals. Again, the creation of a marketing organization was the critical determinant. The first enterprises to build extensive marketing networks abroad were also the first firms to own and operate their own plants and other productive facilities overseas.[29] Table 10 lists the American firms that had by 1914 substantial

Table 10. American multinationals, 1914 (companies with two or more plants abroad or one plant and raw material producing facilities)

Groups 20 and 21: Food and tobacco[a]	*Groups 35, 36, and 37: Machinery and transportation equipment*
American Chicle	American Bicycle
American Cotton Oil	American Gramophone
Armour	American Radiator
Coca Cola	Crown Cork & Seal
H. J. Heinz	Chicago Pneumatic Tool
Quaker Oats	Ford
Swift	General Electric
American Tobacco	International Harvester
British American Tobacco	International Steam Pump (Worthington)
Groups 28, 29, and 30: Chemicals and pharmaceuticals, oil, and rubber	Mergenthaler Linotype
	National Cash Register
Carborundum	Norton
Parke Davis (drug)	Otis Elevator
Sherwin-Williams	Singer
Sterns & Co. (drug)	Torrington
United Drug (drug)	United Shoe Machinery
Virginia-Carolina Chemical	Western Electric
Du Pont	Westinghouse Air Brake
Standard Oil of N.J.	Westinghouse Electric
U.S. Rubber	
	Others
	Alcoa (33)[a]
	Gillette (34)
	Eastman Kodak (38)
	Diamond Match (39)

Source: Mira Wilkins, *The Emergence of Multinational Enterprise* (Cambridge, Mass., 1970), pp. 212–213, 216.

[a] The two-digit groups used by the U.S. Bureau of the Census in its Standard Industrial Classification.

investments abroad. As might be expected, nearly two-thirds of the 41 companies with plants and raw material producing facilities abroad were in the food and machinery industries. Of these food and machinery enterprises, all had at least 2 foreign plants and a dozen of these had 4 or more.

The table does not include any primary metal or metal-fabricating firms, firms that had only small marketing organizations. A small number of metal makers—Bethlehem Steel, International Nickel, and the Guggenhiem's American Smelting and Refining—had overseas sources of raw materials. Only United States Steel and Crucible Steel built extensive sales networks abroad. And only one, American Rolling Mill, had even constructed a single plant more distant than Canada, and only 3 other metal-producing companies had Canadian plants.

In expanding overseas, nearly all these American companies followed the same pattern. They first created their extensive foreign marketing organization, often setting up branch offices abroad at the same time that they did at home. Then because of tariffs, high transportation costs, lower labor costs, and difficulties of coordinating transocean flows, they build factories abroad. Once production and marketing were integrated overseas, purchasing of raw, semifinished and other material could often be obtained locally at less cost and more speed. As a result, well before 1914 a number of American firms were operating fully integrated foreign subsidiaries.

By 1914 American direct foreign investment was impressive. It amounted to a sum equal to 7 percent of the United States gross national product. In 1966 the amount of direct foreign investment equalled precisely the same 7 percent of GNP.[30] And although the food companies had some competition abroad from companies of other nations, most machinery companies controlled their overseas markets as effectively as they did at home. These machinery firms spearheaded what by 1902 the Europeans were calling "the American invasion."[31] Long before World War I these invaders led the field in sewing and office machinery, agricultural machinery elevators, shoe machinery, printing machinery, pumping machinery, and telephone equipment. In electrical machinery and chemicals, where they had rivals (in both cases German), their foreign competitors were comparable integrated enterprises. After World War I, chemical, automobile, and then in the 1930s, oil companies, became as numerous as food companies in the ranks of American multinationals. Throughout the century, however, the machinery firms continued to lead the way in foreign markets. On the other hand, manufacturers with only small marketing organizations or those who relied on middlemen to sell and distribute their goods almost never became multinational enterprises with direct investments overseas.

Integration and the structure of the American economy. By 1917 the large industrial enterprise, the most influential American economic institution abroad, had taken its place at the center of the nation's economy at home. Whereas the country's basic transportation and communication infrastructure had been shaped by the 1890s, its underlying industrial organization had been solidified by World War I.

Table 11 shows that as the twentieth century progressed, the large industrial enterprise continued to operate in much the same industries.[32] In 1929, 88 percent of the largest 81 manufacturing firms were in food

Table 11. The location of the largest manufacturing enterprises, 1929, 1935, 1948, 1960

Group[a]	1929	1935	1948	1960
20 Food	8	8	9	6
21 Tobacco	4	3	3	2
22 Textiles	1	0	2	1
23 Apparel	0	0	0	0
24 Lumber	1	0	1	0
25 Furniture	0	0	0	0
26 Paper	2	5	1	3
27 Printing/publishing	0	1	0	0
28 Chemicals	5	5	10	9
29 Petroleum	19	16	17	18
30 Rubber	4	4	4	4
31 Leather	1	1	0	0
32 Stone/clay/glass	1	1	2	2
33 Primary metals	16	17	15	15
34 Fabricated metal	1	3	2	2
35 Machinery	4	7	6	6
36 Electrical machinery	3	3	3	4
37 Transportation equipment	8	6	5	7
38 Instruments	2	1	1	1
39 Miscellaneous manufactures	1	0	0	1
TOTAL	81	81	81	81

Source: Alfred D. Chandler, Jr., "The Structure of American Industry in the Twentieth Century: A Historical Overview," *Business History Review*, 43:257, 283–284 (Autumn 1969), table 2 by P. Glenn Porter and Harold C. Livesay. United Fruit Company and Cleveland-Cliffs Iron Company were excluded as not manufacturing, and the categories of Koppers, National Lead, American Radiator, and Crane Company were altered.

[a] The two-digit groups used by the U.S. Bureau of the Census in its Standard Industrial Classification.

and tobacco, oil, rubber, chemicals, primary metals, and the three machinery-making groups (35–37). If the integrated paper, glass, can, and
photographic equipment firms are added, the total is over 90 percent. The
overall percentages remain, and the number of firms in each industrial
group is much the same for 1935, 1948, and 1960.

These industries, where the visible hand of management had the greatest opportunity to increase productivity and reduce costs, were the most
critical to the current health and continuing growth of the rapidly industrializing American economy. Robert Averitt in his *Dual Economy* has
defined 41 "key industries" which in 1963 had the maximum impact on the
American economy.[33] These were the industries that led in technological
convergence (that is, disseminating technological advances), in investment in research and development, in capital goods production, and in
interindustrial dependence (having extensive forward and backward
linkages); that had the greatest price/cost and the strongest wage-setting
effects on other industries; that were in leading growth sectors; and that
were full-employment bottlenecks (that is low employment in them,
reduced employment in others). Of these, 5 were electronic and aircraft
industries which were just getting started in 1917. Of the 36 in full operation at that time, all but 3 were in oil, rubber, chemical, and machinery
and metals two-digit SIC groups. These 3 were scientific instruments,
mechanical measuring devices, and sheet pipe and tube. All but 4 of these
36 key industries were concentrated ones, with the 8 largest firms accounting for more than 48 percent of the total value of shipments. And in the
remaining 4 (these included the 3 just listed plus steel foundries) the
largest 8 accounted for between 32 and 42 percent of the total value of
shipments. Of those industries in which the large firm had come to
cluster before 1917, only food and tobacco were not on Averitt's list. And
these may have had a greater impact, in terms of Averitt's criteria, forty
years earlier, when the economy was more agrarian and less industrial.

The leading enterprises in these vital industries continued to grow
both by internal expansion and by merger. After World War I, however,
mergers much more often involved the acquisition of one integrated enterprise by another than, as at the turn of the century, consolidations of many
small single-function firms. Normally the personnel and activities of the
smaller or acquired firms were internalized by the core organization of the
larger or acquiring megacorps.

Very few managerial hierarchies therefore actually disappeared. Of
the 278 largest industrials in 1917 listed in Appendix A, only 14 had been
liquidated, dissolved, or discontinued by 1967.[34] All others that were no
longer independent enterprises had been incorporated into the hierarchies
of existing companies. Of the 14 that no longer existed, only 4 had built

extensive managerial organizations.[35] The other 10 included 3 mining, 3 agricultural, 1 lumber, and 3 manufacturing firms. These 3—2 textiles and 1 shipyard—had remained single-function enterprises.[36] Once an enterprise had set up a managerial hierarchy and once that organization had provided efficient administrative coordination of the flow of materials through the processes of production and distribution it became self-perpetuating.

Nevertheless, these self-perpetuating human organizations appeared and continued to flourish only in industries where the technology of high-volume production and the needs of high-volume distribution offered the greatest potential for the administrative coordination of the flow of goods through the economy. The first of these big businesses were in the food and machinery industries. As the economy continued to industrialize and urbanize, those in oil, rubber, chemicals, and primary metals acquired the same characteristics.

Determinants of size and concentration

The basic institutional arrangements used in the production and distribution of goods in modern America had fully evolved by the 1920s. Salaried managers working in multiunit enterprises had replaced owners in single-unit firms in carrying out these processes in the key sectors of the economy. Where the processes of production were capital-intensive and energy-consuming, and where the creation of a marketing organization assisted in the selling and distribution of mass-produced products, the manufacturers managed these processes and administered the flow. Where the production processes were more labor-intensive and less energy-consuming, and where marketing and distribution did not benefit from specialized scheduling and advertising and other services, the mass marketers and, increasingly, the mass retailers coordinated the flows.

In both cases the visible hand of management replaced the invisible hand of market mechanisms in administering and coordinating day-to-day production and distribution. Yet the difference between the two methods of coordination and control was significant. For where the manufacturer became the coordinator, his firm grew to great size, and the decisions in his industry concerning current production and distribution and the allocation of resources for future production and distribution became concentrated in the hands of a small number of managers. This centralization of decision making, and with it economic power, was of particular importance because it occurred in industries central to the growth and well-being of the economy.

Markets and technology, therefore, determined whether the manufacturer or the marketer did the coordinating. They had a far greater influence in determining size and concentration in American industry than did the quality of entrepreneurship, the availability of capital, or public policy.

Entrepreneurial ability can hardly account for the clustering of giant enterprises in some industries and not in others. The most brilliant industrial statesmen or the most ruthless robber barons were unable to create giant multinational companies in the furniture, apparel, leather, or textile industries. Yet, in other industries the first to try often succeeded. Within the single decade of the 1880s entrepreneurs built giant enterprises that dominated their industries at home and abroad in tobacco, matches, breakfast cereals, meat packing, cotton oil, kerosene, photographic film, sewing machines, office machines, agricultural machinery, electrical equipment, telephone equipment, elevators, boilers, pumps, and other standardized machinery. Once these men had completed their integrated international organizations, the opportunities for empire building in their industries became limited. An entrepreneur might enlarge or combine existing enterprises, but he rarely built a new one. Such an opportunity came again only with changes in technology and major shifts in markets.

Nor can the availability of capital and the nature of the capital markets account for size and concentration in American industry. Enterprises did not grow large and industries become concentrated because the entrepreneurs who built them had privileged access to capital. There is little evidence to document the contention of Lance Davis and others that Rockefeller, Carnegie, and Swift dominated their industries because they had access to sources of outside capital denied to their competitors.[37] And there is no evidence at all that the producers of oil, sugar, cigarettes, sewing machines, and other machines had in the 1880s and 1890s sources of outside capital not available to makers of textiles, clothing, leather, and furniture.

What the enterprises that integrated production and distribution did have was a much greater supply of internally generated capital. The technology of their production permitted them to produce a much higher volume of cash flow than was possible in labor-intensive industries. Internally generated funds financed the expansion of their small number of large plants and paid for the setting up of their branch selling and purchasing offices. It was only when the mergers of the 1890s began to consolidate and rationalize their processing facilities that American industrial enterprises required funds that were not available from local commercial banks and businessmen.

The managers of the mergers of the 1890s had little difficulty in obtaining the capital they needed. By that date the capital markets in the United States, particularly those in New York, were as extensive and sophisticated as any in the world. By that decade New York investment houses were marketing blocks of railroad securities to American and European investors as large as any that would be required for industrial expansion. There was no scarcity. If anything, there was a plethora of capital. Bankers, financiers, and speculators were eager to locate securities to sell. They did not discriminate between industries. They promoted enterprises as enthusiastically in those trades that remained competitive as they did in those that became concentrated. The wishes and decisions of financiers had little to do with the size of American firms and the structure of American industries.

Nor can public policy in the form of specific legislation explain why some firms became large and why some industries concentrated and others did not. Tariffs were as high on the products of industries that remained competitive as they were on those that became concentrated. And, of course, American tariffs had no direct impact on the growth of these enterprises abroad. Even when tariffs of foreign nations were specifically directed against the products of these firms, they did little to slow growth. The companies merely went under the tariff wall by setting up factories within the nations that discriminated against their products.

Patents had a greater effect than tariffs. The products of many of the large industrials were new and protected by patents in the American market. This was particularly true for the machinery makers. Manufacturers paid close and continuing attention to protecting their products, processes, and specialized production machinery with patents. Yet American patents often failed to give protection in foreign markets. Even at home they provided only temporary protection on individual products or processes. Moreover, one manufacturer rarely controlled all the patents in his industry. Singer Sewing Machine Company, for example, was one of twenty-four firms employing the Howe patents. It never had patent protection in its overseas markets. Its monopoly came from the effectiveness of its global organization. A set of patents without such an organization could never assure dominance; an organization, even without patents, could.

As early as the 1890s some of the new integrated industrial enterprises began to shift from relying on patents for even temporary protection to depending on the output of their specialized research departments to help them maintain their dominant positions. As Reese V. Jenkins has written of Eastman Kodak, "patents began to play a diminished role, while continuous innovation became a more effective strategy."[38] In 1896 George Eastman set up his experimental department with managers trained in chemical engineering at Massachusetts Institute of Technology and other universities. By that date companies in less technologically sophisticated industries including American Cotton Oil and National Lead had research departments with their own laboratories separated from those used to test products and control production processes. By the first decade of the new century Western Electric, Westinghouse, General Electric, Electric Storage Battery, McCormick Harvester (and then International Harvester), Corn Products, Du Pont, General Chemical, Goodrich Rubber, Corning Glass, National Carbon, Parke Davis, and E. R. Squibb all had extensive departments where salaried scientifically trained managers and technicians spent their careers improving products and processes.[39] Other companies soon followed suit. The research organizations of modern industrial enterprises remained a more powerful force than patent laws in assuring the continued dominance of pioneering mass production firms in concentrated industries.

Antitrust legislation had a more substantial impact than did patent or tariff legislation on the growth of modern industrial enterprise and on industrial concentration. After all, such legislation was specifically directed at controlling the size and activities of these firms. Yet what antitrust legislation did was to reinforce technological and market imperatives. The passage of the Sherman Act and its intepretation by the federal courts affected the creation and continuing growth of the modern industrial enterprises in two ways.

First, the Sherman Act, which was passed as a protest against the massive number of combinations that occurred during the 1870s and 1880s, clearly discouraged the continuation of loose horizontal federations of small manufacturing enterprises formed to control price and production. The Supreme Court's decisions in the E. C. Knight, Addystone Pipe, and Trans-Missouri Freight Rate cases, by condemning federations and condoning the holding company, hastened the coming of legal consolidation. These decisions provided a powerful pressure for a combination of family firms to merge into a single, legally defined enterprise. And such a legal organization was the essential precondition for administrative centralization and vertical integration. Without the Sherman Act and these judicial interpretations, the cartels of small family firms owning and operating single-function enterprises might well have continued into the twentieth century in the United States as they did in Europe.

In the second place, the existence of the Sherman Act discouraged monopoly in industries where integration and concentration had already occurred. It helped to create oligopoly where monopoly existed and to prevent oligopoly from becoming monopoly. The Court's willingness, as indicated by the Northern Securities case, to dissolve a holding company found guilty of restraining trade acted as a brake on the formation of large mergers of already integrated companies such as had occurred in the steel and harvester industries. Later, federal actions against American Tobacco, Du Pont, and American Can helped to transform monopolistic industries into oligopolistic ones. Antitrust action taken against Standard Oil and American Sugar increased the number of competitors in these already oligopolistic industries. Nevertheless, in these formative years of modern industry, federal action under the Sherman Act never transformed an oligopolistic industry back into a traditionally competitive one. Nor did it prevent the rise of the giant integrated firm where markets and technology made administrative coordination profitable.

The rise of modern business enterprise in American industry between the 1880s and World War I was little affected by public policy, capital markets, or entrepreneurial talents because it was part of a more fundamental economic development. Modern business enterprise, as defined throughout this study, was the organizational response to fundamental changes in processes of production and distribution made possible by the availability of new sources of energy and by the increasing application of scientific knowledge to industrial technology. The coming of the railroad and telegraph and the perfection of new high-volume processes in the production of food, oil, rubber, glass, chemicals, machinery, and metals made possible a historically unprecedented volume of production. The rapidly expanding population resulting from a high birth rate, a falling death rate, and massive immigration and a high and rising per capita income helped to assure continuing and expanding markets for such production. Changes in transportation, communication, and demand brought a revolution in the processes of distribution. And where the new mass marketers had difficulty in handling the output of the new processes of production, the manufacturers integrated mass production with mass distribution. The result was the giant industrial enterprise which remains today the most powerful privately owned and managed economic institution in modern market economies.

The building and managing of the modern multiunit business enterprise was, then, central to the process of modernization in the Western world. The task placed a premium on the ability to create and manage large, complex human organizations. Such abilities became the most needed and often best rewarded of entrepreneurial talents. Of all the new types of business organizations to be formed in the United States after 1840, none were more complex than those that integrated mass production with mass distribution. They carried on a wider range of activities than those created to administer the new means of transportation and communication or those built to handle mass distribution. They operated on a global scale. The creation and continuing administration of such complex human organizations deserve close attention.

PART
five

The Management and Growth
of Modern Industrial Enterprise

In outlining the rise of modern business enterprise in American industry, I have demonstrated that the multiunit enterprise appeared and flourished in those industries where the integration of mass production with mass distribution proved most profitable. But this brief review only hints at the diversity, complexity, and implications of the full story.

In the next two chapters I examine the ways in which large integrated industrial enterprises built and used their operating organizations. I indicate in greater detail how these enterprises competed in the market place, how they maintained their dominance, and how they continued to grow. These chapters review the methods devised by middle management to monitor the performance of the operating units under their command and to coordinate the flow of materials through them. And they analyze how top management evaluated and coordinated the activities of middle management and planned and allocated resources for the enterprise as a whole. In a word, they explain how the visible hand of management carried on the functions hitherto performed by market mechanisms in American industry.

Once this explanation has been made, the purpose of this history has been carried out. Only three more sets of data are needed to complete the story of the rise of modern business enterprise in the United States: a review of the ways in which organizational structures and administrative procedures were perfected; a consideration of the growing professionalism of business managers and the rapid spread of the appurtenances of professionalism—journals, associations, and schools—in the first years of the twentieth century; and finally, a brief summation that brings the story to the present.

To analyze systematically the initial organization, operation, and continuing growth of modern industrial enterprise is a challenging task. Such a study must consider more variables than did the earlier discussion of organization building by the railroads and mass marketers. Although large industrial enterprises had common basic characteristics, their more specific attributes and activities varied from industry to industry. Some sold consumer goods, others producer goods. Some used chemical processes of production, others mechanical, and still others a combination of the two. Some had thousands of suppliers, others only a few. Moreover, industrial enterprises grew by different routes, and the path taken affected their operating organizations. Those that became large through merger had different administrative requirements and different relationships between owners and managers than did those that grew through internal expansion.

The case study provides the most satisfactory way to examine and interrelate these variables. It permits examination of the response of a single enterprise to the changing situation in which it operated over a continuing period of time. If other enterprises operated under much the same conditions—that is, if they used comparable production methods and sold in comparable markets—and did so in the same time period, then they were faced with similar opportunity, needs, and operating problems. So the experience of one company can legitimately be considered as illustrative of the experiences of other firms operating under similar conditions.

Each of the companies whose experiences are related in the following chapters provides such an example. Each was the largest enterprise in the United States in its industrial group and each represents a major group in which the integrated firm dominated. Those in Chapter 12 tell of the organization, management, and continuing growth of the largest and most influential firms in the tobacco, food, and light machinery groups, the groups in which the modern industrial enterprise first appeared. They represent the different types of firms that first adopted a strategy of integration forward into marketing and backward into purchasing and obtaining control of raw materials. Because these were among the first to build functional departments and coordinate product flow between them, they were the first to perfect the new ways of middle management.

The case studies in Chapter 13 describe the organization and management of the largest enterprises in the oil, chemical, rubber, and heavy machinery industries, groups in which the large integrated enterprise became so significant in the twentieth century. These cases deal with firms that initially grew by merger. Each represents a somewhat different type of merger and a differing strategy of growth. Because these firms grew by merger rather than by internal expansion, they were the first to work out the structure and function of top management in American industry.

Taken together these case studies permit a detailed review of the bargaining and early evolution of modern industrial management in the United States. The internal organization, the methods of competition, and the processes of continuing growth so described have been modified and elaborated, but, as Chapter 14 indicates, not basically changed in the decades since World War I.

CHAPTER 12

Middle Management: Function and Structure

The entrepreneurial enterprise

Many of the functions of the visible hand of management were first worked out in what I have termed the entrepreneurial enterprise. The entrepreneurs who created the first large industrial firms by building their own marketing or purchasing organizations had to hire a number of middle managers. Neither the entrepreneurs, their close associates, nor their families could carry on the multitudinous activities involved in producing, marketing, and purchasing a massive volume of goods for national and global markets. Yet because the growth of so many of the early integrated enterprises was internally financed—because both working and fixed capital was obtained from the massive cash flow generated by high-volume production and distribution—the founders rarely had to raise capital by issuing stock. So they continued to own and control their companies. They made the final decisions about the basic policies of operation and strategies of growth and allocated the resources necessary to carry out these plans. Because they continued to look on their business empires as personal property to be personally managed, they felt little need to recruit top managers or develop the systematic, impersonal techniques of modern top management. On the other hand, because their enterprises were the first to integrate mass production with mass distribution, they and their salaried executives pioneered in the new ways of middle management. They were the first to devise the means to administer the new processes of production and distribution and to coordinate the flow of goods between them.

The experiences of four entrepreneurial enterprises—James Buchanan Duke's American Tobacco Company, Armour & Company, McCormick Harvesting Machinery Company, and Singer Manufacturing Company

—have been selected as the case studies to describe and analyze the beginnings of middle management in the United States. American Tobacco is an example of the mass producers of semiperishable, packaged products who built their marketing organizations in order to assure effective advertising and coordination of product flow. Armour & Company is an example of the producers of perishable products who built their own refrigerated or temperature controlled facilities so as to assure a continuing distribution of high-volume output. The last two case studies tell of the experience of the makers of machines whose marketing required specialized services if they were to be sold in the volume in which they could be produced. One—Singer—provided these services by building its own retail network, the other—McCormick Harvesting—did so by pioneering in the use of franchised dealers. Together these four cases give a detailed view of the function and structure of middle management in the nation's oldest, largest, and most successful industrial enterprises.

American Tobacco: managing mass production and distribution of packaged products

Of the innovating entrepreneurs who created modern integrated industrial enterprises few were more successful than James Buchanan Duke of Durham, North Carolina. Duke's swift rise to power in the cigarette trade was not based on his technological skills or his advertising talents. He leased his machines and hired the services of advertising agencies and full-time salaried salesmen. His success resulted from his realization that the marketing of the output of the Bonsack machine required a global selling and distributing organization (see Chapter 9). Duke became the most powerful entrepreneur in the cigarette industry because he was the first to build an integrated enterprise.

Before Duke made his gamble in 1885 on Bonsack's continuous-process cigarette machine, he and his four major competitors were still basically single-function manufacturing enterprises.[1] They had begun to purchase, store, and dry tobacco in their own facilities in the bright-leaf tobacco region of North Carolina and Virginia, but only on a small scale. They continued to buy nearly all their leaf directly from tobacco brokers who had their own storing and curing units. In marketing they depended on wholesalers to distribute their output and on advertising agents to carry on their marketing campaign. Before 1885 none had set up branch sales offices operated by their own salaried personnel and managers.

Duke was the first to do so. Even before he had signed the contract with James Bonsack in June 1885 to use his machine to make all his ciga-

rettes, expensive as well as cheap, he began to set up selling and distributing offices in the leading American commercial centers.[2] Each included,
at a minimum, a salaried manager, a city salesman, a traveling man to
cover the outlying areas, and the necessary clerical staff. As Duke began
to build a nationwide network, his close associate, Richard B. Wright,
made his nineteen-month tour abroad to explore foreign markets. Soon
Duke's firm had contracts with the overseas jobbers and had set up offices
abroad to supply and supervise the sale and distribution of cigarettes to
them. At the same time Duke put together his extensive purchasing network with its own buying, curing, and storing facilities. He expanded his
cigarette factory in Durham and built a large new plant in New York
City. To manage this new empire he then established a large central office,
not in Durham but in New York City, the nation's leading distribution
center.

By 1890 when Duke and four other leading cigarette firms joined to
form the American Tobacco Company, Duke's four competitors had been
forced to build comparable though smaller integrated organizations. For
a brief period after the consolidation, the companies maintained their
separate administrative organizations. Between 1893 and 1895, however,
those of the other four were merged into the structure Duke had fashioned so quickly after 1884.[3] Administrative centralization came first
with the formation of a single purchasing department. Then the several
sales departments were unified.

The resulting worldwide integrated enterprise was managed first from
the company's New York office at 45 Broadway. As business expanded
Duke moved his headquarters to a more spacious building at 111 Fifth
Avenue in 1898.[4] Most of the space in the new building was taken up by
the sales department and the buying or what was called the leaf department. By then the heads of the functional departments at 111 Fifth were
already career specialists. Thus, John B. Cobb, the vice president in charge
of the leaf department, had long worked as a tobacco buyer before joining American Tobacco in 1890.[5] William R. Harris, the chief of the auditing department, had been hired by Duke some years before from the Pullman Palace Car Company; and the head of the legal department had been
with the Duke firm since the 1880s.

Of the major functional departments at 111 Fifth Avenue, manufacturing had the fewest managers. After the merger there had been a consolidation of cigarette-making plants in the New York City area, while those
in Rochester and in Virginia and North Carolina were enlarged.
Throughout the 1890s six factories produced nearly all the company's
output, which by 1898 reached 3.78 billion cigarettes.[6] Two of these six
(one in Durham and the other in Rochester) concentrated wholly on

producing the 1.22 billion cigarettes sold to foreign markets. During the 1890s the two plants accounted for almost 100 percent of the cigarettes exported from the United States. Although Duke testified in 1901 that his company always preferred to manufacture at home for markets abroad, he was willing to build factories overseas if the distance or tariffs significantly affected final price.[7] In 1894 the company set up factories in Australia. In 1899 it purchased a leading Japanese producer, and two years later it bought manufacturing companies in Germany and Britain.

The manufacturing headquarters at 111 Fifth remained small because the processes of production were relatively simple. By the 1890s manufacturing and packaging of cigarettes and most other tobacco products had become fully mechanized and the production technology stabilized. Moreover, the manufacturing office did not have the responsibility either for recording costs or for assuring a steady flow of cured tobacco into the factories and of cigarettes from the factories to the retailers. The auditing department took care of the first of these tasks and the leaf and the sales departments handled the second.

The leaf department supervised and coordinated the activities of the many units responsible for purchasing, drying, and handling the uncured or semicured leaf and for prizing (packaging it in hogsheads, storing, and separating the stem from the leaf) and shipping the cured leaf to the factory.[8] Such coordination and control over the curing process was essential to assure the delivery of the right amounts of tobacco in the proper quality needed for the different types of cigarettes. Tobacco for the more expensive brands required longer curing and used a somewhat different process than that used for the cheaper ones. Specialized volume buying helped to bring down the cost of raw materials. However, as Richard Tennant has pointed out, it did not necessarily give American Tobacco a monopsony position. American bright-leaf tobacco continued to be the major ingredient in British and other foreign made cigarettes.[9]

By the beginning of the century, the company had twelve drying and packaging houses and nineteen large storage warehouses in North Carolina and Virginia. As the company moved into the plug tobacco business in the late 1890s its leaf department built a similar organization in the Burley leaf district of Ohio and Kentucky. Then as cigarettes using Turkish tobacco became popular, it set up facilities in Turkey to purchase, process, and ship tobacco.

In addition to its large leaf department, American Tobacco had another smaller, centralized purchasing department to buy in quantity packing materials and such supplies as licorice, sugar, rum flavoring extract, as well as machinery, tools, furniture, and stationary used at 111 Fifth Avenue.[10] Pasteboard, paper, and tin foil were ordered for the factories through the

New York headquarters. After its expansion into other tobacco products, the company found it profitable to organize or buy companies to produce cotton bags, tin foil, tin, and paper boxes. The company soon began to make its own machinery and to produce its own licorice. In these several ways expansion of output at American Tobacco brought an integration of functions rather than a further specialization and subdivision of labor.

"The sales department of the American Tobacco Company," a 1909 report of the Bureau of Corporations emphasized, "is so organized as to secure a high degree of efficiency. The company has sales agents throughout the United States, each in charge of a specified territory and each devoting his attention to a particular class of product."[11] The branch offices, similar to those set up by Duke in the 1880s, had become larger and more numerous. Salesmen, both city and traveling, regularly visited all of the wholesalers, including those handling grocery and drugs as well as tobacco jobbers and large tobacco retailers. And by the mid-1890s foreign branches also had their own traveling men. The Tobacco Company's salesmen proved to be far more effective than those of the wholesaler who still handled the physical distribution to retailers. Indeed the Bureau of Corporations pointed out that company salesmen "solicited no small part of the orders from the retail trade and turned them over to the jobbers without expense to them."[12] This was particularly true in rural areas. As the company moved into new products, the regional sales offices came to have subordinate managers for products as well as for subregions. Each had its advertising manager who coordinated advertising activities with New York. Still another executive became responsible for inventories and for supervising flow of deliveries to a large number of customers.

Actual control of the flow of 3 to 5 billion cigarettes from factory to retailer via the jobber was retained at 111 Fifth Avenue. Such control was necessary not only to keep the factories operating at a relatively full and steady pace, but also to maintain the quality of the product, for in the days before cellophane wrapping cigarettes quickly became dry and bitter. All orders received by a branch office were telegraphed to New York. Managers there decided which factory would process the order, usually sending it to the one nearest to the customer. Small "mixed orders," that is, those for small numbers of different types and brands, were filled from a large central "depot" in New York. European orders were distributed from a similar depot in London. Normally, however, the central office sent orders directly to a factory. Orders, "especially those coming from retail dealers and made in the form of drop shipments" (those left at the local train stations for customers), were "sent from a single place to avoid unnecessary delay and expense."[13] Therefore the factories had attached to them assembling and distribution depots where their products and those of other factories were gathered for shipment. With its daily reports from the factories and the depots and its daily statements of "sales by brands by towns," the New York headquarters kept a continuous check on the flow of cigarettes and the other tobacco products from the factory to the retailers throughout the country and the world.[14]

The auditing department's major responsibility was to control costs rather than to control flows. According to Duke's biographer, that department's accounts "were in such detail that each brand showed cost per unit, running into five decimal points, of every item entering into its manufacture—tobacco, wrapping of package, casing or sweetening material, shipping cases, down to the straps and nails. Labor in cutting tobacco, operating machines, putting goods in cases, and handling them after they were packed was recorded, carried out to the last decimal, even if it was .00035 per thousand."[15] Comparisons between costs of different factories and within the same factory for a different time period were used by middle managers to evaluate the performance of the different factories and their plant managers and to decide where brands and products could be most cheaply produced.

The Tobacco Company's cost sheets in the 1890s became as sophisticated as those of Andrew Carnegie. In addition to detailed data on prime costs (labor and raw materials used in manufacturing), "cost records" reported advertising and selling costs.[16] Selling costs included salaries and expenses of salesmen and of their office managers. On the other hand, as late as 1915 the company had not yet applied the new techniques of standard costing to the determination of overhead costs. "General & administrative costs" were little more than a percentage of total cost prorated between the selling and manufacturing, but not the leaf departments. In this category, "from 50 to 75 percent," the Bureau of Corporations report noted, was allocated to selling. Still less attention appears to have been paid to accounting for depreciation and obsolescence. The American Tobacco Company continued to use the railroad type of renewal accounting that allocated major repairs and replacements to the operating accounts.

Even so the middle managers at 111 Fifth were by the late 1890s carrying out their tasks of administrative coordination and evaluation in a most effective manner. The prices of cigarettes declined during the decade, and profits remained impressively high. According to Bureau of Corporation's investigators, wholesale prices fell from 1893 (American Tobacco's accounts were first consolidated in 1892) until 1899 in all its markets from an average of $3.02 a thousand to $2.01 (in 1900 it rose to $2.16).[17] In the same period costs dropped from $1.74 per thousand to $.89 (in 1900 they rose to $1.00 per thousand.) In the words of the report: "The proportion of the profits to the net price less tax from 1893 to 1900 ranged from 42.4 percent to 55.7 percent." Duke expected these profits, made possible, in part at least, by the high, steady throughput and stock-turn, to provide him with the basic financial resources he needed to expand the company's activities at home and abroad.

Although the middle managers and their staffs at American Tobacco became numerous enough to fill a large New York office building, top management remained tiny. It was little more than Duke, his brother Benjamin, and their long-time associate, George Watt. The heads of the other companies who had joined the 1890 merger had less and less to say about the affairs of the consolidation.

For Duke the function of top management was strategic. By 1892 he had formulated a straightforward strategy of growth. The organization he had created and the profits it produced were to be used to conquer the rest of the tobacco industry. In the 1890s pipe tobacco, plug or chewing tobacco, snuff, and cigars still commanded much larger markets than cigarettes. Duke's plan was first to acquire factories making these other products. Then by driving prices down and spending heavily for advertising he expected to bring the leading producers into his orbit. Once he had convinced the firms to merge with him, he would consolidate their production facilities and centralize their administration. American Tobacco Company's sales and leaf departments could then take over the marketing of finished products and the purchasing of the leaf and other materials. The resulting high-volume throughput would increase productivity, decrease costs, and enlarge profits.

These plans, enthusiastically endorsed by senior managers, were strongly opposed by the other owners.[18] The major stockholders besides the Dukes were the owners of the companies that had merged with Duke's firm to become American Tobacco in 1890. They, particularly W. H. Butler and Lewis Gintner, saw no reason to sacrifice current dividends in order to expand the existing organization.

Duke first won the fight with his board. He then moved forward to carry out his plans using his economic power with ruthless determination. By 1898, with the formation of the Continental Tobacco Company, capitalized at $75 million, and then with the merger of that company with Liggett & Myers in the next year, Duke was close to his goal. He controlled over 60 percent of the smoking and chewing tobacco business. The formation of the Atlantic Snuff Company in 1898 and in 1900 the larger American Snuff Company, capitalized at $35 million, gave him an even greater dominance in that industry.

This campaign was, however, more expensive than Duke anticipated.

Many of the tobacco manufacturers vigorously resisted his attack. Cigarette profits were not enough to cover the costs. For the first time Duke had to look to the capital markets for funds. In 1895 the company's common stock was listed on the New York Stock Exchange.[19] Early in 1898 Duke allied himself with Oliver H. Payne, one of Rockefeller's early associates. Later that same year when Duke acquired a rival combination headed by leading New York financiers, he took several of these men onto the board of the American Tobacco Company as well as on that of the new Continental Tobacco Company.[20] They included Thomas Fortune Ryan, William C. Whitney, Anthony N. Brady, and P. A. B. Widener, all of whom had made their fortunes in street railways. With Payne, they became Duke's close financial allies. These investors, however, never became involved or took an active interest in the day-to-day operations of the American Tobacco Company.

Duke's enlarged empire was soon being managed out of 111 Fifth Avenue. The leaf department at this time expanded its facilities into the Burley tobacco-growing regions of Tennessee and Kentucky. Of the merged firms only R. J. Reynolds continued to have its own purchasing department. This was because its basic brand of navy sweet plug used a special leaf. The sales department at 111 Fifth Avenue set up separate offices for plug, smoking, and snuff, but American's depot and reporting systems were used to coordinate and control flows of the acquired businesses. The manufacturing department instituted, where possible, continuous-process automatic packing and labeling machinery. And of course the auditing department extended its sway over the recently incorporated properties.

Once these new businesses had been integrated into American's structure, Duke continued to expand his enterprise on two fronts. One was to enlarge his companies' overseas trade, especially in products other than cigarettes. The other was to move into the cigar business, the only domestic American tobacco trade not under the dominance of the American Tobacco Company.

In the first he was successful.[21] He began by frontally attacking his foremost competitor, the British firm of W. D. & H. O. Wills which had been the first European manufacturer to adopt the Bonsack machine. Duke entered Wills's home market by purchasing Ogden's Ltd. for over $5 million. Wills countered by carrying out a merger of thirteen British tobacco producers to form the Imperial Tobacco Company.

After some sharp but brief skirmishes Imperial and American made a deal. Duke sold Ogden's to Imperial. The two firms then formed the British-American Tobacco Company in which American held two-thirds and Imperial one-third of the $5.2 million worth of stock issued. In addition American Tobacco received 14 percent of Imperial's ordinary shares from the sale of Odgen's. This transaction made it the largest stockholder in Imperial, second only to Wills. American and Imperial then gave British-American the world markets. Imperial would continue to sell only in the United Kingdom and American only in the United States and its dependencies. Duke became chairman of the board of British-American, and until he retired as chairman in 1923 concentrated most of his time on enlarging British-American's trade.

These legal and financial arrangements had only a small impact on day-to-day operations. The same men in the same offices and factories continued to purchase leaf, process it, ship it, and sell the American-made cigarettes in foreign markets. As world demand grew British factories came to supply a larger share of production. The new company intensified efforts to replace independent sales jobbers or agents with salaried managers. When coordinating flow from distant factories became difficult, these managers often set up local ones. Thus in China where British-American Tobacco had created an extensive distributing network, the company soon had its own factories. Before 1914 it was using locally grown bright leaf tobacco whose seed it had imported from North Carolina. Despite the legal changes instituted by the Supreme Court's antitrust decision against American Tobacco in 1911, British-American Tobacco remained until the 1920s more of an American than a British owned and managed enterprise and so the worldwide tobacco business stayed more in American than in British hands.

If overseas expansion was a continuing success, the move into the cigar business proved to be a costly failure. As Richard Tennant, the most careful student of the modern American tobacco industry points out: "The struggle for the cigar industry was the one case in which the Trust's methods met with complete defeat."[22] Despite the strongest of marketing efforts, including the creation of an expensive nationwide retailing organization (United Cigar Stores Company with nearly 400 retail stores), and despite the most destructive of price wars, American Tobacco never obtained more than 14 percent of the nation's cigar trade.

Duke's mistake was his failure to appreciate fully that the American Tobacco Company could use little of its existing organization to make and sell cigars. The processes of both production and distribution were different. Plug, smoking tobacco, and snuff all used high-volume continuous processes of manufacturing and packaging. Their leaf came from the same areas in southeastern United States, and they were sold to much the same markets and through much the same jobbers as cigarettes. Cigars, on the other hand, were produced by skilled workmen in small batches. Their leaf came from Cuba, Puerto Rico, and scattered areas in the northeastern

United States. It was cured quite differently from other types of tobacco. Finally, cigars traditionally had been sold by their makers in small lots to retailers. Like wines the many different brands had distinctive tastes and flavors. Each appealed to a different type of customer. Cigars were not a product that could be mass produced and mass distributed, nor could the raw materials be purchased in bulk. Since these processes did not lend themselves to high-volume throughput, administrative coordination did not reduce costs and so raise barriers to entry. Neither massive advertising nor effective organization could bring the dominance of a single firm in the cigar business.

The experience of the American Tobacco Company provides several important lessons for understanding the rise and function of the large entrepreneurial enterprise. First, the massive output made possible by application of continuous-process machinery to manufacturing caused and indeed almost forced the creation of a worldwide, integrated organization. The resulting managerial hierarchy permitted its creator to dominate first the cigarette and then the rest of the tobacco industry, except for cigars. The founder fully realized the importance of his organization. According to his biographer, he always considered that his major task was to find and bring forward competent managers.[23]

The middle managers housed in the central office building at 111 Fifth Avenue formed the core of this integrated enterprise. These salaried executives supervised, evaluated, and coordinated the functional activities under their command and coordinated the work of their departments with others. They made possible a continuing, high-volume throughput from the buying of the leaf to the ultimate consumers. Where the processes of production and distribution permitted such high-volume flows, this type of organization was the key to success and dominance; but where, as in the case of cigars, the processes did not, such an organization provided no special advantages.

The experience of American Tobacco was repeated in the same decade, the 1880s, by other pioneer enterprises that used comparable methods of production to make comparable low-priced packaged products. The makers of matches, breakfast cereals and other grain products, canned soups, milk, pickles and other foods, soap, and photographic film (all the foregoing were semiperishable except matches) built similar organizations. So too, in the 1890s, did Coca Cola, Wrigley's chewing gum, and Fleishmann's yeast. These firms had extensive buying departments, global sales organizations, and manufacturing concentrated in a few large plants. Middle managers at their main offices played much the same role as that at American Tobacco. In all cases top management continued to be the domain of the founder, his close associates, and their descendants. Like the Dukes they concentrated on discouraging competition and expanding their own output by a fuller and more effective use of their existing managers and facilities.

Armour: managing the production and distribution of perishable products

The experience of the first large integrated enterprises in the meat-packing industries differed from that of the American Tobacco Company in two significant ways. First, because the packers' products were perishable, the flow from the purchasing of the cattle to the sale to the consumer had to be even more carefully coordinated and controlled. With the refrigeration techniques of the day, beef was chilled, not frozen, and had to be consumed within three to four weeks of its butchering. This need led to an even heavier investment in capital equipment, particularly storage and transportation facilities, and required an even larger managerial organization than did the maintenance of high-volume flows in cigarettes and other packaged products.

Second, in meat packing, several large integrated organizations were formed almost simultaneously. One enterprise did not become a leader before the others. So the industry became oligopolistic rather than monopolistic. In the dozen or so years after 1881, when Swift began to build a national branch-house distributing network, six integrated packers dominated the trade—two giants, Armour and Swift, and four smaller firms, Hammond, Morris, Cudahy, and Schwartzchild & Sulzberger.[24] The first four all had their central offices in Chicago and had completed their network of branch houses, refrigerator cars, packing plants, and buying units by the mid-1880s. The Cudahy Brothers, former Armour associates, began in 1887 a new enterprise based in Omaha; in the early 1890s Schwartzchild & Sulzberger, a New York firm in the kosher trade, decided to have its own supplies and purchased a packing plant in Kansas City. It then built a national network of branch houses and obtained a fleet of refrigerated cars. By the early twentieth century these six firms (Hammond had become the nucleus of the National Packing Company) provided from 60 to over 90 percent of the dressed meat sold in the large eastern cities and 95 percent of American beef exports. They also handled a large share of the nation's pork, lamb, and other animal products.[25]

The capitalization of "the Big Six" indicates their comparative size. Swift, the largest at the beginning of the century, had a stock issue of $35.0 million; Armour followed with $27.5 million; National (a combination in 1903 of Hammond and several small local firms) had $15.0 million;

Cudahy \$7.0; Morris \$6.0; and Schwartzchild & Sulzberger \$5.0 million.[26] By 1903 Armour was slaughtering 7.3 million animals a year, and Swift 8.0 million.[27] By 1917 Armour had surpassed Swift in volume and assets.

All these companies were directed through large, centralized, functionally departmentalized offices. Swift's Chicago headquarters employed a clerical force of over a thousand.[28] Armour's was much the same size. The organization chart of Armour & Company (figure 8) illustrates the size, complexity, and sophistication of the managerial hierarchy operating that vast integrated enterprise.[29] The chart is for 1907, but Armour's organization had changed little during the previous ten to twelve years.

At Armour the manufacturing departments employed more men and managers than did those at American Tobacco and other producers of packaged goods. In meat packing the technology was less mechanized than in processing other products of the farm. The high volume of flow generated by the organization of a national sales and distribution network led to highly specialized subdivision of labor in the processes of slaughtering and dressing. As the Bureau of Corporations explained after a detailed investigation in 1904, the disassembling of a single steer involved 157 men who killed, dismembered, stored, and loaded the meat and whose work was divided into no less than seventy-eight distinct processes.[30] This extreme subdivision of labor appeared only after a carefully designed administrative arrangement permitted an unprecedented high and steady movement of cattle through the packing plants. Without the replacement of market coordination by administrative coordination there would have been far less subdivision of labor in the meat packing trades.

The plant superintendents of Armour's six great packing plants—at Chicago, St. Louis, Omaha, Kansas City, Sioux City, and Fort Worth— sent daily reports of the slaughtering completed for that day and that planned for the next. They worked closely with the managers from the purchasing division, the sales departments, the transportation department, and the by-products departments, in order to maintain a steady flow of meat through the enterprise.[31] On the basis of orders received from the branch houses, the plant superintendent contacted the purchasing managers in his area. These included the manager in charge of local stockyard buying and the district manager in charge of buying cattle, hogs, and sheep directly from farmers. Normally the neighboring stockyard supplied close to 90 percent of the plant superintendent's needs. Each of the purchasing executives had assistant managers for buying the three different types of animals—cattle, sheep, and pigs. As in the case of American Tobacco, Armour also had housed at its central office a purchasing division that bought in volume and at discount a wide variety of supplies used by all departments within the company.

Again, as in the case of American Tobacco Company, the sales organization was the largest (in terms of the numbers of managers) of the functional departments. It was organized into two large subunits and a small one. One of the large departments distributed beef and the other hog products. Each also handled "offal" (liver, hearts, tongue, brains, and the like). At Armour, the third and much smaller sales organization distributed what were known as "laboratory by-products," such as pepsin, elixer of enzymes, pancreatin, and extract of red-bone marrow.

All three divisions marketed their products through Armour's nationwide branch house organization, which by 1900 numbered 200 houses. At that time Swift was operating 193, Morris 77, Cudahy 57, and Schwartz-child & Sulzberger 44 comparable units.[32] The branch houses, in addition to receiving and storing fresh meat and distributing it to local butchers and other retailers, took orders and arranged for local advertising. Its accountants handled billing and the transfer of funds back to Chicago. Armour and other packers supplemented their branch house networks with "peddler car routes," or "car lines" as they came to be called. These marketing units sold and distributed meat directly from refrigerator cars in hamlets and villages along the railroad lines in rural areas.

Both Armour and Swift had enough branch houses and car lines to group them under some twenty-five district superintendents, and so employed a level of middle managers between the operating units and the Chicago headquarters. The managers in these regional offices supervised the performance of the branches in their territories, coordinated the work of the salesmen soliciting the retailers, and reviewed the advertising of the local branches. They also made direct sales to a small number of independent commission wholesalers. The branch house network, the most significant innovation of the industry's leading innovator, Gustavus Swift, remained the most vital component in these giant food-processing enterprises.

The critical task of coordinating the flow of fresh, very perishable meat was handled at the selling departments' headquarters. In coordinating and controlling this flow Armour and the other packers relied heavily on cost and other statistical figures provided at the packing plants by their accounting division. The nature of and reason for such controls was well expressed in the Bureau of Corporations report published in 1905:

On account of their perishability the handling of fresh meat is a peculiarly delicate business. The packer aims to get as high a price as possible, but he must sell the entire product before it spoils. Differences in quality of animals and of their products are so great that the closest supervision of the central office is necessary to enforce the exercise of skill and sound judgment on the part of the agents who buy stock and the agents who sell meats. With this object, those branches of the

Figure 8. Organization chart of Armour & Company, 1907

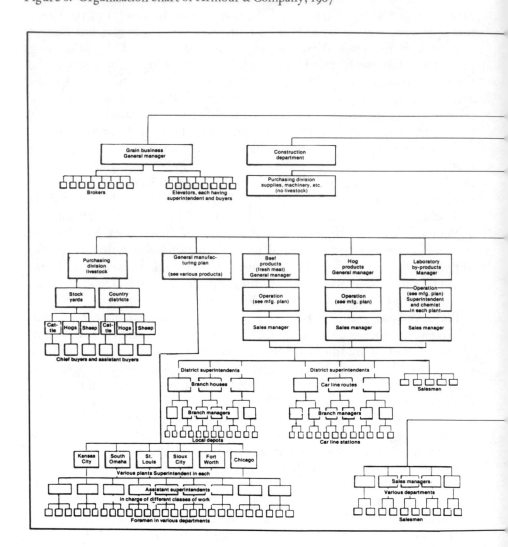

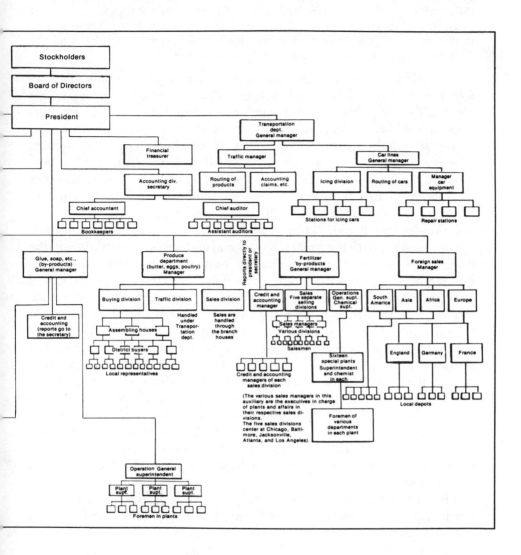

Source: *System*, 12:220 (Sept. 1907).

selling and accounting department of the packing companies which have charge of the purchasing, killing, dressing, and selling of fresh meats are organized in a most extensive and thorough manner. The central office is in constant telegraphic correspondence with the distributing houses with a view to adjusting the supply of meat and the prices as nearly as possible to the demand.[33]

Such administrative coordination was carried out in the following way. Chicago headquarters assigned each branch house and car line a packing plant as their supplier. The managers of each of these distributing units telegraphed their orders daily to their supplying plant, with all orders going through the central Chicago office. If the supplying plant was short, Chicago would fill orders from another plant. If that supplier had surpluses, Chicago allocated such surpluses to branch houses or car lines other than its designated receivers. Even after the beef had left the packing house, its distribution was carefully administered. As the Bureau of Corporations report noted: "The head offices are in constant telegraphic communication with the branch houses and commission agents during the progress of the sale of each carload of beef, obtaining information and giving advice."[34] Not surprisingly, Armour and Swift had expenditures of $200,000 a year for telegraphic service, a large proportion of which came from selling dressed beef. As in the case of railroads a generation earlier, the managers at headquarters were soon employing the data used in coordinating flows to evaluate managerial performance. "The long and elaborate account sales [sic] which the branch house managers and commission agents send in for each car of beef," Bureau investigators reported, "must be carefully checked by the company, not merely to verify the accuracy of the entries, but also for the purpose of criticizing the soundness of the judgment of the branch house manager in his method of disposing of the beef." To collect, collate, and distribute such data, Armour's accounting department set up its branch house and purchasing sections as early as 1889.

The basic figure used in coordinating, supervising, and evaluating the work of the managers as well as in setting prices and regulating flows was what the packers called "dressed" (or sometimes "test" or "red") costs. For each "bunch" of cattle killed, the packing plant recorded the live weight and price paid, labor costs, overhead costs, and the weight and quality of the meat, hides, and fat.[35] These data provided the unit cost for processing or "dressing" that parcel of cattle. The addition of freight charges and overhead gave the "dressed" cost at the branch house. These "dressed" costs were then compared at each market with average sales prices. The resulting margins between costs and sales prices, telegraphed to Chicago headquarters and the packing plants, became a guide to purchasing in the stockyards. If margins dropped, purchasing and slaughtering slowed. If they increased, so did cattle buying and plant output.

Such data, which provided the packers with essential control over flows, gave them an accurate picture of their prime costs but little more. Overhead, administrative, and selling costs appear to have been little more than rough estimates. Selling costs, for example, were simply a flat percentage of sales—"the more common rate being 5 percent."[36] Nor did the packers have a clear view of their assets. They, like American Tobacco, used the current railroad practices of renewal accounting. They charged "to operating expenses, not merely minor repairs, but also from time to time large outlays for reconstruction and improvements."

This concentration on prime costs and the use of renewal accounting meant that the packers had little information on the rate of return they received on invested capital. They did not try to allocate costs to different parts of their businesses and had no way of knowing accurately the profits of their different lines. The Bureau of Corporations admitted that it was "impossible" for their investigators or the companies "to calculate with any approach to accuracy the percentage of return which the large western packers are able to secure on the capital invested in the beef branch of their business." In the packing business the best test of managerial performance continued to be the ability to maintain reasonable margins and to move the goods as quickly as possible. It was not based on the managers' ability to maintain and expand a predetermined rate of return on investment.

The packers differed from other large processors of agricultural products in that they owned and operated much more extensive transportation facilities and exploited more fully these facilities and their processing capacity. Their transportation departments were, in fact, among the largest transportation enterprises in the world. By 1903 Armour's transportation department owned and operated 13,600 refrigerated cars (of which 1,650 were for carrying fruit) and Swift 5,900. The total owned by the Big Six was over 25,000.[37] At an estimated cost of $1,000 a car, this represented a substantial investment. By 1903 Armour's department was operating over 300 million car-miles a year.

Headed by a general manager, the transportation department was divided into two divisions.[38] One maintained and serviced the fleet of refrigerated cars and the icing stations throughout the country. The other, the traffic department, was responsible for scheduling the cars needed to carry the flow of livestock into the plant and the massive movement of dressed and processed meat from the plant to the retailers. In carrying out their task, the managers worked closely with those in the sales, purchasing, and manufacturing departments.

Because the company owned its own rail cars, it was able to schedule flows more precisely and with more certainty than if it had to depend on the traffic departments of railroads to supply them. Therefore, although the packers had been forced originally to build their own cars because of the railroads' refusal to do so, they soon found their control of such facilities invaluable adjuncts to their business. It was for this same reason—to assure a more certain coordination of flows of raw materials and finished goods—that Standard Oil and its smaller competitors had before 1900, and a number of chemical, glass and some other food companies had by 1910, come to own and schedule their own fleets of railroad cars.

The heavy investment in transporting, distributing, processing, and purchasing facilities proved to be a powerful goad to expansion. The process of growth for the purpose of using existing facilities more intensively was more evolutionary at Armour and the other large packers than it was at American Tobacco. Even before 1890 the packers had begun to extend their sales organization overseas, using their own refrigerated ships and setting up depots in major seaports.[39] However, although they had salaried sales and distribution managers abroad, they did not set up a branch office network comparable to those in the United States until the first decade of the twentieth century. In order to make fuller use of their production facilities, they quickly began to process pork, lamb, and other meat products.[40] Almost at once they became leaders in the canned meat industry where small firms had already pioneered, particularly Wilson and Company (which later joined Schwartzchild & Sulzberger) and Libby, McNeil and Libby (which later became associated with Swift). Then Armour and the others began to use their canning facilities for packing salmon, sardines, tuna, evaporated milk, and vegetables. All such canned products were sold through the branch-house distributing organization.

The company set up separate organizations to distribute and market products that could not be sold through their existing marketing facilities. At Armour the largest of these operations was the fertilizer division, where a general manager supervising sixteen plants had his own sales, production, and accounting departments.[41] He thus had all the facilities necessary to operate an autonomous business of his own. Indeed, it was the success of such integrated divisions at Armour and Swift that caused many small fertilizer companies to merge in the 1890s and then to build comparable administrative structures. Other by-products with a smaller volume of production and sales, such as glue, soap, oleo oil, stearin, and other products derived from animal fat, were grouped under the general manager of the by-products department. The marketing men in this department were responsible for coordinating the flow. But precisely because these units did not have large marketing organizations for their own specific products, they had difficulty competing with large integrated enterprises such as Procter & Gamble and American Cotton Oil.

At Armour and its major competitors the desire to make as full use of the facilities in distribution as those in production led to further growth of the firm. The packers began to use refrigerated cars and storage rooms at the branch houses to distribute other perishable products such as butter, eggs, poultry, and fruit. But in order to obtain these products, they had to create new purchasing units. Soon, the company had built, as it had in the fertilizer business, a separate autonomous enterprise to obtain, sell, and coordinate the flow of these perishable items from the farmer to the retailer. This produce department had its own large buying division with a number of refrigerated warehouses which purchased, stored, and assembled its product lines. Its traffic division with offices next to those of the larger transportation department allocated cars; while its sales organization, which used the company's branch-house facilities, handled its own advertising and delivery to retailers, and generated its own daily market orders and buying estimates.

In these ways, then, the pressure to keep the existing facilities fully used caused the managers at Armour and other packers to push the enterprise into obtaining additional facilities. Such expansion, in turn, required the creation of new, autonomous managerial suborganizations to evaluate, coordinate, and plan the activities of these units. This process of growth became an increasingly common one during the twentieth century for the large integrated industrial enterprises in the United States.

During the 1890s, the meat packers had created as complex an organizational structure as those earlier developed by railroad systems. Yet their top management paid little attention to systematic long-term planning and investment decisions. One reason was that such decisions continued to be made by a small number of top executives who spent nearly all their time in day-to-day activities.

Well into the twentieth century the Armours, Swifts, Morrises, and Cudahys continued to manage as well as to own their massive enterprises. Except for the Swifts the founders or their families still held nearly all the stock of their respective companies.[42] Swift was the exception, because the Swift brothers had used stock to obtain branch houses. They paid wholesalers who joined them with shares of Swift & Company. But even the Swift family continued to hold a controlling block of stock in their company.

As owner-managers these entrepreneurs paid little attention to strategic planning and the long-term allocation of resources. In 1907 J. Ogden Armour's daily routine was still totally taken up by reading operational reports and issuing orders to buying, processing, and selling departments.[43] All department heads reported directly to him. In this work he had little or no staff assistance. The only specialized nonoperating officer he consulted was the head of the legal department—an office formally established only in 1897. The senior executives therefore had little time for such things as strategic planning.

Another reason Armour or another of the packers did not plan a strategic campaign of conquest similar to Duke's was that in their industry no single firm had acquired a dominant position. The leaders had built their integrated organizations almost simultaneously. Each realized that he had little chance of driving out the others, except at excessive cost. So like the railroads they decided to cooperate rather than to compete in order to keep their expensive facilities full and running steadily.

As in transportation, cooperation resulted first in informal and then formal pools. The formal cartel operated from 1893 to 1902, with the exception of one year, 1897. Its object was to keep the meat moving from the yards to the retailers as smoothly and evenly as possible and at an acceptable margin between cost and price. It was operated in a personal manner. The president and the heads of the beef departments met every Tuesday in Chicago to decide the coming week's allocations based on costs, output, sales, and margins as reported daily by their accounting departments.[44] In these decisions Swift and Armour took the lead.

After such pooling became clearly illegal, the packers considered merger as an alternative. In April 1902, a month before the government filed a formal suit under the Sherman Act against the Northern Securities Company, the packers began negotiations to merge their enterprises into a giant holding company. The investment banking house of Kuhn, Loeb agreed to finance a $500 million merger to be known as the National Packing Company.[45] After its promoters had opened negotiations with some local companies, the plan fell through. Kuhn, Loeb backed down. One reason was financial. The merger movement by 1902 had pretty well run its course. The market for such a volume of securities was clearly limited. The other was legal. If the government won its case against the Northern Securities Company, the proposed holding company would be particularly vulnerable.

The packers then modified their plans. A National Packing Company was formed, but on a much smaller scale. Made up of Hammond and four small firms, it became an operating rather than a holding company, with its stock owned by Swift, Armour, and Morris. The personnel and activities of the smaller firms were consolidated into the Hammond operating organization. Its three owners used National's headquarters as a central post to disseminate information on "dressed" costs, closing prices, and margins. In pricing and output Cudahy and Schwartzchild & Sulzberger began to follow National's lead, even though they had no formal connection with it.

By 1910, however, the packers decided they no longer needed National Packing. They were quite willing to disband it at the request of the Justice Department without making a court case, even though they had survived an earlier antitrust action. By then they had learned to operate in the domestic market without such formal arrangements. They knew each other's current costs, and they knew the current demand and available supplies and adjusted their flows accordingly. They had the information available and the technique perfected to do without collusion what they had previously done through formal cooperation. The smaller companies now followed the price leadership of Armour and Swift. The packers continued to compete by providing regular, prompt delivery and by advertising rather than by price. And they continued to grow by concentrating on using their manufacturing and distribution facilities more intensively and by enlarging their overseas markets. In other words, during the first decade of the twentieth century the packers learned to compete and grow in the modern oligopolistic manner.

In that decade the owner-managers of Armour and Swift were becoming, like Duke at American Tobacco, more concerned with foreign than domestic business. After 1900 the domestic demand had become so large that the packers no longer had supplies to meet the growing foreign demand. The two packers responded by opening new sources for supplies in South America. During that decade they obtained packing plants in Argentina, Uruguay, and Brazil to process for the European markets.[46] At the same time they acquired the necessary transportation facilities and quickly enlarged branch-house networks in Europe. The largest share of the packers' resource allocation in the years preceding World War I went to building the same type of integrated network to coordinate the flow of meat from the Argentine Pampas to the European cities that they had fashioned two decades earlier in the United States to connect the western plains with the eastern seaboard.

The experience of the packers paralleled that of brewers who competed in the national market, United Fruit, and other processors and shippers of perishable products. The meat packers' story has a wider significance however. It tells much about the competition between and the growth of vertically integrated enterprises that came into being in order to coordinate high-volume flows from the raw materials suppliers to the ultimate consumers. For such firms price leadership without formal collusion became the standard practice. Profits resulted from continued cost cutting, improved administrative coordination, greater use of existing facilities, and expansion overseas. Such growth into new products and new markets often required the building of new suborganizations to coordinate the flow of goods.

Even before the First World War this pattern of competition and growth had appeared in oil, chemical, rubber, glass, fabricated metals, and paper industries, where the nature of the processes of production and distribution made vertical integration and administrative coordination profitable. Whether the new large enterprises integrated after mergers or whether they expanded through internal growth, they maintained their dominance by means of efficient administrative coordination. Like the packers, they purchased and operated their own fleets of tank cars, ships, and other transportation facilities. They developed a full line of products for their major market, energetically developed by-products, and set up new offices to supervise the flow of these goods to new markets. By World War I nearly all had laboratories to improve and develop new and existing products, as well as processes. They, too, expanded overseas. At home and abroad they came to compete in the modern oligopolistic manner, by means of product improvement, product differentiation, service, and improved coordination, rather than by price.

For example, in the oil industry Standard Oil was the price leader before the dismemberment of 1911. After that date, the industry's historians point out, the largest of the former Standard Oil companies, particularly those of New Jersey and New York, "continued to play a leading role in the determination of prices in their respective marketing territories."[47] They rarely resorted to price wars, which the courts had come to define as "predatory practices." And where they led, Texaco, Gulf, Pure, Tidewater, and many others followed. Instead of competing for a share of the market on price, the companies advertised their brands of products with catchy slogans and improved the facilities and services at the growing number of retail gasoline stations which these companies came to own or to franchise. Since the 1880s Standard and the other oil companies had, like the packers, built large by-products trades. And from the beginning of the industry, Standard and its competitors operated in global markets.

Singer and McCormick: making and marketing machinery

The histories of American Tobacco and Armour illustrate the methods of organization, the processes of growth, and the ways of competition for enterprises that grew by integrating high-volume production with national and global mass markets. In such enterprises the marketing organization had the responsibility for maintaining and coordinating transportation, storage, distribution, and sale of goods to a number of widely scattered customers. The experience of Singer Sewing Machine and McCormick Harvester, on the other hand, illustrates organization, growth, and competition in the other type of integrated enterprise—that which depended on its marketing organization to supply specialized services of demonstration, installation, after-sales service and repair, and consumer credit. These enterprises included not only other makers of sewing machines and agricultural equipment but also producers of office equipment, elevators, boilers, pumps, printing presses, electrical equipment, and other standardized heavy machinery. In setting up their marketing organizations, a few machinery makers followed Singer's example by building a network of retail stores. Many more imitated the McCormick Harvester scheme of depending on retail franchised dealers whose activities were coordinated and supervised by the company's sales force.

The place to begin the review of the operations and growth of Singer and McCormick is with the reorganizations of their sales departments in the late 1870s.[48] Before these reorganizations, both companies relied on independent distributors as they expanded their output (see Chapter 9). At Singer, however, Edward Clark had for some time been patiently replacing these agents with salaried employees whenever he found men competent for the task. After he became president in 1876 he and his vice president, George Ross McKenzie, determined to speed up and complete the slow transformation of Singer's marketing network.

Clark outlined the final plan for the reorganization in a circular that went out to all regional offices in November 1878.[49] The sales department was to operate on three levels. At the lowest level were the retail branch offices. Their managers reported to a regional sales office, usually designed a "general agency." The middle managers in these offices in turn were responsible to one of three headquarters, one in the United States and two in Europe.

For Clark the retail branch office remained the core of Singer's marketing and distributing network. The branch manager's salaried staff included at a minimum a general salesman, an instructor, a mechanic, and a bookkeeper. Clark believed that the smallest area covered by a branch office, or "depot" as they became known later, would serve an area with a population of at least 5,000. He hoped to blanket the world with such offices.

The primary task of the branch office manager and his staff was to supervise the work of the canvassers who sold machines, collected payments, and arranged to have customers' machines serviced. These canvassers each received a small weekly salary and commissions of 15 percent on sales and 10 percent on all collections. If the branch office territory was geographically large, small subunits or depots were often set up. The branch manager and his staff assigned the canvassers territories, gave them instructions, and advised and assisted them in their work. It was the canvasser on whom Clark relied to maintain and expand Singer's market.

At the next level of management the salaried "general agent" in the regional office was key man. He had a sizable staff to assist him in monitoring the performance of the branch managers serving under him and in assisting them in carrying out their functions. The regional manager was also responsible for the recruiting and training of new managers and for assuring a steady flow of machines from the factories to the branches and of cash flow from the branches to the main office. His office included a shipping clerk, collector, machinist, lease account clerk, bills receivable clerk, and chief clerk or auditor. In addition a "traveler" helped to keep the manager in close personal touch with the branch managers. In 1879 McKenzie added a "second man" to each of the foreign agencies "so that neither sickness, death, nor any other circumstances may interfere with the smooth working of the business to any great extent."[50]

The establishment of such an organizational structure on a global scale would, McKenzie believed, give the company a maximum coverage by its sales force and provided for "entire control of our men, perfect knowledge of their work, and the power to so direct them that each knows his work, and does it without loss of time or interference." The managerial force would become an "organized, and responsible army, instead of a confused and unmanageable mob." This plan, McKenzie and Clark felt sure, would make the sale of machinery more systematic and effective and collections more regular and certain. Besides assuring a continuing flow of cash, the structure permitted a firmer control over inventory and a more certain delivery of products to the retailing units. Such coordination was essential in preventing the major cause for loss of sales, the failure of the retailer to have the machines in stock or to deliver them at an agreed-upon time.[51] Finally, the new arrangements provided a detailed flow of information into the central office about market and general business conditions throughout the world.

The reorganization at Singer was unhurried. In proposing the scheme Clark urged the "agents to use their judgment in working GRADUALLY into the new organization."[52] The location and performance of each branch office were carefully reviewed. Some were closed, others were consolidated. New ones were established as soon as competent men could be trained. To control the network more effectively, McKenzie had headquarters send out, first abroad, and then in the United States, a force of traveling auditors to provide a direct check on all the business transactions of each branch. These accountants not only reviewed regularly and systematically the accounts of the branch offices but also reported on any new and useful procedures developed by a local unit in order to transmit them to others. This was to assure, McKenzie wrote, "a certain uniformity . . . in the ways of doing business in a most advantageous manner."[53]

The careful attention Clark and McKenzie gave to this reorganization assured their company's dominance abroad as well as at home. Grover & Baker, by not building up a large sales force of its own, had already gone under in the depression of the 1870s. Wheeler & Wilson responded to Singer's initiative by completing its own general agency and branch-office network. Challenged by Singer's success, it moved precipitously, failing to give careful attention to the selection of personnel, the development of procedures, and other organizational matters. The senior executives at Singer were fully aware of their competitor's error. "I am certain," the head of Singer's British office wrote to Clark, "the W & W will lose by these operations this year more than £50,000. This business cannot be made in this slap bang style."[54] He was right. Wheeler & Wilson never developed an organization as effective as Singer's. And in markets unprotected by tariffs and patents, organization remained the key to competitive success. Singer soon had a near monopoly of world markets. In 1906 it absorbed Wheeler & Wilson.

By the first decade of the twentieth century the company's branch offices in the United States had grown from 200 to 1,700, operating under six regional offices.[55] As the number of branches grew, the boundaries of the regions (the general agencies) remained much the same, but were themselves subdivided into eighty-two district offices. Thus, at Singer the sales force had by 1900 two levels of middle management. Abroad, where the growth was comparable, the basic organization perfected in the early 1880s remained much the same. In the 1880s the New York office through its "export agency" supervised the agencies in Latin America, Canada, and the Far East. The Hamburg office had the responsibility for sales in northern and central Europe; while London was responsible for Great Britain and the rest of the world.[56] Then in 1894 New York took over from London the activities it had supervised outside the United Kingdom.

Manufacturing remained concentrated in large plants. Those at Elizabethport, New Jersey, and Kilbowie, Scotland, were by far the largest sewing machine factories in the world. Each had the major responsibility for purchasing its supplies and raw materials. Each maintained close contact with the marketing territories assigned to receive its products. The pattern was repeated when Singer moved into the Russian market after 1897 and set up a third major factory there.[57]

The essence of Singer's economic power thus lay in its organization. That managerial hierarchy recruited, trained, and carefully supervised the canvasser-collector; provided long-term consumer credit; assured continuing servicing of the machines sold; and, finally, permitted a smooth and reliable distribution of the 20,000 to 25,000 machines shipped each week to all parts of the world. It was the underlying reason why Singer was able to maintain and expand world markets for low-priced sewing machines.

Some machinery enterprises such as National Cash Register dominated their businesses by setting up comparable networks of branch retail units administered by regional offices. Most machinery makers, however, decided such a retailing network was too expensive to build and too difficult to staff. They preferred, as did the McCormick Harvesting Machine Company, to use franchised dealers who operated their own retail businesses, usually selling the machines on commission. The manufacturers soon found that such dealers were rarely effective unless they were backed up by a well-organized and disciplined sales department.

When Cyrus McCormick began to reorganize his sales force in the late 1870s, his machines still reached many local dealers through independent distributors. The Chicago office had little control over these distributors and had little information about the work of their salaried "general agents." In 1876, for example, the company did not even have a list of the names of the dealers used by their own agents. By 1881, however, the independent distributing agencies had been replaced by company managers in the midwestern and plains states, and the central office had achieved a much tighter control over these regional offices.[58] By 1885 this was true for newer agencies in other parts of the nation.

During the 1880s the regional or general agency became the central unit in McCormick's sales organization. By the 1890s the salaried general agent normally supervised and evaluated the work of ten to fifteen district managers who maintained direct contact with the dealers in their assigned territory. The regional executive was also assisted by four functional managers for service, traffic, collections, and accounts. The machinists in the servicing office were responsible for assembling the machines, which were sent "broken down" from the factory, and for their maintenance once they had been purchased. The traffic managers worked closely with the transportation department at the Chicago central office, where control of shipments became increasingly centralized. By the 1890s a new central office department, the order and shipping department, had been given the task of receiving orders, seeing that they were properly filled, and arranging for their shipment.[59] The fourth regional executive, the collection manager, kept an eye on bills receivable and on maintaining a continuous flow of payments back to Chicago. The usual payment terms were one-third in the first fall after the purchase, one-third the following fall, and the last third after the third harvest. An interest charge of between 6 and 8 percent was added on the second and third payments. Unlike Singer, McCormick kept collections completely separate from sales. They were either done directly from the collection managers office or by local merchants and banks on commission. A carefully worked-out collections policy assured McCormick, as it did Singer, receipts of cash that flowed in with the same clock-like precision as that of Marshall Field and other mass marketers. These were the ways, then, that the general agents monitored the marketing of the product and coordinated the movement of machines to customers and flows of cash back from them.

In the early 1890s, as competition intensified with the development of the binder, McCormick and other harvester companies expanded their regional offices in order to maintain sales. They hired canvassers to assist the dealers in selling, to make sales of their own, and to maintain ties with customers.[60] By 1900 the McCormick Company employed 2,000 canvassers working for a salary of $50 to $70 a month.[61] The franched dealers, then totaling over 12,000, continued to be paid by commission.

At the turn of the century McCormick's impressive sales network included sixty-five regional offices in the United States and six in Canada. The company's overseas marketing organization was still small, however. The agricultural implement firms began to sell abroad extensively only after the coming of hard times in 1893 reduced demand at home.[62] At first they relied, as they had done earlier at home, on large independent distributors. But by the late 1890s they were beginning to learn that such independents failed to push the sales of their products or to provide satisfactory after-sales service or credit arrangements. In areas where volume of sales permitted, they set up general agencies similar to those in the United States. By 1901 McCormick still sold through distributors who purchased machines outright in Latin America, Africa, New Zealand, and parts of Europe. But in Australia and the major grain-growing areas of Europe, the company already had by 1901 eight general agencies of its own, each with canvassers, machinists, and accountants. These differed from those in the United States only in that the franchised retailers purchased the machines outright, rather than on commission. This had been the practice of the independent distributors and one that the dealers were willing to continue.

As was the case in nearly all of the new large machinery companies, the reorganized and enlarged sales force encouraged expansion of output in the decade of the 1880s. McCormicks annual production rose from 20,000 to 55,000 annually between 1880 and 1884. This increase in turn led to the expansion of the purchasing office and to the buying of sawmills and timber tracts.[63] As a result there were almost as many middle managers at McCormick's Chicago central office building in the 1890s as at the headquarters of American Tobacco, Armour, Swift, and Singer Sewing Machine. The central offices included the domestic and foreign sales departments, two production departments—one for machines, the other for twine—and the purchasing, collection, transportation, and order and shipping departments. An "experimental department," housed in the reaper works, concentrated on improving methods of production and the quality of a product.

The accounting department remained relatively small and concerned itself largely with auditing the accounts of the sales and manufacturing units. McCormick appears to have had a smaller auditing division than Singer. The accounting unit generated detailed and accurate figures on prime costs, but paid relatively little attention to selling costs, and still less to the detailed allocation of overhead costs. Nor did the company, as the Bureau of Corporation investigators discovered, carefully evaluate assets or determine depreciation.[64] It apparently used the same type of renewal accounting as the railroads and other early large industrials.

Like the other early integrated enterprises, top management at both McCormick and Singer enterprises remained small and personal. At McCormick Harvester, where the McCormick family held all the stock, the senior executives throughout the nineteenth century were Cyrus McCormick, his son Cyrus, and the heads of the manufacturing and sales departments.[65] At Singer, where descendants of Clark and Singer controlled the stock, the top group included the president, vice president, and company secretary.[66] In both these machinery companies the top managers concentrated almost wholly on day-to-day activities. Plants were enlarged and, in Singer's case, occasionally new ones set up, but only when a clear demand existed for increased output. With the exception of Clark's building of the sales network, these managers did almost no long-run planning.

The basic difference between top management decisions at McCormick and Singer resulted from the nature of their competition. Whereas Singer, like American Tobacco, dominated its industry, McCormick, like Armour, had one large competitor, Deering, and several small ones.[67] After the 1880s the competition in the harvester business came to be through product improvement as well as aggressive marketing. Competition in the design of the machines led to a series of innovations, including the wire self-binder, the twine binder, the "push type" harvester, and the "header" harvester. Demonstrations, harvesting contests between competing makes, advertising, credit terms, and persistent salesmanship all played a part. Pricing was only one tactic in making sales,[68] and when used, price cutting resulted primarily in the reduction of dealer's commissions. Because competition involved much more than pricing, attempts at cartelization failed and mergers were slow in coming. This was even true when William Deering wanted to sell out and when the McCormicks were tiring of competition. Significantly, the initiative for the first successful merger in

the harvester industry in 1902 came from Judge Elbert Gary, chairman of
the board of Morgan-financed United States Steel Corporation, and not
from the harvester manufacturers. Gary had made his proposal because he
feared plans of McCormick and Deering to integrate backward by building their own rolling mills meant the loss of major customers.[69]

The merger of McCormick, Deering, and three smaller firms, completed in the summer of 1902, created an effective horizontal combination.
The new International Harvester Company controlled close to 85 percent
of the American harvester and reaper market. Like the organizers of other
combinations of the period, the promoters of International Harvester
quickly learned that horizontal combination was not a profitable strategy.
During the fifteen months after merger the company earned less than
1 percent on its net assets.[70] In January 1904 the directors centralized administration under Cyrus McCormick. They failed, however, to unify
the activities of the constituent companies. Finally, in 1906, at the insistence of George W. Perkins, the Morgan partner who was chairman of
the Harvester board, the managers and facilities of the other companies
were consolidated into the core organization of the old McCormick firm.

Once administration had been fully centralized, International Harvester began to develop a full line of agriculture products—plows, har-
rows, seeders, spreaders, and the like—to utilize more fully the company's
facilities. After 1906 the company also began to expand its overseas
operation. Producers of these other types of agricultural implements soon
responded to International Harvester's moves. John Deere, Moline Plow,
J. I. Case, Advance-Rumely, and others began to make and sell harvesters
and reapers and expanded their overseas activities.[71]

By 1917 a number of large vertically integrated, full-line agricultural
machinery makers were competing for the same markets in the United
States and abroad. As in comparable industries, the larger companies—
International Harvester and John Deere—became the price leaders. These
firms continued to contest for their share of the market by advertising,
after-sales service, credit, and aggressive canvassing. They also competed
by improving their products—the coming of the gasoline engine hastened
such product innovation—and by speeding up the processes of production. All enlarged their experimentation or research departments. They
concentrated much more on foreign markets than they did before 1900.
For example, by 1911 International Harvester was operating plants in
Canada, Sweden, France, Germany, and Russia.[72] In Russia it was developing a fully integrated operation comparable to that of Singer. By that
year, Mira Wilkins notes, 40 percent of the International Harvester business and even a higher portion of its net earnings came from foreign sales.

The patterns of growth and competition in the agricultural machinery industry were fully defined well before World War I. The same firms continued to dominate their industry for the rest of the century. They continued to grow by internal expansion and, as did meat packers, by diversifying into markets that made use of their existing facilities and management. Their organizations and their methods of competition differed from those of the packers and the cigarette companies because they produced durable rather than perishable or semiperishable goods; because their products were far more costly and complex; and because both the product and the processes of production lent themselves to continuing technological innovation. The marketing and distribution of such goods required the creation of a disciplined, trained force of salaried employees to make the sales, to provide continuing servicing, to handle the long-term credit arrangements, and to coordinate flows of goods to the customers and of cash to the central office. Their production required close attention to improving the techniques of mass production through the fabricating and assembling of interchangeable parts.

The manufacturers of heavier but relatively standardized machines—generators, motors, streetcars, subway systems, telephonic transmitting equipment, elevators, pumps, boilers, steam engines, printing presses, radiators, shoe machinery, and the like—operated under comparable conditions. The difference was that their processes and products were technologically even more complex. The installation and maintenance of their products were tasks which often only the manufacturer had the necessary skills to handle. Moreover, the makers of the products usually knew more about their potential uses, their standards of performance, and their operating requirements than did the customer. Such machinery was expensive. Payments required long-term arrangements tailored to the customer's needs. So competition in these industries was even less on the basis of price than it was in the light machinery trades.

In these industries, product improvement and innovation became an even more powerful competitive weapon, far more effective than advertising or canvassing. Such product development called for the closest cooperation between the engineers who designed the product and the managers who were responsible for its manufacture. As Harold C. Passer, the historian of the electrical manufacturers, has written about marketing at General Electric and Westinghouse in the 1890s: "The competition in reality was between the engineering staffs of the two companies. If the engineers of one company were able to design a motor that met the customers' wants better than the second company's motor, the engineers of the second company had to improve their motor or run the risk of losing their market."[73] The sales force provided the engineers with information on the customer's specific wants and the types of performance they expected from a machine. The engineers in turn had to be in constant conversation with the managers of the production department if the factory was to have the equipment to manufacture the product desired. In such industries coordination meant more than maintaining a high-volume of flow of goods through the processes of production and distribution. It meant coordination between customers with technologically complex requirements and manufacturers with even more complex producing equipment. The flow of ideas as well as goods had to be coordinated.

The beginnings of middle management in American industry

The pioneering enterprises described above were among the first of many entrepreneurial enterprises to build giant, global business empires. The operations of these integrated companies required the hiring of dozens and in time hundreds of lower and middle managers. The tasks of the managers on the lower level who had charge of the operating units did not differ greatly from those of men who owned and managed a single independent factory or commercial office. But the tasks of the middle managers were entirely new. Middle managers had to pioneer in the ways of modern administrative coordination.

The new middle managers did more than devise ways to coordinate the high-volume flow from suppliers of raw materials to consumers. They invented and perfected ways to expand markets and to speed up the processes of production and distribution. Those at American Tobacco, Armour, and other mass producers of low-priced packaged products perfected techniques of product differentiation through advertising and brand names that had been initially developed by mass marketers, advertising agencies, and patent medicine makers. The middle managers at Singer were the first to systematize personal selling by means of door-to-door canvassing; those at McCormick among the first to have franchised dealers using comparable methods. Both companies innovated in installment buying and other techniques of consumer credit. They devised ways to assure collection and set policies on repossession when the customer failed to keep up his payments. And they were the first to work out ways of providing after-sales service and repair. Whereas they pioneered in the marketing of light machinery, the middle managers at General Electric, Westinghouse, and the heavy-machinery makers did the same thing for heavier producer's goods.

In addition, the middle managers created new and faster channels of distribution. They set up strategically placed warehouses, perfected the use of mixed and dropped shipments, and devised new types of accounting and statistical controls. They developed techniques to purchase, store, and move huge stocks of raw and semifinished materials. In order to maintain a more certain flow of goods, they often operated fleets of railroad cars and transportation equipment.

The middle managers played a comparable role in production. Those in the tobacco and packing companies improved continuous-process machinery and methods, while the heads of manufacturing departments of the sewing machine, typewriter, and other light machinery companies were leaders in perfecting methods in mass production through the fabrication and assembling of interchangeable parts. The latter borrowed from and contributed to the achievements of Frederick W. Taylor and the other practitioners of scientific or systematic management. Not only did these middle managers help to perfect new complex machines and the modern form of factory organization, they also adopted, much more quickly than did American Tobacco, Armour, and other producers of packaged consumer goods, the new techniques of factory cost accounting.

By reshaping the processes of production and distribution the middle managers helped to assure the dominance of their enterprises. They increased output and reduced costs by using more intensively the resources under their command. The lower unit cost in manufacturing and distribution and the trained and experienced sales force created a continuing, sturdy barrier to the entry of smaller firms.

The desire to maintain and expand the use of their facilities brought growth. One reason American Tobacco moved into smoking, plug, and other tobacco was to assure a steady and growing use of its purchasing (leaf) and marketing organization. This was also why International Harvester and other agricultural implement firms developed their full lines. At Armour the decision to exploit by-products of the packing process led to the creation of new marketing organizations, and the decision to use its distribution facilities more fully led to the building of new buying networks. At Armour, integrated suborganizations began to evolve to coordinate flows to the different product markets.

Expansion overseas, for much the same reason, was by World War I having the same results. Increased demand created by the expansion of a sales force overseas led to the building of factories abroad. Often this was the result of transportation costs or local tariffs and other restrictions on imported goods. As often, however, the construction of new factories resulted from the need to assure effective administrative coordination of flows of goods to the customer. For example, of the thirty-seven American companies listed by Mira Wilkins as having two or more factories in Europe by World War I, twenty-three had built plants in Britain, where there was no tariff and where the transportation costs from American plants were the lowest.[74] After factories had been built the imperatives of coordination and costs often led to obtaining supplies locally. Thus by 1914 integrated suborganizations were appearing to serve large regional overseas markets.

Middle managers also determined methods of competition. Oligopolistic competition among the new, modern, multiunit integrated enterprises had little resemblance to the more traditional competition between single-unit manufacturers who bought and sold through middlemen. To the latter the price paid for materials and received for their goods remained an important consideration. For the new industrial corporations pricing was only one of many ways of competing. When more than one large integrated enterprise dominated an industry, competition between them was carried on at every stage of the processes of production and distribution. Such competition was most obvious in marketing and distribution. There it occurred in advertising, in the training and supervision of salesmen, in maintaining prompt deliveries, in credit terms, and in providing satisfactory after-sales service. It also occurred in production. There improved machinery and plants increased productivity and so lowered costs, improvements in products attracted and kept customers, and improved statistical and accounting controls further increased productivity. In addition, competition took place in purchasing. The ability to buy in quantity to close specifications, to be aware of changing sources of supplies, and to schedule flows to avoid unnecessary stockpiling all affected the quality and the cost of the final product.

Competition between these enterprises was, therefore, ultimately between their managers and organizations. The success of a firm depended primarily on the caliber of its managerial hierarchy. Such quality in turn reflected the ability of the top executives to select and evaluate their middle managers, to coordinate their work, and to plan and allocate resources for the enterprises as a whole.

It was precisely here that the administration of these early large integrated enterprises was weak. Coordination of the flow of materials through the enterprise was not tied to a carefully calculated estimate of demand. It was achieved largely by personal cooperation between the heads of functional departments and their staffs. Evaluation and review of departmental performance was rarely systematic. The growth of the enterprise was only occasionally planned with an eye to long-term changes in supply, demand, and technological innovation. Growth came rather as a response to short-term needs and opportunities as perceived by different sets of middle managers.

One reason for this weakness was that owners still managed. The number of top managers remained few, and those few rarely had the time or inclination for objective evaluation and long-range planning. High-volume cash flow had permitted these enterprises to be self-financed. The McCormicks and the Deerings, the Singers and the Clarks, the Procters and the Gambles, the Crowthers and the Stuarts, the Armours and the Swifts, the Pabsts and the Busches, the Dorrances and the Bordens, the Heinzes, Pillsburys, Eastmans, Candlers, Wrigleys, and the entrepreneurs who built Remington Typewriter and National Cash Register, Burroughs Adding Machine and Otis Elevator, all owned the companies they managed. Others such as Duke of American Tobacco and Barber of Diamond Match continued to have a controlling share of the stock in their companies after they had expanded by merger or acquisition.

These entrepreneurs and their families continued to look on their enterprises much as the owner-managers of traditional enterprises did. Where family members were no longer the chief executive or in other top management positions, close associates who had been personally selected by the family usually occupied these posts. The owner-managers prided themselves on their knowledge of a business they had done so much to build. They continued to be absorbed in the details of day-to-day operation. They personally reviewed the departmental reports and the statistical data. They had little or no staff to collect information and to provide expert advice. They promoted, hired, and fired their subordinates as often on personal whim as objective analysis.

Long-term planning was also highly personal. In building their business empires Duke, Swift, Armour, Clark, and the McCormicks were impressive, even brilliant business strategists. But their moves were personal responses to new needs and opportunities. They did not plan systematically for the continuing growth of the enterprise. They rarely adopted formal capital appropriation procedures, rarely asked for budgets. In the more routine expansion of existing operations and facilities they responded to ad hoc requests of middle managers. These they normally approved. As owners—and very wealthy ones at that—they saw little reason to veto such plans for expansion. On the contrary, as owners they had much to gain. What could be a better investment than to plow back profits in order to make existing resources still more lucrative? For these reasons, the enterprises that pioneered in the ways of middle management did very little to develop methods of top management. That contribution was made by the managerial enterprises that grew out of the early industry-wide mergers.

CHAPTER 13

Top Management:
Function and Structure

The managerial enterprise

The practices and procedures of modern top management had their beginnings in the industrial enterprises formed by merger rather than those that built extended marketing and purchasing organizations. The process of merger brought more persons, with more varied backgrounds, into top management. In the new consolidations a family or single group of associates rarely held all the voting stock. It was scattered among the owners of the constituent companies and the financiers and promoters who had assisted in the merger. It became even more widely held after the company sold stock to finance the reorganization and consolidation of facilities. After merger the initial administrative problems were more complex than those in the companies that grew by internal expansion. The facilities of the constituent companies had to be reshaped and their administration centralized. Moreover, a merger, the reorganization that followed it, and then the carrying out of the process of vertical integration all required continued planning.

The shift in strategy from horizontal combination to vertical integration first brought the managerial enterprise to American industry. In the terminology of this study a managerial firm differs from an entrepreneurial one in that full-time salaried executives dominate top as well as middle management. The owners no longer administer the enterprise. The experienced manufacturers, who helped to carry the merger and who, normally with the advice of one or two financiers, rationalized the facilities of a new consolidation, became the core of its top management. Although they were still large stockholders, they rarely controlled the company as did the owners of entrepreneurial firms. Moreover, they hired and promoted managers with little or no stock ownership in the company to head the new functional departments and the central staff offices.

In carrying out the reorganization after the merger, these top managers began to define their specific tasks. The centralizing of administration caused them to institute uniform accounting and statistical controls. In hiring and allocating managerial personnel they began to think more systematically about evaluating managerial performance. And because the reorganization of production and the building of a sales and buying network created numerous and often conflicting claims for capital expenditures, these senior executives were increasingly forced to pay close attention to the systematic long-term allocation of capital and personnel. The methods fashioned during the process of consolidation and integration—and sometimes the process took years—were further refined as the company began to grow and to compete oligopolistically with other large integrated enterprises.

Once administrative centralization and vertical integration had been achieved, the separation of management and ownership widened. The scattered owners of the widely held stock had little opportunity to take part in management decisions at any level; and only a few managers continued to be holders of large blocks of voting stock. Top management in these enterprises, therefore, was more like that of the railroads than that of the industrials that grew by internal expansion.

There were, however, significant differences between the top management of the new industrial consolidations, and that of the large railroad systems. Although investment bankers and other financiers were active in the merger movement, they played a less influential role in the affairs of the new industrials than they did on the railroads. For one thing, many experienced manufacturers who had owned and operated the firms entering the merger often stayed on the board and continued to have an influence on top management decisions. For another, the capital requirements of the industrials were smaller than those of the railroads. In most cases, too, the consolidations were able to generate a higher return than railroads. Because they had less continuing need for outside funds, fewer financiers came on their boards, and those that did rarely had the power—albeit a veto power—that they had on the railroads. In only a few cases where particularly heavy outside financing was required did financiers outnumber managers on the boards of industrials, and such cases became less and less frequent.

Four important consolidations—Standard Oil, General Electric, United States Rubber, and Du Pont—provide detailed case studies of the largest companies in oil, heavy machinery, rubber, and chemicals, four of the nation's most significant industrial groups. They represent differing ways in which the mergers and the shifts in strategy from horizontal combination to vertical integration were carried out and the differing types of offices and practices that resulted.

At Standard Oil the creation of a central headquarters came in an evolutionary, ad hoc manner. Its managers paid little attention to organizational problems. For this reason, possibly, their plan of operating through subsidiaries that were coordinated by committees had only a few imitators. This was true even though theirs was the first and the best known of the modern consolidations. At General Electric, on the other hand, both managers and financiers paid close attention to administrative needs. The managers were aware of the advantages of organizational precision. And the financiers, who there played as important a role as they did in any major industrial merger, advocated the adoption of many administrative methods that had been developed on the railroads. The resulting centralized, functionally departmentalized structure became the basic organizational form used by modern American industrial enterprises.

United States Rubber and the E. I. Du Pont de Nemours Powder Company provide comparable contrasts in an evolutionary and revolutionary restructuring of a consolidated enterprise and with it a major American industry. In neither merger did outside financiers play an important role. The rubber company was even slower than Standard Oil in moving from horizontal combination to vertical integration and paid even less attention to organizational matters, taking over twenty years to build its central administration. Nevertheless, this evolutionary process had by 1917 brought the United States Rubber Company organizational structure close to that of the modern, multidivisional form of administration.

The Du Pont Company completed the administrative organization of its merger in as many months as it took the United States Rubber Company years. In 1903 three du Pont cousins consolidated their small enterprise with many other small, single-unit family firms. They then completely reorganized the American explosives industry and installed an organizational structure that incorporated "the best practice" of the day. The highly rational managers at Du Pont continued to perfect these techniques, so that by 1910 that company was employing nearly all the basic methods that are currently used in managing big business.

The history of these four mergers closely parallels that of most mergers that occurred in American industry before World War I. For some the process was evolutionary; for others the new organization was built with the same speed and care as at General Electric and Du Pont. By 1917, however, the majority of mergers used an organizational structure similar to that devised at those two innovating enterprises. A much smaller number of leading consolidations adopted structures similar to those of Standard Oil and United States Rubber. These four cases therefore can be used as examples of many of the firms that became modern multiunit enterprises by way of merger. They illustrate the merger process in the late nineteenth and early twentieth centuries. They reveal how and why the operating procedures of modern top management came into being.

Standard Oil Trust

The formation of the Standard Oil Trust on January 2, 1882, provided the members of the powerful Standard Oil alliance with a central organization to supervise and coordinate the operations of their constituent companies and to make investment decisions for the group as a whole. Such central direction could not be achieved through a cartel, either formal or informal. Members of the alliance, like those of any pool, cartel, or trade association, could do little more than set price and production schedules and make joint shipment and purchasing arrangements.

In setting up the trust, its creators expected the new central office to administer a group of subsidiary companies. They did not intend to eliminate legally the major companies and then to merge them into a single operating enterprise. Some smaller subsidiaries were amalgamated into the larger existing ones or into the two new state-chartered companies, Standard Oil of New York and Standard Oil of New Jersey. The functions of the trust were to coordinate, evaluate, and plan the activities of operating subsidiaries, whose number grew as the trust moved into new functions and new markets and obtained new sources of crude oil.

The largest processing subsidiaries were those that operated the three great new refineries that together produced two-fifths of the world's supply of kerosene. Standard Oil of New Jersey managed the Bayonne refinery, Standard Oil of Ohio the one in Cleveland, and Atlantic Refining the Philadelphia works. Subsidiaries operating the twenty or so smaller refineries—many of which produced lubricants, paraffin, vaseline, and other specializations—included Pratt, Devoe, Stone & Fleming, Thompson & Bedford, as well as Standard of New York, all located in the New York area. Camden Consolidated had refineries in Baltimore and in Parkersburg, West Virginia, and Central Refining and Acme had refineries in western Pennsylvania and on the seaboard.[1] And from the start the trust relied on the National Transit Company to supervise and plan pipeline activities.

As the trust integrated forward into marketing and backward into crude oil production, it enlarged the number of its operating enterprises. It set up new marketing companies, including Standard Oil of Kentucky, of Iowa, of Illinois, and of Minnesota, and Continental Oil. It also obtained control of the two largest wholesalers in the United States—the Waters, Pierce and the Chess-Carley companies.[2] In the east the trust turned the marketing functions over to existing refining companies—to Standard of New York, of New Jersey, and of Ohio, and to Acme and Atlantic Refining. Abroad the marketing and distribution came to be handled by Anglo-American (a British corporation), American Petroleum (a Dutch corporation), and Deutsch-Amerikanische Petroleum Gesellschaft and some smaller national companies. Each of these subsidiaries was allocated its own marketing territory. Then with the move into crude oil, Standard Oil formed several producing companies—Ohio Oil, South Penn Oil, North Penn Oil, Union Oil, Forest Oil, Midland Oil, and some smaller ones.[3]

To supervise and coordinate the activities of these many functional subsidiaries, the trust relied on committees consisting primarily of senior executives from the larger of these enterprises. These committees, in turn, had the advice and assistance of a permanent staff housed at the trust's central office at 26 Broadway.[4] This system of committees supported by a central staff evolved to meet pressing and continuing needs. It was not the result of any thought-out organizational plan.

The use of committees was a natural way to coordinate the work of managers in different companies carrying out similar functions or activities. Even before the formation of the trust, members of the alliance had representatives on an informal committee on transportation, which reviewed and proposed changes in freight rates negotiated with the railroads. Another early informal committee helped to coordinate the shipping and selling of kerosene in Europe. With the formation of the trust these committees were formalized as the transportation and the export trade committees. As the trust was being organized, its founders formed the manufacturing committee to reorganize and then to supervise the refining capacity. Then came the case and can committee and the cooperage committee to centralize purchasing and to assure uniform specification in the trust's basic packaging materials. The lubricating oil committee appeared in 1885 when the trust decided to centralize the sale of lubricants in New York. Then, as it took on marketing activities, its top executives created in 1886 the domestic marketing committee. In 1889 with the move into crude oil production came the production committee.[5]

Members of these committees found that they required the services of a permanent staff to provide essential information and to check on the implementation of the committee's decisions. By 1886 there were eleven staff departments with offices at 26 Broadway. Five dealt with sales.[6] Two handled domestic trade, one for the east including Ohio and the other for the south and west. A third was responsible for foreign sales. The two others were responsible for lubricants, again one for the west and one for the east. Two other departments were concerned with packaging materials both at the refineries and, after 1886, at a growing number of bulk stations.[7] Still another handled inspection and quality control. In 1886, before Standard began to produce its own crude oil, a "crude stock department" assisted National Transit and the Joseph Seep Agency (the company's purchasing organization) in the buying and shipping of crude oil. The two remaining staff units were the auditing and legal departments. All the staff offices provided information to the operating subsidiaries, the top managers on the board of the trust, and coordinating committees.

Each of these functional committees normally consisted of the senior staff executive for its function, together with a member of the trust's board and the heads of two or three of the major subsidiaries involved in the activity that the committee was to coordinate. In theory, their role was advisory. The subsidiaries and the central board of trustees could reject their advice and decisions. In practice they rarely did.[8]

From the start the most important of these committees was the one responsible for the supervision and coordination of refining operations. The manufacturing committee was expected, according to Ralph and Muriel Hidy, "to assure a regular flow of petroleum through all plants of the combination and to coordinate all manufacturing activities with changing supplies of crude and fluctuations in world-wide markets."[9] In this task it worked closely with the Seep purchasing agency. In addition to the responsibility for coordinating product flow, the manufacturing committee was given the authority "to consider all subjects relative to construction" as well as manufacturing. That is, it became responsible for reviewing proposed expenditures and for keeping an eye on the construction of new facilities and the repair of old ones, once proposals were approved.

As Standard's marketing network and crude oil production expanded, the domestic trade and the crude oil committees appeared to have acquired comparable responsibilities. For pipelines the senior executives of National Transit had the same duties. In this way, then, the functional committees assisted by the staff departments reviewed basic proposals on the allocation of resources and coordinated flow from one basic function to the next.

The responsibility for overall management rested with an executive committee of the nine-man board of trustees. As it worked out, that committee consisted of all trustees who were at 26 Broadway on any given day.[10] From the start the trustees considered their tasks to be evaluating the performance of the operating units, selecting top managers, and making final decisions on long-term plans and allocation of resources to carry them out.

In evaluating performance the trustees relied on accounting and statistical data provided by the operating units. All subsidiary companies were expected to show a profit, with profit defined as a margin between sale price and costs. And in order to have comparable figures on costs, the executive committee ordered, shortly after the formation of the trust, the development of uniform accounting procedures to be used by all subsidiary companies. To assist its members in the evaluation of performance and also to help them keep an eye on output, flows, and sales, the committee also received a constant stream of reports from staff departments. The crude stock department provided a daily "crude oil report" with statistical data on total production in the United States, stocks in storage, Standard's total inventory, runs from tanks and wells, deliveries, new purchases, and information on new wells.[11] The cooperage department had its monthly "barreling and marketing reports" on shipment and sales. The several sales departments sent on information on deliveries and sales, not only of Standard's products but also those of competitors. In addition, the manufacturing committee forwarded monthly cost and yield reports for each of the refineries.

The introduction of uniform accounting procedures, so central to overall evaluation and control, proved, as historians of the enterprise point out, a slow and sometimes painful process. In time, the trust did develop accurate and detailed data on prime manufacturing costs but little on sales, administrative, and other overhead costs. Until well into the twentieth century, earnings, defined as the difference between income and operating costs, continued to be the accepted standard for financial performance. Assets were written down in unsystematic, ad hoc ways. The manner of computing depreciation varied from subsidiary to subsidiary. Efforts "to inaugurate a uniform method of depreciation" were only beginning in 1905.[12] In most cases such write-downs were charged to the subsidiary's profit and loss account. Even with these weaknesses, the trust's control systems were as effective as any used by industrial enterprises of that day. The members of its executive committee, coordinating committees, and staff had more detailed knowledge of operating activities than had the senior executives of entrepreneurial firms.

The executive committee carried out its central task of planning and allocating resources for future production and distribution more systematically than did the top managers of the entrepreneurial enterprises. The committee had to approve all appropriations made by subsidiaries over $5,000 and any salary changes for managers receiving more than $600 a year. These requests came from the manufacturing, sales, and other committees or from the subsidiaries themselves.[13] Such procedures gave the executive committee a regular and continuing review of the size and nature of capital expenditures and the activities and performance of managers, particularly middle and top managers.

Nevertheless, in allocating resources and rewarding personnel, the executive committee acted largely as a ratifying body. It rarely took the initiative and developed its own plans for capital expenditures. The subsidiaries, committees, staff departments, and executive committee itself did not develop capital budgets, or apparently even operating budgets. Nor did they define specific criteria for capital allocation, or forecast for financial needs, or devise a rate of return expected from an investment. No person or unit made long-term analyses of changes in demand, supply, and technology.

This lack of systematic procedures in making appropriations does not mean that the trustees and the heads of operating units did not have long, often heated discussions over the allocation of funds. Nor does it mean that as a ratifying body, the trustees did not have real power. It means rather that long-term investments continued to be determined primarily by middle managers in response to immediate developments in changing markets, sources of supply, and actions of competitors at home and abroad rather than as a result of a long-term plan or strategy.[14]

The primary reason that the executive committee at Standard Oil, the first of the great integrated industrial consolidations, failed to devise systematic procedures for capital allocation and other top management functions was that the trustees were too busy handling other pressing matters. As presidents or senior executives in subsidiary companies, they had to concentrate on the day-to-day operating details of these enterprises.[15] At the same time, as members of functional coordinating committees at 26 Broadway, they had to become specialists in one or another functional activity. Moreover, many of the key trustees became involved in outside business activities. For example, Rockefeller himself in the 1890s purchased large areas in the Mesabi range, helped to start the Colorado Iron and Fuel Company, and obtained a financial interest in American Linseed Oil and other industrials. Henry M. Flagler became increasingly involved in railroads and Florida real estate, H. H. Rogers helped to organize major copper and lead and mining companies, Oliver H. Payne assisted in financing Duke's transformation of the tobacco industry, and Edward T. Bedford became a leader in the corn products refining industry.[16] Too often these men at the top had little time, information, or even inclination to concentrate on Standard Oil's long-range situation. Moreover, the continuing high profits from their existing worldwide business lessened the pressures to systematize procedures for capital allocation or for recruiting senior managers or to define more precisely the activities handled by the subsidiaries, the central staff, and the trustees.

Nor, as time passed, did the trustees make any special effort to improve their top management procedures or their company's overall operating structure. Indeed, as the enterprise's activities expanded, its organization became increasingly complex and even illogical. One reason was that the trust was dissolved in 1893 after it was declared illegal by the Ohio Supreme Court. The holding company, the Standard Oil Company (New Jersey), that legally took its place was not formed until 1899.[17] So for seven years the consolidation had no legal superstructure. Such legal maneuvers had little direct effect on administration. They meant only that the executive committee and the advisory coordinating committees met informally rather than formally. Yet the lack of an overall legal framework did discourage administrative reform. And as the consolidation grew, subsidiaries became larger, more integrated, and more autonomous. In the 1890s Anglo-American Oil, with its affiliate Imperial of Canada, acquired control over the flow of supplies in their regional areas. Then after 1900 with the opening of new fields in the south and far west, Standard of California and Standard of Louisiana developed similar integrated operations.[18] As these subsidiaries became increasingly independent of 26 Broadway, the manufacturing committee ceased to be responsible for coordinating the flow and making capital preparations for the refineries for the enterprise as a whole. It now did so only for subsidiaries in the American northeast. As the committees and staff department became larger, their functions became less clear. In the 1890s, as the Hidys point out:

The staff at 26 Broadway, upon which all executives relied for aid, was an uncommonly heterogeneous mixture. The organization, having developed over time, continued to reflect the melange of companies based on historical precedent, personal predelictions, state corporation requirements, and tax laws. Even such an orderly mind as that of S. C. T. Dodd [the enterprises's general counsel] did not have a complete picture of it. In addition to directors, all the principal manufacturing companies and many of the lesser ones had sales agents at headquarters for refined oil in domestic trade, for refined oil in export trade, for lubricating oil in the West, and for lubricating oil in the East and for export . . . Similarly, other men and units effected economies by performing a specialized function for several corporations . . . The staff departments were not all logically assigned to the parent company . . . Personal preference, historical evolution, and inertia undoubtedly all contributed to the seemingly haphazard arrangement.[19]

Not until the mid-1920s, over a decade after Standard Oil had been dismembered by a Supreme Court decision, were the operating units, the top executives, and the central staff structured in a systematic and rational way.[20] Even then, the massive reshaping of Standard's organizational structure came in an evolutionary, ad hoc manner.

From its very beginning, the central office at Standard Oil was much larger than any of the entrepreneurial enterprises of its day. It had many more top managers and a larger central staff. This was precisely because these offices were created to coordinate, evaluate, and plan for the activities of many subsidiary companies. And the size of the central office, in turn, increasingly required the employment of salaried managers. From the start the central staff was made up of salaried personnel. Before the end of the century, many of the top executives—that is, the trustees (who, after 1899 were directors)—were salaried officials who owned only a very small amount of the securities of the trust or its subsidiaries. Alexander M. McGregor, Thomas C. Bushnell, Frank Q. Barstow, James A. Moffet, A. Cotten Bedford, Orville T. Waring, Lauren J. Drake, and Henry C. Folger were all in this category.[21] At the same time the large stockholders —Oliver H. Payne, Henry M. Flagler, Charles W. Harkness, and John D. and William Rockefeller—were spending less and less time at 26 Broadway. In a period when nearly all American industrial enterprises were still managed at the top in a personal or entrepreneurial way, Standard Oil was rapidly becoming run by salaried employees.

Standard Oil, first as a trust, later as a holding company, created the administrative structure that came to be called the functional holding company form. The employment of subsidiaries to carry out different economic functions and the use of committees and staff departments to coordinate and control the activities of these subsidiaries was a natural and rational way to organize a giant integrated consolidation of many small companies. And although this form was widely used in Europe, surprisingly few American companies followed Standard's example.[22] Two other of the largest oil companies—Sinclair and Pan American—acquired similar structures. The United States Steel Corporation operated through functional subsidiaries (and two or three integrated ones), although it never developed a central staff and coordinating committee comparable to that of Standard. Other companies with assets of $20 million or over (see Appendix A), who were using the functional holding company structure form in 1917, were three other primary metals firms, three mining enterprises, New Jersey Zinc, and an agricultural company.

One reason the new consolidations failed to follow Standard Oil's lead was that they had an even more obvious model, the railroad. During the railroad expansion and reorganization of the 1880s and 1890s, system-builders usually eliminated as legal and administrative entities the companies brought into the system by consolidating them into a single, highly centralized, administrative structure. The new systems did not rely on coordinating committees. They were administered through functional departments, using the line and staff distinction to coordinate activities at the several levels of management. The investment bankers and other financiers who played such a critical role in the final legal and administrative reorganizations of these systems preferred this centralized structure to the more decentralized one of large, self-contained regional divisions.

Even those early trusts that followed Standard Oil's strategy of consolidation, rationalization, and integration looked more to the railroads than to their sister trust in setting up their administrative procedures. At American Cotton Oil this could be expected, for railroad financiers played a major role in financing the merger. There Charles Lanier, of the investment house of Winslow, Lanier & Company, became the chairman of the board, and a junior member of the same house, Edward D. Adams, became its president. They legally eliminated the constituent companies and then transformed the holding company into an integrated, centralized, functionally departmentalized operating company.[23] By 1890 Adams had organized departments at the company's central office at 29 Broadway for domestic sales, foreign sales, purchasing, transportation, and three for processing—the manufacturing, refining, and the cake and meal departments. To meet legal requirements, Adams did set up subsidiaries in the southern states where the company operated over seventy crushing mills, but these mills continued to be administered from 29 Broadway. In addition, in the 1890s the board expanded its chemical laboratory, formed in 1887, into an independent research department.[24] Following railroad practice, the heads of the operating departments reported directly to the president, and the treasurer and the auditing department reported to the finance committee.

At National Lead the adoption of this type of structure was less likely, for there the influence of outside financiers was minimal and its president, William P. Thompson, was a former Standard Oil executive.[25] Thompson began with subsidiaries and coordinating committees, but soon set up a centralized, functionally departmentalized structure. Like Adams, he placed research and development under a separate central department. For some years he retained two formal committees. One, the linseed, linseed oil, and linseed cake committee, coordinated the flow of basic raw materials, which were not only used in the production of paint—its major product—and other final products but also sold directly to wholesalers and retailers. The other, the committee on construction, repair, and manufacturing, became in time the company's capital appropriations committee.

In adopting this structure Thompson and his managers may have been influenced by the example of the new entrepreneurial enterprises as well as the railroad, for by the late 1880s those firms were beginning to work out their departmental structures. However, the experience of Singer, McCormick, Armour, and Duke was little known outside of their own companies, whereas nearly all American businessmen involved in promoting and carrying out mergers dealt with railroads and were aware of their organization. In any case, National Lead, like American Cotton Oil, found the railroad model more relevant to their needs than that of Standard Oil.

General Electric Company

For several reasons the merger that created the General Electric Company was more important to the development of modern industrial management in the United States than were the early trusts. General Electric was the first major consolidation of machinery-making companies and so the first between already integrated enterprises. Its products and processes were as technologically advanced and complex as any of that day. And at General Electric outside financiers played as large a role as they did in any American industrial merger. For this reason the railroad influence was particularly strong. The financiers were important because the electrical manufacturers were the first American industrialists not intimately connected with railroads who found it necessary to go to the capital markets for funds in order to build their initial enterprise.

In the new electrical equipment industry, technological development was much more complex, much more costly, and took more time to achieve than in other industries. Unlike Duke, Crowther, Heinz, Eastman, Singer, or Rockefeller, these manufacturers were unable to exploit the enormous output of a new continuous-process method which provided almost immediately a high cash flow. Instead, Thomas A. Edison, Elihu Thomson, and George Westinghouse had first to fashion an integrated system of power-generating machinery, power stations, lamps, and power-using machines before they could begin to sell their products in volume.

Moreover, once their systems were developed, these enterprises had to help finance the construction of the central power stations that used their products. This they did by taking stock in small, local power companies. Such financing, in turn, forced them to go to Wall Street and State Street. As early as 1878 Thomas Edison was getting help from Drexel, Morgan & Company, then on its way to becoming the foremost investment house in the nation; while Elihu Thomson soon had the backing of Frederick L. Ames, Henry L. Higginson, and T. Jefferson Coolidge, Boston capitalists who were involved in the financing of railroads, the telegraph, and soon the telephone.[26] George Westinghouse, who entered the field somewhat later, in 1886, by developing an alternating current system, grew at a smaller scale than his rivals. At first he attempted to sell his equipment only for cash. By 1889, however, he had to obtain the support of Pittsburgh financiers. And in 1891 he asked August Belmont & Company and Lee, Higginson to refinance his company.[27] The houses of Morgan, Belmont, and Lee, Higginson were, of course, intimately informed about the administrative structures of railroad, telegraph, and telephone companies.

The General Electric Company, incorporated in November 1892, was a merger of two of these three large electrical equipment manufacturers. Both the Edison General Electric Company and the Thomson-Houston Electric Company were themselves the result of mergers. Edison Electric, formed in 1889, was a consolidation of the three manufacturing companies, a patent company owned by the Edison interests, and the Sprague Electric Railway and Motor Company. The latter was a pioneer in the manufacture of electric street railway equipment. Henry Villard, an eminent railroad financier who had helped to finance some of Edison's early developmental work, engineered the merger.[28] Villard had recently returned to the United States after a three-year stay in Germany where he had become closely associated with the powerful Deutsche Bank of Berlin and with Siemens & Halske, the leading German electrical manufacturers who were already beginning to sell in the American market. He planned, according to Edison's biographer, Matthew Josephson, to create a "world cartel."[29]

After the merger, however, Villard concentrated on the new American enterprise. He began to centralize the administration of its manufacturing facilities and to build a nationwide sales organization. He had the new company concentrate its machinery production at the large works at Schenectady and the making of the lamps or light bulbs at Harrison, New Jersey.[30] The working force of these two large factories soon totaled close to 6,000. Young Samuel Insull, a Villard protégé, as second vice president, created a sales force with seven regional offices, each headed by a district manager who supervised and coordinated the work of the salesmen and engineers responsible for sales, contracts, installation, and continuing service and repair. Each reported to Insull, who had on his staff a small "intelligence department." Then two years later Villard began negotiations for a merger with Thomson-Houston.

At that time Thomson-Houston, the largest company in the arc light business and second only to Edison General Electric in assets and output, had the most effective sales force in the industry.[31] The company's president, Charles A. Coffin, had by 1886, four years after its founding, completed a national network of sales offices. In that year Coffin began to move into the production of other electrical products besides arc lights, including a complete incandescent system, a line of direct current motors, railway motors, and alternating current generators and transformers. He did so both by internal expansion and by the acquisition, largely through exchange of stock, of four small companies.[32] The sales department established by Coffin to market these lines differed from Insull's at General Electric in that it had at its Boston headquarters a sales manager for each major product. As Harold C. Passer has pointed out: "These sales managers were charged with the coordination of production and marketing and the development of new markets for the products under their supervision."[33] Soon, too, there were product managers in the branch offices.

Coffin's desire to broaden the company's product line caused him to listen attentively to Villard's proposal for a merger. Both had much the same aim. "Each company desired to expand the lines in which it was weak and to begin the manufacture of those products which showed promise."[34] Patents created a major difficulty. In street railways, Edison General Electric held one set of patents and Thomson-Houston another. This was also true in lamp and arc light equipment.

As the negotiations progressed, J. Pierpont Morgan, whose firm was to be responsible for financing the merger, decided that the Thomson-Houston personnel should manage the new consolidation. Although smaller in capitalization and plant capacity, its executives had the greater administrative and marketing abilities.[35] Almost immediately after the formation of General Electric, Morgan asked Villard to resign and supported Coffin for the presidency. With Villard's departure, Insull left the company and Edison dropped his interest in the electrical business. While three Boston financiers on the Thomson-Houston board continued as directors of the new General Electric Company, the New York financiers, including Morgan, Charles H. Coster (a Morgan partner and long treasurer of the Edison Company), Darius O. Mills, and others, dominated its board.

Coffin amalgamated the organizations of the two companies into a single centralized structure. Nearly all of the twenty subsidiaries or "subcompanies" as Coffin called them, were then liquidated.[36] In its broad outline the new structure followed the railroad model. A first vice president was placed in charge of sales, a second vice president headed the financial department, that is, the treasurer's office and the accounting, collections, and credit departments.[37] In a short time a third vice president took charge of the manufacturing and engineering department. By 1900 engineering, or more precisely, product design, had become a separate department also headed by a vice president of its own.

With the formation of the manufacturing and engineering department,

Coffin concentrated production at the three major works. Lamp production continued to be carried on in Harrison, New Jersey. Schenectady manufactured heavy specialized machinery such as large generators, motors, and turbines. The plant at Lynn turned out smaller mass-produced products including arc lights, small motors, and meters. Because each works handled different lines, each took care of its own purchasing and its own scheduling of flows into the plants. For the same reason each of two larger works had its own engineering offices and soon also its own technical laboratories. The one at Schenectady was headed by a master mathematician, Charles P. Steinmetz, and that of Lynn by Elihu Thomson.[38]

The Thomson-Houston sales organization became the core of the new sales department.[39] The branch offices of the two companies were combined. The central office, now at Schenectady, as well as the branch offices continued to have managers for each product line. In 1892 the product departments included: railway, lighting, power equipment, and supplies (such as fuse boxes, switches, sockets, which were sold to electricians and contractors as well as utilities and manufacturers). A mining division was added in 1895 and the railway one was divided into the traction and the railway division in 1908. In 1895 the company set up an international department to supervise foreign sales carried out by subsidiaries in Britain, France, Germany, and Canada.[40]

Product managers at the district offices and foreign subsidiaries reported to their superiors at headquarters. The heads of the product divisions at Schenectady all had the same function of coordinating production with distribution. For the heavy equipment and large motor departments, this meant close coordination between the sales force and the engineers designing and the plant managers processing the customers' orders. For the small motors unit, it also meant close attention to coordination of product flow. The volume was large at General Electric. By 1895 the company had over 10,000 customers and processed 104,000 separate orders.[41]

At General Electric there were, as at Standard Oil, formal committees, but they played a very different role.[42] In both companies they were used to improve communications between managers carrying out the same functional activities. But at Standard Oil the committees were made up of equals meeting to work out mutually beneficial policies and procedures for their respective subsidiary companies, and those at General Electric consisted of subordinates meeting with their bosses. The manufacturing committee, chaired by its own vice president, included the plant managers, heads of engineering departments at Lynn and Schenectady, and chiefs of the laboratories. The sales committee, also chaired by its vice president, consisted of the product managers, the manager for foreign sales, and the director of advertising. In 1903, after the formation of the central research laboratory, a comparable research advisory council was formed.[43]

At their monthly meetings these committees covered a wide variety of topics. At sales the members considered pricing, competitors' activities, market conditions, customers' needs and concerns, and the processing of major orders. In addition, the committee gave final approval to all sales contracts over $5,000 but under $25,000. The manufacturing committee reviewed the regular factory reports on costs, inventory, and output. Its members discussed product standardization, standardization of machinery, selection of plants for processing new products, and procedures for determining factory costs. In developing the last, the committee probably paid close attention to the work of Frederick W. Taylor and other practitioners of scientific management who were then developing new cost and control procedures based largely on predetermined or "standard" costing.

In addition to the monthly committee meetings, the manufacturing and sales departments also had annual and later semiannual meetings in New York or Schenectady of all the departmental managers, from the field as well as from the central office. These two- or three-day conferences, with their carefully planned agendas, provided a more personal way to maintain communication between the growing ranks of the firm's middle managers who specialized in a single function. Such channels were, in turn, supplemented by a flow of circular letters and bulletins emanating from headquarters and an even greater torrent of statistics, reports, and letters moving from the field to Schenectady.

In this way, then, the new top managers at General Electric structured the organization of the functional departments so as to assure effective communication and control throughout the organization. In the entrepreneurial firms, the departments had been built by the middle managers in an ad hoc fashion to meet current needs. At General Electric order was imposed from the top. Much of this order General Electric clearly borrowed from the railroads. The lines of authority and responsibility were defined in the same way. Railroads used departmental meetings and occasionally committees as means to improve communication between middle managers in the central office and lower-level managers in the field.

The design of top management at General Electric was even closer to that of the railroads than was its middle management. The top managers —the president and the vice presidents in charge of the major functional departments (sales, manufacturing, and finance)—were housed in adjoining offices at the company's headquarters at Schenectady. Each was assisted by a sizable staff, and each reported to a board of directors dominated by outside financiers.[44] As at Standard Oil, the executive committee of the board was the top policy-making body. But as was true on the railroads, but not at Standard Oil, that committee was completely dominated by outsiders. Only two of the salaried managers—Coffin and Eugene Griffin, the vice president in charge of sales—were board and executive committee members.

At the monthly meetings of General Electric's executive committee, it reviewed salaries, approved of organizational changes, and voted on all contracts over $25,000.[45] Although it had to approve salary increases, the selection of all but the most senior executives was left to the department managers. Because of the highly technical nature of the electrical business, only they could fully judge the qualifications of their subordinates. The committee must also have approved capital appropriations. The factories did have budgets. But neither Passer's history nor any of the other literature on that company describes the procedures used for approving budgets or allocating capital funds. The existing evidence does indicate that the executive committee at General Electric functioned much as an executive committee of a late nineteenth-century railroad or as a finance committee of a mid-twentieth-century industrial. Since it met only monthly and relied almost wholly on inside management for information, it must have been more of a policy-approving than a policy-making or planning body. Its members included busy men like J. P. Morgan and Charles H. Coster, who were in the 1890s reorganizing several of the nation's leading railroad systems. From almost its very beginning the key policy makers at General Electric were not the outside directors, not even those who served on the executive committee, but rather its full-time salaried managers, Charles Coffin and his departmental vice presidents.

In carrying out their tasks, the top salaried managers and the members of the executive committee had the assistance of fairly large financial and advisory staffs.[46] As on the railroads, the financial departments included a treasurer's office to handle external financial affairs and a comptroller's office to take care of internal ones. Because of the nature of General Electric's business, its collection and credit departments were larger than those on the railroads. Again, as in the case of the railroads, cost accounting, capital accounting, and financial accounting remained separated. Costing continued to be the province of the manufacturing department and the maufacturing committee and financial accounting that of a central accounting office.[47] In determining its assets and liabilities, as well as its costs, the accounting department continued to rely on the railroad type of renewal accounting. In the words of General Electric's 1896 report: "All expenditures for their [the company's plants] maintenance and repair are charged to operating expenses."[48] The company did, however, refine these accounts so that on the annual balance sheet, book value represented replacement value rather than original costs. After obtaining the evaluation of capital equipment, made at the time of the merger, the company began, after a couple of years, to write-down regularly, using carefully worked out, though arbitrary, depreciation rates. At the same time it added current expenditures that increased the value of plant and equipment. There is no indication that the financial department at General Electric used these figures to compute a rate of return on total investment. At General Electric earnings continued to be considered as margins of sales over costs. And the basic criterion for financial performance continued to be earnings as a percentage of sales, a figure comparable to a railroad's operating ratio. Rate of return was given only as rate of earnings to total stock outstanding.

General Electric's central office staff had a larger number of functions than did the staffs on railroads and other industrial enterprises of that day. In addition to a sizable patent and law department, the company added in 1897 a publicity bureau whose task was to publicize broader developments within the industry as well as within the company. Of more importance, General Electric, like American Cotton Oil and National Lead, came to have its own independent research department.[49] Although Thomson at Lynn and Steinmetz at Schenectady were able to concentrate on broader problems, the laboratories they headed were located at the plant sites. So their technicians were primarily involved in quality control and inspection. In 1895 Coffin set up in Schenectady a standardizing laboratory for the company as a whole. Then in 1901 he and his associates created the research laboratory. The impetus for creating this laboratory came wholly from the top salaried managers and not from financiers on the executive committee, nor from middle managers in the functional departments.[50] Under Willis R. Whitney, a German-trained chemical engineer who was recruited from the faculty of the Massachusetts Institute of Technology, the laboratory was soon doing innovative research in lighting, vacuum tubes, x-rays, and alloys. Its work was to improve products and processes, and its contributions eventually led to the expansion of the company's product line.

At General Electric, therefore, the practices of middle management first developed in the entrepreneurial firms of the 1880s were married to the methods of top management developed by the railroads. Unlike the organizers of the Standard Oil trust, those at General Electric eliminated the existing subsidiaries as units of management, replacing them with a highly centralized administrative structure. Subsidiaries were retained only as legal forms to meet specific legal requirements. The senior executives at General Electric defined the authority and responsibility of the middle managers and the channels of communication between them far more carefully than did the top executives at the entrepreneurial firms. They also built much larger central office financial and advisory staffs. Full-time salaried managers carried out the top management functions at General Electric, but the board, still dominated by outside financiers, continued to have a powerful veto power similar to that of comparable boards on the large railroad systems. Except for this continuing relationship with outside financiers, the structure built at General Electric became and still remains today a standard way of organizing a modern integrated industrial enterprise.

United States Rubber Company

General Electric adopted the centralized, functionally department-alized operating structure even more readily than did American Cotton Oil and National Lead, not only because many senior executives were trained as engineers and its financiers were experienced students of railroad organization, but also because the merger was one of integrated firms that already had functional departments. Except in the metal-working industries, nearly all mergers were between single-unit, nonintegrated manufacturing firms. Integration came only after combination. And many firms moved far more slowly than had Standard Oil, American Cotton Oil, and National Lead from horizontal combination to vertical integration. Directors, like those of American Sugar and the earlier corn products companies, were reluctant to abandon the older strategy of horizontal combination. These efforts to maintain the status quo delayed still longer the adoption of a new administrative structure. Constituent companies continued as operating as well as legal units. The heads of the consolidated enterprise paid little heed to administrative problems and needs and thus rarely looked to other firms or other industries for administrative models.

The United States Rubber Company was just such a merger. Although that company was formed in 1892, eight months before General Electric came into being, its managers took two decades to perfect an organizational structure comparable to that of General Electric. The manufacturers who put together the merger had little engineering training, and the financiers who assisted them had little direct connection with railroad management. Neither paid attention to long-term strategy or organizational structure.

In 1892, after the merger, the many small rubber footwear and glove companies continued to operate much as they had done before consolidation. In the following year, the holding company made a move to centralize purchasing.[51] It then started to tighten its control over the manufacturing plants of its subsidiaries. By 1895 it began to set up its own branch regional sales offices to sell to jobbers. Soon it was buying out large wholesalers and transforming them into branch stores managed by salaried executives. A little later it began to integrate backward by building its own felting, wool boot, and boot hardware plants. Nevertheless, as it inched toward vertical integration and administrative centralization, it continued a policy of buying out competition. Its most important purchase came in 1898 when it obtained control of the Boston Rubber Shoe Company, an aggressive entrepreneurial enterprise that had built an effective national sales organization (with one major office abroad) and had remained the largest independent in the industry.[52]

As the rubber company's annual reports bring out, administrative centralization was often painful. Formerly independent factory owners disliked taking orders from the central office. The heads of selling companies who became salaried managers had the same response. The annual report of 1896, in reviewing the company's policies, noted that: "It may be that thereby some local interests have been antagonized and possibly some feelings of antagonism developed in individuals, but your management has sought to move on lines of general benefit without any personal motives."[53] By 1901, almost a decade after its formation, the United States Rubber Company was still in the process of transition.

With the coming of a new president in May 1901, the company's top management began for the first time to think explicitly about strategy and structure.[54] The new man, Samuel P. Colt, was an honors graduate of the Massachusetts Institute of Technology who, after some legal training and political and industrial experience, took charge of a rubber company that joined the 1892 consolidation. On becoming president, he decided to transform United States Rubber into a modern industrial corporation. In marketing he called for a major expansion of the branch stores that did the company's wholesaling and appointed a manager with a separate office at sales headquarters to administer these units. In purchasing he formed the General Rubber Company in 1904 to buy crude rubber. This organization soon had offices in Liverpool and London and the rubber-growing areas of Brazil and the Dutch East Indies. In 1909 the company obtained the first of its rubber plantations in Sumatra. As early as 1904, the board decided to produce its own sulphuric acid plant for its rubber reclaiming processes and to have its own fleet of tank cars. Then, to house the enlarged company headquarters, Colt moved at the end of 1904 into a large building at 42 Broadway.

The organization chart of September 1902 (figure 9) outlines Colt's first attempt to define the rubber company's organization structure.[55] It emphasizes the company's evolutionary development. The constituent companies still retained operating functions as well as legal status. Middle management at U.S. Rubber was still small in numbers, and the lines of communication and authority were fuzzy. Boston Rubber Shoe had not yet been brought fully into the larger organization. Supervision of the plants was minimal. The company continued to rely on regular meetings of the plant superintendents, started in 1893, to set basic policies and procedures.[56] The central sales staff, larger than that of manufacturing, included an advertising manager and a traffic office responsible for the coordination of the flow of goods from the factories to the wholesalers and in some cases large retailers. Financial accounts were not yet consolidated. Many of the operating units were apparently financially as well as legally autonomous. In 1902 uniform accounting was only beginning to be instituted throughout the company.[57]

Although its top management was still small in 1902, the company's central office organization was becoming like that of General Electric. A first vice president had general supervision of operations, the second vice president of finance. Its financial staffs were growing. An executive committee had become the top decision-making unit. Unlike General Electric's, it consisted of full-time managers. In fact, a majority of the board members were already such "insiders."[58]

Once Colt and his managers had their company well on the road to vertical integration and administrative centralization, they turned to diversification as a way to use fully their existing facilities and organization. The production of belting, hose, insulating and flooring materials, sheeting and other industrial rubber products, and, above all, tires, for the new automobile market promised a different and steadier demand than that for footwear, whose market was seasonal and dependent on the weather. The development of such lines promised to make use of the company's worldwide purchasing organization, its new chemical company, some of its production facilities, and its central office advertising and traffic departments. So, in 1905, United States Rubber purchased the Rubber Goods Manufacturing Company, a merger formed in 1892 and enlarged and reorganized in 1899.[59] Colt quickly consolidated the Rubber Goods Company's manufacturing operations and set up a small, separate sales organization to sell products that went to very different markets than did footwear. Tires were also sold through this same organization. Then, as the demand for tires boomed, the sales network was greatly enlarged.[60]

Not until 1912 did the company form a separate, central Development Department. Headed by Raymond B. Price, a chemist who had been in charge of the testing and control laboratories (the first established in

Figure 9. Organization chart of United States Rubber Company, September 1902

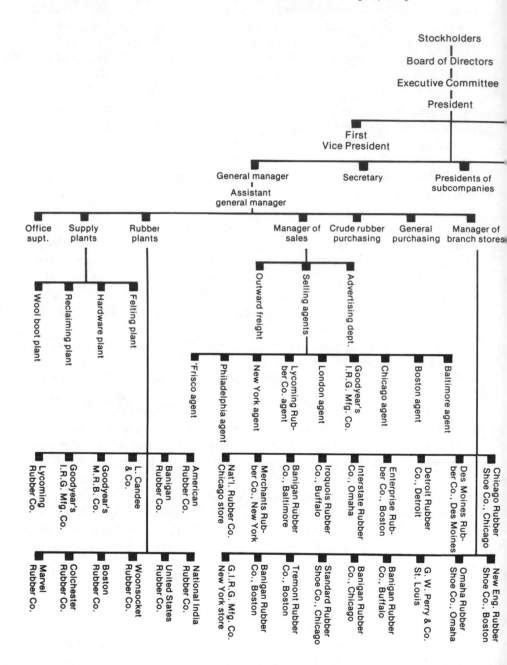

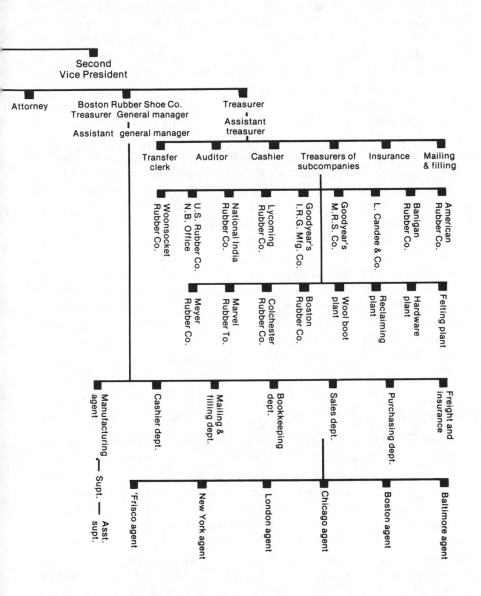

Source: United States Rubber Company Archives.

the industry), the department took over administration of the company's chemical activities. It quickly set up its central research laboratories and then extended its functions to include research in rubber growing, crude rubber processing, as well as product improvement.[61]

The top decision makers at United States Rubber, like those at Standard Oil, rarely thought in terms of organization qua organization. Even after Samuel Colt's appearance, little careful and systematic attention was given to organization problems. Offices were built, managers hired, and responsibilities defined in order to handle immediate and usually pressing needs that resulted first from the company's forward and backward integration and then its expansion into new markets.

As the company's organization chart for 1917 (figure 10) reveals, its structure was moving toward what became defined in the 1920s as the multidivisional form. By 1917 the company managed footwear, its original business, through an integrated division. On the other hand, tires and industrial rubber goods continued to be sold through a single sales force, even though they went to very different markets. The number of top managers had increased and the central staff included offices to handle purchasing, research and development, traffic, advertising, legal affairs, and finance. But the relationships between the central staff and the divisional managers and the staff and the general executives on the executive committee were not yet clear. Overlapping functions and activities existed, as well as confused lines of communication, authority, and responsibility. These remained until the company underwent a complete administrative reorganization in the late 1920s. The experience of United States Rubber, like that of Standard Oil, suggests that unless close attention was paid to organization matters, administrative confusion resulted.

E. I. Du Pont de Nemours Powder Company

At the Du Pont Company, the transformation from horizontal combination to vertical integration and from a loose agglomeration of plants to a centralized functionally departmentalized structure came with speed and precision.[62] Its creators gave careful thought to organizational design. These men were trained engineers who knew firsthand the most advanced administrative practices on the railroads and in the steel, electrical, and machinery industries. Two—Coleman du Pont and Arthur Moxham—had managed the Johnson and Lorain Steel Company that built steel track and electric-powered equipment for street railways. In 1896 Coleman du Pont had hired Frederick W. Taylor to install a new cost and control system at plants in Johnstown, Pennsylvania and Lorain, Ohio.[63] A third, Pierre du Pont, came to appreciate these management procedures when he joined his cousin at Lorain in 1899. Pierre and Coleman, like their cousin, Alfred du Pont, had been educated at the Massachusetts Institute of Technology. Other Du Pont executives—the Haskell brothers (J. Amory and Harry), Hamilton Barksdale, and Major William G. Ramsay—had comparable educations at engineering schools. Their training and experience fitted them exceptionally well for organization building.

The opportunity for the three young du Pont cousins—Alfred, Coleman, and Pierre—to reorganize their family firm, and at the same time the American explosives industry, came early in 1902 with the death of the senior partner, Eugene du Pont. At that time, the Du Pont Company was small indeed. It had only six stockholders, all du Ponts, and it worked closely with a number of other small family firms to control the industry through two horizontal combinations.[64] The first, the Gunpowder Trade Association, had, since its formation in 1872, set prices and output of the traditional product, black powder. That cartel had remained effective for more than a generation, because the larger firms in the association—Du Pont, Laflin & Rand, and Hazard—had purchased each other's stock and also that of the smaller members of the association. In the newer dynamite business these same companies maintained control through another horizontal combination—the Eastern Dynamite Company, a holding company formed in 1895.

After purchasing control of the family firm in 1902, the three cousins discarded the policy of horizontal combination for one of administrative centralization and vertical integration. They agreed that the attempts to control competition by price cutting and buying up competitors were unnecessarily costly. Such a strategy meant that the leading firms in the industry often had to purchase unplanned and unwanted plant capacity that was rarely located in the place best suited to meet market and supply conditions and rarely equipped with the most modern facilities. By early 1903 the cousins had devised a plan to merge the members of the Gunpowder Trade Association and the constituent companies in the Eastern Dynamite Company into a single consolidated enterprise—the E. I. Du Pont de Nemours Powder Company. Once the legal arrangements had been completed, they planned to consolidate manufacturing and then to build their own sales and purchasing organizations.

Their aim was to dominate the industry by running the most efficient mills as fully and as steadily as possible and so to reduce their unit costs to levels that small competitors could not achieve. In carrying out this plan they listened closely to the advice of one of their number, Arthur Moxham, who urged them not to take on more than 60 percent of the industry's capacity. His argument was not based on any legal constraint

Figure 10. Organization chart of United States Rubber Company, January 1917

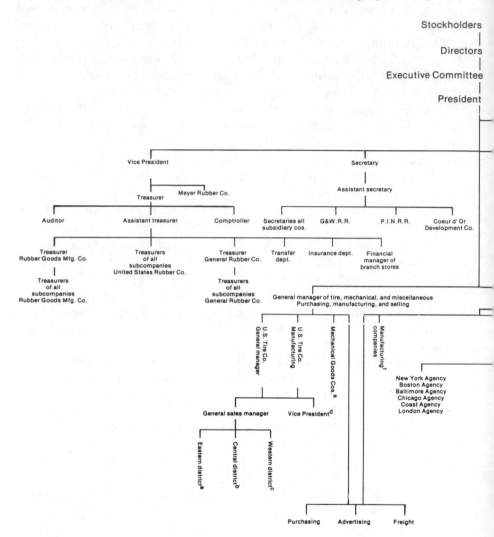

a Atlanta, Ga.; Baltimore, Md.; Birmingham, Ala.; Boston, Mass.: Buffalo, N.Y.; Charlotte, N.C.; Hartford, Conn.: Jacksonville, Fla; Newark, N.J.; New York, N.Y.; Philadelphia, Pa.; Pittsburgh, Pa.; Providence, R.I.; Richmond, Va.; Rochester, N.Y.; Savannah, Ga.; Syracuse, N.Y.; Washington, D.C.; Wilkesbarre, Pa.; Worcester, Mass.

b Chicago, Ill.; Cincinnati, Ohio; Cleveland, Ohio; Columbia, Ohio; Dallas, Texas; Dayton, Ohio; Denver, Col.; Des Moines, Iowa; Detroit, Mich.; Houston, Texas; Indianapolis, Ind.; Kansas City, Mo.; Louisville, Ky.; Milwaukee, Wis.; Minneapolis, Minn.; New Orleans, La.; San Antonio, Texas; St. Louis, Mo.; Toledo, Ohio.

c Butte, Mont.; Fresno, Cal.; Los Angeles, Cal.; Portland, Ore.; Salt Lake City, Utah; San Francisco, Cal.; Seattle, Wash.

d Morgan & Wright; Hartford Rub. Wks. Co.; G. & J. Tire Co.; Revere Rubber Co., Providence, report to Vice President.

e Hartford Rub. Wks. Co.; Morgan & Wright; G. & J. Tire Co.; Peerless Rub. Mfg. Co.; N.Y. Belt & Pack. Co.; Mech. Rub. Co. Cleveland; Mech. Rub. Co. Chicago; Sawyer Belting Co.; Stoughton Rubber Co.; Fabric Fire Hose Co.; Mech. Fabric Co.; Can. Cons. Rubber Co.; Eureka Fire Hose Co.; Revere Rubber Co. Chelsea.

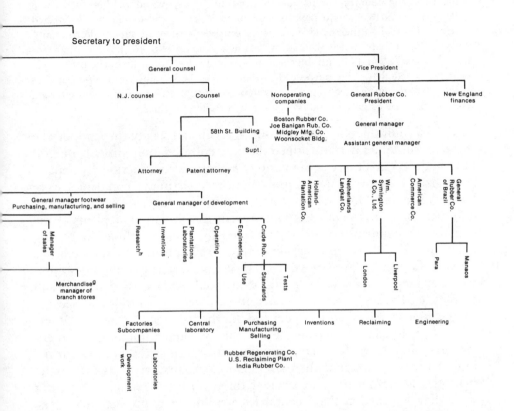

Secretary to president

General counsel

N.J. counsel   Counsel

Vice President

Nonoperating companies   General Rubber Co. President   New England finances

Boston Rubber Co.
Joe Banigan Rub. Co.
Midgley Mfg. Co.
Woonsocket Bldg.

General manager

58th St. Building   Supt.   Assistant general manager

Attorney   Patent attorney

General manager footwear
Purchasing, manufacturing, and selling

General manager of development

Manager of sales

Research[h]   Inventions   Plantations Laboratories   Operating   Engineering   Crude Rub.

Use   Standards   Tests

Holland-American Plantation Co.   Netherlands Langkat Co.   Wm. Symington & Co. Ltd.   American Commerce Co.   General Rubber Co. of Brazil

London   Liverpool

Para   Manaos

Merchandise[g] manager of branch stores

Factories Subcompanies   Central laboratory   Purchasing Manufacturing Selling   Inventions   Reclaiming   Engineering

Development work   Laboratories

Rubber Regenerating Co.
U.S. Reclaiming Plant
India Rubber Co.

[f] American Rub. Co.; Boston Rub. Shoe Co.; L. Candee & Co.; Goodyear's M.R.S. Co.; Goodyear's I.R.G. Co.; Naugatuck Chem. Co.; National Ind. Rub. Co.; N.J. Factory; Woonsocket Rub. Co.; Shoe Hardware Co.; Mishawaka W. Mfg. Co.; Hastings Wool Boot Co.; Can. Cons. Rubber Co.; Lawrence Felting Co.

[g] Amsterdam Rubber Co.; Banigan, Baltimore; Banigan, Boston; Banigan, Buffalo; Banigan, Chicago; Chicago Rubber Co.; Columbus Rubber Co.; Des Moines Rub. Co.; Detroit Rubber Co.; Duck Brand Co.; Enterprise Rubber Co.; G.I.R. Selling Co.; Hubmark, Boston; Hubmark, Detroit; Hubmark, N.Y. City; Inter-State Rub. Co.; Iroquois Rubber Co.; Maryland Rubber Co.; Maumee Rubber Co.; Merchants Rubber Co.; New Eng. Rub. Shoe Co.; Omaha Rubber Co.; George W. Perry; Pittsburgh Rubber Co.; Rochester Rubber Co.; St. Paul Rubber Co.; Springfield Rub. Co.; Stand. Rub. Shoe Co.; Syracuse Rubber Co.; Tremont Rubber Co.

[h] Departments for Colloids; Textiles; Apparatus; Vulcanization; Construction.

Source: United States Rubber Company Archives.

but the judgment that a larger percentage would not permit them to obtain the maximum advantages of vertical integration. Moxham had written Coleman du Pont in June 1903:

> I have been urging upon our people the following arguments. If we could by any measure buy out all competition and have an absolute monopoly in the field, it would not pay us. The essence of manufacture is steady and full product. The demand for the country for powder is variable. If we owned all therefore when slack times came we would have to curtail product to the extent of diminished demands. If on the other hand we control only 60% of it all and made that 60% cheaper than others, when slack times came we could still keep *our* capital employed to *the full* and our product to this maximum by taking from the other 40% what was needed for this purpose. In other words you could count upon always running full if you make cheaply and control only 60%, whereas, if you own it all, when slack times came you could only run a curtailed product.[65]

To carry out this objective of assuring a full and steady throughput, the three cousins quickly transformed the new consolidation into what might be considered an ideal type of integrated, centralized, functionally departmentalized enterprise. Where possible, the constituent companies were legally dissolved. Only in a few cases did minority stockholders or existing contractual arrangements delay or prevent dissolution. The plants of the constituent companies were then placed into one of three "operating departments"—black powder, high explosives (dynamite), and smokeless powder (a product even newer than dynamite). The existing sales agencies were replaced by branch offices, manned by salaried managers and employees. Because the new high explosives were dangerous and because their efficient use required special skill, the salesmen of the du Pont-controlled dynamite companies were usually trained mining or civil engineers. Their sales offices and organization served as the nucleus for the branch office network of the consolidation. At first, three assistant sales managers at headquarters supervised three different regional areas, but soon they became, in the General Electric manner, product managers. Assistant sales managers headed the black powder and dynamite divisions. The district offices were also divided along these two major product lines. A third headquarters unit was responsible for the sale of smokeless powder propellants to the army and navy. A fourth supervised the sale of rifle and shotgun smokeless powder, which were sold to ammunition makers.

The sales department and the three operating departments at Du Pont were organized in much the same way as those at General Electric. They had their vice presidents in charge, their staffs, and their department committees. Each of the operating departments had its own engineering, research, control, personnel, and accounting staffs. The sales department staff included an advertising bureau and an information bureau.[66] The latter provided a constant flow of information on sales of the company and of its competitors. That office, which became the trade record division, also supplied district managers with detailed forms and procedures to record and analyze changing demand. Besides their regular committee meetings, these departments (again following the General Electric pattern) held semiannual meetings of all headquarters and field managers in Wilmington, where papers devoted to a wide range of departmental policies, problems, and concerns were read and discussed.[67]

Because its manufacturing processes were similar to those at United States Rubber and the entrepreneurial firms processing agricultural products, the Du Pont Company purchased relatively few items in massive volume. So, like these other enterprises, it immediately set up an "essential materials department" to do its purchasing. In a short time that department owned and operated mines and other sources of raw material.[68] By 1908, for example, the company was consuming one-third of the glycerine sold in the United States or one-sixth of the world's supply, as well as 30 percent of the Chilean nitrates sold in this country or 5 percent of the total world's supply. By 1911 the company owned its own glycerine and acid-making facilities and had purchased large nitrate fields in Chile. As was true at American Tobacco and the meat packers, it had a smaller purchasing department to buy in volume the supplies and stock other than its basic raw materials. In 1904 it enlarged the traffic department, placing it under an experienced industrialist, Frank G. Tallman.[69] Tallman was soon chartering ships to carry nitrates and purchasing special railroad cars to move acids, nitrates, and finished explosives. Tallman, working closely with the directors of the operating and sales departments, took the major responsibility for coordinating the flow of materials from the nitrate fields of Chile through the processes of production to the customers— building contractors, mining and transportation companies, military buyers, and makers of rifle and shotgun shells.

As in the case of the other mergers, the executive committee of the board ran the company. The consolidation had been financed from within, so, as was the case at Standard Oil, no outsiders sat on the board. That board included the three cousins, members of the older generation of du Ponts who had sold out, and able powder men from other of the merged companies, including J. Amory Haskell from Laflin & Rand, Frank Connable from Chattanooga Powder, and Colonel Edmund G. Buckner from International Smokeless. The committee met weekly rather than monthly as it did at General Electric. It consisted of the president, Coleman du Pont, and the vice presidents in charge of the three operating departments, the sales department, and the smaller departments for development and finance.[70]

The committee members, except for the president, therefore, had two sets of responsibilities. As vice presidents they were accountable for the performance of their respective functional departments. As members of the executive committee, they were charged with managing the company as a whole. Under the original plan of organization outlined by Moxham in 1903, the second task was to have precedence. By this plan each vice president was given a departmental director who was specifically charged with handling the day-to-day departmental operations. The vice president was then to concentrate on overall policy making, planning, and evaluation. Thus the executive committee at Du Pont differed from that at General Electric in that it consisted entirely of full-time, experienced salaried managers. It differed from that at Standard Oil in that its members appreciated the distinction between day-to-day administration and long-term policy making and explicitly expected to devote their attention to the latter.

In carrying out its tasks the executive committee relied not only on the regular detailed monthly reports from the operating and sales departments, and many special departmental reports, but also on a wide variety of data supplied by the development department and increasingly sophisticated information on costs and capital accounts generated by the financial offices.[71] The development department at Du Pont, headed by Arthur Moxham, the most imaginative of the new consolidation's founders, was carrying out by 1904 what United States Rubber was only beginning to achieve in 1917. The Du Pont development department had three divisions. The experimental division supervised the company's control research laboratories set up near Wilmington, and the raw materials division kept a careful eye on the company's basic supplies. In the years after 1903 it provided information for and helped to plan and carry out the strategy of backward integration. A third unit, the competitive division, supplemented and provided a check on the sales department information on markets and competitors. All three of these divisions of the development department provided the executive committee with a source of information that was independent of the marketing and production departments. Finally, the development department was charged with reviewing and suggesting improvements in the company's organizational arrangements.

The new financial offices at Du Pont, similar to those at General Electric, included treasurer's, accounting, auditing, and credit and collection departments, and two smaller units—salary and the real estate departments.[72] Under the command of young Pierre du Pont the financial staff grew rapidly as the consolidation was completed. An office force of twelve in the summer of 1903 had grown to over two hundred a year later. The first tasks that Pierre and his staff faced involved consolidation of the accounts of the firms coming into the merger, development of uniform accounting procedures for all the company's plants and offices, and obtaining firm control of a steady supply of working capital.

In carrying out this work, Pierre du Pont and his division heads pioneered in the ways of modern industrial accounting. They were among the first industrialists to end the long separation between cost, capital, and financial accounting. They did so, in part at least, by replacing renewal accounting with modern industrial asset accounting. By 1910 they had developed accounting methods and controls that were to become standard procedure for twentieth-century industrial enterprises.

In cost accounting the financial office concentrated on obtaining more accurate information on overhead costs.[73] Russell Dunham, Pierre's senior accounting executive, had worked with Frederick W. Taylor at Bethlehem before coming to Du Pont. Pierre and Coleman had become intimately acquainted with Taylor's costing and control methods at Lorain Steel. Using these methods Pierre's subordinates improved their analysis of overhead costs, including such indirect labor costs as those of foremen, managers, and inspectors and such indirect material costs as those of maintenance, depreciation, taxes, power, and light. They also included costs of accident insurance, interest charges on raw materials, stocks, and other inventories, and depreciation on facilities other than plant and equipment. They did not, however, at this time set up a full standard cost system based on a standard volume as a percentage of total capacity. In addition to determining these "mill costs" (the total of direct and indirect costs), the financial staff worked out the administrative costs of maintaining the development, legal, purchasing, and real estate departments and the allocation of these costs to each of the company's products. Next, close attention was paid to determination of actual selling and purchasing costs. The treasurer's office was soon preparing for the executive committee monthly cost sheets that allocated mill, administrative, selling, and transportation (freight and delivery costs) for each of the thirteen products the company manufactured. They used this continuous flow of data on unit costs to monitor the performance of the individual operating units, of the functional departments, and of the company as a whole.

After defining costs carefully, Pierre du Pont and his financial managers turned to a more precise definition of profit and with it a more precise criterion for evaluating financial performance. They considered as inadequate the standard definition of profits developed by General Electric and other new industrials—that is, earnings (revenue from sales minus costs) as a percentage either of sales or costs. (This was, in turn, a modification of the railroads' operating ratio.) Such a criterion was incomplete, they argued, because it failed to indicate the rate of return on capital invested. "The true test of whether the profit is too great or too small," Dunham once wrote, "is the rate of return on the money invested in the business and not the per cent of profit on the cost."[74] For, as Dunham further pointed out, "A commodity requiring an inexpensive plant might, when sold only ten per cent above its cost, show a higher rate of return on the investment than another commodity sold at double its cost, but manufactured in an expensive plant."

To obtain such a rate of return, the basic problem was to develop accurate data on investment in fixed capital. This could not be done by using the renewal accounting procedures employed by the railroads and copied by other new large industrials, for by this practice many capital expenditures were charged to operating expenses. To obtain an accurate picture of capital invested, Pierre carefully reviewed the valuation made of all properties coming into the merger in 1903. He then had these entered into a new general ledger account for "permanent investment." Next, his department devised capital appropriation procedures so that all new construction was charged (any dismantled assets were credited) to this account at cost. At the same time the financial department obtained increasingly accurate data on inventories, accounts receivable, securities, and cash, which made up the working capital account. On the basis of this information on fixed and working capital, Pierre's department was by 1904 presenting the executive committee with monthly figures on costs, income, and rate of return on total capital investment for each of the company's thirteen products. From almost the beginning of the modern Du Pont Company its executive committee was using rate of return on capital invested as a basic management tool for both evaluation and planning.

Before World War I the financial office had further refined this tool so that it reflected more accurately the speed and volume of the flow of materials through the company's facilities. Donaldson Brown, one of Pierre's subordinates, was the first to point out that if prices remained the same, the rate of return on invested capital increased as volume rose and decreased as it fell.[75] The higher the throughput and stock-turn, the greater the rate of return. Brown termed this rate of flow "turnover." He defined it as value of sales divided by total investment. Brown then related turnover to earnings as a percentage of sales (still the standard definition of profit in American industry). He did this by multiplying turnover by profit so defined, which gave a rate of return that reflected the intensity with which the enterprise's resources were being used. This formula devised by Brown (figure 11) is still the method employed by the Du Pont Company and most other American business enterprises to define rate of return.

Figure 11. The Du Pont Company: relationship of factors affecting return on investment

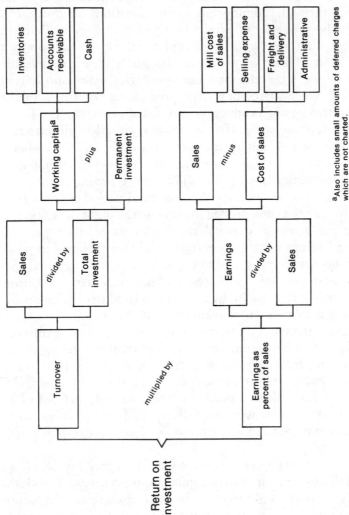

Source: T. C. Davis, "How the du Pont Organization Appraises Its Perform-ance," in American Management Association, *Financial Management Series*, no. 94:7 (1950).

These accounting innovations at Du Pont were significant achieve-ments. They helped to lay the base for modern asset accounting by effec-tively combining and consolidating for the first time the three basic types of accounting—financial, capital, and cost. By devising the concept of turnover, the Du Pont managers were able to account specifically, and again for the first time, for that part of the basic contribution made by modern management to profitability and productivity—the savings achieved through administrative coordination of flows of materials through the processes of production and distribution. With these innovations, modern managers had completed the essential tools by which the visible hand of management was able to replace the invisible hand of market forces in coordinating and monitoring economic activities.

As they were sharpening their procedures for the administration of current processes of production and distribution, the Du Pont managers were also devising and perfecting those required to allocate resources for future production and distribution. As early as November 1904, the executive committee's members decided that they were not appropriating capital systematically enough.[76] They were having increasing difficulty in deciding how best to meet the many and varied calls for funds. By the end of 1904 capital was needed to increase the plant capacity (particularly to meet the growing demand for explosives in the western states), to purchase Chilean nitrate properties, to obtain facilities to produce glycerine and other supplies, and to expand the research laboratories. At that moment an opportunity appeared to obtain subsidiaries in Europe. Capital expenditures in turn had to be carefully related to dividend policy and the continuing availability of working capital. As a result of prolonged discussion and disagreement on how much to allocate to these different alternatives, the executive committee asked the treasurer to formulate detailed capital appropriation procedures. Because Pierre du Pont was out of the country investigating investment opportunities in Europe and Chile during most of 1905, these procedures were not fully defined or acted upon until early 1906. They were not fully applied until the company's financial program recovered from a temporary disarray caused by the panic of 1907.[77]

Under the new procedures, the committee agreed to devote a minimum of one full meeting a month to capital appropriations. Agendas were to be carefully prepared and reports to be as precise as possible. Routine investment decisions, like routine operating ones, were to be turned over to a new operative committee made up of departmental directors. Limits on investment requiring executive committee approval were raised from $5,000 to $10,000. All requests were to have, in addition to detailed information as to estimated rate of return, elaborate blueprints and cost figures. Plant sites required the approval of the sales, purchasing, and traffic departments to assure that the greatest comparative advantage had been obtained in determining the location and design of new facilities. Most important of all, Pierre set up an office in his department under his younger brother, Irénée, with the full-time task of reviewing and coordinating expenditures; reporting regularly to the executive committee and the treasurer on amounts actually expended; and keeping the "permanent investment" account up to date. Irénée's staff was also to make a preliminary review of departmental proposals and budgets before they were presented to the executive committee. Such controls permitted the company to carry out a policy that there "be no expenditures for additions to the earning equipment if the same amount of money could be applied to some better purpose in another branch of the company's business."[78]

After 1906 Pierre and the executive committee continued to systematize the making and approval of both operating and capital budgets. The treasurer's office also began to make long- and short-term financial forecasts. The most important of these, the forecast of the net earnings, determined the maximum amount available for new capital expenditures from retained earnings.[79] Such forecasts were computed by multiplying sales department monthly estimates of sales by the accounting department's estimates of net profit per unit for each product. By combining these data on net earnings with information provided by the office responsible for capital appropriations, the financial office was soon sending to the executive committee monthly forecasts of the company's cash position for each of the next twelve months. These forecasts were, of course, checked regularly against actual results. Such information increased the possibilities for rational choice between alternative investments and alternative methods of financing them.

In 1911, during a minor reorganization of the company's organization structure, Pierre and Coleman du Pont enlarged the central office staff.[80] They set up a central office engineering department to design, build, or contract for major maintenance, repair, and construction of new plants, offices, and other facilities for the company as a whole. Chemical research was taken from the development department and became an independent unit of its own. So, too, did the office handling real estate, which had been in Pierre du Pont's treasurer's office. With the great expansion of production at the beginning of World War I, the executive committee set up a central personnel department to set policies for recruitment, training, and promotion of workers and to administer the company's pension program.[81] Soon a publicity department, the forerunner of the public relations department, was reporting to the president.

With the rounding out of the staff and the perfection of capital appropriations procedures, the Du Pont Company employed nearly all of the basic offices and methods used today in the general management of modern industrial enterprise. Top management at the majority of large industrial firms became, as it had at Du Pont, collegial or group management. It became professional in that it consisted of full-time, salaried managers who spent their careers in the industry in which their company operated. These managers soon came to have the assistance of large central office staffs similar to those at Du Pont. They relied on their central laboratories for innovation in product and process and on their financial offices for the same kind of cost and capital accounting that had been developed at Du Pont. Asset accounting quickly took the place of renewal accounting as the standard form in large industrial enterprises. Rate of return on capital investment became a widely used criterion of performance; and the use of capital budgets and financial forecasts became standard procedure in the allocation of resources. Well before World War I executives at the Du Pont Company had drawn together and perfected methods of business management that had their beginnings on the railroads and were further developed by the mass marketers, by the practitioners of scientific factory management, by the managers of the early entrepreneurial enterprises, and by consolidators of the first mergers.

The growing supremacy of managerial enterprise

In 1917 few American industrial enterprises had as modern a management as Du Pont. Many of the mergers were, in the manner of United States Rubber, still slowly working out such administrative structures and procedures. A number of those enterprises that had grown by internal expansion rather than merger were still controlled by entrepreneurs who created them or by their descendants. Within a generation, however, the type of management begun at General Electric and perfected at Du Pont had become standard for the administration of modern large-scale enterprise in American industry.

The methods developed and perfected by these early mergers were widely adopted because they permitted their managers to perform effectively the two basic functions of modern business enterprise—the coordination and monitoring of current production and distribution of goods and the allocation of resources for future production and distribution. In carrying out the first, Du Pont, General Electric, and to a lesser extent, Standard Oil and United States Rubber, improved on existing methods of administrative coordination. In devising ways to perform the second function, these firms were innovators.

In the administration of current operations, these firms perfected ways to assure a faster and more efficient flow of materials through the enterprise. They did so by defining more precisely the duties of the senior executives of the functional departments, those directly responsible for the performance of the middle managers; by instituting sophisticated accounting and other control systems; and by structuring the departments so as to assure clearer and closer communications between central headquarters and the operating units in the field. These new structures and controls also permitted the top managers to evaluate with more precision the performance of the middle and lower-level managers and to select for top management with more assurance.

In allocating resources for future production and distribution, the new methods extended the time horizon of the top managers. Entrepreneurs who personally managed large industrials tended, like the owners of smaller, traditional enterprises, to make their plans on the basis of current market and business conditions. By setting up budgets and other systematic capital appropriation procedures, the managers at Du Pont and other consolidated firms began to look much farther into the future. The central sales and purchasing offices provided forecasts of future demand and availability of supplies; the treasurer's office did the same for financial conditions; the development department provided information on changing technology. Such planning became more and more indispensable as both the capital investment and the time needed to build mass production plants grew. Investments involving tens of millions of dollars and requiring two to three years to come into production required careful study of long-term trends if they were to provide satisfactory rates of return.

The creation of a large central office of top managers and their staffs further sharpened the distinction between ownership and control. The men who engineered the merger, their close associates, and their families were unable to provide the large number of managers needed to operate the consolidated enterprise. As the early leaders in the enterprise retired, they were replaced by salaried career managers. By 1917 each of the four companies had become, in differing degrees, managerial enterprises. At Standard Oil the transformation was complete. There the Harknesses, Pratts, Rockefellers, and other large stockholders no longer even sat on the board of directors. As the Jersey's legal counsel wrote to a colleague in 1913: "Within a very short time, Harkness and Pratt resign and their places will be filled by people who own very little of the stock. As you know, the Rockefellers, who as large holders of the stock controlled the company as directors for more than thirty years, have absolutely retired, and are simply receiving their dividends and voting at the annual meetings."[82] At United States Rubber the separation between ownership and management was not so sharp. Some representative of large investors still sat on the board; but the inside managers dominated it. The six top salaried managers (the president and the five vice presidents) were all board members, and the executive committee included four of these managers and only one other board member. At General Electric financiers and representatives of major investors still made up the majority of the board. Those from Boston had now outnumbered the New York bankers. But by World War I, Coffin, the veteran professional manager, had become the board's chairman. After the war the number of insiders on General Electric's board grew larger and the number of financiers declined. By 1925 40 percent of the board were professional managers. In the 1930s senior managers of other large industrial enterprises began to take the place of financiers on the board.

At Du Pont, owners still managed in 1917. Pierre and his brothers maintained control through an intricate network of holding companies. Nevertheless, the only du Ponts to serve on the executive committee were experienced managers. Graduates of M.I.T. or other engineering schools, they had spent years with the company. In fact, Pierre's insistence that no du Pont serve in middle or top management unless he was fully qualified helped to bring on a bitter family fight. Even so, the seven men on the executive committee from its beginning included three or four non-family members. By the 1930s top managers outnumbered the family on the Du Pont board.

In recent years Du Pont, so long cited as a preeminent family firm, has become managerial. Today literally hundreds of du Ponts and du Ponts-in-law are eligible to serve as managers. Yet only a tiny handful work for the company. Only one du Pont now serves in the ranks of top management. The family continues to enjoy a substantial share of the company's profits. Five or six members sit on the company's twenty-five-man board of directors. Still owners, du Ponts no longer manage. They no longer make significant industrial decisions.

The story has been similar for the successful integrated enterprise that became large through internal growth rather than through merger. As their markets and output expanded and as they began to compete with better organized managerial enterprises, the entrepreneurial firms began to enlarge their central financial and advisory staff, to restructure their finance departments, and to add new staff offices for development, personnel, and public relations. Members of the families of the founder and builders normally remained active in top management only if they were tested managers with years of experience within the administrative ranks.

In these companies and in the earlier managerial enterprises where families or investment banks or other financial intermediaries held large blocks of stock, the owners and their representatives kept a watch over their investment as members of the board's finance committee. That committee regularly reviewed major capital investments and the general financial condition of the company. But, as in the case of the executive committee on railroads and utilities, its power was essentially negative.

Its members could say no, but they were rarely in the position to propose alternative policies and programs. If the career managers performed poorly, they had little choice but to hire another set of managers. They could not manage the enterprise themselves. Because there were fewer outsiders and more insiders on the boards of industrials than on the boards of railroads, financiers and large investors rarely had even the limited influence representatives of investment banking houses had on the large railroad systems.

By 1917 modern industrial enterprise was flourishing in industries where administrative coordination had proved more efficient than market coordination. By that time the managers of these enterprises had created the organization and devised and improved the procedures required to coordinate and monitor day-to-day production and distribution and to allocate capital for future economic activity. By then these enterprises were becoming managerial. The career managers who were beginning to make decisions at the top as well as middle and lower levels were beginning to look on themselves as professionals.

Nevertheless, in 1917 modern industrial enterprise still had structural weaknesses, and the managerial class was only beginning to become professionalized. The centralized, functionally departmentalized form developed at Du Pont and other early managerial enterprises had two serious faults. Both affected the ability of their managers to carry on the two basic functions of the modern industrial enterprise—coordinating of flows and allocating of resources.

First, administrative coordination of flows was only crudely calibrated to short-term fluctuations in demand. Sudden changes in demand threatened inventory surpluses or shortages at each stage in the flow through the enterprise.

Second, in the centralized, functionally departmentalized organizations, top managers responsible for long-term allocations continued to concentrate on day-to-day operations. This was true even at Du Pont, where the functional vice presidents on the executive committee were specifically responsible for overall company affairs and their directors for those of their functional departments. Despite repeated admonitions from Coleman and then Pierre du Pont, these top managers preferred to give priority to the more immediate problems and issues of departmental operations than to what seemed vague and less pressing concerns—long-term planning and appraisal.[83] As specialists, these top executives nearly always continued to judge company policy from the point of view of their specialties and their departments. In the new industrial enterprises, policy making and planning were thus often the result of negotiations between interested parties rather than responses to overall company needs.

Top managers too often did not have the time, interest, or information required to make effective top management decisions.

Moreover, top executives in some of the nation's leading industrial enterprises did not yet believe that the centralized functionally departmentalized form met their operating needs. Others, who had adopted that structure, felt that they were outgrowing it. The largest American industrials, United States Steel and Standard Oil, had never attempted to place all their operating units under the administrative control of a single set of functional departments, nor had more recent mergers, such as Union Carbide and General Motors. Other companies, including Armour, Swift, and United States Rubber, which had expanded by adding new products for new markets, were becoming constrained by the centralized structure. They had begun to set up semiautonomous, integrated divisions to coordinate the flow of goods to the different markets. In none of these companies, however, had the relationships between the divisions or the subsidiaries and the general office—that is, between top and middle management—been clearly defined. In many cases the top managers were either so intimately involved in supervising and coordinating day-to-day operations that they had only a limited picture of the operations of the company as a whole, or they were so removed from current operations that they had only a vague understanding of activities and performance of the operating units. In neither situation were the senior executives in a position to carry out effectively their top management functions.

In the years after World War I the managers of these large industrials devised and perfected a new form of overall organizational structure to remedy these weaknesses. It permitted the middle managers to focus on managing and coordinating the processes of production and distribution and the top managers to concentrate on evaluating, planning, and allocating resources for the enterprise as a whole. At the same time the training and outlook of these industrial managers was becoming increasingly professional. Both developments further enhanced the economic power of the large industrial enterprises and of the men who managed them.

C H A P T E R 14

The Maturing of Modern
Business Enterprise

By World War I, modern business enterprise had come of age. The giant transportation and communication systems were already a generation or more old. In those industries where the requirements of production and distribution encouraged the visible hand of management to replace existing market mechanisms, the new form of business organization was firmly established. In those industries where the technology did not lend itself to mass production and where distribution did not require specialized services, mass marketers, and increasingly mass retailers, coordinated the flows from suppliers to consumers. And although enterprises in mass marketing were still entrepreneurial, and those in transportation and communication still had boards of directors dominated by financiers, those industrials that had integrated production and distribution were becoming more and more managerial. Many had already acquired all the basic attributes of today's giant corporations.

The development of top management methods and procedures in the early managerial firms marked the culmination of an organizational revolution that had its beginnings in the 1850s with the railroads. The processes of production and distribution, the methods by which they were managed, the enterprises that administered them, and the resulting structure of industries and of the economy itself—all were, by World War I, much closer to the ways of the 1970s than they were to those of the 1850s or even of the 1870s. A businessman of today would find himself at home in the business world of 1910, but the business world of 1840 would be a strange, archaic, and arcane place. So, too, the American businessman of 1840 would find the environment of fifteenth-century Italy more familiar than that of his own nation seventy years later.

The history of the modern multiunit business enterprise after World

War I becomes an extension of the story already told here. It consists of refinements in existing processes and procedures, and the continuation of basic trends that appeared before 1917. This is not to say that these later developments were not complex, innovative, and significant.[1] But World War I marks the proper point for bringing to a close a detailed examination of the beginnings and early growth of modern business enterprise in the United States.

An analysis of three significant but quite different developments completes this history. First, the post-World War I economic recession revealed critical weaknesses that required adjustments in the organizational structures of large, integrated industrial enterprises. The resulting improvements made industrial enterprise more dynamic and spurred its continuing growth by permitting it to carry out more effectively the coordination of current flows and the allocation of resources for the future. Second, the needs of the new large industrial and marketing enterprises brought a professionalization of management in much the way comparable needs had done the same for the railroads during the 1880s and 1890s. Such professionalization encouraged the rapid spread of new administrative techniques, and helped managers to identify themselves as a distinct economic group. Finally, a description in capsule form of the growth of modern business enterprise from World War I to the present emphasizes how profoundly the operation of today's big businesses and today's economy were shaped by the institutional changes described in this history.

Perfecting the structure

The sharp recession following World War I had a shattering impact on many of the new industrial and marketing companies. The majority had been established after the depression of the 1890s. Most industrials that began before 1893, such as the meat packers and American Tobacco, were at the time of that depression still developing their operating procedures. The sudden and continuing drop in demand from the summer of 1920 until the spring of 1922 was, therefore, the first period of hard times that the modern business enterprise had to face. The recession dramatically indicated the need to be able to adjust flows readily to changes in demand. It also made clear, though in a less obvious manner, the failure of top managers to plan effectively. Senior executives, still deeply involved in day-to-day operations, had not foreseen or made plans to handle a slackening of demand.

This slow-down in demand caught both mass marketers and large integrated industrials by surprise. Even enterprises like the meat packers, who coordinated supply and demand by constant telegraph and telephone communication, had difficulties. Few adjusted their inventory quickly enough. Armour's losses in 1920 and 1921 forced J. Ogden Armour, the son of founder Philip D., to lose control of the family firm and to see it transformed from an entrepreneurial to a managerial enterprise.[2] The mass retailers, with their dependence on high stock-turn, had comparable problems. Sears Roebuck was saved from defaulting on payments to suppliers only when its president, Julius Rosenwald, drew on his family's personal fortune to cover these accounts.[3] The large integrated manufacturers and processors in chemical and mechanical industries, where a much longer period of time was required to get costly materials through the processes of production and distribution, had the greatest difficulty of all. Few could, as did Henry Ford, pass the burden of carrying unsold inventory on to their dealers. Ford was able to force his dealers to buy and pay for cars they could not sell by threatening to cancel their valuable franchises if they refused to comply.[4] Far more manufacturers had to follow General Motors' example and drastically write down the value of their overstocked inventory. At General Motors these inventory write-downs in 1921 and 1922 amounted to over $83 million.

General Motors and Sears Roebuck, as well as Du Pont, General Electric, United States Rubber, and other large enterprises, responded to the inventory crisis of 1920–1921 by developing techniques that set and adjusted their flows to carefully forecasted future demand. At General Motors and Du Pont the reorganizers went further. They created what has become known as the multidivisional structure (figure 12). In this type of structure, autonomous divisions continued to integrate production and distribution by coordinating flows from suppliers to consumers in different, clearly defined markets. The divisions, headed by middle managers, administered their functional activities through departments organized along the lines of those at General Electric and Du Pont. A general office of top managers, assisted by large financial and administrative staffs, supervised these multifunctional divisions. The general office monitored the divisions to be sure that their flows were tuned to fluctuations in demand and that they had comparable policies in personnel, research, purchasing, and other functional activities. The top managers also evaluated the financial and market performance of the divisions. Most important of all, they concentrated on planning and allocating resources.

Of the organizational innovations developed at General Motors and Du Pont, those at General Motors are the more illustrative. In automobile production the need to calibrate flows to changing demand was even more pressing and complex than it was in chemicals. At General Motors the

Figure 12. The multidivisional structure: manufacturing

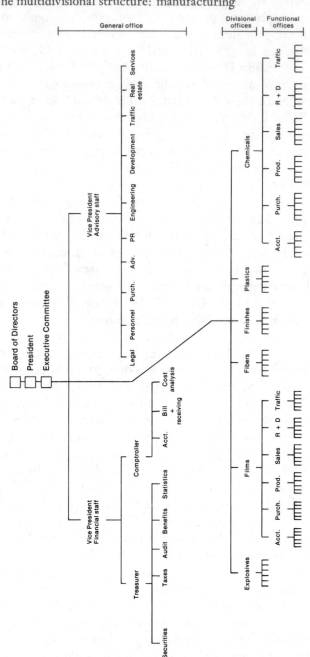

Source: First prepared by the author for "The United States: The Evolution of Enterprise," *Cambridge Economic History*, vol. 7 (Cambridge, Eng., 1977).

general office had to be built from scratch. As many of the reorganizers at General Motors came from Du Pont, the General Motors story also indicates how organizational techniques were transferred from one industry to another and adjusted to meet somewhat differing needs. Moreover, because the executives at General Motors described their achievements in the new management journals, theirs became the standard model on which other enterprises later shaped their organizational structures. For these reasons the history of the post-World War I reorganization at General Motors provides an appropriate final case study in this history of the rise of modern business enterprise in the United States.

The recession of 1920–1921 transformed General Motors from an entrepreneurial to a managerial enterprise.[5] William C. Durant, an entrepreneur of imperial ambitions who formed the company in 1908, had little interest in the processes and needs of management. A prominent carriage maker in Flint, Michigan, Durant had taken over the Buick Motor Company in 1904. By 1908 its production of over 8,000 vehicles made it the largest automobile company in the country. In this expansion Durant's greatest contribution was, according to an early historian of General Motors, the building of a nationwide sales organization.[6]

In carrying out a strategy of growth, Durant preferred buying to building. After the formation of General Motors in 1908 he gained control of a number of enterprises producing and distributing cars, trucks, parts, and accessories. As he enlarged his empire, Durant made little effort to bring these many activities under centralized control. The company's general office remained staffed by Durant, two or three personal assistants, and their secretaries. Durant had neither the time nor information to evaluate, coordinate, and plan the activities of his subsidiaries or the company as a whole. In the boom times immediately following the Armistice of November 1918, the operating divisions quickly expanded production and stocked quantities of inventory, in order to have the supplies to meet what they expected to be an ever-increasing demand. This was why, when the automobile market collapsed in September of 1920, the company had such a costly write-down of inventory values and why it came so close to bankruptcy.

At this same moment Durant was himself having personal financial difficulties. By attempting to hold up the price of General Motors stock, the company's president, by November 1920, owed close to $30 million in brokers' loans. These were secured by General Motors stock, whose value was plummeting. The Du Pont Company and J. P. Morgan and Company, the two largest single investors in General Motors, arranged to take over Durant's debts, and much of the stock he controlled. Pierre du Pont then became president. He did so because the Du Pont Company had, on his recommendation, invested over $25 million of its wartime profits in General Motors in 1917. He now hoped to make the investment once again profitable.

In rehabilitating General Motors, Pierre du Pont worked closely with Alfred P. Sloan, Jr., a talented engineer and administrator who was at that time managing the company's parts and accessory units. At the outset, Sloan and du Pont decided against creating a single centralized functionally departmentalized organization. The company's activities were too large, too numerous, too varied, and too scattered to be so controlled. They agreed to retain the company's integrated car, truck, parts, and accessory enterprises as autonomous operating divisions. They then defined a division's activities according to the market it served. For the five automobile divisions, the market was set by price. Each division sold in a single price class within what Sloan called the price pyramid. Cadillac was the top of the pyramid with the highest prices and lowest volume, and Chevrolet was at the bottom with the lowest prices and highest volume. Once the divisions' markets had been defined, du Pont and Sloan began to replace Durant's tiny personal headquarters with a general office consisting of a number of powerful general executives and large advisory and financial staffs.

At the same time, du Pont and Sloan had executives from the general office devise procedures to coordinate current output with existing demand and to allocate resources in terms of long-term demand. The techniques for improved coordination evolved out of the pressing need in late 1920 to regain control over inventories, especially purchases. The small team of executives given this task first required the divisions to submit for each coming month and the following three months forecasts of material, equipment, and labor needed for each month's production. Only after the general office approved these estimates were the divisions permitted to make their purchases. These forecasts quickly came to include all the inputs required for the anticipated output. By 1924 they were tied to annual forecasts of demand provided by the new financial staff headed by Donaldson Brown from Du Pont. Annual forecasts were prepared for each division by a collaborative effort between divisions and the general staff. These "divisional indices," as they were called, included not only purchases and delivery schedules for materials and capital equipment required and labor to be hired, but also estimated rates of return on investment and prices to be charged for each product. Prices, unit costs, and rates of return were all closely related to the volume permitted by demand. In drawing up these divisional indices, the staff computed the size of the national income, the state of the business cycle, normal seasonal variations in demand, and the division's anticipated share of the total market for each of its lines.

The forecasts on which output and purchases of materials were based were constantly adjusted to actual sales. The data on sales came from reports submitted every ten days by the dealers and from monthly figures on new car registrations collected by the R. L. Polk Company. The latter also provided excellent information on General Motors' market share and on that of its competitors. Besides permitting immediate adjustments of flows to even small changes in demand, this information had other uses. The comparison of actual to estimated results of sales, market share, and rate of return was used to sharpen forecasting techniques. Of more importance, such comparison provided another source of information for the monitoring of divisional performance and the planning and allocating of resources for the future. Similar, though often less complete, techniques were adopted for controlling inventory and coordinating flows and for the evaluation of managerial performance at General Electric, Westinghouse, and Sears Roebuck. Eventually such methods were adopted by nearly all large modern business enterprises in the United States.

As the new financial and advisory staffs were devising statistical information to control, coordinate, and evaluate day-to-day operations, Sloan, du Pont, and their associates were working out ways to further improve long-term planning and the allocation of capital and managerial resources. Here the most significant move was to relieve top managers in the general office of all day-to-day operating responsibilities. Pierre du Pont remembered all too well the difficulties he and his cousin Coleman had had in keeping the attention of senior operating executives on long-term planning and policy making.[7] Sloan recalled even more painfully how the divisions' managers had negotiated with themselves and with Durant over capital expenditures.

On taking over at General Motors, du Pont concentrated top management decisions in the hands of a four-man executive committee. It included himself, Sloan, and two of his most trusted associates at Du Pont, John J. Raskob and J. Amory Haskell. In one of his first directives after taking office, Pierre emphasized: "It is my belief that 90 percent of all questions arising will be settled without reference to the Executive Committee and that the time of the Executive Committee members may be fully employed to study general routine and lay down general policies for the Corporation, leaving the burden of management and the carrying out of instructions to the Line, Staff and Financial Divisions."[8]

Once the crisis was surmounted and the new policies, procedures, and rules for the more routine operations had been laid down, Pierre du Pont enlarged the executive committee. By 1924 it had ten members, including Sloan who had become president, du Pont who was then chairman of the board, the head of the financial and the head of the advisory staffs, one of the two group vice presidents—general executives—who had overall supervision of specific groups of divisions, and four executives without any specific positions. The tenth member was the only manager with operating responsibilities. He was the chief executive of Buick, the company's most profitable automotive division.[9] Although such exceptions were made, the committee continued to consist almost completely of executives who had no day-to-day operating responsibilities. Its tasks were explicitly to approve the divisional indices, to evaluate divisional performance, to set pricing and other general corporate policies on the basis of its evaluations, and most important of all, to plan long-term strategy and the allocation of resources to carry it out. For such planning the committee relied on long-term financial and economic forecasts prepared by trained economists on Brown's financial staff.

In performing its work, the committee used the advisory and financial staff to check on information received from the operating divisions. The functional specialists on the advisory staff were, for example, expected to "audit" divisional activities and policies for their specific functions. Thus staff sales executives reviewed marketing policies, controls, and procedures with the sales managers of the many divisions; those on the manufacturing staff did the same with the divisional production managers; and so with automobile design, advertising, and other comparable activities. At the same time, the staff executives were expected to give specialized expert advice to the operating managers as well as to top executives in the general office.

Sloan soon realized that communication between staff, line, and general executives left much to be desired.[10] Friction between line and staff executives often had serious consequences. It proved most critical in product development, where line managers considered the staff men too theoretical, and staff executives complained that the line managers never looked beyond current production schedules. To bring together the three types of executives—staff, line, and general—Sloan formed interdivisional relations committees for major functional activities: product development, works management, power and maintenance, sales, and institutional advertising. These committees, which had their own salaried staffs, were normally chaired by a member of the executive committee. They had as their secretary the advisory staff's senior executive for that functional activity, and they included functional executives from major divisions.

By these several techniques top management was able to free itself of operating biases and responsibilities, and at the same time keep in touch with the corporation's widespread operations. Policy and planning were no longer made through negotiations between the senior managers of powerful operating departments or divisions. Policy was formulated by general executives who had the time, information, and psychological commitment to the enterprise as a whole, rather than to one of its parts.

This type of structure, with its general office and its autonomous, integrated divisions, began to be adopted, though rather slowly, by other large industrial enterprises in the 1920s and 1930s. It provided a more flexible and effective organizational alternative for mergers than either the holding company or the consolidation of the operations of constituent companies into a single centralized functionally departmentalized structure. Such holding companies as Allied Chemical and Union Carbide adopted the multidivisional structure in the 1920s as did United States Steel in the 1930s. It became even more widely used to manage enterprises which grew, as Armour and United States Rubber were beginning to before World War I, by moving into new product and new regional markets. With the creation of a general office consisting of general executives and a large financial and advisory staff and with the calibration of product flow and day-to-day operating activities to forecasted demand, the basic organizational structure and administrative procedures of the modern industrial enterprise were virtually completed.

These methods would be, of course, constantly polished and adjusted. The most important developments came in the coordination of activities between and within departments.[11] As a company's sales rose from $50 million to $500 million and even $1 billion, product development, coordination of product flow, and marketing became increasingly complex. To assist in such short-term integration of production and distribution and short-term allocation of materials, managers specializing in coordination appeared. "Project program managers," "market program managers," "interface managers," and "scheduling managers" all helped to facilitate flows of materials, funds, and ideas through the enterprise.

Although they developed many variations and although in very recent years they have been occasionally mixed into a matrix form, only two basic organizational structures have been used for the management of large industrial enterprises. One is the centralized, functional departmentalized type perfected by General Electric and Du Pont before World War I. The other is the multidivisional, decentralized structure initially developed at General Motors and also at Du Pont in the 1920s. The first has been used primarily by companies producing a single line of goods for one major product or regional market, the second by those manufacturing several lines for a number of product and regional markets.

The professionalization of management

The techniques of industrial management developed at General Electric, Du Pont, and General Motors spread rapidly. During the 1920s the new accounting, budgeting, and forecasting methods were becoming normal operating procedures. Once the strategy of diversification created or intensified the need for a multidivisional structure, that organizational form was speedily adopted.

One reason for the rapid spread of the new techniques was the growing professionalization of the managers of large industrial enterprises. Such professionalization took much the same form as it had with the railroad managers in the 1870s and 1880s and with mechanical engineers in the 1890s and 1900s. Professional societies were formed, professional journals published, and professional courses established in major American colleges and universities. In the early years of the twentieth century, such societies, journals, and courses appeared first for the functional middle managers, in finance, marketing, and production, and then for general top managers.

Salaried managers in financial offices of the new enterprises were the first to develop such a professional apparatus partly because their activities were the most closely tied to earlier developments in railroad and factory operations. The modern accounting profession in the United States had two roots, the auditors and the cost accountants.[12] Managers in the auditing and accounting departments of railroads had formed their own national association in the 1880s. During the 1880s and 1890s investment bankers had brought certified public accountants to New York from Britain to assist them in railroad reorganization. For example, in 1890 the British firm of Price, Waterhouse & Co. opened a branch in New York, and during that decade other English and Scottish firms followed suit. In 1897 members of these firms helped to form the American Association of Public Accountants, which included railroad comptrollers as well as executives from accounting firms. That association grew quickly after the merger movement created a demand for auditors and certified public accountants in industry as well as in railroads. In 1905 the association that had published the proceedings of its meetings began to support the monthly *Journal of Accountancy*. In 1916 it attempted to broaden its appeal to other types of accountants by changing its name to the American Institute of Accountants in the United States of America, but it continued to be primarily an association for auditors.

The pioneers in cost accounting were, on the other hand, the industrial engineers who developed new techniques as they systematized the factory management and attempted to make it more scientific. During the first decade of the new century these men continued to describe their work primarily in the *Transactions* of the American Society of Mechanical Engineers and in *Engineering News* and the *American Machinist*. Alexander H. Church, Harrington Emerson, H. L. Arnold, L. P. Alford, and other cost accounting innovators were publishing numerous articles in these journals dealing with overhead standard costing, factory burden, and accounting controls.[13]

During the second decade of the century both financial and cost accounting began to be taught extensively in colleges and universities. In 1900 accounting courses were given in only 12 institutions of higher learning, and these courses were little more than surveys of commercial bookkeeping. By 1910, 52 colleges and universities offered accounting courses, and by 1916 the number had risen to 116.[14] By then, these courses included auditing, public accounting, and cost accounting. Significantly, the first association to include cost accountants was the American Association of University Instructors in Accounting, formed in 1915, which became the American Accounting Association after the First World War. In 1926, when that association began to publish *The Accounting Review*, a separate National Association of Cost Accountants had already been formed.

Marketing lagged somewhat behind finance and accounting in developing comparable professional activities. Trade journals had flourished since the 1850s, first in the basic dry goods, hardware, grocery, drug, and other trades, and then in more specialized ones. These journals, however, concentrated on discussing commodities and markets. Then in 1888 *Printers' Ink* was established as a journal for advertising managers and firms. Neither *Printers' Ink* nor the trade journals devoted space to more general methods and procedures of distribution, marketing, and purchasing. On the other hand, such topics made up the agenda of the meetings of the first national marketing association founded in 1915. Articles about these matters appeared in its *Proceedings* and later in the association's *Journal of Marketing*. These themes were also at the core of courses on marketing that had been established by 1910 in the new schools of business. And as was the case with the cost accountants, these teachers formed the first professional marketing association.[15]

Professional organizations and journals for factory and production managers grew out of those originally formed by mechanical, electrical, and other types of engineers. The leaders of the movement for scientific management were particularly anxious to find a more congenial home than the American Society of Mechanical Engineers. The ASME, they complained, paid too much attention to engineering and too little to management.[16] The small American Association of Industrial Management was started in 1899. Then in 1911 Frank Gilbreth formed the Society for the Promotion of the Science of Management which later became the Taylor Society. Still later it merged with the Society of Industrial Engineers to become the Society for the Advancement of Management. Until World War I these management associations were concerned largely with factory management and production engineering.

Immediately after the war, however, general managers formed their own organizations. In 1919 the founding of the Administrative Management Association created a forum for papers and discussion on more general management problems. Its meetings, the contents of its *Proceedings,* and its monthly *Administrative Management Magazine* appealed to managers in both government and business administration. Then in 1925 a small association of specialists in personnel matters reorganized their society to form the American Management Association, which quickly became the leading professional organization for top and middle management in American business corporations. Its meetings and its publications focused on the overall administration, operation, and control of the modern business enterprise.

A major periodical devoted to general management had appeared even before the formation of the American Management Association in 1925. Before the war, *Engineering News* began to carry articles that dealt with more than factory management. In 1916 it changed its name to *Industrial Management.* Earlier, *System,* which Arch W. Shaw had made the most successful periodical devoted to general business affairs, occasionally published pieces on enterprise management. By 1921 the demand for such material led to the founding of *Management and Administration,* a journal designed specifically to meet the needs of corporate management. It was in this periodical that Donaldson Brown, Charles S. Mott, and other senior executives at General Motors in 1924 explained in detail the organizational control and accounting procedures they had devised during the reorganization of their giant enterprise.[17] During the 1920s many of the leading experts on corporate management as well as managers of major corporations contributed to this journal.

Central to the professionalization of management in the new multiunit business enterprises were modern business schools. Their appearance marked an educational development that was at that time unique to the United States. In the late nineteenth century, business education consisted of little more than the teaching of bookkeeping and secretarial skills in small specialized private schools of commerce and, increasingly, in public high schools. Only the University of Pennsylvania's undergraduate Wharton School of Commerce and Finance, founded in 1881, offered courses in business, and these included little more than commercial accounting and law. In the decade after 1899, business education became part of the curriculum of the nation's most prestigious colleges and universities. The University of Chicago and the University of California set up undergraduate schools of commerce in 1899. In 1900 New York University and Dartmouth, with its Amos Tuck School of Administration and Finance, followed suit.[18] By the time Harvard opened its Graduate School of Business Administration in 1908, professional postgraduate business education was already off to a good start.

The initial offerings of the new Harvard Business School indicate a concern from the start with the training of managers for large multiunit enterprises.[19] The three required courses—accounting, commercial law and contracts, and a general course on the commerce of the United States—reflected the older commercial orientation of the American economy. But the electives were on the management of transportation, industrial, and marketing firms. In railroading the electives included Railroad Organization and Finance, Railroad Operation, and Railroad Rate-Making. In finance there was a course in corporate finance as well as one in banking and one in life insurance. By 1914 the required course in American commercial activities had become one in marketing, focusing on management rather than on specific trades or commodities. As the school's historian has explained about this course: "Marketing comprehended the whole process of physical distribution, demand activation, merchandising, pricing, and other activities involved in the exchange of products and services."

From the start Industrial Organization was one of the most popular courses. It always included more than just the study of factory management. The course was set up by Arch W. Shaw, who came to the Harvard Business School after turning over the administration of his Chicago publishing house to subordinates. At first Shaw relied quite heavily on outside lecturers. In 1910 these included Frederick W. Taylor, Harrington Emerson, Carl Barth, Morris Cooke, Charles Day, and C. H. Going, all leading practitioners of the new systematic and scientific management. Also lecturing were two senior managers from General Electric. One, W. C. Fish, spoke on "decentralized management." The other, Russell Robb, had his talks on organization later published.

In the academic year 1911–1912 the school offered a course on Business Policy. Resulting from a series of discussions between Dean Edwin F. Gay and Arch Shaw, "its purpose was to develop an approach to business problems from the top management point of view."[20] At Shaw's urging, this course and others used the case method of instruction in a manner similar to that developed at the Harvard Law School. Business Policy soon became the core course of the curriculum at the Harvard Business School, and the case method its primary method of teaching. In developing cases and in making assignments, the instructors at Harvard and the other new schools of business were able to draw on the wave of books appearing after 1910 on accounting, finance, marketing, and industrial organization, written by Taylor, Going, Robb, Shaw, Paul T. Cherington, Dexter Kimball, Ralph S. Butler, Hugo Diemer, Lewis D. Haney, Edward D. Jones, and many others.

Another evidence of professionalism was the appearance of the management consultant. Before World War I engineering consultants like Taylor, Emerson, and Cooke were giving professional advice on more than just factory management. By the end of the First World War, firms like Arthur D. Little, Inc., Day & Zimmerman, and Frazer and Torbet had become primarily management rather than engineering consultants.[21] As early as 1911, Arthur D. Little was advising General Motors on the creation of a Technical Laboratory. In 1921 Day & Zimmerman had provided, at the request of the bankers who helped the du Ponts refinance General Motors, advice on its internal reorganization. Frazer & Torbet, formed in 1917, advised on the reorganization of both corporate and governmental structures. An early associate and partner, James O. McKinsey, in 1925 set up his own firm which became and remained one of the leading management consulting firms in the world. By the 1920s comparable consulting firms provided expert advice on functional activities, including the newer ones of personnel and public relations.

The appurtenances of professionalism—societies, journals, university training, and specialized consultants—hardly existed in the United States in 1900. By the 1920s they were all flourishing. Even then they were still uniquely American, and did not appear in any strength in other economies until after World War II. They developed in American industry, much as they had in railroading, to provide channels of communication through which managers could review and discuss similar problems and issues. And by providing communication and personal contact they helped to give the corporate managers a sense of self-identification. By attending and participating in the same meetings, by reading and writing for the same journals, and by having attended the same type of college courses, these managers began to have a common outlook as well as common interests and concerns.

The impact of these professional activities was, of course, gradual. In the 1920s the societies were still small, the journals not too widely read, and the business school graduates still in the lower ranks of management. By the mid-twentieth century, however, professionally oriented, salaried career managers were the men who had taken charge of the large multiunit enterprises dominating the critical sectors of the American economy.

Growth of modern business enterprise between the wars

One reason for the continuing spread of the modern enterprise was that the new professional associations, journals, training courses, and consultants made possible a rapid diffusion of the new managerial and administrative procedures. More important, of course, were the advancing technologies and expanding markets that gave the multiunit firm a competitive advantage in an increasingly larger part of the American economy. Where the firm already dominated, it continued to grow by adding new units and by internalizing their activities and the market transactions involved. In other industries and sectors where the multiunit enterprise had not yet become strong, it appeared, grew, and flourished when processes of production and the needs of distribution made administrative coordination more efficient than market coordination.

In transportation and communication, the operations and organization of the railroad, telephone, and telegraph systems remained much the same well into the twentieth century. The boundaries of the large regional railroad systems changed little even though some mergers occurred and some interior lines continued to try, usually unsuccessfully, to obtain their own outlets to the seaboard. Only after World War II, when railroads began to become technologically obsolete in the carrying of passenger and some freight traffic, did the maps of American railroad systems begin to change significantly. In communication, the telephone steadily replaced the telegraph in long-distance service. American Telephone & Telegraph continued to operate much the same way after World War I as it had at the beginning of the century, with its nationwide "long-lines" organization responsible for long distance and twenty or so regional subsidiaries for local operations. The latter were still managed through centralized functionally departmentalized structures.[22]

In the two decades following World War I, the internal combustion engine began to break the railroads' hold, first on the nation's passenger traffic and then in the carrying of freight. By the outbreak of World War II, the place of the large enterprise in the new forms of transportation was becoming clear. In air transport, where precise operational coordination was as essential for safe and efficient operations as it was on the railroads eighty years before, a few carefully structured enterprises were beginning to dominate, with the consent and even assistance of the Civil Aeronautics Board. Truck, bus, and taxi lines, however, required much less precision in operational scheduling, less complex equipment, and a smaller capital investment. Here small firms competed effectively with large ones, even on the long hauls. So, as air transport was becoming oligopolistic, ground transportation was becoming more competitive.

In mass marketing and distribution, retailers continued to expand at the expense of wholesalers. Retail enterprises grew by adding new lines and, even more, by adding new outlets or stores. The chain store became the fastest growing channel of distribution. The existing chain stores expanded more rapidly than other types of retailers. And new chains appeared more often than did new department stores or mail-order houses. Chains moved into the drug, grocery, and other trades that had hitherto been the domain of the wholesaler and the small retailer.[23] Department stores began, albeit most hesitantly, to enlarge their business by building branches in the suburbs.

Mail-order houses did so much more precipitately when their basic rural market ceased to grow. Farm income fell from $14.6 billion in 1919 to $8.6 in 1921; it came back to only $10.5 billion in 1926. As a result, mail-order firms, large and small, began to build chains of retail department stores to provide outlets in urban and, particularly, the fast-growing suburban markets. Between 1925 and the onslaught of the great depression at the end of 1929, Sears and Montgomery Ward both created a large nationwide chain. By the end of 1929, Sears had opened 324 retail stores and Montgomery Ward nearly 500.[24]

This expansion, by internalizing more market transactions, permitted the enterprises to make fuller use of their buying, traffic, and operating organizations. Sears, Montgomery Ward, and some chains integrated backward, obtaining factories to assure themselves of a constant supply of goods in certain lines. But, as was true before World War I, manufacturing remained only a small part of their total operations. They always preferred to buy when they could and to manufacture only when it was absolutely necessary in order to obtain stocks of desired specifications. In one area they did develop new facilities—when they began to sell, in volume, appliances, sewing machines, and other "big tickets," as they were called, which required specialized marketing services. The chains soon found that if they were to compete with the producers of such machinery, they too would have to have their own organizations to service and repair the machines as well as to provide credit and to make collections.[25]

Because the mass retailers did not need to invest in large amounts of costly capital equipment, they continued to rely on the high-volume, internally generated cash flow to provide for most of their working and fixed capital. Sears, Roebuck and Montgomery Ward did obtain some outside funds to build new mail-order plants before World War I and to get through the inventory crisis of 1920–1921. On the other hand, the great expansion of retail stores after 1925 was, despite the costs of buying land and building stores, entirely self-financed.[26] So the Rosenwalds of Sears and the Thornes of Wards remained in control of their enterprises. So, too, did the families of the builders of many department stores and those that created the Atlantic & Pacific, Woolworth's, Penney's, and other chains. They began to relinquish control only when they wished to lessen their business responsibilities or to diversify their holdings.[27] The nature of the chains' financial needs permitted the mass retailers to remain entrepreneurial enterprises much longer than did the integrated industrials.

Although this study has not examined the continuing growth and internal organization of financial enterprises, it is worthwhile to point out that they too expanded by becoming multiunit. The insurance companies were the first financial firms to become modern business enterprises. In their early years, the life insurance firms had specialized marketing needs that were similar to those of the mass producers of machinery.[28] For actuarial reasons they had difficulty in becoming viable business enterprises until they had enough policyholders to spread the risks widely. Then the large volume of their business permitted them to lower the unit cost of writing insurance by internalizing and routinizing the transactions involved. The maintenance of the volume of business, in turn, depended on direct canvassing by salesmen and on maintaining a close continuing relationship with the customer. Like the early machinery companies, most insurance firms began in the 1880s and 1890s to replace large sales agencies with branch offices operated and administered by salaried employees. Nearly all came to be managed through three basic functional departments: sales, operations, and investment.

Well before 1900 the structure of the American insurance industry showed similarities to the agricultural implement and meat-packing trades. The Big Three—Mutual, Equitable, and New York Life—dominated the industry, and the smaller, though still large, enterprises—Metropolitan, John Hancock, Aetna, Connecticut Mutual, Northwestern Mutual, and Pennsylvania Mutual—followed their lead. The Big Three immediately built extensive marketing organizations overseas. By the beginning of the twentieth century they were among the largest insurance companies operating in many European countries. The smaller enterprises tended to stay closer to home. Again, as in the case of the marketing companies and those industrials which were financed by high cash flow, these enterprises were controlled by the founders and their families.

In the twentieth century the structure of the enterprise and the structure of the life insurance business remained relatively unchanged. As state regulation increased and as companies adopted a mutual form of corporate organization by which policyholders became share owners, these firms became managerial. Even before World War I, the Big Three had begun to contract their overseas business as European states passed regulations against foreign and particularly American insurance companies doing business in their territories. While concentrating on the home market, the insurance firms did come to carry a full line of policies. However, they made no attempt to diversify into other fields. They remained, as did most transportation and communication companies, large bureaucratic enterprises carrying out a single major activity through a centralized functionally departmentalized organizational structure.[29]

Commercial banks, unlike insurance companies, did not build national organizations. This was because banks could normally do business only in the state in which they were chartered. Moreover, the National Banking Act of 1864 and laws in many states forbade the banks within their jurisdictions to have branches. During the nineteenth century, commercial banks, except those of New York and Chicago, looked on themselves as local institutions serving a single community. After 1900, however, as the economy, particularly the cities, grew, the demand for banking services became more acute. In 1913, for example, the Federal Reserve permitted national banks to open branches abroad.[30] When state and national laws were modified, American banks then began to grow by building branches. And where local laws continued to limit branches, banks created multiunit enterprises by merging and forming chains. Like the marketing firms, they found that they could make more intensive use of their central office facilities and reach more customers by setting up geographically dispersed outlets. In 1900 fewer than 100 American banks operated in more than one office. By 1919, 464 banks operated 1,082 branches, and by 1929, 816 had 3,603 branches. The share of bank resources held by the multiunit enterprises rose from 16 percent in 1919 to 46 percent in 1929. By then, many banks had also set up branches overseas. While remaining solely banking enterprises, American banks did, like the insurance companies, soon offer a full line of services and so had departments for checking and savings accounts, foreign exchange, and fiduciary trusts, as well as for commercial banking.

After World War I the most important developments in the history of modern business enterprises in the United States did not come from enterprises involved in carrying out a single basic activity such as transportation, communication, marketing, or finance. Nor did they come from firms that only manufactured. They appeared rather in large industrials that integrated production with distribution. In the years after 1917 these enterprises continued to grow in size and number. As regional and national markets expanded and as technological advances permitted an increase in the speed and volume of throughput and stock-turn, the integrated enterprises moved into industries where they had played a smaller role before World War I. These industries, however, were nearly all in those larger industrial groups where the integrated enterprises had clustered from the start. As the firms became integrated, the industries in which they operated became more concentrated.[31]

In the years after the First World War, large integrated firms began to expand by moving into new products for new markets. This strategy of diversification evolved from the concept of the "full line," which many early integrated enterprises had adopted well before 1917. Many American companies, following the example of pioneering big businesses in tobacco, grain, soap, meat packing, cotton oil, rubber, and lead processing, added lines that permitted them to make more effective use of their marketing and purchasing organizations and to exploit the by-products of their manufacturing or processing operations. As in the case of the meat packers and others, the intensified use of their marketing organization led to the addition of new production facilities, and expansion in the output of by-products led to the addition of new marketing facilities and personnel.

It was not until the 1920s, however, that diversification became an explicit strategy of growth. Before the war, acquisitions of new products had been ad hoc responses of middle managers to fairly obvious opportunities. After the war, top managers began to search consciously for new products and new markets to make use of existing facilities and managerial talent. The Du Pont Company, one of the very first to diversify in this manner, did so in order to employ the managerial staff and facilities which had been so greatly enlarged by the demands of World War I. Others soon followed. Their goal was, like that of the Du Pont executive committee and the managers at the meat-packing firms, to use more intensively all or part of the existing organization. The leveling off of the national income in the mid-1920s and its drastic decline in the 1930s intensified the search for new products.

The new strategy was aimed at assuring the long-term health of an enterprise by using more profitably its managers and facilities. In nearly all cases, the plans were formulated and carried out by salaried and professional managers. And in nearly all cases they were financed from retained earnings. Without such expansion, current dividends would certainly have been higher.

The strategy of diversification of the industrial managers, therefore, raised the possibility of internal controversy much as system-building did in railroading. The conflicting goals of maintaining current profits and assuring long-term organizational stability may have led to arguments within boards of directors of industrials, as they did earlier on railroads.

Much more research is needed before reliable information exists on this point. Nevertheless, it seems unlikely that such conflicts became as overt as they did on the railroads. The large industrials, unlike the railroads, were able to maintain dividends while carrying out their strategy of growth. Their oligopolistic position helped them to make profits and to absorb losses even during the great depression of the 1930s. Moreover, such expansion required smaller amounts of capital expended over longer periods of time than did railroad system-building. As long as the managers of these enterprises continued to pay modest dividends regularly, the bankers or representatives of the founder's family or of the large stock-holders who sat on the finance committee of their boards could view such growth with equanimity and even enthusiasm. Expansion financed by retained earnings, and not by large issues of stocks and bonds, promised to increase substantially the value of their holdings.

In undertaking the new strategy of diversification, managers occasionally purchased or merged with a company that provided a new or complementary line. Much more often such expansion resulted from internal growth. The managers looked to their research organizations, originally set up to improve product and process, to develop the new products that might be particularly suitable to their production processes or marketing skills.

Not surprisingly, therefore, this new use for industrial research was first developed in the same industrial groups where the large enterprise had come to cluster by World War I. In 1929 over two-thirds of the personnel employed in industrial research were concentrated in five groups: electrical with 31.6 percent; chemical with 18.1 percent; non-electrical machinery with 6.6 percent; metals, also with 6.6 percent; and rubber with 5.9 percent.[32] Although food and oil companies employed somewhat fewer researchers, they still had many more than did firms in labor-intensive, small-unit, competitive industries. As Michael Gort has pointed out in a detailed study of product diversification, chemical companies were the major diversifiers during the 1930s—that is, they added more new product lines than did enterprises in any other industrial group. They were followed by those in electrical machinery, transportation equipment, primary metals, and rubber.[33] Moreover, the industries into which these diversifying enterprises moved were, in order, chemicals, machinery, fabricated metals, electric machinery, food, and stone/glass/clay. This pattern of interweaving diversification continued well beyond World War II.

The histories of individual firms emphasize Gort's more general points.[34] In the 1920s, chemical firms like Du Pont, Union Carbide, Allied Chemical, Hercules, and Monsanto all entered new industries. Each did so from its own specific technological base (for example, the Du Pont base was nitrocellulose chemistry, and Union Carbide's was carbon chemistry). In the same decade, the great electrical manufacturers—General Electric and Westinghouse—which up to that time had concentrated on manufacturing light and power equipment, diversified into the production of a wide variety of household appliances, as well as radio and x-ray equipment. During the depression decade of the thirties, General Motors (and to a lesser extent, other automobile companies) began to make and sell diesel locomotives, appliances, tractors, and airplanes. By using organizational and operating techniques developed in the automobile industry for the production and distribution of diesels, General Motors helped to make the steam locomotive a historical relic within a single decade. Metal makers, particularly copper and brass companies, followed the example of the Aluminum Company of America by producing kitchenware and household fittings. Some rubber companies started to develop the potentialities of rubber chemistry. Others used their distribution networks to sell a wide variety of products often made by other manufacturers. In the 1930s, too, food companies began to use their marketing facilities to handle new lines of goods which they then processed themselves.

These firms found that the new multidivisional structure met the administrative needs of the new strategy. In fact, the managers at Du Pont had first fashioned such a structure during the recession of 1920–1921 as an answer to the new administrative challenges created by their diversification program.[35] Their move into paints, dyes, film, fibers, and chemicals overloaded the company's existing centralized, functionally departmentalized organization. That structure broke down under the strain of attempting to coordinate the flow of goods of several lines of products sold in a variety of markets and to allocate resources among these dissimilar kinds of businesses. As a result, Du Pont's performance in the new ventures had been so poor that in 1921 only the long-established explosives business showed a profit. The creation of separate integrated autonomous divisions to handle the production and distribution of explosives, dyestuffs, celluloid products, fabrics and film, paints and chemicals, and rayon made these major lines profitable. Since Du Pont had long had large and efficient top management, its organizational effort was not concentrated, as was General Motors', on building the general office, but rather on setting up and defining the functions and structure of the new product divisions.

The multidivisional structure adopted by General Motors, Du Pont, and later by United States Rubber, General Electric, Standard Oil, and other enterprises in technologically advanced industries institutionalized the strategy of diversification. In so doing, it helped to systematize the processes of technological innovation in the American economy. The research department in such enterprises tested the commercial viability of new products generated either by the central research staff or by the operating divisions or even developed outside the company. The executives in the general office, freed from day-to-day operational decisions, determined whether the company's managers could profitably process and distribute these new products. If they decided that the managers could not, then they normally licensed the new product to some other firm. If they agreed that they could, and that the potential market was similar to one in which the firm currently sold, then its production and sale were given to an existing division. If the market was quite different, a new division was formed. By the outbreak of World War II, the diversified industrial enterprises using the divisional organization structure were still few, but they had become the most dynamic form of American business enterprise.

Modern business enterprise since 1941

In many sectors of the American economy, but above all in the central sectors of production and distribution, World War II put the capstone on the institutional developments of the interwar years and set the stage for the impressive growth of the modern business enterprise and of the economy itself in the postwar years.[36]

In the first place, wartime demands for new, technologically complex products such as synthetic rubber, high octane gasoline, radar, electronic antisubmarine devices, and a wide variety of weapons brought a pooling of scientific and technological knowledge and led to a major expansion in the systematic application of science in American industry. As a result, petroleum, rubber, metals, and a number of food companies developed new capacities for producing a variety of chemicals and synthetic materials. Electrical and radio companies, small as well as large, old as well as new, acquired the facilities for producing a wide range of electronic products.

Second, the requirements of mobilizing the economy led to the pooling and expansion of managerial procedures and controls whose use was still largely concentrated in the large, departmentalized and divisionalized integrated enterprises. During the war, small firms (usually as subcontractors for the larger concerns) learned about the modern methods of forecasting, accounting, and inventory control.

In addition, the war brought full employment for the first time since 1929. The continuance of a vast national mass market was further assured when, early in 1946, Congress passed the Employment Act, which committed the federal government to maintain maximum employment and with it a high-level aggregate demand. This commitment to support the mass market, together with the spread of industrial technology and the increased knowledge of administrative techniques, all promised a postwar economic expansion which the large integrated and diversified industrial enterprise was in the best position to exploit.

Indeed, the years after World War II mark the triumph of modern business enterprise. Aided by the new federal commitment, aggregate demand grew steadily at a healthy rate for twenty years after the war, with the gross national product (in constant dollars) rising from $309.9 billion in 1947 to $727.1 billion in 1969.[37] This growth provided a mass market far greater than any previously known in history; regional markets became as massive as the national market had been in the late nineteenth century. In technology, the electronics revolution (including automation), the high-speed computer, the development of new plastics, artificial fibers, and metal alloys, and the continuing systematic application of science to industry all increased the speed and volume of production and distribution and so expanded the needs and opportunities for applying the visible hand of management.

In finance and distribution, as well as in many consumer services, the great postwar market was probably more important than technological change in stimulating the spread of modern business enterprise. New electronic machinery did allow greatly increased speed and volume of work performed. As important was the increasing internalization of market transactions by the building or buying of branches. In banking, the enterprise grew by adding branches and by consolidating many small units within major urban, suburban, and state areas into large administrative networks. In food retailing, chain stores had a continuing boom, with new grocery stores and supermarkets enjoying immense popularity. Hotels, restaurants, even rent-a-car services spread their networks across the land. The older mass retailers—merchandise chains, mail-order houses, and department stores—became large enough to adopt the multidivisional structure. This was done largely by defining the divisions along regional rather than product lines (see figure 13). As a result of this massive growth of chains, the number of small, single-unit jobbers and retailers, and also of hotels and restaurants, has declined more rapidly since the Second World War than before it.

In manufacturing and communications, technology had the greatest impact. Automation, the computer, and the new materials (such as plastics) increased output of existing large-batch and continuous-process plants and factories and permitted the introduction of these mass produc-

Figure 13. The multidivisional structure: retailing

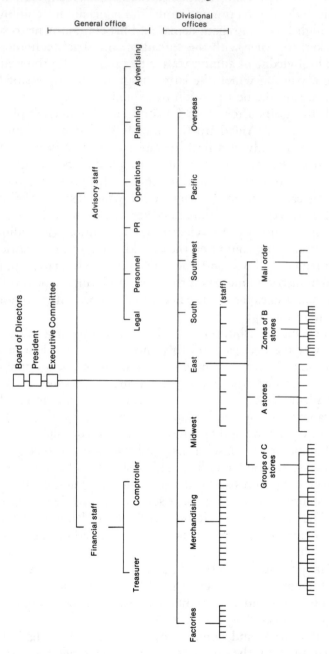

Source: First prepared by the author for "The United States: The Evolution of Enterprise," *Cambridge Economic History*, vol. 7 (Cambridge, Eng., 1977).

tion techniques in many of the older industries where they had not yet been adopted. Thus, the technological advances in production encouraged the continuing spread of the integrated enterprise, and with it, oligopoly in man-made fibers, paper, glass, and some metal-fabricating industries. Technology also changed the mass communications and entertainment industry as television replaced both motion pictures and radio as the most popular mass medium. Because of the huge capital requirements and the complex scheduling needed, a few large television broadcasting chains (usually an outgrowth of radio chains) quickly dominated the industry. In transportation, the pre-World War II trends initiated by earlier technological innovations accelerated. Airline companies grew in size and complexity but not in number. More large firms appeared in the movement of goods by trucks, but large and small companies continued to compete side by side.

Technology was all-important in the rapid postwar growth and spread of the diversified multi-industry firms. The obvious rewards of research and development turned more and more integrated enterprises to a strategy of expansion through diversification. It also encouraged firms which had already diversified to move into still other product lines. By the 1960s, nearly all of the leading companies in chemicals, rubber, glass, paper, electrical machinery, transportation vehicles, and many food companies were making products in ten or more different SIC four-digit industries.[38] Most of the large metal, oil, and machinery firms operated in from three to ten such industries. In order to obtain the maximum return from their new investments, nearly all of these enterprises had by the 1960s adopted the multidivisional structure with its autonomous operating divisions and its evaluating and planning general office.

During the 1950s, the divisionalized firms further refined their strategy of diversification by exploiting what became known as the product cycle.[39] Strategies became designed to obtain the maximum return from a new product as it moved through the cycle from its initial commercialization to full maturity. An effectively diversified enterprise attempted to have a number of product lines, each at a different stage of the product cycle.

The multidivisional structure which helped to institutionalize product innovation also made it easier for the large integrated enterprise to meet the demands of the federal government for military and advance scientific hardware and to reach the rapidly growing overseas markets. During the years of the cold war, the government required a wide variety of weapons —ranging from aircraft carriers, missiles, and submarines, to conventional guns and tanks, as well as nuclear reactors for the Atomic Energy Commission and spaceships, with all their accoutrements, for the National

Aeronautics and Space Administration. To handle these markets companies merely added a separate division or group of divisions for atomic energy, weapons, or government business in general.

More significant in the recent evolution of modern enterprise than the postwar governmental demand were foreign markets. The large integrated food and machinery companies that built their overseas domains before 1914 continued to maintain and often to expand them after the First World War. During the 1920s, a relatively small number of oil, chemical, rubber, and automobile companies followed the pioneering firms overseas. The depression of the 1930s slowed, and the Second World War almost stopped, expansion abroad. Then in the 1950s and early 1960s, particularly after the opening of the European Common Market, came a massive drive for foreign markets. Direct American investment in Europe alone rose from $1.7 billion in 1950 to $24.5 billion in 1970.[40] This second "American challenge" in Europe was spearheaded by the two hundred firms that accounted for more than half of the direct investment made by United States companies abroad. These two hundred were clustered in the capital-intensive, technologically advanced industries that had integrated, diversified, and then adopted the multidivisional form of organization.[41]

Overseas investment, in turn, had an impact on the structure of the diversified enterprise.[42] When a company first began to move abroad, it usually created an international division to supervise and coordinate overseas activities and to recommend investment decisions to the corporation's senior executives. However, as the operations and investment decisions grew larger and more complex, the international division began to disappear. Where the product divisions were strong, they took over the international business of the lines they were already handling domestically. For those companies which still concentrated on one dominant line of business, such as oil, copper, some food, and drink (for example, Coca-Cola), the operating divisions became geographical, each covering a major area of the globe. A few multinationals developed a matrix form of structure in which overseas managers reported to regional divisions on some matters and to product divisions on others. In all cases, the multidivisional form was extended from a national to a worldwide basis, with long-term allocation decisions continuing to be made at the general office, and day-to-day coordination of throughput continuing to be handled by the divisions.

During the 1960s a major variation of the diversified, multidivisional enterprise appeared on the American business scene. This was the conglomerate. The conglomerate differed from the older, multi-industrial, multinational enterprise in its strategy (and, therefore, in the nature of its

capital investments) and in its organizational structure. The large, diversified enterprise had grown primarily by internal expansion—that is, by
direct investment of plant and personnel in industries related to its original
line of products. It moved into markets where the managerial, technological, and marketing skills and resources of its organization gave it a
competitive advantage. The conglomerate, on the other hand, expanded
entirely by the acquisition of existing enterprises, and not by direct investment into its own plant and personnel, and it often did so in totally unrelated fields. With the exception of a few large relatively undiversified oil
companies looking for profitable investments, the acquiring firms were
not usually in the capital-intensive, mass production, mass distribution
industries. They were, rather, in industries such as textiles and ocean
shipping, where small enterprises remained competitive, or they were in
those industries producing specialized products for individual orders, such
as the machine tool and defense and space industries.[43] The creators of the
first conglomerates embarked on strategies of unrelated acquisition when
they realized that their own industries had little potential for continued
growth, and when they became aware of the value of a diversified product
line and a strategy based on the product cycle. Tax considerations played
a part in the making of specific acquisitions but were rarely the basic
reason for embarking on the new strategy. The acquiring firm tended to
purchase relatively small enterprises in industries that were not yet oli-
gopolies. Because many of these small enterprises had not become wholly
managerial, the acquiring firms were in some cases able to provide them
with new administrative and operational techniques.

The structure of the new conglomerates reflected their strategies of
growth.[44] Their general offices were small and the acquired operating
units were permitted more autonomy than the divisions of the large
diversified firm. The difference in the general office of a conglomerate
was not in the size of its financial or legal staff or in the number of general
executives. Indeed, many conglomerates had even more general executives
than did the older, diversified majors. The difference came in the size and
functions of its advisory staff. The conglomerate had no staff offices for
purchasing, traffic, research and development, sales, advertising, or production. The only staff not devoted to purely legal and financial matters
was for corporate planning (that is, for the formulation of the strategy to
be used in investment decisions). As a result, the conglomerates could
concentrate more single-mindedly on making investments in new industries and new markets and withdraw more easily from existing ones than
could the older, large, diversified companies. On the other hand, the
conglomerates were far less effective in monitoring and evaluating their
divisions and in taking action to improve divisional operating performance.

They had neither the manpower nor the skills to nurse sick divisions back to health. Moreover, because conglomerates did not possess centralized research and development facilities or staff expertise concerning complex technology, they were unable to introduce new processes and products regularly and systematically into the economy. The managers of conglomerates became almost pure specialists in the long-term allocation of resources. They differed, however, from the managers of banks and mutual funds in that they made direct investments, for whose management they were fully responsible, rather than indirect portfolio investments, which rarely carried responsibility for operating performance.

As the history of the conglomerate suggests, changes in the operation and organization of the large business enterprise since World War I have had more of an effect on the formulation of long-term strategy and resource allocation than on short-term, day-to-day operations. The techniques for managing the functional departments within an integrated business organization (either a division or firm) continued to be improved, but not basically changed. Methods to coordinate product flow and information have become increasingly sophisticated. But neither interdepartmental nor intradepartmental activities have been fundamentally changed. On the other hand, as the diversified enterprises that adopted the multidivisional form expanded their activities, they enlarged these top management offices by appointing group executives who became responsible for a number of operating divisions. The new conglomerates set up comparable general offices, though assisted by smaller staffs. Even those few industrials that did not diversify and the large, single-function, mass marketing and service enterprises enlarged their top management. In the second half of the twentieth century top management had become collective. It concentrated increasingly on long-term resource allocation.

The dominance of modern business enterprise

In the years after World War II the large managerial enterprise became ever more powerful. It acquired control of an increasing share of the nation's economic activities, as well as a growing part of the industrial production of Europe and the rest of the world. In 1947, the two hundred largest industrials in the United States (many of which were not yet fully diversified or divisionalized) accounted for 30 percent of the value added in manufacturing and 47.2 percent of total corporate manufacturing assets. By 1963, after most of these enterprises had adopted the new strategy and the new structure, they were responsible for 41 percent of the value added and 56.3 percent of assets. By 1968, that last figure had risen to 60.9 percent.[45] These giant enterprises generated by far the largest share of nongovernment funds and provided most of the nongovernment personnel involved in industrial research and development. These same firms were the prime contractors used by the government in World War II and in the two decades of the cold war. They were the companies that provided the hardware for its atomic energy and space programs. They, too, were the same enterprises that continued to present the "American challenge" to European and other businessmen overseas.

This brief review of the spread of modern business enterprise after World War I can only hint at the diversity and complexity of the process. It cannot indicate the responses—some successful and others much less so—of individual enterprises or even of the institution as a whole, to the coming of the great depression, World War II, the cold war, or the continuing fluctuations of the business cycle. Nor does it attempt to delineate the costs as well as the benefits of efficient, high-volume exploitation of resources.

The purpose of this review has been only to emphasize the fact that modern business enterprise had reached its maturity in the United States by the 1920s. It continued to flourish and to spread in those sectors of the economy where administrative coordination proved more profitable than market coordination—in those sectors where the visible hand of management had demonstrated its value. The fundamental changes in the organization of American business enterprise and of the economy came before World War I; and they came as a response to profound market and technological changes that began in the middle of the nineteenth century.

Conclusion: The Managerial Revolution in American Business

This study does more than trace the history of an institution. It describes the beginnings of a new economic function—that of administrative coordination and allocation—and the coming of a new subspecies of economic man—the salaried manager—to carry out this function. Technological innovation, the rapid growth and spread of population, and expanding per capita income made the processes of production and distribution more complex and increased the speed and volume of the flow of materials through them. Existing market mechanisms were often no longer able to coordinate these flows effectively. The new technologies and expanding markets thus created for the first time a need for administrative coordination. To carry out this function entrepreneurs built multiunit business enterprises and hired the managers needed to administer them. Where the new enterprises were able to coordinate current flows of materials profitably, their managers also allocated resources for future production and distribution. As technology became both more complex and more productive, and as markets continued to expand, these managers assumed command in the central sectors of the American economy.

General patterns of institutional growth

The significance of the coming of this new function and class for an understanding of American economic history can be pinpointed by briefly summarizing the general patterns of growth. Such a summary demonstrates how historical experience substantiates the general propositions

484

outlined in the introduction to this study. It suggests areas of research for economists concerned with industrial organization and the theory of the firm and for historians concerned with the new class and its growing power in the American economy. Although this summary deals only with the institution in the United States, it can provide a set of ideas for analyzing and explaining its history in other economies as well.

The multiunit business enterprise, it must always be kept in mind, is a modern phenomenon. It did not exist in the United States in 1840. At that time the volume of economic activity was not yet large enough to make administrative coordination more productive and, therefore, more profitable than market coordination. Neither the needs nor the opportunities existed to build a multiunit enterprise. The few prototypes of the modern firm—textile mills and the Springfield Armory—remained single-unit enterprises. The earliest multiunit enterprise, the Bank of the United States, became extremely powerful and, partly because of its power, was short-lived. Until coal provided a cheap and flexible source of energy and until the railroad made possible fast, regular all-weather transportation, the processes of production and distribution continued to be managed in much the same way as they had been for half a millennium. All these processes, including transportation and finance, were carried out by small personally owned and managed firms.

The first modern enterprises were those created to administer the operation of the new railroad and telegraph companies. Adminstrative coordination of the movement of trains and the flow of traffic was essential for the safety of the passengers and the efficient movement of a wide variety of freight across the nation's rails. Such coordination was also necessary to transmit thousands of messages across its telegraph wires. In other forms of transportation and communication, where the volume of traffic was less varied or moved at slower speeds, coordination was less necessary. There the large enterprise was slower in coming. When steamship and urban traction lines did increase in size, they had little difficulty in adapting procedures perfected by the railroads. And when the development of long-distance technology permitted the creation of a national telephone system, the enterprise that managed it became organized along the lines of Western Union.

The new speed and volume of distribution brought a revolution in marketing. Multiunit enterprises began to coordinate the greatly expanded flows of goods from producers to consumers. The commodity dealers, the large full-line wholesalers, and the new mass retailers (department stores, mail-order houses, and chains) pushed aside the existing commission merchants. The administrative coordination they provided permitted them to lower prices and still make profits higher than those of the merchants they replaced. As time passed, the mass retailers supplanted the wholesalers because they internalized one more set of transactions and so coordinated flows more directly and efficiently.

In production, the first modern managers came in those industries and enterprises where technology permitted several processes of production to be carried on within a single factory or works (that is, internalized). In those industries, output soared as energy was used more intensively and as machinery, plant design, and administrative procedures were improved. As the number of workers required for a given unit of output declined, the number of managers needed to supervise these flows increased. Mass production factories became manager-intensive. Nevertheless, as long as the output of these factories was distributed efficiently by the new mass marketers, the manufacturing enterprise remained small. Only a score of managers were needed to manage even the largest of the new factories.

On the other hand, where the mass marketers were unable to provide the services needed to distribute the goods in the volume in which they could be produced, the enterprise became large. The modern industrial enterprise began when manufacturers built their own sales and distribution networks, and then their own extensive purchasing organizations. By integrating mass production with mass distribution, they came to coordinate administratively the flow of a high volume of goods from the suppliers of the raw materials through the processes of production and distribution to the retailer or ultimate consumer.

In all these new enterprises—the railroads, the telegraph, the mass marketers, and the mass producers—a managerial hierarchy had to be created to supervise several operating units and to coordinate and monitor their activities. The railroads, in managing their huge regional systems, and Western Union, in administering its national one, had to recruit large managerial staffs that included several levels of middle managers. On the other hand, in the marketing and the nonintegrated mass producing enterprises and in all but the largest steamship, traction, and utilities companies, the managerial hierarchy remained relatively small. But when an enterprise integrated mass production with mass distribution, its management became even larger than those in transportation and communication.

Once such a hierarchy had successfully taken over the function of coordinating flows, the desire of the managers to assure the success of their enterprise as a profit-making institution created strong pressures for its continuing growth. Such growth normally resulted from two quite different strategies of expansion. One was defensive or negative and stemmed from a desire for security. Its purpose was to prevent sources of supplies or outlets for goods and services from being cut off or to limit entry of new competitors into the trade. The other strategy was more positive. Its aim was to add new units, permitting by means of administrative coordination a more intensive use of existing facilities and personnel. Such positive growth might be considered as productive expansion and negative or defensive growth as nonproductive expansion. One increased productivity by lowering unit costs, the other rarely did.

In the growth of railroad and telegraph enterprises, both positive and negative motives were significant. Expanding the system by building or buying lines into another major commercial center helped to assure fuller use of existing facilities and personnel. This was particularly true if connecting lines were not adequate to handle the full flow of current traffic. Such expansion was also used to prevent a basic source or outlet of traffic from being taken over by a rival road or to prevent a rival from obtaining access to sources of traffic. Once the nation's basic transportation network had been completed, defensive rather than productive growth became the norm. Where lines already existed with capacity to carry current traffic, the building or buying of additional roads resulted almost wholly from defensive measures. The costs of such expansion were far greater than any savings that might be achieved from more efficient coordination of flows. For this reason, the building of the giant systems during the 1880s and 1890s resulted in nonproductive rather than productive expansion of railroad enterprises.

Defensive motives were less significant to the modern marketing enterprises. Because the marketers normally had a number of suppliers, they were rarely threatened by the possibility of having their stocks cut off. Nor was there much opportunity to keep stocks out of competitors' hands. The marketers went into manufacturing only on those relatively rare occasions when processors were unable to provide the goods at the price, quality, and quantity desired. The cost of obtaining expensive manufacturing plants normally outweighed any gains to be achieved by more effective coordination. Nor were there defensive reasons to integrate forward. The wholesalers had little to gain by purchasing their customers, and the retailers were, of course, at the end of the distribution line.

The basic strategy of growth for the mass marketers was, then, one of productive expansion. They expanded by adding new outlets and new lines that permitted them to make more complete use of their centralized buying, goods handling, and administrative facilities. A comparable strategy of productive expansion was carried on in the twentieth century by banks and other financial and service enterprises. They became large, managerial firms by adding new branches or outlets that permitted them to make more intensive use of their centralized services and facilities.

For those manufacturers who moved into mass distribution when they found existing marketers inadequate for their distribution needs, the motives for expansion were both defensive and productive. The initial reasons for building their marketing and then their purchasing organizations were positive; in the beginning the creation of a buying and selling network was essential to insure the administrative coordination needed to keep their production facilities fully employed. Necessary for the mass production and mass distribution of their products, the administrative coordination made possible by obtaining such selling, buying, and transportation facilities provided these enterprises with a powerful barrier to competition.

Integration backwards into the control of materials, on the other hand, tended to be more defensive than productive. It was productive where, as in the case of food and tobacco companies, suppliers were numerous and scattered. Then the creation of an extensive buying network made possible the maintenance of a high-volume flow of perishable or semiperishable products into processing plants. But where supplies were limited or could be easily controlled by a small number of enterprises, expansion was defensive. Mass producers wanted to have assured control over at least some of the sources of raw or semifinished materials. They also found it advantageous to bar others from access to these supplies. The savings from improved scheduling hardly covered the heavy cost of such investments.

Positive motives appeared and played a larger role than did defensive ones in the *continuing* growth of the large integrated industrial enterprise. Like the marketers, the industrialists continued to set up new branch sales offices at home and abroad. Increases in sales, in turn, brought expansion in manufacturing facilities and enlarged purchasing organizations. These industrial firms also added new lines to make more intensive use of their buying, selling, and processing facilities. Such additions, in turn, required the creation of new facilities. The sale of by-products in markets different from those of the primary line called for the creation of new marketing departments. Lines taken on to make fuller use of a distributing network often required the development of new manufacturing and purchasing units. In time such enterprises found it profitable to produce and market products that made use of only their technological capacities and managerial experience. Such moves into new product lines for new markets were not done to protect their own sources or outlets, or to take preventive action against others. They were to permit the continuing use of existing resources as well as to develop new ones.

Because large integrated industrial enterprises carried on a wider variety of functions over a wider geographical area than did marketing, transportation, and communications enterprises, they had greater potential for continuing growth. The facilities and administrative skills of the railroad and telegraph companies could not be easily transferred to other economic activities. The marketers, with their small investment in and little pressure to buy into manufacturing, remained marketers. Their expansion was limited to the number of outlets that could make effective use of their centralized purchasing and other facilities. Much the same was true of financial firms and a variety of such enterprises.

On the other hand, the large integrated industrial enterprises, with their extensive marketing, manufacturing, purchasing, raw-materials producing, transportation, and research facilities, had a wider variety of resources that could be transferred to the production and distribution of other products for other markets. The executives in these large managerial hierarchies were trained in different types of economic activity and so were better equipped to take on the manufacture and sale of new products in new markets than were those in enterprises that carried out only one basic function—finance, marketing, transportation, or communication. Moreover, because the large integrated industrial had more and different types of operating units than other kinds of business enterprises, the likelihood that units might be underutilized was greater. It was rare for all units in such an enterprise to be operating at the same speed and capacity. Such disequilibrium provided constant pressure for the growth of the firm.[1] Whether the enterprise was pushed by the need to use existing physical and human resources or pulled by the coming of new markets that might use its facilities, it tended to move into areas where existing demand and technology created the needs and opportunities for administrative coordination. Such productive expansion was inherently more profitable than defensive expansion, and so set the direction in which the enterprise grew. And the distance the enterprise moved in this direction was closely related to the nature of its resources, the skills of its managers, and the transferability of these resources and skills to new products, services, and markets.

In those industries where administrative coordination of mass production and mass distribution was profitable, a few large vertically integrated firms quickly dominated. Concentration and oligopoly appeared as a consequence of the need for and the profitability of administrative coordination. Where markets and technology did not give the manufacturing or processing enterprises a competitive advantage, large mass retailers came increasingly to coordinate flows. Because of the number and complexity, of these flows, many small suppliers and distributors, including brokers and freight forwarders, continued to fill-in and even-out the flows. Their functions, however, supplemented, and were integrated into, the larger economy by the coordinating activities of the mass producers and mass marketers.

Although administrative coordination has been a basic function in the modernization of the American economy, economists have given it little attention. Many have remained satisfied with Adam Smith's dictum that the division of labor reflects the extent of the market. Like George Stigler, they see the natural response to improved technology and markets as one of increasing specialization in the activities of the enterprise and vertical disintegration in the industries in which these enterprises operate.[2] Such an analysis has historical validity for the years before 1850 but has little relevance to much of the economy after the completion of the transportation and communication infrastructure. Besides ignoring the historical experience, such a view fails to consider the fact that increasing specialization must, almost by definition, call for more carefully planned coordination if volume output demanded by mass markets is to be achieved.

Economists have also often failed to relate administrative coordination to the theory of the firm. For example, far more economies result from the careful coordination of flow through the processes of production and distribution than from increasing the size of producing or distributing units in terms of capital facilities or number of workers. Any theory of the firm that defines the enterprise merely as a factory or even a number of factories, and therefore fails to take into account the role of administrative coordination, is far removed from reality.

In addition, administrative coordination helps to account for a significant segment of what economists have defined as a residual, that is, the proportion of output that cannot be explained by the growth of input. Certainly the speed and regularity with which goods flow through the processes of production and distribution and the way these flows are organized affect the volume and unit cost. Until economists analyze the function of administrative coordination, the theory of the firm will remain essentially a theory of production. The institution through which the factors of production are combined, which coordinates current flows, and which allocates resources for future economic activities in major sectors of the economy deserves more attention than it has yet received from economists.

The ascendancy of the manager

Historians as well as economists have failed to consider the implications of the rise of modern business enterprise. They have studied the entrepreneurs who created modern business enterprise, but more in moral than in analytical terms. Their concern has been more whether they were exploiters (robber barons) or creators (industrial statesmen). Historians have also been fascinated by the financiers who for brief periods allocated funds to transportation, communication, and some industrial enterprises and so appeared to have control of major sectors of the economy. But they have paid almost no notice at all to the managers who, because they carried out a basic new economic function, continued to play a far more central role in the operations of the American economy than did the robber barons, industrial statesmen, or financiers. When they have looked at the development of the American economic system, historians have been more concerned about the continuing of family (that is, entrepreneurial) capitalism or of financial capitalism than about the spread of managerial capitalism.

At the beginning of this century the American economic system still included elements of financial and family capitalism. Managerial capitalism was not yet fully dominant. Where the initial cost of facilities was high, as was the case with the railroad, the telegraph, urban traction lines, and other utilities, investment bankers and other financial intermediaries who had played a major role in raising funds for the enterprise continued to participate in decisions on the allocation of resources for the future. Where, as was the case with the mass marketers, initial capital costs were low and high volume output generated funds for expansion, the entrepreneurs who created the firm and their families continued to have a say in top management decisions. But by 1917 representatives of an entrepreneurial family or a banking house almost never took part in middle management decisions on prices, output, deliveries, wages, and employment required in the coordinating of current flows. Even in top management decisions concerning the allocation of resources, their power remained essentially negative. They could say no, but unless they themselves were trained managers with long experience in the same industry and even the same company, they had neither the information nor the experience to propose positive alternative courses of action.

The relationship between ownership and management within the integrated industrial firm reflected the way in which it became large. The experience of those that expanded initially by building an extensive marketing and purchasing organization paralleled that of the mass marketers. Because internally generated funds paid for the facilities and financed continued growth, the founder and his family retained control. Even when the enterprise went to the money markets for funds to supplement retained earnings for expansion, the family continued to own a large minority and nearly always controlling share of its stock.

Nevertheless, members of the entrepreneurial family rarely became active in top management unless they themselves were trained as professional managers. Since the profits of the family enterprise usually assured them of a large personal income, they had little financial incentive to spend years working up the managerial ladder. Therefore, in only a few of the large American business enterprises did family members continue to participate for more than two generations in the management of the companies they owned.

The descendants of the founders of and early investors in such industrial enterprises continued to reap the profits of successful administrative coordination. Indeed, the majority of American fortunes came from the building and operation of modern business enterprises. These families remain the primary beneficiaries of managerial capitalism, but they are no longer involved in the operation of its central institution. By mid-twentieth century few had any direct say in the decisions concerning current flows and future allocations so essential to the operation of the American economy.

A comparable pattern occurred in those industrial enterprises that grew large through merger rather than through internal growth. The financiers who provided or arranged to obtain funds to rationalize and centralize production and to create new marketing and purchasing organizations remained on the boards of consolidated industrial enterprises. They rarely, however, had as strong an influence on the boards of directors of industrial enterprises as they had on the boards of railroad companies. The capital needed for the initial reorganizations was less than that required for railroad system-building, and the profits for internal financing generated by these industrials was higher. In a few of the largest and best-known mergers—General Electric, United States Steel, International Harvester, and Allis Chalmers—outside directors from the financial community outnumbered insiders taken from management. But on the boards of a much greater number of food, machinery, chemical, oil, rubber, and primary metals enterprises, outside financiers were very much in the minority. Their influence was significant only when the enterprise decided to go to the money markets to supplement retained earnings. With a few notable exceptions, such as United States Steel, managers soon came to command those enterprises where financiers were originally influential. Financial capitalism in the United States was a narrowly located, short-lived phenomenon.

By mid-century even the legal fiction of outside control was beginning to disappear. A study of the 200 largest nonfinancial companies in 1963 indicates that in none of these firms did an individual, family, or group hold over 80 percent of the stock.[3] None were still privately owned. In only 5 of the 200 did a family or group have a majority control by owning as much as 50 percent of the stock. In 26 others a family or group had minority control by holding more than 10 percent of the stock (but less than 50) or by using a holding company or other legal device. In 1963, then, 169 or 84.5 percent of the 200 largest nonfinancial companies were management controlled. In 5 of these firms families did still have influence, but because they were professional, full-time salaried executives, not because of stock they held. Thus by the 1950s the managerial firm had become the standard form of modern business enterprise in major sectors of the American economy. In those sectors where modern multiunit enterprise had come to dominate, managerial capitalism had gained ascendancy over family and financial capitalism.

As the influence of the families and the financiers grew even weaker in the management of modern business enterprise, that of the workers through representatives of their union increased. Union influence, however, directly affected only one set of management decisions—those made by middle managers relating to wages, hiring, firing, and conditions of work. Such decisions had only an indirect impact on the central ones that coordinated current flows and allocated resources for the future.

Except on the railroads, the influence of the working force on the decisions made by managers of modern business enterprises did not begin until the 1930s. Before then craft unions had some success in organizing the workers in such labor-intensive skilled trades as cigar, garment, hat, and stove marking, shipbuilding, and coal mining—trades in which modern business enterprise rarely flourished. They organized the workers in the shops of small, single-unit, owner-managed firms into local, city, and state unions. These regional organizations were represented in a national union which was, in turn, loosely affiliated with other craft unions in the American Federation of Labor.

The craft unions, however, made little effort to unionize those industries where administrative coordination paid off. Workers in the mass production industries, where the large modern industrial enterprises clustered, were primarily semiskilled and unskilled workers. Those industries employed few skilled craftsmen. With the coming of the modern factory, the plant manager and his staff took over from the foreman the decisions concerning hiring, firing, and promotion, as well as those on wages, hours, and conditions of work. As the enterprise grew, such decisions were placed in the hands of middle management. Policy matters were determined by executives in new personnel departments housed in the central office. And until the 1930s, these middle managers were rarely forced to consider seriously the demands of labor unions to represent the workers in making such decisions.

Even with the strong support of the Roosevelt administration, the American Federation of Labor was unable to meet the challenge of organizing the mass production industries.[4] The success of such an organizing drive required the restructuring of its unions along industrial—plant and enterprise—rather than geographical—city and state—lines. In addition, the craft unions had difficulty in devising a program that appealed to the semi- and the unskilled workers and still met the needs of their skilled members. Only in 1936 after the creation of the Committee for Industrial Organization, after its split from the A F of L, and after the resulting "civil war" in the ranks of labor, did the mass production industries begin to be extensively unionized. Only then did the managers of large enterprises in the automobile, machinery, electrical, chemical, rubber, glass, and primary metals industries begin to share their decisions with representatives of their working forces.

Even so, union leaders, during the great organizing drives of the late 1930s and immediately after World War II, rarely, if ever, sought to have a say in the determination of policies other than those that directly affected the lives of their members. They wanted to take part only in those concerning wages, hours, working rules, hiring, firing, and promotion. Even the unsuccessful demand "to look at the company's books" was viewed as a way to assure union members that they were receiving a fair share of the income generated by the company. The union members almost never asked to participate in decisions concerning output, pricing, scheduling, and resource allocation.

A critical issue over which labor and management fought in the years immediately after World War II was whether the managers or the union would control the hiring of workers. With the passage of the Taft-Hartley Act of 1947, the managers retained control over hiring, a prerogative that has never been seriously challenged since. And since that time the unions have made few determined efforts to acquire more of "management's prerogatives."

The actions of government officials, particularly those of the federal government, have had an increasingly greater impact on managerial decisions than have those of the representatives of workers, owners, or financiers. By and large, however, their impact has been indirect. They have helped to shape the environment in which management makes its decisions, but, except in time of war, these officials have only occasionally participated in the making of the decisions themselves. And since the market has always been the prime factor in management decisions, the government's most significant role has been in shaping markets for the goods and services of modern business enterprise.

Prior to the depression and World War II, the impact of the state and federal government on the modern corporation was primarily through taxes, tariffs, and regulatory legislation. Taxes remained low until the war and had a minimal impact on the direction and rate of growth of the modern managerial enterprises and the sectors they administered. Tariffs, which protected all industries, were of more help in maintaining small-unit, competitive enterprises than in assisting those that exploited the economies of speed and sold their products on a global scale. Antitrust legislation and, since its founding in 1914, the Federal Trade Commission have continued to discourage monopoly and encourage oligopoly. The Federal Reserve Board, formed in 1914, has affected the interest rates and money markets and therefore the managers' financial environment. The wave of regulatory legislation passed during the New Deal reduced the choices open to management in transportation, communications, and utilities enterprises. However, except in the issuance of securities, the new legislation placed few limitations on the discretionary power of mass marketers and mass producers to coordinate flows and allocate resources.

The government's role in the economy expanded sharply in the 1930s and 1940s. With the coming of World War II, the federal government became for the first time a major customer of American business enterprise. Before that time, except for a brief period during World War I, government buyers, including the military forces, provided only a tiny market for the food, machinery, chemical, oil, rubber, and primary metal companies that made up the roster of American big business. The suggestion that the *rise* of big business has any relation to government and military expenditures (or for that matter to monetary and fiscal policies) has no historical substance. Only during and after the Second World War did the government become a major market for industrial goods. In the postwar years, that market has been substantial, but it has been concentrated in a small number of industries, such as aircraft, missiles, instruments, communication equipment, electronic components, and shipbuilding.[5] Outside these industries, output continues to go primarily to non-government customers.

Far more important to the spread and continued growth of modern business enterprise than direct purchases has been the government's role in maintaining full employment and high aggregate demand. Again, it was only after World War II that the government inaugurated any sort of systematic policy to maintain demand and thereby support the mass market. One reason the federal government took on this responsibility was that the depression clearly demonstrated the inability of the private sector of the economy to maintain continuing growth of a complex, highly differentiated mass production, mass distribution economy. In the 1920s, the new corporate giants had begun to calibrate supply with demand. They had no way, however, of sustaining aggregate demand or of reviving it if it fell off. In the middle and later part of the decade, when national income stopped growing, the larger firms maintained existing output or cut back a bit. When the 1929 stock market crash dried up credit and further reduced demand, they could only roll with the punches. As demand fell, these enterprises cut production, laid off workers, and canceled orders for supplies and materials. Such actions further reduced purchasing power and with it aggregate demand. The very ability to effectively coordinate supply with demand intensified the economic decline. The downward pressure continued relentlessly. In less than four years, the national income was slashed in half. The 1931 forecasts of General Motors and General Electric for 1932, for example, were horrendous. At best they might operate at about 25 percent of capacity.

The only institution capable of stopping this economic descent was the federal government. During the 1930s, it began to undertake this role, but with great reluctance. Politicians and government officials moved hesitantly. And managers and businessmen, those who had the most to gain, were among the most outspoken critics of the few moves that were made. Until the recession of 1937, President Franklin D. Roosevelt and Secretary of the Treasury Henry Morgenthau still expected to balance the budget and bring to an end government intervention in the economy. Roosevelt and his cabinet considered large-scale government spending and employment a temporary expedient. When Roosevelt decided in 1936 that, despite high unemployment, the depression was over, he reduced government expenditures. National income, production, and demand immediately plummeted. By then, a few economists and government officials and still fewer business managers began to see more clearly the relationship between government spending and the level of economic activity. Nevertheless, the acceptance of the government's role in maintaining economic growth and stability was still almost a decade away.

During World War II attitudes changed. The mobilization of the war economy brought corporation managers to Washington to carry out one of the most complex pieces of economic planning in history. That experience lessened ideological anxieties about the government's role in stabilizing the economy. Then the fear of postwar recession and consequent return of mass unemployment brought support for legislation to commit the federal government to maintaining full employment and aggregate demand. While a few managers and businessmen favored such legislation, most continued to oppose what they considered government interference in the processes of business. The Employment Act of 1946 passed only through the concerted efforts of liberal and labor groups.[6] By the 1950s, however, businessmen in general and professional managers in particular had begun to see the benefits of a government commitment to maintaining aggregate demand. They supported the efforts of both Democratic and

Republican administrations during the recessions of 1949, 1957, and 1960 to provide stability through fiscal policies involving the building of highways and shifting defense contracts.

In carrying out these policies, the government officials had no intention of replacing the managers as the coordinators of current demand and allocators of resources for the future. They acted only when the activities of the corporate managers failed to maintain full employment and high demand. The federal government became a coordinator and allocator of last resort.

In the United States, neither the labor unions nor the government has taken part in carrying out the basic functions of modern business enterprise as it has been defined in this study. They had had as little *direct* say as the representatives of the owners or financiers in decisions coordinating current flows and allocating resources for future production and distribution. Such decisions remain market-oriented. They continued to reflect the managers' perceptions of how to use technology and capital to meet their estimates of market demand.

The appearance of managerial capitalism has been, therefore, an economic phenomenon. It has had little political support among the American electorate. At least until the 1940s, modern business enterprise grew in spite of public and government opposition. Many Americans—probably a majority—looked on large-scale enterprise with suspicion. The concentrated economic power such enterprises wielded violated basic democratic values. Their existence dampened entrepreneurial opportunity in many sectors of the economy. Their managers were not required to explain or be accountable for their uses of power.

For these reasons the coming of modern business enterprise in its several different forms brought strong political reaction and legislative action. The control and regulation of the railroads, of the three types of mass retailers—department stores, mail-order houses, and the chains—and of the large industrial enterprise became major political issues. In the first decade of the twentieth century, the control of the large corporation was, in fact, the paramount political question of the day. The protest against the new type of business enterprise was led by merchants, small manufacturers, and other businessmen, including commercial farmers, who felt their economic interests threatened by the new institution. By basing their arguments on traditional ideology and traditional economic beliefs, they won widespread support for their views. Yet in the end, the protests, the political campaigns, and the resulting legislation did little to retard the continuing growth of the new institution and the new class that managed it.

The United States: seed-bed of managerial capitalism

Modern business enterprise has appeared in all technologically advanced market economies. Comparable protests, even stronger ideological and political opposition, has not prevented its emergence and spread in western Europe and Japan. In recent years the same type of multiunit enterprises, using comparable administrative procedures and organizational structures, have come to dominate much the same type of industries as in the United States.[7] In these industries a new managerial class has become responsible for coordinating current flows of goods and services and allocating resources for future production and distribution. The study of the past history and present operations of modern business enterprise in Europe and Japan provides as significant a challenge to economists and historians as the analysis of the American story.

In Europe and Japan, however, the new institution appeared in smaller numbers and, at least until after World War II, spread more slowly than it did in the United States. Because it came slower and later, its builders and administrators have often looked to the American experience for models and precedents. Therefore one of the most significant questions for economists and historians studying modern business enterprise in its international setting is to explain why the institution appeared so quickly and in such profusion in the United States.

An obvious, though still untested, reason why the United States became the seed-bed for managerial capitalism was the size and nature of its domestic market. In the second part of the nineteenth century the American domestic market was the largest and, what is more important, the fastest growing market in the world. In 1880, the nation's national income and its population were one and a half times those of Great Britain. By 1900, they were twice the size of Britain's and, by 1920, three times the size.[8] As Simon Kuznets's carefully drawn data reveal, the rate of growth of the American population and national product was consistently much higher than that of other technologically advanced nations—France and Germany, as well as Britain—during the years between the American Civil War and World War I.

The American market was not only larger and faster growing than in these other nations; it was also more homogeneous. Income distribution appears to have been less skewed than in other nations. Markets were less defined by class lines than they were in Europe. The newness of the American market—much of which had been unsettled wilderness a few decades earlier—also meant that business enterprises were new and business arrangements had not had time to become routinized and rigid.

The existence of such a fast-growing, homogeneous, open market did more than encourage the rise of mass marketers. It hastened the adoption of new technologies. This market stimulated the rapid spread of fundamental innovations—the railroad, the telegraph, and the new coal technologies in the furnace, foundry, and refining industries. It then encouraged Americans to pioneer in the machinery and organization of mass production. They developed machinery (often based on European innovations) to mass produce a wide variety of products. Of even more importance, they were the first to manufacture standardized machines by mass production methods.

Smaller and slower growing domestic markets in Western Europe and Japan lessened the interest of manufacturers in adopting new mass production techniques and also reduced the incentive to build large marketing and purchasing organizations. In Britain and France producers continued to rely on middlemen to handle their more traditional wares, which in turn were produced in a more traditional craft fashion. Where large, integrated enterprises did appear, they remained small enough to be managed at the top by a small number of owners. So the entrepreneurial enterprise and with it family capitalism continued to flourish. In Germany and Japan, where the integration of production and distribution was more common, smaller markets and cash flows reduced the opportunity to rely on internal financing and so increased the dependence on outside financiers—the large banks in Germany and the major financial groups (the Zaibatsu) in Japan. Managers continued to share top management decisions with financiers. There financial capitalism continued to hold sway.

Cultural and social differences also may have played a role in delaying the coming of the large managerial enterprise and with it managerial capitalism. Legal differences based on cultural values were of particular significance. The Sherman Act by prohibiting cartels of small family firms hastened the growth of big business in the United States. In Europe a family firm federated with other family firms, through holding companies in Britain or through cartels in Germany, to assure continuing profit. Even when European firms merged into integrated holding companies, they did so primarily for the defensive purpose of assuring outlets and supplies. Such companies remained essentially federations that employed neither middle nor top managers to coordinate flows of goods or allocate resources. Owners or their representatives made decisions on price, output, and coordination at weekly or monthly conferences. In the United States, such federations were illegal. The Sherman Act and its interpretation by the courts provided a powerful pressure that did not exist elsewhere to force family firms to consolidate their operations into a single, centrally operated enterprise administered by salaried managers.

In Europe, class distinctions may have made a difference. Families identified themselves more closely with the firm that provided the income with which to maintain their status more than did families in the United States. In those large enterprises that did integrate mass production and mass distribution and in which the owners hired middle managers to coordinate flows, the family continued to dominate top management. Often the family preferred not to expand the enterprise if it meant the loss of personal control.

Since World War II, such restraints have diminished, and the spread of managerial enterprise has accelerated within western Europe and Japan. The war and postwar needs have encouraged the adoption of new mass production technology. Domestic markets have grown rapidly as gross national output rose and as income became more equitably distributed. The coming of the European Economic Community further enlarged markets. Laws against monopoly and restrictive business practices have discouraged the continuance of holding companies and cartels of family firms. Class distinctions have blurred. Large enterprises with salaried top as well as middle managers have grown in size and increased in numbers. They have clustered in much the same industries as in the United States—those in which administrative coordination pays the best. With the spread of modern managerial business enterprise in Europe and Japan, all the paraphernalia of professional management has appeared—the associations, the journals, the training schools, and the consultants.[9]

Such comparisons between the development and operation of modern multiunit enterprise at home and abroad are only tentative. Much more information is needed to test these suggested hypotheses. Nevertheless, readily available data underline the central importance of administrative coordination and allocation to modern technologically advanced, urban, industrial market economies and emphasize the value of further study of the institution and class of managers.

The comparative approach is surely the proper one for such a continuing work in the history of modern business enterprise. Describing and analyzing the history of the new institution and the ways in which it has carried out its basic functions in different nations can help to define the organizational imperatives of modern economies and reveal much about the ways in which cultural attitudes, values, ideologies, political systems, and social structure affect these imperatives. As important, such studies can provide clues to ways to answer a critical issue of modern times. They may suggest how narrowly trained managers, who must administer the processes of production and distribution in complex modern economies, can be made responsible for their actions—actions that have far-reaching consequences.

Appendixes, Notes, and Index

Appendix A. Industrial enterprises with assets of $20 million or more, 1917

Rank[a]	Firm	Assets ($ millions)	Type[b]	Structure[c]	Comment[d]
Groups 10 and 12: Mining companies[e]					
29.	Chile Copper Co.	136.0	—	—	(Insuf.) Possibly a sales force
32.	Consolidation Coal Co.	127.8	I	FD	
42.	Pittsburgh Coal Co.	112.9	I	FD	
50.	Philadelphia & Reading Coal & Iron Co.	100.0	I	FD	(Inc.)
60.	Calumet & Hecla Mining Co.	85.8	I	FD	(Inc.)
67.	Lehigh Coal & Navigation Co.	81.4	I	FD	Subsidiaries for utilities & transportation
68.	Utah Copper Co.	80.8	SF	Ex.	
85.	Greene Cananea Copper Co.	59.1	SF	Ex.	
91.	United Verde Extension Mining Co.	55.4	SF	Ex.	
100.	United Verde Copper Co.	50.0	SF	Ex.	
102.	Calumet & Arizona Mining Co.	49.4	SF	Ex.	
105.	Cleveland-Cliffs Iron Co.	46.9	I	FD	
113.	Glen Alden Coal Co.	45.0	—	—	(Insuf.)
116.	Inspiration Consolidated Copper Co.	44.6	SF	Ex.	
119.	Cerro de Pasco Copper	43.9	SF	Ex.	
125.	Lehigh Valley Coal Co.	42.7	I	—	Functional sales subsidiary
133.	Lehigh & Wilkes-Barre Coal Co.	40.4	I	FD	
148.	Goldfield Consolidated Mines Co.	36.7	I	FD	
152.	Ray Consolidated Copper Co.	35.9	SF	Ex.	
157.	Bunker Hill & Sullivan Mining and Concen. Co.	35.0	SF	Ex.	
175.	Nevada Consolidated Copper Co.	32.7	SF	Ex.	
177.	Miami Copper Co.	32.4	SF	Ex.	
189.	Berwind-White Coal Mining Co.	30.0	—	—	(Insuf.)
200.	Homestake Mining Co.	28.6	SF	Ex.	
209.	Elk Horn Coal Corp.	27.4	SF	Ex.	(Inc.)
233.	Clinchfield Coal Corp.	24.7	I	—	Functional subsidiaries
240.	Chino Copper Co.	24.3	SF	Ex.	
254.	Pocohontas Fuel Co.	21.9	I	FD	

Appendix A. *Continued*

Ranka	Firm	Assets ($ millions)	Typeb	Structurec	Commentd
271.	Federal Mining & Smelting Co.	20.2	SF	Ex.	
275.	Jamison Coal & Coke Co.	20.0	SF	Ex.	
Group 13: Petroleum and gas extraction					
48.	Prairie Oil & Gas Co.	102.6	SF	Ex.	
61.	Ohio Oil Co.	85.4	SF	Ex.	
151.	California Petroleum Corp.	36.0	SF	Ex.	
162.	Texas Pacific Coal & Oil	35.0	SF	Ex.	Moving toward integration
168.	Houston Oil Co. of Texas	34.1	SF	Ex.	Oil and timber
205.	South Penn Oil Co.	27.9	SF	Ex.	(Inc.)
278.	Skelly-Sankey Oil Co.	20.0	SF	Ex.	Planning to integrate
Group 20: Food and like products					
4.	Armour & Co.	314.1	I	FD	
5.	Swift & Co.	306.3	I	FD	
28.	American Sugar Refining Co.	137.3	I	FD	
43.	Corn Products Refining Co.	112.0	I	FD	
49.	Wilson & Co.	102.0	I	FD	
57.	Morris & Co.	91.1	I	FD	
76.	National Biscuit Co.	73.5	I	FD	
79.	Cudahy Packing Co.	64.7	I	FD	
90.	Distillers Securities Corp.	55.7	I	—	Legal delay. Toward FD
93.	Great Western Sugar Co.	54.0	—	—	(Insuf.)
97.	Cuban American Sugar Co.	51.4	I	HC(f)	
103.	Borden's Condensed Milk Co.	47.5	I	FD	Two divisions
126.	American Cotton Oil Co.	42.4	I	FD	Subsidiaries for by-products
130.	E. Anheuser Brewing Assoc.	41.5	I	FD	
134.	Quaker Oats Co.	40.0	I	FD	
155.	American Ice Co.	35.2	I	—	Functional and regional departments
165.	Fleischmann Co.	34.5	I	FD	
169.	California Packing Corp.	33.7	I	FD	
186.	American Beet Sugar Co.	30.5	I	FD	(Inc.)
194.	Royal Baking Powder Co.	30.0	I	FD	
196.	Standard Milling Co.	29.3	I	FD	(Inc.)
207.	Booth Fisheries	27.5	I	FD	
212.	Coca Cola Co.	27.0	I	FD	
214.	Utah-Idaho Sugar Co.	26.7	I	FD	

Appendix A. *Continued*

Rank[a]	Firm	Assets ($ millions)	Type[b]	Structure[c]	Comment[d]
220.	Libby, Mcneill & Libby	26.0	I	FD	
223.	Southern Cotton Oil Co.	25.9	I	—	(Insuf.)
226.	H. J. Heinz Co.	25.0	I	FD	
228.	Jos. Schlitz Beverage Co.	25.0	I	FD	
236.	Ward Baking Co. of NY	24.6	—	—	(Insuf.)
242.	Federal Sugar Refining Co.	23.8	I	—	(Insuf.)
246.	Wm. Wrigley Jr. Co.	23.0	I	FD	
247.	Pittsburgh Brewing Co.	22.9	I	FD	
259.	Loose-Wiles Biscuit Co.	21.3	I	FD	
279.	Washburn-Crosby Co.	20.0	I	FD	
357.	American Chicle Co.[f]	15.1	I	FD	

Group 21: Tobacco manufactures

18.	American Tobacco Co.	164.2	I	FD	
44.	Liggett & Meyers Tobacco Co.	111.2	I	FD	
81.	P. Lorillard Co.	63.4	I	FD	
111.	American Cigar Co.	45.0	I	FD	
146.	R. J. Reynolds Tobacco Co.	37.4	I	FD	
153.	General Cigar Co.	35.7	I	FD	

Group 22: Textile mill products

36.	American Woolen Co.	123.0	I	FD	Foreign sales by branch office, domestic sales by commission agents
128.	Pacific Mills	42.4	SF	Mfg.	
195.	American Thread Co.	29.8	SF	Mfg.	
237.	Arlington Mills	24.4	SF	Mfg.	
238.	Plymouth Cordage Co.	24.4	I	FD	
249.	American Manufacturing Co.	22.3	I	FD	(Inc.)
263.	Fall River Iron Works	20.6	SF	Mfg.	Former iron works plant used for textile printing

Group 23: Apparel and related products

163.	Cluett, Peabody & Co.	34.9	I	FD	
213.	Hart, Schaffner & Marx	26.9	I	FD	(Inc.)
235.	National Cloak & Suit Co.	24.7	—	—	(Insuf.)

Group 24: Lumber and wood products, excluding furniture

21.	Weyerhaeuser Timber Co.	153.2	I	FD	
221.	Red River Lumber Co.	26.0	I	FD	
232.	Long-Bell Lumber Co.	24.8	I	FD	

Rank[a]	Firm	Assets ($ millions)	Type[b]	Structure[c]	Comment[d]
257.	Potlach Forests	21.6	—	—	(Insuf.)
265.	Great Southern Lumber Co.	20.5	I	FD	
Group 26: Paper and allied products					
70.	International Paper Co.	77.6	I	FD	
131.	American Writing Paper Co.	41.3	I	FD	
139.	Bemis Bros. Bag Co.	39.2	I	FD	
193.	Great Northern Paper Co.	30.0	I	FD	
199.	West Va. Pulp & Paper Co.	28.7	I	FD	
243.	Crown Willamette Paper Co.	23.6	I	FD	(Inc.)
274.	Brown Co.	20.0	I	FD	
Group 27: Printing and publishing					
158.	Hearst Publications	35.0	SF	Mfg.	
166.	Curtis Publishing Co.	34.2	SF	Mfg.	
269.	Butterick Co.	20.3	—	HC	(Inc.)
Group 28: Chemicals					
8.	E. I. du Pont de Nemours & Co.	263.3	I	FD	
20.	Union Carbide & Carbon Corp.	155.9	I	HC	Product divisions
55.	Va.-Carolina Chemical Co.	94.4	I	FD	(Inc.)
66.	American Agricultural Chemical Co.	82.1	I	FD	Some integrated subsidiaries
73.	New Jersey Zinc Co.	75.0	I	HC(f)	With centralized sales
83.	Procter & Gamble Co.	62.8	I	FD	
86.	National Lead Co.	58.7	I	FD	With integrated subsidiaries for downstream products
88.	General Chemical Co.	56.9	I	FD	
104.	United Drug Co.	47.4	I	FD	
114.	Barrett Co.	44.9	I	FD	
117.	National Aniline & Chemical Co.	44.2	I	FD	
122.	U.S. Industrial Alcohol Co.	43.5	I	HC(i)	
138.	American Linseed Oil Co.	39.4	I	FD	
150.	International Agricultural Corp.	36.4	I	FD	(Inc.)
154.	Semet-Solvay Co.	35.6	I	—	Two divisions; moving toward divisional structure
176.	Hercules Powder Co.	32.5	I	FD	

Appendix A. *Continued*

Rank[a]	Firm	Assets ($ millions)	Type[b]	Structure[c]	Comment[d]
180.	United Dyewood Corp.	31.9	I	HC(i)	Regional integrated subsidiaries
192.	Grasselli Chemical Co.	30.0	I	FD	
197.	Aetna Explosives Co.	29.0	I	FD	
217.	Atlas Powder Co.	26.1	I	FD	One integrated, regional subsidiary
266.	Sherwin-Williams Co.	20.4	I	FD	

Group 29: Petroleum refining and coal products

Rank[a]	Firm	Assets ($ millions)	Type[b]	Structure[c]	Comment[d]
2.	Standard Oil Co. of N.J.	574.1	I	HC(f&i)	Integrated and non-integrated subsidiaries
14.	Standard Oil Co. of N.Y.	204.3	I	FD	No crude
24.	Texas Co.	144.5	I	FD	
26.	Gulf Oil Co.	142.9	I	FD	
34.	Standard Oil Co. of Ind.	126.9	I	FD	Moving into crude
35.	Standard Oil Co. of Cal.	126.9	I	FD	
37.	Magnolia Oil Co.	122.8	I	FD	No crude
45.	Ohio Cities Gas Co.	110.0	I	FD	(Inc.) Has utilities; Pure Oil core enterprise
56.	Sinclair Oil & Refining Corp.	93.8	I	HC(f)	
64.	Pan American Petroleum & Transport Co.	83.0	I	HC	Functional and regional subsidiaries
69.	Associated Oil Co.	80.6	I	FD	
71.	Union Oil Co. of Cal.	77.5	I	FD	
72.	Vacuum Oil Co.	76.1	I	FD	No crude
84.	Atlantic Refining Co.	60.7	I	FD	
95.	Midwest Refining Co.	52.4	I	FD	
106.	Pierce Oil Corp.	46.7	I	FD	
110.	Cosden & Co.	45.5	I	FD	
124.	Tide Water Oil Co.	42.7	I	FD	Production and pipe line subsidiaries
132.	General Asphalt Co.	40.9	I	FD	
160.	Shell Co. of Cal.	35.0	I	FD	
178.	General Petroleum Corp.	32.2	I	FD	
229.	Sun Co.	25.0	I	FD	
261.	Producers & Refiners Corp.	20.9	I	FD	Sales primarily through outside marketing units
262.	Standard Oil Co. (Ohio)	20.7	I	FD	No crude

Appendix A. *Continued*

Rank[a]	Firm	Assets ($ millions)	Type[b]	Structure[c]	Comment[d]
Group 30: Rubber products					
9.	U.S. Rubber Co.	257.5	I	FD	Integrated divisions
22.	B. F. Goodrich Co.	146.1	I	FD	
65.	Goodyear Tire & Rubber Co.	82.5	I	FD	
96.	Firestone Tire & Rubber Co.	51.6	I	FD	
129.	Fisk Rubber Co.	41.9	I	HC(f)	
Group 31: Leather and its products					
23.	Central Leather Co.	145.3	I	FD	(Inc.)
112.	Endicott, Johnson & Co.	45.0	I	FD	
120.	American Hide & Leather Co.	43.9	I	FD	
149.	International Shoe Co.	36.6	I	FD	
Group 32: Stone, clay and glass products					
127.	Harbison-Walker Refractories	42.4	I	FD	
142.	Pittsburgh Plate Glass Co.	38.7	I	FD	
188.	Atlas Portland Cement Co.	30.0	I	FD	
208.	Lehigh Portland Cement Co.	27.5	I	FD	
230.	Owens Bottle Machine Corp.	24.9	I	FD	
272.	American Window Glass Co.	20.0	I	FD	
Group 33: Primary metal industries					
1.	U.S. Steel Corp.	2,449.5	I	HC(f & i)	
3.	Bethlehem Steel Corp.	381.5	I	FD	
6.	Midvale Steel & Ordnance Co.	270.0	I	FD	
10.	Phelps Dodge Corp.	232.3	I	FD	
12.	Anaconda Copper Corp.	225.8	I	FD	
13.	American Smelting & Refining Co.	221.8	I	FD	With geographical divisions
19.	Jones & Laughlin Steel Co.	159.6	I	FD	
27.	Kennecott Copper Corp.	142.4	I	—	(Insuf.)
39.	Republic Iron & Steel Co.	122.3	I	FD	Two regional, integrated divisions
40.	Lackawanna Steel Co.	117.3	I	FD	
47.	Aluminum Co. of America	104.0	I	FD	
53.	Youngstown Sheet & Tube Co.	97.0	I	FD	
54.	Colo. Fuel & Iron Co.	95.3	I	FD	
58.	Crucible Steel of America	90.3	I	FD	
59.	U.S. Smelting, Refining & Mining Co.	88.7	I	HC(f)	
82.	International Nickel Co.	63.1	I	FD	

Appendix A. *Continued*

Rank[a]	Firm	Assets ($ millions)	Type[b]	Structure[c]	Comment[d]
87.	Inland Steel Co.	57.4	I	FD	
107.	La Belle Iron Works	46.5	I	FD	
109.	Brier Hill Steel Co.	45.9	I	FD	(Inc.) Probably a small sales force
135.	M. A. Hanna & Co.	40.0	I	HC(f)	
137.	Trumbull Steel Co.	40.0	SF	Mfg.	(Inc.)
141.	American Steel Foundries	38.9	I	FD	
164.	Pittsburgh Steel Co.	34.7	I	FD	
179.	Woodward Iron Co.	32.0	I	FD	
184.	U.S. Cast Iron Pipe & Foundry	31.3	I	FD	
187.	American Rolling Mill	30.3	I	FD	
203.	United Alloy Steel Corp.	28.0	I	FD	
206.	Sloss-Sheffield Steel & Iron Co.	27.8	I	FD	
211.	St. Joseph Lead Co.	27.1	I	FD	
241.	Mark Mfg. Co.	24.0	I	FD	
248.	Wheeling Steel & Iron Co.	22.4	I	FD	
250.	Rogers Brown Iron Co.	22.3	I	FD	
251.	Otis Steel Co.	22.3	I	FD	
253.	American Metal Co.	22.0	I	HC(f)	
268.	American Zinc, Lead & Smelting Co.	20.3	I	FD	
270.	Donner Steel Co.	20.2	I	FD	Integrated through billets and bars
276.	Lukens Steel Co.	20.0	I	—	(Insuf.)
277.	John A. Roebling Sons Co.	20.0	I	FD	
280.	Whitaker-Glessner Co.	20.0	I	FD	

Group 34: Fabricated metal products except ordnance, machinery, and transport equipment

31.	American Can Co.	133.1	I	FD	
94.	Crane Co.	53.8	I	FD	
101.	Weirton Steel Co.	50.0	I	FD	
108.	American Brass Co.	46.1	SF	Mfg.	Small sales force
143.	National Enameling & Stamping Co.	38.6	I	FD	
172.	Scovill Mfg. Co.	33.5	—	—	(Insuf.)
183.	National Acme Co.	31.3	I	FD	
222.	Continental Can Co.	25.9	I	FD	(Inc.)
244.	Gilette Safety Razor Co.	23.5	I	FD	
256.	Standard Sanitary Mfg. Co.	21.7	SF	Mfg.	(Inc.)
267.	American Brake Shoe Co.	20.3	I	FD	

Appendix A. *Continued*

Rank[a]	Firm	Assets ($ millions)	Type[b]	Structure[c]	Comment[d]
Group 35: Machinery, except electrical					
7.	International Harvester Co.	264.7	I	FD	
15.	Singer Mfg. Co.	192.9	I	FD	
74.	United Shoe Machinery Corp.	74.1	I	FD	Legal delay
77.	Deere & Co.	69.9	I	FD	
92.	Allis-Chalmers Mfg. Co.	54.8	I	FD	
136.	H. Koppers Co.	40.0	I	FD	(Inc.)
140.	J.I. Case Threshing Machine Co.	39.2	I	FD	
144.	Winchester Repeating Arms Co.	37.8	I	FD	
147.	Niles-Bement-Pond Co.	37.3	I	FD	
156.	Babock & Wilcox	35.1	I	FD	
167.	Ingersoll-Rand Co.	34.2	I	FD	
173.	Advance-Rumely Co.	33.2	I	FD	
181.	Worthington Pump & Machinery Corp.	31.9	I	FD	
182.	Remington Typewriter Co.	31.6	I	FD	
190.	Burroughs Adding Machine Co.	30.0	I	FD	
198.	Moline Plow Co.	28.9	I	FD	
201.	American Radiator Co.	28.1	I	FD	
202.	Otis Elevator Co.	28.0	I	FD	
210.	Emerson-Brantingham Co.	27.4	I	FD	(Inc.)
227.	Remington-Arms-Union Metallic C'tr Co.	25.0	I	FD	
239.	E. W. Bliss Co.	24.4	I	FD	(Inc.)
252.	Computing-Tabulating- Recording Co.	22.2	I	FD	
255.	Underwood Typewriter Co.	21.8	I	FD	
264.	Mergenthaler Linotype Co.	20.6	I	FD	
285.	Fairbanks Morse & Co.[f]	19.6	I	FD	
286.	National Cash Register Co.[f]	19.6	I	FD	
Group 36: Electrical machinery					
11.	General Electric Co.	231.6	I	FD	
17.	Westinghouse Electric & Mfg. Co.	164.7	I	FD	
38.	Western Electric Co.	122.6	I	FD	
174.	Victor Talking Machine Co.	33.2	—	—	(Insuf.)
234.	Electric Storage Battery Co.	24.7	I	FD	(Inc.)
Group 37: Transportation equipment					
16.	Ford Motor Co.	165.9	I	FD	

Appendix A. *Continued*

Rank[a]	Firm	Assets ($ millions)	Type[b]	Structure[c]	Comment[d]
25.	Pullman Co.	143.3	I	FD	(Inc.)
30.	General Motors Corp.	133.7	I	—	Integrated divisions
33.	American Car & Foundry Co.	127.2	I	MD	
41.	Willys-Overland Co.	113.2	I	FD	
51.	Chevrolet Motor Co.	97.2	I	FD	
62.	American Locomotive Works	84.1	I	FD	
75.	Baldwin Locomotive Works	73.8	I	FD	
78.	Studebaker Corp.	69.6	I	FD	
89.	United Motors Corp.	56.3	I	FD	
98.	Maxwell Motor Co.	50.8	I	FD	
99.	Dodge Bros.	50.0	I	FD	
115.	Pressed Steel Car Co.	44.7	I	FD	
118.	Westinghouse Air Brake Co.	44.0	I	FD	
121.	Packard Motor Car Co.	43.6	I	FD	
123.	Railway Steel Spring Co.	43.0	I	FD	
145.	New York Shipbuilding Corp.	37.7	SF	Mfg.	
161.	Standard Steel Car Co.	35.0	I	FD	(Inc.)
171.	American Ship Bldg. Co.	33.6	SF	Mfg.	
185.	Newport News Shipbuilding & Dry Dock Co.	31.1	SF	Mfg.	
204.	Union Tank Line Co.	28.0	I	Transp. with some mfg.	
215.	Curtiss Aeroplane & Motor Co.	26.3	SF	Mfg.	
216.	Todd Shipyards Corp.	26.3	SF	Mfg.	
218.	Standard Parts Co.	26.1	SF	Mfg.	
219.	Pierce Arrow Motor Car Co.	26.0	I	FD	
224.	White Motor Co.	25.5	I	FD	
245.	New York Air Brake Co.	23.4	I	FD	(Inc.)
260.	Wm. Cramp & Sons Ship & Engine Bldg. Co.	21.1	I	FD	No sales
273.	Briggs Mfg. Co.	20.0	I	FD	(Inc.)

Group 38: Instruments and related products

80.	Eastman Kodak Co.	63.9	I	FD	

Group 39: Miscellaneous manufacturers

231.	Aeolian-Weber Piano & Pianola Co.	24.8	—	—	(Insuf.)
258.	Diamond Match Co.	21.5	I	FD	

Agricultural

46.	United Fruit Co.	109.8	I	FD	

Appendix A. *Continued*

Rank[a]	Firm	Assets ($ millions)	Type[b]	Structure[c]	Comment[d]
63.	Cuba Cane Sugar Corp.	83.3	SF		
159.	Miller & Lux	35.0	SF		
170.	Intercontinental Rubber Co.	33.7	SF	HC	Regional subsidiaries
225.	Atlantic Fruit and Sugar Co.	25.0	I	HC(f)	No sales subsidiary

Transportation and distribution (therefore not included above)

52.	W. R. Grace & Co.	97.0			
191.	Famous Players-Lasky Corp.	30.0	I	HC(f)	

Source: This list of 278 companies was taken from a compilation of the 500 largest industrials in the United States made by Thomas R. Navin in *Business History Review* (Autumn 1970). Data and comments are from company reports and Moody's *Manuals of Industrial Securities*.

[a] By size of assets among the 278 largest industrial enterprises.

[b] I indicates integrated; SF indicates single function.

[c] FD, functional departments; HC, holding company; HC(f), holding company with functional subsidiaries; HC(i), holding company with integrated subsidiaries; Ex., single department, extractive; Mfg., single department, manufacturing.

[d] (Inc.) means information incomplete but enough to suggest type and structure. (Insuf.) means not enough information to indicate type or structure. Other comments provide supplementary data on type and/or structure.

[e] The two-digit groups used by the U.S. Bureau of the Census in its Standard Industrial Classification.

[f] Enterprise mentioned in the text with assets less than but close to $20 million.

Appendix B. Railroad systems with assets in excess of $200 million, 1917

Road	Mileage[a] (length of line)	1917 assets ($ millions)
New York Central, including Cleveland, Cincinnati, Chicago & St. Louis and Michigan Central	12,413	1,786
Pennsylvania	12,129	2,663
Atlantic Coast Line, including Louisville & Nashville	12,090	756
Atchison, Topeka & Santa Fe	11,291	847
Southern Pacific, including Central Pacific	11,208	1,788
Chicago, Milwaukee & St. Paul	10,313	691
Chicago, Burlington & Quincy, including Colorado & Southern	9,373	729
Chicago, Rock Island & Pacific	8,297	402
Great Northern	8,264	761
Chicago & Northwestern	8,095	593
Union Pacific	8,003	1,034
Missouri Pacific	7,302	405
Southern, including Mobile & Ohio	6,983	716
Northern Pacific	6,534	736
St. Louis—S.F.	5,165	359
Baltimore & Ohio, including Cincinnati, Hamilton & Dayton	4,949	841
Illinois Central, including Central of Ga.	4,766	566
Missouri, Kansas & Texas	3,869	284
Seaboard	3,461	221
Denver & Rio Grande	2,610	263
Wabash	2,519	224
Chesapeake & Ohio	2,478	398
Erie	2,259	600
Norfolk & Western	2,086	343
N.Y., New Haven & Hartford	1,995	694
Lehigh Valley	1,449	201
Reading	1,127	500

Source: Moody's *Analysis of Investments: Part I—Steam Railroads, 1918* (New York, 1918). Mileage is the length of line operated, as defined by Moody. Assets are the sum of the figures given for each parent company and its subsidiaries.

[a] The first track mileage operated by the above roads (171,028) was 65 percent of the total first track mileage operated in the United States (259,705) in 1917.

Notes

Introduction: The Visible Hand

1. Lance E. Davis and Douglass C. North, *Institutional Change and American Economic Growth* (Cambridge, Eng., 1971) and Douglass C. North and Robert Paul Thomas, *The Rise of the Western World* (Cambridge, Eng., 1973).

2. John Higham, with Leonard Kreiger and Felix Gilbert, *History* (Englewood Cliffs, N.J., 1965), pp. 231–232.

3. Richard Coase, "The Nature of the Firm," *Economica*, n.s., 4:386–405 (1937) provides a pioneering analysis of the reasons for internalizing of operating units. His work is expanded upon by Oliver Williamson, particularly in his *Corporate Control and Business Behavior* (Englewood Cliffs, N.J., 1970), p. 7. Useful articles on coordination and allocation within the enterprise are Kenneth J. Arrow, "Control in Large Organizations," *Management Science*, 10:397–408 (April 1964); H. Leibenstein, "Allocative Efficiency Versus X-Efficiency," *American Economic Review*, 56:392–415 (June 1966); A. A. Alechian and H. Demsetz, "Production, Information Costs, and Economic Organization," *American Economic Review* 62:777–795 (December 1972); and G. B. Richardson, "The Organization of Industry," *Economic Journal*, 83:883–896 (Sept. 1972).

4. Werner Sombart, "Capitalism," *Encyclopedia of Social Sciences* (New York, 1930), III, 200. Though there is very little written on the nature of coordination and allocation of resources and activities within the firm, there is a vast literature on the bureaucratic nature of modern business enterprise and on the goals and motives of business managers. Almost none of this literature, however, looks at the historical development of managerial hierarchies or the role and functions of managers over a period of time.

5. James Burnham, who in his *Managerial Revolution* (New York, 1941) was the first to describe and analyze that phenomenon, gives in chap. 7 a definition of the managerial class in American business but makes no attempt to describe the history of that class or the institution that brought it to power.

1. The Traditional Enterprise in Commerce

1. Adam Smith, *Wealth of Nations*, Modern Library ed. (New York, 1937), p. 423.

2. Stuart Bruchey, *Robert Oliver, Merchant of Baltimore, 1788–1819* (Baltimore, 1956), pp. 370–371.

3. Douglass C. North and Robert Paul Thomas, *The Rise of the Western World* (Cambridge, Eng., 1973), pp. 53–55, 134–143, 149–150, 155–156, for a thumbnail sketch; for more details see Raymond de Roover, "The Organization of Trade," M. M. Postan and H. J. Habakkuk, *The Cambridge Economic History* (Cambridge, Eng., 1963), III, 49–58, and Herman Van der Wee, *The Growth of the Antwerp Market and the European Economy* (The Hague, 1969), pp. 323–324, 328–368.

4. Unless otherwise indicated, statistics in this chapter come from U.S. Bureau of the Census, *Historical Statistics of the United States, Colonial Times to 1957* (Washington, 1960).

5. Sam Bass Warner, *The Private City* (Philadelphia, 1968), pp. 5–6. Still a most useful source for colonial manufacturing is Victor S. Clark, *History of Manufacturers in the United States*, vol. 1, *1607–1860* (New York, 1928), esp. chaps. 8 and 9.

6. U.S. Bureau of the Census, *Historical Statistics*, p. 761, and Howard N. Eavenson, *The First Century and a Quarter of the American Coal Industry* (Pittsburgh, 1942), pp. 32–34.

7. The business activities of colonial merchants are best viewed in Stuart Bruchey, *The Colonial Merchant* (New York, 1966), esp. parts III and IV, and his *The Roots of American Economic Growth* (London, 1965), pp. 55–63. Also valuable are Bernard Bailyn, *The New England Merchants in the Seventeenth Century* (Cambridge, Mass., 1955), chap. 7; Virginia D. Harrington, *The New York Merchant on the Eve of the Revolution* (New York, 1935), pp. 51–73; and James B. Hedges, *The Browns of Providence Plantation: The Colonial Years* (Cambridge, Mass., 1952).

8. Particularly useful, in addition to Bruchey, *The Colonial Merchant*, part III, is Aubrey C. Land, "Economic Behavior in a Planting Society: The Eighteenth Century Cheasapeake," *Journal of Southern History*, 35:464–485 (Nov. 1967), and James H. Soltow, "Scottish Traders in Virginia, 1750–1775," *Economic History Review*, 12:83–99 (1959).

9. Warner, *Private City*, p. 18, shows that in Philadelphia's Middle Ward in 1774 those in trade included twenty-three shopkeepers, nineteen merchants, two druggists, two tobacconists, and one grocer. Harrington, *The New York Merchant*, pp. 58–70, describes the beginning of commercial specialization in New York City.

10. Arthur H. Cole, *Industrial and Commercial Correspondence of Alexander Hamilton* (Chicago, 1928) provides a detailed view of manufacturing in the United States in 1791.

11. This story is succinctly traced in Douglas C. North, *The Economic Growth of the United States, 1790–1860* (Englewood Cliffs, N.J., 1961). Stuart Bruchey, *Cotton and the Growth of the American Economy, 1790–1860* (New York, 1967) provides documents on these developments and an excellent set of statistics on cotton production and trade. The statistics here come from his tables 3A and 3H. Robert G. Albion, *Rise of New York Port* (New York, 1939), p. 99, lists the 1821 U.S. exports as totaling $54 million. Of these, cotton accounted for $20 million, tobacco $5 million, and flour $4. D. M. Williams, "Liverpool Merchants and the Cotton Trade, 1820–1850," in John R. Harris, ed. *Liverpool and Merseyside, 1820–1850* (Liverpool, 1969), p. 184, gives volume of the U.S. share of Britain's total cotton imports. Bruchey's table 2B indicates that the percentage was even higher.

12. The significance of the plantation as a market for western crops has, of course, been a topic of major debate among American economic historians. Useful reviews of this debate are: Diane L. Lindstrom, "Southern Dependence Upon Interregional Grain Supplies: A Review of Trade Flows, 1840–1860," in William N. Parker, ed., *Structure of the Cotton Economy of the Antebellum South* (Washington, 1970), pp. 101–113; and Albert Fishlow, *American Railroads and the*

Transformation of the Antebellum Economy (Cambridge, Mass., 1965), pp. 275–288. Controversy focuses on the years after the 1830s, when the southern plantation had become relatively self-sufficient. But evidence still suggests that until the 1830s the coming of the cotton plantation to the lower Mississippi Valley provided a market for the provisions, horses, and mules of the northwest, particularly as the new plantation owners concentrated their energies on clearing land and planting cotton. There was a large flatboat trade down the river, and there is little evidence that these provisions were shipped to the east. Produce seems to have been sold along the way. John G. Clark points out that in 1820 about one-half of the recorded shipments of flour and provisions actually went to New Orleans. Much was shipped to the West Indies and the new plantations of Alabama and Georgia. On the other hand, tobacco, lead, and hemp appear to have been sent via New Orleans to the east, with consignments going to merchants in both New Orleans and the east. Also, much of the trade from the west to the south was from Kentucky and Tennessee to the lower south. This trade is considered by the economists carrying out the debate as intra- rather than interregional. See John G. Clark, *New Orleans, 1718–1812: An Economic History* (Baton Rouge, La., 1970), pp. 301–303; and his *The Grain Trade in the Old Northwest* (Urbana, 1966), chap. 2, esp. pp. 47–48; also Lewis E. Atherton, "The Pioneer Merchant in Mid-America," *The University of Missouri Studies*, 14:90–102 (April 1, 1939).

13. Albion, *New York Port*, esp. chaps. 2–6.

14. Albion, *New York Port*, pp. 40–41, 99–104, 114–115; Harold Woodman, *King Cotton and His Retainers* (Lexington, Ky., 1968), chaps. 1–2. John R. Killick, "Bolton Ogden & Co.: A Case Study in Anglo-American Trade, 1790–1850," *Business History Review*, 48:501–519 (Winter 1974) provides a close view of an enterprise that began as an agency for British textile manufacturers. The story of a New Hampshire village storekeeper who became a trader in Boston, and, in order to find an export to pay for imports of dry goods from Britain, moved into the cotton trade in 1804 is told in Frances Gregory, *Nathan Appleton: Merchant and Entrepreneur, 1779–1861* (Charlottesville, Va., 1975), chaps. 2–5. Again, Stuart Bruchey in his *Cotton and the Growth of the American Economy* provides an excellent set of documents and readings.

15. Norman S. Buck, *The Development of the Organization of Anglo-American Trade, 1800–1850* (New Haven, 1925), p. 16. The census figures given in this paragraph are from Buck. Figures given in Allan R. Pred, *Urban Growth and the Circulation of Information: The United States System of Cities, 1790–1840* (Cambridge, Mass., 1973), p. 195, are comparable. Pred lists 918 commission houses and 417 commercial houses for New York, 375 and 8 for New Orleans, and 89 and 142 for Boston.

16. The following is from Woodman, *King Cotton*, chaps. 2–6; see particularly p. 19. Bruchey, *Cotton and the Growth of the American Economy*, pp. 255–263, provides letters, accounts, and other documents of the day-to-day work of the cotton factors.

17. Woodman, *King Cotton*, pp. 34–35. Woodman concludes that: "It is doubtful if any firm in the United States—North or South—or abroad refused a requested advance." See also Buck, *Anglo-American Trade*, pp. 13, 17–19, 89–91. The commission merchant's statement is on p. 13.

18. Woodman, *King Cotton*, p. 119.

19. Woodman, *King Cotton*, p. 25–26.

20. The storekeeper's role is well described in Lewis E. Atherton, *The Southern Country Store, 1800–1860* (Baton Rouge, 1949). See also Woodman, *Cotton Kingdom*, chap. 7, and Clarence H. Danhof, *Change in Agriculture: The Northern United States 1820–1870* (Cambridge, Mass., 1969), pp. 29–31, 39–41, which indi-

cates how the general store played a similar role in the distribution system in the north.

21. Clark, *New Orleans*, pp. 302–304. Clark notes, p. 303, that in his *Grain Trade* he had spoken "incorrectly of these developments as advancing through clearly defined stages from the simple to the more complex. Actually, there are elements of all stages present in the early 1800s." This seems to have continued to be the case almost up to the 1840s, with the storekeepers and farmers continuing to flatboat down the river. At the same time the network of marketing middlemen extending from the Mississippi Valley to the eastern ports had become fully developed.

22. Clark, *Grain Trade*, p. 54; also tables on pp. 44, 61 (flour converted from wheat at five bushels to the barrel). For additional information see Thomas Odle "Entrepreneurial Cooperation on the Great Lakes: The Origin of the Methods of American Grain Marketing," *Business History Review*, 38:440–443 (Winter 1964). Stuart Bruchey, "The Business Economy of Marketing Change, 1790–1840: A Study of Sources of Efficiency," *Agricultural History*, 46:211–226 January 1972), and Morton Rothstein, "Antebellum Wheat and Cotton Exports: A Contrast in Marketing Organization and Economic Development," *Agricultural History*, pp. 91–100 (April 1966), both make useful comparisons of the development and efficiencies of the cotton and grain trade.

23. Clark, *Grain Trade*, pp. 119–120. See also Ralph W. Hidy, *The House of Baring in American Trade and Finance* (Cambridge, Mass., 1949), pp. 257–258, and Rothstein, "Antebellum Wheat and Cotton Exports," pp. 94–95.

24. The annual average for selected imports during the decade of 1821–1830 as estimated by Douglass North was $8.3 million for cotton textiles, $1.8 million for rolled and bar iron, $0.5 million for other metal products, $5.1 million for coffee, $4.3 million for sugar, $2.2 million for molasses, $2.4 million for tea, $1.5 million for wine, and $1.5 million for distilled spirits. North, *Economic Growth*, p. 287.

25. A good example of this type of trader was Bolton Ogden & Co., an American agency for the British textile manufacturers. This firm began by importing a general line of goods from Europe and trading extensively with the West Indies, but after 1815 it concentrated wholly on the United States–British trade. Exporting cotton became its major business. It also imported high-grade dry goods, some earthenware, and metals, but left standardized dry goods to jobbers. Killick, *Bolton Ogden & Co.*, pp. 501–519. The Browns followed somewhat the same pattern. Edwin J. Perkins, *Financing Anglo-American Trade: The House of Brown, 1800–1880* (Cambridge, Mass., 1975), chaps. 2–4.

26. The information for this paragraph is from Elva Tooker, *Nathan Trotter, Philadelphia Merchant, 1787–1853* (Cambridge, Mass., 1955).

27. Albion, *New York Port*, pp. 238, 248–249, and P. Glenn Porter and Harold Livesay, *Merchants and Manufacturers: Studies in the Changing Structure of Nineteenth Century Marketing* (Baltimore, 1971), p. 57.

28. Quoted in Arthur H. Cole, *The American Wool Manufacture* (Cambridge, Mass., 1926), I, 214.

29. Ira Cohen, "The Auction System in the Port of New York, 1817–1837," *Business History Review*, 45:488–510 (Winter 1971) has a most useful account on the rise and decline of auctions and the resulting implications for trade. See also Albion, *New York Port*, pp. 276–280. The statistics given here are from Albion, p. 279 and Cole, *Woolen Industry*, I, 156, II, 216. As Cohen points out (p. 495), the great expansion system in New York came between 1818 and 1826. In 1818, 10 percent of all imports in the United States sold at auctions and, in 1826, 26 percent of all imports. In 1826 nearly 53 percent of all imports into the port of New York were sold at auction.

30. Albion, *New York Port*, p. 410. In 1835, of a total of $23.8 million worth of goods sold at auction in New York City, $15.2 were textiles (of which $2.5 million were American made); $3.1 million were groceries, hardware, and drugs, nearly all from Europe; $4.2 million were teas and silks from the more distant seas; $0.9 million were wines and spirits, largely from Europe; and $0.4 were miscellaneous items. Coffee, sugar, and molasses were apparently not sold extensively at auction and normally went to the Mississippi Valley via New Orleans rather than New York and the other eastern ports. In the 1830s auctions had become less important and by 1840 accounted for 13 percent of U.S. imports and 22.5 percent of New York imports. Cohen, "Auction System," p. 496.

31. Dogget's *New York Business Directory for 1846 and 1847* (New York, 1947), part II; Albion, *New York Port*, pp. 421–422; and *Dogget's Directory* for 1840 and 1841; *O'Brien's Philadelphia, Pennsylvania Directory* for 1850; and *Green's St. Louis Directory* for 1850. The list for St. Louis, the largest and oldest city in the interior, indicates that there were, in 1850, 108 commission merchants, 29 dry goods wholesalers, 80 "dry goods wholesalers and retailers," and 101 "fancy grocers." The specialization between retailer and wholesaler was thus only beginning to appear in St. Louis in 1850. Porter and Livesay, *Merchants and Manufacturers*, pp. 27–34, 52–53, give excellent descriptions of the role of jobbers in different types of products.

32. James B. Hedges, *The Browns of Providence Plantation: The Nineteenth Century* (Providence, 1968), chap. 9. Here the author describes the promotion of banks, insurance companies, turnpikes, and canals as "Private Enterprise in the Public Interest." This chapter also provides an excellent case study of how the older resident general merchant moved into banking and transportation. In addition see Fritz Redlich, *The Molding of American Banking, Men and Ideas* (New York, 1951), I, 7–8, 31; and Stuart Bruchey, "The Historical Development of the Corporation in the United States," *Encyclopaedia Britannica* (Chicago, 1963), pp. 525–528.

33. Hedges, *The Browns, the Nineteenth Century*, p. 135.

34. Redlich, *The Molding of American Banking*, II, 68–69; Tooker, *Nathan Trotter*, chap. 10; Albion, *New York Port*, p. 249.

35. Other important British houses included Isaac Low & Company and Ewart, Meyers & Co. of Liverpool; Anthony Gibbs & Company of London; and Dennistown & Company and Pollock Gilmore & Company of Glasgow. See D. M. Williams "Liverpool Merchants and the Cotton Trade," pp. 192–196, 200–201. For the Barings and other London companies see Hidy, *House of Baring*, esp. chaps. 4 and 5, and Perkins, *House of Brown*, chaps. 2–5.

36. Quoted in Redlich, *Molding of American Banking*, I, 47.

37. Statistics on banks are given in U.S. Bureau of the Census, *Historical Statistics*, p. 623, and Bruchey, *Roots of American Growth*, p. 145.

38. Herman E. Krooss and Martin R. Blyn, *A History of Financial Intermediaries* (New York, 1971), pp. 57–63.

39. *House Reports* no. 460, 22d Cong., 1st Sess. (1832), p. 316.

40. Catterall, *The Second Bank*, pp. 112–113, 502. Profits for those same three selected months were $49,800, $190,750, $741,800. "The total discounts of bills of inland exchange from July 1827, to July 1828," Catterall notes, "were $22,084,222, and the profits $451,203.17, as against profits in 1822 of $95,240.25." Thomas P. Govan, *Nicholas Biddle, Nationalist and Public Banker, 1786–1844* (Chicago, 1959), provides useful information, while Peter Temin, *The Jacksonian Economy* (New York, 1969), chap. 11, gives an incisive brief analysis of the role of the bank in the American economy as viewed by a modern economist. Redlich, *Molding of*

American Banking, 127–145, outlines Biddle's role as an early central banker in the United States. In vol. 2, pp. 337–343, Redlich describes Biddle's pioneering role as an investment banker after his bank became state chartered in 1836.

41. These developments are particularly well described in Perkins' study of the Browns, esp. chap. 4.

42. North, *Economic Growth,* p. 50; Albion, *New York Port,* pp. 270–274; George Rogers Taylor, *Transportation Revolution, 1815–1860* (New York, 1951), pp. 322–323, and R. Caryle Buley, *The American Life Convention, 1906–1952* (New York, 1953), pp. 26–50.

43. James F. Shepard and Gary M. Walton, *Shipping, Maritime Trade and the Economic Development of Colonial North America* (Cambridge, 1972), esp. chaps. 4 and 9.

44. For the coming of the regular traders and then the packet lines see Robert G. Albion, *Square Riggers on Schedule: The New York Sailing Packets to England, France and the Cotton Ports* (New York, 1938), chaps. 1–3.

45. An excellent example of "a budding specialist in ship owning, agency, and management" was Charles Morgan. Connecticut born, Morgan began as a ship's grocer and chandler in 1815 and owned shares of ships and packet lines after 1819. Between 1819 and 1846, he was a partner in eighteen packets, serving ten different packet lines, and also in at least fifteen tramps, primarily in the coastal trade. His partners were young men like himself from New York or Connecticut. James P. Baughman, *Charles Morgan and the Development of Southern Transport* (Nashville, 1968), pp. 8–13. See also Albion, *Port of New York,* pp. 243–250, and Robert G. Albion, "Early Nineteenth Ship Owning: A Chapter of Business Enterprise," *Journal of Economic History,* 1:1–11 (May 1941). Albion notes that "every vessel was regarded as a separate business entity" (p. 2).

46. Williams, "Liverpool Merchants and the Cotton Trade," pp. 199–201.

47. Taylor, *Transportation Revolution,* chap. 4, and Louis C. Hunter, *Steamboats on the Western Waters* (Cambridge, Mass., 1949), chap. 1, esp. pp. 24, 33, and pp. 308–313. See also Albion, *New York Port,* chap. 8, and Wheaton J. Lane, *Commodore Vanderbilt* (New York, 1942), pp. 29–38.

48. Taylor, *Transportation Revolution,* pp. 24–26, 48–52, and Carter Goodrich, *Government Promotion of American Canals and Railroads, 1800–1890* (New York, 1960), chaps. 2–4.

49. Harry N. Scheiber, *Ohio Canal Era* (Athens, Ohio, 1969), p. 252; Odle, "Entrepreneurial Cooperation," pp. 443–444.

50. Pred, *Urban Growth,* esp. chaps. 3–5, indicates the growing efficiency of the transaction sector in terms of reducing the time and cost of information flows and transportation.

51. By 1840, according to estimates of Robert E. Gallman, the United States had a per capita income that was 40 to 65 percent larger than France and was close to that of Britain. Paul David estimates that the real per capita domestic product increased at a rate of 55 to 62 percent between 1800 and 1840. Robert E. Gallman, "Gross National Product, 1834–1909," National Bureau of Economic Research, *Output, Employment, and Productivity in the United States After 1860* (New York, 1969), pp. 5–7, and Paul David, "New Light on a Statistical Dark Age: U.S. Real Product Growth Before 1840," *American Economic Review,* 57:294–306 (May 1967).

52. Pred, *Urban Growth,* p. 51.

53. Perkins, *House of Brown,* pp. 40–43; Killick, "Bolton Ogden Co." p. 5. For Astor see Kenneth W. Porter, *John Jacob Astor, Businessman* (New York, 1931), II, 741–751. A chart on p. 750 indicates the changing partnership arrangements within the American Fur Company during its existence. It was incorporated largely

because it carried on international negotiations with the large British trading companies—the Hudson Bay Company and the Northwest Company.

54. Quoted in Albion, *New York Port,* p. 264. Professor Morison estimates that the busiest merchants in Boston in the 1790s rarely spent three hours a day in the counting house. Samuel Eliot Morison, *The Maritime History of Massachusetts* (Boston, 1920), pp. 190–191. This view is supported by Arthur H. Cole, "The Tempo of Mercantile Life in Colonial America," *Business History Review,* 33:277–300 (Autumn 1959).

55. The counting house and its organization and the activities of the partners that managed it are well described in Albion, *New York Port,* pp. 260–265. The work of a merchant at the beginning of the nineteenth century is told in great detail by Bruchey, *Oliver,* esp. chaps. 2 and 3.

56. Albion, *New York Port,* p. 264.

57. This information comes from John Mair, *Book-Keeping Methodized: or A Methodical Treatise of Merchant-Accounts According to the Italian Form,* 8th ed. (Edinburgh, 1765). This was one of the most widely read textbooks at the end of the eighteenth century and the beginning of the nineteenth, and that the methods described by Mair were generally used is supported by a check on the records of firms of that period in Baker Library, Graduate School of Business Administration, Harvard University, and elsewhere. The item Mair refers to as a waste book, or, occasionally, a journal, was generally known as a day book in early nineteenth-century America. I am indebted to Professor Bruchey for the Mair citation and for his comments on accounting based on his wide knowledge of mercantile book-keeping.

58. Mair, *Book-Keeping Methodized,* p. 17.

59. This and the following quotation are from Mair, *Book-Keeping Methodized,* pp. 1–2.

60. Bruchey, *Oliver,* pp. 136–139.

61. Sidney Pollard, *The Genesis of Modern Management* (Cambridge, Mass., 1965), p. 213; Roy J. Sampson, "American Accounting Education, Text Books and Public Practices Prior to 1900," *Business History Review,* 34:459–464 (Winter 1960).

62. Bruchey, *Oliver,* p. 141.

63. The more specialized merchants appear to have paid closer attention to recording interest charges than did the earlier general merchants. *Woodman, King Cotton,* pp. 363–367, and the Nathan Trotter manuscripts, Manuscript Division, Baker Library, Graduate School of Business Administration, Harvard University.

64. Mathew A. Crenson, *The Federal Machine* (Baltimore, 1975), pp. 104–115; and Albion, *New York Port,* pp. 217–218.

65. Pred, *Urban Growth,* chap. 2. Albion, *New York Port,* pp. 281, 329, 331, gives examples of such commercial news, including the publication of prices current. North and Thomas, *Rise of the Western World,* p. 136, indicates the initial development of prices current in Europe.

66. Redlich, *Molding of American Banking,* I, 55, II, 11–12. By the 1850s, country bankers followed those in eastern cities by delegating the authority for making decisions on discounts or loans to the president or cashier, instead of the boards.

67. There are several sets of accounts of banks in the Manuscript Division of Baker Library. The most complete is that for the Plymouth Bank (the journal is actually a day book and the cash journal is the journal). Also valuable are those of the first National Bank of Massachusetts.

68. N. S. B. Gras, *The Massachusetts First National Bank of Boston, 1784–1934* (Cambridge, Mass. 1937), pp. 62–63, 80, 93.

69. Baker Library has a complete set of books for the Commercial Insurance Company of Boston for the years 1823–1827.

70. Albion, *New York Port*, pp. 270–274; quotation on p. 272.

71. N. S. B. Gras and Henrietta M. Larson, *Casebook in American Business History* (New York, 1939), p. 179. Perkins, *House of Brown*, p. 238 (also p. 36) gives profits of the interlocking partnerships in terms of annual changes in their combined capital accounts of the five senior partners in the several partnerships.

72. Redlich, *Molding of American Banking*, I, 113–124. See also Reginald C. McGrane, *The Correspondence of Nicholas Biddle* (New York, 1919), pp. 34–40.

73. Hunter, *Steamboats on the Western Rivers*, p. 308, also pp. 110–112.

74. Lane, *Commodore Vanderbilt*, p. 67.

75. Hunter, *Steamboats on the Western Waters*, p. 362.

76. Albion, *Square Riggers on Schedule*, pp. 100–101, and chap. 6. On the other hand, ocean-going steamships in the late 1840s and 1850s cost as much as $400,000.

77. Ronald E. Shaw, *Erie Water West: A History of the Erie Canal, 1792–1854* (Lexington, Ky., 1966), p. 198. Shaw estimates that horses cost from $25 to $80 each and hay was $5 a ton.

78. Hunter, *Steamboats on the Western Waters*, p. 311. Albion, "Early Nineteenth-Century Shipowning," gives an excellent summary of the pattern of joint ownership in the coastal and ocean trades. Of the sailing ships permanently registered in New York in 1850, 24 percent had a single owner, 47 percent were owned by two to five men, and 29 percent by five or more. Of these, 3 percent were wholly owned by the captain and 35 percent partly owned (p. 4). For steamboats, the proportion of single owners was larger with 44 percent, 41 percent had two to four owners, and 15 percent had five or more owners, of which two-thirds were corporations. Of these (except for the last category), 13 percent were fully owned and 34 percent partly owned by the ship's captain. Albion's *Square Riggers on Schedule*, pp. 108–109, describes the operating procedures of the packet lines.

79. Hunter, *Steamboats on the Western Waters*, pp. 322–325, 342–347.

80. Lane, *Vanderbilt*, chap. 4.

81. Albion, *Square Riggers on Schedule*, pp. 28–35, 45–48, Appendix X.

82. Scheiber, *Ohio Canal Era*, p. 252, refers to freight forwarders who owned one or two boats and others who had "large fleets." Large fleets, mentioned in Shaw, *Erie Waters West*, pp. 198–199, 216–217, operated from ten to twelve boats.

83. Daniel H. Calhoun, *The American Civil Engineer* (Cambridge, Mass., 1960), pp. 54–78.

84. Calhoun, *The American Civil Engineer*, p. 71; Shaw, *Erie Waters West*, pp. 90–91; Scheiber, *Ohio Canal Era*, pp. 70–72. For the Chesapeake and Ohio Canal Company see Walter S. Sanderlin, *The Great National Project: A History of the Chesapeake and Ohio* (Baltimore, 1946), pp. 126–127. The working force on the Chesapeake and Ohio included many Irish, besides "Dutch and country borns," pp. 117–122. The total number of workers, or the proportion of native to foreign-born, are not given.

85. Scheiber, *Ohio Canal Era*, p. 70; also Roberts, *The Middlesex Canal*, chap. 5.

86. The resident engineer was seldom the man who located the canal and supervised construction. Calhoun, *American Civil Engineer*, pp. 73–74.

87. The administration of the Erie is described well in Shaw, *Erie Waters West*, chap. 13. The quotation is from p. 245. By the Canal Act of 1819, the financing of the construction of the canal was turned over to the Commissioners of the Canal Fund, including the comptroller, secretary of state, attorney general, treasurer, and lieutenant governor of the state. Nathan Miller, *The Enterprise of Free People* (Ithaca, N.Y., 1962), p. 71.

88. Shaw, *Erie Water West*, p. 250.

89. Shaw, *Erie Waters West*, p. 245. In the late 1840s a more elaborate procedure of accounting on contracting for large-scale repairs was developed. The Erie was divided into twelve sections, each under a superintendent of repairs, reporting to the state engineer and surveyor as well as to the canal board (p. 252).

90. Shaw, *Erie Waters West*, p. 253. The larger role of the comptroller and the canal fund is indicated in Miller, *Enterprise of A Free People*, esp. chaps. 5–8.

91. Louis Hartz, *Economic Policy and Democratic Thought: Pennsylvania 1776–1890* (Cambridge, Mass., 1948), pp. 148–160; Scheiber, *Ohio Canal Era*, chaps. 3, 7; Sanderlin, *The Great National Project*, pp. 135–137, 184–186, 208–209. Maryland, as the controlling stockholder in the Chesapeake and Ohio, appointed the board. Sanderlin stresses the complete lack of an effective administrative structure for the C. & O.

92. Pred, *Urban Growth*, p. 93. In 1839, with the opening of the railroads in Georgia, the New York–New Orleans mail run could be completed in nine days.

93. Thomas C. Cochran, in his "The Business Revolution," *American Historical Review*, 79:1449–1466 (January 1975), describes these institutional changes as revoluntary and as an essential base for the Industrial Revolution that occurred in the United States after 1840. Yet a close reading of his article emphasizes the point that this revolution consisted of improving existing and not devising new types of business institutions, practices, and procedures, such as occurred in the distribution as well as in the production of goods after 1840.

2. The Traditional Enterprise in Production

1. Before the coming of the mechanical harvester, twenty acres in the east and thirty acres in the west was the maximum a single man could operate. Full-time hired hands were scarce. They were usually men trying to earn enough to start farming for themselves. The possibility of obtaining extra hired labor for the harvest was always uncertain. Clarence H. Danhof, *Change in Agriculture: The Northern United States, 1820–1870* (Cambridge, Mass. 1969), esp. chap. 6. The standard study of labor shortage in the United States and its impact on technological change is H. J. Habakkuk, *American and British Technology in the Nineteenth Century* (Cambridge, Eng., 1967).

2. Victor S. Clark, *History of Manufacturers*, vol. 1 *1607–1860* (New York, 1929), pp. 438–440. Danhof, *Change in Agriculture*, pp. 16–22.

3. Albert Gallatin, *Report on Manufacturees Communicated to the House of Representatives*, April 19, 1810, 11th Cong., 2d Sess., reprinted in the *New American State Papers, Manufacturers* (Wilmington, Del., 1972), I, 126, also 125, 127, 136–137.

4. Clark, *History of Manufacturers*, I, 440–442, provides a summary, while Arthur H. Cole, *Industrial and Commercial Correspondence of Alexander Hamilton* (Chicago, 1928) gives a detailed documentation of American manufacturing in 1791. Volume I of *American State Papers, Manufacturing*, does the same up to 1817. James P. Baughman, *The Mallory's of Mystic* (Middletown, Conn., 1972), chap. 1, provides an excellent picture of the work as an artisan sailmaker and his shop in the period after 1816.

5. Howard Eavenson, *The First Century and a Quarter of the American Coal Industry* (Pittsburgh 1948), chaps. 5–7.

6. Few studies have been made of the construction industry of the early nineteenth century. Useful for shipbuilding are Robert C. Albion, *Square Riggers on Schedule* (Princeton, 1938), chap. 4, esp. pp. 93–95, and his *Rise of New York Port* (New York, 1939), chap. 17, and John G. B. Hutchins, *American Maritime Industries and Public Policy, 1789–1914* (Cambridge, Mass., 1941), chap. 4. A

good source on building construction are the accounts of New England building contractors in Baker Library, Harvard University.

7. George Rogers Taylor, *The Transportation Revolution* (New York, 1951), pp. 216–220.

8. Blanche Hazard, *The Boot and Shoe Industry in Massachusetts Before 1875* (Cambridge, Mass., 1921) is still the best book on the shoe industry and the only detailed study on the putting-out system as it was practiced in this country. The book is summarized in "The Organization of the Boot and Shoe Industry Before 1875," *Quarterly Journal of Economics*, 27:236–262 (February 1913), reprinted in Alfred D. Chandler, Stuart Bruchey, and Louis Galambos, *The Changing Economic Order* (New York, 1968), pp. 167–184. The citations to her article in this and later notes are from the pages in this reprinted article.

9. Hazard, "Organization of the Boot and Shoe Industry," pp. 175–177.

10. Hazard, "Organization of the Boot and Shoe Industry," p. 178.

11. U.S. Bureau of the Census, *The Eighth Census of the U.S., Manufactures* (Washington, D.C., 1853), pp. xc–xcii, also U.S. Congress, House, *Executive Document* no. 208, 22d Cong., 1st Sess., "Documents Relative to the Manufacturers in the United States," collected by the Secretary of Treasury (Louis McLane), 2 vols. (Washington, D. C., 1833); hereafter cited as the *McLane Report*. This report indicates the widespread use of the domestic system in the making of straw goods.

12. For example, Hazard, *Boot and Shoe Industry in Massachusetts*, pp. 51–52, 58–63.

13. Clark, *History of Manufacturers*, I, 179–181, for milling and I, 467–476, for woodworking. Nathan Rosenberg, "America's Rise to Woodworking Leadership," in Brook Hindle, ed., *America's Wooden Age* (Tarrytown, N.Y., 1975), pp. 37–55 provides detail on the latter.

14. John Joseph Murphy, "Entrepreneurship in the Establishment of the American Clock Industry," *Journal of Economic History*, 26:169–186 (June 1966). The two quotations are from pp. 173, 180. John T. Kenney, *The Hitchcock Chair* (New York 1971), chap. 3, describes comparable operations in chair-making.

15. For example, William Lathrop, *The Brass Industry in the United States* (Mt. Carmel, Conn., 1926), chap. 3, and Theodore F. Marburg "Management Problems and Procedures of a Manufacturing Enterprise 1802–1852," Ph.D. diss., Clark University, 1942.

16. From the *McLane Report*. I am indebted to Edwin J. Perkins for collecting the material on the number of blacksmiths in Maine and other states. The situation in the metal-making and metal-working industries before the 1840s is in Alfred D. Chandler, Jr., "Anthracite Coal and the Beginnings of the Industrial Revolution in the United States," *Business History Review*, 46:143–181 (Summer 1972), esp. pp. 145–148, 159–165.

17. The difference in costs of transportation and fuel was analyzed by a contemporary Swedish expert E. G. Danielsson, *Anteckningar om Nora Amerika Fri-Statenas jerntillverkning samt handel med jeronch stalvaror* (Stockholm, 1845), p. 72. His findings are summarized in Chandler, "Anthracite Coal," pp. 160–163.

18. Peter Temin, *Iron and Steel in Nineteenth Century America* (Cambridge, Mass., 1964), p. 15.

19. Louis C. Hunter, "Heavy Industries Before 1860," in Harold F. Williamson, ed., *The Growth of the American Economy* (New York, 1951), p. 178.

20. Chandler, "Anthracite Coal," p. 147.

21. This is particularly well documented in the *McLane Report*. For a review of finished products see James E. Walker, *Hopewell Village: A Social and Eco-*

nomic History of an Iron Mining Community (Philadelphia, 1961), esp. pp. 153–154.

22. The story of the Browns, Slater, and the introduction and spread of machine spinning is best told in James B. Hedges, *The Browns of Providence Plantation: The Nineteenth Century* (Providence, 1968), pp. 158–172. A more general view is given in Caroline F. Ware, *The Early New England Cotton Manufacture* (New York, 1931), chap. 2. Also valuable is "Samuel Slater and the American Textile Industry, 1789–1835," N. S. B. Gras and Henrietta M. Larson, eds., *Case Book in American Business History* (New York, 1939), pp. 217–221.

23. Gallatin, "Report on Manufacturers, 1810," pp. 125, 136–137. See also Clark, *History of Manufacturers*, I, 535–536.

24. Gallatin, "Report on Manufacturers, 1810," pp. 125, 132–133. For the expansion of the industry during the war and embargo see Ware, *Early New England Cotton Manufacture*, chap. 3, and Hedges, *Browns, the Nineteenth Century*, pp. 170–174.

25. Hedges, *The Browns, the Nineteenth Century*, p. 172.

26. Hedges, *The Browns, the Nineteenth Century*, p. 173.

27. The formation of the Boston Manufacturing Company is well told in Ware, *New England Cotton Manufacture*, chap. 4, and in Nathan Appleton and Samuel Batcheler, *The Early Development of the American Cotton Textile Industry*, ed. George Rogers Taylor (New York, 1969), pp. xviii–xx, 7–16. See also George S. Gibb, *The Saco-Lowell Shops* (Cambridge, Mass., 1950), pp. 7–14 and chap. 2, and Frances W. Gregory, *Nathan Appleton, Merchant and Entrepreneur, 1779–1861* (Charlottesville, Va., 1975), chap. 10.

28. Ware, *New England Cotton Manufacture*, pp. 66, 140–141.

29. For the building of Lowell see Ware, *New England Cotton Manufacture*, pp. 80–85; Gibb, *Saco-Lowell Shops*, chap. 3; Appleton and Batcheler, *American Cotton Industry*, pp. 17–30; and Gregory, *Nathan Appleton*, chap. 11.

30. U.S. Bureau of the Census, *The 8th Census of the United States, Manufactures* (Washington, 1865), pp. xviii–xxi, has a good brief description of the spread of the large integrated mills. See also Clark, *History of Manufacturers*, I, 551–552.

31. Ware, *New England Cotton Manufacture*, pp. 148–151. As time passed the stock ownership became disbursed but control was largely retained by the families of the founders and their heirs.

32. Cost was not a factor in holding back the spread of weaving machinery. The power loom was available and by 1820 was being sold for as low as $70. The Blackstone River could not supply the power needed to move a battery of weaving as well as spinning machines. Hedges, *The Browns, the Nineteenth Century*, p. 182; Ware, *New England Cotton Manufacture*, pp. 72–77, 85–86; Gibb, *Saco-Lowell Shops*, pp. 42–48.

33. Arthur H. Cole, *The American Wool Manufacturer* (New York, 1926), I, 97–107, 113–117. Cole lists nine firms given in the *McLane Report* with more than 100 employees, pp. 256–257. He describes marketing on pp. 156–160, 210–212.

34. This paragraph follows closely Chandler's "Anthracite Coal," pp. 143–146, which provides more detailed documentation. I am indebted to my son Alfred D. Chandler III for compiling the list of all enterprises in the *McLane Report* with assets of $50,000 or over. He listed for each enterprise its name, location, product made, source of power, legal form, fixed assets, working capital, number of employees, and date founded.

35. A review of the documents collected in the four-volume edition of the *American State Papers, Manufacturing* mentions only a few large manufacturing enterprises not in the 1832 *McLane Report*. These include the unsuccessful glass

works of John Amelung, a tannery at Cambridge, Massachusetts, with a capitalization of $100,000, and a soap works at Roxbury, Massachusetts, with the same
capitalization. Also mentioned are two hat makers (one in Danbury, Connecticut,
and one on the Charles River in Massachusetts). These were clearly central shops
using hand labor and traditional tools, pp. 39–42, 125–127.

36. Peter Temin, "Steam and Water Power in the Early Nineteenth Century,"
Journal of Economic History, 26:189 (January 1966).

37. One competent observer, writing in 1828, estimated that the cost of operating
a steam engine in England was two-fifths that of operating one on the American
seaboard, "while at Pittsburgh, on the contrary, from the wonderful abundance of
coal, steam power is actually available at about three-fourths of the expense required in England." Zachariah Allen, *The Science of Mechanics* (Providence, 1829),
p. 351.

38. For example, Baughman, *Mallory's of Mystic*, chap. 1, provides an excellent
description of such production and accounting methods in the sail-making trade.
See esp. pp. 17–18. In the 1850s, at the height of the American shipbuilding boom,
the average work force of an American shipyard was fourteen workers; see U.S.
Senate, 35th Cong., 2d Sess., Exec. Doc. no. 39, "Digest of the Statistics of Manufacturers According to the Returns of the Seventh Census," p. 141.

39. Sidney Pollard, *The Genesis of Modern Management* (Cambridge, Mass.,
1965), pp. 30–37, and Raymond de Roover, "A Florentine Firm of Cloth Manufacturers," *Speculum*, 16:3–33 (January 1949).

40. Good examples of such accounts in Baker Library, Harvard University, are
those of Howard and Niles (#641), Captain John Belcher (#642), and Ebenezer
Belcher (#427).

41. Pollard, *Genesis of Modern Management*, p. 214.

42. Hazard, *Boot and Shoe Industry*, pp. 175–176.

43. Ware, *New England Cotton Manufacture*, p. 50–51.

44. Ware, *New England Cotton Manufacture*, p. 51.

45. Pollard, *Genesis of Modern Management*, pp. 25–30.

46. Mark Schmitz, "Economic Analysis of Antebellum Sugar Plantations in
Louisiana," Ph.D. diss., University of North Carolina, 1974, pp. 124–127, points
out that in 1850 only 5.8 percent of 329 Louisiana sugar plantations were "truly
absentee" owners—that is, excluding widows and those held intestate. Schmitz says
(p. 160): "The 1860 figure implies a total of just over one hundred true absentee
owners in the total population of sugar planters. This would be an upper limit due
to probable over-representation of large farms that had a higher degree of absentee-
ism." Both Schmitz and Joseph N. Menn, in his study of large slave holders in
Louisiana, emphasize the contiguous nature of the southern plantation.

47. Robert William Fogel and Stanley L. Engerman, *Time on the Cross* (Boston,
1974), I, 211. Because many plantations had no white resident overseers, Fogel
and Engerman conclude that "on a majority of large plantations the top non-
ownership management was black." They give little evidence to demonstrate that
such management was not carried out by the planters themselves who could easily
arrange to be on their plantations during the period requiring careful supervision.
If accurate, the findings of Fogel and Engerman emphasize that the white owners
were as willing to have black "drivers" as well as white employees assist them in
carrying out these managerial functions. They also show that plantation owners
left the control of the plantation and its work force in the hands of trusted slaves.
However, the statistical validity of their findings have been seriously challenged.
See Paul David and others, *Reckoning with Slavery* (New York, 1976), pp. 83–86.

48. William K. Scarborough, *The Overseer: Plantation Management in the
South* (Baton Rogue, 1966), pp. 10–11. Stanley Engerman, using a computer tape

prepared by William Parker and Robert Gallman on southern agriculture taken from the manuscript schedules of the census for 1850, provided me with a print-out of the sample of 5,229 farms producing cotton in the south. Of these, only 21 had assets (land, buildings, machinery, and livestock) of over $100,000 excluding slaves. Of these, 16 were in Louisiana. Only 8 had assets of over $200,000 and, of these, 2 over $300,000. On large plantations the value of slaves was usually, according to Engerman, equal to or less than the value of total assets. A plantation with non-slave assets of $100,000 would then have at most a total value of $200,000. Of the plantations in this sample 11 had over 100 slaves and, of these, 5 over 150 and 1 over 300.

49. Scarborough, *The Overseer*, p. 10. On pp. 68–70, Scarborough provides an excellent example of rules for governing plantations. Another set of rules, coming from the Mississippi plantation of Alexander Telfair, who continued to reside in Georgia, is printed in Ulrich B. Phillips, ed., *Plantation and Frontier* (New York, 1958), and is reprinted in Stuart Bruchey, *Cotton and the Growth of the American Economy* (New York, 1967), pp. 180–182. In this set, twenty-three out of thirty-five rules dealt with the handling of slaves and ten with the working of the land. One calls for sending a detailed monthly letter to Savannah and the other for maintaining a regular plantation journal or diary. One reason that little was said about machinery may have been that its operation was left to skilled slave artisans.

50. Scarborough, *The Overseer*, p. 74. Similar statements by other southern plantations are given in Bruchey, *Cotton and the Growth of the American Economy*, pp. 183–188.

51. Scarborough, *The Overseer*, pp. 80–81.

52. Scarborough, *The Overseer*, p. 71.

53. Thomas P. Govan, "Was Slavery Profitable?" *Journal of Southern History*, 8:516–535 (November 1942).

54. Both the early iron plantations and some of the James River coal mines were managed in much the same way as the southern commodity producing plantations. For the first see William A. Sullivan, *The Industrial Workers in Pennsylvania* (Harrisburg, 1955), pp. 59–71; and for coal, Eavenson, *American Coal Industry*, chap. 6.

55. Gibb, *Saco-Lowell Shops*, pp. 32, 37–38, 47, 261. The ring-spinning frame replaced the throstle in the 1850s (p. 192).

56. David J. Jeremy, "Innovation in American Textile Technology during the Early Nineteenth Century," *Technology and Culture*, 14:40 (January 1972). See also Lance E. Davis and H. Louis Stettler III, "The New England Textile Industry, 1825–1860, Trends and Fluctuations," *National Bureau of Economic Research, Output, Employment and Productivity in the United States after 1800* (New York, 1966), pp. 227–232. The quotation is from p. 230.

57. Francis W. Gregory, "The Office of the President in the American Textile Industry," *Bulletin of the Business Historical Society*, 26:122–134 (September 1952). This was also true in textile machinery making (see Gibb, *Saco-Lowell Shops*, pp. 183–186, 220–221).

58. Henry A. Miles, *Lowell, As It Was and As It Is* (Lowell, 1845), pp. 76–84. This floor arrangement quite often changed because of the weight of machinery and the power needed. Sometimes weaving was done in the subbasement, carding on the first floor, spinning on the second, and finishing and storing on the third. I am indebted to Merritt Roe Smith for this information.

59. This and the following two quotations are from James Montgomery, "Remarks on the Management and Government of Spinning Factories," in *The Carding and Spinning Masters Account; or the Theory and Practice of Cotton Spinning* (Glasgow, 1832), reprinted with an introduction in *Business History Review*,

42:219–226 (Summer 1968), pp. 221, 224. This piece was widely read in the United States and was partly responsible for an invitation from the York Manufacturing Company at Saco, Maine, to have Montgomery "come to the United States to improve their plant and its methods" (p. 219). Montgomery's best known work was *A Practical Detail of Cotton Manufacturers of the United States* (Glasgow and New York, 1840).

60. The generalizations in this and the following paragraphs result from a review of the accounts of a number of the leading New England textile companies (records in Baker Library, Harvard Business School). They include those of the Slater Mills, the Boston Manufacturing Company, and the Lawrence, Hamilton, Tremont, Suffolk, Amoskeag, Nashua, Lancaster, Dwight, Lyman, Pepperell, and Dover mills. Paul F. McGouldrick has written an excellent set of "Notes on Cotton Textile Records at the Baker Library," dated December 26, 1958, a script of which is kept by the director of the Manuscript Division at Baker. Harry C. Bentley and Ruth S. Leonard, *Bibliography of Works on Accounting by American Authors* (Boston, 1934), vol. 1, list nothing at all dealing with textile accounting until the very end of the nineteenth century.

61. Where piecework was used, the amounts paid out were determined by the use of "clocks . . . on the speeders, throstles, wrappers and dressers . . . which marked the quantity of work done." At the end of the week, a contemporary report continued, "the overseer transfers the account to a board which hangs in the room in sight of all the operatives. From this board the monthly wages of each operative are ascertained." Miles, *Lowell*, pp. 80–81.

62. McGouldrick, "Cotton Textile Records," p. 3.

63. Paul F. McGouldrick, *New England Textiles in the Nineteenth Century: Profits and Investments* (Cambridge, Mass., 1968), p. 116, states that the write-offs, when they were made, did come quite close to reality. See also Ware, *Cotton Manufacture*, pp. 155–156.

64. H. Thomas Johnson, "Early Cost Accounting for Internal Management Control: Lyman Mills in the 1850s," *Business History Review*, 46:472 (Winter 1972) points out that the raw material for such data at the Lyman Mills was not available until 1875. However, John Lozier has shown me a statement of cost per yard for labor, cotton, and repairs for the Lyman Mills in the first nine months of operation in 1850. The computation for unit cost on this sheet from the Lyman Mills collection (Baker Library) for April through December 28, 1850, was the total cash cost for each item divided by the yards produced. Also, by 1852, Lyman Mills had information on yards per pound of cotton and yards per loom produced by each loom weekly.

65. Of all the records of the textile companies at Baker Library, only one has the regular treasurer's reports to stockholders, and that is the only company with copies of bylaws in Baker Library where the bylaws require the making of such reports.

66. McGouldrick, *New England Textiles*, p. 144. The *McLane Report* emphasizes that the operating expenses were high compared with fixed costs in textile enterprises. For the Lowell mill, annual working capital was 35 to 55 percent of total capital investment. Therefore, every two or three years the enterprises spent in operating costs an amount equivalent to that which had been paid out of their construction and machinery.

67. Ware, *New England Cotton Manufacture*, pp. 142–145. In 1845, two leading market partnerships, including A. A. Lawrence and J. L. Page & Company, purchased the oldest and largest textile machinery company in the United States, the Lowell Machine Shop (see Gibb, *Saco-Lowell Shops*, pp. 183–185).

68. Ware, *New England Cotton Manufacture*, pp. 178–188. The Mason &

Lawrence account is given on p. 186. A good review of the role of the marketing agency in the textile industry is in Hansjorg Siegenthaler, "What Price Style? The Fabric Advisory Function of the Dry Goods Commission Merchant, 1850–1880," *Business History Review*, 41:36–39, 59–60 (Spring 1967).

69. Gregory, *Nathan Appleton*, pp. 242–251, 258–261. Mills overextended himself and went bankrupt in 1857.

70. The following account of the small arms industry and the organizational innovations of the Springfield Armory relies heavily on Paul Uselding, "An Early Chapter in the Evolution of American Industrial Management, 1795–1833," in Louis P. Cain and Paul Uselding, eds., *Business Enterprise and Economic Change* (Kent State, Ohio, 1973), pp. 51–84. Also valuable is a seminar paper given at Johns Hopkins University, May 1967, by Russell I. Fries, "Springfield Armory, 1794–1820: An Early Industrial Organization." Felicia Deyrup, "Arms Makers of the Connecticut Valley," *Smith College Studies in History*, 33 (1948), pp. 43, 48, 220–221 describes the early private contractors. See also *McLane Report*, I, 1030–1031.

71. Merritt Roe Smith. "The Harpers Ferry Armory and the 'New Technology' in America, 1794–1854," unpublished, pp. 67–68.

72. This and the following quotation are from Colonel James Dalliba, "Armory at Springfield," November 5, 1819, *American State Papers, Military Affairs*, II, 548. I am indebted to Merritt Roe Smith for this citation.

73. From 1817 to 1833 the output of "musket equivalents" per production worker was only a little under sixty a year. During those years between 1815 and 1833, when the number of workers remained steady between 231 and 250, output per production worker increased to sixty-five a worker in only four years. See Uselding "American Industrial Management," p. 60. As Springfield did not have the need, and as no other enterprise had the volume of output nor the complexity of production, no American firm appears to have developed cost-accounting techniques as detailed and sophisticated as those devised by Josiah Wedgwood in 1772. See Neil McKendrick, "Josiah Wedgwood and Cost Accounting in the Industrial Revolution," *Economic History Review*, pp. 45–66 (April 1970). Wedgwood's methods appear to have had little impact on accounting practices in British manufacturing— at least McKendrick gives no evidence that they did. Deyrup, "Arms Makers," p. 119, points to the "dubious means" used by the government armories and private contractors to determine costs.

74. Joseph W. Roe, *English and American Tool Builders* (New Haven, 1916), chaps. 11 and 15, esp. pp. 139 and 187, depicts "genealogies" of arms manufacturers and their descendants. These charts show how personnel went from the armories to the gun factories and then to sewing machines and machine toolmaking establishments.

75. The new economic historians have emphasized that demand was the major factor in encouraging industrial expansion in the first half of the nineteenth century: for example, Robert Zevin, "The Growth of Cotton Textile Production after 1815," and Robert William Fogel and Stanley L. Engerman, "A Model for the Explanation of Industrial Expansion During the Nineteenth Century: With Application to the American Iron Industry." Both articles are in Robert William Fogel and Stanley L. Engerman, *The Reinterpretation of American Economic History* (New York, 1971), pp. 122–146, 148–162.

76. Deyrup, "Arms Makers of the Connecticut Valley," pp. 120, points out that only one of the private arms-making factories—that of Eli Whitney—active before 1830 survived to the Civil War. See also Thomas C. Cochran, "The Business Revolution," *American Historical Review*, 79:1452 (December 1974).

77. Chandler, "Anthracite Coal," esp. pp. 149–174. The statistical data on output,

prices, and transportation from Philadelphia to Boston are on pp. 153–158. A useful supplementary analysis on the industrializing of a single town in these years is Carol E. Hoffecker, *Wilmington, Delaware: Portrait of an Industrial City* (Charlottesville, Va., 1974), esp. pp. 14–35.

78. Temin, *Iron and Steel*, pp. 87–90, 264–266.

79. Roe, *English and American Tool Builders*, pp. 138–140, 173–185, 202–215, 247–252, and sketches of James T. and Nathan P. Ames and William and Colman Sellers in Dumas Malone, ed., *Dictionary of American Biography* (New York, 1946) I, 248–250, XVI, 574–577.

80. By 1850 the average number of workers was sixty-two for glass as compared with ninety-two in cotton textiles, sixty in iron rolling, and fifty-one in iron furnaces. "A Digest of the Statistics of Manufacturers . . . According to the Returns of the Seventh Census," U.S. Senate, 35th Cong., 2d Sess., Exec. Doc. no. 39, pp. 138–140.

3. The Railroads: The First Modern Business Enterprises, 1850s–1860s

1. For example, as Walter S. Sanderin, the historian of the Chesapeake and Ohio pointed out, the directors of that canal "refused to have any connection with the business of transportation." *The Greater National Project: A History of the Chesapeake and Ohio Canal* (Baltimore 1946), p. 190. The Middlesex Canal had a fleet of six to nine boats in commission from 1808 to 1818 when they were sold. Christopher Roberts, *The Middlesex Canal, 1783–1860* (Cambridge, Mass. 1938), pp. 137–138. The important exceptions to this generalization were the anthracite coal companies of eastern Pennsylvania.

2. These developments can be followed in Edward C. Kirkland, *Men, Cities and Transportation* (Cambridge, Mass., 1948), I, chap. 4; and in Julius Rubin, "Canal or Railroad?" *Transactions of the American Philosophical Society*, n.s., vol. 51, part 7 (November 1961). Rubin stresses that the railroad was a serious alternative to the canal for overland transportation, even before the steam locomotive had been proved practical. One reason that the Pennsylvania legislators decided in 1825 to build a state system of canals rather than railroads was "insufficient experience with the general-purpose railroad to justify a large-scale project." It was a "risky step into the unknown" (p. 56). Also some legislators expressed concern at the possibility of having the state operate common carriers.

3. George Rogers Taylor, *The Transportation Revolution* (New York, 1951), pp. 24–26, 48–52.

4. Particularly useful on the railroad technology of this period is Kirkland, *Men, Cities and Transportation*, I, 284–313.

5. For example, Patrick Tracy Jackson, one of the founders of the mill complex at Lowell, estimated that the time and cost saved by rail over canal transportation were equivalent to moving Lowell within ten miles of Boston. George S. Gibb, *The Saco-Lowell Shops* (Cambridge, Mass., 1950), p. 74.

6. U.S. Bureau of the Census, *Historical Statistics of the United States, Colonial Times to 1957* (Washington, D.C., 1960), pp. 427–429; Taylor, *Transportation Revolution*, p. 32.

7. Taylor, *Transportation Revolution*, p. 53, indicates that canals cost somewhat less than railroads on moderate terrain. Rubin, "Railroads and Canals," p. 30, notes that contemporaries emphasized how much railroad transportation shortened distances between towns. All accounts of canals stress high maintenance costs, particularly with the reoccurrence of freshets; for example, Sanderlin, *The Great National Project*, pp. 191–193.

8. Stanley Legerbott, "United States Transport and Externalities," *Journal of Economic History*, 26:444–446 (December 1966); italics added. Robert William Fogel, in his pioneering work, *Railroads and American Economic Growth: An Econometric History* (Baltimore, 1964), argues that the railroads were not indispensable for economic growth. By 1890 the social savings "attributed to the railroad for all commodities . . . is well below 5 per cent gross national product" (p. 223). Fogel's findings have been strongly challenged by new economic historians in such articles as that of Legerbott given above; Peter D. McClelland, "Railroads, American Growth and the New Economic History: A Critique," *Journal of Economic History*, 28:102–123 (March 1968); and Paul David, "Transportation and Economic Growth: Professor Fogel On and Off the Rails," *Economic History Review*, 20:507–525 (December 1969). Fogel concentrates almost wholly on estimating the differences between rail and canal transportation in the seasonal movement of crops and on the impact of railroads on the demand for iron. In estimating the cost differences between rail and water he develops only the grossest estimates of cargo losses in transit, transshipment costs, costs resulting from time lost in slow movement, the closing down of waterways in the winter months, and capital costs. Fogel's handling of inventory costs is particularly disconcerting. David points out that to maintain inventory at Union Stock Yards in Chicago in 1890 would have required 10,000 acres, or a half of all privately utilized land in Chicago in that year (p. 512). Fogel has little analysis of the barriers to the expansion of factory production created by the need to maintain costly inventories and an idle working force during winter months.

9. Kirkland, *Men, Cities and Transportation*, pp. 161, 162.

10. Roberts, *Middlesex Canal*, p. 160.

11. Harry N. Scheiber, *Ohio Canal Era* (Athens, Ohio, 1969) pp. 302, 304. Scheiber's chap. 11 has an excellent analysis of the swift railroad victory in the 1850s. Hartz indicates a comparable failure of the Pennsylvania Canal system in his *Economic Policy and Democratic Thought*, pp. 161–180. U.S. Bureau of the Census, *Historical Statistics*, p. 455, gives the freight carried on the Erie. See also Sanderlin, *The Great National Project*, chaps. 11, 12.

12. Louis C. Hunter describes the way that the railroads took over trade from the steamboats in the 1850s in *Steamboats on the Western Rivers* (Cambridge, Mass., 1949), chap. 12.

13. U.S. Bureau of the Census, *Historical Statistics*, p. 484. The story of the telegraph and telephone is given in more detail in Chapter 6.

14. Carter Goodrich, *Government Promotion of American Railways and Canals, 1800–1890* (New York, 1960), p. 270. The railroad figures come from Henry Varnum Poor's carefully compiled stock and bond list in Alfred D. Chandler, Jr., *Henry Varnum Poor, Business Editor, Analyst and Reformer* (Cambridge, Mass., 1956), pp. 207–210. See, for example, *American Railroad Journal*, 32:784 (December 3, 1859).

15. Alfred D. Chandler, Jr., ed., *The Railroads: The Nation's First Big Business* (New York, 1965), p. 16.

16. Evelyn H. Knowlton, *Pepperell's Progress: A History of a Cotton Textile Company* (Cambridge, Mass., 1948) p. 32.

17. The triumph of New York over Philadelphia and Boston in becoming the nation's financial center is reviewed in Alfred D. Chandler, Jr., "Patterns of Railroad Finance, 1830–1850," *Business History Review*, 28:248–263 (September 1954). The resulting institutionalizing of the national capital market is told in more detail in Chandler, *Poor*, chap. 4. Dorothy R. Adler, *British Investments in American Railways* (Charlottesville, Va., 1970), chaps. 1–3, has additional information on the return of the British investors to the American market.

18. Herman E. Krooss and Martin R. Blyn, *A History of Financial Intermediaries* (New York, 1971), pp. 56–57, 86–87.

19. For the appearance of the large contractor see Chandler, *Poor*, pp. 112–113, 313, and Thomas C. Cochran, *Railroad Leaders, 1843–1899* (Cambridge, Mass., 1953), pp. 99–100, 111–114. For specific contractors see John B. Jervis, *Railway Property* (New York, 1861), chap. 4; Henry W. Farnum, *Henry Farnum* (New York, ca. 1889), esp. pp. 41–45, 54–55.

20. *American Railroad Journal*, 26:488 (July 30, 1853). Seymour and Morton had formed a construction company shortly before the former's death. In 1855 and 1856 the firm advertised in the pages of the *American Railroad Journal* that it was "prepared to contract for the construction and equipment of railroads in any part of the country; also to furnish Corps Engineers and contractors; Locomotive Engines, Cars; Railroad Iron, Chairs, Spikes, Switch-Irons, etc." The firm would also "sell and negotiate loans on all kinds of railroad securities . . . [and] dispose at private sales, in amounts to suit persons desirous of investing, a large amount of valuable Railroad and other Securities." *ARJ*, 28:509 (August 11, 1855). The firm listed regularly in the *Journal* the securities of the roads which it was constructing and had for sale.

21. Brief backgrounds (and sources of information) on Latrobe, McCallum and Thomson are given in Alfred D. Chandler, Jr., "The Railroads: Pioneers in Modern Corporate Management," *Business History Review*, 39:16–40 (Spring 1965); and on Haupt, Jervis, McClellan, and Whistler, in Dumas Malone, ed., *Dictionary of American Biography* (New York, 1946), VII, 400, XI, 59–60, 581–582, XIX, 72.

22. Quoted in Kirkland, *Men, Cities and Transportation*, I, 338. The operations of many early roads are described in detail in J. Knight and Benjamin H. Latrobe, *Report on the Locomotives and the Police and Management of Several of the Principal Railroads in the Northern and Middle States* (Baltimore, 1838), pp. 4, 13–19. Knight and Latrobe point out that the Boston & Worcester employed fifty-one operating workers (that is, those not involved in construction work).

23. Stephen Salsbury, *The State, the Investor, and the Railroad: Boston & Albany, 1825–1867* (Cambridge, Mass., 1967), pp. 182–184. The succeeding pages in chap. 9, "The Western Railroad in Crisis: An Operating Man's Nightmare," cover the crisis and the organizational response to it.

24. Salsbury, *Boston & Albany*, pp. 186–187.

25. Ibid., p. 187.

26. Ibid., p. 157.

27. The comparisons of the two roads and the sources of information are given in Chandler, *Poor*, p. 320; also Edward H. Mott, *Between the Ocean and the Lakes: The Story of the Erie* (New York, 1899), p. 483.

28. Daniel C. McCallum, "Superintendent's Report," in *Annual Report of the New York and Erie Railroad Company for 1855* (New York, 1856), quoted in Chandler, *The Railroads*, p. 101, where much of McCallum's report is reprinted.

29. *Organization of the Service of the Baltimore & Ohio R. Road, under the Proposed New System of Management* (Baltimore 1847), p. 3; and the *Twentieth Annual Report of the President and Directors to the Stockholders of the Baltimore & Ohio Rail-Road Company* (Baltimore, Md., 1846), pp. 11–14. Much of the following on the creation of the first management structures on railroads appeared in Alfred D. Chandler, Jr., "The Railroads: Pioneers in Modern Corporate Management," *Business History Review*, 39:16–40 (Spring 1965).

30. *Twenty First (1847) Annual Report* of the Baltimore & Ohio, p. 13.

31. This and the following quotation are from the *Organization . . . of the Service of the Baltimore & Ohio Rail-Road, 1847*.

32. *Twenty-First (1847) Annual Report of the Baltimore & Ohio Rail-Road*, p. 13.

33. This and the following quotations are from the *Organization . . . of the Service of the Baltimore and Ohio Rail-Road, 1847.*

34. *Report of the Directors of the New York and Erie Railroad Company to the Stockholders in November 1853* (New York, 1853), p. 47–48.

35. It included five divisions and two short branches of just under twenty miles apiece.

36. This and the following quotations are from McCallum, "Superintendent's Report" in the *Erie Annual Report (1855)* reprinted in Chandler, *The Railroads*, pp. 102–105.

37. Chandler, *Poor*, pp. 147–148.

38. This and the following quotations are from McCallum's "Superintendent's Report" in *Erie Annual Report (1855)*, p. 79.

39. Quoted in Chandler, *Poor*, p. 147, from *American Railroad Journal*, 27:549 (September 2, 1854).

40. Chandler, *Poor*, pp. 148, 153; *American Railroad Journal*, 29:280 (May 3, 1856); *Atlantic Monthly*, 2:641, 651–54 (November 1858).

41. Sidney Pollard, *The Genesis of Modern Management* (Cambridge, Mass., 1963), chap. 7, and "The Genesis of the Managerial Profession: The Experience of the Industrial Revolution in Great Britain," *Studies in Romanticism*, 4:57–80 (Winter 1965). Pollard, by stopping his analysis at 1830, does not consider the impact of the operation of railroads on management in Great Britain. *Genesis of Modern Management*, p. 132.

42. *Fifth Annual Report of the Pennsylvania Rail-Road* (1851), pp. 42–85, and James A. Ward, "Herman Haupt and the Development of the Pennsylvania Railroad," *Pennsylvania Magazine of History*, 95:73–97 (January 1971), esp. 78, 86.

43. The activities of these departments are described in *Pennsylvania Rail-Road Company: Organization for Conducting the Business of the Road, Adopted December 26, 1857* (Philadelphia, 1858), pp. 9–16.

44. *Pennsylvania Rail-Road Company: Organization . . . 1857*, p. 7. In addition, the manual defined the relations between the financial and operating departments. "Orders issued by the Accounting Department to Officers or Agent of the Transportation Department will be sent to the General Superintendent, and by him immediately distributed and enforced" (p. 11).

45. For example, *By-Laws and Organization for Conducting the Business of the Pennsylvania Rail-Road Company, to Take Effect June 1, 1873* (Philadelphia, 1873), pp. 20, 25–26. When construction was completed, the chief engineer at the head of the department of maintenance of way became explicitly a staff officer to "act as a consulting engineer."

46. The information on the operating structure of these roads comes from their annual reports in the 1850s. There is very useful information, including an organization chart, in David Lee Lightner, "Labor on the Illinois Central Railroad, 1852–1880," Ph.D. diss., Cornell University, 1969, pp. 68–73.

47. The departmental organization of the British railroads is described in detail in Ray Morris, *Railroad Administration* (New York, 1920), chap. 6.

48. A description of the more informal departmental structure of the New York Central, a road created by consolidation of several small roads and headed by merchants and financiers, is given in Chandler, "The Railroads: Pioneers in Modern Corporate Management," pp. 38–39.

49. For example, in 1856 the Illinois Central had 44 officers and 3,501 employees (about 800 of which were involved in new construction). Lightner, "Labor on the Illinois Central Railroad," p. 72. In 1852, before its western division had been fully

opened for operations, the Baltimore & Ohio already had 63 managers, 4 in top management (the president, general superintendent, treasurer, and chief engineer), 9 in middle management, and 50 in the lower levels, including foreman of shops and repair gangs and full-time freight and passenger agents. These data were compiled by Harold W. Geisel for an honors thesis at Johns Hopkins University in 1967.

50. *Pennsylvania Railroad Company: Organization . . . 1857*, p. 11. The accounts are itemized on pp. 21–23.

51. The *Fourth (1851)*, the *Fifth (1851)*, the *Seventh (1853)*, and the *Tenth (1856) Annual Report(s) of the Pennsylvania Rail-Road*, pp. 60–61, 103–104, 74–76, respectively.

52. See Chandler, *Poor*, p. 139, for use of the operating ratio in the 1850s, and William J. Ripley, *Railroads: Finance and Organization* (New York, 1915), pp. 112–115, for its use well into the twentieth century.

53. Kirkland, *Men, Cities and Transportation*, I, 340–344, II, 332–335. One of Poor's earliest editorial campaigns in 1849 urged roads to set aside funds for renewal and replacement. Chandler, *Poor*, p. 50.

54. This and the following quotations are from the *Ninth Annual Report of the Pennsylvania Rail-Road (1855)*, p. 15.

55. This phrase and the following quote are in the *Tenth Annual Report of the Pennsylvania Rail-Road (1856)*, p. 12.

56. "Proceedings of the Convention of Railroad Commissioners Held at Saratoga Springs, New York, June 10, 1879," Appendix 21, a pamphlet in Baker Library, Harvard University. For background of the movement for uniform accounting that led to this meeting, see Kirkland, *Men, Cities and Transportation*, II, 335–339.

57. As one accounting historian has emphasized: "Over time, replacement accounting understates capital consumption." Richard P. Brief, "Nineteenth-Century Accounting Era," *Journal of Accounting Research*, 3:21 (Spring 1968). Brief gives an excellent analysis of replacement accounting in this article which can be supplemented by his "The Evolution of Asset Accounting," *Business History Review*, 40:1–23 (Spring 1966). Useful too is L. E. Andrade, "Accounting Thought in the United States, 1815–1860," in J. Van Fenstermacher, ed., *Papers Presented at the Annual Business History Conference, February 26–27, 1965* (Kent, Ohio, 1965), pp. 113–120.

58. McCallum, "Superintendent's Report," in the New York and Erie's *Annual Report (1855)*, reprinted in Chandler, *The Railroads*, p. 107.

59. *Dictionary of American Biography*, VI, 387–388.

60. See especially Albert Fink, *Cost of Railroad Transportation, Railroad Accounts and Government Regulation of Railroad Tariffs* (Louisville, Ky., 1875), reprinted in Chandler, *The Railroads*, pp. 108–117. See also Fink, *Investigation into Cost of Transportation on American Railroads, with Deductions for its Cheapening* (Louisville, 1874), and his *Cost of Railroad Transportation, Railroad Accounts, and Governmental Regulation of Railroads* (Louisville, 1875). Charles Ellet, another competent engineer, had made a detailed analysis of railroad costs in the early 1840s which he published in the *American Railroad Journal*. His work appears to have had much less impact than that of McCallum or Fink, possibly because he had much less practical experience than the other two and because he wrote before American railroads had developed large operating units with extensive traffic. Chandler, *Poor*, pp. 38, 296.

61. Quoted in Chandler, *The Railroads*, p. 115. The percentages of expenses on the different divisions are given on pp. 110–111.

62. Published in New York in 1879. Kirkman also published such books as

Railway Disbursement (New York, 1877); *Railroad Revenue and Its Collection* (New York, 1877, revised 1887); and *Railroad Service: Trains and Services* (New York, 1878).

4. Railroad Cooperation and Competition, 1870s–1890s

1. George Rogers Taylor and Irene D. Neu, *The American Railroad Network, 1861–1890* (Cambridge, Mass., 1956), pp. 52, 93.

2. Joseph Nimmo, Jr., *Report of the Internal Commerce of the United States* (Washington, 1879), pp. 9, 97–98. Nimmo reports that by 1875 the Mississippi River was bridged at twelve places between St. Louis and St. Paul.

3. As early as 1854 the three railroads entering Troy, New York, had built and jointly operated a belt line. Information on belt lines can be gleaned from Henry Varnum Poor, *Manual(s) of the Railroads of the United States* for the late 1870s and early 1880s.

4. *American Railroad Journal*, 27:532–539, 605, 663–664, 810 (August 26, September 23, October 21, December 23, 1854), and 28:197–198 (March 31, 1855).

5. *Eighth Annual Report of the Directors of the Pennsylvania Rail Road Company to the Stockholders, February 5th, 1855* (Philadelphia, 1855), p. 13. Hereafter only the date of submission of the Pennsylvania Annual Reports will be given.

6. Stephen Salsbury, *The State, the Investor, and the Railroad: The Boston & Albany, 1825–1867* (Cambridge, Mass., 1967), pp. 127–130.

7. *Tenth Annual Report of the Pennsylvania Rail Road* (1857), pp. 74–75; Edward C. Kirkland, *Men, Cities and Transportation* (Cambridge, Mass., 1948), I, 352.

8. General Superintendent's report in *Fifth Annual Report of the Pennsylvania Rail Road* (1852), pp. 82–83, 104. Kirkland, *Men, Cities and Transportation*, I, 353–354.

9. Taylor and Neu, *American Railroad System*, p. 69; Alden Hatch, *American Express: A Century of Service* (New York, 1950), pp. 15–54.

10. One reason for the change was that the express company provided a way to finance the increase in equipment for carrying war-expanded traffic. Another was that the New York road's express line allies had been charging below the official rates. *Twenty-Sixth Annual Report of the Pennsylvania Railroad Co., March 11, 1873*, p. 28; pages 28 to 31 review in detail the decision to sponsor the Union line. See also *Nineteenth Annual Report of the Pennsylvania Railroad Co., February 20, 1866* pp. 22–23, and the annual report for the following year dated February 19, 1867, pp. 27–29.

11. William B. Wilson, *History of the Pennsylvania Railroad Company* (Philadelphia, 1899), II, 66–69; *Report of the Investigating Committee of the Pennsylvania Railroad Company Appointed by Resolution of the Stockholders at the Annual Meeting held March 10, 1874* (Philadelphia, 1874), pp. 121–122. Page 122 describes the size of the Empire Transportation Company as does the company-published *The American Fast Freight System Presented by the Empire Transportation Company* (Philadelphia, 1876), pp. 16–23. That pamphlet gives 1863 as the date of the forming of the Union line, and 1865 as the date of the Empire. (Rack cars were used by the Empire Company to carry oil barrels and cases.)

12. The information for this and the next two paragraphs comes largely from Taylor and Neu, *American Railroad System*, pp. 69–76. The quotation from a congressional committee is given on p. 72. Also valuable is Kirkland's *Men, Cities and Transportation*, I, 500–501, and Louis C. Hunter, *Steamboats on Western Rivers* (Cambridge, Mass., 1949), p. 349.

13. Of the four remaining companies, two retained ties with railroad enterprises,

the U.S. Express with the Baltimore & Ohio, and Wells Fargo with the Erie. [Nicoll & Roy Company], *The Manual of Statistics, 1895* (New York, 1895), pp. 256, 257, 279, 280.

14. Taylor and Neu, *American Railroad Network*, pp. 74–75, 97. The first through bill of lading was used in 1853 between Cincinnati and the Atlantic ports. See also Kirkland, *Men, Cities and Transportation*, I, 497–498.

15. Nimmo, *Internal Commerce*, pp. 148–149, 196–197.

16. John B. Jervis, *Railroad Property* (New York, 1861), pp. 206–208. See also Marshall Kirkman, *Railroad Revenue* (New York, 1887), book III, chap. 7.

17. The activities of the car accountant office can be best seen by reviewing the notices about the Car Accountant's Association in the *Railroad Gazette*—for example, 22:202, 421, 475 (1890). This association was formed in 1876. See also Stover, *American Railroads*, p. 156.

18. Stover, *American Railroads*, pp. 152–159, provides an excellent brief summary of such standardization. Edward C. Kirkland, *Industry Comes of Age: Business, Labor and Public Policy, 1860–1897* (New York, 1961), pp. 47–51, is also a first-rate review. For the coming of uniform accounting through the cooperation of the Association of Railroad Accounting Officers, railroad commissioners, and the Interstate Commerce Commission see Alfred D. Chandler, Jr., *Henry Varnum Poor: Business Editor, Analyst and Reformer* (Cambridge, Mass. 1956), pp. 262–263. Frederick Warner Allen, "The Adoption of Standard Time in 1883—An Attempt to Bring Order into a Changing World," Yale undergraduate honors thesis, 1970, provides a useful case study of the critical role middle management on the railroads played in initiating and carrying out a change that affected the lives of all Americans.

19. *Railroad Gazette*, 17:378 (1885). The next quotations are on pp. 413, 589. Examples of meetings of other associations can be found in the index to the *Railroad Gazette* and other railroad journals during the 1870s and 1880s. Particularly useful for discussion about standardization, safety, and economy in plant, equipment, accounting, traffic, and train movements are *Railroad Gazette*, 17:394–395 (1885) for Master Mechanics; 677–678 for Roadmasters; 378 for Master Car Builders; 300 and 764 for Railroad Agents; 589 for Railroad Traveling Auditors; 475 for Car Accountants; 15:193–194 (1883) for General Passenger and Ticket Agents; 22:458 (1890) for Railroad Telegraph Superintendents; 22:693–694 (1890) for Railroad Superintendents. See also Stuart Morris, "Stalled Professionalism: The Recruitment of Railway Officials in the United States, 1885–1940," *Business History Review*, 48:317 (Autumn 1973).

20. Morris, "Recruitment of Railway Officials" has excellent information on this point. His sample of 500 general officers in 1885 indicates that 18.4 percent began their railroad career in senior positions; 29.6 percent as clerks; 6.2 percent as messengers and office boys; 8.0 percent as telegraph operators; 5.8 percent as agents (station, freight, passenger, and so on); 11.6 percent as "assistant engineers" (mainly roadmen and chainmen); 6.2 percent as mechanist apprentices; 4.2 percent as brakemen and firemen; 2.8 percent as laborers and sectionmen; 0.2 percent as attorneys; and 7.0 percent as miscellaneous (p. 323).

21. Daniel H. Calhoun, *The American Civil Engineer: Origin and Conflict* (Cambridge, Mass., 1960), pp. 182–190, describes earlier attempts to form the society before the Civil War. Calhoun points out that before 1843 regular academic training for American engineers was given only at West Point and at two smaller institutions—Rensselaer Polytechnic Institute and Norwich University (pp. 37–46).

22. Albert Fishlow, "Productivity and Technological Change in the Railroad Sector, 1840–1910," in National Bureau of Economic Research, *Output, Employ-*

ment and Productivity in the United States After 1800 (New York, 1966), p. 629.

23. Fishlow, "The Railroad Sector," p. 626. The next quotations are on pp. 629, 633.

24. Fishlow, "The Railroad Sector," pp. 644–645.

25. For example, see Albert Fink, "Classification of Operating Expenses," from the annual report of the Louisville & Nashville Railroad for the year ending June 30, 1874, and reprinted in Alfred D. Chandler, Jr., *The Railroads: The Nation's First Big Business* (New York, 1965), pp. 110–111.

26. Maury Klein, "The Strategy of Southern Railroads," *American Historical Review*, 73:1052–1068 (April 1968), and *The Great Richmond Terminal* (Charlottesville, Va., 1970), pp. 16–26.

27. *Eleventh Annual Report of the Pennsylvania Railroad Company, February 1, 1858*, p. 14. Other western connections whose securities the Pennsylvania purchased included the Maysville & Big Sandy and the Springfield, Mount Vernon & Pittsburgh; see Henry Varnum Poor, *History of the Railroads and Canals of the United States* (New York, 1860), pp. 471–474; *Sixth Annual Report of the Pennsylvania Railroad Company, February 7, 1853*, pp. 21–26; *Seventh Annual Report of the Pennsylvania Railroad Company, February 6, 1854*, pp. 6–7, 18–20. Its holdings in both these roads were sold off in 1858. George H. Burgess and Miles C. Kennedy, *Centennial History of the Pennsylvania Railroad* (Philadelphia, 1949), pp. 236–237. For the Baltimore & Ohio's and New York Central's investment in western connections see Poor, *History of Railroads*, pp. 580–582, and Edward Hungerford, *The Story of the Baltimore & Ohio Railroad, 1827–1927* (New York, 1928), II, 68, 110–111. For the western roads see Richard C. Overton, *Burlington Route: A History of the Burlington Lines* (New York, 1956), chaps. 3, 4; Thomas C. Cochran, *Railroad Leaders, 1845–1890: The Business Mind in Action* (Cambridge, Mass. 1953), pp. 35–41; *Annual Report of Michigan Central Railroad Company to the Stockholders, June 1855* (Boston, 1855), pp. 7–8, 10; Arthur M. Johnson and Barry E. Supple, *Boston Capitalists and Western Railroads* (Cambridge, Mass., 1967), chaps. 8, 11; Alvin F. Harlow, *The Road of the Century: The Story of the New York Central* (New York, 1947), pp. 251–252, 255–259 (these pages review the early history of western lines that ultimately became part of the New York Central); Carlton J. Corliss, *Main Line of Mid-America: The Story of the Illinois Central* (New York, 1950), pp. 23–25, 38–41, 143–149; W. H. Sennett, *Yesterday and Today—A History of the Chicago & Northwestern Railway System* (Chicago, 1910), pp. 9–42. By 1853 the Georgia Railroad had invested close to $1.0 million in western connections. John F. Stover, *Railroads of the South* (New York, 1961), p. 27. The Central had spent a comparable amount. Klein, *Richmond Terminal*, pp. 73–74.

28. See citations in n. 4.

29. Chandler, *Poor*, p. 151; Cochran, *Railroad Leaders*, p. 164.

30. *Twenty-Fourth Annual Report of the Pennsylvania Railroad Company, February 21, 1871*, p. 17.

31. Paul W. MacAvoy, *The Economic Effects of Regulation: The Trunk Line Railroad Cartels and the Interstate Commerce Commission Before 1900* (Cambridge, Mass., 1965), pp. 26–27.

32. Klein, "Strategy of Southern Railroads," pp. 1055–1057.

33. Julius Grodinsky, *The Iowa Pool* (Chicago, 1950), p. 17, and Nimmo, *Internal Commerce*, pp. 175–177.

34. Nimmo, *Internal Commerce*, pp. 161–183; Lee Benson, *Merchants, Farmers and Railroads* (Cambridge, Mass., 1955), pp. 39–40; Gabriel Kolko, *Railroads and Regulation, 1877–1916* (Princeton, N.J., 1965), chap. 1; and MacAvoy, *Economic Effects of Regulation*, pp. 39–41.

35. This and the preceding quotation are from the *Twenty-Eighth Annual Report of The Pennsylvania Railroad Company, March 9, 1875*, pp. 41–42. See also MacAvoy, *Economic Effects of Regulations*, p. 39.

36. Kirkland, *Men, Cities and Transportation*, I, 498–500.

37. Benson, *Merchants, Farmers and Railroads*, pp. 41–54; MacAvoy, *Economic Effects of Regulation*, pp. 50–56.

38. Kirkland, *Men, Cities and Transportation*, I, 508–510; D. T. Gilchrist, "Albert Fink and the Pooling System," *Business History Review*, 34:34 (Spring 1960); *Thirty-First Annual Report of the Pennsylvania Railroad Co. March 25, 1878*, pp. 69–70.

39. Stover, *Railroads of the South*, pp. 151–152; Kirkland, *Men, Cities and Transportation*, II, 176–179; Maury Klein, *History of the Louisville & Nashville Railroad* (New York, 1972), pp. 76–78.

40. Fink describes his tasks in some detail in *The Railroad Problem and Its Solution: Argument of Albert Fink before the Committee on Commerce of the U.S. House of Representatives, in Opposition to the Bill to Regulate Interstate Commerce, January 14, 15, and 16, 1880* (New York, 1882), pp. 44–46. See also Gilchrist, "Albert Fink and the Pooling System," p. 35, and MacAvoy, *The Economic Effects of Regulation*, pp. 53–56.

41. Gilchrist, "Albert Fink and the Pooling System" (the quotation in the next sentence is from p. 36); and *Testimony of Albert Fink (before) United States Senate Committee on Labor and Education, New York, September 17, 1883* (np, nd), pp. 344–345; also MacAvoy, *Economic Effects of Regulation*, p. 58.

42. Fink, *The Railroad Problem*, p. 21.

43. Nimmo, *Internal Commerce*, pp. 174–175, and "Information furnished by J. W. Midgley Esq.," dated April 28, 1878. See also "Supplementary statement by Mr. J. W. Midgley (June 21, 1879), printed as Appendices 4 and 5 of *Internal Commerce*, and Riegel, *Story of Western Railroads*, pp. 157–159, 165–170, 199–200, 208–211, 217–220. *Testimony of Albert Fink . . . Sept. 17, 1883*, pp. 5–8; T. Addison Busbey, *Biographical Directory of the Railroad Officials of America* (Chicago, 1906), II, 412.

44. Fink, *The Railroad Problem*, p. 24.

45. This and the following quotation are from Fink, *The Railroad Problem*, p. 21. The several published testimonies before congressional committees indicate how Fink kept up his plea for a law that would make pooling agreements legally enforceable as contracts. G. R. Blanchard, *Traffic Unity, Popularly Called "Railway Pools"* (New York, 1884), pp. 19–20, 30, indicates the widespread support for legalized pooling and the arguments used for it. See also Benson, *Merchants, Farmers and Railroads*, pp. 233–235, and Kolko, *Railroads and Regulation*, pp. 26–29.

46. Grodinsky, *Jay Gould*, chaps. 11, 16, 18; Gilchrist, "Albert Fink and the Pooling System," pp. 41–42.

47. Quoted in Kirkland, *Men, Cities and Transportation*, I, 512–513.

48. Gilchrist, "Albert Fink and the Pooling System," p. 43; Grodinsky, *Jay Gould*, pp. 368–369.

49. Quoted in Gilchrist, "Albert Fink and the Pooling System," p. 46. Midgley's difficulties are described in Riegel, *The Story of Western Railroads*, pp. 165–170, 199–200, 208–211.

50. Kolko, *Railroads and Regulation*, chap. 4. Kolko argues that railroads have been slow to recognize their inability to bring stability to their industry through their own efforts; that most railroad leaders supported the act of 1887 to regulate interstate commerce; and that they derived from it the benefits of stability they hoped for. These stimulated fresh investigations into the significant subject, but they have been seriously challenged. For example, Edward A. Purcell, Jr., "Ideas

and Interests: Businessmen and the Interstate Commerce Act," *Journal of American History*, 54:561–578 (December 1967) demonstrates that railroad men were hardly unanimous on the question. Albro Martin, "The Troubled Subject of Railroad Regulation in the Gilded Age—A Reappraisal," *Journal of American History*, 61:339–371 (September 1974) shows that if railroad men wanted or expected any help from government, it was in making pooling contracts enforceable by law. But the act of 1887 did just the opposite by outlawing pooling, and the Sherman Antitrust Act of 1890 (as interpreted by the Supreme Court in the Trans-Missouri and Joint Traffic decisions of 1897 and 1898) further outlawed even unenforceable agreements to uphold official tariffs in the absence of pooling. Martin indicates that when these avenues to stability were shut off, the only alternative—formal consolidation—was eagerly resorted to. In his *James J. Hill and the Opening of the Northwest* (New York, 1976), 296–297, 409–410, 537, Martin confirms that as early as the mid-1880s key railroad men like James J. Hill of the Great Northern and investment bankers like Henry L. Higginson placed little faith in pools or rate associations, and looked forward expectantly to rapid consolidation of the railroads into a limited number of balanced systems. The best effort to resynthesize scholarship on the subject of the origins, enforcement, and accomplishments of government regulation is Thomas K. McCraw, "Regulation in America: A Review Article," *Business History Review*, 49:159–183 (Summer 1975).

51. Martin, "Troubled Subject of Railroad Regulation," pp. 350–351, 358.

5. System-Building, 1880s–1900s

1. In the Appendix to his *Railroad Leaders, 1845–1900: The Business Mind in Action* (Cambridge, Mass., 1953), Thomas C. Cochran summarizes the careers of sixty railroad presidents. Of these, twenty-eight were managers who had spent nearly all their working lives as railroad executives and thirty-two were men who had moved into senior positions without working up the managerial ladder. Nearly all the latter were stockholders or representatives of stockholders. For reasons to be pointed out shortly, this ratio changes over time. In the 1850s many more presidents were representatives of stockholders, and in the 1890s many more were career managers. See n. 2, chap. 4.

2. The term was coined by Alfred S. Eichner, *The Emergence of Oligopoly: Sugar Refining as a Case Study* (Baltimore, 1969), p. 2.

3. Julius Grodinsky, *Jay Gould: His Business Career, 1867–1892* (Philadelphia, 1957), chap. 3; Wheaton J. Lane, *Commodore Vanderbilt: An Epic of the Steam Age* (New York, 1942), chaps. 9–10.

4. The data for this and the following paragraph are from Grodinsky, *Gould*, chap. 3; Lane, *Vanderbilt*, chap. 11; George H. Burgess and Miles C. Kennedy, *Centennial History of the Pennsylvania Railroad Company, 1846–1946* (Philadelphia, 1949), pp. 198–200; and Charles Francis Adams, Jr., and Henry Adams, *Chapters of Erie and Other Essays* (New York, 1871), pp. 398–406.

5. Grodinsky, *Gould*, pp. 56–65. Burgess and Kennedy, *Centennial History of the Pennsylvania Railroad*, p. 46. The quotation is from the *Twenty-Third Annual Report of the Board of the Pennsylvania Railroad Co. to the Stockholders*, February 15, 1870 (Philadelphia), p. 17. Hereafter only the number and date of the Pennsylvania Annual Reports will be given.

6. Grodinsky, *Gould*, pp. 65–66. The quotation in the next paragraph is from p. 65. Lane, *Vanderbilt*, pp. 264–270.

7. *Report of the Investigating Committee of the Pennsylvania Railroad Company Appointed by Resolution of the Stockholders at the Annual Meeting Held March 10th, 1874* (Philadelphia 1874), p. 45.

8. *Report of the Investigating Committee,* p. 161. The rise of managerial dominance on the Pennsylvania board is effectively described and analyzed in James A. Ward, "Power and Accountability on the Pennsylvania Railroad, 1846–1878," *Business History Review,* 49:37–59 (Spring 1976).

9. For the strategies of expansion and the following legal reorganization see Ward, "Power and Accountability on the Pennsylvania," pp. 45–61; *Twenty-Third Annual Report . . . of the Pennsylvania Railroad Co. . . . February 15, 1870,* pp. 15–20; *Twenty-Fourth Annual Report . . . of the Pennsylvania Railroad Co. . . . February 21, 1871,* pp. 17–27; *Twenty-Fifth Annual Report . . . of the Pennsylvania Railroad Co. . . . February 20, 1872,* pp. 14–20; and Burgess and Kennedy, *Centennial History of the Pennsylvania Railroad,* pp. 195–240.

10. *Twenty-Fourth Annual Report of . . . the Pennsylvania Railroad Co. . . . February 21, 1871,* pp. 18–21; *Twenty-Eighth Annual Report of the Pennsylvania Railroad Co. . . . March 9, 1875,* p. 38.

11. *Twenty-Fifth Annual Report of . . . the Pennsylvania Railroad Co. . . . February 20, 1872,* pp. 27–28. The American Steamship Company's president was H. J. Lombaert, a Pennsylvania vice-president. The investments in the International Navigation Company are given in the *Thirtieth Annual Report of . . . the Pennsylvania Railroad Co. . . . March 13, 1877,* p. 37.

12. *Twenty-Sixth Annual Report of . . . the Pennsylvania Railroad Co. . . . March 11, 1873,* pp. 29–32.

13. An annual report of the Philadelphia and Reading Railroad Company cited in Dumas Malone, *Dictionary of American Biography* (New York, 1946), VII, 461. This policy led in time to financial difficulties for the Reading and also for the Central Railroad of New Jersey and the Delaware and Lackawanna. Edward C. Kirkland, *Industry Comes of Age: Business, Labor and Public Policy 1860–1897* (New York, 1961), pp. 82–83.

14. *Twenty-Seventh Annual Report of . . . the Pennsylvania Railroad Co. . . . March 10, 1874,* p. 28.

15. Ibid, p. 46. Later the Pennsylvania made a small investment of $25,360 in the Standard Steel Works Company. *Thirtieth Annual Report of . . . the Pennsylvania Railroad Company . . . March 17, 1877,* p. 40. By then the investment in the Pennsylvania Steel Works was listed at $735,100, and in the Pullman Palace Car Company at $770,000.

16. *Twenty-Third Annual Report . . . of the Pennsylvania Railroad Co. . . . February 15, 1870,* p. 18, stressed that: "We have no interest in any line beyond the Mississippi."

17. This quotation is from *Report of the Investigating Committee of the Pennsylvania Railroad . . . by Resolution of . . . March 10, 1874,* p. 75. Pages 75–77 describe the Pennsylvania's interest in the lines south of Washington and Cairo. *Twenty-Seventh Annual Report of . . . the Pennsylvania Railroad Co. . . . March 10, 1874,* pp. 34–35; Burgess and Kennedy, *Centennial History of the Pennsylvania Railroad,* pp. 279–281; and Maury Klein, *The Great Richmond Terminal* (Charlottesville, Va. 1970), pp. 61–64, add some further details. In bringing together a number of southern roads connecting Richmond and Atlanta, the Pennsylvania formed a holding company, the Southern Railway Securities Company to hold stock of several roads. The Pennsylvania then took $783,734 worth of stock in the holding company, as well as stock and bonds in the individual operating concerns.

18. *Dictionary of American Biography,* XVI, 500–501; Grodinsky, *Jay Gould,* pp. 115–117. Thomson's interest in western roads is suggested by the fact that he became for a brief period the president of the Dubuque and Pacific. Carlton Corliss, *Main Line of Mid-America* (New York, 1950), p. 146.

19. *Twenty-Eighth Annual Report of . . . the Pennsylvania Railroad Co. . . .*

March 9, 1875, p. 43; Ward, "Power and Accountability on the Pennsylvania," pp. 54–55. Scott continued to retain his personal holdings in the Texas Pacific, remaining its president until 1880, when he also retired as president of the Pennsylvania, a post he took on after Thomson's death in June 1874.

20. This information comes from the treasurer's reports included in the *Annual Reports of the Pennsylvania Railroad* from that dated February 15, 1870, through the one dated March 10, 1874.

21. Burgess and Kennedy, *Centennial History of the Pennsylvania Railroad,* p. 303.

22. Henrietta M. Larson, *Jay Cooke, Private Banker* (Cambridge, Mass., 1936), pp. 315–317; Fritz Redlich, *The Molding of American Banking: Men and Ideas* (New York, 1951), II, 360.

23. Burgess and Kennedy, *Centennial History of the Pennsylvania Railroad,* pp. 219–222, 279–281.

24. James Dredge, *The Pennsylvania Railroad: Its Organization, Construction and Management* (London, 1879) gives the number of employees on the Pennsylvania Railroad Company (that is the lines east of Pittsburgh) as 18,000 in 1877, the worst year of the depression of the 1870s. The lines west of Pittsburgh operated about three times the mileage of the lines east. In 1877 the first operated 1,071 miles of road and the second 3,407 miles. Henry Varnum Poor, *Manual of Railroads for the United States for 1878* (New York, 1878), pp. 309, 340. The lines west were, however, less heavily used than those to the east of Pittsburgh, therefore 32,000 workers would be a conservative estimate for the number of workers on the lines west. In more normal economic times the employees on the Pennsylvania system must have numbered at least 55,000. The first figure on employment on the Pennsylvania Railroad (the lines east) given in Burgess and Kennedy, *Centennial History,* p. 807, is 44,000 in 1889. By then the total number of employees for the system as a whole must have been at least 100,000. In 1910, the first year Burgess and Kennedy give the employees for the system as a whole, the number was 215,000.

25. Henry Varnum Poor, *Manual of the Railroads of the United States for 1870–1871* (New York, 1870), p. 169; Edward Hungerford, *The Story of the Baltimore & Ohio Railroad Company, 1827–1927* (New York, 1928), II, 68, 106–108, 155, 220–227; Grodinsky, *Jay Gould,* pp. 169–332.

26. Hungerford, *Story of the Baltimore & Ohio,* II, 125–127 and 74–79.

27. Hungerford, *Story of the Baltimore & Ohio,* II, 126.

28. *Dictionary of American Biography,* IV, 132–133; Lane, *Vanderbilt,* pp. 270–273; Grodinsky, *Jay Gould,* pp. 105–106; Alvin F. Harlow, *The Road of the Century: The Story of the New York Central* (New York, 1947), pp. 283–284, 370.

29. Lane, *Vanderbilt,* pp. 273–274; Harlow, *Road of the Century,* pp. 290–293. It is not certain when Vanderbilt sold his stock in those roads, but it is clear that he had little stock interests in the Ohio and Mississippi and the Wabash when they went into receivership during the depression of the 1870s.

30. Grodinsky, *Gould,* p. 209.

31. Grodinsky, *Gould,* pp. 154–158.

32. Harlow, *Road of the Century,* pp. 237–258.

33. Frederick Lewis Allen, *The Great Pierpont Morgan* (New York, 1949), pp. 43–45; N.S.B. Gras and Henrietta M. Larson, *Casebook in American Business History* (New York, 1939), pp. 552–553.

34. Cochran, *Railroad Leaders,* pp. 130–132, 307, 335, 433; Grodinsky, *Gould,* p. 229; Richard C. Overton, *Burlington Route: History of the Burlington Lines* (New York, 1965), p. 154.

35. Grodinsky, *Gould,* pp. 226–229; Overton, *Burlington Route,* pp. 166–169;

and Julius Grodinsky, *Transcontinental Railway Strategy, 1869–1893* (Philadelphia, 1962), chaps. 5, 7.

36. Quoted in Grodinsky, *Gould*, p. 229.

37. Quoted in Cochran, *Railroad Leaders*, p. 433. A month later on December 30, 1879, Perkins wrote Forbes: "Sooner or later the lines West of the Missouri will extend, and they will by degrees become allied with lines East of the River and pooling will become a thing of the past, a step merely, in the solution of the railroad conundrum." For Forbes's opposition to Perkins see Cochran, *Railroad Leaders*, pp. 337–338.

38. Grodinsky, *Gould*, chaps. 7, 8; Overton, *Burlington Route*, pp. 154–158.

39. Grodinsky, *Gould*, chaps. 9–13, 16–21; *Transcontinental Strategy*, chaps. 8–11; Overton, *Burlington Route*, pp. 166–175; Robert E. Riegel, *Story of Western Railroads* (New York, 1926), chap. 11.

40. Grodinsky, *Gould*, p. 354.

41. Grodinsky, *Gould*, chaps. 22, 26–27, 29.

42. Harlow, *Road of the Century*, chap. 13, as well as Grodinsky, *Gould*, chap. 18.

43. Cochran, *Railroad Leaders*, pp. 29, 478.

44. Harlow, *Road of the Century*, chaps. 13, 16, 17; Allen, *Morgan*, pp. 50–55.

45. Edward Hungerford, *Men of the Erie* (New York, 1946), pp. 204–205. The Erie obtained its own trunk line into Chicago in 1884. Close ties with the Cincinnati, Hamilton & Dayton assured the old Atlantic & Great Western branch of the Erie an entrance into the Cincinnati.

46. Quoted in Cochran, *Railroad Leaders*, p. 137.

47. The expansion and consolidation of the Burlington roads are covered in Overton, *Burlington Route*, chaps. 10–11; Arthur M. Johnson and Barry E. Supple, *Boston Capitalists and Western Railroads* (Cambridge, Mass., 1967), chap. 13.

48. These interacting strategies of expansion of the Burlington, Milwaukee, Rock Island, and Northwestern are best covered in Grodinsky, *Transcontinental Strategy*, esp. chaps. 8, 15, 16; also August Derleth, *The Milwaukee Road: Its First Hundred Years* (New York, 1948), pp. 126–128, 133–137; Grodinsky, *Transcontinental Strategy*, p. 126, emphasizes that Merrell was "the guiding hand in the expansion of the property."

49. Again the best sources are Grodinsky's chapters cited in the previous note. Stuart Daggett, *Railroad Reorganization* (Boston, 1908), pp. 214–317, provides additional information.

50. Besides Grodinsky's chapters see William H. Sennett, *Yesterday and Today: The History of the Chicago & Northwestern Railway System* (Chicago, 1910), pp. 63–69.

51. Grodinsky, *Gould*, p. 526.

52. Richard C. Overton, *Gulf to Rockies: The Heritage of the Fort Worth and Denver-Colorado and Southern Railways, 1861–1898* (Austin, Texas, 1953), chap. 10, has an excellent summary of the Union Pacific strategy in this period. Also invaluable is Grodinsky, *Transcontinental Strategy*, chaps. 14, 16. During the Adams administration 3,000 miles of railroad were added to the Union Pacific system.

53. For the Santa Fe's history and its relation to the Southern Pacific see Riegel, *Story of the Western Railroads*, ch. 12; Grodinsky, *Transcontinental Strategy*, chaps. 10–12, 14–16; Johnson and Supple, *Boston Capitalists and Western Railroads*, chaps. 14–15; and Leslie L. Waters, *Steel Trails to Santa Fe* (Lawrence, Kans., 1950).

54. Riegel, *Story of the Western Railroads*, p. 179.

55. In explaining to his stockholders why he took still another costly step, Strong pointed out that the roads best situated to act as connectors into Chicago "already

invaded our territory in Kansas." Any satisfactory agreement would be difficult to arrange. "A traffic agreement, at best is always uncertain and unsatisfactory, and generally becomes neglected or odious . . . And it is the history of such contracts that they are effective only so long as it is to the interest of the parties concerned to make them so, and broken as soon as they become burdensome to either party. It is, moreover, more than doubtful if such an agreement however carefully drawn and attended with severe penalty for breach could be enforced against the party breaking it, since the law looks with disfavor upon such contracts as contrary to the public interest which demands the utmost freedom of action on the part of transportation companies." *Fifteenth Annual Report of the Atchison, Topeka and Sante Fe Railroad Company for 1886*, p. 27. Two pages later the report added: "It would seem to be a fact that we tempted these invasions by our own inertia rather than challenged them by an aggressive disposition." Perkins through Forbes had without success tried to convince the Sante Fe's directors not to build still another road into Chicago but to use the Burlington tracks. See Overton, *Burlington Route*, pp. 188–190.

56. Grodinsky's *Transcontinental Strategy* is the best source, esp. chap. 17.

57. Klein, *The Great Richmond Terminal*, p. 24. This study and Klein's *History of the Louisville & Nashville Railroad* (New York, 1972), provide the best picture of system-building in the 1880s in the south. His basic findings are expertly summarized in his "Strategy of Southern Railroads," *American Historical Review*, 78:1052–1068 (April 1968). Also useful is John F. Stover, *The Railroads of the South, 1865–1900* (Chapel Hill, N.C., 1955), esp. chaps. 10, 11, and pp. 198–203, 220–221.

58. Stover, *Railroads of the South*, pp. 203–204, 261–273; E. G. Campbell, *The Reorganization of the American Railroad System, 1893–1900* (New York, 1938), pp. 214–216; Joseph T. Lambie, *From Mine to Market Place: The History of Coal Transportation on the Norfolk and Western Railway* (New York, 1954), esp. chaps. 1, 5–7.

59. Edward C. Kirkland, *Men, Cities and Transportation: A Study in New England History* (Cambridge, Mass., 1948), I, 368–376, 381–386, for the Boston & Albany, chap. 16 for the Boston & Maine, chap. 17 for the New York & New England, and chap. 18 for the New Haven.

60. Kirkland, *Men, Cities and Transportation*, II, 31.

61. Stuart Daggett, *Railroad Reorganization*, p. v.

62. Harvard Business School, "J. P. Morgan, 1837–1913," Case No. 4-371-572, BH 202, p. 23.

63. Paul M. MacAvoy, *The Economic Effects of Regulation: The Trunkline Railroad Cartels and the Interstate Commerce Commission Before 1900* (Cambridge, Mass., 1965), pp. 111–119; Gabriel Kolko, *Railroads and Regulation, 1887–1916* (Princeton, N.J., 1965), chap. 3.

64. MacAvoy, *Economic Effects of Regulation*, pp. 123–125.

65. Quoted in Harvard Business School case, "J. P. Morgan," p. 22.

66. Overton, *Burlington Route*, p. 221, notes that after the withdrawals in 1892 "The Western Traffic Association virtually passed out of existence, and with it vanished the most ambitious attempt at self-regulation without the benefit of pooling."

67. MacAvoy, *Economic Effects of Regulation*, p. 144. MacAvoy reveals cartel performance from 1887 to 1890 on pp. 125–144 and 1889 to 1893 on pp. 144–164. Railroad freight revenues fell in 1894 to $699 million from $829 million the previous year and did not rise to over $800 million again until 1898. U.S. Bureau of the Census, *Historical Statistics of the United States, Colonial Times to 1957* (Washington, D.C. 1960), p. 431. The pattern was the same for passenger revenues which

were at $301.5 million in 1893 and failed to return to even that of 1891 ($281.2 million) until 1899 (p. 430).

68. MacAvoy covers the destruction of regulation and cartelization between 1897 and 1899 in *Economic Effects of Regulation*, pp. 183–191. See also Kolko, *Railroads and Regulation*, pp. 80–83.

69. Cited in William Z. Ripley, *Railroads: Finance and Organization* (New York, 1915), p. 461.

70. Ripley, *Railroads*, pp. 480–485; Klein, *Louisville & Nashville*, pp. 311–314; Daggett, *Railroad Reorganization*, chap. 9.

71. The story of Harriman and Hill is well presented in Overton, *Burlington Route*, chap. 14, Campbell, *Reorganization of American Railroad System*, chaps. 6–7, Ripley, *Railroads*, pp. 491–516, and most recently and expertly in Albro Martin, *James J. Hill and the Opening of the Northwest* (New York, 1976), chaps. 15–17.

72. These figures are from Stover, *American Railroads* (Chicago, 1961), p. 135, and Ripley, *Railroads*, chaps. 14–15, modified by table 4. John Moody in his *Truth about the Trust* (New York, 1904), pp. 431–442, described six such groups (Hill's lines are included in the Morgan group). He computes the total mileage of their lines at 164,000 miles and then lists the independent mileage as 37,500, of which 5,532 belong to the two New England roads (p. 440).

73. Kolko, *Railroads and Regulation*, pp. 88–101.

74. *United States Congress, Senate Document*, 243, III (1905) from vol. 16 intermittently to vol. 19, p. 3291. Kolko in *Railroads and Regulation* (pp. 118–144) argues that, although railroad men did oppose the strong Esch-Townsend bill, they supported the milder Hepburn Act. But the only railroad managers he cites as supporting the bill are Cassett of the Pennsylvania and Stickney.

75. John M. Blum, *The Republican Roosevelt* (Cambridge, Mass., 1954), pp. 87–105; Kolko, *Railroads and Regulation*, p. 147; and Ripley, *Railroads*, pp. 481–483.

76. Gabriel Kolko maintains that postdepression merger movement failed, as had the earlier attempts at pooling, "to establish operational control over falling rates." He continues that "When *all* lines are taken into account, it is the diffusion rather than concentration of the American railroad system that is of greatest significance to the political behavior of the major railroads" (Kolko's italics). *Railroads and Regulation*, p. 88. He supports this assertion by indicating that the number of operating railroads increased from 1,224 to 1,564 between 1900 and 1907, and that the number of independent roads declined only from 847 to 829 in the decade after 1900. Yet clearly he knows that size in terms of mileage and capitalization and not number of firms determines concentration. In the same paragraph he points out that "the larger railroads and banking houses had for several years owned or controlled nearly two-thirds of the mileage." He presents no data at all to contradict Moody, Ripley, Daggett, and the detailed reports by the Interstate Commerce Commission that massively document the concentration of the American railroad system before the passage of the Hepburn Act. The greatest weakness in Kolko's pioneering study is his failure to recognize the importance of system-building as an alternative to pooling in railroad competition after the early 1880s. He appears to assume that competition in the first decade of the twentieth century was much the same as that in the early 1880s.

77. C. E. Perkins, Memorandum on railroad organization, May 1883 (C. E. Perkins Letter Book #6, p. 341–342). Unless otherwise indicated, letters of Perkins and other Burlington personnel cited here are from the company's files. I am indebted to Richard C. Overton for the opportunity to use these files.

78. S. F. Van Oss, *American Railroads as Investments* (New York 1893), p. 235.

79. *Report of the Investigating Committee* (1874), pp. 48–53. The eastern sys-

tem also operated 408 miles of canals. The Pennsylvania executives found it convenient to have some connecting lines at the edges of the new system "worked by their own organizations."

80. *Twenty-Fifth Annual Report . . . the Pennsylvania Railroad Co. . . . February 20, 1872*, p. 16.

81. *By-Laws and Organization for Conducting the Business of the Pennsylvania Railroad Company . . . to Take Effect June 1, 1873* (Philadelphia, 1873), pp. 13–15; *By-Laws and Organization for Conducting the Business of the Pennsylvania Company* (Philadelphia, 1881), pp. 10, 22. At first the general manager of the Pennsylvania also had the title of vice president. Later, as the system grew, it had a vice president for operations as well as a general manager.

82. *Organization . . . of the Pennsylvania Company* (1881), pp. 10–11, 14. A comparison of the list of officers of the Pennsylvania Company and the Panhandle listed in Henry Varnum Poor, *Manual of the Railroads of the United States for 1872–1873* (New York, 1872), pp. 255–256, 561–562, indicates that T. D. Messler and William Thaw served in the same posts on both roads.

83. Information for the following paragraphs comes from *Organization . . . of the Pennsylvania Railroad Company* (1873), *Organization . . . of the Pennsylvania Railroad Company* (1881), and "The Relations of the Pennsylvania Railroad Company to Other Organizations in which it holds an Interest," *Railroad Gazette,* 15:45–46 (1883), reproduced in Leland H. Jenks, "Multi-Level Organization of a Great Railroad," *Business History Review,* 35:339–343 (Autumn 1961).

84. *Organization . . . of the Pennsylvania Railroad Company* (1873), p. 14.

85. "Historical Development of the Organization of the Pennsylvania Railroad," *Railroad Gazette,* 14:766ff (1882) reproduced in Leland H. Jenks, "Early History of a Railroad Organization," *Business History Review,* 35:163–179 (Summer 1961). The quotation is from p. 174.

86. For example, *Organization . . . of the Pennsylvania Railroad* (1873), pp. 16–17, 20, and *Organization . . . of the Pennsylvania Railroad Company* (1881), p. 26.

87. Described in *Organization . . . of the Pennsylvania Railroad Company* (1873), pp. 9–11. All quotations in this paragraph are from pp. 10–11.

88. "Historical Development of . . . the Pennsylvania Railroad" in Jenks, "Early History," p. 174.

89. *Organization . . . of the Pennsylvania Company* (1881), p. 5; "Relations of the Pennsylvania Railroad," in Jenks "Multiple-Level Organization of a Great Railroad," p. 342.

90. *Report of the Investigating Committee* (1874), p. 167. The following quotation is from Frank H. Spearman, *The Strategy of Great Railroads* (New York, 1904), p. 25.

91. This and the following quotations are from a memorandum Perkins wrote in May 1883 in C. E. Perkins, Letter Book #6, pp. 348–349, from the Burlington files. Overton, in his *Burlington Route,* pp. 177–182, summarizes Perkins' ideas on management, pp. 170–171; he gives the outline of initial reorganized structure. Alfred D. Chandler, Jr., *The Railroads: The Nation's First Big Business* (New York, 1965), pp. 118–125, partially reprints a memorandum of Perkins on the "Organization of Railroads," written in 1885. In a memorandum to T. J. Potter of June 4, 1883, Perkins strongly opposed the concept of a traffic manager for the whole system.

92. C. E. Perkins to T. J. Potter, June 4, 1883, Burlington records.

93. Perkins, "Organization of Railroads" (1885), p. 25. To assure as much local authority as possible, Perkins continued to maintain a careful line and staff distinction down to the lowest level of management, same memorandum, p. 7.

94. C. E. Perkins to T. J. Potter, May 12, 1883, Burlington records.

95. Perkins' memorandum on executive personnel policy, undated but written in May 1883 (C. E. Perkins, Letter Book #6, pp. 338–340). Other railroad presidents fully agreed. See quotations in Cochran, *Railroad Leaders*, pp. 81, 138.

96. This and the following quotations are from C. E. Perkins' second memorandum on the duties of third vice president, May 1883. Perkins sent this memorandum to T. J. Potter, who was to take over the vice presidency a few days later. After Potter had reviewed the memorandum and suggested some modifications and changes, Perkins had the revised draft typed up; C. E. Perkins to T. J. Potter, May 12, 22, 1883. In the memorandum the wording was "third" rather than "second vice president," but the title third vice president was only a temporary one. His duties were soon to be carried out, as Perkins had originally planned them to be, by the second vice president. But in the spring of 1883 Perkins had appointed J. C. Peasley as second vice president, for he wanted to train him to take the place of either Potter or A. E. Touzalin, who was then the first vice president in Boston. Cochran, *Railroad Leaders*, pp. 434–435. In time, Peasley became the first vice president in charges of finances, and the second vice president carried out the tasks Perkins had outlined in these memoranda.

97. C. E. Perkins, "Organization of Railroads" (1885), p. 17, also pp. 15–16. Important too is C. E. Perkins, memorandum on railroad organization, May 1883 (C. E. Perkins, Letter Book #6, pp. 341–342). Kirkman presents a penetrating analysis of the difficulties of obtaining efficient administration in a large railroad system. He describes how the resulting breakdown encouraged the growth of a much less efficient informal structure. See Kirkman, *Railroad Expenditures*, I, 238–243.

98. Perkins, "Organization of Railroads" (1885), p. 17. Perkins added: "This is a consideration of importance and is another good reason for not making a unit too large. Personal acquaintance promoted good understanding and people like to see those in authority."

99. C. E. Perkins to T. J. Potter, March 3, 1883, Burlington records.

100. The quickest method to determine whether a railroad had a decentralized structure was to check Henry Varnum Poor, "List of Officers of Operating Railroads in United States and Canada, and of the Chief Railroads in Mexico," which first appeared in the 1891 edition of *Poor's Manual*. This gives a full list of executives on all lines and their titles. A road was considered to have a "decentralized" structure when it had at least two units, each with their own general managers or superintendents who had a traffic officer directly under them, and if it had no traffic officer in the general office except for a vice president. See also Henry Varnum Poor, *Manual of the Railroads of the United States for 1891* (New York, 1891), pp. 916–944, 1365–1369. The structure of the Plant lines is given in Henry S. Haines, *American Railway Management* (New York, 1897), pp. 157–160.

101. Cochran, *Railroad Leaders*, p. 29; Harlow, *Road of the Century*, pp. 332–333. In so doing William Vanderbilt followed the example of his father, the Commodore, who after obtaining the Lake Shore had made his son-in-law Clark its president, but had given the "entire control of the Railway, its business, its maintenance and improvements" to his general manager, James H. Devereux. Devereux handled all activities including financial. The treasurer reported to him. (Cochran, *Railroad Leaders*, p. 313.) After Clark's death, the Commodore placed finances under the treasurer and comptroller of the New York Central; then he put the four members of its single Executive and Finance Committee—himself, William, and Richard and Augustus Schell—on the board of the Lake Shore Line. Lane, *Commodore Vanderbilt* (New York, 1942), pp. 272–274.

102. Quoted in Cochran, *Railroad Leaders*, p. 478. The interconnection between

financial departments and directors of these roads can be seen by comparing the names of the roads' officers as listed in *Poor's Manual* for these years.

103. The relationship of the senior executives of the major operating roads in the New York Central system with each other and with the New York headquarters can be seen by reviewing the correspondence of Henry B. Ledyard and James H. Rutter in Cochran, *Railroad Leaders*, esp. pp. 370–391, 393–394, 398, 400, 456. The H. J. Hayden in this correspondence is the third vice president of the New York Central.

104. An excellent analysis of the development of standardization of procedures and equipment on the Burlington is given in Sherry H. Olson, "Economies of Reorganization in Railroad Consolidation," unpublished manuscript, Johns Hopkins University, 1970. For the work of the Pennsylvania Railroad laboratory see Howard R. Bartlett, "The Development of Industrial Research in the United States," in National Resource Planning Board, *Research—A National Resource* (Washington, D.C., 1938–1941), II, 26–27.

105. Harlow, *Road of the Century*, p. 337; also Cornelius Vanderbilt (the younger) to John Newell, in Cochran, *Railroad Leaders*, pp. 409, 476–477.

106. Riegel, *Western Railroads*, p. 151. See also Grodinsky, *Gould*, pp. 598–599.

107. Ray Morris, *Railroad Administration* (New York, 1920), pp. 54–63.

108. Several of Morgan's reorganizations are described in detail in Campbell, *Reorganization of the American Railroad System*, esp. chaps. 5 and 6. Particularly useful on Morgan's reorganizations is John W. Brackett, "Morgan's Reorganized Railroads: How They Were Controlled," unpublished paper, Massachusetts Institute of Technology, 1959. Klein, *Richmond Terminal*, pp. 269–284, has additional information; and the Harvard Business School case, "J. P. Morgan," pp. 23–26, summarized Morgan's procedures. For Kuhn, Loeb, see Campbell, *Reorganization of American Railroad System*, pp. 209–211, 245–247; and Klein, *Louisville & Nashville*, pp. 220–221, 241–243, 252–258. For Kidder, Peabody see Vincent P. Carosso, *Investment Banking in America* (Cambridge, Mass., 1970), pp. 34–37. As indicated by Poor's "List of Officers Operating Railroads" in the *Manual of Railroads for the United States for 1898*, the Erie, the Reading, the Chesapeake & Ohio and the Southern all had a centralized form of organization.

109. Cochran, *Railroad Leaders*, pp. 46–48, has a brief summary of the road's history in these years, and p. 317 gives the positions held by Fish. More details can be found in Corliss, *Main Line of Mid-America*, pp. 206–225.

110. Minutes of the Executive Committee Meeting, April 5, 1888. Unless otherwise indicated, all documents on the Illinois Central are from the company archives in the Newberry Library, Chicago, Illinois. See also B. F. Ayer and S. Fish to E. T. Jeffery, June 6, 1888; E. H. Harriman to S. Fish, June 11, 1888; J. Dunn to E. T. Jeffery, June 7, 1888. The following spring the drafting of the final definition of a new structure was turned over to a separate group of general financial and legal executives. As the minutes of the meeting of the board for May 15, 1889, stated: "A board consisting of the President, Vice President, Treasurer, two General Solicitors, General Manager and General Auditor, is hereby created and required to immediately prepare a classification into departments of business of the Company; a specification of the chief officers or agents in each department and their titles; a description of the powers and duties of each; and that the President shall cause the same to be printed, and a copy sent to each Director."

111. A. W. Sullivan (acting general superintendent) to J. C. Welling, Oct. 12, 1889; C. A. Beck (acting general manager) to J. C. Welling, Oct. 24, 1889.

112. T. J. Hudson to J. C. Welling, Oct. 5, 1889. See also J. Dunn (assistant to the president) to A. F. Barnard, Oct. 21, 1884, and Corliss, *Main Line of Mid-America*, pp. 215–216.

113. The final structure was described in a text entitled "Code of Rules for Conducting the Business of the Illinois Central Railroad Company," which was accepted by the board on Dec. 16, 1889, Minutes of Board of Directors, Dec. 16, 1889. The Baltimore & Ohio, after its reorganization under Kuhn Loeb, had installed a very similar structure in the preceding year. See *Annual Report of the Baltimore & Ohio for 1889*. Morris, *Railroad Administration*, pp. 50–52, provides a useful organization chart and a description of such a structure on the Norfolk & Western.

114. The use of budgets for the operating departments as early as 1881 is described in Haines, *American Railway Management*, pp. 159–167. Nevertheless, a review of the procedures which the managers on the Harriman lines used early in the twentieth century to have their operating expenditures approved indicates that on these roads only past, not anticipated, expenditures were reported and that capital was allocated in a personal, ad hoc way. See Morris, *Railroad Administration*, pp. 236–239.

115. Ripley, Ray Morris, and other authorities on railroad finance and organization writing in the early 1920s including Cleveland and Powell and Stuart Daggett, make no references to systematic capital appropriation procedures. Morris, *Railroad Administration*, pp. 61–62, describes the ad hoc informal, personal way that capital was allocated on the Harriman lines.

116. Morris, "Stalled Professionalism," pp. 330–332.

6. Completing the Infrastructure

1. Robert G. Albion, *The Rise of New York Port* (New York, 1939), chap. 15; John G. B. Hutchins, *The American Maritime Industries and Public Policy, 1789–1914, an Economic History* (Cambridge, Mass., 1941), pp. 343–368. The first firm to operate a steamship on the transatlantic run was Britain's Great Western Railway. Samuel Cunard began making scheduled trips between Liverpool and Boston in 1840. In 1847 an American sponsored, German financed and owned line began services between New York and Bremen. In 1849 a steamship line to Le Havre was inaugurated.

2. Hutchins, *American Maritime Industries*, p. 486.

3. Hutchins, *American Maritime Industries*, chap. 16.

4. Hutchins, *American Maritime Industries*, p. 539.

5. Hutchins, *American Maritime Industries*, pp. 567–570, 573; James P. Baughman, *The Mallorys of Mystic: Six Generations in American Maritime Enterprise* (Middletown, Conn., 1972), pp. 179–200; William L. Taylor, *A Productive Monopoly: The Effect of Railroad Control on New England Coastal Steamship Lines, 1870–1916* (Providence, 1970), esp. chaps. 7 and 8.

6. Baughman, *Mallorys of Mystic*, p. 204.

7. Baughman in *Mallorys of Mystic*, pp. 202–206, 221–224, describes the operating organization of the Atlantic, Gulf & West Indies Lines.

8. Hutchins, *American Maritime Industries*, pp. 537–539; and N.S.B. Gras and Henrietta M. Larson, *Casebook in American History* (New York, 1939), pp. 566–590.

9. For example, Taylor, *Productive Monopoly*, pp. 88–89.

10. This section on urban transportation relies primarily on Charles N. Cheape III, "The Evolution of Public Transit, 1880–1912: A Study of Three Cities," Ph.D. diss., Brandeis University, 1975. The most useful supplementary information came from Harold C. Passer, *The Electrical Manufacturers, 1875–1900* (Cambridge, Mass., 1953), chaps. 16–17.

11. Cheape, "Evolution of Public Transit," pp. 12–13, has the figures on per-

centage of street railway mileage operated by the different forms of transportation in 1890 and 1902.

12. Cheape, "Evolution of Public Transit," pp. 241–242, describes the organization of the West End Street Railway Company in Boston, and Passer, *Electrical Manufacturers*, pp. 247, 252–253, tells of its formation. Cheape, pp. 110–112, depicts the organization of New York's Metropolitan Street Railway Company. An organization chart of the latter is given in *Street Railway Journal*, 12:515 (Sept. 1896).

13. The relationships between municipal bodies, financial houses, and traction company managers are considered for New York, Philadelphia, and Boston in Cheape, "Evolution of Public Transit," and for Chicago in Paul Barrett, "Public Policy and Private Choice: Mass Transit and the Automobile in Chicago between the Wars," *Business History Review*, 49:491–494 (Winter 1975).

14. This information comes from the *Report of the Postmaster General for 1847, December 6, 1847*, Exec. Doc. no. 1, p. 1311; and *Report of the Postmaster General for 1857, December 1, 1857*, p. 863. The reports for these years are bound in a volume in Pusey Library, Harvard University.

15. U.S. Bureau of the Census, *Historical Statistics of the United States, Colonial Times to 1957* (Washington, D.C., 1960), p. 498. Postage stamps were first introduced in 1847. In 1851 the Post Office Department sold 1,246 stamps, and in 1852, 54,136 (p. 497).

16. Matthew A. Crenson, *The Federal Machine: Beginnings of Bureaucracy in Jacksonian America* (Baltimore, 1975), pp. 104–115. Under Kendall, Barry's successor, the third unit was divided into a contract office and an inspection office. Leonard White, *The Jacksonians: A Study in Administrative History, 1829–1861* (New York, 1963), chaps. 11–12, and Gerald Cullinan, *The Post Office Department* (New York, 1968) chap. 4, adds only a little about the management of the postal service. The best analysis of the operation of the postal service before 1840 is Allan R. Pred, *Urban Growth and the Circulation of Information: The United States System of Cities, 1790–1840* (Cambridge, Mass., 1973) chap. 3. None of these studies consider the changes in the organization of the Post Office Department in the 1850s.

17. U.S. Bureau of the Census, *Historical Statistics*, p. 497.

18. *Report of the Postmaster General for 1849, December 3, 1849*, Exec. Doc. no. 5, 798.

19. *Report of the Postmaster General, December 4, 1850*, Exec. Doc. no. 1, pp. 424–426. The quotation is from pp. 425–426.

20. *Report of the Postmaster General, December 5, 1854*, p. 617, states: "Many of the railroads, desirous of properly serving the public, devote a car exclusively for mail services; but in the great majority of cases, a car is divided between the government and the express companies, or a space is apportioned off for the route agent, the mail being placed with the baggage at one end, and the balance of the car appropriated for a smoking room." Pages 618–619 describe the new distribution system.

21. The information for this paragraph came from Robert L. Thomson, *Wiring a Continent: The History of the Telegraph Industry in the United States, 1832–1866* (Princeton, 1947), p. 241, chaps. 20, 27; also White, *The Jacksonians*, pp. 456–457.

22. *Annual Report of the Western Union Company for 1869*, pp. 16–18. See also *Western Union Telegraph Company, Rules, Regulations and Instructions . . .* (Cleveland, 1866).

23. The information for this paragraph comes from Grodinsky, *Gould*, pp. 148–158, 203–205, 269–285, and chap. 23, and Mira Wilkins, *The Emergence of Multi-*

national Enterprise (Cambridge, Mass., 1970), pp. 47–48. Elisha P. Douglass, *The Coming of Age of American Business: Three Centuries of Enterprise* (Chapel Hill, 1971). Chap. 34 provides us with a useful summary of the business history of the telephone and telegraph companies in the nineteenth century.

24. These changes can be traced in the Annual Reports of the president of the Western Union Company for 1880 through 1883. Gould took no executive position for himself. He permitted Norwin Green to continue as president and made his son George Gould a vice president. Green remained little more than a figurehead.

25. Lester G. Lindley, "The Constitution Faces Technology: The Relationship of the National Government to the Telegraph, 1866–1884," Ph.D. diss., Rice University, 1970, provides the best description and analysis of government–industry relations in the telegraph business.

26. Information about the telephone comes from Albert B. Paine, *In One Man's Life: Being Chapters of the Personal and Business Career of Theodore N. Vail* (New York, 1921), chaps. 12–15, 18–31, 36–39; Arthur S. Pier, *Forbes, Telephone Pioneer* (New York, 1953), chaps. 10–16; Alvin F. Harlow, *Old Wires and New Waves* (New York, 1932); N. R. Danielian, *AT&T: The Story of Industrial Conquest* (New York, 1939); Robert V. Bruce, *Alexander Graham Bell and the Conquest of Solitude* (Boston, 1973), chaps. 22–23; and Rosario J. Tosciello, "The Birth and Early Years of the Bell Telephone System, 1876–1880," Ph.D. diss., Boston University, 1971. Particularly useful was Donald T. Jenkins, "A Schumpeterian Analysis of the Origins of the American Telephone Industry," seminar paper, Harvard, 1974. This study is based in part on a 1938 report of the Federal Communications Commission, *Proposed Report, Telephone Investigation* (Washington, D.C., 1938), and correspondence from the files of the American Telephone & Telegraph Company. John Brooks, *Telephone: The First Hundred Years* (New York, 1976) effectively summarizes the published studies cited here and others.

27. Harlow, *Old Wires*, p. 382; Jenkins, "Schumpeterian Analysis," pp. 21–30.

28. Jenkins, "Schumpeterian Analysis," pp. 47–59.

29. FCC *Report*, Exhibit 1130 A, p. 91; Jenkins, "Schumpeterian Analysis," pp. 59–61, for post-1902 expansion; also FCC, *Report*, pp. 96–103. A reading of Danielian, *A.T. & T., The Story of Industrial Conquest*, pp. 46–49, suggests that "the Traction Kings," Widener and Elkins, in making a grab for the Bell System played a role comparable to Gould's with many railroads by pushing the Boston investors into accepting Morgan financing.

30. This organization is fully described in AT&T *Annual Report* for 1911, pp. 27–29, 36–46. In this report Vail made a careful distinction between the role and function of Central Administration and those of the Associated Companies. The AT&T's *Annual Report* of 1911 noted:

"Administration" [AT&T] is centralized, it is legislative determination of general subjects, supervisory and judicial, acts alike for all branches and divisions and may be located apart from the seats of action.

"Operation" [the Associated Companies] is executive. It is the action, the operation supreme as to local questions but responsible to the central administration. It may be separated into divisions or departments each having operating relations with the other but no lines of authority between them (pp. 36–37).

31. In 1917 the generating capacity of private utility companies was 8.41 million kilowatts and that of the municipally owned power stations 0.58 million (6.0 percent). U.S. Bureau of the Census, *Historical Statistics*, p. 510.

32. Forrest McDonald, *Insull* (Chicago, 1962), pp. 138–145, 149–156, 225–228, 231–232, 248–252, provides instructive examples of system-building in the electrical utilities industries.

33. In 1906 Western Union was capitalized at $96.6 million and American

Telephone & Telegraph at $276.0 million. In that year the New York City Railway Company (by then one of the largest urban transit companies in the world) was capitalized at $114.1 million (assets of $150.6 million) and Consolidated Gas Company of New York had a capitalization of $80.0 million. For the capitalization of the railroads in the same year see table 4.

34. George H. Burgess and Miles Kennedy, *Centennial History of the Pennsylvania Railroad Company* (Philadelphia, 1949), p. 807 gives the number of employees on the lines east of Pittsburgh for 1891 as 51,750. The lines west with their greater mileage must have employed more than this number. See chap. 5, n. 24. For the 1893 statistics on the Pennsylvania see table 3 and *47th Annual Report for the Year 1893 of the Board of Directors of the Pennsylvania Railroad to the Stockholders, March 15, 1894* (Philadelphia, 1894), p. 27. Those for the U.S. government are from U.S. Bureau of the Census, *Historical Statistics,* pp. 718, 721.

7. Mass Distribution

1. John G. Clark, *Grain Trade of the Old Northwest* (Urbana, Ill., 1966), p. 120.

2. By 1876 only 32.5 million of the 224.7 million bushels reaching the seven principal seaports came by water. Joseph Nimmo, *First Annual Report of the Internal Commerce of the United States* (Washington, D.C., 1877), pp. 118–119. Later large railroad systems revived lake shipping, which they operated through their integrated networks.

3. Guy E. Lee "History of the Chicago Grain Elevator Industry, 1840–1890," Ph.D. diss., Harvard University, 1938, p. 38. The information on grain elevators comes from this dissertation, esp. chaps. 2–5.

4. Clark, *Grain Trade,* p. 259.

5. S. S. Huebner, "Functions of Product Exchanges," *The Annals of the American Academy of Political and Social Sciences,* 38:1–2 (Sept. 1911), gives the dates of the founding of the grain exchanges. See also "The Exchanges of Minneapolis, Duluth, Kansas City, Mo., Omaha, Buffalo, Philadelphia, Milwaukee and Toledo," no author listed, in same vol. of *Annals,* pp. 237, 245, 250.

6. Morton Rothstein, "The International Market for Agricultural Commodities, 1850–1873," in David T. Gilchrist and W. D. Lewis, eds. *Economic Change in the Civil War Era* (Charlottesville, Va., 1966), pp. 67–69.

7. Thomas Odle, "Entrepreneurial Cooperation on the Great Lakes: The Origin of the Methods of American Grain Marketing," *Business History Review,* 38:451–454 (Winter, 1964). The quotation from the New York Legislative Report is given in Odle, p. 453.

8. For futures and hedging in the grain trade see Rothstein, "International Market," pp. 68–71. S. S. Huebner, "Functions of Produce Exchanges," 24–32, gives an excellent brief summary of the process of hedging against loss through price fluctuations in grain, cotton, and other trades.

Hedging may be defined as the practice of making two contracts at about the same time of an opposite, though corresponding nature, one in the *trade* market, and the other in the *speculative* market. A purchase in the actual grain market of a certain amount of grain at a certain price is promptly offset by a short sale in the speculative market on some large exchange of the same amount of grain for some convenient future month's delivery, with a view to cancelling any losses that might result from fluctuations in price. As soon, however, as the *trade* transaction is terminated by a sale, the speculative short sale must also be terminated, i.e., covered by a purchase on the exchange. Both contracts are entered into at about the same time, and both must be terminated at about the same time if the hedger wishes to avoid speculation (p. 24).

9. Lee, "Chicago Grain Elevator Industry," chaps. 8–10, 13, documents these regulations in detail, while Jonathan Lurie, "Private Association, Internal Regulation and Progressivism: The Chicago Board of Trade, 1880–1923," *Journal of American Legal History*, 26:219–222 (1972) summarizes well the beginning of internal regulation.

10. Rothstein, "International Market," pp. 66–67, and Rothstein's Ph.D. diss., "American Wheat and the British Markets, 1860–1905," Cornell University, 1960, pp. 267–272.

11. Harold D. Woodman, *King Cotton and His Retainers: Financing and Marketing the Cotton Crop of the South, 1800–1925* (Lexington, 1968), p. 273. The following information comes largely from Woodman's chap. 23, "The Decline of Factorage."

12. Besides Woodman's account of the cotton exchanges and futures buying, pp. 289–294, see Arthur R. Marsh, "Cotton Exchanges and Their Economic Functions," *The Annals of the American Academy of Political and Social Sciences*, 38:253–280 (Sept. 1911).

13. Woodman, *King Cotton*, p. 293.

14. Woodman, *King Cotton*, pp. 288–289.

15. For example, E. H. Carhart, "The New York Produce Exchange," *The Annals of the American Academy of Political and Social Science*, 38:215–221 (Sept. 1911).

16. S. S. Huebner, "The Coffee Market," *The Annals of the American Academy of Political and Social Sciences*, 38:296–302 (Sept. 1911), and Thomas D. Clark, *Pills, Petticoats and Plows* (Indianapolis, 1944), p. 167.

17. Lewis E. Atherton, *The Frontier Merchant in Mid-America* (Columbia, Mo., 1971), p. 98.

18. Quoted in Fred M. Jones, "The Middleman in the Domestic Trade of the United States, 1800–1860," *Illinois Studies in Social Sciences*, XXI, no. 3 (Urbana, Ill., 1937), p. 15.

19. Robert W. Twyman, *History of Marshall Field & Co.* (Philadelphia 1954), p. 31.

20. Twyman, *Marshall Field*, pp. 51–56.

21. Clark, *Pills, Petticoats and Plows*, chap. 1, best describes the relationship between the jobbers of the border commercial centers and the southern country storekeepers and has the most detail on the rise of the country store in the south. Joseph Nimmo, *Report on the Internal Commerce of the United States* (Washington, D.C., 1879), pp. 86–96, is particularly useful on the wholesale trade of St. Louis, Cincinnati, and Louisville.

22. Glenn Porter and Harold C. Livesay, *Merchants and Manufacturers: Studies in the Changing Structure of Nineteenth Century Marketing* (Baltimore, 1971), pp. 137–147. See also, Alfred D. Chandler, Jr., and Stephen Salsbury, *Pierre S. du Pont and the Making of the Modern Corporation* (New York, 1971), pp. 71–72, 140–141; William H. Becker, "The Wholesalers of Hardware and Drugs, 1870–1900," Ph.D. diss., Johns Hopkins University, 1969, p. 31.

23. Elva Tooker, *Nathan Trotter, Philadelphia Merchant, 1787–1853* (Cambridge, Mass., 1955), pp. 64–65, 225.

24. Harry E. Resseugie, "Alexander Turney Stewart and the Development of the Department Store, 1823–1876," *Business History Review*, 39:315, 320 (Autumn 1965).

25. Twyman, *Marshall Field*, p. 54.

26. Twyman, *Marshall Field*, pp. 29–30, for Field's sales and pp. 47, 55–56, for the activities of his competitors.

27. For Hood, Bonbright and Company see N. S. B. Gras and Henrietta M.

Larson, *Casebook in American Business History* (New York, 1939), pp. 495–496. For the two large hardware jobbers see Becker, "The Wholesalers of Hardware and Drugs," pp. 70–71, 85–86, and his "American Wholesale Hardware Trade Associations, 1870–1900," *Business History Review*, 45:194–195 (Summer 1971); Fred C. Kelley, *Seventy-five Years of Hibbard Hardware: The Story of Hibbard, Spencer and Bartlett & Co.* (np, 1930); for Shieffelin Brothers & Co. and McKesson & Robbins see Edwin T. Freedley, *Leading Pursuits and Leading Men: A Treatise on the Principal Trades and Manufacturers of the United States* (Philadelphia, 1854), pp. 119–121. Names of leading wholesalers in the jewelry, grocery, and drug trades are given in Chauncey Depew, ed., *1795–1895: One Hundred Years of American Commerce* (New York, 1895), pp. 591, 598, 617–619.

28. The physical size and shape of the central offices of these establishments are described in Twyman, *Marshall Field*, pp. 46–47, 96–97; Becker, "The Wholesalers of Hardware and Drugs," pp. 70–71, 85. Harold F. Williamson and Arnold R. Daum, *The American Petroleum Industry: The Age of Illumination, 1859–1899* (Evanston, Ill., 1959), pp. 543–544, provide an excellent contemporary description of the full-line petroleum jobber in St. Louis in 1878.

29. Freedley, *Leading Pursuits and Leading Men*, p. 156, writes in 1854: "Many jobbers keep one or more young men as drummers at each of the principal hotels . . . They watch for customers as a cunning animal does for his prey . . . The country merchant is booked on his arrival, is captivated by courtesy, is attracted by appeals to each of his appetites and passions, is coaxed, decoyed, and finally ensnared and captured."

30. The role and functions of the salesman are described in Clark, *Pills, Petticoats and Plows*, chap. 6; Becker, "The Wholesalers of Hardware and Drugs," pp. 118–124, 249–255; and Twyman, *Marshall Field*, pp. 11–12, 52–53, 92–95.

31. Twyman, *Marshall Field*, pp. 27, 99.

32. Resseugie, "Alexander Turney Stewart," p. 316.

33. Twyman, *Marshall Field*, p. 65; also Becker, "The Wholesalers of Hardware and Drugs," pp. 85–86.

34. Twyman, *Marshall Field*, pp. 98, 102–103, 110; Resseugie, "Alexander Turney Stewart," p. 319; Gras and Larson, *Casebook in Business History*, p. 481.

35. Becker, "The Wholesalers of Hardware and Drugs," chaps. 3 and 5.

36. Francis J. Reynolds, *American Business Manual*, vol. 1, *Organization* (New York, 1914, first edition 1911), pp. 179–187, describes fully the internal organizational structure of a wholesale jobber at the beginning of the twentieth century; also useful is Becker, "The Wholesalers of Hardware and Drugs," pp. 93–94, 232–234.

37. Twyman, *Marshall Field*, pp. 33–37; Becker, "The Wholesalers of Hardware and Drugs," pp. 104–107, 229.

38. James Madison, "The Evolution of Commercial Credit Reporting in Nineteenth Century America," *Business History Review*, 48:167–168, 174–176, 184 (Summer 1974). [Dun & Bradstreet], *Dun & Bradstreet: The Story of an Idea* (New York, 1966) adds little.

39. Twyman, *Marshall Field*, p. 36.

40. Reynolds, *American Business Manual—Organization*, pp. 237–242.

41. Theodore N. Beckman, *Wholesaling* (New York, 1926), chap. 19, has a useful analysis of the technical definition and uses of stock-turn; see also Paul D. Converse and Harry H. Huey, *The Elements of Marketing* (New York, 1940), pp. 610–618.

42. Twyman, *Marshall Field*, pp. 50–51.

43. Twyman, *Marshall Field*, pp. 118–119.

44. Harry E. Resseugie, "The Decline and Fall of the Commercial Empire of

A. T. Stewart," *Business History Review*, 36:268–270 (Autumn 1962), pp. 260–286.

45. Becker, "American Wholesale Hardware Trade Associations," p. 197, and "The Wholesalers of Hardware and Drugs," pp. 61, 226, also pp. 55, 57. During the 1880s the wholesale druggists numbered about 200; the number in the hardware trade was higher, while the number of dry goods jobbers was still greater, probably closer to 500. One of the earliest accurate counts of wholesalers, made forty years later in 1925, lists the number of dry goods wholesalers at 3,200, hardware at 2,800, and druggists at 1,680. Grocers, as always, were the largest, with 8,200. By then wholesalers in confectionary with 3,200, jewelry with 2,000, and boots and shoes with 1,738, had become proportionately larger than they were in the 1880s. These data for the 1880s are from Becker, "American Wholesale Hardware Trade Association," p. 197, and "The Wholesalers of Hardware and Drugs," pp. 55, 57, 61, 226. See also Beckman, *Wholesaling*, p. 7. The 1925 figures are from a survey made by R. L. Polk Company for the J. Walter Thompson Company. Beckman cites another survey made in 1922 by the Crowell Publishing Company where figures are much higher for each category. As Polk specialized in getting this type of data, its figures were probably the more accurate.

46. Harold Barger, *Distribution's Place in the American Economy Since 1869* (Princeton, 1955), pp. 69–71. Barger says on page 11, "For all practical purposes . . . in 1879 there were no department stores." The articles and books cited below, most of which were written after the publication of Barger's book, show that such stores were firmly established by that date.

47. Herbert A. Gibbons, *John Wanamaker* (New York, 1926), I, 238–239. For Stewart see Resseugie, "The Decline and Fall . . . of A. T. Stewart," pp. 268–270, and "Alexander Turney Stewart," p. 320. See also Twyman, *Marshall Field*, pp. 175–177.

48. Information on the dates of the beginning of department stores comes from John William Ferry, *A History of the Department Store* (New York 1960), chap. 3, plus the two articles by Resseugie, cited in the previous note.

49. Ralph M. Hower, *History of Macy's of New York, 1858–1919* (Cambridge, Mass., 1943), p. 43.

50. U.S. Bureau of the Census, Ninth Census, vol. 1, *The Statistics of the Population of the United States* (Washington, D.C., 1872), p. 380.

51. Ferry, *The Department Store*, chap. 4; Hower, *Macy's*, p. 211, for R. H. White and Woodward & Lothrop. Richard W. Edwards, *Tales of the Observer* (Boston 1950), chaps. 1–2, has some information on Jordan Marsh.

52. Twyman, *Marshall Field*, pp. 43–44, 108–111.

53. Hower, *Macy's*, pp. 102–103, 161–162.

54. Resseugie, "Alexander Turney Stewart," pp. 302–322; Hower, *Macy's*, pp. 48–57; J. H. Appel, *The Business Biography of John Wanamaker* (New York, 1930), pp. 43–48, 107–119; Gras and Larson, *Casebook in American Business History*, pp. 482–483 (for Chicago's The Fair and Washington's Woodward and Lothrop) and pp. 483–496 (for Wanamaker).

55. Ralph M. Hower, *The History of an Advertising Agency, N. W. Ayer & Son at Work, 1869–1939* (Cambridge, Mass., 1939), pp. 58, 214.

56. Resseugie, "Alexander Turney Stewart," p. 302. Reynolds, *American Business Manual—Organization*, pp. 187–200, has an excellent review of the internal structure of the department store at the beginning of the twentieth century.

57. Hower, *Macy's*, p. 117.

58. Hower, *Macy's*, p. 115.

59. Hower, *Macy's*, pp. 220–230.

60. Twyman, *Marshall Field*, pp. 26–27.

61. See Hower, *Macy's*, pp. 112, 242–243, for Macy's purchasing organization and

pp. 244-251 for manufacturing. Besides clothing and other cloth products, Macy's became involved in the manufacturing of cigars, cards, and perfumes and, for a time, even leased a bicycle shop. Nevertheless, the value of goods manufactured at Macy's was never as high as 10 percent of its overall sales (p. 247).

62. Twyman, *Marshall Field*, pp. 118-119, 175-176; Hower, *Macy's*, pp. 185-188. This rate of stock-turn was on Macy's wholly owned (and not leased) departments.

63. Gras and Larson, *Casebook in Business History*, pp. 483.

64. Twyman, *Marshall Field*, p. 120; Hower, *Macy's*, p. 156; Barger *Distribution's Place*, p. 117. Excellent examples of the nature of protest against the department stores and the arguments made in their defense can be found in testimony given before the Industrial Commission in 1899: see *Report of Industrial Commission* (Washington, 1901), VII, 451-465, 697-698, 736 (for defense); 705-711, 723-727 (for attack).

65. Boris Emmet and John E. Jeuck, *Catalogues and Counters: A History of Sears, Roebuck and Company* (Chicago, 1950), pp. 19-22. The following review of the early history of Sears Roebuck and Company comes almost completely from Emmet and Jeuck's excellent study. W. L. Braham, *The Romance of Montgomery Ward and Company* (New York, 1929) has little of value on that enterprise. Because of the excellence of the Emmet and Jeuck study and the lack of information on Montgomery Ward and Company, the analysis here of the rise of the mail-order enterprise in the United States focuses on Sears, a story that repeated the comparable experience of Wards in the 1870s and 1880s.

66. For example, Macy's began as early as 1879 to sell through catalogues, but such sales were small: see Hower, *Macy's*, pp. 164-177. Two other mail-order houses, Speigels and National Cloak and Shoe, followed Sears into that business. See Orange A. Smalley and Frederick D. Sturdivant, *The Credit Merchants: A History of Speigel, Inc.* (Carbondale, III., 1973), chaps. 3-5; Emmet and Jeuck, *Catalogues and Counters*, p. 171.

67. Emmet and Jeuck, *Catalogues and Counters*, p. 104.

68. Emmet and Jeuck, *Catalogues and Counters*, p. 172.

69. Emmet and Jeuck, *Catalogues and Counters*, p. 127.

70. Emmet and Jeuck, *Catalogues and Counters*, pp. 39, 119, 240-244. The value of sales of goods produced in Sears-controlled factories rarely reached 10 percent of net sales.

71. Emmet and Jeuck, *Catalogues and Counters*, p. 128.

72. Emmet and Jeuck, *Catalogues and Counters*, p. 132.

73. Emmet and Jeuck, *Catalogues and Counters*, p. 172; Hower, *Macy's*, p. 332; and Twyman, *Marshall Field*, pp. 175-177.

74. Emmet and Jeuck, *Catalogues and Counters*, p. 163.

75. Emmet and Jeuck, *Catalogues and Counters*, pp. 150-163, 187-189.

76. Daniel Bloomfield, *Chain Stores* (New York, 1931), suggests the nature of the attack before the onslaught of the depression and the coming of the New Deal strengthened still more the protest against the chain store. Also useful is Godfrey M. Lebhar, *The Chain Store: Boom or Bust?* (New York, 1932).

77. The A&P's early history is reviewed by the editors of Progressive Grocers Magazine, *A&P: Past, Present and Future* (New York, 1971), pp. 2-21; and in Godfrey M. Lebhar, *Chain Stores in America, 1859-1962* (New York, 1963), pp. 25-27. On pp. 27-30 Lebhar describes A&P's imitators and competitors.

78. The story of Woolworth and its imitators is given in Lebhar, *Chain Stores*, pp. 36-43, also pp. 15-18.

79. Lebhar, *Chain Stores*, pp. 43-47; Barger, *Distribution's Place*, p. 140; Smalley and Sturdivant, *Credit Merchants*, pp. 42-43.

80. The information on the organization and management of chain stores comes

largely from William J. Baxter, *Chain Store Distribution and Management* (New York 1928), esp. pp. 132–137, 143–145, 155, 161–164.

8. Mass Production

1. Albert Fishlow, *American Railroads and the Transformation of the Ante-Bellum Economy* (Cambridge, Mass., 1965), pp. 141–149.

2. Victor S. Clark, *History of Manufacturers in the United States*, I, *1607–1860* (New York, 1916), p. 574, and II, *1860–1893* (New York, 1929), p. 447.

3. Carroll D. Wright, "The Factory System of the United States," U.S. Bureau of the Census, *Report of the United States at the Tenth Census (June 1, 1880)* (Washington, 1883), p. 548.

4. H. Thomas Johnson, "Early Cost Accounting for Internal Management Control: Lyman Mills in the 1850's," *Business History Review*, 46:466–474 (Winter 1972). It is possible that other mills had comparable accounts but there is still little evidence of this in available literature and accounts.

5. David J. Jeremy, "Innovation in American Textile Technology during the Early 19th Century," *Technology and Culture*, 14:40–76 (Jan. 1973) shows that the major period of innovation was before 1850 and came with the rapid growth of the integrated mills. Clark, *History of Manufacturers*, II, 101–102, 111–112, 386–389; the estimate on increasing output at the end of the paragraph is from p. 388.

6. For a useful discussion of the increase in productivity in New England textiles as a result of the increased skills of workers see Paul A. David, "Learning by Doing and Tariff Protection: A Reconsideration of the Case of the Ante-Bellum United States Cotton Textile Industry," *Journal of Economic History*, 30:421–601 (Sept. 1970) and his "The 'Horndal Effect' in Lowell, 1834–1865: A Short-Run Learning Curve for Integrated Cotton Textile Mills," *Explorations in Economic History*, 10:131–150 (Winter 1973).

7. Edwin T. Freedley, *Leading Pursuits and Leading Men* (Philadelphia, 1856), pp. 111. For a description of the carriage works in Flint, Michigan, in the 1890s see Carl Crow, *The City of Flint Grows Up* (New York, 1945), pp. 29–36, and Lawrence R. Gustin, *Billy Durant, Creator of General Motors* (Grand Rapids, Mich., 1973), pp. 41–48.

8. These included circular saws, cross saws, mortisers, planers, borers, lathes, and tenoning machines. Polly Anne Earl, "Craftsmen and Machines," in Jan M. G. Quimby and Polly Anne Earl, *Technological Innovation and the Decorating Arts* (Charlottesville, Va., 1974), pp. 307–329. See also Nathan Rosenberg, "Americans Rise to Woodworking Leadership," in Brooke Hindle, ed., *America's Wooden Age* (Tarrytown, N.Y., 1975), pp. 37–55.

9. Richard B. Tennant, *The American Cigarette Industry* (New Haven, 1950), pp. 17–20. Nannie May Tilley, *The Bright-Tobacco Industry, 1860–1929* (Chapel Hill, N.C., 1948), pp. 575–576. B. W. E. Alford, *W.D. & H. O. Wills and the Development of the U.K. Tobacco Industry* (London, 1973), pp. 143–149.

10. See Chapter 9 for the history of these three companies.

11. This quotation is the title of chap. 16 of John Storck and Walter D. Teague, *Flour and Men's Bread* (Minneapolis, 1952). Chaps. 14–16 describe the revolution in American milling, which started with the adoption of French and Hungarian technology, particularly the purifier, to American needs, was advanced by the coming of rollers and gradual reduction, and was completed by the development of the automatic, all-roller, gradual-reduction mill. A brief analysis is given by Charles B. Kuhlman, "Processing Agricultural Products after 1860," in Harold F. Williamson, ed. *The Growth of the American Economy*, 2d ed. (New York, 1951), pp. 437–440.

12. Kuhlman, "Processing Agricultural Products," p. 439.

13. Earl C. May, *The Canning Clan* (New York, 1937), pp. 350–351. For other canners see Chapter 9.

14. Jacob Schmookler, *Invention and Economic Growth* (Cambridge, Mass., 1966).

15. The technological development can be followed in detail in the superb study of the industry's history by Harold F. Williamson and Arnold R. Daum, *The American Petroleum Industry: The Age of Illumination 1859–1899* (Evanston, Ill., 1959), particularly chaps. 9, 11, and 18.

16. Williamson and Daum, *American Petroleum Industry*, p. 285.

17. Williamson and Daum, *American Petroleum Industry*, p. 282.

18. Allan Nevins, *Study in Power: John D. Rockefeller, Industrialist and Philanthropist* (New York, 1953), I, 70–75.

19. Alfred S. Eichner, *The Emergence of Oligopoly: Sugar Refining as a Case Study* (Baltimore, 1969), pp. 32–39.

20. Williams Haynes, *American Chemical Industry: Background and Beginning*, I (New York, 1954), 253; chap. 16 describes revolutions in making of sulphuric acid. See also Williamson and Daum, *American Petroleum Industry*, p. 284. For white lead, cotton, and linseed oil see Chauncey DePew, ed., *One Hundred Years of American Commerce* (New York, 1895), pp. 438–440, 451–453. Haynes, *American Chemical Industry*, I, 200, is also good on white lead.

21. Thomas C. Cochran, *The Pabst Brewing Company* (New York, 1948), pp. 54, 73–74, for output figures and chap. 5 for production technology.

22. Williamson and Daum, *American Petroleum Industry*, p. 616.

23. Ralph W. Hidy and Muriel E. Hidy, *Pioneering in Big Business, 1882–1911* (New York, 1955), pp. 71–73, 100–107.

24. Cochran, *Pabst Brewing Company*, p. 95.

25. Peter Temin, *Iron and Steel in Nineteenth Century America: An Economic Inquiry* (Cambridge, Mass., 1964), p. 112.

26. Temin, *Iron and Steel*, p. 109. Advertisements in the *American Railroad Journal* state that Cambria Iron Works was capitalized at $1.0 million.

27. They were the Albany Iron Works of Erastus Corning and John Winslow in 1865, the rail-making subsidiary of the Pennsylvania Railroad, the Pennsylvania Steel Company, in 1866, followed by Cleveland Rolling Mill Company (A. B. Stone) in 1868. Five mills opened between 1871 and 1873. They included the Cleveland Rolling Mill Company's Chicago works, and those of North Chicago Rolling Mill (E. P. Ward), Cambria (Morrell), Joliet Iron & Steel, and Bethlehem Iron Works. Three opened in 1875–1876—Edgar Thomson (Carnegie), Lackawanna (W. W. Scranton), and Vulcan. Temin, *Iron and Steel*, p. 171.

28. Joseph Frazier Wall, *Andrew Carnegie* (New York, 1970), pp. 312–313. Holley designed six of the eleven converters and was consulted on three others. The remaining two were copied directly from those he had designed. Temin, *Iron and Steel*, p. 133.

29. Temin, *Iron and Steel*, p. 135.

30. *Metallurgical Review*, 1:332–333 (Dec. 1877), italics added. Robert Longsbon was Henry Bessemer's partner and brother-in-law.

31. *Engineering*, 26:21–22 (July 12, 1878).

32. *Engineering*, 25:295 (April 19, 1878); italics added.

33. Temin, *Iron and Steel*, p. 159.

34. These two quotations are from Temin, *Iron and Steel*, pp. 164–165. Carnegie's commitment to technological innovation is summarized effectively in Harold Livesay, *Andrew Carnegie* (Boston, 1974), pp. 114–117.

35. Figures for capital investment, output, and employment are from Temin,

Iron and Steel, pp. 166–167. Those on coke are from Sam H. Schurr, Bruce C. Netchert, and others, *Energy in the American Economy* (Baltimore, 1960), p. 73. Coke was the largest single use of coal next to that of the railroads. Railroad consumption stood at 29.3 million tons in 1895 and 109.3 million in 1905.

36. John Fritz, *The Autobiography of John Fritz* (New York, 1912), p. 126.

37. The best summary and evaluation of Carnegie's railroad career is Livesay, *Carnegie,* pp. 29–42, as told in more detail in Wall, *Carnegie,* chaps. 6–7; also useful is Andrew Carnegie, *The Empire of Business* (Garden City, N.J., 1933), pp. 291–296.

38. Temin, *Iron and Steel,* p. 174.

39. Wall, *Carnegie,* pp. 314–316, 329. The overall organization of Carnegie enterprise is best described in James H. Bridge, *The Inside History of the Carnegie Steel Company* (New York, 1903), chap. 18.

40. Wall, *Carnegie,* p. 329. Wall states that Shinn was vice president of the Allegheny Valley Railroad. In Henry Varnum Poor, *Manual(s) of the Railroad of the United States* for those years, Shinn is listed from 1871 until 1874 as "the general agent of the Pennsylvania Company." Poor also lists him as an officer of the Allegheny Valley Railroad.

41. Bridge, *Inside History,* pp. 84–85. Bridge reports that the Standard Oil Company used this system of accounting.

42. Wall, *Carnegie,* p. 342.

43. Bridge, *Inside History,* p. 95, also 84–85, 106–107; George A. Wood, *The Voucher System of Book Keeping* (Pittsburgh, 1895) gives examples of the vouchers used at Carnegie Steel and Allied A. C. Frid Company as well as the Pennsylvania Company and the Westinghouse Electrical and Manufacturing Company.

44. Wall, *Carnegie,* p. 342.

45. Wall, *Carnegie,* p. 336.

46. Bridge, *Inside History,* p. 85.

47. Livesay, *Carnegie,* pp. 110–114; Bridge, *Inside History,* pp. 84–85; Wall, *Carnegie,* pp. 337–345.

48. Bridge, *Inside History,* p. 97.

49. Livesay, *Carnegie,* pp. 99, 110–111; Andrew Carnegie, *Autobiography of Andrew Carnegie* (Boston, 1920), p. 182. The engineers include a civil, a resident, and a chief engineer. *Bulletin of the American Iron and Steel Association,* 9:274 (Sept. 10, 1875).

50. Bridge, *Inside History,* pp. 95–102; Wall, *Carnegie,* 635.

51. The details for organization of factories in some of these industries can be found in Charles H. Fitch, "Report on Manufacture of Hardware, Cutlery and Edge Tools," in the *Tenth Census* (1882), and Fitch, "Report on Manufacture of Interchangeable Mechanisms," also in the *Tenth Census.* A similar analysis for a stove-making establishment is suggested in Henry Metcalfe, "The Shop Order System of Accounts," *Transactions, American Society of Mechanical Engineers,* 7:439–468 (1886).

52. Fitch, "Report on Manufacture of Interchangeable Mechanisms," p. 33.

53. John W. Roe, *English and American Tool Builders* (New Haven, 1916), chaps. 14–16; especially useful are the "genealogies" of the New England gun makers and of other metal-working establishments, pp. 139, 187. Charles H. Fitch, writing in 1882, in his "Report on Manufacture of Interchangeable Mechanisms" in the *Tenth Census,* pp. 25–26, noted "The general manufacture of milling machines dates back only twenty-five or thirty years, and twenty years ago there were but three extensive manufactures of milling machines. The demand for them in the rapid growth of gun and sewing machine manufacture after 1855 was very largely supplied by George S. Lincoln and Co. of Hartford, the Lincoln pattern

being a well-known and standard machine." Robert S. Woodbury, *History of the Milling Machine* (Cambridge, Mass., 1960), helps document the points made by Fitch and Roe with useful illustrations. Many machines which Woodbury describes were developed between 1848 and 1855. He ascribes the coming of the universal milling machine to John R. Brown of Brown and Sharpe, who improved on the one designed by Frederick W. Howe of Robbins and Lawrence in 1852 (pp. 38–50). This machine was improved in the 1870s to do heavier work such as that required for locomotives and steam engines. Woodbury's other volumes suggests the importance of the clock and gun industries in bringing in the extensive use of gear-cutting and grinding machines. *History of the Gear Cutting Machine* (Cambridge, Mass., 1959), part III, *History of the Grinding Machine* (Cambridge, Mass., 1959), pp. 31–71.

54. For inside contracting and its use in connection with piece and day rates see Fitch, "Report on Manufacture of Hardware, Cutlery and Edge Tools," in *Tenth Census*, p. 4; Felicia Deyrup, "Arms Makers of the Connecticut Valley," *Smith College Studies in History*, 33 (1948), pp. 101–102; Alden Hatch, *Remington Arms* (New York, 1956) pp. 188–189; Fitch, "Report on Manufacture of Interchangeable Mechanisms," in *Tenth Census*, pp. 33–35; Harold Williamson, *Winchester: The Gun that Won the West* (Evanston, Ill., 1952), pp. 85–91, 136–138; and John Buttrick, "The Inside Contract System," *Journal of Economic History*, 12:205–221 (Summer 1952). It was also used in the making of ships and mining. Edward C. Kirkland, *Industry Comes of Age* (New York, 1961), p. 347. The contract system was also employed to some extent in shoemaking but did not last long. Blanche Hazard, *The Boot and Shoe Industry in Massachusetts Before 1875* (Cambridge, Mass., 1921), pp. 122–123. Constance M. Green, "Light Manufacturers and the Beginning of Precision Manufacture," in Williamson, *Growth of the American Economy*, p. 208, states that the contract system was occasionally used in the finishing departments of textile mills, but gives no citation for this point.

55. Williamson, *Winchester*, p. 87.

56. Fitch, "Report on Manufacture of Interchangeable Mechanisms," pp. 33–34.

57. Henry R. Towne, "The Engineer as an Economist," *Transactions, American Society of Mechanical Engineers*, 7:429–430 (1886). The society was founded in 1880.

58. Metcalfe, "Shop Order System of Accounts," pp. 440–441. Metcalfe's talk summarized his book, *The Cost of Manufactures and the Administration of Workshops, Public and Private*, published the year before in New York. His ideas are placed in a larger setting in Joseph A. Litterer, "Systematic Management: Design for Organizational Recoupling in American Manufacturing Firms," *Business History Review*, 37:378–379 (Winter 1963).

59. Metcalfe, "Shop-Order System of Accounts," p. 451.

60. Metcalfe, "Shop-Order System of Accounts," pp. 463–465, and *Cost of Manufactures*, pp. 142–143. See also S. Paul Garner, *Evolution of Cost Accounting to 1925* (University, Ala., 1954), pp. 244–245, 256–257, 325–326.

61. Oberlin Smith, "Inventory Valuation of Machinery Plant," *Transactions, American Society of Mechanical Engineers*, 7:433–439 (1886). Smith's background and interests are described in Monte A. Calvert, *Mechanical Engineer in America, 1830–1910* (Baltimore, 1967), pp. 81–83, 114, 153–154, 170–178.

62. For Taylor, pp. 475–476, for Anderson, pp. 471–475, for Fitch, p. 471 in vol. 7 of *Transactions*. Fitch described a comparable system used in the Wilson Sewing Machine Company in "Manufacture of Interchangeable Mechanisms" in the *Tenth Census*, p. 35. For Taylor's debt to railroad accounting see n. 79 below.

63. For example, Henry L. Binsse, "A Short Way to Keep Time and Cost," *Transactions, American Society of Mechanical Engineers*, 9:380 (1888).

64. Williamson, *Winchester*, p. 91; also Buttrick, "Inside Contract System," pp. 209–210. In metal working, the forge and furnace work was usually done by skilled labor on a piecework basis, while assembling was done on a day rate. Williamson, *Winchester*, pp. 88, 490. An exception to this rule appears to have been stove-making, where the assemblers rather than the parts-makers worked under contract, while the moulders were paid by the piece. Metcalfe, "The Shop-Order System of Accounts," p. 466.

65. Henry R. Towne, "Gainsharing," *Transactions, American Society of Mechanical Engineers*, 10:600–620 (1889).

66. Daniel Nelson, *Managers and Workers* (Madison, Wis., 1975), pp. 52–53.

67. Taylor, who had worked at the Midvale Steel Company (makers of heavy specialized machinery, machine tools, interchangeable bridge structures, and other steel shapes), had instituted a shop-order system of control in that company during the late 1870s and had in 1884 organized a "rate-fixing department." Much has been written about Frederick W. Taylor and his work. The standard biography, Frank B. Copley, *Frederick W. Taylor, Father of Scientific Management*, 2 vols. (New York, 1923) is quite uncritical and unanalytical. A good brief summary of his ideas and career can be found in David A. Wren, *The Evolution of Management Thought* (New York, 1972), chap. 6. The best analysis of the development and implications of the Taylor system is Hugh C. Aitken, *Taylorism at Watertown Arsenal: Scientific Management in Action, 1908–1915* (Cambridge, Mass., 1960), chap. 1. A useful account is Daniel Nelson, "Scientific Management, Systematic Management, and Labor, 1880–1915," *Business History Review*, 49:479–500 (Winter 1974). Calvert, *Mechanical Engineer*, pp. 9–10, 173, 176, suggests the important role that William Sellers, Taylor's mentor, played as an innovator in the machine tool industry and as a leader in the mechanical engineering profession.

68. Frederick W. Taylor, "A Piece-Rate System, Being a Step toward Partial Solution of the Labor Problem," *Transactions, American Society of Mechanical Engineers*, 16:856–883 (1895).

69. Frederick W. Taylor, *Shop Management* (New York, 1911), pp. 41–43 and "Piece Rate System," pp. 865–866.

70. Frederick W. Taylor, "Shop Management," *Transactions, American Society of Mechanical Engineers*, 24:1337–1456 (June 1903). The ideas presented here were fully developed in his *Shop Management*, pp. 95–105.

71. Taylor, *Shop Management*, p. 104.

72. Taylor, *Shop Management*, pp. 110–111. The concept of the planning department came directly out of the work done at Midvale by the rate-fixing department (Taylor, "Piece Rate System," pp. 877). Taylor described the functions of the Planning Department on pp. 112–120 of *Shop Management;* see also pp. 64–66. Other activities of the Planning Department included the operation of an information bureau, messenger system, and post office delivery, a mutual accident association, and a rush order department.

73. Taylor, *Shop Management*, pp. 116–117. One man was to have a full-time job devising improvements in the system (p. 120).

74. For the concern of these early writers on factory management for integration and coordination see Joseph A. Litterer, "Systematic Management: The Search for Order and Integration," *Business History Review*, 35:472–474 (Winter 1961). Church's statement is given on p. 472. Litterer in his "Systematic Management" (1963), pp. 385–387, suggests how the rise of the new specialized functions led to the emergence of a factory staff. Wren provides an excellent brief sketch of the writings of Alford, Robb, and Church in *Management Thought*, pp. 183–184, 188–189, 191–192. The fruition of Church's experiences and ideas appear in his *The Science and Practice of Management* (New York, 1914). Useful too for

Church is Joseph A. Litterer, "Alexander Hamilton Church and the Development of Modern Management," *Business History Review*, 34:211–225 (Summer 1961). The quotation is from p. 213.

75. Daniel Nelson, *Managers and Workers* (Madison, Wisc., 1975), p. 72, examines the application of Taylor's system in twenty-nine establishments and finds that functional foremen were instituted in only six, and then only on a partial basis.

76. Harrington Emerson, *Efficiency as a Basis for Operations and Wages* (New York, 1911) (a compilation of articles) and *Twelve Principles of Efficiency* (New York, 1913). Wren, *Management Thought*, pp. 169–172, has a useful summary of Emerson's ideas. The quotation and the paragraph is from the first of these books, quoted in *Management Thought*, pp. 170–171.

77. Hugo Diemer, *Industrial Organization and Management* (New York, 1914), pp. 39–41.

78. [Yale and Towne Manufacturing Company], *Fifty Years of a Successful Industry, 1868–1918* (Stamford, Conn., 1919), pp. 46–47.

79. Taylor and others saw these innovations as improvements on current railroad practice. As Taylor wrote in Sept. 1898, describing a cost accounting system he was introducing at Bethlehem Steel: "The method of bookkeeping which the writer believes to be the best is in general the modern railroad system of accounting adapted and modified to suit the manufacturing business." Copley, *Taylor*, II, 360–361, and Litterer, "Systematic Management" (1963), pp. 381–382.

80. Garner, *Evolution of Cost Accounting to 1925*, chap. 5. For Church's series of articles, entitled "Proper Distribution of Establishment Charges," see pp. 129–130, 148, 212–213, 223, 227. For Gantt's contribution see Alex W. Rethe, ed., *Gantt on Management* (New York, 1961), pp. 152–164.

81. Copley, *Taylor*, I, chaps. 7–8; Aitken, *Taylorism at Watertown*, pp. 29–32, 102–104.

82. The story of the introduction of the moving assembly line is dramatically told in Allen Nevins and Frank E. Hill, *Ford: The Times, The Men and The Company* (New York, 1954), chap. 18. Also Horace L. Arnold and Fay L. Faurote, *Ford Methods and the Ford Shops* (New York, 1915), pp. 129–140 and 360–370.

83. Calvert, *Mechanical Engineer*, chap. 6, and pp. 210–211.

84. Calvert, *Mechanical Engineer*, chap. 9, has an excellent discussion of the move toward standardization in mechanical engineering from the 1870s on. As Wren points out, one of Taylor's basic goals was to standardize methods and procedures. *Management Thought*, p. 146.

85. Calvert, *Mechanical Engineer*, pp. 135–138.

86. Calvert, *Mechanical Engineer*, chaps. 3–5.

9. The Coming of the Modern Industrial Corporation

1. Robert H. Wiebe, *The Search for Order, 1877–1920* (New York, 1967), esp. chaps. 2–3, 5–6.

2. The history of the early cigarette industry and the role played by James B. Duke in its development are well documented. Particularly useful are Richard B. Tennant, *The American Cigarette Industry* (New Haven, 1950), esp. chap. 2, and Nannie M. Tilley, *The Bright-Tobacco Industry* (Baltimore, 1948), esp. chaps. 7, 8, and 13; Glenn Porter and Harold Livesay, *Merchants and Manufacturers: Studies in the Changing Structure of Nineteenth Century Marketing* (Baltimore, 1973), chap. 13; and Patrick G. Porter, "Origins of the American Tobacco Company," *Business History Review*, 43:59–76 (Spring 1969).

3. Tilley, *Bright-Tobacco Industry*, pp. 559, 573–576, and Tennant, *Cigarette Industry*, pp. 19–24.

4. Porter, "Origins of the American Tobacco Company," pp. 65–67, describes the beginnings and continuing growth of Duke's purchasing and sales organization. Their operations are described in Chapter 12.

5. Tennant, *Cigarette Industry*, pp. 24–26, and Porter, "Origins of the American Tobacco Company," pp. 71–74, describe the interfirm competition and the formation of the American Tobacco Company.

6. The story of the American Tobacco Company is best summarized in Tennant, *Tobacco Industry*, chap. 3.

7. Herbert Manchester, *The Diamond Match Company* (New York, 1935) is the primary source of information on this company, supplemented by Ohio Columbus Barger, "The Match Industry," in Chauncey Depew, *One Hundred Years of American Commerce* (New York, 1895), pp. 465, and Diamond Match, *Commemorating the 75th Anniversary of the Diamond Match Company, 1881–1956* (np, 1956), pp. 4–8.

8. Manchester, *Diamond Match Company*, p. 64; Barber, "The Match Industry," p. 462. Barber gives an excellent description of automatic matchmaking machinery.

9. Barber, "The Match Industry," p. 462, and Mira Wilkins, *The Emergence of Multinational Enterprise* (Cambridge, Mass., 1970), pp. 100, 177.

10. Dumas Malone, ed., *Dictionary of American Biography* (New York, 1946), XIII, 143, and John Moody, *Manual of Industrial and Miscellaneous Securities, 1900* (New York, 1900), p. 630.

11. See Chapter 8.

12. Arthur E. Marquette, *Brands, Trademarks and Good Will* (New York, 1967), p. 33. This book provides most of the information used on the oatmeal industry; especially useful were pp. 18–19, 30–33, 40–44, chap. 4, and p. 80. Harrison J. Thorton, *The History of the Quaker Oats Company* (Chicago, 1933) adds some information, esp. chaps. 4 and 5, as does Richard E. Day, *Breakfast Table Autocrat: The Life and Times of Henry Parsons Crowell* (Chicago, 1946); see also John Stork and Walter D. Teague, *Flour for Man's Bread* (Minneapolis, Minn., 1952), p. 274.

13. See esp. Marquette, *Brands, Trademarks, and Good Will*, chap. 4. Chap. 5 describes the growth of the American Cereal Company.

14. Bell's plans and accomplishments are noted in Gray, *Story of General Mills*, chap. 4. Storck and Teague, *Flour for Man's Bread*, p. 254, indicates Pillsbury's backward integration.

15. Earl C. May, *The Canning Clan* (New York, 1937), pp. 351–353. See also Robert C. Alberts, *The Good Provider: H. J. Heinz and His 57 Varieties* (Boston, 1973), p. 49.

16. The best book on Heinz is Alberts, *The Good Provider;* see esp. pp. 62, 91–94. E. D. McCaffery, *Henry J. Heinz: A Biography* (New York, 1923) adds little, but pp. 106–107 give useful statistics on the size of activities at Heinz on the founder's death in 1919. The firm then included 6,323 employees; there were 25 branch factories, including one each in Canada and Spain, 87 raw product stations, 85 pickle salting stations, 258 railroad cars owned and operated (car loads of goods handled in 1919 numbered 17,011), 952 salesmen, and 55 branch offices and warehouses. The company owned its own bottle, box, and can factory, as well as its own seed farm. May, *Canning Clan*, pp. 341–346, provides some information on Campbell.

17. The information on canners of milk is in Joe B. Franz, *Gail Borden, Dairymaker to a Nation* (Norman, Okla., 1951), chaps. 15–16; Martin L. Bell, *A Portrait*

of *Progress: The Business History of the Pet Milk Company from 1885 to 1960* (St. Louis, 1962), chap. 2; and Jean Heer, *World Events, 1866–1966: The First Hundred Years of Nestle* (Rivaz, Switzerland, 1966), chap. 6, esp. pp. 72–77.

18. James W. McKie, *Tin Cans and Tin Plate* (Cambridge, Mass., 1950), pp. 103–107.

19. Charles Wilson, *History of Unilever* (London, 1959), pp. 17, 203–204, and Hower, *N. W. Ayer & Sons*, p. 58. Marquette, *Quaker Oats*, p. 21, indicates that besides Ivory soap other brand names were Babbitt and Fairy in the 1880s.

20. Williams Haynes, *American Chemical Industry*, VI, *The Chemical Companies* (New York, 1949), 342–344; the company-sponsored *Into a Second Century with Proctor & Gamble* (Cincinnati, 1934), esp. pp. 8–19, 31–36; and Alfred Lief, *"It Floats," The Story of Proctor and Gamble* (New York, 1958), chaps. 1, 4–7.

21. Samuel Colgate, "American Soap Industry," in Depew, *One Hundred Years of American Commerce*, p. 426.

22. Reese W. Jenkins, "Technology in the Market: George Eastman and the Origin of Amateur Photography," *Technology and Culture*, 16:1–19 (Jan. 1975). For more detail see his *Images and Enterprise: Technology and the American Photographic Industry, 1839–1925* (Baltimore, 1975), chaps. 4–6.

23. Oscar Edward Anderson, Jr., *Refrigeration in America* (Princeton, 1953), pp. 49–50. The best brief review of the rise of the dressed beef industry is Mary Yeager Kujovich, "The Refrigerator Car and the Growth of the American Dressed Beef Industry," *Business History Review*, 44:460–482 (Winter 1970), Kujovich's Ph.D. diss., "The Dynamics of Oligopoly in the Meat Packing Industry, an Historical Analysis," Johns Hopkins University, 1973, provides most of the information used here. Some data can be had from Lewis F. Swift in collaboration with Arthur Van Vlissington, *The Yankee of the Yards: The Biography of Gustavus Franklin Swift* (New York, 1928), and R. A. Clemen, *The American Livestock and Meat Industry* (New York, 1923). The best of the government reports for historical purposes is the U.S. Bureau of Corporations, *Report of the Commissioner of Corporations on the Beef Industry, March 3, 1905* (Washington, 1905). As part of his operating network Swift built ice stations along the railroad routes and also obtained ice harvesting rights on the Great Lakes. Kujovich, "Refrigerator Car and American Dressed Beef Industry," p. 467.

24. Kujovich, "Refrigerator Car and American Dressed Beef Industry," pp. 473–481, and Thomas C. Cochran, *Railroad Leaders, 1845–1890* (Cambridge, Mass., 1953), pp. 156, 387–391. Useful for the Armour story is "Armour & Company, 1867–1938," in N. S. B. Gras and Henrietta Larson, *Case Book in American Business History* (New York, 1939), pp. 623–643, and a major revision of this case written by James P. Baughman in 1966 and listed as Harvard Business School Case ICH 13G 231 BH 138. After the death of its founder, George H. Hammond, in 1886, that company stopped expanding at home and began to specialize in overseas shipments of refrigerated ships.

25. Thomas C. Cochran, *The Pabst Brewing Company* (New York, 1948), pp. 171–173. Other information for this paragraph comes from Cochran's history, esp. chaps. 4, 6–7 (for advertising agencies see pp. 129–131).

26. By 1894 the Pabst Company had over $2 million invested in such properties. Cochran, *Pabst*, p. 144.

27. U.S. Bureau of Corporations, *Report . . . on Beef Industry*, pp. 50–51. See also Baughman, "Armour & Co.," pp. 11 and 6, and Cochran, *Pabst*, pp. 83–86.

28. The information on the sewing machine industry comes from Andrew B. Jack, "The Channels of Distribution for the Innovation: The Sewing Machine Industry in America," *Explorations in Entrepreneurial History*, 9:113–141 (February 1957) and Robert B. Davies, "Peacefully Working to Conquer the World:

The Singer Manufacturing Company in Foreign Markets, 1854–1889," *Business History Review*, 43:299–346 (Autumn 1969), and a book published in New York in 1976 with same title except for the dates, 1854–1920. Davies kindly let me review the much lengthier manuscript on which the book is based. Also useful is Wilkins, *Multinational Enterprise*, pp. 37–45, and Daniel Boorstin, *The Americans: The Democratic Experience* (New York, 1973), pp. 193–196.

29. The Grover & Baker branches are listed in Edwin T. Freedley, *Leading Pursuits and Leading Men* (Philadelphia, 1857), p. 537, and those of Singer in Jack, "Channels of Distribution," pp. 116–124.

30. Jack, "Channels of Distribution," p. 129; Davies, *Singer in Foreign Markets*, p. 21. In this manuscript Davies reported that in 1859 *Hunt's Merchants' Magazine* estimated that twenty-five companies produced 37,000 machines, with Wheeler & Wilson manufacturing 40 percent, Singer 27 percent, and Grover & Baker 24 percent, and that in 1862 *Scientific American* reported a total production of 195,000 machines.

31. Wilkins, *Multinational Enterprise*, pp. 43, Davies, *Singer in Foreign Markets*, pp. 62–66.

32. Davies, *Singer in Foreign Markets*, pp. 58–61, Wilkins, *Multinational Enterprise*, pp. 42–44.

33. I am indebted to Professor Frederick V. Carstensen for data on the number of Singer branch offices. The figures are for 1879, except for Hamburg, which is 1880.

34. Quoted in Wilkins, *Multinational Enterprise*, p. 41. For plant construction, Davies article "Singer in Foreign Markets" pp. 314–317, and book, pp. 78–80.

35. According to an American trade journal in the 1880s, of the five American sewing machine companies competing in Great Britain, Singer had "made the greatest effort to perfect an organization"; quoted in Davies, in the manuscript on which the book was based, p. 134 (also see book p. 83).

36. Cyrus Hall McCormick III, *The Century of the Reaper* (New York, 1933), p. 60. This study and the careful and detailed two-volume biography of Cyrus Hall McCormick, by William T. Hutchinson (New York, 1930 and 1935), based on the voluminous records of the McCormick Company, provide the general information on this man, his firm, and his competitors. For the sales organization see vol. II, pp. 704–718, and McCormick, *Century of the Reaper*, pp. 45–53, 81–83. Professor Carstensen has provided invaluable additional information including the figures on factory output.

37. Hutchinson, *McCormick*, II, 698–700, 728; McCormick, *Century of the Reaper*, pp. 75–77.

38. Hutchinson, *McCormick*, II, chap. 25, and U.S. Bureau of Corporations, *The International Harvester Co.* (Washington, 1913), pp. 335–340, 370–371.

39. Information in this paragraph comes from references to these companies in McCormick, *Century of the Reaper;* U.S. Bureau of Corporations, *International Harvester*, esp. pp. 45–56, 188–189; a company-written brochure, "The Story of John Deere"; and annual reports and listings in *Moody's Manuals*. All but the first of the harvester companies listed here became part of International Harvester.

40. [Fairbanks, Morse & Company], *Pioneers in Industry: The Story of Fairbanks, Morse & Company* (Chicago, 1945), pp. 28–36, 41–42, 53–56.

41. For NCR, Samuel Crowther, *John H. Patterson, Pioneer in Industrial Welfare* (New York, 1926), esp. chaps. 6–7, 16. See also Isaac F. Marcosson, *Wherever Men Trade* (New York, 1945), esp. pp. 33–46, 60. Marcosson points out (p. 39) that only 64 registers were sold in 1885, 5,400 were in operation in 1887, and 16,400 in 1890.

42. Alden Hatch, *Remington Arms* (New York, 1956), chap. 24. The quotation is from p. 169.

43. The company changed its name in 1893 when it absorbed two small firms to become the Union Typewriter Company. It retained Remington as a trade name. In 1913 it took back its old name as the Remington Typewriter Company.

44. Information on the electrical companies comes from Porter and Livesay, *Merchants and Manufacturers*, pp. 184–192; Harold C. Passer, *The Electrical Manufacturers* (Cambridge, Mass., 1953), esp. chaps. 9, 17, 19–20; and Passer, "Development of Large Scale Organization: Electrical Manufacturing around 1900," *Journal of Economic History*, 12:378–395 (Fall 1952).

45. For Otis Elevator see L. A. Peterson, *Elisha Graves Otis, 1811–1861* (New York, 1945), pp. 13–16; David Shannon, "The Annals of Vertical Transportation," an unpublished manuscript completed in 1953 in the Baker Library, Harvard University; and Wilkins, *Multinational Enterprise*, p. 46. For Western Electric see Wilkins, *Muntinational Enterprise*, pp. 51, 200, and for the Johnson Company, Michael Massouth, "Technological and Managerial Innovation: The Johnson Company, 1823–1898," *Business History Review*, 50:46–48 (Spring 1976).

46. Data on Babcox and Wilcox and Link Belt Machinery are from Porter and Livesay, *Merchants and Manufacturers*, pp. 182, 183; Moody's *Manuals;* and the Davies manuscript of *Singer in Foreign Markets*, p. 148. For Worthington see Moody's *Manual*, 1900, pp. 616–617, and for Norton later *Manuals*, also Wilkins, *Multinational Enterprise*, pp. 212–213. (Worthington became International Steam Pump Company in 1899.)

47. Jenkins' review of the creation and growth of Eastman Kodak's organization (*Images and Enterprise*, chaps. 8–11) provides a revealing and detailed case study of the advantages such marketing and research organizations also conferred on the makers of more complex consumer goods.

48. Charles M. Wilson, *Empire in Green and Gold* (New York, 1947), pp. 99, 168–173.

49. Information on these companies comes from data in Moody's *Manuals* and Harris E. Starr, ed., *Dictionary of American Biography*, supp. I (New York, 1946), p. 715.

50. Charles H. Candler, *Asa Griggs Candler* (Atlanta, Ga., 1950), chaps. 4–5. The first branch plant was in Dallas, Texas; then came one in Philadelphia and one in Los Angeles. By 1906 plants had been built in Chicago, Havana, and Toronto.

51. Besides Moody's *Manuals* and annual reports, see for A. B. Dick Company and the Burroughs adding machine firm, Boorstin's *The Americans*, pp. 400, 204–205, and Porter and Livesay's *Merchants and Manufactures*, pp. 183, 193. (In 1895 Burrough's sold 284 adding machines; by 1906 sales were 5,000 annually.)

52. For these companies see Moody's *Manual*, 1900, pp. 677, 624, and 305–306, respectively. There is further information in later *Manuals* and in Wilkins, *Multinational Enterprise*, pp. 212–213.

53. Boorstin, *The Americans*, pp. 341–342, summarizes the achievement of Libbey and Owens. Libbey had invented his bottling machine in the factory of Michael J. Owens. Later inventions brought the Libbey-Owens enterprise into the plate glass industry.

54. For example, Harold F. Williamson, *Winchester: The Gun that Won the West* (Evanston, Ill., 1952), pp. 177–183. Information on other companies come from Moody's *Manuals* and annual reports.

55. Porter and Livesay, *Merchants and Manufactures*, pp. 144–145.

56. Porter and Livesay, *Merchants and Manufactures*, pp. 140–144, and Joseph Frazier Wall, *Andrew Carnegie* (New York, 1970), pp. 667–671.

10. Integration by Way of Merger

1. William Letwin has pointed out that: "The Sherman Act went far beyond the common law when it authorized the Attorney General to indict violators of the Act, and gave the injured persons the power to sue them, thus making it possible to enforce competition actively. The Act was therefore much more an innovation than its authors realized. It did not, as they thought, merely declare the common law. It can almost be said to have helped create the common law, insofar as its author's convictions helped spread the belief that the common law always expressed as much antagonism to monopoly as they wrote into the Sherman Act." *Law and Economic Policy in America: The Evolution of the Sherman Act* (New York, 1965), p. 52.

2. Milton Friedman and Anna J. Swartz, *A Monetary History of the United States, 1867–1960*, (Princeton, 1963), chap. 2, provides the most authoritative account of this interaction. "Whichever estimate of national product one accepts, the major conclusion is then the same: an unusually rapid rise in output converted an unusually slow rate of rise in the stock of money into a rapid decline in prices" (p. 41). The price data are from the U.S. Bureau of the Census, *Historical Statistics of the United States, Colonial Times to 1957* (Washington, 1960), p. 115. For these indices 100 was equal to 1910–1914 prices.

3. William H. Becker, "American Wholesale Hardware Trade Associations, 1870–1900," *Business History Review*, 45:182–185 (Summer 1971); Henry Demerest Lloyd, "Lords of Industry," *North American Review*, 31 (June 1884), reprinted in Peter d'A. Jones, ed., *The Robber Barons Revisited* (Boston, 1968), pp. 1–9; Hans B. Thorelli, *Federal Antitrust Policy*, (Stockholm, 1954), pp. 73–76.

4. Examples of the operation of such cartels can be found in William J. Ripley, *Trusts, Pools, and Corporations* (Cambridge, Mass., 1905), chap. 1 (salt), chap. 2 (whiskey), chap. 3 (wire nails), chap. 4 (iron and steel); and in Alfred D. Chandler, Jr., and Stephen Salsbury, *Pierre S. du Pont and the Making of the Modern Corporation* (New York, 1971), pp. 57–62, The index to Victor S. Clark, *History of Manufacturers in the United States, 1869–1893*, vol. II (New York, 1929) has many listings for the trade associations.

5. Ralph W. Hidy and Muriel E. Hidy, *Pioneering in Big Business* (New York, 1955), pp. 40–49; Thorelli, *Federal Antitrust Policy*, pp. 76–83. See also Thomas R. Navin and Marion V. Sears, "The Rise of a Market for Industrial Securities, 1887–1902," *Business History Review*, 24:112–116 (June 1955); Alan Nevins, *Study in Power: John D. Rockefeller, Industrialist and Philanthropist* (New York, 1953), I, chap. 21.

6. Thorelli, *Federal Antitrust Policy*, pp. 84–85; Alfred S. Eichner, *The Emergence of Oligopoly: Sugar Refining as a Case Study* (Baltimore 1969), pp. 148–150; James C. Bonbright and Gardner C. Means, *The Holding Company* (New York, 1932), pp. 56–57. In the 1890s New York, Pennsylvania, and Delaware followed New Jersey's example in liberalizing general corporation laws.

7. There were probably more trusts operating on a national scale but the number was certainly few. And some smaller regional trusts may have carried on interstate business. The only regional trusts whose certificates were traded on any stock exchange of any major city were those of the Chicago and the St. Louis Gas Trusts. Letwin, *Law and Economic Policy*, p. 70, mentions the envelope, salt, oil-cloth, paving-pitch, school-slate, paperbag, and New York meat trusts. Although there were associations to operate cartels in these industries (except for New York meat), I have not yet run across evidence that such associations adopted the legal form of a trust.

8. The story of the beginnings of Standard Oil has often been told. The most useful accounts are Hidy and Hidy, *Pioneering in Big Business,* pp. 14–23, and Harold F. Williamson and Arnold R. Daum, *The American Petroleum Industry: The Age of Illumination, 1859–1899* (Evanston, Ill., 1959), chaps. 14, 16. Nevins, *Rockefeller,* I, chaps. 3–12, adds much detail. None of these accounts, however, suggest that the building of the transsectional pipeline precipitated the formation of the Trust. The quotation in the next paragraph is from Nevins, *Rockefeller,* I, 175. For Standards' negotiations with the Lake Shore see Nevins, *Rockefeller,* I, 89, and Williamson and Daum, *American Petroleum Industry,* pp. 305–306.

9. Williamson and Daum, *American Petroleum Industry,* pp. 416–421, and Hidy and Hidy, *Pioneering in Big Business,* pp. 18–19, 40–41, 46–47.

10. Williamson and Daum, *American Petroleum Industry,* p. 473, gives 89.7 percent.

11. Williamson and Daum, *American Petroleum Industry,* pp. 489, 509, 519.

12. Williamson and Daum, *American Petroleum Industry,* chap. 17, has the best account of the building of the transregional pipelines, first by Tidewater and then by Standard Oil.

13. The charter was obtained by the Pennsylvania Railroad's Thomas Scott as a possible instrument to use in controlling that railroad's southern lines. Williamson and Daum, *American Petroleum Industry,* p. 452; Bonbright and Means, *Holding Company,* pp. 58–61.

14. Hidy and Hidy, *Pioneering in Big Business,* pp. 40–46. The Hidys mention forty-one firms coming into the Trust, but list only forty.

15. Nevins, *Rockefeller,* I, 393.

16. Williamson and Daum, *American Petroleum Industry,* pp. 474–475, 483–484.

17. Hidy and Hidy, *Pioneering in Big Business,* pp. 87–88; Williamson and Daum, *American Petroleum Industry,* pp. 558, 619–620.

18. Williamson and Daum, *American Petroleum Industry,* chap. 25; and Hidy and Hidy, *Pioneering in Big Business,* pp. 108–121.

19. Williamson and Daum, *American Petroleum Industry,* pp. 637–661.

20. Williamson and Daum, *American Petroleum Industry,* chap. 22; Hidy and Hidy, *Pioneering in Big Business,* chap. 7.

21. For Tidewater see Williamson and Daum, *American Petroleum Industry,* pp. 452–456, 581–582; John Moody, *Moody's Manual of Industrial and Miscellaneous Securities, 1900* (New York, 1900), p. 1011.

22. For Pure Oil see Williamson and Daum, *American Petroleum Industry,* pp. 576–581.

23. Information on American Cotton Oil comes from its surprisingly detailed annual reports which *The Manual of Statistics—Stock Exchange Handbook, 1894* (New York, 1894), p. 257, characterizes as "distinguished by the full and frank exhibition afforded of its operations and finances." See also Clark, *History of Manufactures,* II, 519–523, and R. Chaney," "The Cotton Seed Oil Industry," in Chauncey Depew, ed., *One Hundred Years of American Commerce* (New York, 1895), pp. 452–455. One of the soap works acquired was the pioneering firm of N. K. Fairbanks.

24. For the Southern Cotton Oil Company see Clark, *History of Manufacturers,* II, 521–522, and for Lever, Jurgens, and Van den Berg, see Charles Wilson, *The History of Unilever* (London, 1954), I, 203–204, II, chap. 11.

25. William P. Thompson, "The Lead Industry," in Depew, ed., *One Hundred Years of American Commerce,* p. 440; Hidy and Hidy, *Pioneering in Big Business,* pp. 60–69; Mira Wilkins, *The Emergence of Multinational Enterprise* (Cambridge, Mass., 1970), p. 185, and the annual reports of that enterprise.

26. Clark, *History of Manufacturers*, II, 371, 523–524, and his *History of Manufacturers*, III, *1893–1928* (New York, 1929), 284, and summaries of operation in the annual volume of *Manuals of Statistics* for the 1890s, particularly 1894 and 1899.

27. Annual report of the American Linseed Company for fiscal year ending July 31, 1900.

28. The story of the whiskey trust and its corporate successes comes from Jeremiah W. Jenks and W. E. Clark, *The Trust Problem* (New York, 1917), pp. 141–149, and the companies' annual reports. The story is summarized in Alfred D. Chandler, Jr., "The Beginnings of Big Business in American Industry," *Business History Review*, 33:10–11 (Spring 1959).

29. Eichner, *Emergence of Oligopoly*, chaps. 5, 7, and 8.

30. Clark, *History of Manufacturers*, III, 274, and Eichner, *Emergence of Oligopoly*, p. 344. The 1907 figure includes 49.9 percent of the share produced by the American Sugar Refining and 10.8 percent by National Sugar, a firm controlled by American.

31. Eichner, *Emergence of Oligopoly*, pp. 226–228.

32. Eichner, *Emergence of Oligopoly*, chaps. 9, 10, and pp. 264–273. For American Sugar's moves into Cuba see Wilkins, *Emergence of Multinational Enterprise*, p. 115, and Eichner, *Emergence of Oligopoly*, p. 309.

33. Eichner, *Emergence of Oligopoly*, chap. 11, and pp. 345–349. As Eichner points out: "The government's objectives in the suit had, to a certain extent, already been accomplished through the death in 1907 of the American Sugar Refining Company's first president" (p. 307). At this time, American Sugar sold, besides its holdings in the beet sugar companies, its holdings of 12 percent in Cuban-American Sugar, a cane sugar firm formed in 1906 (pp. 309–311). On pp. 325–328, Eichner describes the completed integrated enterprise. By 1917 there were 13 independent competing sugar companies.

34. Gene M. Gressley, *Bankers and Gentlemen* (New York, 1966), pp. 259–266.

35. Arthur S. Dewing, *Corporate Promotions and Reorganizations* (Cambridge, Mass., 1914), chap. 5; Clark, *History of Manufacturers*, II, 461–462.

36. Dewing, *Corporate Promotions and Reorganizations*, chap. 6.

37. Navin and Sears, "Market for Industrial Securities," pp. 116–121.

38. The first handled American Cotton, the second American Sugar, the third National Cordage, and the fourth American Linseed. Annual reports of American Cotton Oil for the 1890s, esp. for 1891; Eichner, *Emergence of Oligopoly*, p. 151; Dewing, *Corporate Promotions*, pp. 121–122 (National Cordage used also Vermilye and Company); and *Manual of Statistics*, 1894.

39. Because the legality of the pure holding company (one that held stock only and did not have operating facilities) had not been tested in the courts, most of the mergers of the early 1890s were achieved by purchasing properties of the companies coming into the merger with the stock issued specifically for that purpose. Later in the decade the pure holding company became more widely used. Bonbright and Means, *Holding Company*, pp. 67–72.

40. Navin and Sears, "Market for Industrial Securities," pp. 116–126.

41. Thorelli, *Federal Antitrust Policy*, pp. 294–303.

42. Ralph Nelson, *Merger Movements in American Industry, 1895–1956* (Princeton, 1959), pp. 33–34.

43. Thorelli, *Federal Antitrust Policy*, reviews key cases referred to in this paragraph and also the Northern Securities case, pp. 445–448, 458, 462, 466–475. See also Eichner, *Emergence of Oligopoly*, pp. 184–187, and Letwin, *Law and Economic Policy*, pp. 152–155, 161–181, 207–227.

44. Navin and Sears, "Market for Industrial Securities," pp. 129–136.

45. For example, Chandler and Salsbury, *P. S. du Pont*, pp. 112–114.

46. The annual report of the National Biscuit Company for the year ending December 31, 1901, and dated January 3, 1902. The company's experience is summarized in Chandler, "Beginnings of Big Business," pp. 11–13.

47. Ralph M. Hower, *The History of an Advertising Agency* (Cambridge, Mass., 1939), pp. 115–116, indicates the importance of this account to the Ayer Company and shows well how a new national advertising campaign was mounted.

48. The history of the starch and glucose combinations is covered in Dewing, *Corporation Promotions*, chaps. 3–4.

49. Hidy and Hidy, *Pioneering in Big Business*, pp. 318–319.

50. Shaw Livermore, "The Success of Industrial Mergers," *Quarterly Journal of Economics*, 50:94 (Nov. 1935).

51. *Moody's Manual of Industrial Securities*, 1900, pp. 682–683.

52. Livermore, "Industrial Mergers," pp. 68–95. In listing his rejuvenations Livermore appears to include only those that continued under the same name. He occasionally does not indicate failures that became successful after being reorganized under a new name. All rejuvenations have been indicated on table 6. In table 6 Livermore's outstanding successes have been listed with successes, and early and late failures are combined into one category, failure. I have not included mergers on Livermore's list that became part of other mergers before 1905.

53. Described in Navin and Sears, "Market for Industrial Securities," p. 123.

54. Only one occurred in tobacco, but that one, the American Tobacco Company, monopolized its industry; in these four groups thousands of small firms continued to compete.

11. Integration Completed

1. Thomas R. Navin, "The 500 Largest American Industrials in 1917," *Business History Review*, 44:360–386 (Autumn 1970). Navin searched diligently for firms whose stock was closely held by a few individuals and not listed on stock exchanges. He checked the antecedents of all companies on the *Fortune* 500 list for 1968 and searched Poor's *Register of Corporations, Directors and Executives*. However, he may have missed a few. The only obvious omissions on Navin's list are the Campbell Soup Company owned by the Dorrance family, and the A. B. Dick Company, makers of the mimeograph machine. The information in Appendix A is from Moody's *Manual of Industrial Securities* and company annual reports. Unless otherwise indicated, these are the sources of information for the companies mentioned in this chapter.

2. The third firm was Weyerhaeuser Lumber.

3. According to S. J. Prais and C. Reid, the 100 largest companies in the United States in 1919 already produced 22 percent of net output in manufacturing. See Leslie Hannah, ed., *Management Strategy and Business Organization in Britain: A Historical and Comparative View* (London, 1976), pp. 5–6. It may be assumed that the other 178 companies in Appendix A added at least another 5 percent.

4. Dean Witten & Company, *California Packing Corporation: A Study of Impressive Progress* (np, nd), pp. 13–14.

5. Mira Wilkins, *The Emergence of Multinational Enterprise* (Cambridge, Mass., 1970), pp. 120, 212, 216. In the candy and confectionery business the pattern was much the same. National Candy and New England Confectionery, after building marketing organizations, competed successfully against Baker Chocolate, Whitman's, and Hershey, firms which had grown initially through vertical integration. Lewis Untermeyer, *A Century of Candy Making, 1849–1949* (Cambridge, Mass., 1947), pp. 82–88; Glenn Porter and Harold C. Livesay, *Merchants and Manufacturers* (Baltimore, 1971), p. 220, and company annual reports.

6. Richard B. Tennant, *The American Cigarette Industry* (New Haven, 1951), pp. 80, 94–95.

7. A useful summary of integration in the oil industry in this period is Harold F. Williamson and Ralph L. Andreano, "Competitive Structure of the American Petroleum Industry, 1880–1911: A Reappraisal," in Ralph W. Hidy, ed., *Oil's First Century* (Cambridge, Mass., 1960). See also Harold F. Williamson and others, *The American Petroleum Industry: The Age of Energy, 1899–1959* (Evanston, Ill., 1963), chap. 1. The details of the story are most ably chronicled and analyzed in chaps. 2–7 of this volume. John C. McLean and Robert William Haight, *The Growth of Integrated Oil Companies* (Boston, 1954), chap. 3, adds some further information.

8. George S. Gibb and Evelyn H. Knowlton, *History of Standard Oil Company (New Jersey), The Resurgent Years, 1911–1927* (New York, 1956), pp. 8–9.

9. Ralph L. Nelson, *Merger Movements in American Industry, 1895–1956* (Princeton, 1959), pp. 43–45.

10. Williamson and others, *American Petroleum Industry*, p. 165. Of the list of thirty companies cited on this page, twenty-two are the same as that on table 7. There is only one company on table 7 that is not in the Williamson list, the Producers and Refiners Corporation. The total refining output of the Williamson list is 71.6 percent. The total of those eight firms not on table 7 is 3.8 percent. As the one not on Williamson's list accounted for at least 0.5 percent, the total for those refining companies on table 7 would be 68.3 percent.

11. Williamson and others, *American Petroleum Industry*, p. 63 for 1919 figures, and p. 564 for 1931 figures.

12. Two other major oil companies—Phillips Petroleum and Continental (the latter was a former Standard company)—were large enterprises in 1917 but do not appear on table 7 because their assets were under $20 million.

13. Wilkins, *Emergence of Multinational Enterprise*, chap. 10; Mira Wilkins, *The Maturing of Multinational Enterprise* (Cambridge, Mass., 1974), pp. 84–88, 113–122.

14. Wilkins, *Emergence of Multinational Enterprise*, pp. 141, 188, 214, and 216.

15. American Writing Paper was, according to Livermore, a financial failure, and Union Bag and Paper (number 288 on Navin's list) was a marginal success.

16. Navin, "500 Largest American Industrials," pp. 375–376.

17. There are historical sketches of all chemical companies listed here in Williams Haynes, *American Chemical Industry: The Chemical Companies* (New York, 1949), vol. VI, except for United Dyewood. The information on that firm is from *Moody's Manuals*. Some industrial chemical companies sold goods to consumers. For example, the General Chemical Company, makers of heavy chemicals and sulphuric acid, also sold grocery specialties and a branded baking powder, "Ryson."

18. The histories of Du Pont, Virginia-Carolina Chemical, and Semet-Solvay provide excellent examples of such backward integration. Wilkins, *Emergence of Multinational Enterprise*, pp. 98–99; Alfred D. Chandler and Stephen Salsbury, *Pierre S. Du Pont and the Making of the Modern Corporation* (New York, 1971), esp. chap. 9; and Haynes, *The Chemical Companies*, pp. 10–11. See also company reports of Virginia-Carolina and Semet-Solvey.

19. Harris E. Starr, ed., *Dictionary of American Biography*, supp. 1 (New York, 1946), p. 345, and company annual reports.

20. James W. McKie, *Tin Cans and Tin Plate* (Cambridge, Mass., 1959), pp. 83–92. American Can's share of industry fell from 90 percent in 1901 to 50 percent of sales in 1913. It then shifted from a strategy of horizontal combination to one of vertical integration (p. 86).

21. Mira Wilkins, "An American Enterprise Abroad: American Radiator Company in Europe, 1895–1914," *Business History Review*, 43:326–346 (Autumn 1969) provides an excellent description of how one company built its overseas organization. F. A. McKenzie, *The American Invaders* (London, 1901), pp. 49–52, indicates the success of United Shoe Machinery in dominating the British market by 1902.

22. One exception was Todd Shipyards, which operated two yards in the New York area and one in Seattle, Washington.

23. Walter Adams, *The Structure of American Industry* (New York, 1954), pp. 163–164.

24. Joseph F. Wall, *Andrew Carnegie* (New York, 1970), chap. 20, esp. pp. 767–773. Henry R. Seager and Charles A. Gulick, *Trusts and Corporation Problems* (New York, 1929), chap. 13, has a good brief summary of the formation of the United States Steel Corporation. Pages 216–219 indicate how the strategy of integration served as a stimulus to this giant consolidation of several mergers.

25. Gertrude G. Schroeder, *The Growth of the Major Steel Companies* (Baltimore, 1953), chaps. 2–4, and Alfred D. Chandler, Jr., *Strategy and Structure: Chapters in the History of the Industrial Enterprise* (Cambridge, Mass., 1962), pp. 331–337. Schroeder considers twelve "major" companies—the "Big Three" (U.S. Steel, Bethlehem, and Republic) and nine smaller independents. All but one, Sharon Steel, is in table 8, and that firm was founded in 1900. Schroeder does not include Colorado Fuel & Iron or Lukens.

26. Edward L. Allen, *Economics of American Manufacturing* (New York, 1952), pp. 114–115, and Chandler, *Strategy and Structure*, pp. 327–330.

27. Wilkins, *Emergence of Multinational Enterprise*, pp. 87–89, 185, 212, 215–216; Chandler, *Strategy and Structure*, pp. 337–340.

28. For a more detailed analysis see Alfred D. Chandler, Jr., "The Structure of American Industry in the Twentieth Century: A Historical Overview," *Business History Review*, 43:293–298 (Autumn 1969).

29. Wilkins, *Emergence of Multinational Enterprise*, pp. 211–217.

30. Wilkins, *Emergence of Multinational Enterprise*, p. 201.

31. In less than two years the following three books were published in London: Fred A. McKenzie, *The American Invaders* (1901); B. H. Thwaite, *The American Invasion* (1902); and W. T. Stead, *The Americanization of the World* (1902). Wilkins, *Emergence of Multinational Enterprise*, p. 71.

32. Information on table 9 is from Chandler, "Structure of American Industry in the Twentieth Century," pp. 255–298, particularly tables prepared by P. Glenn Porter and Harold C. Livesay. These tables used the Kaplan list of the 100 largest enterprises for these years. A number of Kaplan's firms are not industrials. But all his lists have at least 81 industrials, so the tables are of the 81 largest industrials for these specific years. The same point is made in an excellent article by Richard C. Edwards, using another list of large companies, "Stages in Corporate Stability and Corporate Growth," *Journal of Economic History*, 35:428–457 (July 1975).

The data on concentrated industries in Chandler, "Structure of American Industry," pp. 258–259 for 1929, 1939, 1947, and 1963, are similar to that in G. Warren Nutter and Henry A. Einhorn, *Enterprise Monopoly in the United States: 1899–1958* (New York, 1969), p. 78. The only major difference is petroleum, which Nutter and Einhorn list as unconcentrated. This may be because they list petroleum with coal products. Detailed information in Williamson's history and Federal Trade Commission reports emphasized the concentrated nature of the oil refining and particularly the gasoline business.

33. Robert T. Averitt, *The Dual Economy: The Dynamics of American Industry Structure* (New York, 1968), pp. 38–44. The establishment of the widespread

use of the large integrated industrial enterprise may have increased the productivity of the manufacturing sector. John W. Kendrick, *Productivity Trends in the United States* (Princeton, N.J., 1961), pp. 70-71, points to "a remarkable acceleration in manufacturing productivity in the 1920's." He suggests several reasons for this acceleration: the adoption of mass or "flow" production techniques, the spread of the scientific management movement, the expansion of college and graduate work in business administration, the beginning of organized industrial research and development, and the increased average education of the labor force. Except for the last, all these factors were an integral part of the modern industrial enterprise, the institution which brought these activities together by administering and coordinating the processes of production and distribution within a single enterprise.

34. Navin, "500 Largest American Industrials in 1917," pp. 369-385.

35. The four were Central Leather, American Linseed Oil, Pierce Oil, and Emerson-Brantingham, an agricultural implement firm.

36. Navin, "500 Largest American Industrials in 1917," pp. 369-385.

37. Lance Davis, "The Capital Markets and Industrial Concentration: The U.S. and U.K., a Comparative Study," *Economic History Review*, 19:255-272 (August 1966). Nelson, *Merger Movements*, pp. 89-100, stresses that his (Nelson's) "findings provide positive though not decisive support for the theory that the development of a large-scale capital market was necessary to support the merger movement" (p. 94). He adds: "However, in view of the earlier and important role played by railroad reorganizations in these changes in the capital market, industrial mergers were probably the beneficiaries of the changes in the capital market rather than the cause of them" (p. 99).

38. Reese V. Jenkins, *Images and Enterprise: Technology and the American Photographic Industry 1839-1925* (Baltimore, 1975), p. 184. Eastman summarized the problem and the strategy in this manner in a memorandum written April 23, 1896: "I have come to think that the maintenance of a lead in the apparatus trade will depend greatly upon a rapid succession of changes and improvements, and with that aim in view, I propose to organize the Experimental Department in the Camera Works and raise it to a high degree of efficiency. If we can get out improved goods every year nobody will be able to follow us and compete with us. The only way to compete with us will be to get out original goods the same as we do."

39. The historical sketches of these companies in Haynes, *The Chemical Companies*, describe the establishment of these departments. The study made at Johns Hopkins by Leonard S. Reich on scientists with Ph.D.'s working in American companies has additional information.

12. Middle Management: Function and Structure

1. Nannie Tilley, *The Bright-Leaf Tobacco Industry, 1860-1929* (Chapel Hill, 1948), pp. 303-306; Glenn Porter and Harold C. Livesay, *Merchants and Manufacturers* (Baltimore, 1971), pp. 203-204.

2. P. Glenn Porter, "Origins of the American Tobacco Company," *Business History Review*, 43:65-70 (Spring 1969) outlines Duke's sales, purchasing, and manufacturing procedures. Richard Tennant, *The American Cigarette Industry* (New Haven, 1950), pp. 19-25, has an excellent brief review on the formation of the American Tobacco Company. Robert F. Durden, *The Dukes of Durham, 1865-1929* (Durham, N.C., 1975) adds important details based on family papers. Useful, too, is Maurice Corina, *Trust in Tobacco* (New York, 1975), chaps. 3-4, 6-8.

3. Porter and Livesay, *Merchants and Manufacturers*, pp. 203-204, 207-208; U.S. Bureau of Corporations, *Report of the Commissioner of Corporations, Report on*

Tobacco Industry, Part I . . . February 25, 1909 (Washington, 1909), pp. 256–257 (hereafter cited as B. of C. *Report on Tobacco Industry*).

4. The first year that the company was listed at 111 Fifth Avenue was 1898. *Manual of Statistics 1899* (New York, 1899). Prior to that date the manual listed 45 Broadway as American Tobacco's address.

5. For Cobb see Tilley, *Bright-Leaf Tobacco Industry*, pp. 298–299; for Harris see John B. Jenkins, *James B. Duke, Master Builder* (New York, 1929), p. 163; for W. W. Fuller, chief counsel, see Jenkins, *Duke*, pp. 163, 165–168.

6. B. of C. *Report on Tobacco Industry*, pp. 165, states that 1.22 billion cigarettes were exported in that year and *Report of the Commissions of Corporations on the Tobacco Industry, Part III, Prices, Costs and Profits, March 18, 1915* (Washington, 1915), p. 155, shows domestic output for 1898 at 2.56 billion. See also Tennant, *Cigarette Industry*, pp. 40–41.

7. Mira Wilkins, *The Emergence of Multinational Enterprise* (Cambridge, Mass., 1970), pp. 91–92; B. of C. *Report on Tobacco Industry*, I, 69–70, 83–84, 88, and chap. 8. Also B. W. E. Alford, *W. D. & H. O. Wills and the Development of the U.K. Tobacco Industry* (London, 1973), pp. 217–220.

8. There is an excellent description of the company's Leaf Department in B. of C. *Report on Tobacco Industry*, I, 252–256. See also Livesay and Porter, *Merchants and Manufacturers*, pp. 207–208.

9. Tennant, *American Cigarette Industry*, pp. 52–53. In April 1894, Wills, the largest British Tobacco manufacturer, became concerned about American Tobacco Company's increasing power in the leaf market, but after an investigation George Wills decided that "the American Tobacco Company was not in a position to dictate prices on its own purchases of leaf." Alford, *Wills*, p. 251.

10. The purchasing organization was given the legal status of a corporation under the name of the Amsterdam Supply Company. Its activities are described in B. of C. *Report of Tobacco Industry* I, 265–266, also 259. The Supply Company charged a commission of 2 percent on all its purchases; after 1906 this was reduced to 1 percent.

11. B. of C. *Report on Tobacco Industry*, I, 256–258, outlines the organization of the Sales Department. The quotation is from p. 257. Also Porter and Livesay, *Merchants and Manufacturers*, pp. 205–210. For travelers working out of foreign branch office see Alford, *Wills*, p. 215.

12. B. of C. *Report on Tobacco Industry*, III, 171.

13. B. of C. *Report on Tobacco Industry*, I, 257.

14. Jenkins, *Duke*, pp. 168–169.

15. Jenkins, *Duke*, p. 169.

16. The data on costs came from B. of C. investigators who had "full and complete access to their [the company's] books and accounts including their cost records." B. of C. *Report on Tobacco Industry*, III, 32, and also xxv.

17. B. of C. *Report on Tobacco Industry*, III, 158. The quotation is from p. 160.

18. Corina, *Trust in Tobacco*, pp. 56–57; Tennant, *Cigarette Industry*, pp. 33–34. Tennant has an excellent summary of Duke's conquest of the industry, pp. 26–39, and Durden, *Dukes of Durham*, chap. 4, has the best detailed account. For Cobb's support see pp. 64–65.

19. Jenkins, *Duke*, p. 94. Some nonvoting preferred stock has been sold before 1895 by the industrialists forming the enterprise. Thomas R. Navin and Marion V. Sears, "The Rise of a Market for Industrial Securities, 1887–1902," *Business History Review*, 39:131 (June 1955). At the time of the formation of American Tobacco the new company was capitalized at $25 million, $15 million in common and $10 million in preferred. By 1895 $10 million more was issued to use in Duke's conquest of the industry.

20. Jenkins, *Duke*, chap. 8; Durden, *Dukes of Durham*, pp. 66–70; and Mark O. Hirsch, *William C. Whitney, Modern Warwick* (New York, 1948), pp. 544–550.

21. Details of the move into Britain are given in Jenkins, *Duke*, chap. 10; Corina, *Trust in Tobacco*, chaps. 5–6; and B. of C. *Report on Tobacco Industry*, I, chap. 8. Alford, *Wills*, pp. 255–277, tells the British side of the story. See also Wilkins, *Emergence of Multinational Enterprise*, pp. 92–93. Sherman G. Cochran "Big Business in China: Sino-American Rivalry in the Tobacco Industry, 1890–1930," Ph.D. diss., Yale University, 1975, provides a carefully detailed account of the coming of the cigarette trade and the growth of British-American Tobacco in China.

22. Tennant, *Cigarette Industry*, p. 31, and B. of C. *Report on Tobacco Industry*, I, chap. 23, II, 10. The largest share ofthe market which the Cigar Company was able to obtain was 14.6 percent in 1903 (I, 420–423).

23. Jenkins, *Duke*, p. 90.

24. The most detailed analysis of the large packers and their role in the industry in the late 1880s and 1890s is Mary Yeager Kujovich, "The Dynamics of Oligopoly in the Meat Packing Industry: An Historical Analysis," Ph.D. diss., Johns Hopkins University, 1973, chap. 4.

25. Bureau of Corporations, *Report of the Commissioner of Corporations on the Beef Industry*, March 3, 1905 (Washington, 1905), pp. 65–70.

26. B. of C. *Report on Beef Industry*, p. 25. Armour was capitalized at $20.0 million and the Armour Packing Company at $7.5 million. Swift also had $5.0 million in bonds.

27. B. of C. *Report on Beef Industry*, p. xix. In 1903 Swift slaughtered 1.6 million cattle, 4.1 million hogs, and 2.3 million sheep, while Armour slaughtered 1.3 million cattle, 3.5 million hogs, and 1.5 million sheep. Morris killed .8 million cattle, 1.2 million hogs, and .8 million sheep.

28. B. of C. *Report on Beef Industry*, p. 209.

29. Arthur Graydon, "The Second Generation of Business, II: From One-Man Power to Organization," *System: The Magazine of Business*, 12:220 (Sept. 1907) has useful comments on this chart.

30. B. of C. *Report on Beef Industry*, pp. 17–18.

31. B. of C. *Report on Beef Industry*, pp. 15–16. *Report of the Federal Trade Commission on the Meat-Packing Industry* (Washington, 1919), III, 88ff, has an excellent description of the buying procedures.

32. [James P. Baughman], "Armour & Co., 1868–1914," Harvard Business School case No. ICH 13G 231 (1966), p. 12. See also Kujovich, "The Meat Packing Industry," pp. 133–134, 167–168, 294–295.

33. B. of C. *Report on Beef Industry*, p. 21.

34. This and the following quotations are from B. of C. *Report on Beef Industry*, pp. 207–209.

35. B. of C. *Report on Beef Industry*, pp. 208, 251–253; also 160–167, 181–188.

36. B. of C. *Report on Beef Industry*, p. 253. The following quotations are from pp. 210 and 269.

37. B. of C. *Report on Beef Industry*, pp. 270–271, 277–278.

38. This is best depicted in the organization chart in *System*. See also B. of C. *Report on Beef Industry*, pp. 21–24, 115–118.

39. Kujovich, "The Meat Packing Industry," p. 310.

40. Baughman, "Armour & Co.," Harvard Business School case, p. 9. The packers did not go into leather making, but when the leather processors began to consolidate, J. Ogden Armour helped to organize one of the leading combinations in the Central Leather Company in order to protect its markets.

41. As indicated on the organization chart in Grayden, "Second Generation," p. 220.

42. B. of C. *Report on Beef Industry*, pp. 50–51. Louis F. Swift and Arthur van Vilissingen, Jr., *Yankee of the Yards: The Biography of Gustavus Franklin Swift* (New York, 1927), pp. 80–81.

43. Graydon, "Second Generation," p. 224.

44. Kujovich, "The Meat Packing Industry," p. 200, 216–237. Packers who sold over their quota paid an "average" charge to the pool that went to those selling less than their quotas.

45. Kujovich, "The Meat Packing Industry," chap. 5, tells the story of National in detail, and (pp. 359–362) reviews the bringing of the suit against the packers in April 1902.

46. Wilkins, *Multinational Enterprise*, pp. 189–190; Kujovich "The Meat Packing Industry," pp. 308–317.

47. Harold F. Williamson and others, *The American Petroleum Industry: The Age of Energy, 1899–1950* (Evanston, Ill., 1963), pp. 235–240, describes competition between the integrated firms in the oil industry before World War I with its reliance on price leadership, advertising, and service facilities.

48. The continuing story of Singer comes from Wilkins, *Multinational Enterprise*, pp. 37–45; Andrew B. Jack, "Channels of Distribution for an Innovation: The Sewing Machine in America," *Explorations in Entrepreneurial History*, 9:113–141 (February 1957); and Robert B. Davies, "Peacefully Working to Conquer the World: The Singer Manufacturing Company in Foreign Markets, 1854–1889," *Business History Review*, 43:299–346 (Autumn, 1969), or his book with same title but with dates, 1854–1920 (New York, 1976).

49. Davies, *Singer in Foreign Markets*, p. 59–65.

50. Wilkins, *Multinational Enterprises*, p. 44. The next quotation is Davies, "Singer in Foreign Markets," p. 311 and the third is from the manuscript on which Davies book was based, p. 130.

51. Carstensen shows that the failure of delivery on schedule was a major cause for lost sales later when Singer began to expand into the Russian market. Frederick V. Carstensen, "American Multinationals in Russia," Ph.D. diss., Yale University, 1976, p. 115.

52. Davies, *Singer in Foreign Markets*, p. 59. The full quotation is from Davies manuscript, p. 130.

53. Davies, *Singer in Foreign Markets*, p. 77, and Wilkins, *Multinational Enterprise*, p. 44.

54. Quoted in Wilkins, *Multinational Enterprise*, p. 43.

55. Information on Singer for 1910 is from Lynn G. Wright, "A Study of the Singer Agency Organization," *Printers' Ink*, 72:3–7 (July 28, 1910).

56. Wilkins, *Multinational Enterprise*, p. 44; Davies, *Singer in Foreign Markets*, pp. 110–114, 128–129.

57. Carstensen, "American Multinationals in Russia."

58. McCormick's sales organization is described in William T. Hutchinson, *Cyrus Hall McCormick, Harvest, 1856–1884* (New York, 1935), pp. 704–718. Carstensen has provided me with essential additional information.

59. U.S. Bureau of Corporations, *International Harvester Company* (Washington, D.C., 1913), p. 331, for traffic and pp. 278–280, 340–342, for credit and collections; hereafter cited as B. of C., *Harvester Co.*

60. Cyrus McCormick, *The Century of the Reaper* (New York, 1931), pp. 98–99; B. of C., *Harvester Co.*, pp. 336–339. See p. 327 for 1902 figures.

61. An excellent description of the McCormick sales force and the organization

and operation of its central office is given in "Statements Made by Mr. Stanley McCormick and Mr. Bentley to Mr. Perkins, July 27, 1902, in New York City" and "Statement Submitted to Bankers by McCormick Harvester Machine Co. in 1902," Exhibits I & II, B. of C., *Harvester Co.*, pp. 327–342.

62. Hutchinson, *McCormick, Harvest*, chap. 15; Carstensen, "American Multinationals In Russia," pp. 171–172. The McCormick's overseas marketing organization is succinctly described in the company's statement to bankers in 1902. B. of C., *Harvester Co.*, pp. 333–342. By 1910 the company had twenty distributors in Latin America, three in Africa, one in New Zealand, and twenty-one in Europe. As yet they had none in Asia.

63. Hutchinson, *McCormick, Harvest*, pp. 698–700. In 1883 the purchasing office "handled annually about fifteen thousand tons of iron and malleable castings, eighteen miles of wrough-iron pipe, one hundred and thirty miles of chain, 241,000 yards of canvas, and 48,000 gallons of linseed-oil, turpentine, varnish, and lard oil. Steel from Birmingham and Sheffield, England, had been supplanted in favor by the output of Pittsburgh mills, deemed to be of equal quality."

64. B. of C., *Harvester Co.*, pp. 190–194. In 1902 Stanley McCormick wrote George W. Perkins that the company was at work "getting a more accurate system of ascertaining the cost of manufacture" (p. 329).

65. B. of C., *Harvester Co.*, p. 67.

66. Navin and Sears, "The Market for Industrial Securities," p. 168, says that Singer's holdings were held by the Clark family. Davies indicates that the Singer family continued to control blocks of the company's stock.

67. B. of C., *Harvester Co.*, p. 96, has the appraised value of the companies that joined the 1902 merger. McCormick's value was estimated at $29.5 million, Deering at $28.5 million, and the smaller companies just between $3.5 million to $9 million. In 1902 McCormick estimated Massey-Harris' value at $9.0 million (p. 331). Wood (p. 491) appears to have been relatively small.

68. Helen M. Kramer, "Harvesters and High Finance: Formation of the International Harvester Company," *Business History Review*, 38:283–301 (Autumn 1964); McCormick, *Century of the Reaper*, pp. 70–73, for technological competition and chap. 6 for market competition.

69. John R. Garraty, *Right-Hand Man: The Life of George W. Perkins* (New York, 1957), pp. 127–128.

70. B. of C., *Harvester Co.*, p. 238; Carstensen, "American Multinationals in Russia," p. 238; Garraty, *Perkins*, pp. 143–148.

71. B. of C., *Harvester Co.*, pp. 49–55. For Allis-Chalmers see Alfred D. Chandler, Jr., *Strategy and Structure* (Cambridge, Mass., 1962), pp. 370–371.

72. Wilkins, *Multinational Enterprise*, pp. 102–103, 208, 212–213. Carstensen, "American Multinational Enterprise in Russia," tells the International Harvester story in admirable detail.

73. Harold C. Passer, *The Electrical Manufacturers, 1875–1900* (Cambridge, Mass., 1953), p. 263.

74. Wilkins, *Multinational Enterprise*, pp. 212–213.

13. Top Management: Function and Structure

1. Ralph W. Hidy and Muriel E. Hidy, *Pioneering in Big Business, 1882–1911* (New York, 1955), pp. 40–51, for the formation of the trust and constituent companies.

2. Hidy and Hidy, *Pioneering in Big Business*, pp. 112–116, 144–153, 193–200; Harold F. Williamson and Arnold P. Daum, *The American Petroleum Industry: The Age of Illumination, 1859–1899* (Evanston, Ill., 1959), pp. 687–689.

3. Hidy and Hidy, *Pioneering in Big Business*, pp. 182–185.

4. The evolution of the committee system is described in Hidy and Hidy, *Pioneering in Big Business*, pp. 59–68, 90, and Ralph W. Hidy, "Large Scale Organization: The Standard Oil Company (New Jersey)," *Journal of Economic History*, 12:411–429 (Fall 1952), esp. pp. 416, 419.

5. Hidy and Hidy, *Pioneering in Big Business*, pp. 68–75, 88, 197.

6. Hidy and Hidy, *Pioneering in Big Business*, pp. 70, 191.

7. By the end of the 1880s two departments on barrels, case, cans, and other packaging materials were combined under George H. Hopper.

8. Hidy and Hidy, *Pioneering in Big Business*, pp. 61–62.

9. This and following quotations are from Hidy and Hidy, *Pioneering in Big Business*, pp. 62, 87–88.

10. Hidy and Hidy, *Pioneering in Big Business*, pp. 57–59, 66–68, 71–75.

11. Hidy and Hidy, *Pioneering in Big Business*, pp. 72–73.

12. Hidy and Hidy, *Pioneering in Big Business*, pp. 612–638, provide a good picture of Standard's accounting practices to 1911. The quotation is by that company's comptroller (pp. 624–625).

13. Hidy and Hidy, *Pioneering in Big Business*, pp. 58, 72, on approval of salaries and capital appropriations.

14. For example, Hidy and Hidy, *Pioneering in Big Business*, pp. 195, 198. See also Williamson and Daum, *American Petroleum Industry*, chap. 22.

15. Hidy and Hidy, *Pioneering in Big Business*, p. 229.

16. Hidy and Hidy, *Pioneering in Big Business*, pp. 26, 197, 228, 231, 316.

17. Hidy and Hidy, *Pioneering in Big Business*, pp. 218–232.

18. Hidy and Hidy, *Pioneering in Big Business*, pp. 324–325.

19. Hidy and Hidy, *Pioneering in Big Business*, pp. 329, 331.

20. Alfred D. Chandler, Jr., *Strategy and Structure* (Cambridge, Mass., 1962), chap. 4.

21. Hidy and Hidy, *Pioneering in Big Business*, pp. 314–322.

22. For the widespread use of the functional holding company in Europe see Bruce R. Scott, "The Industrial State: Old Myths and New Realities," *Harvard Business Review*, 51:133–149 (March–April 1973).

23. Annual reports for American Cotton Oil Company, esp. those that were dated Nov. 5, 1891, p. 16; Nov. 3, 1892, p. 17. The information on E. D. Adams comes from *Who Was Who* (New York, 1942).

24. Williams Haynes, *American Chemical Industry: Background and Beginnings*, I (New York, 1954), 196.

25. Annual reports of the National Lead Company, particularly for 1894. Unfortunately, the annual reports for National and then American Linseed have little information about that company's organization and management.

26. Harold C. Passer, *The Electrical Manufacturers, 1875–1900* (Cambridge, Mass., 1953), pp. 28–29, 85–86, 101–102, 104, 322; Matthew Josephson, *Edison* (New York, 1959), pp. 358, 383. Coolidge had been treasurer of the Amoskeag Mills and president of the Atchison, Topeka, and Santa Fe. Allen Johnson, ed., *Dictionary of American Biography* (New York, 1946), IV, 395.

27. Passer, *Electrical Manufacturers*, chap. 9; H. G. Prout, *A Life of George Westinghouse* (New York, 1922), pp. 275–276; Arthur S. Dewing, *Corporate Promotions and Reorganizations* (Cambridge, Mass., 1914), pp. 167–175. The U.S. Electrical Company, which Westinghouse purchased in 1889, had early financial support from the Equitable Life Insurance Company. Passer, *Electrical Manufacturers*, p. 147.

28. Passer, *Electrical Manufacturers*, pp. 85–86, 102–104, 219–221, 248–249, 321–322; Forrest McDonald, *Insull* (Chicago, 1962), pp. 39–42.

29. Josephson, *Edison*, p. 353.

30. Harold C. Passer, "Development of Large Scale Organization: Electrical Manufacturing around 1900," *Journal of Economic History*, 12:379–381 (Fall 1952); McDonald, *Insull*, p. 42.

31. Passer, *Electrical Manufacturers*, pp. 26–31.

32. Passer, *Electrical Manufacturers*, pp. 52–57, 233.

33. Passer, "Large Scale Organization," p. 382.

34. Passer, *Electrical Manufacturers*, p. 325.

35. Josephson, *Edison*, pp. 362–366; McDonald, *Insull*, pp. 49–51.

36. The Annual Report for General Electric Company dated Jan. 31, 1894, pp. 8–9.

37. Passer, *Electrical Manufacturers*, pp. 322–324; "Large Scale Organization," pp. 382, 383; and General Electric Annual Reports dated Jan. 31, 1895, 1896, and 1897. The Annual Report of Jan. 31, 1900, indicates that the electrical and manufacturing department was separated into two autonomous departments during that year, each still reporting to the vice president in charge of manufacturing. I am greatly indebted to James Baughman for providing me with information on General Electric's organization and accounting procedures.

38. Kendall Birr, *Pioneering in Industrial Research: The Story of the General Electric Research Laboratory* (Washington, D.C., 1957), p. 31.

39. Passer, "Large Scale Organization," pp. 385–386; Passer, *Electrical Manufacturers*, pp. 323; and Annual Report, dated Jan. 31, 1894. For the additions of later sales office see the Annual Reports for those years.

40. Mira Wilkins, *The Emergence of Multinational Enterprise* (Cambridge, Mass., 1970), pp. 95–96; John W. Hammond, *Men and Volts: The Story of General Electric* (Philadelphia, 1941), pp. 57, 69–76.

41. Passer, "Large Scale Organization," p. 386.

42. For the operation of the sales and manufacturing committees see Passer, "Large Scale Organization," pp. 384–389, and for the research council see Birr, *Pioneering in Industrial Research*, p. 69.

43. Birr, *Pioneering in Industrial Research*, pp. 68–69.

44. Passer indicates the role and makeup of its board and its executive committees in *Electrical Manufacturers*, pp. 322–323, and "Large Scale Organization," pp. 382–383.

45. Passer, "Large Scale Organization," p. 384.

46. [G.E.], *Professional Management in General Electric* (np., 1953), p. 55.

47. The company took over and further developed cost accounting procedures initiated at Thomson-Houston. Passer, *Electrical Manufacturers*, p. 324.

48. General Electric's Annual Report, dated Jan. 31, 1896, p. 18. That report states that by that year the "write-downs" were completed and the account did then represent replacement value. The company continued to use this replacement accouting system until at least World War I.

49. Birr, *Pioneering in Industrial Research*, pp. 31–33; John A. Miller, *Workshop of Engineers* (Schenectady, 1919), pp. 1–20; [G.E.], *Professional Management*, p. 57. For publications bureau see Passer, "Large Scale Organization," p. 384.

50. Birr, *Pioneering in Industrial Research*, pp. 30–31.

51. U.S. Rubber Company's Annual Reports, dated April 17, 1894, pp. 4–7, May 21, 1895, pp. 4–5, May 25, 1896, pp. 3–8, and Glenn D. Babcock, *History of the United States Rubber Company* (Bloomington, Ind., 1966), chap. 2.

52. Babcock, *U.S. Rubber*, pp. 26, 38–39.

53. U.S. Rubber Company Annual Report, May 25, 1896, p. 8.

54. Babcock, *U.S. Rubber*, pp. 53–60, 67–70, 87–89, and U.S. Rubber Company's annual reports May 26, 1902, esp. pp. 5–8, and May 17, 1904, pp. 8–11.

55. Babcock, *U.S. Rubber,* pp. 64–65.

56. U.S. Rubber Company Annual Report, April 17, 1894, p. 4.

57. Babcock, *U.S. Rubber,* pp. 128–129; U.S. Rubber Company Annual Report, May 17, 1904, p. 10.

58. Of the three outside directors, two, Elias C. Benedict and Anthony N. Brady, were financiers but neither of them had been involved in railroad finance. U.S. Rubber Company's Annual Reports list the directors and officers of the company as well as the members of the executive committee. Information on Benedict and Brady comes from *Who Was Who.*

59. Babcock, *U. S. Rubber,* pp. 44–48, 73–75; U.S. Rubber Company Annual Report, May 16, 1911, pp. 8–10.

60. In 1911 U.S. Rubber formed the United States Tire Company, a wholly owned subsidiary. Babcock, *U.S. Rubber,* p. 115. The organization chart for 1917 (see figure 10) indicates how the subsidiary fitted into the company's administrative arrangements.

61. Babcock, *U.S. Rubber,* pp. 133–135.

62. The information on the merger that created the modern Du Pont Company comes almost wholly from Alfred D. Chandler, Jr., and Stephen Salsbury, *Pierre S. du Pont and the Making of the Modern Corporation* (New York, 1971), chaps. 3–5. That analysis was based on the Du Pont Company archives and the full collection of the papers of Pierre du Pont, Coleman du Pont and other Du Pont Company executives at the Eleutherian Mills Historical Library, Greenville, Wilmington, Del.

63. Chandler and Salsbury, *P. S. du Pont,* p. 62; Daniel Nelson, "Scientific Management, Systematic Management and Labor, 1880–1915," *Business History Review,* 48:484n (Winter 1974); and Michael Massouh, "Technological and Managerial Innovation: The Johnson Company 1883–1898, *Business History Review,* 50:66–67 (Spring 1976).

64. Described in Chandler and Salsbury, *P. S. du Pont,* p. 93.

65. Quoted in Chandler and Salsbury, *P. S. du Pont,* p. 93.

66. The creation of the Operating and Sales Department is described in Chandler and Salsbury, *P. S. du Pont,* pp. 137–141; also Chandler, *Strategy and Structure,* p. 59.

67. Ernest Dale and Charles Meloy, "Hamilton Macfarland Barksdale and the Du Pont Contributions to Systematic Management," *Business History Review* 36:127–152. In 1911 Pierre and Coleman du Pont set up a series of functional committees made up largely of men on the executive committee to help set policy for the functional departments. This experiment was, however, short-lived. Chandler and Salsbury, *P. S. du Pont,* pp. 304–315.

68. Chandler and Salsbury, *P. S. du Pont,* pp. 141–142, and chap. 9, esp. pp. 232–233, 238–240, 244.

69. Tallman had worked at the Corliss Steam Engine Shops, Carnegie Steel, Yale & Towne, and the Brown Hoisting Company. Chandler and Salsbury, *P. S. du Pont,* p. 641.

70. The beginnings of the executive committee as described in Chandler and Salsbury, *P. S. du Pont,* pp. 125–137.

71. Chandler and Salsbury, *P. S. du Pont,* pp. 142–143.

72. Chandler and Salsbury, *P. S. du Pont,* pp. 143–147.

73. Chandler and Salsbury, *P. S. du Pont,* p. 151–155, and in Thomas Johnson, "Managerial Accounting in an Early Integrated Industrial: E. I. du Pont de Nemours Powder Company, 1903–1912," *Business History Review,* 49:184–204 (Summer 1975). Johnson's excellent article places the accounting developments at Du Pont in their larger setting. Michael Chatfield, *History of Accounting Thought* (Hins-

dale, Ill., 1974), chaps. 8, 12, 13, indicates the significance of the types of accounting innovations made at Du Pont.

74. This and the following quotation are given in Johnson, "Managerial Accounting," p. 188.

75. Chandler, *Strategy and Structure*, p. 67; Alfred P. Sloan, Jr., *My Years with General Motors* (New York, 1964), pp. 140–148. The best exposition of the Brown formula is in T. C. Davis, "How the Du Pont Organization Appraises Its Performance," American Management Association, *Financial Management Series*, no. 94, pp. 3–7 (1950).

76. Chandler and Salsbury, *P. S. du Pont*, pp. 132–133.

77. Chandler and Salsbury, *P. S. du Pont*, pp. 164–168, 203–204, 251–255.

78. Johnson "Management Accounting," p. 187.

79. Johnson, "Management Accounting," pp. 189–190.

80. Chandler and Salsbury, *P. S. du Pont*, pp. 303–306, 310–311.

81. Chandler, *Strategy and Structure*, pp. 73–75, 127; Chandler and Salsbury, *P. S. du Pont*, pp. 470–471.

82. George S. Gibb and Evelyn H. Knowlton, *History of Standard Oil Company (New Jersey): The Resurgent Years 1911–1927* (New York, 1956), p. 38; Chandler and Salsbury, *P. S. du Pont*, pp. 343, 357–358; and company annual reports for General Electric and United States Rubber. The nine-man executive committee appointed at Du Pont in 1919 included only two members of the clan. Chandler, *Strategy and Structure*, p. 73.

83. Chandler, *Strategy and Structure*, pp. 61, 64–65, 105–106, 294–297.

14. The Maturing of Modern Business Enterprise

1. I have devoted a volume to one set of these developments, and that study, *Strategy and Structure*, reviews only a small part of the story.

2. N. S. B. Gras and Henrietta M. Larson, *Casebook in American Business History* (New York 1939), pp. 630–640.

3. Boris Emmet and John E. Jeuck, *Catalogues and Counters: A History of Sears, Roebuck and Company* (Chicago, 1950), pp. 198–215.

4. The responses of Ford and General Motors to the inventory crisis of 1920–1921 are outlined in Lawrence H. Seltzer, *A Financial History of the American Automobile Industry* (New York, 1929), pp. 114–118, 197–202.

5. The reorganization at General Motors is told in detail in Alfred D. Chandler, Jr., *Strategy and Structure: Chapters in the History of the Industrial Enterprise* (Cambridge, Mass., 1962), chap. 3; Alfred D. Chandler, Jr., and Stephen Salsbury, *Pierre S. du Pont and the Making of the Modern Corporation* (New York 1971), chaps. 19–21; and Alfred P. Sloan, Jr., *My Years with General Motors* (New York, 1969), chaps. 3–8. Comparable problems and responses at Du Pont are given in Chandler, *Strategy and Structure*, pp. 91–113; at Sears, Roebuck in Emmet and Jeuck, *Catalogues and Counters*, pp. 201–202 and Chandler, *Strategy and Structure*, pp. 231–232; at General Electric and Westinghouse, in Chandler, *Strategy and Structure*, pp. 363–369.

6. Arthur Pound, *The Turning Wheel* (Garden City, N.Y., 1934), pp. 87, 364–365.

7. Chandler and Salsbury, *P. S. du Pont*, pp. 303–315; Chandler, *Strategy and Structure*, pp. 61, 64–65, 105–106. These two books review du Pont's experience. Sloan, *My Years with General Motors*, pp. 27–29, recalls his experience.

8. P. S. du Pont to Officers, Directors, Heads of Departments, Dec. 29, 1920, quoted in Chandler, *Strategy and Structure*, p. 140.

9. Chandler, *Strategy and Structure*, pp. 157–158. In late 1924 members of the

executive committee without an explicit executive title included Raskob and three Fisher brothers who had recently come on the General Motors board as a result of its purchase of the controlling shares of the Fisher Body Company in 1924. Chandler and Salsbury, *P. S. du Pont*, pp. 576; Sloan, *My Years with General Motors*, p. 161. When Lawrence Fisher took over the Cadillac division he remained a member of the executive committee. On the other hand, the general manager of Buick soon left the committee. See General Motors' organization chart dated January 1925 and April 1927. Defense Exhibit G.M.2 and 3, *United States v. E. I. du Pont de Nemours & Company, General Motors Corporation, et al.*, U.S. District Court for the Northern District of Illinois, Eastern Division, Civil Action No. 49C–1071 (1953). The personnel listed on the January chart was almost exactly the same as for 1924.

10. Sloan, *My Years with General Motors*, chaps. 5, 7.

11. A comprehensive study of recent organizational changes within the operating divisions of large industrial enterprises is E. Raymond Corey and Steven H. Star, *Organization Strategy: A Marketing Approach* (Boston 1971).

12. Michael Chatfield, *A History of Accounting Thought* (Hinsdale, Ill., 1974), pp. 125–126, 150–153; Michael Chatfield, ed., *Contemporary Studies in the Evolution of Accounting Thought* (Belmont, Calif., 1968), chaps. 12, 15 16, all by James Don Edwards, and chap. 15, by C. A. Moyer.

13. Chatfield, *History of Accounting Thought*, chap. 12; Chatfield, ed., *Evolution of Accounting Thought*, chap. 17, by S. Paul Gardner.

14. Chatfield, *History of Accounting Thought*, p. 153.

15. J. E. Hagerty, "Experiences of an Early Marketing Teacher," *Journal of Marketing*, 1:20–27 (July 1936). Hugh E. Agnew, "The History of the American Marketing Association," *Journal of Marketing*, 5:374–379 (April 1941). I am indebted to Joseph d'Cruz for these citations.

16. Monte A. Calvert, *The Mechanical Engineer in America* (Baltimore, 1967), pp. 275–276; Daniel A. Wren, *The Evolution of Management Thought* (New York, 1972), p. 165.

17. Chandler, *Strategy and Structure*, pp. 421–422.

18. Melvin T. Copeland, *And Mark an Era: The Story of the Harvard Business School* (Boston, Mass., 1958), pp. 15–16.

19. The information for this paragraph comes from Copeland, *And Mark an Era*, pp. 21–26; Herbert Heaton, *A Scholar in Action: Edwin F. Gay* (Cambridge, Mass., 1952), pp. 77–78; and the annual reports of the Dean of the Graduate School of Business Administration to the President of the University which are available in Baker Library, Harvard Business School. Particularly useful are listings on pp. 115–117 of the report for the academic year 1910–1911. The quotation at the end of the paragraph is from Copeland, *And Mark an Era*, p. 43. For the development of Paul Cherington's course in marketing see Hagerty, "An Early Marketing Teacher," pp. 21–22.

20. Copeland, *And Mark an Era*, p. 43.

21. Specific tasks carried out by Arthur D. Little, Inc., Frazier Torbet, and Day & Zimmerman are indicated in Chandler, *Strategy and Structure*, pp. 121, 240–243; Chandler and Salsbury, *P. S. du Pont*, p. 514. George E. Frazer's autobiography, *First Forty Years* (np, 1957) provides useful information on the beginnings of the specialty of the management consultant.

22. Until very recent years the Bell companies were organized into functional departments including accounting, directory, traffic, engineering, plant, commercial, and sales. Only since the late 1960s were alternative structures experimented with. See AT&T, Executive Department, Corporate Planning Studies Division, "Organization Issues: Fall Presidents' Conference," November 1973, pp. 34–39. By 1973,

AT&T controlled all shares of all but seven of the twenty-two regional subsidiaries, and in five of these seven it owned from 88 percent to 99 percent of the stock. In addition, it still owned and operated Western Electric and the Bell Telephone Laboratories. Annual Report for 1973, p. 17. But in 1920 it sold all of Western Electric's international activities to International Telephone and Telegraph. Mira Wilkins, *The Emergence of Multinational Enterprise* (Cambridge, Mass., 1970), p. 50, and Mira Wilkins, *The Maturing of Multinational Enterprise* (Cambridge, Mass., 1974), p. 71.

23. Godfrey M. Lebher, *Chain Stores in America, 1859–1962* (New York 1963), chap. 4.

24. Emmet and Jeuck, *Catalogues and Counters*, p. 345. For the decline in farm income, ibid., p. 315. See also Jim Potter, *The American Economy Between the World Wars* (New York, 1974), pp. 27–30, 32–33.

25. Emmet and Jeuck, *Catalogues and Counters*, pp. 503–520.

26. Emmet and Jeuck, *Catalogues and Counters*, pp. 656–659.

27. For example, in 1929, in order to diversify risks and investments, the families controlling Filenes of Boston, Abraham & Straus of Brooklyn, New York, and Lazarus of Columbus, Ohio, formed the Federated Department Stores. No attempt was made to put these into centralized control. There was no central purchasing and, indeed, no overall central planning and evaluation until after World War II. Then Fred Lazarus recognized the value of using the multidivisional structure to transfer the company into more of an operating managerial enterprise with a general office coordinating, evaluating, and planning the activities of the different regional offices. These, in turn, began to grow fast through the building of branches. Richard Hamermesh, "Federated Department Stores Inc.: A Historical Analysis of Strategy and Structure from 1945 to 1960," unpublished seminar paper, Harvard Business School, Fall 1973.

28. These developments are recorded in Morton Keller, *The Life Insurance Enterprise, 1885–1910* (Cambridge, Mass., 1963), chaps. 1, 4–5. For overseas expansion and then contractions see Keller, ibid., chaps. 6 and 7; Wilkins, *The Emergence of Multinational Enterprise*, pp. 64–65, 103–107; and Wilkins *The Maturing of Multinational Enterprise*, pp. 43–44. John A. Garraty, *Right-Hand Man; The Life of George W. Perkins* (New York, 1957), chap. 3, describes in detail the creation of the branch office system at New York Life; see chap. 4 for its expansion into Europe.

29. The centralized functionally departmentalized structure of Equitable Life is described in R. Carlyle Buley, *The Equitable Life Assurance Society of the United States, 1859–1964* (New York, 1967), pp. 853–857, 1250–1252, 1293–1295. The structure was little changed throughout the twentieth century, even with what was considered a major reorganization between 1953 and 1958.

30. Wilkins, *The Maturing of Multinational Enterprise*, p. 19. Herman E. Krooss and Martin R. Blyn, *A History of Financial Intermediaries* (New York, 1971), pp. 159–160, 229–230. U.S. Bureau of the Census, *Historical Statistics of the United States, Colonial Times to 1957* (Washington, D.C., 1957), p. 635, gives higher figures for banks with branches: 119 in 1900; 1,281 in 1920; and 3,353 in 1929.

31. Alfred D. Chandler, Jr., "The Structure of American Industry in the Twentieth Century," *Business History Review*, 43:255–297 (Autumn 1969), esp. table 1, prepared by P. Glenn Porter and Harold C. Livesay, pp. 283–290, summarized on pp. 258–259.

32. Nester E. Terleckyj, assisted by Harriet J. Helper, *Research and Development, Its Growing Composition* (New York, 1963), quoted in *Economic Conventration Hearing before Subcommittee on Antitrust and Monopoly of the Committee of the Judiciary*, United States Senate, 89th Cong., 1st Sess. (Washington, 1965),

part III, p. 1139. The pattern of investment has remained much the same for expenditures, as well as personnel employed in research and development. The only industries to acquire heavy expenditures and personnel since the 1930s have been the aircraft and missile and scientific instruments. National Science Foundation, *Research and Development Industry, 1973* (Washington, 1975), table B-36, p. 51; National Science Foundation, *Science Indicators, 1974* (Washington, 1975), figures 4–5, p. 88.

33. Michael Gort, *Diversification and Integration in American Industry* (Princeton, 1962), pp. 42–45.

34. Chandler, *Strategy and Structure,* pp. 342–378. Table 2 by Porter and Livesay in Chandler, "Structure of American Industry," pp. 290–298, illustrates the pattern of diversification for about eighty of the nation's largest enterprises in 1909, 1919, 1929, 1935, 1948, and 1960.

35. Chandler, *Strategy and Structure,* pp. 78–113.

36. This section follows closely the final pages of Alfred D. Chandler, Jr., "The United States: The Evolution of Enterprise," Peter Mathias, ed., *Cambridge Economic History,* vol. 7 (Cambridge, Eng., 1977).

37. *Economic Report of the President: Transmitted to the Congress, February, 1971* (Washington, 1971), p. 198.

38. Chandler, "Structure of American Industry," pp. 297–298.

39. A useful analysis of how one diversified enterprise has exploited the product cycle by use of a sophisticated version of the multdivisional structure is William C. Goggin, "How the Multidivisional Structure Works at Dow Corning," *Harvard Business Review,* 52:55–56 (Jan.–Feb. 1974). Louis T. Wells, "A Product Life Cycle for International Trade?" *Journal of Marketing,* 32:1–6 (July 1968) suggests how the concept of the life cycle can have strategic implications for multinational enterprise.

40. Wilkins, *Maturing of Multinational Enterprise,* p. 330.

41. Lawrence E. Fouraker and John M. Stopford, "Organizational Structure and Multinational Strategy," *Administrative Science Quarterly,* 13:110–113 (June 1968).

42. John M. Stopford and Louis T. Wells, Jr., *Managing the Multinational Enterprise* (New York, 1972), chap. 5.

43. Staff Report of the Federal Trade Commission, *Economic Report on Corporate Mergers* (Washington, D.C., 1969), chap. 5. Most useful is Neil H. Jacoby, "The Conglomerate Corporation," *The Center Magazine,* 2:40–53 (July 1969).

44. Norman Berg, "Corporate Role in Diversified Companies," Harvard Business School Working Paper (HBS 71–2, BP2) provides an excellent comparison of the structure of large diversified industrials and conglomerates.

45. Federal Trade Commission, *Corporate Mergers,* p. 176. The figures for the share of the 200 largest in manufacturing and mining assets are, for 1947, 44.2 percent; in 1963, 55.3 percent; and 1968, 58.6 percent. Oliver F. Williamson, *Corporate Control and Business Behavior* (Englewood Cliffs, N.J., 1970), pp. 6–8, provides comparable figures for sales and employment.

Conclusion: The Managerial Revolution in American Business

1. Edith T. Penrose, *The Theory of the Growth of the Firm* (New York, 1959), chap. 5.

2. George Stigler, "The Division of Labor Is Limited by the Extent of the Market," *Journal of Political Economy,* 59:185–193 (June 1951).

3. Robert J. Larner, "Ownership and Control in the 200 Largest Non-Financial Corporations, 1929 and 1963," *American Economic Review,* 56:777–787 (Sept.

1966). Larner's later book, *Management Control and the Large Corporation* (New York, 1970) expands his survey to cover almost all the 500 largest companies. There he finds the same basic patterns of management control as he did for the 200 largest. A rebuttal to Larner—Philip J. Burch's *The Managerial Revolution Reassessed: Family Control in America's Large Corporations* (Lexington, Mass., 1972)—does little to contradict the hypothesis that the managers operate the central sectors of the American economy. By using the criteria that 4 to 5 percent of stock means control, Burch finds that of the 200 largest firms on *Fortune*'s list of 500 largest industrials in 1965, 43 percent were probably management controlled, 17.5 percent were possibly family controlled, and 39.5 percent were probably family controlled. Under the possibly family controlled category, he lists, for example, Standard Oil of New Jersey, Socony Mobil, Standard of California, and Standard Oil of Indiana as possibly controlled by the Rockefeller family (the last with the Blaustien family), although there were no Rockefellers on the board or among the top and middle managers. Burch gives little indication how a "family, group of families, or some affluent individual," who holds 4 to 5 percent of the stock affects the decisions in that enterprise that coordinate flows and allocate resources, except to point out that in a large percentage of family firms, family members have over the years "served in major executive capacities." These are not defined but clearly include serving on the board of directors. What Burch's data does show is that wealthy Americans invest in the securities of large corporations, that some families of the entrepreneurs who helped to found a company still retained as much as 5 percent of the stock in those companies, and that members of those families often have jobs in that enterprise. Burch helps to document the fact that wealthy families, particularly those of the founders of modern business enterprises, are the beneficiaries of managerial capitalism, but gives little evidence that these families make basic decisions concerning the operations of modern capitalistic enterprises and of the economy in which they operate.

4. The paragraphs on labor organization and the coming of the commitment to maintaining aggregate demand follow those in Alfred D. Chandler, Jr., "The Role of Business in the United States: A Historical Essay," *Daedalus*, 98:35–38 (Winter 1969).

5. *Report of President's Committee on the Impact of Defense and Disarmament* (Washington, D.C., 1965), chap. 1, reprinted in James L. Clayton, *The Economic Impact of the Cold War* (New York, 1970), pp. 54–64. Of the eighty-one largest industrials in 1960, only twelve were among the twenty-five largest military contractors during the 1960s. Of these, four aircraft companies and General Dynamics had from 57 to 88 percent of sales in military contracts. Sperry-Rand sold 35 percent of its output to the government. Three electrical and electronic companies (General Electric, Westinghouse, and RCA) sold from 13 to 19 percent of their output to the government. (In addition, IT&T and AT&T, which is not on the list, made 19 and 9 percent respectively of their sales to the military.) Of the remaining three, IBM sold 7 percent to the military, General Motors 3 percent, and Ford's Philco Division 3 percent. The list of 81 companies is from Alfred D. Chandler, Jr., "The Structure of American Industry in the Twentieth Century," *Business History Review*, 43:297–298 (Autumn 1969) and the list of leading contractors is in Clayton, *Economic Impact of the Cold War*, table 12, p. 44. For the impact of military spending on industrial research and development see Clayton, pp. 147–164.

6. See Stephen K. Bailey, *Congress Makes a Law* (New York, 1950), chaps. 2, 5.

7. See Leslie Hannah, ed. *Management Strategy and Business Development: An Historical and Comparative Study* (London, 1976); Herman Daems and Herman van der Wee, eds., *The Rise of Managerial Capitalism* (The Hague, 1974); Keiichiro

Nakagawa, *Strategy and Structure of Big Business* (Tokyo, 1976); Derek F. Cannon, *The Strategy and Structure of British Enterprise* (Boston, 1973); Robert J. Pavan, *Strutture Strategie delle Impresse Italiane* (Bologna, 1976); G. P. Dyas, "The Strategy and Structure of French Enterprise," Ph.D. diss., Harvard Business School, 1972; and H. I. Thanheiser, "The Strategy and Structure of German Industrial Enterprise," Ph.D. diss., Harvard Business School, 1972.

8. Simon Kuznets, *Economic Growth of Nations: Total Output and Production Structure* (Cambridge, Mass., 1971), pp. 38–40, and W. S. and E. S. Woytonsky, *World Population and Production* (New York, 1973), pp. 383–385.

9. Alfred D. Chandler, Jr., "The Development of Modern Management Structure in the U.S. and the U.K.," in Hannah, ed., *Management Strategy and Business Development*, chap. 1, briefly reviews the British experience.

Index

587